INVENTING TIMES SQUARE

INVENTING TIMES SQUARE

COMMERCE AND CULTURE
AT THE CROSSROADS
OF THE WORLD

EDITED BY

William R. Taylor

THE JOHNS HOPKINS UNIVERSITY PRESS
Baltimore and London

Originally published in a hardcover edition by Russell Sage Foundation, 1991. This edition published by arrangement with Russell Sage Foundation, New York, N.Y., U.S.A.
Johns Hopkins Paperbacks edition, 1996
05 04 03 02 01 00 99 98 97 96   5 4 3 2 1

The Johns Hopkins University Press
2715 North Charles Street
Baltimore, Maryland 21218-4319
The Johns Hopkins Press Ltd., London

Library of Congress Cataloging-in-Publication Data will be found at the end of this book.

ISBN 0-8018-5337-0 (pbk.)

To Warren I. Susman (1927–1985)

PHOTO CREDITS

Prologue: Courtesy of The New-York Historical Society, New York City. Part I: Courtesy of The New-York Historical Society, New York City. Part II: *Theatre Magazine*, July 1923, page 10. Courtesy of The New York Public Library Picture Collection. Part III: Courtesy of The New-York Historical Society, New York City. Part IV: Courtesy of The New-York Historical Society, New York City. Afterword: Rockefeller Plaza West. Courtesy of Kohn Pederson Fox Associates, P.C.

CONTENTS

ACKNOWLEDGMENTS

THOSE OF US who have gone the distance on this project have accumulated a great many obligations along the way. Our lengthiest debt is to the New York Institute for the Humanities at New York University. For the past fifteen years the Institute has provided an array of activities focusing on the historical study of urban cultures. Two of the early directors, Richard Sennett and Thomas Bender, themselves urbanists, provided encouragement and support when it was first needed. Two postdoctoral colloquia were especially important. The *Culture of Cities* seminar that Thomas Bender and I coordinated from 1981 to 1984 and the *Commercial Culture* seminar that Peter Buckley, William Leach, Daniel Czitrom, and I organized during 1985–87 brought some of the authors of this volume together for the first time and helped to direct our focus to the Times Square phenomenon. Many scholars from the Northeast participated in these colloquia and helped to lay the groundwork for the project.

The Times Square Conferences, sponsored by the Institute and held at New York University during 1988–89, were decisive in giving shape to this study. Brendan Gill, Neil Harris, David Harvey, J. B. Jackson, Laurence Senelick, and the late Kate Simon gave keynote lectures. Scholars from many disciplines, some from the earlier colloquia, attended the six conferences and provided us with their insight and guidance. The Institute's current director, Richard Turner, did everything a director can to make the conferences a success. During the whole course of the project he provided leadership, funds, and an unfailingly sympathetic ear. Jocelyn Carlson, administrator of the Institute, and the Institute staff—Claude Dorsinville-Leman, Dana Kinstler, and Cristina Lourosa—willingly accepted the added burdens imposed by the project and with unfailing good will provided day-to-day support. All of us associated with the project are indebted to Jocelyn Carlson for her attentive management and the hospitable and decorous amenities she provided while the work of the conferences went forward. New York University, through its support of the Institute; the Humanities Council at NYU, administered by deputy vice-president for academic affairs Leslie Berlowitz; the Daniel Rose family; and the Russell Sage Foundation provided the necessary funding.

We feel a special indebtedness to Mr. and Mrs. Daniel Rose for guarantee-
ing support to the project before other donors were in sight. The Russell
Sage Foundation, under the presidency of Eric Wanner, helped to fund the
project and provided me with a fellowship at the Foundation where,
among other work, I was able to complete the editorial tasks connected
with publication. I am grateful to the dean of social sciences at Stony
Brook, Andrew Policano, for providing me with a research assistant for the
year and to the chair of the history department, Fred Weinstein, for the
constant encouragement and support I received as a faculty member who
was often away and preoccupied during the long period of this study.

Members of the project's planning and editorial committee gave
generously of their time and counsel through a succession of meetings
before the conferences began. These meetings, which took place over the
course of a year, provided the structure necessary to giving coherent shape
to our individual research. The committee included Peter Buckley, Ada
Louise Huxtable, Barbara Kirshenblatt-Gimblett, Margaret Knapp,
William Leach, Brooks McNamara, and myself. Members of this committee, in one way or another, have also made substantial contributions as the
project wound down. In particular, William Leach and Peter Buckley
willingly shared the more onerous editorial tasks. Minda Novek, out of her
resourcefulness and New York expertise, has served the project in many
different ways. She provided on-site research to many of the out-of-town
scholars and provided invaluable guidance to others of us. She has also
done the photo and graphic research for the book. Throughout the
publication process Lisa Nachtigall, director of publications of Russell
Sage Foundation, has been everything an editor could be. It was good to be
reminded of how much an experienced and perceptive editor can add to the
quality of a manuscript. Charlotte Shelby, managing editor, with wisdom
and judiciousness has seen the book through the complications of copy
editing and production. My research assistant from Stony Brook, Gina
Grossfeld, helped at every point in preparing the Times Square manuscript. Jennifer Parker at Russell Sage provided tireless and efficient help
in arranging the public meeting on Times Square in the fall of 1990 and in
the final stages of manuscript preparation. William Kornblum helped
organize and chair the fall meeting on Times Square today. Provost Steven
Cahn and Marvin Carlson of the Program in Theatre History agreed to
have this meeting cosponsored by the CUNY Graduate Center. Through
their participation all three helped to make it a success.

INTRODUCTION

William R. Taylor

W HEN EDWARD Bernays located his publicity firm in Times Square at
the close of World War I, he thought of it as "the center of the
universe." Allowing for Bernays's cosmic exaggeration, there is some truth
to his claim, as the following chapters demonstrate.

Those of us who met in a succession of conferences on Times Square
during 1988–89 took the "crossroads" dimension of the subject seriously,
although none of us realized at the time how much we still needed to know.
We began our work with hunches not certainties, questions not answers.
What significance, we wondered, did the development of Times Square as
a central entertainment district hold for New York? For the rest of the
country?

To answer these questions we have put together a cultural history that
is national as well as local. Basically, as John Agnew tells us, it is the "story
of the rise and fall of a distinctive American popular culture in the city,"
but it is also more than this. Americans have a tendency to isolate New
York from the mainstream of national culture and to see its preoccupations
as peripheral. We felt, on the contrary, that Times Square developed as an
integral part of cultural changes taking place nationally; that it was both an
indicator and a cause of those changes. We suspected from the outset that
a Broadway style, including everything from neon lights and publicity
hype to dress and manner of speech, had somehow worked its way beneath
our skin as a nation by sometime in the 1930s. How did it get there? We
knew a little about this question when we began. We soon learned much
more. We knew that Broadway was the center of American theater during
the entire period of the study, that it was the center of a music industry that
had serenaded American cities and towns with over a million songs since
the turn of the century. We quickly became aware that syndicated
journalism, network radio, and Hollywood studios—all national media—
had used the entertainment district as a base of operations after the 1920s.
We recognized that Broadway, as a result, was perceived almost everywhere as the hub of show business; that, in Neil Harris's term, it was
"imaged" as a kind of city of night where the drumbeat of commerce never

relents and the lights never go out. In short, it had become for Americans what Brooks McNamara calls a "nostalgic generalization."

It is amazing, as John Agnew suggests in his Prologue, that it has taken cultural historians so long to get to Broadway as a national event or chain of events, especially given the new work on urban cultures that has recently appeared. Working singly, our perspectives have been limited. It may have required a collaborative study of this kind to mount the assault. We probably, as he says, have Warren Susman among others to thank for reminding us that our cities hold out a rich store of myths and fantasies at least as germane to our identity as a nation as the countryside. To interpret them as we do here is therefore part of a larger inquiry into who we are.

We approached our study of New York as part of a larger subject. We sensed from the outset that we needed to know more than any of us did about the organization and chemistry of such a central entertainment district; we needed to know specifically about the kinds of popular culture generated by New York's expansive commercial life. Many of the resulting chapters are devoted to explicating the genres of popular culture that developed in the city. We have tried to strike a balance between such studies and essays which, in one way or another, are more devoted to historical context. The chapters in the opening section of the book, for example, examine the historical circuitry of Times Square, while those in the following three sections tend to focus on particular features of Times Square and to analyze the colorful configuration of institutions and cultural practices that brought it to national and, finally, to international prominence.

As we pursued particular strains of change through the early twentieth century, we found that Times Square functioned as a kind of historical prism that did, in fact, refract elements of a changing national culture. The chapters that follow therefore have something new to say, we believe, not just about Times Square but about the character of this larger transformation.

The title alludes to "inventing" Times Square. This emphasis on invention is designed to focus attention on the many different kinds of initiatives that brought such a central entertainment district into being. We hoped that by stressing invention, we could steer attention to the deliberate tactics and strategies that were employed to shape the cultural productions of the area. The bustling cultural scene of the 1920s and 1930s was not inevitable; it was contrived. It appears to have resulted from many different kinds of business decisions which, in turn, succeeded in giving the area its concentrated commercial energy and visual distinction. Its colorful commercial character, too, was not predetermined. When the *New York Times* gave its name to the area in 1905, it foresaw the Square's development as the city's public center rather than the gaudy entertainment center it soon became. We are reminded each New Year's Eve that another, competing idea of the area as a central public square still survives.

This approach to the subject has exacted a price. Any hope that our study, long as it is, would touch upon every important aspect of Times Square had to be tempered by the need to stress the interrelatedness of developments and their relevance to larger changes in the culture. We systematically sought out investigators and topics of investigation that would stress interrelationships, sometimes in preference to expertise on a particular facet of the local scene.

The first section of the book, "Structural Changes," places Times Square in the context of national changes in economics, culture, and religion. These chapters, taken together, illuminate the changes in each area which, we concluded, made Times Square possible. Eric Lampard, in his "Introductory Essay," describes the emergence of a new interest in mass-produced goods and standardized consumption by the end of the nineteenth century. The twentieth century meaning of consumption, he points out, did not even exist in 1900. The ensuing changes in production, distribution, and consumption style, fired by the unleashing of consumer credit, created the first consumer culture during the 1920s. This new consumer world ran into a brick wall in 1929 only to resume its revolutionary development on a worldwide scale in the decades after World War II, finally bringing the blue jean revolution to Red Square itself.

The colorful segment of midtown that we have been calling Times Square, with its concentration in the years before World War I of entertainment, promotion, and display, was seen as an epicenter of these new promotional and consumption styles. This Times Square, according to Lampard, also refracted the stepped-up brokering activities on Wall Street and New York's new concentration of corporate headquarters, especially in the new advertising and communications industries. It also reflected the rapidly increasing centrality of New York in world markets.

The appearance at a critical moment of the "broker" figure, according to William Leach, launched consumer culture. Through their intervention at all levels of the economy, brokers were so successful in rationalizing the promotion and marketing of goods that by the 1920s they had helped create what one of them called "a staggering machine of desire." Consumers, it appears, often without any conscious recognition, had been living in a heady atmosphere of promotion, advertisement, and enticement that must have penetrated into every corner of the culture, and which succeeded in altering the perceived reality of everyone who was exposed to these transforming new experiences.

Neil Harris shows how a developing tourist industry, employing these new marketing strategies of "tie-ins" between rail companies, hotels, and other purveyors, offering discount fares and massive promotions, was able to target cities as attractive places to visit and vacation in, thereby helping to reverse an older, nineteenth century assumption that cities were pestilential, noisy, and unattractive—places to avoid rather than to seek out. Picture postcards, in turn, helped to pinpoint distinctive urban sites worthy of a visit, which led to the creation of the kinds of urban Baedeker itineraries we take for granted in modern travel. The street became a center of attraction for those who came to find their recreation in observing the life of large cities. City residents inevitably followed suit. In a sense, the consumer revolution came to feed upon itself, since, as Harris points out, the busy commercial life of the modern city turned out to be one of its principal tourist attractions.

In these developments there was a marked enhancement of the visual as opposed to the older moral assessment of urban experience. More and more, in interpreting what they saw and felt, urban people believed their eyes rather than scripture: They read the city in new and exciting ways. Besides printed ads, corridors of illuminated signs by night and colorful billboards by day created visual excitement about the products and locations they promoted. Strategies in advertising, such as the tie-in, encouraged consumers to see products in relation to other desired objects or constructs. Consumer products thus assumed their modern place in personal aspirations, personal dreams.

Christian churches, well into the nineteenth century, had roundly condemned such aspirations for visual pleasures and worldly goods, dancing and entertainment, just as they had viewed almost everything about the commercial life of cities as little better than John Bunyan's Vanity Fair. At the end of the nineteenth century liberal churches elected in a startling shift in direction to "take on" the world rather than to reject it. The result was a gradual shift in perspective within Protestant churches, which encouraged properly circumspect worldly recreation and pleasure. Richard Fox's account of this important transformation adds a further dimension to the analysis of the more general structural changes underlying the development of Times Square.

Why the headquarters and marketing center of theater and entertainment should have been located in New York, and why and how this concentration of commercial entertainment became lodged in Times Square, are questions raised by David Hammack. During the nineteenth century New York became the marketing center of the nation, the largest entrepôt for overseas trade. As its commercial volume grew and heavy manufacturing moved west, New York retained its stronghold on credit, banking, and market-sensitive manufacturing in women's clothing, luxury goods, fashion, and publishing. As a major center of publishing and market information and as the nation's largest seaport and the terminus of a national railway network, New York very early became an important destination for commercial travelers and a national barometer of what was fashionable, what was exciting, and what was new.

The process through which Times Square, or the area surrounding the intersection of Broadway and Seventh Avenue just above Forty-second Street, became the focus of commercial entertainment and nightlife is more complicated. Such concentrations had earlier been located successively off City Hall Park along Broadway in lower Manhattan, on the Bowery, around Union Square, and at the turn of the century, from Madison Square up Broadway to what is now Herald Square. Several developments, according to Hammack, led to the rapid development of the area farther north—what we have been calling Times Square. The development of a transportation network between 1900 and 1920 was a major factor. In particular, a major rail terminus in the vast new Grand Central Station at Forty-second Street and Fourth Avenue concentrated commercial activity in midtown, and the construction of a subway system after 1904 eventually funneled movement both north and south through Times Square. The existence of the Garment District just to the north of Thirty-fourth Street led entertainment entrepreneurs and other developers associated with such activities to skip over the intervening blocks just to the north of Herald Square and concentrate their efforts on the stretch of Broadway on either side of Forty-second Street and in surrounding side streets.

In her chapter in this section, Betsy Blackmar raises a number of interesting questions about real estate development in midtown after about 1910. Her argument calls into question linear thinking about the "predestined" concentration of entertainment in Times Square. She argues that a zigzagging sequence of risky decisions by theatrical producers and others distinguishes midtown development from previous real estate transactions. The development of Times Square, she argues, revolutionized the real estate market by substituting commercial prospects over the moral character as the new measure of value. Times Square thus became a threshold of modernism in the real estate market and a harbinger of much that was to follow, especially in the speculative redevelopment of other deteriorating neighborhoods.

It is this midtown area which, for convenience, we have been referring to as "Times Square." Strictly speaking, Times Square refers to the open space created by the convergence of Broadway cutting diagonally across Seventh Avenue in front of the new *Times* building that was constructed in 1905 at Forty-second Street. Once known as Longacre Square, it was not a "square" at all but an important commercial axis resembling the junction a few blocks to the south of Sixth Avenue and Broadway at Thirty-fourth Street which, after the location there of the *New York Herald*, became known as Herald Square. Both areas became important commercial districts, Herald Square, finally, for department store retailing and Times Square for entertainment.

Historically, this area around Forty-second Street has gone by many different names and its parameters have changed correspondingly. The New York theater district was called the Rialto even before it moved uptown from Union Square. In the opening decades of the century it was known simply as "Broadway," the designation that appears most often to have carried the area into song and myth. "Times Square" was the name given to the subway stop, at the insistence of the *Times*, when the subway was brought in. Few locals adopted the name, preferring "Broadway" for the stretch of Broadway between Thirty-seventh and Fifty-second streets that contained the largest concentration of theaters and related activities. Few habitués called it Times Square, preferring such labels as "The Main Stem," or for Forty-second Street itself, "The Deuce."

The extent of this territory is also in dispute. Those principally concerned with theater and vaudeville tend to limit the focus of their attention to the area that contains the largest concentrations of theaters and support institutions, from just south of Forty-second Street up Broadway through the Forties and into the Fifties. For those with more musical interests, it extended from the original Metropolitan Opera House on Thirty-ninth Street to Carnegie Hall on Fifty-seventh Street. The sporting scene, on the other hand, was located after 1925 near the new Madison Square Garden at Eighth Avenue in the block between Forty-ninth and Fiftieth streets. The music industry was more widely dispersed, but a major center after its completion in 1931 was the Brill Building at Broadway and Forty-ninth Street just to the east, with Irving Berlin's office a block to the south. Nightlife was even more widely dispersed with the largest clubs, cabarets, and speakeasies slightly to the north of the theaters in a district reminiscent of the old Tenderloin (an area of cheap and seamy bars, dives, and rooming houses in west midtown at the turn of the century). It is probably more instructive, in reading the following chapters, to visualize Times Square as a hub centered at Broadway and Forty-second Street with axes radiating in all directions than it is to try to conceive of it as a precise area.

It was the commercial dynamic of this entertainment district, meanwhile, that assured its popular outreach and its persisting challenge to propriety and to authority, as well as its seemingly unquenchable grip on our imaginations, as the chapter by Philip Furia on Irving Berlin and Tin Pan Alley and my chapter on Damon Runyon and the origins of slang illustrate. No figures demonstrate the power of this dynamic better than Irving Berlin and Damon Runyon, two brilliant entrepreneurs who tapped the linguistic resources of the area and in the course of doing so brought Broadway national and international fame.

Irving Berlin arrived on the Broadway scene just as the sheet music business was beginning to expand into a booming national industry. His career embodied almost every imaginable role in the history of Tin Pan Alley, from plugger and boomer and singing saloon waiter promoting popular songs by others to composer-lyricist, musical publisher, and theatrical producer. By 1915, according to Furia, he had invented the generic form of popular song that was to characterize the music industry for almost half a century. Berlin songs were characterized by the short line, ragged meter, and a slangy, often comic, phraseology drawn from the locality. Jerome Kern once said that Berlin *was* American music, but he was also New York. Born in Russia of Jewish parents and brought up on the Lower East Side, he had worked in saloons in Chinatown and Union Square before he moved his operations from Twenty-eighth Street up to Times Square, just as the area was booming. He soon acquired the Music Box as a theater for staging musical drama. He so thoroughly institution-alized popular music that, as Furia shows, he finally set up separate offices for handling sheet music, compositions for Broadway shows, and his Hollywood musical scores.

In 1910 Damon Runyon arrived in New York as a seasoned journalist from the West and, after his Broadway years of writing for Hearst's *American*, left for a new career of writing and producing films in Holly-wood. Runyon's years as a reporter working the area brought him in touch with the volatile linguistic world surrounding Times Square, which I describe as having become a "language funnel" for the special tongues that had developed in the area. The sporting world (especially horse racing and boxing), bootlegging, the underworld more generally, and the worlds of vaudeville, carnival, and show business had all developed rich and expressive argots by the twenties.

Journalists like Runyon, Ring Lardner, and Jack Conway of *Variety* were quick to exploit the vitality of these languages in forging new journalistic styles for themselves. In doing so they were in the vanguard of the creation of an American slang that rapidly spread through the local then to the national press; in magazines like the *Saturday Evening Post*, which published Runyon's Broadway stories; and finally, during the thirties, through national network radio and Hollywood films to the rest of the country. Walter Winchell, writing for *Vanity Fair* in 1927, included a list of slang expressions from the area and called New York "the slang capital of the world." Ten years later the list of slang expressions he included had, thanks to the work of Runyon and others, become part of a national slang that was quite generally employed. A whole cast of Broadway characters out of *Guys and Dolls* with their colorful monikers and vivid speech had found a place in some national dramatis personae. The authority challenged by his soft-hearted gangsters and gamblers was less the law than the formalities of written English and Emily Post, the same authorities challenged in Irving Berlin's lyrics. One revolution that Times

Square had helped to bring off was a revolution in vernacular speech, a revolution that a sometime habitué of the area, H. L. Mencken, had labored to track in the various editions of *The American Language*.

In her useful historical survey of theatrical activity in the area, Margaret Knapp has traced the evolution of theatrical entertainment into a large-scale national business based in, and operated out of, Times Square. She points out that by 1915 both theater and vaudeville were on course toward their peak of expansion in the twenties. Some 50 theaters were producing over 150 new shows. The full range of support institutions, such as costume, wig, and scenery makers, as well as hotels, restaurants, and cabarets, were then in place and expanding. The big, splashy musical revues produced by Florenz Ziegfeld and others had begun to make their appearance. Road companies were "touring" successful plays through "chains" of theaters across the country. Motion pictures, which were to dominate entertainment in the area after the Depression, had only begun to make their appearance.

Theater, in fact, taking its cue from the economy at large, proved to be a lucrative investment in this period. This expansive vitality was largely the result of a new breed of theatrical producer who, seeing a market opening, mobilized and organized the industry and thereby succeeded in attracting the capital necessary for expansion. Two of the following chapters in the section on theater examine industry organization. Robert Snyder's chapter discusses the role of Keith's United Booking Office in the kind of vaudeville circuitry that developed within the city itself and, more extensively, on a regional basis around the country. A subsequent chapter by Peter Davis argues that it was the adoption of modern corporate management by the Shuberts that enabled them to win out over the theatrical Syndicate, which had employed the pool as a less flexible way of accumulating venture capital.

These studies of New York theater show that the adjacent commercial culture of the city had an even more pervasive influence on the development of theatrical entertainment. The fact that American theater was unsubsidized, unlike most European national theaters, meant that success depended entirely on the volume of tickets sold. Market forces therefore encouraged an ever-widening appeal to fresh audiences. Broadway theatrical entertainment through the twenties, Knapp points out, was therefore not unlike primetime television programming today. The number of new productions expanded through the peak years of 1927–28, when 264 shows were produced. Every effort was made to entertain and satisfy this broadening audience for theater. In an earlier period, vaudeville had succeeded where legitimate theater had failed through the age-old vaudeville device of fitting acts to local audiences' tastes, as Snyder shows. Theater expanded its appeal, like vaudeville, by recourse to the "road"; but it also was forced to limit theatrical repertory to the sure thing. Theatrical fare on Broadway during the twenties therefore strikes us today as formulaic and repetitive, tailored to the moment and the need to be constantly entertaining and undemanding. Controversial and serious themes were seldom aired.

Meanwhile, what modern marketing was referring to as the tie-in turned out to be a built-in feature of the Times Square area. Theater, both formally and informally, spilled over into the surrounding blocks every night, as Lewis Erenberg indicates in his essay on Broadway nightlife. Stars of Oscar Hammerstein's shows made late-night appearances at his Roof Garden; Ziegfeld's *Midnight Frolic* included stars from his *Follies* downstairs. Later during the thirties Ziegfeld dancers performed at the large clubs run by Granlund, Billy Rose, and others. Certain hotels, restaurants, cafés, and informal hangouts were also theatricalized by the frequency with which they entertained celebrities from the stage. In other ways, too, they appear to have operated as extensions of Broadway theater. By the thirties Billy Rose, adopting marketing techniques then in use, used discounts and special arrangements with hotels and conventions in the city to fill large clubs like his Diamond Horseshoe, which could provide 700 patrons with a show and a five-course meal nightly.

The revocation of the Volstead Act and the introduction of huge dinner clubs brought many other changes in the thirties. Most striking perhaps was the rapid decline of legitimate theater, especially on the stretch of Forty-second Street that had once contained the principal theaters. No new theaters were built after 1929, and most of the existing theaters were rented out as radio studios or converted to cheap "grinder" movie houses that ran continuous showings. The movie palace and the motion picture premiere replaced the theatrical "opening" as the signature activity.

By the thirties, crowds still thronged to Times Square for entertainment, as Brooks McNamara notes in his chapter on the period. On Forty-second Street only the New Amsterdam was the scene of regular theatrical production, and four out of five theaters stood vacant. The Palace, once the capital of vaudeville, had been made into a movie theater. For a decade during the thirties, burlesque proved to be a major attraction in the area. The Minskys and others, reworking an old tradition of "naked dancing" to audiences of sporting males, struck a very different note from the sophisticated *Follies* of Ziegfeld, White, and Carroll. Outside of structured entertainment, different tastes also prevailed. Fancy restaurants and luxury hotels went into permanent decline during the Depression, replaced by cheap eateries, peep shows, taxi dance halls, penny arcades, and dime museums—a series of related changes that turned the area into a midtown version of the classic midway.

As early as 1905 there had been indications about where Times Square was heading as an entertainment center. There is no better indicator than the opening in April of that year of Fred Thompson's vast Hippodrome, which occupied an entire block between Forty-third and Forty-fourth streets along Sixth Avenue. Thompson, the architect and entertainment entrepreneur who had created the immensely successful Luna Park in Coney Island the previous year, attempted to redirect the course of show business in the area. As William Register points out in his chapter on Thompson in the section on aesthetics, he conceived of the Hippodrome as an immense machine for entertainment of "the masses," which he called (in a reference to new, large-scale retailing) "a department store in theatricals." Encompassed in one building was to be everything in the way of entertainment that the ordinary citizen could want and at prices (from 25 cents to a dollar per seat) most could afford.

At the center of this palladium of fun were to be huge spectacles like the opening "A Yankee Circus on Mars." Thompson's credentials went back to the Midway of Chicago's 1893 Columbian Exposition and included several amusement parks before the opening of Luna Park. With the Hippodrome he clearly hoped to open an entertainment beachhead in a city center, a midway as theater and a theater as midway, or, as the advance publicity put it, "a city within a city." Its amusement park lineage was apparent in everything from its blocklong electrified billboard facade to the intricate technology of the inner working of its machinery for moving staging areas. As it turned out, it was an idea ahead of its time: Thompson lost control of his creation after a mere fourteen months. The Hippodrome, nonetheless, provides a brilliant premonition of an entertainment future that was to depend increasingly upon catering to an expanding popular appetite for amusement and employing ever more striking visual and spectatorial fare in the effort to do so.

What these changes were to mean, culturally, apart from a rejection of older, elitist notions about entertainment and decorum, is one of the most interesting questions raised in the book. Clearly, something important was happening, *had* happened, to ideas of recreation and entertainment, fun and enjoyment. Pleasure and enjoyment, once conceived of as subversive, began to be more openly accepted. Older religious conceptions of recreation as rational and instructive were giving way to notions that derived from sensory pleasure and astonishment. Americans had traditionally kept delight and astonishment at a distance because of their association with childhood. But toward the end of the century adults were given furtive opportunities to experience these emotions through the eyes of children. At the circus, in the growing volume of children's literature, and in the new amusement parks, new forms of what were once thought to be childish pleasures and delights were experienced by adults. A classical instance from the new juvenile literature with this ambivalent appeal is Huck Finn's innocent astonishment at the antics of a circus clown as described by Twain. Fred Thompson, as the impresario of amusement parks, appears to have embodied this quality himself, a point underscored by Register, who characterizes the Hippodrome as "New York's gigantic toy" and reminds us that Thompson was considered by contemporaries to be a Peter Pan, "the child who never grew up," a description that helps to explain his successes as well as his failures.

There is probably no better benchmark of such a shift in values than the extraordinary success of L. Frank Baum's *Wizard of Oz*, which became a long-running Broadway show soon after its publication in 1900. That a book by a former department store window display designer could become such a theatrical success is testament to the widespread acceptance of a new commercial aesthetic of color and light and supplies important evidence of its provenance. One whole section has accordingly been devoted to an effort to analyze the aesthetic values of these new forms of entertainment and display. As William Leach points out in his introduction to this section, the sudden appearance of color, glass, and light in commercial display worked an arresting revolution that not all Americans welcomed. Thorstein Veblen, for example, saw in all this the usurpation of religious inconography for mercenary ends. Transformed by new technologies in illumination, Times Square became the "white light district," and the "Great White Way." It is estimated that over one million Americans daily raised their eyes to take in the half-block-long sign of the Dodge Brothers mounted on top of the Strand Theatre in the center of the Square. Register's analysis of the Hippodrome provides an interesting insight into the rapidly changing aesthetics of outdoor entertainment.

Indoors as well as out-of-doors, the art of display underwent a dramatic change between 1900 and the end of the twenties. Another part of the process through which new technologies in illumination and a fresh interest in color were refined into a new commercial aesthetic is illustrated in the career of Vienna-born Joseph Urban, as recounted by Gregory Gilmartin.

It would be hard to think of two figures within the world of commercial culture farther apart than Fred Thompson and Joseph Urban. Thompson, a manufacturer's son from the Midwest, was self-taught while Urban, from the Hapsburg court and the personal patronage of Franz Joseph, was trained at the Viennese Academy of Art. Thompson's milieu was the incandescent midway, Urban's the cooler medium of the musical stage and the sophisticated urban drawing room. The first sought to astonish and delight, the second sought the gratification expressed by the archly lifted eyebrow. Together, they define the outer limits of the new commercial aesthetic. The influence they exerted, moreover, illustrates a point made by Gilmartin about an evolving commercial aesthetic. Commercial art, he points out, has difficulty innovating from within like other art since market pressures tend toward homogeneity and what Thorstein Veblen has called marginal differentiation. Significant changes in a commercial aesthetic therefore are obtained only through a process of cannibalizing ideas and forms from the world of art and architecture outside the commercial sphere. For Thompson the area to raid was the rich store of design implicit in the forms of the new industrial technology; for Urban it was the cooler vision of European modernism with its utopian *Jungstil* dream of redesigning everyday life.

Urban, trained as an architect/designer in the spirit of craft, had acquired a varied background in design and especially in stage and production design by the time he arrived in New York in 1915 and became associated with Florenz Ziegfeld and the *Follies*. For the next seventeen years, until Ziegfeld's death in 1932, he functioned as the "eye" of the *Follies*, designing everything from costumes and sets to the interior and exterior of theaters. Beyond this work, he served as the personal architect and interior designer for Ziegfeld. He designed houses, nightclubs, and hotels for Ziegfeld and his friends in and around Palm Beach and in New York. His success lay in his ability to bring to society the same sense of sophisticated theater and drama he had introduced to the *Follies*. The linear, stylized aesthetic that Urban brought from the fringes of European modernism to American commercial design revolutionized musical theater on Broadway. For a generation, Americans appeared unwilling to carry their newly acquired taste for modern design beyond the musical stage and its cabaret environs. The next generation of European-trained designers, such as Raymond Loewy, succeeded in carrying this same aesthetic revolution into a much wider vector of modern consumer life. By such a reckoning Broadway becomes the American threshold of modernism in architecture and design a generation before the arrival of the more authentic Bauhaus structures in the 1940s.

Something resembling a blind taste test must have brought Urban from the supervision of the Imperial Jubilee of 1908 and the patronage of Count Carl Esterhazy, for whom he had built a hunting lodge in 1904, to Florenz Ziegfeld and his circle of wealthy friends in New York and Palm Beach, to whom he was to devote the balance of his career. Urban's move and comfortable relocation in the latter milieu was a tacit recognition of the analogous power exercised in America by the leading figures in the new world of commercial entertainment.

Peter Buckley, in his introduction to the final section of the book, "Boundaries of Respectability," has called attention to the political implications of the efforts after the turn of the century to redefine the boundaries of propriety and respectability. In these efforts the interests of those who dominated commercial entertainment were a formidable if often contested factor.

No one would have disputed the fact that by World War I these boundaries were in disarray. Nightlife of the kind that had been developing in Times Square was an obvious factor in the breakdown of the social conventions that had governed the behavior of middle-class Americans in cities like New York, as Lewis Erenberg points out in his chapter earlier in the volume. There is a solid basis for the association of theater, night, and vice that had governed earlier standards of behavior. Timothy Gilfoyle's essay on prostitution in New York shows the close proximity of theater life and brothel life throughout the nineteenth century and suggests how coordinated the two activities were in the move uptown from the Bowery and Union Square to their adjacent location side by side in Times Square and in the Tenderloin directly to the west, which had become the center of brothel life by the turn of the century.

By the end of the nineteenth century prostitution had a recognized place in the life of the city and operated, in Buckley's description, as part of a "semi-public economy of vice and amusement." The brothel world was a gender-specific world of sporting male patrons employing the services of prostitutes. During much of the century it operated openly, if discreetly, in the rows of brownstones lining the side streets of the area, largely tolerated by those city officials and police who shared in its profitability. Income from vice and gambling was, in fact, a major source of funding for political machines. A succession of changes placed strains on this older state of affairs. The appearance of large numbers of women in public—first in the new department stores and at matinee performances of the theater and, in the years immediately before World War I, escorted at night in the lobster palaces, cabarets, and other places where the new craze in ballroom dancing could be enjoyed—challenged convention in a way that was bound to bring resistance.

This resistance came initially not from governmental authority, either state or local, but from what has been characterized as "a private state": voluntary organizations and committees of citizens who took it upon themselves to bypass existing authorities and exercise power. During the nineteenth century the power of the private state was often exercised directly and was immediately influential. Gilfoyle gives an analysis of such groups as the Society for the Suppression of Vice (SSV) and the Society for the Prevention of Cruelty to Children (SPCC). After the turn of the century the private state surrendered its responsibilities to enhanced public authority, state and local, with organizations such as the State Liquor Authority (SLA) rather than the SSV superintending the moral character of the area. Committees such as the powerful and long-lived Committee of Fourteen, whose tenure lasted until 1932, became powerful agents of reform. Peter Buckley sees strong links in the rationale and objectives of these groups to the objectives of Progressivism in the country at large. Their agenda was largely one of making the city safe for the new commercial culture and making commercial entertainment safe for the city.

In the struggle between vice and propriety, major entrepreneurs of commercial entertainment like Ziegfeld appear to have played a mediating role. Their undertakings thrived on probing the boundaries of what was acceptable, packaging and repackaging sexuality in forms that expanded its acceptance as well as its market. European sophistication of the kind embodied in the very conception of the *Follies* and fortified by the stylized elegance of Urban's designs was one of many ways of reaching into the population for an enlarged nightlife clientele.

The effect on the area of this regulation by the private state was not a suppression of sexuality but a shift from participation to what Laurence Senelick, in the last chapter on boundaries, has called "spectation," from the flesh-peddling of prostitution to various forms of refined and not-so-refined voyeurism implicit in commercial entertainment and other forms of nightlife. Even prostitution, which seemed to have disappeared by World War I, soon resurfaced as part of a large and increasingly complex sexual underground in the city.

How such a sexual underground is organized and functions in the city, the politics of sexuality, so to speak, is the subject of George Chauncey's chapter on the ways in which gay men, a criminalized minority, created social space for themselves in the Times Square area after World War I. Chauncey discusses the many-layered world of homosexuality in the area, the social and geographical divisions within the gay world, the places and ways of meeting, communicating, coding, and decoding. He describes the particular forms of entertainment, like the later concerts of Judy Garland and Bea Lillie, which drew gay men and created a sense of collective responsiveness. He also analyzes the highly organized street culture that governed male hustling and other forms of sexual exchange in public. The degree to which an underground can exist almost invisibly becomes clear from his analysis, as in his example of gay clients occupying one side of the Astor Hotel bar unbeknownst to most of the people sitting around them.

By the 1930s, surveillance in places selling liquor was regularly exercised by the State Liquor Authority on the premise that gays, as "undesirables," were a disorderly element. Chauncey also clarifies how much the responsibility for constraint rested with those who managed commercial entertainment. Market forces acted in both directions with gay clients, acting against their "obvious" behavior in peak hours and acceptingly, even invitingly, in slack times when their patronage added to profitability, as it did after midnight in the local Automat or in Childs.

By the end of the thirties the ground had been laid for the civic revulsion that underlies current efforts to restructure the area. An old elitist neighborhood built by the Astors had gone through a series of transformations that had carried it from silk hat brothels discreetly serviced by carriages and cabs through a period as a glittering center of legitimate theater and vaudeville through its location as the center of a gaudy carnival of popular show business and a greater and greater array of commercialized sexual entertainment. Burlesque, for example, arrived late and spread rapidly after the Depression had taken its toll on theater, as one way of filling empty houses. The "rough trade" of male hustlers along Forty-second Street, memorialized in John Schlesinger's *Midnight Cowboy*, was another fallout from the Depression when unemployed men from the West took to hustling as a way of surviving hard times. As Chauncey makes clear, the layered and complex social organization of the Times Square world was capable of accommodating and providing protective coloration to a varied population, from inside and outside the area, with different stakes in its economic and entertainment life.

Beyond such changes, the invention of Times Square points to a striking transformation, one might call it a revolution, in the spatial arrangement of cities. Historically, the center of the city had always been either City Hall or the central market, the forum or the agora. Times Square, located in the transportation hub of New York, was neither. The *New York Times* had hoped in 1905 that its new tower would preside over the square as a civic presence, a kind of journalistic *hôtel de ville* or *rathaus* rather than as a center of misrule of the kind that eventually developed.

The modern commercial city as represented by New York had developed an unanticipated inclination to locate its entertainment and amusement industries where they were most accessible. In the full rein they gave to urban society's appetites and fantasies, these commercial activities challenged and defied the norms of behavior that prevailed elsewhere in the city. Cities had always contained districts that served analogous needs, but these districts did not occupy the city and media center. Their influence on the general population, moreover, was muted by the discretion and reticence that surrounded them. The modern city was unique in its convergence upon such commerce in recreation at its very core. It was also unique in giving the site of such commerce center stage in a national cultural marketplace.

The historical model provided by New York of a great metropolis radiating such cultural signals from its inner core required a timing and a unique configuration of institutions that cannot be reimposed upon the city today. Changes in theater and in other popular forms of entertainment have delivered a fatal blow to such central entertainment districts. Wigmakers and costume and scenery production firms have fled the high rentals in the area along with the other support institutions that once made up the complex overlay of theatrical activities. The newspapers, so vital to creating the legendary Broadway, no longer play their former role. Hollywood studios, which once provided a visual and musical conduit to Broadway for the rest of the nation, have long since turned their attention elsewhere. Tin Pan Alley, along with other changes, has lost its heart to Nashville. Gone, too, are most of the structures and visual effects that once gave Times Square its distinctive appearance. The trophy for brilliant nighttime illumination has passed to Tokyo's Ginza district.

Because the historical Times Square was a creature of its time, no imaginable redevelopment of the area could bring back what was once there. Given the high value of midtown real estate, it was inevitable that developers would pick up the slack created by deteriorating nightlife and the encroachment of cheap sexual entertainment that had moved in after the heyday of theater and prime moviegoing. Efforts on the part of developers, which purport to restore the past or even a feeling of the past, have led to farcical results—office buildings displaying neon ribbons reminiscent of the "Great White Way," as Ada Louise Huxtable in her Afterword, "Re-Inventing Times Square," so clearly shows. The campaniled *Times* tower, which once provided a visual center to the Square, has been deconstructed into a piece of "junk architecture." The bulldozer revolution that swept away the large hotels and the one- and two-story surrounding structures with their lacework of massive signs has ushered in a generation of dull new hotels and unimaginative skyscraper towers whose sheer bulk has forever altered the scale, the daytime exposure to sunlight, and the overall feeling of the area.

Times Square, Huxtable points out, was never the site of great architecture. An Italian campanile tower for the *Times*, mansard roofs on the two large hotels, here and there emblems of French renaissance design, and ornate, riotously eclectic, historicist interiors provided an architectonic background for those who cared to peer behind the glitzy bauble. In her eloquent tribute to five towers rising several blocks north of the Square, Huxtable has located still another and final irony in the history of the area. Times Square in redevelopment has finally found architectural distinction not in theaters, hotels, or other structures associated with its vernacular entertainment past but rather in sleek, modern office towers. These towers, presumably soon to be occupied by a substantial portion of the city's legal profession and brokerage houses that have decamped from Wall Street, herald a new and different future for the area. *Plus ça change. . .*

Broadway, gashing the city like a lava-stream,
Crowned with shower of sparks, as a beaten fire,
Blazing theatres, brazen restaurants, smell of talc,
Movie mansions, hock-shops, imitation diamonds,
Chorus girls making rounds of the booking-agencies
Music-factories blatting from twenty-five pianos
And all the hectic world of paint and shirt-front. . .

From John Reed, *America 1918*

PROLOGUE

TIMES SQUARE: SECULARIZATION AND SACRALIZATION

Jean-Christophe Agnew

I F TIMES SQUARE no longer serves as the Crossroads of the World, it can still provide a place where minds may meet, as this volume shows so well. The Square is a singularly fascinating place, and these chapters deepen our sense of that singularity and its fascination. Indeed, whatever else the chapters may be said to be about, they are about fascination; in one way or another, they all take up the question of the Square as an attraction, as a point of intense interest upon which Americans have banked for a century. A hundred years is a respectable run for any show, so it is no surprise that the story of the Square's wonders can fill a volume. In fact, if there is a surprise in all of this, it is the time it has taken historians to shed any light on a world whose own lights have at one time or another held so many of them all in thrall.

It is all the more surprising that historians should come to the Square so late when one considers how much important and exciting historical work has been done on urban commercial culture in the last decade. Theater, vaudeville, cabaret, nickelodeons, movie palaces, amusement parks, saloons—all have come under the appreciative scrutiny of a new generation of social and cultural historians. Drawing on previously unexamined sources, these scholars have pointed to the presence in America of a vital, socially heterogeneous world of urban leisure and entertainment lasting from the mid-nineteenth to the mid-twentieth century.[1] In that world, their argument runs, Americans, especially immigrant Americans, improvised and patronized entertainments whose forms anticipated mass culture but whose scale conformed more closely to neighborhood enterprise. Bounded yet free, exploitative yet liberating, familiar yet exotic, the new pleasure zones of the American city offered their customers the scenery, props, and idiom with which to translate the potentially explosive tensions of class, race, gender, and ethnicity into energy and that energy,

2

in turn, into spectacle. Theater, Margaret Knapp tells us, was "the television of its day." Vaudeville, Robert Snyder adds, knit local audiences together "into a modern audience of national proportions."

In sum, these and other studies have taught us that urban commercial entertainments offered privileged spaces wherein immigrants and their children might acquire cultural citizenship on terms far more generous and hospitable than those laid down by church and state. Furthermore, these historians suggest, it was on those terms and not those of church and state that most urban Americans endured a Depression, fought a war, and embraced the mass-mediated modernity of the late twentieth century. When television first entered into American homes in the late forties and fifties, its producers looked back for models not to Main Street but to Broadway.[2] But in thus memorializing the Great White Way, television was also writing Times Square's obituary, or so it seemed.

Given this compelling narrative of the rise and fall of a distinctively American popular culture in the city, one may well ask why it has taken the historians of commercial culture so long to look at Broadway—and Times Square—as a phenomenon in itself? This volume begins to answer that question, and it does so, I think, by virtue of the singularity of its subject and the multiplicity of its vision. By confining the story of commercial culture's Golden Age within the dramatic unities of action, time, and, most importantly, place, we throw that new narrative of American commercial culture and its attractions into sharper relief. We see our own storytelling differently when we subject it to the bright lights of Forty-second Street. For this reason, the two principal questions I raise will be less historical than historiographical.

First, and in keeping with the secular spirit of so many of the other chapters in this volume, I would ask: What has been the payoff— intellectual, spiritual, political—of our own interest in the history of commercial culture? I raise that question partly in response to the stark and somewhat defamiliarizing juxtaposition of saints and sinners in the articles by Richard Fox, Laurence Senelick, and others. Oscillating between the upbeat homiletics of liberal clergymen and the weary wisdom of pimps and prostitutes, these particular essays offer views of commercial culture that stand apart from the image we've most recently come to accept of the historic Times Square and its analogues—an image, that is, of a vibrant sociocultural mix of unabashedly earthy and poignantly utopian fantasies. In place of that intriguing and inclusive image, we are given the polarities of piety and prurience, of clergy and impresarios, of gimlet-eyed reformers and starry-eyed performers—each using the other for inspiration.

To see these two poles of feeling as subliminally yoked together is scarcely new, of course, and we do not need the structuralism of a Mary Douglas or the poststructuralism of a Michel Foucault to appreciate the dialectic of disgust and desire that has energized the discipline of amusement, not to mention the amusement of discipline—in Times Square as elsewhere. But if there is nothing particularly new about this dialectic, how do we then square its seeming universality with the particular history of New York City's premier pleasure zone? Conversely, what happens to the timebound story of commercial culture's golden age when the story is set within a frame bounded by Thirty-eighth and Fifty-seventh streets, Sixth and Eighth avenues, and the years 1890 and 1990? That is the second question the essays have raised for me.

Though Richard Fox's discussion of liberal Protestantism treats figures and a period at some distance from this particular frame, he nonetheless contextualizes and complicates our received notions of the religious response to amusement in a way that makes it difficult to take avid Comstockery as its representative face. What is more, he argues that the liberals' gradual accommodation to the city and its pleasures should be understood not as a desperate remedy for their own felt displacement from the urban landscape but rather as a measure of their confidence in the powers of cultural colonization. Clearly, Protestant leaders had to respond to the new facts of Times Square, he writes. "But it is no less true," he adds, "that Times Square was itself a response . . . to powerful religious forces, which helped call it into being."[3]

That is as strong and, on the face of it, as counterintuitive a proposition as we might imagine for the historical origins of Times Square's commercial culture. But even without evidence of real Arthur Dimmesdales pouring off the city's subways and buses to sample the pleasures of the Square at the turn of the century, we may still recognize that the cultural interplay between the theater and the liberal clergy was as intense as the opposition between the theater and the fundamentalist ministers. Perhaps because Fox keeps to the writings of his clergymen, their own embrace of theatricality—its forms and energies—seems a bit pallid and fainthearted. True, we can look to Harold Frederick's best-selling novel of 1896, *The Damnation of Theron Ware*, and find a vindication of the staginess of American revivalism. And we could, if we wished, trace such staginess as far back as the evangelical minister Charles Grandison Finney, not to mention the Grand Itinerant of eighteenth century America, George Whitefield. But could we imagine a more theatrical figure than the liberal clergyman Henry Ward Beecher? It was Beecher, after all, who had Brooklyn's Plymouth Church redesigned as a theater-in-the-round, with himself as the cynosure. "I want them to surround me," he said of his congregants, "so that they will come up on every side, and behind me, so that I shall be in the center of the crowd, and have the people surge all about me."[4] It need only be added that such designs aimed to produce roughly the same kind of structured intimacy that Lewis Erenberg has written of in relation to the design of the Times Square cabarets, and with the same cult of personality as its result.[5] "In Mr. Beecher," one British observer wryly noted, "the Stage suffered as great a loss as the Pulpit enjoyed a gain. He would have made a revolution in stage history."[6]

Of course it is Fox's argument that liberal clergymen like Beecher did effectively occasion a revolution in stage history, if only by their willingness to apply stage values to pastoral practice. During this period churches grew in tandem with theaters, enlarged and ornamented their structures, paid their performers, and serviced increasingly anonymous crowds of congregants, a good proportion of whom were themselves tourists on any given Sunday. The temptation toward spectacle must have felt irresistible. I, for one, find Washington Gladden's inspirational image of three thousand proper Cleveland women gathered at the People's Tabernacle to watch the methodical disassembly of five "whole carcasses of animals," a curiously Foucauldean moment of intense, almost parodic domesticity: the opening scene, perhaps, for a study of nineteenth century cuisine entitled *Discipline and Garnish*.

But to allude to Henry Ward Beecher and Washington Gladden is to move only part of the way toward Fox's hypothesis that religious forces, "among other things," helped call into being such distinctively urban institutions as Times Square. To flesh that proposition out requires a more deliberate movement from the church into the Square itself. As it happens, one figure who made that step—though he never quite reached the Square—was James Steele MacKaye, whom William Register discusses briefly in his essay. Born into the social and intellectual elite of antebellum New York, MacKaye ignored his businessman-father's wishes in order to become an actor, director, playwright, and stage designer. Yet this act of defiance concealed a deeper loyalty to his father's social and moral values, for MacKaye looked upon the theater in much the same way that Washington Gladden and his colleagues looked upon amusements in general, which is to say as an empire to colonize and a vehicle for that colonization. "Our faith in prayers is waning," MacKaye once wrote a friend, "our faith in performances is strengthening."[7] Backed by his father's grudging and sporadic subsidies, his wife's forbearance, and a seemingly boundless reserve of energy, MacKaye bent his efforts to the discipline of amusement.

MacKaye wrote, or rather rewrote, plays, invented stage machinery, and in 1879 entered into a partnership with George and Marshal Mallory to renovate and reopen the Madison Square Theatre (at Fifth Avenue and Twenty-fourth Street) as a small repertory company. He hired Daniel Frohman as his business manager and designed and installed the first double-elevated stage, indirect lighting, and an elaborate system of ventilation. This venture marked the beginning of a pattern of grander and grander designs, culminating in MacKaye's campaign to finance and construct his Spectatorium at the Chicago Exposition of 1893—one of the prototypes (as Register notes) of the "Great Toy" that Frederick Thompson would build in Times Square a decade later. A huge, hippodrome-style theater with twenty-five telescoping stages, the Spectatorium was built to perform the spectacle of America's discovery for an audience of some 8,000. MacKaye's aim, as he put it, was nothing less than "the education and inspiration of the masses, while affording them at moderate prices, an entertainment as irresistibly fascinating as it was ennobling."[8] This was cultural colonization without apology and, as it turned out, without money as well. Initially financed by Chicago's leading business-men, the steel skeleton of the Spectatorium began to rise outside the Columbian fairgrounds, only to halt midway under the accumulated financial pressures of the Panic of 1893.

Though the colonizing ambitions of Steele MacKaye's project aligned it with the imperial self-image of the Chicago Exposition's organizers, they did not necessarily set his project apart from other popular spectacles mounted outside the Exposition fence. For example, Imre and Bolossy Kiralfy's "Columbus and the Discovery of America," a touring spectacle, likewise promised "Bewildering scenes of dazzling splendor, hundreds of radiant damsels in flashing costumes, with myriads of vari-colored Lan-terns."[9] And as if these thousand points of life were not enough, there were the spectacles to be seen in vaudeville palaces and the ingenious stage machinery installed in structures like that of Samuel French's American Theatre at Eighth Avenue and Forty-second Street.

Less than a year after the Chicago World's Fair closed its gates, Steele MacKaye died, broke. Although he had authored one of the longest-running and most profitable dramas of the late nineteenth century, *Hazel Kirke*, the play never bore his name while it ran, nor put a penny in his pockets while he lived—all because MacKaye had unwittingly signed over all his rights to the play to his obliging partners, the Mallory brothers. His oversight was pardonable, if regrettable, for George Mallory was at the time the pastor of the Episcopal church at Madison Square. Two years before he met the Mallories, MacKaye had written of his dream of a time when the church would grasp "the hand of the theatre in hearty and honest fellowship."[10] And grasp it the church had, without God perhaps, but not without greed.

What seemed a gross betrayal to Steele MacKaye would scarcely have raised the eyebrows of the sporting types and sex workers whose collective story Timothy Gilfoyle and Laurence Senelick trace with such care in their chapters. These are bracing accounts of the world of Times Square, but bracing in much the same way that a sharp tap on the skull can be to someone who has fallen asleep during the sermon. Gilfoyle's and

Senelick's unblinking treatment of the varied yet tirelessly repetitive transactions of the Square's sexual subcultures, William Leach's account of urban cultural brokerage, Peter Davis's analysis of the theater syndicates, and Brooks McNamara's treatment of the institutional support system of the Square—all may be said to parallel Betsy Blackmar's and David Hammack's equally even-toned considerations of Manhattan real estate. In almost all of these chapters, we find the same "infrastructural" determinacy of capital balanced by the same "superstructural" indeterminacy of cultural value; the same single-minded drive for profit challenged by the same mercurial and impulsive voices of demand. And it is to this chorus of customers that the many historians have been most attentive. As a result, the "curious silence" about commercial districts that Betsy Blackmar detects in the "early twentieth century planning literature" finds its match in the curious silence on economic value typical of many current histories of commercial culture. What historians like Gilfoyle and Senelick offer, then, is an answer from the point of view of sexual labor to Blackmar's call to explore the social processes that translate cultural value into profit. Again and again, we see this alchemical transmutation performed as one after another erotic or merely exotic fantasy is made to walk the streets of Times Square, a walk that seems to accelerate over time.

Of course from the vantage point of the Forty-second Street sidewalk, most "cultural value" does begin to look *merely* superstructural, and the more nostalgic reminiscences about Times Square begin to meld imperceptibly into the more calculated effusions of the Mallory brothers over at Madison Square. And as with the Mallories, Gilfoyle's and Senelick's studies of sexual work strengthen one's impression of the impregnable confidence (as opposed, say, to the divided or repressed sensibility) of Richard Fox's amusement-minded clergymen. Indeed, what is perhaps most striking about the liberal ministers' changing attitudes toward entertainment is the overweening sense of power and responsibility their call for cultural colonization presumed. These spokesmen for liberal Protestantism appear to have treated the social control of desire with roughly the same regard for class prerogative that the sporting elites treated its social indulgence.

Not surprisingly, from the days of vaudeville and cabaret to the days of the movie palace and video parlor, Times Square regularly changed its face in order to flatter the class authority, real or imagined, of its customers. Here, the impresarios and performers spoke as with one voice: "We consider our audiences first," Frederick Thompson declared at the turn of the century. "The customers are boss," Jimmy Durante echoed, "and you have to please them, no matter how it hurts." "You lived by the reaction of the audience," George Jessel recalled. Maybe so, but this was not to say that the effort, much less the "hurt," of a life thus lived was not occasionally recouped by the performers' delight in having put something

7

"over" as well as "on" for the customers. So Billy Rose backhandedly acknowledged when he assured customers that at his establishments there would be no tolerance for the "Broadway password: Never give a sucker an even break." Tourists, audiences, johns—all may have come to the Square in search of something "real" or "organic" or "experiential," but, as these chapters remind us, that reality, that organicism, and that experience were invariably staged.

To be sure, there were always customers who approached this world with the ingenuousness of a Theron Ware, but it would be naïveté on our part to ignore the convention of disingenuousness framing the theatricality of the theater district: the convention, that is, of the consumer's willing suspension of disbelief. When "cultural value" is transformed into profit along the Great White Way, or the Deuce, what is bought is both the fantasy and the *right* to the fantasy, and it is over against the customer's (actual or potential) claim upon that right that the self-mocking and self-ironizing gestures of the entertainment industry have both to assert and disguise themselves. Amusement may indeed require a collaborative or collusive relation between performer and customer, but what makes it collusive is precisely the double invitation the customer accepts: first, to use the price of his admission to conceal from himself the extent of the work and risk he must contribute; and second, to use the offered fantasy to conceal from himself the price of admission. In other words, sex-work, and in some measure all commercial cultural work, must both appeal to and deny the power of purchase.

It is that same power, purchasing power, which we hear asserted in the alternating middle-class instructions to raise or lower the skirts of Times Square throughout its long history, just as it is that same power—this time in the form of real estate interests—that we see claimed in the alternating efforts to enlarge or reduce the physical boundaries of the Square itself. There is nothing archaic about this claim: Restatements of it can easily be found in almost any edition of the *New York Times*, which not surprisingly looks down upon its square with an especially proprietary air. But there is nothing particularly new about it either, for we can find equally vehement expressions of the customer's right in the century-old polemics of social reformers. Take, for example, the progressive economist Simon Patten, who once wrote, "We must make of our streets an Institution that shall express, direct and gratify men's thwarted necessities for vital excitement as definitely as the church has been used to express his longings for spiritual excitement." A Methodist seminarian turned prophet of abundance and a man marked (according to his biographer) by a "lifelong distaste for sexuality," Patten wrote those words in a little book of 1909 called *Product and Climax*.[11] Even then many Americans could see— whether from the pulpit, the proscenium, or the planning department—

that urban entertainment offered a new set of cultural compass points for twentieth century Americanism: a new plane of action and a new horizon of desire.

Simon Patten's *Product and Climax* has another interest for me, however, for it was that book and indeed those particular words that the late Warren Susman used in his eloquent defense of America's new urban, commercial culture, a defense gathered together in a collection of articles he revealingly labeled *Culture as History*. There, in one of his lesser noticed essays, "The City in American History," Susman offered a revision of Frederick Turner's famous frontier thesis in a manner that speaks to (where it does not actually underwrite) the current inquiry into nature and meaning of twentieth century commercial culture. Beginning with "the relatively unnoted" announcement of the 1950 census that the epoch of the bounded city—as distinguished from the more amorphous "urbanized" or "metropolitan" area—had ended, Susman launched into an impassioned and characteristically astute debunking of the myth of intellectual antiurbanism in America.[12] By his lights earlier American writers and critics had rarely singled out the city for their contempt and certainly not in sufficient numbers to constitute a tradition. By thus depriving contemporary critics of modernity of a convenient intellectual genealogy in which they might insert themselves, Susman, like Arthur Schlesinger before him, no doubt hoped to reclaim a genealogy for his own, conspicuously urban, ethnic reading of twentieth century culture. To accomplish this he boldly resurrected one of the classic figures of antimodern communitarianism, namely, John Winthrop's image of the City on a Hill, but only to use it as a mythic charter for a much more dynamic and democratic ideal of abundance, variety, and vitality *within* the bounds of the American city.

Here Susman did something more than merely push the terminal point of the frontier thesis beyond 1890 to the mid-twentieth century or transplant its setting from outside to inside the modern city. He also redefined the character of Turner's environmentalism by shifting from a social and material determination to an emphatically cultural one—not the city as such but the city as imagined, or more precisely, the city as a convergence point of discrete and collective fantasies. Throughout the essay Susman's vision remained as fixed upon the City on a Hill as Perry Miller's had once been, but with the important stipulation that this vanishing point, this ever-receding horizon of social expectation, be understood as the property of millions of urban immigrants and not just of a few genteel intellectuals. For him, I suspect, the notion of the American city as an object of collective fascination—a locus of material desire, social aspiration, and utopian longing—was the basis for his even deeper conviction that culture could indeed *be* history. That urban commercial culture (and eventually mass culture) came down to a set of attractions, then, was exactly the point.

As a response to the Turnerism, not to say pastoralism, implicit in the postwar critique of mass society, status anxiety, and the lonely crowd, Susman's essay was a brilliant, heartfelt, and timely rejoinder. "There is something more important," he argued, "than a hunger for an idyllic rural past."[13] His city on a hill was always, in some measure, other-directed, so it is not surprising to see how his essays have inspired the historical inquiry into the spectacle of urban commercial culture that has, at long last, landed us in Times Square. Obviously, it is more satisfying to explore a guidebook to the Square, or even to Disneyland, when we are assured in advance that the terrain there charted is not a cultural wasteland. Warren Susman assured us that it was not.

To the contrary, he intimated that it was about as close to the City of God as we were likely to get in this world. In the closing pages of his essay on the city, Susman quoted liberally from Kenneth and Ethel Miller's study of the New York Mission Society.

> For the people are the city, the shape of the physical assemblage of brick and mortar is the outward expression of the city's material success, the symbols of civilized living. Within, invisible, but all-vital, is the spirit and the soul of the real city, its treasury of people. The city is a sacrament, instituted of God.[14]

If Warren Susman did not openly endorse this sentiment, he did not qualify it either, save perhaps to place it in a tradition of American thought "at least from 1830 to 1930 [that] built in large part on a structure that assumed the growth of the ideal of a great city."[15] In that tradition of thought, I would submit, we may place *Culture as History*, and, with it, the inquiry into urban commercial culture its essays helped bring into being; for the century to which Susman referred—1830 to 1930—almost exactly delineates the boundaries of the urban commercial culture that the new generation of historians has rescued from the condescension of previous interpreters.

It is that mission of rescue—in which every historian is always in some way implicated—that led me to pose my first question: What is the payoff, crudely speaking, of our historical interest in urban commercial culture? And it is the preservationist language in which that mission has so often been couched that leads me to borrow and, in a sense, to invert Lawrence Levine's recently developed notion of cultural sacralization.[16] For if it can be said, as Levine and others do, that the nineteenth century bourgeoisie canonized high culture, then it could also be said that twentieth century historians have now canonized popular culture. Indeed, I would suggest that we have begun to reproduce in our own work the same gradual, outward displacement of the "sacred" into the world of amusement that Richard Fox traces in the late nineteenth and early twentieth century career of liberal Protestantism. Commercial culture has become for many of us what Emile Durkheim meant by the "social church."

Naturally, this sacralization of commercial culture is a descriptive, not a prescriptive, affair. It does not announce itself in the exultant tones of the New York Mission Society, but it is intermittently and obliquely present nonetheless. Even in the various essays collected in this volume, we can find frequent references to theaters as "cathedrals," to Times Square as a "mecca," to sexuality as "pneuma," and to entertainments as "redemptive." Granted that these terms are often deployed ironically or in tacit paraphrase of the self-advertisements of commercial culture, nonetheless this very ambiguity of inflection suggests a deeper uncertainty over the play between spiritual longing and commodity fetishism at the heart of those processes transforming cultural value into profit.

That uncertainty is visible, for example, in the historian's temptation to see the relation of the American city (and its culture) to the hinterland in much the same fashion in which Walter Benjamin once described the aura of an original work of art in relation to its mechanical reproductions. As Robert Snyder, Lewis Erenberg, Peter Davis, and Brooks McNamara show, tourists, or "pilgrims," repeatedly journeyed to Times Square's vaudeville palaces, cabarets, and theaters in order to see the authentic, original, or "showcase" entertainments of which the road shows, recordings, and films were but copies. But it is not always easy to tell whether that aura, that attraction, sprang out of the Square's presentations of the Other or out of others' representations of it. Aware that nostalgia is but one of the many impulses that the Square has stood ready to service, historians have struggled to find a way to describe the experiential meaning of the place. "I want to know what consumers [got] out of a particular amusement," Lewis Erenberg writes, "why they put so much energy into it." In other words, he wants to write the history of the "culture of abundance" in the manner that Susman demanded—on its own terms. But I'm not exactly sure how we can manage that task, for as this volume shows so well, those terms have always been negotiable.

So where does this leave us? The study of urban commercial culture (and, by extension, of Times Square's place in it) began as a skeptical response to the airy dismissal by the acolytes of modernism and high culture of all popular culture—original and copy—as so many vulgar anticipations or forms of mass consumer culture. Now it promises to end not so much by redeeming that mass culture as by enlarging the historical "moment" of its local forerunner: extending the life of commercial culture, that is, from 1830 to 1930, and perhaps even to 1950. Whatever the particular genre or form of entertainment a historian takes up, his or her

11

story usually concludes in the deepening shadow of mass-cultural incorporation, domestication, sentimentalization, and exploitation.[17] Even Laurence Senelick's hardboiled history of Times Square's sexual marketplace closes with the undeniably dispiriting image of "original" sexual acts replaced by their mass-manufactured copies in the ultimate discipline of amusement: the image, that is, of meek, silent, joyless, white-collar masturbators working in mechanical rhythm to the jump-cut schedule of an average 30-second commercial: the pleasure principle and the performance principle merged.

All of this returns me to my second question: How to reconcile the seemingly universal sacred and secular longings to which Susman and Senelick allude with the particular history of Times Square? Here, it seems to me, one of the main virtues of this volume's unflinching gaze upon a single and indeed singular *place* over time is the light it throws on the sacred narratives we as historians may be bringing to our subject; for it is far easier to tell a story of rise and fall or of efflorescence and eclipse when one's subject is a vanished genre, technology, or milieu. But the longevity of Longacre Square defies any effort to assimilate it to a favored narrative of progress or decay; the *New York Times* may have renamed it, but it has yet (fully) to remake it.

If we look at any particular chapter, then, we see that the peak moment in the Square's history hangs, or so it seems, on which kind of entertainment the author has chosen. But having read *all* the chapters, we realize that the Square has outlived each of the entertainments that were once thought to be the indispensable wellsprings of its existence. And being thus confined to the "specialized commercial neighborhood" of the Square—as Brooks McNamara so plainly puts it—we are constrained to recognize the forces that our own symbolic and sacred investments in commercial culture have repressed; namely, the holy trinity of political economy—land, labor, and capital. That trinity has not just underwritten the amusements of Times Square; it has survived them, supplying ready substitutes the moment any particular attraction faltered. One suspects that our own inclination to nostalgia draws strength from the fact that art has never lasted much longer than life in the Deuce.

Lest it seem that I, as an historian, stand somehow outside this tendency to romanticize, if not sacralize, the story of commercial culture in America, I should add that though I have not researched or written much, if anything, about such culture between 1830 and 1930, I have certainly taught it. And I have taught it exactly in the mode and in the moods I have described. Moreover, my investment in the bell-curve narrative of vernacular culture is not just intellectual, but, if you will, "lived." I discovered as much some years ago when attending, of all things, the annual convention of the American Historical Association. The meeting was held in the new and as yet uncompleted Marriott Marquis Hotel in Times Square. The hotel is itself a nasty piece of business, an altogether sinister tower that squats over the street sheathed in materials that quietly breathe the words "maximum security" to passersby. I was told that the hotel had been designed in accordance with earnest promises made to the city to keep the structure open to the bustling, Bakhtinian streetlife of the entertainment district. But as far as I could see, the formidable combination of mirrors and darkened glass and of floor-upon-floor of yawning, undifferentiated, and impersonal, pseudopublic space seemed more deliberately arranged to sift out all but the most doggedly determined street people before they reached the eighth floor, where the postmodern, climate-controlled micro-world of the hotel (atrium and all) actually began.

As if this coy architectural strategy were not bad faith enough, there was the added touch of bland, institutional camp in the name cards that had been hurriedly tacked to the doors of the convention meeting rooms—O'Neill, Williams, Belasco, Shubert, and so on. An apt commemoration, the owners probably thought, to the theatrical rubble and memories upon which the hotel had been built. I remember, then, sitting in one of the Marquis's overheated and overcrowded meeting rooms, half-listening to another convention paper and half-musing as to the ways in which this suddenly odd and inexplicable academic ritual might be disrupted. As my fantasy developed, it took the shape of an exceptionally resolute street person bursting into the room, lurching toward the podium, and demanding to know, more or less, where was the speaker's evidence.

On whose terms, we might ask, was I consuming the hotel's attractions? Was I drawing on the "negative vitality" of the Square in order to act out, imaginatively and vicariously, my own alienation effects? Was I registering the defamiliarizing consequences of the different subcultures of the Square itself? Or was I merely responding to the suggestibility of the room itself, so thoughtfully named for Berthold Brecht?

I

STRUCTURAL CHANGES

INTRODUCTORY ESSAY

Eric Lampard

> Apollo astronauts returning from their moonflight were greeted by a Times Square sign flashing "Welcome Back to Earth, Home of Coca-Cola."
>
> *The Chronicle of Coca-Cola Since 1886*

ONTRIBUTORS to this section—Structural Changes—have shown that, in one way or another, the inherited regional varieties of American life and livelihood were being changed in the direction of a so-called consumer culture well before the end of the nineteenth century. Even before the severe Depression of 1893–97, the trend was set *via* the marketplace toward a mass consumption of more uniform semiperishable and semidurable goods, which climaxed in the consumer durable goods revolution of the 1920s. At that time the consumer culture seems to have been firmly, if not finally, established as "The American Way."

A new cultural climate had emerged in the larger cities from the 1880s, according to Neil Harris. It involved a new work and leisure discipline, as Richard Fox points out, and by the early twentieth century, according to Betsy Blackmar, had given rise to a new style of cosmopolitan living of which midtown Manhattan became the symbol, and in which Times Square by the 1920s would be, as David Hammack suggests, the largest, brightest stage for the presentation and sale of commercial culture.

Old New York City-Manhattan was, according to Harris, itself already imaged and packaged by the railroad-hotel-entertainment complex as a place which "a new American social type"—tourist *genus urbanus*—would want to visit on business or pleasure. The same economic and political forces that shaped the nation had, Hammack tells us, brought the market for commercial culture to New York City. But it was the confluence of these agencies with local economic and political interests which determined the location of both long-distance and citywide public transport facilities in midtown Manhattan—not least important was the "Broadway subway" of the banker August Belmont's Independent Rapid Transit Co.—which after 1904 finally centered the market for commercial culture in Times Square.

In that year Adolph Ochs and Mayor George McClellan had agreed upon a new name for William H. Vanderbilt's old American Horse Exchange—"The Longacre"—an item of "news" which most New York City newspapers deemed unfit to print. But the real inventor of the new Rialto was Oscar Hammerstein I. Almost a decade before Belmont's subway or Ochs's newspaper tower disrupted the local scene, Hammerstein had "crossed the line" of Forty-second Street into the dismal and, at night, dangerous Longacre, to construct "the grandest amusement temple in the world," the Olympia. When the Olympia opened after many delays on November 25, 1895, it occupied an entire block on the east side of Broadway between Forty-fourth and Forty-fifth streets, and contained three theaters and an exotic roof garden.

Hammerstein was bankrupt by 1898, but in two years he had built two more theaters at Broadway and Forty-second Street, linked by the fabulous glass-domed Paradise Roof Garden with ponds, swans, and a rock grotto populated by monkeys—for the delectation of drinkers, diners, and dancers. New York City had long been, at least in its own ample mirror, "the crossroads of the world" and, since electric street lighting, Broadway was "The Great White Way."[1] In the years between 1904 and the United States entry into the Great War in April 1917, however, Times Square would be promoted by its developers and denizens alike as "the crossroads within the crossroads": the entertainment and amusement hub of Greater New York City, itself only six years old in 1904 and a product of many of the same business and political forces as had squared the triangle in the same year.

There is about all this a certain "midtown Manhattanite's view" of the United States and its business economy around the turn of the century. Insofar as New York City stood preeminent in the interactive "system of cities," the real powerhouse was not midtown and Longacre/Times Square but Lower Manhattan and "Wall Street," where in varying manifestations it had always been and still is (or what remains of it after the reckless 1980s asset inflation).

Over the last three decades of the nineteenth century the growing involvement of private bankers and their syndicates in issues of securities had turned the Wall Street financial district into a kind of corporate headquarters for the nation. The number of listings on the New York Stock Exchange had doubled to more than one thousand by 1900. Wall Street had enjoyed its first "million share day" in 1886 and scored a "three million share day" by 1901. Since the 1880s the number of head offices of large mercantile and manufacturing firms with assets of more than a million dollars each had risen to 298 in 1895—a period of secular price decline—a greater number than the next four largest metropolitan centers combined. By 1900, in the middle of the first great merger wave, the twelfth U.S. Census showed that New York City was the headquarters location for 70 of the largest industrial combinations (45 controlling more than six plants across the country) compared with only 54 in the eight other metropolitan centers with two or more headquarters. Certainly, Lower Manhattan's investment bankers were behind many of the holding companies and outright mergers across the United States.

With their mounting stake in business integration and stability after the Depression of the 1890s, it is not surprising that some Wall Street houses recognized an opportunity for underwriting the capacity "to sell." Midtown rather than downtown was where the powerhouse situated its expanding commercial colony for advertising in print media and business publications, public relations, and from where, in the mid-1920s, it was to organize the commercial hijacking of radio broadcasting: a symbiosis of commercial advertising and commercial entertainment prophetically juxtaposed in the glittering theater marquees and extravagant electrical billboards of Times Square.[2] The first clarion call to the "great Buy-and-Buy" was sounded across the nation from midtown Manhattan.

Advertising and commercial entertainments had lengthy histories—mostly independent of each other—long before "multiservice" agencies or theatrical syndicates were formed a decade or so before the invention of Times Square. Theater (legitimate, musical, and illegitimate), together with its associated night life, had likewise been ambling up Broadway to beyond Greeley Square decades before Oscar Hammerstein "crossed the line" in 1895 or the new subway from the East Side made its end run along Forty-second Street in 1904. Midtown *north* of Forty-second Street, particularly on the West Side, was still on the periphery of commercial "improvement," while new areas for desirable residence had recently been capitalized *north* of West Sixty-first Street after the penetration of the Sixth–Ninth Avenue "EL" in the early 1880s.

Thus, the coming together of advertising and entertainment among the throngs of people in midtown in the vicinity of Times Square turned out to be an historic conjuncture that could hardly have taken place elsewhere at any earlier time. Their capitalized confluence would play a decisive role in determining the character and content of American consumer culture in its first abortive flowering during the 1920s and again—with mounting input from Washington, D.C., and Los Angeles—over the third quarter of the twentieth century when it reached its full efflorescence. Its marketed "image," albeit in the California style, would go on to change the world: finally laying the specter that had haunted Europe and, more recently, America and its "free world," since 1848.

During the nineteenth century's third quarter, large-scale standardization in certain lines of production was creating the need for more standardized "consumption." As Andrew Carnegie was among the first to remark: the condition for cheap manufactures was "running full." By the close of the century this shift toward standardization of products had rendered traditional notions of retail patronage by discriminating customers almost a contradiction in terms, except perhaps among metropolitan elites who characteristically favored imported "quality wares." Yet despite this change, a standard dictionary definition of the word "consume" as late as 1894 emphasized the destructive, burning, squandering, using-up connotations of the verb, although it allowed that the word had taken on a secondary use in political economy where a "consumer" might be "either productive or unproductive," the latter "using up some exchangeable value in serving his own wants." Persons who used up such values producing other, presumably enhanced, values were seemingly the ones who made the world go round, but why they bothered is not clear. Consumption was still "destructive," although political economists recognized that clothing and food could be "used up. . .in use or useful expenditure. . .by the people." Expenditure on the part of the user seems critical since it was never enough on the distributive side to move goods to places where potential "consumers" might be thought to reside. Unless the products were sold with equal dispatch and efficacy at retail, inventories would pile up at great expense in warehouses, orders would be cancelled, and the great engine of production run down. Such was indeed the effect of the short-period business or "inventory" cycle that plagued the process of industrialization; the phenomenon of producers alternately overshooting and undershooting prevailing levels of effective demand.

This recurring "boom and bust" was becoming insupportable for many large businesses by the close of the nineteenth century. Their operations were based on increasing ratios of *fixed* to variable costs, all in a cruelly competitive market environment. Their enlarged capital stakes in plant and equipment had, in many instances, compelled them to buy into vital sources of raw materials, transport, and fuel, lest any of the latter fall into the hands of more aggressive competitors or rogue speculators. Such commitments on the production side, however, only heightened a firm's sense of vulnerability on the marketing side, a vulnerability to its competitors and no less to its own internal imperative to "run full." Such marketing structures could ultimately result in steadier, occasionally greater, "economies of scale" than mass production itself, but forward investments into marketing meanwhile might merely raise the fixed cost factor still further, leaving the business not much more secure than before. Combined with more forceful and effective *sales* competition rather than price reductions, however, the enlarged enterprises might hope not only to meet their pressing obligations to bondholders and private bankers, but even to pay out regular dividends to stockholders in a more stable and, hence, "manageable" market environment.

Aggressive selling was often the best form of business defense.

Large-scale productive enterprises had to take over the channels for marketing their goods or risk others moving in ahead of them. Manufacturers, for example, felt the need to capitalize long chains of "independent" small-scale jobbers, dealers, and other wholesalers on whom, with few exceptions, they had hitherto depended to get their products to market. This defensive capitalization of small intermediaries—operating for the most part on small margins—into large-scale distributive organizations enabled the latter to regulate the flow of their more standardized and packaged goods toward retail destinations.

If nineteenth century mass production had required "running full," it also necessitated "selling fast"—at predictable, but unprecedented, twentieth century rates. The ensuing capitalization of consumption, moreover, demanded rapid social and moral engineering—unprecedented, even in cities—during the long, drawn-out adaptation of society to industrialization. The glad tidings of consuming as a way of life had to be evangelized nationwide much as the market for spiritual goods had been propagated over the antebellum decades by Methodists, Mormons, spiritualists, and other enthusiasts with fervor, theatricality, and an unaccustomed concern for the needs of women. Even the old testament of economics—the dismal science of original scarcity and abstinence—was hieratically extended, with no compromise of allocative resolve or rigor, to reveal in the fullness of time an adjunct palmy side of abundance and pay-later prodigality. The new testament of consumer indulgence was mediated *urbi et orbi* by a new group of brokers who, according to William Leach, promoted themselves as designers, consultants, and missionaries of "the desire for goods." They were the harbingers of the coming order of coast-to-coast consumption of which Times Square was the most brilliant symbol.

"Live From New York!" made the "ether advertising" of network radio a public license to print money after 1926–27.[3] Except for the CBS Radio Theaters 1 and 2 on West Forty-fifth Street near Eighth Avenue in the 1930s, neither NBC nor CBS ever moved into Times Square. They eventually located their network headquarters farther uptown, from Forty-eighth through Fifty-second streets, between Sixth and Madison avenues. After the 1929 Crash, the proposed site of "a magnificent new opera house" was converted into the huge 12-acre Rockefeller Center development project of 1930, "the largest construction project in the world's history." Over a quarter of its enclosed space was to be allocated as the offices, studios, and theaters of three or four major entertainment corporations, affiliates, and their like. Subsequently, *Time-Life* and Associated Press "news" brokers were admitted to the precincts of Radio City's towering cathedral. A few blocks east, the clustering effect of CBS Radio's presence made "Madison Avenue" a collective trope for the power and influence of advertising agencies and other mass-selling media.

But the stratagem of selling fast by artfully stimulating desire was still

20

a one (supply)-sided panacea: it was psychology not economics. To convert the latent energy of awakened desire into effective demand—getting a targeted consumer to put his hard-earned cash where the pitchman's mouth was—turned out to be quite a different and more difficult order of business. It was never enough to use early radio—as Julius Klein, Ph.D. (Harvard), of the U.S Commerce Department, was wont—to remind millions of hyphenated and not-yet hyphenated Americans of their country's "morbidly unhappy" Puritan past, of its utilitarian ugliness, of a people "starved" for beauty and conveniences, which was giving way before a fun-loving people who pursued their happiness to the point of "Persian luxury" in an "everyday world of beauty," courtesy of American business, as Leach points out. What if American consumers, now duly massing, still did not earn enough to clear the market at "the rate of stock turn" decreed by the accountants of corporate fixed cost? Did Dr. Klein propose that the same American business should pay still higher wages? Meanwhile, if most members of the public were to buy more of this, many of them, a majority, would have to buy less of that. There could be no rapid upsurge in flows of goods to consumers out of current production, *ceteris paribus*, without corresponding declines in business investment and/or government spending. To be sure, desire was necessary, but demand consummated in the deal was the only procreant urge sufficient to satisfy the growing volume producers of "big" and "little ticket" items.

The banker Paul Mazur of Lehman Brothers, who before October 1929 brokered the creation of Federated Department Stores, was himself consumed by fears of "glut." In moving from merchandising to banking early on in his career, his mission was to further the expansion of consumer business; a new frontier for capitalization by some of New York's smaller investment houses. To keep the business of department stores, retail chains, or new movie palaces expanding—if only to cover interest and taxes—the selling had to increase. Every enticement of fashion, style, design, and service had to be exploited. But members of the public were ordinarily spending most of their disposable incomes on current consumption. As a simplistic socialist pamphlet, obtainable for five cents at the Rand bookstore, put it boldly: "People cannot pay a decent price for the goods and services" on offer. And, despite the shocking source, Samuel Gompers and Henry Ford would have agreed!

The revelation of built-in obsolescence as an "ally of business" was vouchsafed to Paul Mazur about the same time as to Alfred P. Sloane in Detroit. It was surely worth a try. For Sloane the idea, like any fashion change, was "to create demand for a new value" and through the "vast used-car market" to beat Henry Ford at his own game, without reducing *new* car prices. Annual retooling, especially in the automobile industry, proved so costly, however, it almost blunted the point of mass production, until it was reduced to cosmetic matters of styling and appearance.

Meeting such costs was beyond the capacity of most surviving small manufacturers, many of whom either became insolvent or were merged into the oligopolistic structure of a market in which the price leader was able to *raise* prices for new cars by passing the remodeling costs on to those who could afford to buy. But was it the answer? Automobile advertising budgets meanwhile rose from $3.5 million in 1921 to $9.27 million in 1927—"one of the heaviest users of magazine space"— but by the latter year the buying public was no longer able to absorb new cars (or, by implication, the cheaper hand-me-downs) at the rate that the industry needed to run them off the assembly lines.

Mazur was similarly unable to get from "needs to desires," to the acceleration of sales necessary to sustain the costs of capitalization. Although the capital-forming impetus in a dozen or more major manufacturing categories appears, in retrospect, to have been slackening by 1926, he went on blissfully recommending further mergers and consolidations which were supposed to "rationalize" business, and which enabled the likes of Lehman Brothers or Goldman Sachs to continue receiving comfortable brokers' commissions. A few months before his Federated Stores coup, Mazur seemed to have overcome his fears of "glut" when he published his paean to profit making, *American Prosperity* (1928). His book celebrated the sportsmanlike motives of businessmen in the great game of marketplace. There was so much more to it, Mazur insisted, than just money making! To a great degree Americans "play the game of business for the sake of play and they measure their effort—like other sportsmen—by their success." Business had created American prosperity almost as a by-product of the sporting life: America merely kept score in dollars. Businessmen had done it, he disclosed, by "forceful advertising and selling methods," which had "imposed upon each family the buying standards of its neighbors." As for retailing automobiles, electric refrigerators, radios, or appliances—the new "consumer durables," as accountants would later call them—this feat had been accomplished by the "sugar-coated pills of partial payments."

It is not clear that Mazur understood much at the time about the magic pill he prescribed. Advertising and selling were his forte, not how retail customers paid their bills. Besides, many current transactions in those simple times allowed 90 days to settlement. Like commercial bankers and economists, most private bankers knew little or nothing about consumer credit except that they disapproved of it. "Charging it" was immoral; people should not live beyond their incomes: it was akin to stealing. There was a rich lore of the impoverishment of the honest farmer by the country storekeeper, the racking of the humble workman at the company store, and the misery inflicted on those caught in the loan shark's razor teeth. Even in the early automobile showrooms, purchases on "the never, never," as they were called in Britain, were still deplored, although widely practiced.

Such arrangements had come too slowly and hesitantly during the 1920s to transubstantiate the awakened desires of "consumer culture" into easy credit sales, especially for low- and moderate-income families whose credit training and "worthiness" could not easily be certified, especially by banks.[4] Yet by 1928–29 the banks were thought by Wall Street pundits to have eliminated the costly business cycle that drove enterprises into receivership and rendered so many potential consumers jobless. "With the assistance of the Federal Reserve System," concluded Mazur, "we may expect freedom from the unwarranted and annoying financial panics of the past"—a prediction which, even by standards of economics, must rank among the most famous last words.

The Wall Street Crash of October 1929 marks the end of the beginning. The nascent "consumer culture" appeared to wither in the agricultural hunger of England, Arkansas, and the breadlines and municipal bankruptcy of Detroit, Michigan. Yet the notion that the Federal Reserve System had cured the business cycle was one that appealed to most financiers and monetarists in the 1920s. The severe liquidity crisis that had followed the Crash of 1907, when many banks stopped payment on their business depositors' accounts, had finally led to the creation of a more flexible system at once formally centralized in Washington, D.C., under a coordinating Federal Reserve Board and regionalized in a dozen reserve districts, each managed by its own reserve bank and financed by its member bank, representing local and regional productive interests.

The Federal Reserve Act of December 1913 had been intended to break the hold of New York City's legendary "money trust" on the rest of the country, at the same time as it put in place an "elastic" money supply, no longer curbed by the formal restrictions imposed by the old national banking legislation, a relic from the Civil War years. Under the new system, each district bank would act *inter alia* as "lender of last resort to its members, and credit would henceforth be available in amounts appropriate for financing *real* commodity production and commerce, as opposed to fueling "unproductive speculation" in already existing properties. The emphasis was clearly on "productive industry" and new production, although "the real bills doctrine" did recognize the historic role of banks in facilitating commerce in such products. Thus, the nineteenth century had finally solved its "problem" of business fluctuations. What is no less clear, from the standpoint of "consumer culture," is that the Federal Reserve was wholly geared toward "producer culture," since the latter by experience and definition accounted for "consumption."

The economic history of the nineteenth century United States has largely been written from the supply side: the "growth" of the nation's productive capacity. The eye of the historian, like that of the classic entrepreneur, is on commodity production: agriculture, mining, lumber, manufactures, and even construction when it comes to the building of canals and railroads. Entrepreneurs had displaced the eighteenth century merchants as the movers and shakers of material progress, the artisan gave way to "industry," commerce to business. By the end of the War of 1812, raw cotton from the South became the nation's export base. Cotton textiles and light manufactures furnished an opening for water and, later, steam-powered factory development in the Northeast; and steamboats on Western rivers expedited the spread of grain farming across the Old Northwest, although the New York and Ohio canals had pulled the West away from the South by the 1840s—even before the steam railroad reinforced the bond.

Comparatively little attention has been given to consumption; i.e., how and where people ultimately "used up" "exchangeable values in serving [their] own wants." Even contemporary accounts rarely went beyond the wholesale channels. Supply thus created its own demand through payments for labor and property services, and the profits of entrepreneurs, out of which income aggregate would also come most of the savings "plowed back" into investment in further expansion. Subsequent expenditures by private enterprises *and* households would virtually clear the market. Not surprisingly, the earliest national income and product estimates for the 1840s have confirmed the amplitude of private consumption—a "people of plenty"—in the very seedtime of "the producer culture."

These classical certainties—most elegantly expressed in J. B. Say's "law of markets"—acknowledged that all producers (even slaves) required food, clothing, shelter, some services and amenities for themselves and their dependents. Such needs were converted to demand *via* the market-place, especially in the burgeoning towns and more fertile countrysides, whose residents were no longer independent or as self- sufficient as they, and their less specialized village ancestors, may once have imagined themselves to be. Households bought whatever assortment of available goods they could afford in public (or periodic) markets and accessible stores (a very different-looking "market basket" from that purchased in the brave new consumer world of the 1920s). Other services and amenities, if any, were "delivered" in some fashion outside the allocative mechanisms of the market by voluntary associations, charitable corporations, and church missions from their own collective resources or, in default, by the scant provision of local magistrates out of their meager property tax revenue. No "free lunches" could yet be charged by men of business to the taxpayers' account. During the nineteenth century's second quarter, therefore, the consumption end appears to have taken care of itself. Compared with the real business of raising output and exporting staple commodities, most other business, especially retail and custom business, was taken for granted. Except for highly competitive, under-capitalized middlemen, final distribution at retail was an undertaking of no more than local capitalist concern. Needless to add, the resource requirements for "industrialization" did not normally impose any noteworthy sacrifice of consumption on the public, beyond the inexorable rationing by price that enforced nature's "law of supply and demand."

The prepossession with production—commonly found in all industrializing countries—amounted in the United States to a cultural bias. Nevertheless, the concentrations of population and "exchange power" were no longer confined to three or four "great towns" along the Atlantic seaboard and a few interior enclaves draining downriver to New Orleans. Agglomeration was almost literally taking place along the main-traveled water and rail routes across the continent *via* an integral array of different-sized centers which, for financial, informational, and most other communications and control purposes, was still anchored to "the great metropolis" of New York. Indeed, the preferential rate agreement in 1866 between the newly consolidated Western Union Telegraph Co. and the New York (Associated) Press consortium not only confirmed that city's preeminence in "the circulation of information" but gave its newsbrokers the power—with a little help from their friends at Reuters—"to shape the picture of the world delivered to editors and their readers" in the restored republic's provinces. Despite some perfunctory competition in the 1880s from (and eventual merger in 1893 with) the first United Press newswire, no effective supplement to the AP's characteristic "New York news touch" emerged—even while briefly managed out of Chicago—before Scripps-McCrae's new UP and Hearst's INS in 1907 and 1909, respectively. Transactions within and among this evolving system of metropolitan regions—centering on Chicago, Philadelphia, Boston, St. Louis, Cincinnati, Pittsburgh, Kansas City, and San Francisco—had not only reduced space/time frictions from weeks to days, annihilating any remaining protections of distance, but had thereby extended the *potential* market for goods and services unnecessary or unknown in the smaller, more localized, exchanges of the midcentury.[5]

During the century's protean last quarter, for all the inertial motion of industrialism, the future was already rushing into competition with the present. The very accomplishments and agencies of the expansive, market-driven, "producer culture" would—as noted at the outset—compel reorganization of "the consumption end" along the same highly capitalized, integrative lines as had already industrialized so much of transport and production. Customers were out there—as A. T. Stewart's or J. A. Wanamaker's "new kind of [department] store" or A. M. Ward's "diversified" advertising mail-order businesses had shown since the 1860s and 70s—but henceforth volume *producers* would also have to cultivate and fashion *consumption* according to much the same canons of business as had been prompting competitive enlargement of production, with its mounting incubus of "fixed costs." Since, despite the abundance, a "consumer culture" did not exist, one had to be invented under the same auspices, to further similar ends, as the industrial form of "producer culture" itself.

By retailing standards of the day, the metropolitan department stores and centralized mail-order businesses—even more than early "chains" such as Gilman's Great Atlantic Tea Co. (from 1 to 11 stores, 1862–70) or F. W. Woolworth (1 to 10, 1879–86)—were highly capitalized enterprises already pushing volume sales. As "big business" interlopers, they were much resented as unfair competition for the smaller, more specialized, retailers in big cities and country towns alike. Compared with developments from the 1880s, however, these early retailing "giants" were only beginning to explore the possibilities of "mass merchandising." They were soon outclassed when large volume producers of staple items, like sugar, beer, lead paint, distilled liquors, and salt moved *forward* into distribution. Aggressive Chicago meatpackers and Milwaukee and St. Louis brewers absorbed lesser rivals and built up their own costly interregional networks of cold storage facilities, railroad refrigerator cars, and large-city warehouses. Others took a more economical course, perhaps, by tightening up existing wholesale channels for their semiperishable, brand-named, packaged goods—Diamond Matches, Borden's Condensed Milk, or such novelties as Kodak Cameras and exotically labeled packs of W. Duke & Sons' machine-made cigarettes (1885). These producers closely monitored the rates of their products' flows to final retail outlets and themselves undertook the massive advertising and promotional campaigns necessary to affect consumer choices and heighten the selling enthusiasm of increasingly adjunct retail merchants.

The reputation of the advertising business in the first light of the consumer era was no better than that of its principal stock in trade for the previous forty years—patent medicines. Otherwise, most "agencies" (as they chose to style themselves) were still largely involved in placing scores of short-running notices on behalf of local retailers, direct sellers of dry goods or clothing, books and printed cards, cheap jewelry, tableware and napery, nursery stock, household hardware, and (curiously) a wide variety of schools and colleges. It is not surprising that the advent of potentially large-volume "clients" (as they were dubbed after 1900) coincided with the further extension of large-scale production/distribution or with efforts by leading "professional" agencies—Rowell (Boston/New York), Ayer (Philadelphia), Carlton & Smith (New York), or Lord & Thomas (Chicago)—to clean up their puffing act. The large distributors of consumer staples and novelties were compelled by the logic of *competitive* expansion, almost without regard to mode of marketing, to push the rates of sale at retail. The brand name, trademark (federally protected after 1905), package recognition, the slogan, were often potent techniques for enlarging a market and ensuring repeat sales coast to coast. Ivory Soap, "99⁴⁴/₁₀₀ per cent. pure,"

1885; H:O Hornby's Oatmeal, ". . .you can obtain power," 1891; Fairy Soap, "Have you a little fairy in your home?," 1891; Prudential's "Rock of Gibraltar," 1896; and the incomparable "Uneeda Biscuit," 1899; were but the earliest among many to proliferate in the American cultural environment.[6]

Present at the creation, so to speak, was one destined by Mammon and modern merchandising to become the most universal beverage since the darkness was upon the face of the watery deep. Between 1886 and 1888 Dr. John S. Pemberton, a pharmacist, recommended his "new and popular soda fountain drink" as "Delicious and Refreshing," but only on a few occasions within the narrow confines of the *Atlanta Journal*'s circulation. On May 1, 1889, that paper revealed the sale of Coca-Cola to Asa Candler & Co.—already the exclusive owner of the Great Tooth-Wash "Delecta-lave"—for $2,300. Three years later the Candlers formed a provincial Georgia corporation with a capital stock of $100,000, and apparently backed "Coke" over "Delectalave," the better to serve the gums of a parched world. Within five years Candler's promotional budget was ten times the original purchase price of 1889, equal to the amount that George Eastman in Rochester, N.Y., had spent in the latter year to kindle customer interest in his Kodak. In the crisis year 1893 Royal Baking Powder put half a million dollars directly into newspaper ads. In the same year, the recently formed American Newspaper Publishers Association offered a 15 percent discount to advertisers on all puffs placed through agencies to cut their members' heavy clerical costs, maintain rate structures, and meet competition from the "new" magazine medium.

The circulations of general magazines had soared since the mid-1880s, when Cyrus H. Curtis of Philadelphia first sought a wider distribution for his *Ladies Home Journal* (1883). Popular "weeklies" and "monthlies" (*Munsey's Magazine*, 1889, and *McClure's*, 1893) disseminated the metropolitan "way of life" and its consumer iconography into every provincial town and hamlet in competition with the enticements offered by local newspapers and direct mail advertisers (the latter reinforced after 1893 by the single most powerful sales instrument in U.S. history, the decidedly unmetropolitan Sears Roebuck *Catalogue*). The greatly enhanced visual appeal of uncluttered magazine ads—even before the regular "full page" layout (*c.* 1906) or half-tone color processes (*c.* 1910)—had in turn led to greater emphasis on more pithy and persuasive written copy to drive the pitch home. So great was the impact of the "new" magazine medium (in which the J. Walter Thompson agency of New York had specialized) that by 1896 N. W. Ayer & Son and several other leading firms moved more decisively into the field. In 1903 Ayer opened its New York branch office—connected by private long-distance wire to Philadelphia—in order to maintain closer relations with more promising and demanding "clients."

The growth and urbanization of output and incomes, along with

27

population, were necessary sinews of a consumer culture. But the conversion of wary customers into ardent consumers, and their subsequent cultivation by producers, were alike the special office of the metropolitan agencies and their print media. Outlays on advertising in all media doubled in real terms during the 1880s and, partly as a consequence of the magazine explosion, rose by 50 percent again over the ensuing decade despite the severe Depression after 1893. By 1900 the *Ladies Home Journal* had 850,000 subscribers, while *Munsey's* exceeded 650,000. From 1890 through 1905 aggregate circulation of *monthly* magazines and periodicals increased by 256 percent to 64 millions, compared with a *daily* newspaper increment of 161 percent to 21 millions. U.S. population increased by less than a third over the same span, although its urban sector had risen by more than half to 42 percent of the whole.

The general magazine was the last great innovative medium before the commercialization of radio broadcasting in the later 1920s. Such other salients as Carlton & Kissam's streetcar advertising empire, which reached from New York to 54 other cities (9,000 cars) by 1905, or the increasingly spectacular electrical billboard displays in Times Square and other great crossroads a decade later, could not compare with either of these extensive print or sound media in terms of "billings" potential, no matter how great the impact of their presence on the urban scene.

There was little by way of direct selling evidence to show for the vast dollar outlays on advertising—as reported by the *Printers' Ink* series for all media—either before 1900' or after. From the 1870s, increases were enormous in the absolute flow of goods and services to consumers as well as other components of Net National Product (NNP)—there were so many more potential consumers with higher average incomes and somewhat greater amounts of leisure time as well. Real average annual expenditures per capita by advertisers meanwhile increased at roughly two-and-a-half times the average annual rate of real consumer flows per capita ($1929), with the latter holding at around 85 percent of NNP per capita through 1900. Rates of consumer flows and NNP per capita retard somewhat (as does consumer advertising) over the second decade before rebounding after the war at increased velocities, especially 1922-29. Only after 1920 did per capita consumer flows proceed at a perceptibly faster rate than NNP per capita (3 or 4 percentage points net shift), while the unprecedented surge in real per capita outlays on advertising certainly affected the *composition* of consumer purchases, even if they did little for their magnitude. Given the increases in real average personal incomes over time as a consequence of industrialization, however, even the changing "market basket"—from food and other perishables and semidurable goods towards consumer durable goods *and* services—of consumables may simply have reflected the operation of one or more of Ernst Engel's "Laws of Consumption" concerning observed regularities between income changes and household expenditure patterns.[7]

Clearly, advertising was a costly, although highly acceptable, form of *non-price* competition among available goods and services rather than a potent stimulus to aggregate consumption (over business or public spending). Notwithstanding the "consumer durable goods revolution" much advertised in history and economics textbooks, of greater moment in *reshaping* early twentieth century consumer spending is the category of consumer *services*, which forms a consistently rising share of all consumer spending after 1900. It surpasses even the proportional weight of *perishables* before 1920 (40 percent), and it is only briefly surpassed in *rate* of increase by the "new" *durables*, although not in magnitude (10.8 percent durables to 41.4 percent *services*) during the short-lived "New Era," 1922–29.

Entertainment, amusement, and recreational services spending—a special interest of contributors to this volume—comprised but a segment of this unsung "consumer services revolution." Nevertheless, were nonbusiness spending on transportation, hotel, restaurant, and other tourist services added to outlays on entertainment, amusement, and other recreational activities, the aggregate would be very large indeed over the early decades of this century. It sufficed to justify the capitalization by bankers and others of both the provision of amusements and diversions and their relentless self-advertisement; for example, by the movie industry, which itself never became a successful medium for other advertising (unless, for better and for worse, the two-dimensional "American Way," Hollywood style).[8] Entertainment, amusement, and recreational services in certain instances, moreover, may have directly stimulated choices of collateral retail goods purchases; e.g., phonograph disks, musical instruments, sheet music, sporting goods, and the like, from early in the century. Such buying impulses would, in any case, have already been imparted to a small public at least by enthusiastic amateur and voluntary involvements countrywide as well as by exemplary professional or commercial variants emanating from the metropolitan centers.

Spending on plays, operas, and concerts climbed steadily across the country, even as they lost audience share, to crest around 1927. The moving picture box office, however, had surpassed that of older theatrical entertainments by World War I and continued to expand through the introduction (1927) of "talkies"—and the deepening Depression—in 1930. Somewhat surprisingly, spending on spectator sports did not catch up with theatrical and musical entertainments before 1933 when the latter were shrinking fast (not to recover even their current dollar gross until late in World War II).

Insofar as more than 40 percent of spending on newspapers, magazines, books, maps, and sheet music (including funny papers, comics, and scandal sheets) since 1909 has been classified by a Twentieth Century Fund Survey as *entertainment* rather than *educational* expenditure, the confluence of selling and "the passing show" in print media may have prefigured the physical convergence of advertising and show biz in Times Square. The reporting of theatrical, musical, sports, and other celebrity doings in such media—as well as by the collateral advertising they purveyed—may represent the symbiotic linkage over an extended period of entertainment, diversions, and selling importunity well before the advent of radio commercials as a potentially intrusive advertising tool. The first challenging jingle, "Have You Tried Wheaties?" was placed by General Mills on the "Jack Armstrong" radio show just prior to the 1929 "Crash."[9] Commercial radio did not have to invent show biz, since it already existed. But radio broadcasting in the United States depended on show biz as no other medium or mode of selling since diversionary fairground maneuvers to hawk some life-enhancing compound or balm to an audience of nineteenth century rustic producers.

Certainly, advertising had come a long way since James Gordon Bennett's "fixed rate" penny-press puffs or P. T. Barnum's first spectacular "ballyhoo" promotions in the late 1830s. But if businessmen were to undertake the "forceful selling and advertising" necessary to keep running full in 1928 without conjuring up the nemesis of "glut," was advertising up to the job? Advertising was to help remove money from people's pockets but it did not put it there unless you were a producer or an advertising agent! The credit-creating capacity of the Federal Reserve likewise was not designed to finance consumers. Earnest Elmo Calkins produced his *Business the Civilizer* in 1928 as a vigorous counterblast to such "carping" criticisms of advertising and consumption as Stuart Chase's *Tragedy of Waste*, and to trumpet the Emersonian virtues of "selfish, huckstering trade." Although he had to concede that "about everything is now sold on the deferred payment plan," Calkins nevertheless devoted only two short sentences to "installment selling"—Paul Mazur's "sugar-coated pill"— and he clearly did not understand the reluctance of bankers to "finance consumption" on grounds of cost and risk, as well as of "dubious morality." As late as 1938, however, Roger Babson, an upstanding economic writer, greatly esteemed as a prophet of the 1929 Crash, was widely praised in financial circles for his trenchant exposure of *The Folly of Installment Buying*.

Yet, in the 1920s some others had gone beyond a stock market Crash to proclaim the limits of advertising and the certain consequence of a serious Depression—when "business" might find itself "without a buyer." One such Jeremiah was Waddill Catchings, a president of Goldman, Sachs, who had chaired the finance committee of Warner Brothers, and described himself as "a capitalist." From 1925 through 1928, in successive articles and pamphlets, Catchings and his associate William Trufant Foster, a former president of Reed College, had gone to the crux of an impending crisis: the mass of would-be consumers simply *lacked* the means in income or credit to continue purchasing durables and other goods *at the rates* at which manufacturers were compelled to produce and sell them. "Industry does not disburse to consumers—as wages, interest, dividends, rent, and the rest—enough money," they argued, "to buy its products." Thus "industry has resorted more and more to the device of handing them the goods, to be paid for out of future incomes."[10] Most bankers, however, continued to oppose capitalized consumption in the interwar years, missed out almost entirely on its application to automobile retailing, and contributed little or nothing to the flowering of "the consumer culture" thereafter before the prosperous 1950s.

The strange career of consumer credit—keystone of the financial arch spanning twin piers of producer and consumer cultures—lay altogether outside the smiling pharisaical world of bankers. It was conjured in the interest of selling from social depths lower even than those of the hucksters and shlockmeisters who banged out the first radio commercials in dim offices and studios from Tin Pan Alley to Times Square. Consumer credit came from a dark and despised demimonde of chattel mortgagees, note shavers, pawnbrokers, loan sharks, and other usurers.

Commercial bankers knew little about events unfolding in the barely legitimate nether precincts of money lending. They were too preoccupied with their own problems after "the Panic of '07," solutions to which resulted in the Federal Reserve System in December 1913. No more than a handful among them—such as the lawyer-banker Clarence Hodson, who founded the Beneficial Loan Society in Newark, N.J. in 1914—had any notion that low finance was on the rise, that *personal loans* to Tom and Dick, if not Henrietta, would soon be "big business," or that credit charge plates and store cards would be issued even to creditworthy ladies by 1915. The advent of mass-produced consumer durables during the century's second decade turned luxury into necessity and heightened the urgency of selling.

The names of the founding fathers of personal loan and sales finance enterprises should surely be added to a Consumer Culture's Hall of Fame along with John A. Wanamaker, Frank W. Woolworth, Thomas A. Edison, Richard W. Sears, and Henry Ford. Henry Ittelson of St. Louis founded the Commercial Credit and Investment Co. (later CIT Financial Corporation) in 1908. Alexander Duncan was the proprietor of the Manufacturers Finance Co. of Baltimore (1909), and in 1912 launched the Commercial Credit Co., soon to be one of the Big Three automobile finance companies. The San Francisco motor car dealer L. F. Weaver was probably the first, comparatively small-time, enterpriser (1913) to finance the purchase of automobile time-payment paper. The first sales finance company in New York City was the Guaranty Securities Corporation (1916), which housed itself in the new Equitable Building at 120 Broadway. It had been established only the previous year in Toledo, Ohio, to finance sales of Willys Overland models, but the sheer rush of business from a variety of dealers drove it to reorganize in New York where, on April 8, 1916, in the *Saturday Evening Post*, it placed its famous two-page announcement: "Time Payments: The First Organized National Service to Help Dealers Sell Automobiles." Guaranty Securities (later absorbed by CCC) offered to finance twenty-one makes of U.S. cars, and gave as references to its "soundness" the names of two New York City and three Chicago banks. By 1919 the General Motors Acceptance Corporation was hurriedly launched by the manufacturers to compete with CIT and CCC in financing the postwar automobile boom.[11]

During "the New Era," sales finance companies became the effective "bankers" of automobile retailers by purchasing the sales contracts of which the dealers were guarantors. With few exceptions, they were able to avoid confrontation with state usury laws by representing their markups on the contracts as "charges" rather than "interest," a legal stratagem not generally open to the forerunners of HFC or Beneficial on the personal loan side. Although a few metropolitan banks did become interested in lending to personal loan companies—First National of Chicago's relationship with HFC may have been the first (and it certainly was among the first to endorse Guaranty Securities in 1916)—only one major money center bank, National City of New York, organized a "personal loan" department, a short-lived effort (from May 1928) to cash in on the anti-loan shark investigations being conducted by the N.Y. State Attorney General. Not before so many other speculative avenues were closed did the chastened banks become more actively interested in doing business with the resilient sales finance companies still riding out the storm despite an initial drop of 41 index points for all consumer credit between 1929 and 1933. Personal finance corporations, increasingly legitimized by tighter state regulations, also came back slowly, but maintained their standing (and supported their "outstandings") not so much with commercial bank support as through the capital market itself. HFC's participating preference shares were listed on the N.Y. Stock Exchange as early as 1928, while Beneficial successfully sold some $7 millions of convertible debentures and listed its common during the trough of the Depression in 1933.

Americans were only too ready and willing to go on converting themselves into a "nation of time buyers." The institutional fulfillment of the age-old dream of living beyond one's means in "happiness"—without the misery which Mr. Micawber and the common folk everywhere knew to be reality—was the last miracle performed for "consumer culture" in the marketplace before the American earthquake of October 1929. Although retail consumer credit, *pace* the "under-consumptionists," could not alone have prevented the Depression, it was no less a wonderwork performed by new nonbank intermediaries, while the speculative practices of "sound" professional bankers—still almost exclusively credit wholesales—were contributing to economic disaster for producers and consumers alike. Once the momentum of capitalization had failed, the "commercial culture" of the 1930s lost much of its inventive dynamism and the hot air went out of advertising's facility to affect consumer choice. The effects of the new credit machinery, however, could not be reversed; consumers had seen the future and wanted it to work. The shift from "small miscellaneous consumption" into "the purchase of substantial equipment," as Robert S. Lynd put it, "meant. . .primarily a qualitative change in current consumption rather than an increase in total volume."[12]

This chapter defines the context of "consumer culture" and, in exploring its content, the authors of the following chapters show some of the ways in which Times Square and its environs manifested the change in current consumption brought about by the capitalization of entertainment and tourism, "showcasing" promotions, public relations, and advertising. The confluence of show biz and selling determined the character of this midtown colony of Lower Manhattan's money engine, culminating just before the Crash in William S. Paley's lucrative discovery of Gresham's Law of Broadcast Programming. By that time, all but one of the five most highly assessed blocks of Manhattan real estate were situated within an area bounded by Fifth and Seventh avenues between Thirty-seventh and Forty-second streets. The exception was still located in the Wall Street vicinity but when Times Square received its name (1904), the top three block valuations had still been in the financial district south of Fulton Street, followed in fourth and fifth places by commercial blocks on Broadway north of Herald Square, between Thirty-seventh and Fortieth streets. Many of the greatest gains in residential properties, meanwhile, had been achieved on Fifth and Eighth avenues bordering Central Park. No doubt some of these "improvement" values had splashed over into the brightly lit entertainment district around Times Square, despite the damper of Prohibition, but the "overcentralized" and "undercapitalized" commercial theater in New York, even at its peak (c. 1927), was in a worse financial condition relative to its costs than in the days before the Frohman Syndicate, when independent stock companies had furnished the bulk of the nation's theatrical entertainment. For all of its technical and artistic attainments, theater had been losing "market share" of the growing audiences over the first three decades of the century, but even in Times Square the theater had never been "industralized," and remained, as Jack Poggi suggests, an expensive "hand made item in a mass production society."[13] Nevertheless, the iconic luster of Times Square never shone more brightly across America's heartland—even when dimmed above street level—than in the dark winter months following Pearl Harbor. The "consumer culture" had been mobilized for war.

Capitalization of this "new American," *homo consumens*, had made the brief life of "the consumer durable goods revolution" possible, but "the mass consumption society" was itself still uncertain. Installment selling of the motor car was scarcely known before 1917, yet by that time enough had been learned to gainsay an earlier president of Princeton's claim that "the arrogance of wealth" manifested in the automobile was the most potent force to "spread socialistic feeling" across the nation. Some 75 percent of automobiles purchased (1922–29) after that same president left the White House were sold on the basis of installment contracts purchased by nonbank intermediaries. Even Henry Ford was not averse to such a source, although Roger Babson attributed "the present state of the nation's morals" in 1938, as well as its economy, to the "crime of installment selling" of motor cars! Between 75 and 80 percent of phonographs, mechanical refrigerators and other appliances, radios, and almost as much of pianos and home furniture among the older durables, went by "the sugar-coated pill." Yet when the twenties ceased to roar, and after diligently "emulating the buying standards of. . .neighbors," only 40 percent of families possessed a radio; 30 percent, a vacuum cleaner; 24 percent, a washing machine; and 8 percent, a mechanical refrigerator (as distinct from an ice box). One in 6 persons owned a new or secondhand car, but 1 in 7 a nonbusiness telephone. Such levels of consumption, no matter how rapidly or recently achieved, could not lick the business cycle—not to mention more profound structural imbalances. The volume of short-term personal loans actually increased through the early Depression years: a few commercial banks got into the act.[14] The shift from older patterns of expenditure (except for a return to unprocessed foods) went on fitfully as consumers confirmed their "qualitative" commitment to refrigerators, ranges, and radios, to rayon goods, toiletries and cosmetics, personal care, entertainment, schooling, coffee, and condensed milk. But there was to be no consumer-led recovery.

Almost two decades of Depression and war intervened before a restyled "consumer culture" could flourish again in the context of a hardening "Cold War" consensus, financed and managed out of Washington, D.C. Only from around midcentury did the public-private partnership for "economic growth and political stability" in the form of an institutionalized "military-industrial complex" lift consumption to heights and breadths undreamed of in the 1920s. The "American Way" became the envy (and the dream model) for "the free world" during the *embourgeoisement* of consumer expectations in the third quarter of the century. This great transformation at home was now powered by a public spending commitment to containing "Communism" and a massive invasion by commercial banks—with "instant cash," "privilege checking," and ubiquitous credit cards—into the fields of personal and sales finance, stimulated by media penetration of every household.

Although the costs of overseas adventures and domestic price inflation combined with cartelized energy prices from 1973 to undermine the Times Square-Levittown model of postwar consumerism after the cultural and civil rights revolutions of the later sixties, the world had been converted by magazines, movies, radio, and television to "the American Way." The acceptance of consumption as a global ideal—the most universal ideal in human history—had been accomplished even as "the consumer culture" in its homeland was segmenting into packages of "alternate life styles"—from the Los Angeles County to green Vermont models—and disintegrating under the self-destructive asset inflation and debt burdens of the deregu-lated Carter-Reagan years. When the no longer, if ever, monolithic Marxist Empire began to collapse under the strain of its own competitive military adventurism and industrial incompetencies, the conquest of "consumer culture," in aspiration at least, was complete. The starry-eyed youth in their uniform blue jeans poured through the breaches in the Berlin Wall in search of the VCRs, color TVs, and foreign travel by plane and automobile. By the late 1980s, the barely century-old "consumer culture," however diminished at home—reflected in the honky-tonk decline of Times Square—had converted the masses everywhere to the global creed of a plastic cargo cult.

1

DEVELOPING FOR COMMERCIAL CULTURE

David C. Hammack

T IMES SQUARE became America's great central marketplace for commercial culture between 1900 and 1929. With its garish lights, large and numerous theaters, close proximity to movie and radio headquarters, and stacked office warrens, it flourished as the great national showcase for popular music, vaudeville turns, plays, mass-market fashions, and consumer goods through the 1920s and, even as it was challenged by Hollywood, for many years thereafter. Times Square did not create its market. Indeed, the products of commercial culture were important to the nation's economy long before Times Square emerged on the scene. But by the early 1920s Times Square provided the largest, brightest stage for the presentation and sale of commercial culture in the United States. And to the extent that Americans increasingly defined themselves through the items they bought on the market rather than through inherited or workplace identities, the commercial fashions and icons marketed through Times Square took on added importance.

Why did Times Square come to take on this shape and play this role? The answer has four parts. National decisions gave the United States a market economy; geographic circumstances and local actions made New York City its great central place. Within New York City, local geography and disjointed decisions combined to make mid-Manhattan the great transit crossroads. Private and public land-use policies determined that within mid-Manhattan commercial entertainment would be concentrated in Times Square. And the entertainment industry's response to market opportunities (constrained by such national developments as Prohibition and the Depression) gave Times Square its classic shape—large office buildings fronted and interspersed with great theater marquees.

Two infrastructures developed Times Square for commercial culture.

The market economy and fragmented polity that characterized both the nation at large and New York City in particular provided the institutional infrastructure that allowed Times Square to take on its classic role. This in turn produced decisions that shaped the transportation system and the built environment of the nation and the city, providing the physical infrastructure that located and defined Times Square. These bases combined to put the national market for commercial culture in Times Square by the early 1920s and to keep it there for several decades.

That there would be a single central marketplace for commercial culture in the United States was determined long before the rise of Times Square. It was determined first by the nation's Revolutionary hostility to strong, active government, then by the commitment to national unity after the Civil War. That the commercial culture marketplace of the United States would be located in New York City was also determined by the time of the Civil War. By the mid-1860s New York was already well established as the central market for the entire nation. Since about 1780, as historical geographer Allan Pred has shown, the metropolis had been *the* central place in the circulation of information.[1] It was also the great center for commerce with Europe: in 1870 some 57 percent of all imported and exported goods passed through the port of New York. Although New York's share of the goods trade declined to just under 50 percent in 1900, its volume grew rapidly. And the metropolis moved much further ahead of its rivals, Boston and Philadelphia, in the import and export of fashions, ideas, credit, and other intangibles.[2]

In the last third of the nineteenth century, manufacturing also changed in ways that reinforced the market for commercial culture in New York. Heavy manufacturing moved toward the sources of raw materials around the Great Lakes, but the manufacturing industries most closely tied to the shifting fashions of commercial culture—women's clothing, publishing, and luxury goods of all descriptions—flourished in New York. As one manufacturer explained in 1910, "Those industries which produce products of a standard pattern can locate anywhere . . . but industries whose products differ with each particular order must be located in or very near their market, in order to be under the constant supervision of their customers." New York was located in the midst of the largest regional population in the United States, in the center of the East Coast and at the terminus of one of the best sets of rail and canal routes to the interior. It was also at the central point for imports and exports from Europe. New York provided the market.

New York's intensely urban qualities also provided special support for the women's wear, fashion, luxury, and publishing trades. Its uniquely large and varied population offered a great variety of specialties and skills and every conceivable sort of service or supply, at a moment's notice and in any quantity. And New York's many publications—its many local newspapers, trade journals ranging from *Variety* to *Women's Wear Daily* to *Advertising Age* to the *Wall Street Journal* to the *Real Estate Record and Investor's Guide*, and its national magazines and press services—all reinforced its position as the national market for every sort of fashion.

Together, the information and goods markets and the myriad specialties of New York provided an unmatched environment for all the industries that were increasingly ruled by fashion. This infrastructure of market, market information, support services, and the press also supported aspiring writers, performers, and theatrical producers as well as producers of commodities in the equally fickle and fashion-dominated field of commercial culture.[3] From the 1870s, and perhaps earlier, the popular music of Tin Pan Alley, the "serious" music of opera and operetta, vaudeville and variety acts of all descriptions, theater—classic and contemporary, tragic and comic—and, when they appeared, film and radio all found their central American markets in New York.

The economic infrastructure of both the nation and the metropolis created the conditions that brought the market for commercial culture to mid-Manhattan. The market for commercial culture had to be accessible to the largest and most diverse audience possible to test and validate vaudeville acts, plays, films, songs, singers, and performers of all kinds. By 1918 local and national transportation networks brought such an audience together in just one place: mid-Manhattan. Here, more than anywhere else in the United States, city residents of modest as well as ample means, affluent suburbanites, and visitors from other regions and from Europe could easily assemble to view the latest offerings on the stages of American popular culture. A long, complex, and fragmented process of economic and political decision-making had centered the transportation networks that served these three groups in mid-Manhattan. The location of the market for commercial culture in that district was simply a by-product of these decisions.

Grand Central Station, at Forty-second Street and Fourth (now Park) Avenue, was the first of mid-Manhattan's transport facilities, with a railyard in the 1840s, a terminus in 1871, enlargements in 1884–86 and 1900, and construction of the present vast structure between 1903, when plans were announced, and 1913. Elevated railroads followed: by 1876 their lines ran up Second and Third avenues on the East Side, up Sixth Avenue in the middle of Manhattan Island, and up Ninth Avenue on the West Side. All of these lines had stations at the major cross streets, including Thirty-fourth and Forty-second streets.[4] But because these lines were slow and dirty, they did not provide "real rapid transit," and they failed to spur midtown development.

The transportation infrastructure for mid-Manhattan, and for Times Square in particular, was built between 1900 and 1920. "Real" rapid transit arrived in 1904, with the opening of the first IRT line up what is now Lafayette Street and Park Avenue South to Grand Central Station at Forty-second Street, across Forty-second Street to Seventh Avenue, and north up Seventh Avenue and Broadway to the Upper West Side and, through a branch at 103rd Street, to Harlem and the Bronx.[5] Rail connections to the New Jersey and Long Island suburbs followed, with the construction between 1908 and 1909 of the Hudson Tubes from Newark, Jersey City, and Hoboken to the Battery, Wall Street, and under Sixth Avenue as far north as Thirty-third Street.[6] Pennsylvania Station, the Manhattan terminal for the Pennsylvania and the Long Island railroads, opened its vast structure in 1910 on the double block between Thirty-first and Thirty-third streets and Seventh and Eighth avenues.[7] By 1920 the IRT had completed its projected H-plan, with the Seventh Avenue line south from Times Square and the Lexington Avenue line north from Grand Central Station; and the BMT had completed its line up Broadway from Brooklyn and Wall Street to Times Square, then up Seventh Avenue to Fifty-seventh Street and across to Queens.[8]

Economic and political factors were intricately mixed in the many decisions that produced this tightly woven though often poorly coordinated transport net. And sometimes it was difficult to distinguish between the economic and the political factors. Economic elites—bankers, great merchants, leading real estate investors—often dominated the political decision-making process. But they had to work with the funds provided by the masses of ordinary consumers—the fares of straphangers, the tolls of bridge-crossers.

Economic elites dominated the political decision-making process in late-nineteenth century New York. The 1857 ban on steam-powered locomotives below Forty-second Street, for example, reflected an effort by the owners and insurers of large commercial buildings to control smoke and fire pollution in the city's chief business and residential districts. This decision forced the New York Central to build its Grand Central Station at that point; and by concentrating transfers from the northern suburbs and from long-distance travel here, it had the effect, 40 or 50 years later, of making Forty-second Street the most important of mid-Manhattan's wide cross streets. Times Square—a triangle above the intersection of Forty-second Street with Broadway and Seventh Avenue—developed rapidly only after the first rapid transit subway opened in 1904 with a key stop at Forty-second Street and Broadway. Times Square thus owes its significance as a transit intersection and assembly point to the location of the subway as well as of the railroad.

The IRT subway was the product of a protracted decision-making process in which—as often in New York City—"private" and "public" interests and powers were thoroughly intertwined. A public commission planned the subway, but every member of that commission was also a leader of the Chamber of Commerce of the State of New York. A private corporation, put together by some of the nation's leading bankers and railroad men, built and operated the subway, but a municipal franchise defined its powers, and a municipal guarantee subsidized the bonds that financed it. The commission and the corporation recognized political reality by awarding construction contracts to a company that enjoyed warm relations with Tammany Hall and by accepting the preferences of a variety of private business interests in defining the first subway's route.

The Chamber of Commerce itself insisted that one of the most important tasks of the first subway was to connect Grand Central Station with the long-established downtown business centers at Wall Street, City Hall/Brooklyn Bridge, Canal Street, and Fourteenth Street. Such a connection was essential, Chamber leaders insisted, because congestion in the streets impeded access to warehouses and delayed shipments, increasing the cost of doing business in New York.[9]

But if merchants needed rapid transit to speed the movement of their goods and messages, owners of already-developed properties put severe constraints on the possible locations of rapid transit lines. The East Side was relatively well supplied with elevated railroads (on Second, Third, and Sixth avenues). These were slow and, until their small steam engines were replaced with electric motors after 1902, dirty, but their franchises preempted alternative improvements on their thoroughfares. The New York Central already controlled Fourth Avenue, but in 1887 and thereafter it was cool to a proposal to use its lines as part of a rapid transit scheme that would extend both downtown and uptown from Forty-second Street. Property owners along the lower portions of Broadway had put a clause forbidding the construction of a railroad over, under, or on the street in the Rapid Transit Act of 1879, and even into the early twentieth century feared the disruption that would accompany the construction of rapid transit on their streets. Fifth Avenue property owners secured a clause in the Rapid Transit Act of 1891 that forbade any railroad construction on their thoroughfare.

Owners of less well developed property had different interests. In the 1880s and 1890s, owners of property on the Upper West Side insisted that the absence of adequate rapid transit facilities was unfairly holding their district back. They lobbied hard for the location of the first subway on Broadway above Fifty-ninth Street. When the N.Y. State Public Service Commission chose that route, Upper West Side property owners worked hard to help it gain the necessary legislative support. Ultimately, the IRT subway line connected the Wall Street/Broadway/Canal Street business district with Grand Central Station, then ran under Forty-second Street to the West Side at Broadway, and up Broadway to the Upper West Side. To provide "real" rapid transit, the IRT would provide express as well as local service, on four tracks. The projected volume of traffic dictated the location of express stops at Forty-second Street and the other major crosstown streets. Altogether, the IRT's route met the needs of several key economic interest groups, and accommodated others by avoiding the avenues and boulevards they wished to protect. That the IRT gave a great locational advantage to Times Square, at a time when theatrical entrepreneurs were on the move, was incidental.

After the turn of the century, mass-market economic factors and popular politics played more direct roles in the location of transport facilities in mid-Manhattan. Pennsylvania Station and the Hudson Tubes were planned, financed, built, and operated by private corporations (though with the permission of public authorities); they brought travelers from New Jersey as far north as Thirty-third Street and as near the center of Manhattan as Sixth and Seventh avenues, largely because they had concluded that was where the largest numbers of passengers wished to go. The new IRT and BMT subway lines built under the Dual Contracts[10] were also designed to serve the largest possible number of passengers, including passengers from Brooklyn and Queens, for two overriding reasons: to generate the largest possible flow of fares and to gain the greatest possible number of votes for the city officials who negotiated them. Broadway property owners now relented, and the BMT followed that street from Wall Street to Forty-second Street, then up Seventh Avenue (with another stop at Forty-ninth) to Sixtieth Street as it connected Brooklyn, Manhattan, and Queens. This route strongly reinforced Times Square's place at the center of the city's rapid transit network.

After World War I, political considerations delayed additional subway construction for many years. Federal policy had allowed wage inflation but forced transit companies to retain the five cent fare during the war; afterwards, it was politically impossible to raise the fare. As a result, private interests were unwilling to invest in rapid transit franchises or in bonds guaranteed only by transit fare revenues. New subways would require large subsidies that could be provided only by tax revenues, and the taxpayers balked. Construction of the projected IND subway under Eighth Avenue was delayed throughout the 1920s. The locational advantages that mid-Manhattan and particularly Times Square had accumulated remained unchallenged.

New York's rail and subway lines served suburban as well as city neighborhoods. Before 1920 transportation planners paid little attention to the automobile; indeed, until the late 1940s New York's suburbs depended far more on rail than on road connections with Manhattan. And since the rail terminals were at Grand Central and Pennsylvania stations, mid-Manhattan remained a logical place for the location of entertainment for suburbanites. The development of facilities for automobiles and buses came later. Unlike the rail facilities, all roads, bridges, and tunnels were designed, financed, built, and operated by government agencies, usually agencies of the state and federal governments, rather than by the city government or private corporations. Since many of these were special-purpose agencies (state highway departments, the Port of New York Authority (1921), and the Triborough Bridge and Tunnel Authority (1933, powers greatly expanded, 1937), however, they operated with some of the independence and secrecy—and with some of the ability to choose those with whom they would deal—that characterize private businesses.

Such agencies produced the Holland Tunnel (a special interstate commission, 1927), the George Washington Bridge (the Port of New York, 1931), and the Triborough Bridge (1936), which brought traffic into the far ends of Manhattan; and the West Side Highway (as far north as mid-Manhattan, 1903), the Lincoln Tunnel (New York Port Authority, 1937, 1945), and the Queens-Midtown Tunnel (a special commission, then the Triborough Authority, 1940), which brought traffic closer to midtown. Despite their distinct institutional forms, these agencies were influenced by political and economic considerations similar to those that shaped rapid transit. Investor skepticism, property-owner protests, Regional Plan Association advocacy of comprehensive transportation and recreational planning, and Port Authority plans for the rival Lincoln Tunnel, for example, combined to kill a proposal for a road and rail bridge over the Hudson to New Jersey that was seriously advanced by bridge-builder Gustav Lindenthal and several mid-Manhattan real estate groups in 1929.[11] During the 1930s and 1940s, their actions did more to reinforce than to displace the centrality of Times Square.

So, from the moment that Adolph Ochs celebrated the completion of Times Tower and the renaming of Longacre Square with a New Year's Eve Spectacular in 1905, Times Square has been New York City's great crowd-center. But the square plays this role only because it sits at the center of the city's transport facilities—the second crucial infrastructure for New York's commercial culture marketplace.

National political and economic forces brought the American market for commercial culture to New York City; local transportation decisions brought it to mid-Manhattan. The local economic and government decisions that defined the city's land-use districts finally centered the market for commercial culture in Times Square. Retail, manufacturing, corporate office, and mass communication activities also sought to take advantage of mid-Manhattan's central location. Economic calculation based on the reputations of certain streets as well as on accessibility governed location decisions for most of these activities; "sound business," as a spokesman for the Forty-second Street Property Owners and Merchant's Association asserted in 1929, "is both Czar and Dictator here."[12] Political decisions also played a significant role, however: the nation's first comprehensive zoning ordinance, enacted in 1916, was designed to control land-use patterns in mid-Manhattan. In its first period of intensive development after 1900 the area was also controlled, far more than lower Manhattan during its intensive development in the nineteenth century, by government regulation of factories, tenement houses, theater safety, electric signs, and building heights. The economic and political forces that defined land-use districts in Manhattan provide a third infrastructure of power for Times Square.

Specialized land-use districts are as old as cities; in ancient Athens, the port district at Piraeus, the market and civic facilities of the Agora, and the temples of the Acropolis were widely separated. In nineteenth and twentieth century cities in Western Europe and the United States the commercial and industrial districts expanded out of all proportion to the rest of the city and developed finer and more complex internal differentiations. As early as the eighteenth century, Dorothy George tells us, "The London watchmaking trade was minutely subdivided," and "the working part of the trade located itself in Clerkenwell and the neighbouring parish of St. Luke's," while "the watchmakers and clockmakers of repute . . . were to be found in the chief streets for shops, such as Cornhill, Cheapside, or the Strand."[13]

A similar process occurred in New York City. Retailing increasingly separated from manufacturing, and activities that once required only a few lots grew to occupy many large buildings over several entire city blocks. Mid-Manhattan became a sort of permanent World's Fair, with particular streets reserved for the display and sale of clothing, housewares, jewelry, appliances, automobiles, books—as well as for the music, arts, fashions, and theatrics of commercial culture.

Mid-Manhattan also became a major center for garment manufacture, business services, and the offices of business firms and professionals. The location of each of these activities affected the location of others. The commercial culture district might have located in any of several areas that afforded good access to Grand Central and Pennsylvania stations. Transport considerations attracted commercial culture to Times Square; competing land-use districts pushed it away from Fifth Avenue and up from the West Side between Thirtieth and Fortieth streets.

The changing land-use patterns of Manhattan were stimulated by the expansion of the market for ready-made women's wear, an expansion that was well under way in the 1880s and which exploded after 1900. New York's retail stores grew, with some becoming more specialized and others emerging as vast department stores. The garment manufacturing industry grew as well, producing for the national as well as the regional market. By the early twentieth century these two parts of the industry were in conflict.

For decades, dry goods and department stores had sought lower rents and better access to their affluent customers by moving up Broadway, away from the expanding financial and government office district below Canal Street. As the retailers moved, garment manufacturers, seeking to minimize their own transport costs and to maximize their access to buyers and market information, moved with them. In New York, as in London, retailers sought streets with fashionable reputations. Broadway provided that asset in the nineteenth century. Macy's, which successfully appealed to a broad middle-class market, moved up on Broadway to Thirty-fourth Street in 1902, displacing Koster & Bial's Music Hall and a large part of the notorious red-light district known as the Tenderloin. But stores that sought a narrower, more wealthy clientele, including Lord & Taylor, B. Altman, Stern Brothers, and Arnold, Constable & Co., moved to Fifth Avenue, seeking to associate themselves with the prestige left by an earlier generation of fashionable homes, churches, and clubs.

The extraordinary growth of New York's garment manufacturing business created problems as the fashionable stores themselves grew and moved toward mid-Manhattan. The loft buildings used by the garment industry did not fit Fifth Avenue's fashionable pretensions, and by 1907 the retailers had created a Fifth Avenue Association to find ways to keep the lofts off Fifth Avenue. Many of the lofts were "cheap in construction and appearance," the Association's representative complained in 1913, and they were "crowded with their hundreds and thousands of garment workers who swarm down upon the avenue for the lunch hour . . . and as work ends at the close of the day." Uncomfortable in what seemed like an industrial district, "women shoppers tended to avoid the section."[14] The terrible 1911 fire in the Triangle Shirtwaist Company's loft on Washington Place at Broadway made shoppers painfully aware of the "cheap" and "crowded" conditions in the lofts, intensifying their sense of discomfort.

Stanislaw J. Makielski, Jr., has described how the Fifth Avenue Association succeeded in protecting the Avenue above Thirty-fourth Street from the invasion of garment industry loft buildings. Its first instrument was economic power: a threat by dry-goods stores to boycott any manufacturer who located in a loft above Thirty-fourth Street, and by the Metropolitan Life Insurance Company (and perhaps other lenders) to refuse loans for such a purpose. Government action was still more effective: New York City's Zoning Resolution of 1916, which received key support from the Fifth Avenue Association and several other business groups, excluded industrial activities from districts designated as commercial, and specified Fifth Avenue (and Broadway) as commercial districts.

Makielski does not note another source of support for the Zoning Resolution: the alliance of Charity Organization Society leaders, social workers, and politicians which successfully supported legislation to improve housing and working conditions between 1911 and 1914.[15] The Zoning Resolution pushed garment manufacturing away from Fifth Avenue. Government (and private) incentives pulled the industry into a new area on the West Side, between Broadway and Eighth Avenue and Thirty-fifth and Fortieth streets. By 1929 this area constituted the "foremost manufacturing center of the metropolis." Entirely created in the years after the enactment of zoning, the new Garment District provided space for over 25,000 workers in buildings that contained "every modern convenience to meet the needs of the trade," including adequate fireproof stairways and toilet facilities.[16] It is likely that some of the key planners and investors in the Garment District were the same people who pushed for the exclusion of manufacturing on Fifth Avenue, and who supported efforts to strengthen the regulation of tenement houses and factories. Some of them may well have been leaders of the German Jewish community which was struggling to retain a leading position after the massive influx of Jews from Russia and Poland.

The rapid development of the Garment District after 1920 had in turn the effect of pushing away the many theaters that were then located on and just off Broadway in the thirties—which might have remained in a cluster near the grand, new Pennsylvania Station. It would have been impossible to have matinee performances on weekdays or Saturdays in a district where the sidewalks, narrowed to allow the construction of larger buildings, were "wholly inadequate to accommodate the crowds of workers" who overflowed from those buildings onto the sidewalks and into the streets, clogging vehicular traffic, interfering with the movement of garment racks, and delaying the movement of the "buyers for whose benefit the district has been so closely concentrated."[17] The Pennsylvania Railroad and the proprietors of adjoining hotels no doubt welcomed the buyers but regretted the decision to locate the manufacturing activities of the Garment District on their doorsteps.

At the end of the nineteenth century, New York's theaters had been scattered in clusters on Second Avenue, the Bowery, East Fourteenth Street, on 125th Street in Harlem, and along Broadway "from Union Square to Forty-second Street," with concentrations at Madison Square and Herald Square. In the next 25 years many of these theaters closed, and almost 80 new theaters were built in and around Times Square.[18] The theaters followed their audiences to mid-Manhattan's transportation nexus. Within mid-Manhattan, informal and formal zoning pressures then pushed the theaters away from Fifth Avenue and up to Times Square.

Early in its career as a theatrical center, Times Square became known for the spectacular quality of its productions and for the great size of its theaters. Because New York lacked the subsidized state theaters of the great cities of Europe, these buildings were designed to the specifications of entrepreneurs driven by the market. Commercial forces, organized in a succession of business arrangements, were in control.

The entertainment industry was in constant flux between 1880 and

1930 as entrepreneurs sought more efficient ways to create salable products for customers throughout the United States. Their changing strategies established a continuous history from the lyceum, chautauqua, vaudeville, and opera-house circuits to the theatrical road shows to movies and radio—and eventually to television. After 1900 each set of demands brought new building forms to Times Square.

Entrepreneurial strategies and building forms evolved more or less continuously in response to market opportunities between 1900 and 1930. Twice, however, national policy dramatically intervened. Prohibition made roof gardens and many restaurants unprofitable just at the time when improved transportation facilities were driving up rents in Times Square; thus it strongly reinforced the rise of the great movie palaces. The Federal Reserve's high-interest policy discouraged construction after the Crash of 1929, helping to bring on the Depression and incidentally freezing Times Square into the shape created during the 1920s. In the 40 years that followed 1920, only five major new theaters were opened in mid-Manhattan—all of them between Forty-ninth and Sixty-third streets.[19] Working within the constraints imposed by Manhattan's transit system, by land-use controls, and by federal efforts to regulate alcohol and interest rates, entrepreneurial strategies constituted the fourth infrastructure of power that shaped Times Square.

Through most of the nineteenth century the theatrical business was in the hands of freewheeling entrepreneurs. Before the 1860s, New York theaters provided showcases for plays, star performers, and vaudeville and other acts. Box office receipts, shaped by the reviews and reported in the news and gossip columns of metropolitan and trade papers, determined success. Successful plays and performers became available through booking agents located in New York for tours to other American cities. Some plays and large productions often did not travel. Instead, theater managers in other cities used their own stock companies, sometimes augmented by stars, to produce seasons that included scripts recently successful in New York as well as classics and unprotected English material which did not require royalties.[20]

The completion of the national railroad system and the growth of cities across the nation made it possible, after the Civil War, for touring shows to challenge and largely displace resident stock companies outside New York. The touring shows provided complete productions, including not only entire casts but also scenery and props, freeing provincial theater managers from the onerous tasks of maintaining companies of actors and producing their own shows. In the 1880s more than 100 separate companies were touring the nation; by 1904 there were 420. All these companies worked out of New York, using its theaters to establish their productions and to demonstrate their merits to booking agents in New York and to visiting theater managers from other cities.[21]

So long as the show-touring business remained fragmented, it was well served by the small and medium-sized theaters around Union Square and up Broadway, especially at Madison Square and Herald Square along Broadway. At the end of the nineteenth century, Brooks Atkinson once asserted, "the section of Broadway between Thirty-seventh Street and Forty-second Street was known as the Rialto," because, like the Venetian promenade of the same name, it provided a great marketplace. "Theatre people gathered there or promenaded there," Atkinson wrote. "Producers could sometimes cast a play by looking over the actors loitering on the Rialto; and out-of-town managers, gazing out of office windows, could book tours by seeing who was available."[22]

After the mid-1890s, however, much larger organizations sought to create order and to increase profit by gaining control of national chains of theaters as well as the shows that toured through them. The first of these organizations, the Theatrical Syndicate, was organized in 1896; by 1904, according to a competitor's estimate, it was managing 500 theaters across the country. The Syndicate relied heavily on independent producers, but it also produced its own shows. By 1900 it was developing shows and acts on its own, testing and improving them on Broadway, and sending them on national tours. Some theater historians suggest that the Syndicate's control of so many theaters on the road enabled it to establish something close to a monopoly by 1900, but this seems exaggerated. Oscar Hammerstein and other major "independent" producers continued to produce road shows in competition with the Syndicate. And as early as 1901, the Shubert Brothers were mastering the theater business; within a few years they would have their own national chain of theaters. Other entrepreneurs, meanwhile, were applying similar methods to the declining genres of vaudeville and burlesque.[23]

The Syndicate, independents like Hammerstein, and the Shuberts all sought national publicity for their New York productions; to get it, they built showcase theaters in Times Square. To attract the attention of audiences and the theatrical press, they made these theaters large and ornate. When the Syndicate's flagship New Amsterdam Theatre opened on Forty-second Street in 1903, it was one of the most impressive examples of art nouveau interior decoration in the United States; for more than twenty years it provided the perfect stage for Central European operettas like *The Merry Widow* and for the Ziegfeld Follies. The great theatrical entrepreneurs also used dozens of less impressive theaters to launch shows for the road. As Lee Shubert put it in 1912, "The rivalry of the theatrical factions" led them to build or lease an "excessive number of playhouses . . . in other cities." So long as these playhouses had to be supplied with shows "direct from New York," producers would demand large numbers of theaters whether New York audiences showed up or not. The Syndicate fell apart in 1916, but the Shuberts—who enjoyed stronger financial backing—took over a large part of its theater chain and carried on into the Depression years.[24]

Even as the Shuberts were mastering the national market for theatrical entertainment, movies were changing that market and, with it, the shape of New York's theater district. By 1909 leading vaudeville houses, including Hammerstein's Victoria, were incorporating movies into their programs; by 1912, moviemakers were expanding their offices in Times Square.[25] D. W. Griffith opened *Birth of a Nation* on Forty-second Street in 1915; with two performances a day at prices ranging from twenty-five cents to two dollars, he grossed $14,000 a week, comparable to the income of a successful stage production. In 1916, at the very moment when the Shuberts were picking up some of the pieces left by the Syndicate's collapse, S. L. Rothafel, "Roxy," was tearing down Hammerstein's Victoria Theatre, the greatest of all vaudeville houses, to erect the Rialto, designed exclusively for movie programs.[26]

Henceforth, the movie business would shape much of what happened on Times Square. Theatrical producers would continue to look for theaters. Their aim, however, was less and less to put together a show they could take on the road: more often, they hoped to gain national exposure—and wealth—by developing scripts that could be sold to a movie producer. Between 1910 and 1925, according to one estimate, the number of legitimate theaters in the United States declined from 1,549 to 674, and the number of road companies collapsed from 236 to 39.[27] In New York the prospect of selling material to the movies, the vast available audience, and speculative greed all encouraged the continued increase in the number of legitimate theaters to about 80 in 1925.

The national triumph of the movies affected Times Square in several ways. Movie producers tried to get each show off to a good start by presenting it first in Times Square, with its unparalleled access to mass audiences and to the metropolitan and theater press. Roxy's Rialto and such later picture palaces as the Strand, the Paramount, the Roxy, and the Capitol were built for this purpose.[28] Since the movie palaces housed larger audiences than did the legitimate theaters, and their programs were repeated several times a day, they produced much larger revenues.

The rise of the movies brought new groups of managers and producers, as well as new, larger theaters, to New York's theater district. They came in large part to see the talent of all kinds—writing, directing, designing, and performing—that was constantly on display before the live audiences of Times Square and of "Broadway" in general. After 1912 the movie industry established offices on Forty-second Street and in Times Square itself and some production facilities in the industrial district west of Eighth Avenue. Famous Players-Lasky and other film production companies produced live shows in their own theaters, then made them into films. Although most film production soon moved to Hollywood, many movie

offices, including the headquarters of several producing companies, remained in or near Times Square because New York continued to provide
much of the talent—as well as most of the capital—for the new industry.

The growth of radio during the 1920s brought still another communications industry to Times Square. According to Walter Zvonchenko,

> As late as 1926, every important aspect of the radio industry was
> located on Broadway just above or below City Hall, with the
> exception of facilities which the Radio Group (a term used often to
> identify General Electric, Westinghouse, and the Radio Corporation
> of America) had installed in Aeolian Hall at 33 West 42nd Street and
> in the Waldorf-Astoria Hotel at Fifth Avenue and 34th Street. But
> within two years time, as network radio became big business,
> virtually every operation of primary importance in the radio industry
> was in midtown Manhattan.[29]

Most of these operations were located on Sixth and Fifth avenues near
Times Square. Radio executives, like movie producers, were eager to
evaluate theatrical talent—and to make it easy to bring performers and
newsmakers to their studios. By the early 1920s radio programs were also
originating from the stages of several theaters or from their studios. The
explosive expansion of the radio industry in turn persuaded hard-nosed
investors to build the Radio City complex in Rockefeller Center, on the
edge of the Times Square district.

Land-use regulations imposed by local government could not hold
Times Square steady. Indeed, there were no such regulations. The New
York Zoning Resolution of 1916 did not create a district for the exclusive
use of the entertainment industry. It created only three kinds of land-use
districts: residential, business, and unrestricted. The resolution excluded
industrial activities, such as garment-making, from business districts, but
it did not segregate the various kinds of commercial businesses from one
another. As the theater district developed around Times Square, property
owners continued to be free to use their land and buildings for the
commercial uses that offered the highest income.[30]

Nor did New York City's zoning regulations protect the theater
district by limiting the heights of buildings in the Times Square area, a
limitation that would have retarded the intrusion of large office buildings.
The core supporters of zoning in New York City were very much
concerned with reducing what they saw as the excessive "congestion of
population" in the city. They firmly believed, as the *Regional Plan of New
York and Its Environs* put it, that the Times Square district was congested,
"due primarily to the concentration of theaters," which was in turn "both

a cause and an effect of the concentration of transit facilities."[31] But they could not use zoning to reduce congestion, because mid-Manhattan already contained "buildings of excessive height on the street line," some occupying "their entire lot areas." The *New York Times* tower itself exceeded the zoning guidelines, and because such structures already existed in 1916, the author of the zoning resolution later wrote, "There was danger that the courts would declare more drastic regulations discriminatory and therefore unreasonable and void."[32]

So as the transportation network that served Times Square improved and as real estate developers bid up the price of land, nothing prevented property owners from raising their rents. Small, two-story legitimate theaters with no rentable office or shop space, limited to eight or nine performances a week, began to find it difficult to stay open. As early as 1920, continuous-play movie houses and a flea circus had moved onto Forty-second Street, and most new theaters on Times Square itself were designed to show movies to large audiences several times a day. By 1925 many proposed theaters like the Paramount were combined with office buildings. Or they were to be joined, like the Roxy proposed for a site on Broadway at Fiftieth Street, with hotels.[33] When the final plans for Radio City (with its Music Hall) were announced in 1928, that vast project was simply the culmination of tendencies that had already been at work for several years. It was only the Depression, the restrictions on construction during World War II, and then the vastly changed postwar markets for transportation, Manhattan office space, and popular entertainment that delayed the reshaping of Times Square along the lines of Rockefeller Center. Already projected in the *Regional Plan of New York* during the 1920s, that reshaping was delayed for more than 60 years—and when it finally arrived at the end of the 1980s, Times Square no longer served as popular culture's great American market.

2

UPTOWN REAL ESTATE AND THE CREATION OF TIMES SQUARE

Betsy Blackmar

REAL ESTATE investment is an enterprise that builds on omens and prophecy. In 1900, the editor of the *Real Estate Record and Building News* greeted the new century by divining the signs of the "Present and Future of Forty-second Street." Three "complex" and "vigorous" developments were already at work to shape the street's future "character." Theaters near Broadway were forming the core of the city's "amusement center" and the "very heart of [its] night life." A second "influence," plans for the New York Public Library (along with exclusive clubs, expensive restaurants, and large retail stores) promised to establish "a rather more selective character" for Forty-second Street near Fifth Avenue as "a center of metropolitan life." And a "third great influence," Grand Central Station, had begun to attract hotels and shops to the midtown district. With these institutions already in place, the *Record*'s editor announced, the future development of rapid transit could only make "the neighborhood of Forty-second Street much more valuable for purposes of retail trade and amusement."[1]

The *Record*'s editor was not a bad prophet, although the process of Forty-second Street's "destined" development encountered many snags along the way. In 1903, for example, investors worried that hotels and theaters had been "overbuilt" because an economic downswing kept "industrial adventurers and promoters . . . sitting at home . . . wondering where and how they can best economize."[2] When speculation drove up the price of midtown land, the *Record*'s seers added office buildings to the catalog of "improvements that [would] pay sufficiently" to offset the costs of development.[3] And in 1916, Fifth Avenue merchants had to turn to zoning laws to enforce the "selective character" of their end of the street.

Whatever the trials and uncertainties of investors at the time, later historians have read the "influences" of the *Record*'s prophecy, and particularly its predictions of the propelling power of rapid transit, as explanations for the formation of one of the nation's great commercial districts. For historians, no less than for real estate investors themselves, profit determined the logic of location and hence the creation of a new kind of social space.

We can readily see the economic advantages that a mid-Manhattan location offered commercial entrepreneurs. By locating in (or relocating to) the area between Herald Square and Fifty-ninth Street, proprietors of theaters, hotels, restaurants, and retail establishments paid lower rents for more space, built new "modern" facilities, and captured increased customer traffic. Midtown's commercial entrepreneurs promoted and reinforced one another (encouraging, for example, comparison shopping, or theatergoers' sense of being "on the town"); and together they created an address that became increasingly important with the emergence of a national market that relied on certified and credentialed "metropolitan culture."

Profit also supplied an underlying motive for the economic and political cooperation that sustained midtown's commercial development. Downtown businesses welcomed the uptown relocation of stores, theaters, and hotels in order to relieve traffic on lower Manhattan streets and open up space for new corporate headquarters and financial institutions. Real estate investors throughout the city calculated their own interests in supporting the rapid transit system that converged on and radiated from midtown. And taxpayers and politicians saw in the district's commercial expansion the means to spread the city's tax base.

Lest such self-serving motives seemed too crude, business groups throughout the city joined in insisting that the true beneficiary of midtown's development was a broadly defined consuming "public." For families who worked and lived further uptown, in the boroughs, in New Jersey or Westchester County, midtown represented the heart of the city, an easily accessible and relatively contained district that could accommodate a wide range of personal needs and desires. For tourists and business visitors, Times Square created what J. B. Jackson has called "the stranger's path," an exotic home away from their own and New York City's homes.[4] To both local and national audiences, midtown Manhattan became the symbol of a new style of cosmopolitan, modern living. We are less clear as to what Times Square in the period 1900 to 1930 offered New Yorkers living and working at the district's and the city's margins, or how they fit into the development of a neighborhood that was thought to benefit the "public" as a whole.

In stressing the benefits of Times Square's development, promoters sought to establish the unproblematic commensurability of economic and cultural value. In a capitalist economy the material benefits of a particular location can be calculated by measuring land costs, distances, and the volume and flow of traffic. The utilitarian logic that informs so much of public policy-making, moreover, seldom misses a beat in linking these measures of growth to an expansively but vaguely defined social "well-being." But, as the *Real Estate Record*'s prophecy suggests, these equations of space, time, and money also rest on the cultural value that people assign to the "character" of a particular place in relation to the larger city. Whatever the seeming locational advantages of a district, developers must also capitalize on the perceptions, behaviors, and prescriptions associated with it in order to translate cultural value into profit.

What was the relation between cultural and economic values in the shaping of Times Square into a profitable social space? How do we link the economic and political forces that David Hammack has identified to the process (and tensions) of cultural change? Although some historians have outlined the overarching economic and institutional logic of Times Square's development as a commercial center, we must also consider the illogic—and the indeterminacy—of the district's social transformation. The development of Times Square, the city's most rapidly appreciating land in the period we are examining, broke with earlier conventions of real estate investment which associated the value of a neighborhood with the moral "character" of its users and which sought to control space by restricting access. But Times Square also departed from the contemporary progressive-era preoccupation with the establishing social order (and value) through spatial uniformity and predictability. By contrasting the "investment logic" of nineteenth century New York real estate development with that which governed the production of Times Square, we can see how cultural and economic changes intersected to create new ways of interpreting the value of social space.

The creation of any district as a new and desirable location requires coordination. In midtown Manhattan, as David Hammack shows, real estate interests and commercial institutions helped establish and then claimed a new territory by undertaking extensive political negotiations with taxpayers, downtown merchants, manufacturers, and borough politicians over the location of subway lines and stops, street widenings, sidewalk narrowings, zoning regulations, and building codes (including fire laws that initially restricted the construction of theaters within multipurpose buildings). At the center of these negotiations, we can see the continuing power of a coalition that had dominated the city-building process in the nineteenth century: commerce and real estate. Yet a shift in the identity and interests of the dominant actors within these sectors also transformed the nature of their collaboration in the production of social space. In the nineteenth century, merchants consumed the cultural values produced by real estate developers who created new "respectable neighborhoods." In the twentieth century, real estate investors consumed the economic values produced by commercial entrepreneurs who dissolved the older spatial boundaries of respectability. This shift in initiative reflected a larger change in the source and deployment of income which carried with it the power to shape social space.

In one sense, commerce has always held the upper hand in negotiations over land use in New York because the first determinant of location remains economic power—the ability to pay. New York's nineteenth century import and export merchants claimed the territory of lower Manhattan for business simply by virtue of commanding more money than anyone else in the city. Merchants' ability to pay higher rents for "prime" downtown space initially reflected the volume and value of the commodities that passed through the port; by the second half of the century, bankers and brokers, who treated money itself as a commodity, reinforced the commercial monopoly of downtown space. Similarly, Times Square is the product of commercial capital's ability to pay for the space it wants. Yet, one of the most remarkable aspects of Times Square's formation is the way its institutions—theaters, department stores, restaurants, and the like—amassed their purchasing power less from the value of commodities as such than from capturing and channeling millions of New Yorkers' earnings into ephemeral pursuits that sustained new levels of rent.

With the ability to pay determining land use, real estate investors operate as parasites of commerce. But as merchants themselves, real estate developers also seek to enhance their own commodities of land and location. Profits from developing land lie not simply in selling or renting to the highest bidder but also in the jump in price and rents, the speed with which land values rise with the conversion to new use. The quickest jumps generally occur at a periphery of development when vacant land is first brought into "productive use." Alternatively, values increase rapidly with the wholesale conversion of old neighborhoods to new use. But either way, to collect this gain, developers must persuade customers of the advantages (indeed, the necessity) of new locations. That persuasion appeals as much to cultural as to economic definitions of need. Through much of the nineteenth century, the cultural and economic values of location were expressed in the same moral language. But this language of social and spatial order had to be recast for Times Square to establish its cultural as well as economic value.

The first arena of concerted capitalist real estate development in Manhattan was the production of respectable residential neighborhoods, which included as part of their value a new cultural institution—the home—and a new sense of the importance of a social address. Having claimed the territory of lower Manhattan for business, merchant families worried that the "exposed" activities of trade subverted the canons of respectability. In the first half of the nineteenth century, developers tapped this concern (as well as the expanding wealth) of the city's predominantly merchant bourgeoisie by promoting the link between respectability and the controlled social space of new and exclusive neighborhoods.

Developers cashed in on new desires for social refinement, certification, and insulation by building private residential parks like St. John's and Gramercy and by coordinating development in the vicinity of such public spaces as Washington and Union squares. Restrictive covenants, uniform architecture, and government subsidies (for example, modifications of the grid street plan) set these territories visually apart from the larger city. In seeking both customers and political favors, developers readily drew on a republican rhetorical tradition to define the public interest in promoting interchangeable moral and economic qualities of "character" and "improvement." The reputation of the entire city as a mercantile capital, they claimed, rested on the tastes, manners, and conduct of its leading citizens. Elite residential neighborhoods would offer a clear statement of the close relation between the larger city's economic and cultural "progress."[5]

Precisely because the luxury of new housing could be associated with republican virtues, homes in such neighborhoods solved the question of what citizens should do with new wealth, and sanctioned new levels and modes of consumption. The ideological definition of the home as a realm set apart from the economy, of course, disguised the tensions of its market acquisition and of its labor relations—between husbands and wives, and householders and servants. But such a definition also trained propertied New Yorkers in a habit of mind that could disassociate the pleasures of enjoying new goods and services from the social relations of their production. Indeed, part of the cultural value of such spaces rested on the ideological erasure of the necessity and activities of "productive labor."

In contrast to the real estate developers' coordinated production of elite residential neighborhoods, the formation of the city's first retail commercial districts operated primarily on the purchasing power of individual entrepreneurs. When John Jacob Astor sought the "convenience" of a lower Broadway address for his new hotel, he bought out the prior residents, like Philip Hone, who were willing, for a price, to be persuaded that they too needed the social certification of an uptown address.[6] By the second half of the century, however, the requirements of cultural respectability had spilled over to environs of commercial institutions that catered to the city's wealthy and professional classes. The conversion of Union Square to commercial use built on its prior elite residential identity, and the Ladies' Mile between Fourteenth and Twenty-third streets assumed its "character" in relation to the parallel Fifth Avenue housing district.[7]

Antebellum real estate developers' promotion of cultural values to realize new economic value culminated with the creation of Central Park in the 1850s. The movement to create it came from a coalition of merchants and uptown landowners who had little trouble projecting their interests and needs onto the city as a whole. As a new kind of public place for moral leisure activity in the mid-nineteenth century, a large landscaped park would enhance land values and attract and keep well-to-do New Yorkers —as well as visiting traders, tourists, customers— within the city. If the commercial benefits lay primarily in demonstrating that the republican city could match European capitals in its attractions, real estate expectations lay in the development of the park's borders as an elite residential enclave. Within the vision of the park's promoters, housing and leisure were understood to be "compatible" and logically linked land uses.[8]

This perception of the interlocking social and economic benefits of creating a new kind of social space rested on the cultural values of the predominantly Yankee merchants, bankers, and lawyers who advocated and controlled the park in its first two decades. The coalition that supported Central Park assumed that leisure was properly a pursuit (in the words of Frederick Law Olmsted, part of the "moral capital") of wealthy New Yorkers, who not only knew how to behave but could influence the behavior of others. For all the rhetoric devoted to the park's democratic character, it is clear that those who first had charge of regulating behavior within the park and those who owned land on its borders preferred a space that would accommodate respectable citizens' desire to have a place where they could "see and be seen" by one another without confronting "uncouth" or "rowdy" city residents. One of the park's selling points was that it promised to eliminate the unpleasant, unexpected interactions that wealthy New Yorkers encountered on the lower Broadway promenade.

The merchant and real estate interests that dominated the process of city building through most of the nineteenth century met with relatively little resistance. Small shopkeepers and artisans went on the defensive as middle-class residential development pushed up land prices, rents, and with them the costs of gaining and maintaining an independent livelihood. The nascent manufacturing sector, especially clothing manufacturing, developed through the outwork system, which saved entrepreneurs' factory rents even as it required workers to contribute to overhead through their domestic rents. Cultural polarization and conflict accompanied the process of nineteenth century class formation. Native-born artisans and journeymen heard democratic republican values transformed into utilitarian justifications of the "public interest" of class-based institutions, from private residential parks to Central Park. Wage-earning New Yorkers— increasingly immigrant—faced repeated attacks from temperance, Sabba-

tarian, and anti-Catholic groups who pointed to the institutions of working-class neighborhoods as evidence of moral and economic failure. Spatial
separation seemed to offer one "solution" to these conflicts, and the logic of
large-scale real estate investment centered on drawing and maintaining
cultural boundaries.

What happened in the last quarter of the nineteenth century to
transform merchants' and real estate developers' shared interests in organizing social space around the interlocking principles of cultural and
economic "improvement"? Why did some Manhattan developers abandon
the key antebellum strategy of creating socially exclusive neighborhoods in
order to maximize real estate profits and stabilize investments? Why, we
might ask, did Forty-second Street itself not emerge as a convenient,
stable, and respectable residential neighborhood, a use that was as possible
as any other in, say, 1880, and one which surely would have presented a
barrier to its future commercial development?

Developers themselves asked these questions as the real estate market
(like the rest of the economy) entered the era of erratic business cycles and
unrestrained competition. Four forces drove a wedge into the nineteenth
century real estate investment logic that linked profits to the creation of a
neighborhood's exclusive, moral character. The first was the unequal
distribution of income: there were not enough rich people who could
afford to purchase single-family dwellings and exclusive social addresses.
And if the city's social stratification undermined effective demand for
spatial respectability, real estate investors' own greed contributed to the
problems of supply: land speculation pushed up the costs of development
beyond what the city's middle-class families could afford to pay in support
of the wholesale production of "respectable neighborhoods" across the vast
territory of uptown Manhattan.

The second force undermining the antebellum paradigm for ordering
social space followed from the first: real estate investors who could not
make a profit by developing exclusive residential neighborhoods turned to
other sources of rent or profitable sale. Throughout the antebellum period,
hundreds of small speculative builders (as opposed to developers) had
operated at the margins of the real estate industry, producing buildings
rather than "neighborhoods." The city's tenement districts, which represented the sum of small investors' uncoordinated efforts, reinforced the
antebellum city's cultural as well as residential bifurcation. After the Civil
War, while large-scale developers confidently marched up the center of the
island, building Chelsea and Murray Hill on either side, the city's
tenement builders followed the shorelines. But by the third quarter of the
nineteenth century, smaller real estate investors had also moved into the
central territory north of Fortieth Street, where social boundaries had yet

to be established. Because they could not afford to leave land undeveloped, these smaller operators and their tenants introduced "temporary" (often wood) improvements ranging from manufactories and barracklike tenements to saloons.

Divided real estate interests within the same territory disrupted a previous generation's strategy for profitably controlling (and marketing) social locations defined through uniform land use. Forming themselves into neighborhood associations, large landowners and developers attacked the competitive anarchy of smaller investors whose cheap projects undermined uptown's potential "highest and best use" as an elite residential district. These residential developers, who had used restrictive covenants to establish neighborhood uniformity and stability for half a century, were the first real estate group in the city to fully articulate the investment logic that linked profit to spatial and social order, and they did so at the point when they were losing control over the real estate market. Real estate journals, themselves a symptom of the felt need for coordination, rehearsed the dangers of "encroachment" and incompatible land uses in terms that would gain currency with the calls for zoning two decades later.[9]

Although real estate developers devoted most of their attention to controlling land use and battling small operators at the city's periphery, by the 1890s they also took cognizance of another danger, one that came from outside their own ranks. The ascendancy of manufacturing represented a third force that pushed a reconceptualization of the relation of cultural and economic value in the production of social space and promoted new alliances within the city's properties classes.

In the last quarter of the nineteenth century the number and size of the city's manufacturing establishments dramatically expanded, as did the diverse immigrant work force. New York's full emergence as an industrial city had two consequences for the earlier assumptions governing land use. First, economic power permitted manufacturers to claim new space within the city. As Hammack points out, part of the impetus for the relocation of department stores, hotels, clubs, and theaters uptown was the pressure of new loft construction in the vicinity of Fourteenth Street. This pressure arose from economic competition—small clothing manufacturers renting out separate floors generated new levels of rent that prompted real estate investors to build more lofts. But the pressure was also cultural, and it undermined nineteenth century categories of spatial and social order: whatever the respective rent-paying capacities of the two modes of land use, the presence of manufacturing *devalued* Union Square and the Ladies' Mile for respectable shopping and leisure.

A last force disrupting the nineteenth century equation of economic and cultural value in the production of social space came from the recreational pursuits of the working families whose labor sustained the expansion of manufacturing. Working-class New Yorkers expanded the audience for commercial amusements within the city, altered the patterns of class interaction within particular territories, and ultimately prompted entrepreneurs to reshape social spaces in order to "pool" the rent produced by numerous undifferentiated customers. These developments were prefigured even in the "noncommercial" space of Central Park in the late nineteenth century. As more and more immigrant families found their way to the park (particularly on Sunday), for example, the park's zoo became a "commercial entertainment" center. However much elite New Yorkers choreographed their own use of the park in order to limit and regulate interaction, they could not escape its increasingly "popular" character. And working-class New Yorkers who formed part of the park's crowds saw in the carriage parade less a model of moral leisure than a celebration of personal fashion that displayed money—however obtained—as the dominant standard of cultural value.[10]

Alongside the forces of income stratification, competition within the real estate sector, and the rise of manufacturing, the emergence of new practices and geographic patterns of mixed-class socializing undermined the nineteenth century real estate strategy for producing exclusive social space. As Peter Buckley, Tim Gilfoyle, Kathy Peiss, and others have shown, patterns of class interaction changed within such older theater and amusement centers as the Bowery and Union Square and within newer territories like the Tenderloin district. Even where different institutions sorted their clienteles by price, proximity bred familiarity. But in contrast to an earlier generation's contempt, the demimonde of the Tenderloin district courted the novelty of such exposure. As was true in the use of Central Park, the erosion of the link between wealth, leisure, and moral rectitude laid the groundwork for a new "cosmopolitan" tolerance of diversity and ambiguity of boundaries.

As these cultural changes reached into the ranks of respectability, they produced contradictory tendencies within the social spaces that had most clearly marked out the logic of interlocking economic and moral order. Developers worried that Central Park's very popularization, for example, would undermine the reputation of its surrounding neighborhoods for exclusivity. By the end of the century, uptown builders met the economic pressure of land speculation by successfully promoting apartments as a new, respectable housing form. At the same time, however, it is not clear that New York's wealthy and middle-class families continued to regard a territory set aside for "moral leisure" as itself a desirable real estate amenity.

Even as the "convenience" of apartment living offered women in particular more leisure time, the constraints of domestic space prompted middle-class New Yorkers to abandon home hospitality in favor of new commercial centers for socializing.[11] By the end of the century, articles in the *Real Estate Record* gave less attention to the advantages of the Central

Park in promoting the Upper West Side's exclusive social development than to the "convenience" of the area to new midtown commercial institutions, particularly to the theater district.[12] And in explaining the location of the theaters themselves, the *Record* observed that the "greater theater going population lives" on the city's West Side.[13] As Richard Fox suggests, by the end of the nineteenth century respectable families could confidently attend the theater with little fear for either their own character or that of the district they visited. This cultural reorientation encouraged experiments in creating new kinds of social space.

The instability of late nineteenth century real estate investment, the emergence of new kinds of (industrial and commercial) purchasing power, the accompanying uncertainty of commercial, industrial, and domestic institutions' respective claims on particular territories, and New Yorkers' own disregard for cultural boundaries shaped the dynamics of Times Square's formation. In contrast to their eager promotion of Central Park, however, real estate investors took a back seat in the initial process of Times Square's development. Much of midtown land remained in the hands of family estates that left development to leaseholders who, in a significant departure from nineteenth century strategies, often abandoned the constraining influence of restrictive covenants in their ground leases. Yet, the most active and profitable arena of Forty-second Street real estate investment before the 1920s was land speculation rather than development. Landowners and brokers knew (and hoped to persuade buyers) that midtown was valuable, but they were less certain of its "best" uses.

In the face of an unstable real estate market, commercial entrepreneurs introduced new patterns of land use that departed from nineteenth century strategies which featured uniformity of both use and users as the key to "reliable" investment. Unlike domestic or industrial rents, commercial rents could skim off and pool a portion of thousands of New Yorkers' and visitors' disposable income, relying on volume and turnover rather than the stable "character" and predictable habits of particular users. Furthermore, commercial districts extended both the "working day" and the physical space of this rent collection: they operated day and night, in some cases changing their social "character" with the hour or with the story of the building. The impact of transportation on Times Square's development tells us more about the scale and volume of commercial transactions that drove midtown land values to new levels than about the revolution in cultural values that created these new patterns of land use.[14]

The development of midtown marked the ascendancy within the commercial sector of retail and entertainment businesses over importers and wholesalers in shaping the city landscape. Thus, although the coalition that supported subways and zoning included downtown merchants interested in reducing lower Manhattan congestion (and promoting the city's overall image as a place to do business), commercial entrepreneurs who were willing to throw over older definitions of locational advantage—even in the face of uncertainty (and often bankruptcy)—took the initiative in reshaping midtown. Unlike real estate developers, they did so with little concern for the character of their neighbors. As Margaret Knapp has shown, when T. Henry French and Oscar Hammerstein built theaters on or near Forty-second Street in the 1890s, the neighborhood's coal yards, shops, tenements, and cafés offered little reinforcement for the creation of a "pleasure district." Nor, for that matter, did the area have particular advantages of convenient access. But it did offer relatively low land prices and the opportunity to experiment in the organization of social space. Indeed, French, Hammerstein, and other entrepreneurs built theaters which themselves placed a premium on the fluidity of social character by combining legitimate playhouses, roof gardens with dance and music halls, and billiard rooms and cafés in the basement. Their audiences and their programs changed from one season to the next.[15]

In creating Times Square, these entrepreneurs encountered and negotiated a particular set of contradictions that seem to have stood at the heart of the midtown district's ambiguous and unstable cultural identity. One of these contradictions lay in the persistence of older mixed patterns of land use. As part of the process of creating Central Park, the state had used its powers of eminent domain to clear out the "incompatible" presence of poor laboring families who gained a subsistence from "nuisance" land uses such as pig farming. When uptown "squatters" settled outside the park's boundaries, West Side landowners continued their campaigns for the removal of "public nuisances." By contrast, the prior occupants of Forty-second Street, particularly those who held long-term leases, were only gradually displaced by new commercial institutions. The carriage-making trades that had sprung up in the area (to meet the new cultural need created by Central Park) appear to have been the first to go; but tenements, flats, saloons, and small shops remained interspersed among the new theaters, hotels, and restaurants. Thus, the uneven process of Times Square's formation established its mixed-class character from the outset. Although Eighth Avenue formed something of a social border (with Hell's Kitchen at the edges), the West Side residents of the territory between Thirty-fourth and Fifty-ninth streets themselves formed part of the constituency (as well as the labor force) for new commercial institutions. Similarly, the elite Murray Hill residential district fed the enterprise of Fifth Avenue merchants.

The *Real Estate Record*'s efforts at prophecy marked out midtown's general tendencies, but in contrast to their investment advice on the necessity of enforcing uniform development in *residential* districts to preserve land values, the journal's editors were less certain of the logic that should govern investment in a commercial district. In place of exclusion and uniformity, they turned to "modernization" as the key to realizing and maintaining the investment values of Forty-second Street. Again in contrast to the goals of attaining stability in residential development, this strategy valorized change for its own sake and extended even to the new commercial institutions, which repeatedly changed their facades, interiors, and utilities in order to preserve their value. "Of course no city can put in new and better machinery without displacing some of the older equipment," one editor noted of the need to replace "some of the dingier and badly situated theaters." Nor did the journal's editors waste any affection on the short lives of these buildings: investors who lost money from failing to renovate simply paid "the penalty of not keeping abreast of contemporary conditions and standards."[16]

Yet even modernization did not stand as a uniform principle for the district's development. Although real estate investors complained of the "resistance" of prior occupants who stood in the way of commercial conversion (including elite families who were reluctant to give up Fifth Avenue), commercial proprietors themselves appear to have been far less concerned with residual occupants of the territory than with the threat of new competition from industrial users, particularly the clothing manufacturers.[17] In response, entrepreneurs both adopted and altered the older principles of social exclusivity by pushing zoning regulations that preserved their own powers to define and control commercial space, albeit in new and fluid ways.

Zoning legislation built on nineteenth century investment logic of class separation to promote specialized land-use districts, which stabilized both real estate competition and the character of particular neighborhoods. Fifth Avenue merchants' political power in claiming (in effect) a public subsidy in the form of monopoly rights over a territory probably drew on the commercial and real estate coalitions' longstanding upper hand in negotiations with the city's industrial capitalists. Similarly, residential zoning institutionalized earlier generations' use of restrictive covenants to insulate domestic land use from commercial as well as industrial competition.

But there was a selective character in zoning's application of nineteenth century real estate investment logic. While the coalition that supported zoning defined the problem of manufacturing lofts as one "congestion," they embraced a new kind of congestion by promoting midtown as a transportation entrepôt. A simple resolution of this contradiction is that crowds of industrial wageworkers subverted, whereas crowds of shoppers, theatergoers, office workers (and by the 1920s, apartment dwellers) supported the higher and better cultural uses of commercial property. The distinction, however, seems to lie more in the character of the economic activity than in social identity of the people; that is, wageworkers were welcomed to Forty-second Street at night when they were prepared to spend money. This selective exclusion drew on the nineteenth century conviction that what made social spaces both attractive and valuable was the invisibility of "productive labor." But once industrial labor as such had been excluded, there was little concern with the uniformity, predictability, or social order of development within territories that were zoned for "commercial" use. By distinguishing between desirable and undesirable crowds, planners and proprietors modified the nineteenth century project of drawing class boundaries to establish locational value.

There is a curious silence in the early twentieth century planning literature about commercial districts. They are presented as one of the city's "ecological" features, and their location, rapid expansion, and command of territory are explained as a logical consequence of regional transportation systems. But planners devoted volumes to advocating uniform residential districts that enshrined a particular set of moral values, as well as to discerning "rational and efficient" rules for industrial location. By contrast, the commentary on the formation of new commercial districts is limited to recommending the steady, unobstructed flow of traffic (which also creates new kinds of mixed-class crowds). Was it simply a concession to market power that prompted the 1929 Regional Plan to devote most of its discussion of Forty-second Street to the advantages of the subway system and the accompanying rapid rise of property values? Were these districts' cultural problems or benefits (their contribution to the city national image, the promotion of consumption) so obvious or irrelevant as to not require discussion or rules? Or did commercial districts reverse traditional hierarchies of cultural and economic value and dissolve the very equation of social and spatial order, even as they dissolved functional land-use categories on which planning theory rests?[18]

Zoning placed the coordinated interests of real estate investors in establishing land-use predictability and stability above individual competition. But different rules came to govern commercial districts that mixed entertainment, services, office work, transient residence (hotels), and permanent housing (apartments). At the same time that midtown merchants and real estate interests were coordinating campaigns to restrain the both individualistic and sectoral competition that created "incompatible" land uses elsewhere in the city, they were shaping a district that said to investors *and* users "let yourself go," experiment with the conventions of spatial and social order, test the value of new arrangements. In contrast to the institutional consolidation of other sectors of New York's economy, real estate remained a highly entrepreneurial field of investment through the 1920s, and within Forty-second Street, principles of "risk" (rather than "improvement") bridged the distinction between cultural and economic value.

It would seem that New York's commercial proprietors saw little advantage in distinguishing or managing the character or cultural expressions of the crowds that created midtown Manhattan's profitability. Through struggles that secured shorter hours and higher real income, some working-class New Yorkers had constituted themselves as a desirable (hence respectable) market. At the same time, part of the district's appeal for well-to-do New Yorkers, as well as for out-of-towners, may have been its abandonment of the cultural equation of desirability and respectability. Furthermore, commercial proprietors who themselves came from immigrant backgrounds had little investment in Yankee constructions of respectability which looked for (and placed a price tag on) manifestations of moral worth in particular tastes and manners.

Times Square was not without its own internal locational logic. Within the midtown commercial district—reaching more than a mile— particular institutions clustered on particular streets and blocks, and the Fifth Avenue merchants sought to preserve their reputation for exclusivity. One question we need to examine further is how different groups— both New Yorkers and the city's visiting "strangers"—used, moved through, and interpreted the territory as a whole. But whatever particular paths visitors might take, the architecture, spatial arrangements, and social traffic of department stores, hotels, theaters, office buildings, apartments, and subways worked together to create and define the midtown ambience that we associate with new styles of cosmopolitan or modern city life. The novelty, spontaneity, and crowds promoted by commercial districts were geared to courting impulse, inviting people to spend their time and money freely, to indulge themselves, and to condone the indulgences of others.

Yet surely there were social tensions—even contradictions—in the formation of Times Square and the elevation of undifferentiated social "traffic" over the fixed associations of "place." One of these tensions was expressed in the uneven efforts to restrain and police behaviors that the neighborhood itself seemed to welcome. And another tension arose from the very activity that zoning sought to erase as part of the commercial district's defining attributes—from labor. In 1919, Kristin Miller has shown, when members of Actors' Equity went on strike, they used their theatrical talents to make a new open-air pitch to Times Square's "public." "Crowds seemed amazed," a reporter noted, "that actors and actresses should actually have taken steps which aligned them with striking harbor workers, railroad men and trolley employees." And after shutting down the Hippodrome, one Equity organizer proclaimed that the managers "haven't got the stagehands, the chorus or the audience. They lack the audience in particular. Back of the first few rows and boxes sits the laboring class. They are with us."[19] So even Times Square's identity as a fluid place of entertainment was not fixed when its players raised the curtain on its work relations, recast their relation to the audience, and asserted that all social spaces were workplaces

The instability of cultural and economic activities concentrated in the area affected the process of Times Square real estate development by opening the district to rapid innovation and novel definitions of its cultural identity and appeal as a social space. By the twenties, however, the district was losing the economic edge that arose from cultural unpredictability, impulse, and risk. The soaring land prices of speculation prompted developers to trade impulse back in for predictability. As had been true with uptown apartments, new midtown office and residential buildings maximized and stabilized rents through building height, through fixed capital investment in construction. Yet real estate investors also learned something from the gambles of the first generation of commercial proprietors that would make and keep the district culturally attractive. Developers incorporated the experimental and flexible principles of mixed land use and ambiguous boundaries into multifunctional buildings.[20]

By the 1920s, the territory operated simultaneously as a shopping, entertainment, and residential center, as well as corporate headquarters for the entertainment industry, which capitalized on the district's image as well as the locational conveniences of production and labor recruitment. Yet by the end of that decade, commentators observed that Times Square had "peaked" as both the city's and the nation's cultural center. Zoning helped preserve Fifth Avenue's "character," Rockefeller Center and corporate development east of Sixth Avenue established midtown's new value as a "clean" workplace, the theater district preserved the value of entertainment through movies, and Herald Square department stores became fixed features of city life. But real estate journals in the 1930s began to speak of the area's "decline," its inability to attract new capital and promise new levels (and rates) of profit. The revolution in cultural valuation that shaped midtown's formation retained its currency but it lost its local economic power—its drawing power as a location to attract new crowds and with them new levels of investment capital. After the Depression the "new money" went to the periphery, leaving behind the increasingly ambiguous legacy of a territory that dissolved the boundaries of class in undifferentiated crowds. And as the institutions of commercial culture themselves dispersed in the postwar era, Times Square "ripened" for redevelopment to a culturally as well as an economically defined higher and better use. It seems that we are on the eve of the reassertion of the cultural value of class exclusion as the source of economic value in the shaping of Manhattan's social space. With further investigation, perhaps we will come to understand how that principle survived in the shadows of Times Square's initial development.

3

URBAN TOURISM AND THE COMMERCIAL CITY

Neil Harris

ETWEEN the 1890s and the 1920s the creation of a new American social type would have particular meaning for the invention of Times Square: the domestic tourist, city genus. The urban tourist would do much more than help shape amusement centers, however. The physical character, systems of representation, and collective self-consciousness of many of our cities would never be quite the same thereafter. Both the imaging of New York in this period and the effort to define its special personality were stimulated by the heady experience of becoming this country's major tourist center. Anticipated for many decades, by the 1890s mass tourism would provide an increasing share of the city's income, some of its reputation, and even more of its self-image.

In his pioneering book on the subject, Dean MacCannell suggests that tourism has become a "way of attempting to overcome the discontinuity of modernity, of incorporating its fragments into unified experience." It is as tourists that many contemporaries "attempt to discover or reconstruct a cultural heritage or a social identity." Entire cities and cultures, MacCannell argues, "have become aware of themselves as tourist attractions."[1] To some extent this is what happened in New York.

This chapter title's reference to the commercial city is meant to suggest several things. First, that tourism in the late nineteenth and early twentieth centuries was intimately connected to New York's growth as a business center. Second, that tourism itself was becoming a rationalized industry, slower to achieve self-consciousness than some others, but moving toward marketing sophistication. And third, that the urban tourist was increasingly attracted to and stimulated by business, by merchandisers, both as a consumer and as a visitor. Commercial tourism was, in part, the tourism *of* commerce. New York's success in nurturing the enterprise confounded many expectations and ran counter to much received wisdom about city planning.

After a brief discussion of the evolution of domestic tourism, I will examine some of New York's special appeals (and special limitations) as a visitor center; some local efforts to promote and define tourist rituals; and will suggest some effects of tourism on New York and New Yorkers, perhaps its most important contribution to the growth of that city's commercial culture.

Like many another important national experience, the expansion of pleasure travel took root in a transatlantic context. For a long time travel, when listed in the indexes of American magazines and newspapers, meant travel abroad rather than at home. During much of the nineteenth century New York had been an important stopping point for Europeans and Americans. But it was not perceived as a typical vacation spot nor as part of a system of sightseeing movements. Domestic pleasure travel to Americans invariably meant recreation, and recreation consisted of trips to the mountains, the seashore, the Far West, or the health spa. Such activities seemed to possess both economic significance and seasonal logic.[2]

But by the end of the last century foreign tourism began to seem somewhat less exotic as a model for domestic action, particularly to expectant capitalists in this country. The decreasing costs of Atlantic steamship travel, increasing prosperity in the late 1890s, and rationalization of travel services combined to expand the numbers of Americans going abroad, and the financial rewards of serving them.

They did not go unnoticed. Thus in 1903 a major American religious journal, the *Independent*, mulled over what it called the "tourist industry," and more particularly the three million people who visited Switzerland each year.[3] Despite a series of apparently inauspicious conditions—infertile soil, rigorous climate, intimidating mountains—Switzerland had succeeded in plucking $50 million annually from its visitors. At least 10 percent of that amount was deposited by Americans. One reason, of course, was the modern taste for savage scenery, for climbing and Alpine walking, a sensibility championed by Victorian poets and essayists. Another was the charm of Swiss towns and cities and the color of their national past.

But neither their scenery nor their history sufficed to explain why the Swiss had become so effective as international hosts. Their prosperity was based on the self-conscious development of foreign tourism, a cooperative endeavor linking hotels, railroads, and guidebook publications. Trips to Switzerland were more convenient, more predictable, and more economical, albeit more standardized. There was a reason why Swiss travel guidebooks resembled one another so closely; their authors went to school,

67

along with waiters, cooks, and hotel managers. Tourism, the *Independent* concluded, was entitled "to the rank of a distinct profession."

In the United States similar observations were being made, many of them suggesting the systematic and large-scale broadcasting of national attractions. Concern with redressing the international tourist balance of trade and local promotional efforts surfaced when the great international expositions began to appear here. The vigorous competition among American cities to host these spectacles, particularly the Columbian quadricentennial in the early 1890s, indicated awareness that a range of economic benefits awaited the winner. It was symbolically appropriate, therefore, that Chicago's Columbian Exposition of 1893 should have inspired thoughts of publishing the first Baedecker guide to America. British travel agencies, like Thomas Cook, had been operating for more than a generation by this time, certainly since the 1840s.[4] Cook's Continental operations were stimulated by another world's fair, this the Paris Fair of 1855. Eleven years later, in 1866, Thomas Cook organized his first tour of America. And only two years before the Columbian Exposition, in 1891, another traveler's convenience surfaced as the American Express Company introduced its famous traveler's cheque, more valuable for international than for domestic excursions, yet a symbol of the new levels of organized preparation.[5]

But the Columbian Exposition had more tourist significance for the United States than simply as the occasion for new guidebooks. As the most successful and dramatic of the period's fairs, it highlighted the sort of institutional coordination that impressed Americans when they looked abroad to places like Switzerland: cooperative efforts among hotelkeepers, railroad managers, newspaper publishers, and city officials to ensure that a huge mass of visitors could be moved around, housed, fed, and entertained in an efficient as well as a profitable manner.[6]

The fair also represented an effort to provide a landscape worthy of international comparison, a tourist draw that could compete with the imperial capitals exciting so much American envy—Paris, London, Vienna, Berlin. Planning reformers like Charles Rollinson Lamb pointed in the 1890s to the worldwide "competition of capitals," their claims for national greatness coming with new parliament houses, monuments, museums, and opera houses.[7] In creating a temporary extravaganza of fountains, statuary, gardens, lagoons, boulevards, palaces, and plazas, the architects of the exposition had launched a well-tested formula for civic distinction, well-tested, at least, in the Old World. If contemporary American cities lacked the polish, planning, and institutions that attracted tourists abroad, these momentary complexes formed one quick response. After the fairs had closed and the buildings been taken down, American cities could then turn to the serious business of beautification and create a permanent analogue to the exposition in their own civic structures, museums, and public squares.

That was the course of the City Beautiful movement that followed the Columbian Exposition, although there had been such interest even before 1893. But there was a tourist motive in promoting such improvements. It was clear to city plan promoters that urban beautification could benefit behavior, civic pride, political morals, real estate values, and business efficiency.[8] But some of them also believed that these reforms represented an appropriate investment in tourism as well, particularly in great centers like Chicago, Philadelphia, and New York.

This was part of Daniel Burnham's message when he concluded the presentation of his fabled 1909 Chicago Plan. In the penultimate paragraph, after having reviewed his many-layered proposal—the park-lined lakefront, the great civic center, the widened streets, the forest preserves, the coordinated railroad stations—Burnham pointed to one last justification. "People from all over the world visit and linger in Paris," he observed. "No matter where they make their money, they go there to spend it. . . . The cream of our own earnings should be spent here," he continued, talking about Chicago, "while the city should become a magnet, drawing to us those who wish to enjoy life. The change would mean prosperity, effective, certain, and forever continuous." If his plan was good, its realization would produce a better, more enjoyable life. "Then our own people will become home-keepers," Burnham declared, "and the stranger will seek our gates."[9]

Thus, in the 1890s American cities seeking visitors had, as one option, beautification programs which could assign to them the conveniences and elegance associated with Europe. New York City, by then the most visited place in the country, already contained major tourist shrines, many of them recently created. Its two major museums were, by this decade, established on either side of the great park, which was itself a significant attraction. A zoo in the park increased sightseeing opportunities. The Statue of Liberty and the Brooklyn Bridge, both added during the previous decade, were Manhattan's peripheral markers, while a new piece of construction, many years in the making, created another tourist mecca in the 1890s: Grant's Tomb. The eagerness with which city officials sought to keep Ulysses S. Grant's body in their midst after his 1885 death indicated their appreciation of the role of relics in strengthening metropolitan claims to national attention.[10] The granite mausoleum rising on the heights above the Hudson was dedicated with elaborate civic ceremonies. It would become the city's most popular monument after the Statue of Liberty.

New York's symbolic landscape, its vocabulary of popular imagery, was in the process of formation in the 1890s. It was not yet fixed, and contemporary images reveal its tentativeness. One popular photographic anthology of American scenes, George Cromwell's *America*, appeared in 1894 with several hundred photographs taken all over the United States; it revealed the available local options.[11] After Central Park, the Statue of Liberty, and the Brooklyn Bridge, all of which had become clearly recognized places to visit and icons of New York, the other plates were dominated by street scenes and squares, now unfamiliar because of subsequent construction, and even then in the process of change. The overwhelming impression these images offer is a sense of picturesqueness, an irregularity, a multilayered assymetry which reflects a setting that still bore marks of its historic past, betraying villagelike origins alongside more recent mushroomlike growth. The photographs often resemble older paintings of the city, which delighted in contrasting the smaller, ramshackle structures of the early part of the century with the new behemoths arising around them. There are ship masts and greenery and odd assortments of business enterprises, leavened by an occasional evidence of planned symmetry or the neoclasssical monuments that were beginning to dot the landscape. Like other American cities, New York had already been the subject of a whole series of lithographed views, some of them bird's-eye vistas done from atop a church steeple, others as if viewed from a balloon on high, or set within some section of the city, emphasizing busy streets and fearsome traffic.[12] The famed lower skyline was just beginning to emerge as an icon, still competing with a variety of other possibilities to catch the identity of the place.

Such renditions, on canvas, in lithographic prints, or in photography, had a documentary aspect, in keeping with a revived interest in the city's history that began to show itself at this time, spasms of nostalgia for vanishing churches, inns, houses, and other links to the past. *Old New York*, a journal relating to the history and antiquities of the city, began publication in the summer of 1889, focusing on famous events, forgotten travelers, old engravings, and ancient institutions. When Frank Moss published his *American Metropolis* in 1897, a survey from Knickerbocker days to the present, it was one of a string of histories that had appeared since the 1860s.[13] New York in the 1890s was, after all, older than Chicago is today, or Detroit, Denver, or San Francisco, and these cities are now struggling with their own preservation movements. In the 1890s, writers for magazines and newspapers, amateur historians, journalists, genealogists, and photographers began to express concern about the city's vanishing heritage, and indulged themselves in reveries about the days of Dutch settlement, the era of hosting the national capital, or the Knickerbocker city of Washington Irving and Fenimore Cooper. Since the Jacksonian era at least, New Yorkers had been voicing their anxiety over rapid shifts of population within the city, the taking down of houses and warehouses for replacement by larger structures, the disappearance of ancient customs and neighborhoods. Such meditations had attained almost existential status by this time. But the citizenry of the 1890s, faced with improvements in photography and printing, assumed a more activist role in fixing their attention on this moment of transition in the imaging of the city. Then, and for the next twenty years or so, a whole series of illustrators projected this delight in picturesqueness and craving for nostalgia, as they documented the great new structures around them in books and magazine essays, incorporating the new buildings—from Stanford White's Madison Square Garden and the Washington Arch to the Wall Street skyscrapers and new university campuses—into this aesthetic. By 1911 the *New York Times* could poll artists like Jules Guerin, Paul Cornoyer, Henry Reuterdahl, William Ordway Partridge, Colin Campbell Cooper, and others who, with the Ashcan School, were evoking a new concern with the urban landscape. The *Times* asked, "What is the most beautiful spot in New York?" and received many enthusiastic answers. We were once taught, said the *Times*, that "the prettiest spot in New York was an eastward-bound ocean liner. We became convinced that when business entered the door beauty flew out of the window."[14] Now the sense of bustle and the new construction could be incorporated into traditional vocabularies.

But the 1890s also introduced some fundamental changes to the imaging process, as new growth in the city's tourist industry helped set the scene for a different landscape of visitor interest. Although New York did not host the Columbian Exposition (despite an intensive lobbying effort to capture it), although the city never would experience the special planning legacy of a great beaux-arts world's fair, it did demonstrate its tremendous appeal and considerable skill at hosting giant gatherings in a series of massive crowd pageants. They began with the funeral of Ulysses S. Grant in 1885, continued with the centennial of George Washington's inaugural as president in the spring of 1889, the celebration of the quadricentennial of Columbus's voyage in a three-day festival during October 1892, the Sound Money parade for McKinley in the 1896 campaign, the dedication of Grant's Tomb in 1897, and the Dewey Celebration of 1899, all climaxing in the city's biggest and most elaborate such event, the extraordinary Hudson-Fulton Celebration of 1909.

These occurrences were largely unprecedented in New York's history. They attracted millions of visitors from elsewhere, who taxed the city's transportation, hotel, and amusement facilities to the utmost as they viewed the land and water parades, the pageants, the assemblies of dignitaries, and not incidentally, spent some money.

One million sightseers crowded in to celebrate the Washington Centennial. "Never before was there so vast a concourse of spectators in an American city to witness a patriotic event," boasted the *New York Tribune* in 1889.[15] The Columbian parade was witnessed by two million people.[16] When Grant's Tomb was dedicated in April 1897, the *New York Times* observed that New Yorkers had once looked with "good-natured superiority" on the efforts of provincial cities to draw trade from festivals and holidays. This stance, the *Times* pointed out, however dignified, was certainly not profitable. It applauded a newly formed merchants' association which had helped get special excursion rates from the railroads. The railroads not only offered cheap fares, they permitted visitors time to transact some business in the city. The *Times* wanted both a permanent merchants' association and semiannual excursion arrangements for visitors to New York, allowing them to stay up to 30 days with their cheap tickets. These hopes would eventually be realized.[17]

Two years later, when the city celebrated Admiral Dewey's triumphal return from world conquest, there were hints of caution about the scale of the festivities. "Well developed as is New York's appetite for strangers," the *Times* commented, "and remarkable as are its powers of quick and easy assimilation, the present outlook threatens the city with a serious attack of indigestion." Crowds and delays may be "part of the fun for the festival visitor," but local residents who had to go about their ordinary business faced unpleasant problems.[18] Still, when a letter writer observed that city visitors needed to learn how to walk briskly and keep to the right hand side of the street, so as not to interfere with "the comfort and movement of residents," the *Times* responded that such advice was ultimately worthless. "New York is proud and happy" to host the Dewey triumph, and presumably was willing to put up with inconveniences for both glory and profit.[19]

Even without a great world's fair, New York had become practiced at exploiting the presence of major events, indeed cultivating them, in the interests of extensive visitation. Souvenir venders could now offer a range of plates, spoons, pennants, ashtrays, buttons, paperweights, and other objects bearing city scenes and mottoes on their surfaces. And well before the Hudson-Fulton celebration, they could also select from an even more significant instrument shaping the image of the city—the picture postcard. It is difficult to exaggerate the role played by postcards in fashioning urban reputations, and their distribution through the mails aided the expansion of the tourist trade immeasurably.

In 1909 the American picture postcard was only 15 years old, having gotten its start during the Columbian Exposition. Its true growth came after July 1, 1898, when Congress granted privately printed postcards the same mailing privileges given government cards, one cent. The pioneer postcards of these earlier years were sold primarily to tourists. The American Souvenir Card Company produced in the late 1890s dozens of sets, twelve cards each, devoted to major cities and tourist sites like Niagara Falls. Other publishers did the same. According to postcard historians George and Dorothy Miller, no city was better represented by these view cards than New York.[20]

The postcard makers clearly faced the same set of choices confronting the book publishers, that of selecting popular and easily recognizable sights from the vast range of possibilities that the city offered. But the enormous circulation that these cards and their successors enjoyed made the selections influential by shaping popular expectations about what was important to see in the city. The postcard explosion after the turn of the century brought many other categories into prominence, such as holiday greetings, artist scenes, patriotic, political, humorous, religious, ethnic, news, among other subjects. But the view card remained a fundamental part of the tourist experience and the postcard world.

The urban postcards covered a great variety of settings. For New York the possibilities, given the amount of building going on, seemed limitless. To the traditional scenes hallowed by published books, Central Park, the Lower East Side, the Statue of Liberty, and the Brooklyn Bridge, were now added hundreds of buildings and vistas—hotels, skyscrapers, office buildings, churches, stores, stations, clubhouses, street scenes, beaches, squares, restaurants, bridges, tunnels, schools, monuments, stadiums, amusement parks—a seemingly endless parade of highlights, many of them organized, apparently, around some kind of tourist constituency. Who bought the cards? Some were collected by locals or were distributed by proud owners for advertising purposes. Others were used for holiday greetings or to send personal messages. But the majority ended up in the hands of visitors as testimony to their trips, evidence of where they stayed, what they saw, or what they liked.

It is possible to isolate certain repeated formulas in these cards—the bridge-girdled rivers encircling Manhattan, the skyline from Brooklyn or the Narrows, the sweep of north-south avenues lined with tall buildings, and, of course, the sign-cluttered view of Times Square itself, a view that retained its classic outline through many changes of building and promotional message. But determining just which shots were most popular is a sampling job of awesome proportions. Most significant is that the postcard ordered the urban landscape unlike anything that had preceded it—a landscape filled with commercial structures and human transactions. Nothing was too insignificant or trivial or personal to go on a postcard, and the choice was becoming large enough, by 1910 or so, to permit the individual purchaser an expression of individuality, something that had not been possible when working with the pages of books or magazines.

Periodicals were also fundamental to the popularization of New York images in the early twentieth century and helped advertise the city to potential tourists. The number of major American magazines published in the city had been impressive for some decades by now. Many of the most significant were creations of local publishing houses—Scribner, Lippincott, Harper, Century—and reflected New York's increasing monopolization of literary culture.[21] It was therefore inevitable that news pieces, documentaries, and fiction alike should betray some local bias. In the

1890s particularly, as New York prospered and expanded, stories on the city's growth, accompanied now by artist illustrations as well as photographs, obtained particular prominence. To this must be added the traditional absorption with theatrical culture, a national obsession, the largest and most intense celebrity following of the day. The stars of the American theater lived and worked in New York, and their pictures, along with scenes from their major vehicles, the theaters themselves, stories of producers, directors, playwrights, set designers, all added to the city's physical allure.[22]

Many of the magazines claimed national and international coverage and were not specifically about metropolitan culture. Inevitably, however, they served to make claims for New York, particularly when it came to international comparisons. There were special New York issues offered from time to time, issues devoted almost entirely to outlining the city's accomplishments in art, commerce, industry, and entertainment. At times the language was as smug as the loudest booster could wish.

Thus *Harper's Weekly* could declare, in late 1902, that the city's outer appearance daily "startles the eye and dazzles the brain" with some "new manifestation of the conquering American spirit. The city is simply bursting its bonds. It is as if some mighty force were astir beneath the ground, hour by hour pushing up structures that a dozen years ago would have been inconceivable."[23] In 40 years New York would become, *Harper's* promised, the largest city in the world, unrivaled in magnitude, splendor, and power. "One might almost fancy that the town had been bombarded by a hostile fleet, such rents and gashes appear everywhere in the solid masonry," Randall Blackshaw wrote that same year in the *Century*, breathlessly summarizing the dozens of gigantic new structures that had been erected in the previous couple of years, everything from libraries and hotels to theatres and hospitals.[24] "Upon us is the responsibility never before laid on a people," John DeWitt Warner wrote in *Municipal Affairs*, "of building the world's capital for all time to come."[25]

The city's building program was so vast as to defy imagination, and its transformation so extensive that returning visitors might find it almost unrecognizable just a few years later. With all this publicity it did not at first seem necessary for New York to advertise itself as a tourist attraction, in the manner of southern and western resorts. With the help of railroad companies, these latter sites produced a host of elaborately illustrated brochures promoting their healthy climates and natural beauty.[26]

And yet, there were unappeased appetites for more visitors to New York, as well as unanswered questions about tourism itself. Prosperity and building growth testified to power and influence, but these were not necessarily tourist attractions. What could New York do to increase its visitation? And when did systematic efforts begin to stimulate more activity?

It seems clear that the 1890s was the take-off decade. For it was then that New York learned to imitate the efforts of smaller commercial centers in other parts of the country. Nothing helped tourism as much as reduced travel fares, and several recent experiences emphasized the lesson. The enormous success of the Columbian Exposition rested in large part on railroad discounts. Understanding the implications of this, major western roads began to offer special rates to merchants and buyers, encouraging travel to their terminal cities—Chicago, New Orleans, St. Louis, among them. New York merchants persuaded eastern roads to offer excursion rates good for 14 days, purchasable through the Merchants' Association.[27]

Then some of the railroads began to establish summer rates for those going to New England during July and August, and railroads with outlets to the New Jersey shore began to follow suit. The Erie Railroad, which had no resort communication, did have a New York terminus. So the Erie instituted summer rates to New York and, sensing the almost unlimited possibilities, the New York Merchants' Association, a prime mover of civic advertisement, persuaded other railroads to declare the city, much to the surprise of many natives, a summer resort. Local residents might complain about heat and humidity, but many in the South and West found New York's July and August a relief from even more torrid climates. Louisville editor Henry Watterson declared New York the country's greatest summer resort, and others were soon trumpeting its seasonal attractions. "Manhattan entertains more holiday visitors in the summer months than do all the other Atlantic coast resorts combined," Edward Townsend told readers of *Harper's Weekly* in 1900.[28] By this time the Merchants' Association, now a permanent group, was campaigning to convince American buyers not to stop at San Francisco, Denver, or Chicago, but to come all the way to New York and to bring their wives and daughters with them. Alluringly illustrated literature emphasized the city's appeals. According to Townsend, the Merchants' Association used dignified and restrained prose to describe the uplifting art galleries, historical monuments, parks, and ocean breezes awaiting the strangers.

The newcomers, however, knew what they wanted and art museums were not high on the list. The many visitors patronizing the hotels, restaurants, and roof gardens of midtown New York, the summer buyers and their entourages, had other things on their minds. And these were dominated by pleasure rather than by culture.[29] Townsend accepted their modifications with good grace. If "one who comes from Nebraska to buy calico and revel in historical monuments, chances to stray upon a roof [garden]" and finds in such a place attractive feminine company, "why, the object of the Merchants' Association is not defeated." The point, after all, was to make "New York to America what Paris is to Europe," and visitors to the City of Light "have been known to extend their sight-seeing beyond the elevating influences of the Louvre and the Luxembourg."[30]

Two years later the summer tourists had become an established fact, whetting the local appetite for more. The Hotel Association of New York sought $100,000 to advertise the city's attractions in southern and western newspapers, pointing out that New York lagged behind her rivals in boosting energy and civic pride. Whether it was the advertisements or not, summer tourism increased still further. *Harper's* noted the "men of Dixie" doing business under electric fans, making hotel owners happy in July and August, while their wives and daughters went shopping which, said the magazine, "is the chief end of woman if the woman happens to be a Southern woman and in New York." Most people who come to New York for pleasuring, *Harper's* admitted, care as little for sightseeing as do New Yorkers. They came to the city once or twice a year "to see good plays, hear good music, and buy good clothes. . . . Though they often use business as pretext for these frequent visits, their real object is to have a good time."[31]

It was not that traditional tourist stops had disappeared. Earlier in its review *Harper's* had covered them: Grant's Tomb ("mecca of all tourists"), Central Park, the Metropolitan, the Eden Musee, Chinatown, the Brooklyn Bridge, the Statue of Liberty. For some visitors these sights remained imperative parts of a larger ritual like watching the clock strike on the Herald Building and writing down the dimensions of local monuments in those omnipresent little notebooks that every conscientious tourist seemed to possess. Only then could such visitors return home with a sense they had explored New York to the fullest. And local boosters could claim by this time that there "is no American so lowly in condition, or so remote geographically, but cherishes in his heart the ambition to see New York at least once before he dies."[32]

But there were many kinds of visitors to New York by century's end, visitors with differing agendas. How to distinguish them from each other, count them and categorize their various wants and habits, became something of a parlor game for journalists and magazine writers. By 1910 it was estimated that New York had, on a daily basis, something between 100,000 and 200,000 visitors who neither worked nor lived within its borders. With only a few hundred automobiles entering or leaving the city each day, train arrivals furnished a fairly reliable statistical base, supplemented by New York's hotel registers.[33] The growing importance of the tourist industry was reflected in these increasingly precise visitor studies, analyzing where they came from, how much cash they spent and where they spent it, and just what they needed that was not yet available.

One active force behind these investigations, along with the Merchants' Association, was a group of businessmen whose interest was vital to expansion of New York's entertainment district. These were the entrepreneurs and managers who ran the city's hotels, whose locations and services were linked to the fundamental needs of the tourist: food, transport, information, and entertainment. Hoteliers were natural local boosters, and their professional organizations, journals, and lobbying efforts focused attention on tourist traffic. By 1910, reflecting national trends, the American Hotel Association had been founded—a federation of state and local groups. New York State's own hotel group was more than 25 years old by this time.[34]

In addition, by the early twentieth century, New York City contained a group of particularly ambitious and energetic hotel men: Frederick and William Muschenheim, together supervising the Hotel Astor, whose 1905 opening was so crucial to Times Square's future; Frederic Sterry of the Plaza, which opened 2 years later; George C. Boldt of the Waldorf-Astoria; Gustave Baumann of the Holland House, who would help create the Biltmore as part of the Grand Central Complex; his successor, John Bowman, who went on to control the Commodore, among others; Lucius Boomer, of the McAlpin and later the Sherry-Netherland and the new Waldorf-Astoria of the 1930s. In the years following the opening of the Astor, New York hotel construction was huge in quantity and enormous in scale. The Astor, Plaza, and Gotham hotels, all large for their day, were followed, within ten years or so, by the Vanderbilt, the Biltmore, the Commodore, the McAlpin, the Pennsylvania or Statler, and the Ritz Carlton. Most of these hotels had more than 1,000 rooms; when it opened in 1912 the McAlpin's more than 1,500 rooms made it the largest in the world, only to be outdone a few years later by Statler's Pennsylvania.[35]

New York already possessed large and splendid hotels catering to the carriage trade, as well as myriads of boardinghouses and cheap lodging places. But the new hotels, with some high-priced exceptions, offered luxury for less cost, and were often geared specifically for business travel and for small family groups visiting the city for a short time. Some offered "quiet floors," for those whose jobs required them to sleep during the day. Others included special display facilities for salesmen and their samples. And the enormous hotels constructed after 1910 often had some relation to the two new railroad terminals, forming concentrations just to the east and the south of the Times Square area. Long doomed to one inadequate structure, Manhattan just before World War I could glory in two of the greatest and most complex stations in the world.[36] Both the Pennsylvania and the Grand Central stations received national publicity, much of which emphasized the marvels of engineering that had gone into their creation. Amid all the boasting about size, elegance, and convenience, it was their capacity to service train travelers which seemed most impressive—tunnels and elevators carried passengers directly up to the lobby of the Biltmore or across the street from Penn Station to the Statler. The Grand Central area benefited from its proximity to half a dozen giant new hotels which fed off the station's expansion, along with the new Grand Central Palace, an exposition center that complemented and in some cases replaced the activities of the old Madison Square Garden.[37] Whole tourist districts developed around the two stations, natural sources for the clients of Times Square.

The new hotels now not only handled the dinners, parties, banquets, and civic events which had been hosted for many decades; they also boasted of special facilities and meeting rooms for another growing aspect of the travel program: the convention and trade show. Business, fraternal, professional, veteran, and other associations were now major parts of the municipal economy. The largest such events—automobile, flower, boat, and electrical shows—drew several hundred thousand visitors to New York. With them came the annual get-togethers of the National Association of Piano Tuners, the American Posture League, the Traveling Hat Salesman's Association, and the Dancing Masters of America, all of which met in New York. There were, even before World War I, thousands of such conclaves annually throughout the United States.[38]

But though the convention visitors were important, New York was less dominant in this area than in several others. The long travel times of the railroad era meant that conventions had to be chosen for regional convenience. Before World War I Chicago, for example, was approaching the number of conventions New York would host 20 years later. In 1905 Chicago held 310 conventions involving a quarter of a million people; in 1911 it was luring almost 400,000. In some 6 years the city had drawn almost 1,600 conventions.[39] Fifteen years later New York estimated it was attracting half a million convention delegates annually, and that they were spending more than $40 million.[40] The Merchants' Association had created a convention bureau to monitor the activity. But important as New York was, Cleveland, San Francisco, Boston, Philadelphia, and dozens of other places had also become popular convention sites.

The conventions, the buying trips, and the trade associations were not fundamental. It was the combination of business contacts which, when pushed by the search for pleasure, brought New York so many tourists. A range of local institutions appeared to meet the demand. Before 1905 omnibus companies were offering tours of Manhattan, leaving several times daily from the Flatiron Building. There were boat excursions around the island; by the teens several lines competed for the trade.[41] Then the tour buses started and a myriad of maps and guidebooks appeared in print. Many were published by the businesses dependent on active tourism: hotels, transportation companies, department stores like John Wanamaker, which not only printed guides to the city but escorted visitors around its own establishment. The Stock Exchange conducted its tours; great newspaper plants like the *Times* organized their own special programs. And tall buildings increasingly turned to observation decks, whose panoramic views made them obvious targets for sightseers. This was not high culture, but in its concern for information, mundane experience, corporate celebration, and broad urban vistas, it reflected a set of metropolitan values that were easily comprehensible.[42]

It was inevitable that so large and continuous an influx of visitors should eventually produce a reaction from New Yorkers. And just as inevitable that the reaction would be mixed. Some tourists headed for exactly those uplifting institutions that had traditionally justified the act of travel—museums, monuments, parks, churches, libraries. But others did not, and their descent upon the city's pleasure zones raised a number of problems.

In 1904 one writer in *Outlook* magazine exposed the new realities.[43] He claimed to have escorted a series of family visitors to the city. One set of cousins happily trudged through the Metropolitan and Natural History museums, Central Park, the Statue of Liberty, and Grant's Tomb. These aspects of New York, the writer reported, filled him "with pride and public spirit," even though his ignorance of them was much greater than "that of the cousin from Kankakee." But while these relatives sought culture and patriotism, others came for luxury and pure diversion, heading for the great new hotels and nightspots, the fleshpots of the Tenderloin and the variety theaters. He worried about their experiences on several grounds.

One was their impression of the city and its people. When tourists came to the entertainment zone they frequently saw, according to the *Outlook*, not the New Yorkers they hoped to spot, but other visitors like themselves. Peacock's Alley "as a place for the native to see strangers, and for strangers to see one another," offered "unparalleled opportunities," but "it might as well have been the Bowery" as a site from which to observe fashionable New Yorkers. This was a New York of strangers, in 1904 a city of "cafes, with their gilding and looking-glasses and bands of music, the theaters, the big department stores in winter holiday trim, the opera," and similar institutions.

This city, gayer than Paris, was not only dominated by strangers, it was also expensive, far beyond the reach of most locals. Rich visitors could afford lavish tips and high prices, forcing Manhattanites to relinquish favorite spots in favor of pilgrims from "Peoria and Portland." When the proprietor added gilding and doubled prices he was sure of the newcomer's patronage, but the visitor never guessed that "the intimate city" he sought "forever recedes before him." New York was enough of a tourist center by the first decade of the century for locals to feel both part of the attraction and also to sense they inhabited a very different and more conventional world than the frenzied tourist city—a reaction that Parisians and Londoners and Berliners were experiencing at much the same time. "The stranger's New York is a surface New York," concluded the *Outlook*.[44] This was the major comfort metropolitan residents could take, increasingly locked out of such lavish pleasures. No matter how humble his lot in life, no matter how recent his arrival in America, no matter how poor his English, the New Yorker lived within the imperial center, knowledgeable and blasé about things that took away the breath of the visitors. The presence of the tourist underscored the splendid misery of the locals, superior to the out-of-towners who didn't know how to behave in the big city.

The sense of an expensive, isolated, artificial tourist cylinder, shared by a special group of resident high rollers and social butterflies, found expression among contemporary journalists like Julian Street, particularly when writing about the Tenderloin, the term he applied in 1910 to Times Square. Amidst the noisy congestion of theaters, hotels, restaurants, and advertising signs, New York put on its big spending manners. "Broadway eats French better than it speaks it," Street noted of the Cafe dell' Opera, a local night spot, and pointed out how restaurateurs exploited Broadway's "hysterical loathing of cheapness, and of feeling cheap."[45] Indeed, Street's depiction of the tourist's service society was filled with angry indignation directed against the local sharpies. Any welcome to the city was actually a request for money, he argued. The Pullman porter's clothes brush announced the things to come "so that when our parasitic population pounces on you with all sorts of services you don't desire, you'll follow the metropolitan custom and reach for your change pocket instead of your gun pocket." The porter, the taxi driver, the carriage starter, the bellboy, the barber, the newsstand girl, the head waiter, the washroom attendant—the list went on and on. "Conceal, as best you can," Street warned visitors, "your hatred of the countless people who come bumping into you in the congestion of the city's life; for they try to conceal their hatred from you. Remember that New York is that national parlour for the painless extraction of ideals; get a new set made of gold."[46]

Just as in Europe, lavishness and generosity earned the tourists no gratitude from the natives. "It is the custom of the Tenderloin to look with pity and amusement at those who are not of it," wrote Street. "People from out of town are jokes." Why? Street wondered. Why was it more droll to be ignorant of New York than of Omaha or Lhasa? New Yorkers loved to look about restaurants and declare that certain diners must have come from Kankakee or Keokuk. They accuse them of "rubbering." Why not? Street answered. "They stare at New York as a New Yorker stares at Coney Island. For New York is, after all, the Coney Island of the nation."[47]

Other guides were less hard on the resident population, and seemed almost defensive about the entertainment district. "A great part of the people who move along the 'Great White Way' are not New Yorkers, but visitors," wrote Robert Shackleton in 1920, "and it is these who furnish the chief support of much of the more vicious and vivacious features." Most New Yorkers had daily jobs and needed to retire early to be clearheaded at work the next day. But the visitor was different, with money to spend and in no hurry to get to sleep. "At his home in some distant city," Shackleton acknowledged, the average tourist was probably respectable enough, "but on Broadway he is likely to get a fifty cent cigar between his teeth and fling extravagant tips, and become arrogant and boastful, and make it clear that he 'has the price.' It is this class of men who, inviting and receiving the attentions of swindlers and robbers and sharpers, gets into the police courts and gives New York more of a reputation for wickedness than it deserves."[48] For most New Yorkers were neither victimizers nor victimized. New York contained 50 theaters exclusive of movies, Franklin P. Adams pointed out in 1916, but it hosted 2,000 churches. New Yorkers live "as normal, healthful, conventional, and regular a life as the average American anywhere else." Visitors, on the other hand, concentrating on the Broadway of Fortieth to Fiftieth streets, on shopping and restauranting, on late breakfasts, hotels, theaters, and cabarets, are different. "It is possible that visitors to New York, just because they are away from home, go out between the acts for drinks. . . . In fact, most of the actions of the visitor are those of the young boy."[49]

Extravagant, naive, perhaps even wicked, visitors were also accused of threatening some of the city's major institutions. The so-called New York theater audience, wrote *Harper's Weekly* in 1902, was not local at all. With a daily tourist visitation in six figures, most of whom apparently were theatergoers, it was easy to understand why not. After a day spent in business or shopping, tourists took their evenings at the playhouse. "It is not possible always to pick them out," *Harper's* continued, "but it is often quite easy to do so. It may not always be clear that this theatre party or that comes from Chicago, Boston, or Philadelphia, but a discriminating observer can, if he be so minded, justifiably reach the conclusion that their habitat is not Manhattan Island, Brooklyn Borough, or Queens." This charge relieved New York of responsibility for any degeneration in the drama. Its theater was simply a port of entry for all dramatic ships to enter, "and if sporadic cases of diseased taste appear," Father Knickerbocker was not to blame.[50]

The urban tourist, in short, out for fun, free-spending, gullible, more caught up by department stores than museums and libraries, simultaneously caricatured and nurtured the local sensibility. The tourist presence flattered New York as a world center, and demonstrated the knowledgeability and sophistication of the natives. But the tourist was also the whipping boy for aspects of commercial culture that residents were not proud of, and which excited occasional envy, contempt, and indignation. Fame brought inconvenience (and traffic jams), and spectatorship meant playing for the crowd. New York was on stage and Times Square had become the centerpiece. One's attitude to tourists was, in short, a touchstone of one's attitude to the new commercial culture generally. The strident pace, electric atmosphere, life under tension, scurry for space, towering skyscrapers, and ethnic neighborhoods that constituted so much of New York's tourist appeal did not fit the "city beautiful" recipe that true believers in municipal destiny had composed. Their vision of an imperial capital, graced by magnificent buildings, squares, broad avenues, unhurried promenaders, celebrated cultural institutions, resurfaced from time to time in architectural competitions and planning proposals. But it was not the consensual image of the city. Some postcard makers tried, as best they could, to shape the city's structures to this vision, but they also could not contend against the cacophony of tall buildings bordering narrow canyons, bright lights, ethnic festivals, crowds, and commercial promotion that dominated the imaging process.

Such images could be worrisome. Arguing that "great masses of men fall easily to a low moral level if their idealism is not continually stimulated," the *Independent* in 1910 cast a baleful eye on some of the new improvements. "The present age is characterized by an almost pathological passion for the startling, the staccato, the freakish, the bizarre," the *Independent* confided. "These are the qualities of the newspaper headline, of the electric advertisement, of the skyscraper office building, of the monstrous apartment house." Manhattan Island's peculiar topography enforced a standard of dizzy heights, but the new structures required no fantastic or meaningless accessories, the journal argued. In the end this "abnormal taste will have its day," it predicted, and yield to a love for the "dignified and suitable."[51]

The prediction was wrong. In the contest for control of New York's landscape, commercial extravagance rather than aesthetic discipline set the prevailing tone. And it was that which the tourists seemed to savor most. In their descent upon New York City in the early twentieth century the Little Old Lady from Dubuque and the rubbernecker from Peoria between them helped shape the debate over its reputation for the next 50 years. On the horizon stood the city of the tourist caricature—only New Yorkers would wonder whether the caricature was not actually being realized. In the end, the entertainments were redemptive. Wondering how he would respond to the umpteenth visitor he heard saying, "It's a fine place to visit, but I'd hate to live there," Franklin P. Adams had an answer. "Well, I'd reply cheerily, maybe the other towns aren't even great places to visit."[52]

4

THE DISCIPLINE
OF AMUSEMENT

Richard Wightman Fox

T HE FIVE-MEMBER subcommittee of New York's Society for the Prevention of Vice and Crime was "amazed, shocked, and astounded" by a performance at the Shubert Theatre on a November evening in 1923. The musical variety show, "Artists and Models," was in many respects "beautiful and fine," and the audience "enjoyed most" and "generously applauded" those parts of the show that were "devoid of rottenness." But in the first scene they were subjected to "a parade of women entirely nude from the waist up, and with very little, flimsy veiling from the hips down. The breasts of these women were completely exposed. The torsos of these women were exposed." In their report to the Committee for a Clean Stage, the two ministers and three Presbyterian laypeople did not hesitate to conclude that the opening scene "was manifestly a sex appeal."

The "downright nakedness" of the prologue was not the most serious infraction of the evening—indeed, the visitors implied that posed nudity of the sort found "in sculpture or painting" would be unobjectionable in a show depicting an artist's studio. Nor was the "sinister, slimy trail of smut" in several skits the show's worst offense. "Particularly nauseating," for example, was a chorus sung by three brothers who could not manage, despite repeated attempts, to slay their fourth brother: "You can't kill the bastard!" they sang. Nor was the Hawaiian scene, which featured "the most degraded type of dancing we have ever seen" and "absolutely the most forward sort of sex-stimulating gyrations," at the top of their list of complaints. The "most reprehensible" part of the show was the burlesque *All Wet*, in which a female impersonator stripped to corset and undergarments, then withdrew seductively to a hotel room, setting off a stampede that included a group of soldiers, the hotel keeper, and a wavering minister who had observed the whole exhibition and finally, after "a most suggestive struggle with his emotions," set his conscience aside.

All Wet was not just "an offense against the morals of both young and old of the city," but in its heartless satire on the minister "an offense against churches, regardless of creed, for we believe the churches to be united on this one thing, the greatly-needed decency in our theatre." It was unthinkable that the sincere ecclesiastical commitment to decency should be mocked. *All Wet* was in fact more than an attack on the churches in general; it was an implicit attack on moral critics in the audience itself, whose scruples it depicted as surface-deep. Moralists might parade their high-mindedness, but like the watchful minister on stage, they were seducible by flesh and artifice. The subcommittee may not have realized how they were targeted in the skit, but they knew the church had been maligned, and recommended legal action to force the manager to "eliminate the undue nakedness, the suggestive lines, and to take out completely the burlesque." By the time a judge had been dispatched to view the show the following week, however, "the beauties who formerly had appeared almost naked . . . were more properly clad." The newspaper report doesn't indicate whether *All Wet* was cut out of the show, but apparently no further legal steps were taken.

It is easy to read the subcommittee's tale of their night at the theater as one more vain Puritan attempt to turn back the moral clock or as a typically pinched conservative campaign to regulate other people's private lives. But the notable thing about this report for anyone familiar with the long history of Protestant attitudes toward the theater is the subcommittee members' fundamental endorsement of it. They are attacking "Artists and Models" not because it embodies vices intrinsic to theater, but because it fails to live up to the promise of theater. These subcommittee members bear only the palest resemblance to the generations of Protestant moralists who, from the sixteenth century to the late nineteenth, assailed theater as a deadly threat to virtue. In the case of "Artists and Models" they did not call for a shut down: their rallying cry was simply "clean it up."[1]

A decisive transformation in the American Protestant sensibility took place during the nineteenth century. Some "amusements" that were roundly condemned for much of the century, such as the theater, dancing, and card playing, were—along with new commercial entertainments such as baseball, amusement parks, and moving pictures—routinely accepted by the early twentieth century.

The usual explanation for this shift focuses on secularization: A modernizing society becomes more rationalistic and worldly, and as the people learn a new work discipline, they also imbibe a new leisure discipline. They give up cockfighting, bear and bull baiting, long bouts of drinking, and in return they get approved forms of this-worldly entertainment. "Having a good time," a late-nineteenth century phrase that turn-of-the-century writers were still putting in quotation marks, becomes a respectable personal goal.

This explanation has much to recommend it. American culture *was* secularized over the course of the nineteenth century. But the secularization thesis overlooks the major role of religion in carrying out the secularization. Liberals in the mainstream denominations—especially the Congregationalists, Episcopalians, Presbyterians, Methodists, and northern Baptists—told Americans it was all right to embrace the world, even enjoy it. Not in order to recline in it, of course, but to improve it. One could only reform the world if one was of the world. Secularization in the United States was not an anticlerical movement. The paradox is that since secularization took place within an enduringly religious culture, it became all the more deeply rooted. And the religion itself was transformed in the process. But the fully successful secularization required active religious sponsorship.

Catholics and Jews also played decisive roles in the rise of secular values. Both Catholicism and Judaism were heavily immigrant religions in nineteenth and early twentieth century America, and both had a very different relationship to the "world." As religious traditions, they were much more comfortable with the things of this world, including dramatic representation and the dance. But the concrete American "world" was one in which they were alien. Their very distance from the respectable Protestant world of moral striving may have made them less reticent than Protestants about embracing new forms of worldly amusement. In a sense, then, nineteenth and early twentieth century Protestant converts to the world of amusements were catching up with Catholics and Jews. But it was the Protestant conversion that made America a securely secular society, since it was only the Protestants who could put the stamp of bourgeois legitimacy on the new cultural regime.[2]

Changes in ideas do not follow mechanically upon changes in other social phenomena. People learn new modes of thought as they experience the world in new ways—and one important form of experience is listening to their moral teachers. Nineteenth century Americans had to decide to give up inherited modes of thought and action and, to make that decision, many needed advice from those they trusted. Many persisted in viewing amusements as a terrible corruption of republican virtue and a deadly threat to Christian morals. It took an active campaign by liberal Protestant authorities to persuade them that they were wrong.

By the late nineteenth century liberal Protestants were preaching a new "discipline" of amusement—a discipline with two apparently contradictory parts. Amusements needed to be disciplined, regulated, "cleaned up." Church committees would accept the burden of policing the arena of popular entertainment. But amusements needed to be embraced: Christians were called to accept a new regime of enjoyment. Only those who knew the world could improve it. Only those who "re-created" themselves could maintain their strength in the "fast" urban environment. What seems clear is the interrelationship between the two parts of the discipline of amusement. Vigorous patrolling of popular culture to clean up its abuses helped legitimize mass entertainment. Church people could relax in tasting the fruits of the world since the proper authorities were vigilantly scrutinizing them for signs of rottenness.

In the case of the theater, in the mid-nineteenth century liberal Protestants took the lead in rethinking the church's historic war on dramatic artifice. By 1920 most of the mainstream liberal churches had not only sanctioned attendance at theatrical events but even brought theatrical programming into the church. Church people, and not just conservative preachers of doom, continued to lambaste the theater for immorality. But protected by the barrage of anti-smut artillery, the faithful could get about the business of enjoying themselves. [3]

By the 1920s an urban entertainment mecca such as Times Square could become a proper middle-class destination because it was a place where even church people need not fear to tread. In 1923, the year that "Artists and Models" shocked the subcommittee at the Shubert, 700,000 people a day patronized the theaters of New York, at least a quarter of them (by one 1923 estimate) pilgrims from outside the city. They made the journey, not just because transportation and communication networks made it easy, not just because they had succumbed to the blandishments of modern urban society, but because they felt called to experience the world. Their zeal for novel experience—for living in the world and even for pushing back the frontiers of respectability—was one major precipitating cause for the explosion of popular cultural entertainments around the turn of the century. The Times Square area, where no fewer than 80 theaters were constructed between 1900 and 1930, was the crest of a wave that rose up out of urban areas, small and large, all over the country. Certainly Times Square and all it represented was a fact of modern life to which religious forces had to respond. But it is no less true that Times Square was itself a response to, among other things, powerful religious forces, which helped call it into being. [4]

The nineteenth century Protestant accommodation to the world of amusements had its roots in the Puritan viewpoint itself. For all their fulminating against trifling diversions and profane activity—especially the theater—the Puritans made a point of calling for a life that balanced work and leisure. They made a careful distinction between "recreation," which restored a person in body and mind, and "amusements" that were either idle and frivolous or overly "exciting" and therefore exhausting. If made habitual, amusements ate away at one's sense of calling and ended in dissipation.

The theater was the most diabolical of amusements, especially for seventeenth century Puritans such as William Prynne, who was outraged by the low moral tenor of the post-Elizabethan stage. His *Histrio-Mastix* (1633) catalogued the whole history of anti-theater arguments from Plato on: Stage productions were immoral in content, actors were dissolute characters who were no better than beggars, the theater mirrored the Catholic Church in tricking (and entertaining) the people with dramatic mysteries rather than the Word of God. Even when the stage kept "the wanton enticements" under control, Prynne urged, it was still based on hypocrisy and deception. Actors were not who they seemed to be: play-acting eroded selfhood, both in actor and audience. Neither actors nor viewers could avoid being influenced by the characters—amoral, immoral, or simply foolish—depicted and frequently lauded on the stage.[5]

In early nineteenth century America the mainstream Protestant denominations still echoed the Puritan message. Indeed, in the post-disestablishment free market in religion, in which fine points of doctrine were less important than well-publicized demonstrations of social purity, Methodists, Baptists, Presbyterians, and Congregationalists outdid one another in denouncing worldly aberrations. But they also became more vehement in their attacks because growing numbers of self-described "liberals," mostly Unitarians and Universalists in Massachusetts, were beginning to lament the Calvinist rejection of amusements, just as they castigated the Calvinist fixation on original sin and predestination.

Henry Ward Beecher's 1844 "Lectures to Young Men" in Indianapolis was typical of the traditionalists' perspective (unlike the "liberals," the conservatives—those who resisted accommodation with the world of amusements—did not choose a consistent label for themselves). People needed amusement, Beecher granted, but let them enjoy the beauties of nature and attend to the great dramas of life itself. Young men arriving in the city were especially at risk, since "jockeys and actors and gamblers" and other "lynx-eyed procurers" lay in wait. These confidence men "know the city, they know its haunts, they know its secret doors, its blind passages, its spicy pleasures, its racy vices, clear down to the mud-slime of the very bottom." Naturally they met with much success, since the raw young newcomer did have "an intense curiosity to *see* many things of which he has long *heard* and *wondered*, and it is the very art and education of vice to make itself attractive. It comes with garlands of roses about its brow, with nectar in its goblet, and love upon its tongue."

The theater was deeply mired in the cesspool of city life. In the pit, Beecher noted, one "may sit down among thieves, blood-loving scoundrels, swindlers, broken-down men of pleasure"; in the gallery one can carouse with "the quarrelling, drunken, ogling, mincing, brutal women of the brothel." Meanwhile, on the stage "flourishes every variety of wit, ridicule of sacred things, burlesques of religion, and licentious double-entendres." For Beecher the theater was a representation of urban degeneracy. Yet the drama of his prose, his own verbal rush at the city's profligate flair, signaled the theater's appeal for those young men who wished to "see," "hear," and "wonder." "Secret doors" were meant to be opened, "blind passages" illuminated. Beecher's text was at cross-purposes with itself. He described actors who had the most intimate knowledge of the urban scene, yet he insisted they did not belong to the city. They were outside amusers, "a floating population" who "wander up and down without ties of social cohesion," yet manage to "invade our town and destroy our children." They had infiltrated the garden, but were not of the garden.

Beecher bewailed the stranglehold of the theater over community morals, but then labeled the theater an alien intrusion that "is in its dotage, as might be suspected from the weakness of the garrulous apologies which it puts forth." That pious hope flew in the face of his own analysis. He had already shown that the theater was rooted structurally in the city's core and emotionally in the curiosity of the young (and rhetorically in the preacher's jeremiad). It was one thing to deny the theater's legitimacy, to warn it out on the grounds that it embodied a nontraditional moral viewpoint. He could not, after his breathless account of its vitality, deny its continued potency.[6]

Beecher revealed, against his expressed intention, the magnetic pull of worldly existence. The antebellum Unitarian and Universalist apologists for the theater agreed with him about the natural human curiosity to discover that world. But where Beecher perceived a moral precipice, they saw a bright horizon of growth toward salvation. As they did in theology, these "liberals" challenged Calvinists in matters of social practice. In 1830 Boston's Unitarian *Christian Examiner* regretted the "singular inaptitude in our people to amuse themselves." Americans were so worried about "public opinion," so in dread of "imputed indecorum," that they froze at the prospect of "innocent and useful" diversion. Of course the best amusement was "domestic," yet the theater—"a fountain of so much ruin, the receptacle of such infamy"—was "wrong only in the abuse."[7]

"New England Christianity has been severe and stern," the *Examiner* noted in 1848. "Its frown has done much to scare away the lighter graces and pleasures of life. It delights in 'Old Hundred,' acquiesces in an oratorio, but regards an opera as a device of the Adversary." Let us learn from the children, the *Examiner* intoned in a standard Romantic appeal. "God has made the child, for wise purposes, to have a strong craving for social pleasures." It was precisely in their amusements that children learned self-control and disinterestedness. Indeed, "reasonable amusements" were as favorable to religion as "money-making." Although they could be abused, amusements would wreak more havoc if banned. The church should instead reform institutions like the theater. Above all, it was time to bury "the ascetic spirit." "To the calculating question, put in doleful tones, Of what use are amusements? we answer, their use is that they give enjoyment, and this is enough."[8]

The goal of the church, as the *Examiner* put it in 1857, was to take on the world, not withdraw from it in proud isolation. The Calvinist attitude of "touch-not, taste-not, handle-not" was antithetical to Jesus' own example. If the theater was immoral—and it "has been in general steadily purifying itself, since the grossness of two centuries ago"—let good Christian men purify it by appointing "a firm committee of supervision." If dancing too often encouraged, as the independent *Monthly Religious Magazine* feared in 1859, "voluptuous movements" that "heat the blood," then let the church take over dancing. Boston's Warren Street Chapel, which had gathered "exposed children" under its "joyous and cheerful discipline" since the 1830s, did just that: Wednesday afternoons it taught dancing in its "pretty parlors," and it regularly put on "dancing parties."[9]

The liberal argument on amusements was a minority position in the antebellum period, since the groups most likely to embrace it—the Unitarians and Universalists—were themselves a tiny minority in the Christian community. But as concerned traditionalists regularly noted by the 1850s, the accommodationist viewpoint was increasingly popular in the more mainstream denominations too. The world was not to be dismissed as doomed, more and more Christians agreed, but colonized by spirit and redeemed. The liberal view was both idealist and realist. It was idealist in its conviction that human beings could grow and improve themselves in harmony with their environment: human nature was good at its source, even if it took discipline to transcend the lingering taint of original sin. And it was realistic in its observation, as the *Examiner* put it, that "in all large towns, where the fast habits of our modern life are crowding in," the people needed (and would get) public, commercial amusements. Quoting with approval an English cleric, the *Examiner* asserted that "the quietude and rest of the last generation are gone forever, and people must take, in other forms and in a condition of concentration, the recreation which they need more than ever. . . . The people themselves feel this, and with the same haste and energy that they are required to work with, seek their pleasures." Concentrated leisure meant cricket and rowing clubs, magic lantern shows, and "first-rate speaking," not lyceum lectures, oratorios or "scientific music."[10]

And as the *Universalist Review* stressed in 1860, it meant a rejuvenated theater. The people would have their drama; Christians must help mold it. Although, according to the *Review*, Boston had no facility devoted solely to theater in 1860, its dramatic presentations were far better than twenty years earlier because "a more exemplary class of citizens have given their support." True, there had been occurrences on the stage "the particulars of which it would sully these pages to write: words have been spoken which chaste ears cannot hear without calling up a tingle of shame; and spectacles . . . which pure eyes can never desire to look upon." But these were accidents, not essence. It made no sense to criticize the theater as such. The only logical rejection of the theater would entail a rejection of all theatricality, all impersonation designed "to move the sympathies and excite the imaginations of the spectator." But such an argument "would be strangely inconsistent for meeting-going Christians, . . . for with them nothing else is so acceptable in the pulpit. The popular preacher in every communion, save the Catholic, and perhaps the Episcopal (in which communions the effect depends more especially upon scenic representation), is he who can most vividly *act* his sermon." Here as elsewhere the liberals reconciled themselves to the world: just as they chose to embrace the pleasures of earthly existence, and grant the world its causal independence ("modern" urban life inevitably exacted its particular demands), and take on the institutions of the world as projects for reformation, so they admired the agile calculations of the performing entertainer who strove for vivid "effect."[11]

Liberal ideas did not spread through the nineteenth century churches like some slow and irresistible contagion. Liberal and traditional ideas spread simultaneously. Northern Baptists became more liberal, Methodists (the largest denomination of all, with about 800,000 members in the Northern states in 1855) more conservative: as late as 1872 the Methodists added to their *Discipline* a formal prohibition on "intoxicating liquors, dancing, playing at games of chance, attending theaters, horse races, circuses, dancing parties, or patronizing dancing schools." This itemizing of vices suggests that more and more Methodists may have been lapsing into worldliness; perhaps in earlier years a more obedient flock needed no such list. Congregationalists and Presbyterians went both ways at once: the internal polarization of opinion on amusements contributed to the factionalism that erupted in bitter heresy trials in the late nineteenth century.[12]

Both sides could gather strength because both were able to appeal to a new social fact, the explosion by mid-century of urban commercial amusements. Liberals could embrace it as a challenge, conservatives could record it as further evidence of worldly degeneration. In New York City the theater, like other commercial amusements, was thriving by the 1850s. At the National Theater (in the view of *Putnam's Monthly Magazine* one of the "lowest" of the six established theaters in 1854) "Uncle Tom's Cabin" was a booming success: it was still showing twice a day to a mixed house of high- and low-class customers after a six-month run. *Putnam's* could not contain its joy at the new respectability of the stage. Not only was "the elite of our society" turning out—"enduring all the inconveniences [of the National Theater] for the sake of enjoying an emotion, such as neither the preaching of their clergy, nor the singing of Italian artists could create." Actors themselves were of a new breed. "Actors are, generally, when off the stage, the most matter of fact and serious people to be seen; many of them have other callings, they engage in trade or manufacturing, and. perform the parts of good citizens with as much success as those of the stage villains and heroes whom they personate for a living."[13]

Liberals in the churches were confident of their ability to discipline the theater for the very reason that middle-class patrons were turning out in growing numbers. Conservatives continued to insist that the theater could never be reformed, that it would always defeat well-meaning attempts to tame it. Their argument went beyond the very reasonable prediction that commercial calculation would always dominate the stage and impose the lowest common denominator of dramatic fare, no matter how many sensitive souls bought tickets. As the *American Church Monthly* explained in 1857, even those sensitive souls would be at risk. The theater would remake them, not vice versa. They would sooner or later be seduced by "the theatrical taste," by the need to see "a piece which, although not strictly the proper thing, is not so *very objectionable*. This would by degrees break down the line between plays."[14]

The conservative Christians' fear of a spreading "theatrical taste" deserves our attention because it is a complex perception. They deplored a dawning culture of self-indulgence, but not in the simple sense that they wanted people to be serious instead of frivolous, to work instead of lounge. The *American Church Monthly* made a point of rejecting that dichotomy: "The age has a double tendency—towards over-exertion and towards self-indulgence." It was meaningless to preach self-control in amusements if one didn't also preach it in "the pursuit of wealth." Production and consumption were both out of control. "The great lesson for all is to believe that human beings are sent into this world for other purposes than the gratification of their own desires and fancies." Men should seek "a subsistence, or at most a competency, instead of a fortune"; women should "find their happiness in steady employment, and not in alternate idleness and excitement." The problem was a boundless national appetite for both more capital and more stimulating experience.[15]

This antebellum Christian critique of amusements was continuous with a long tradition of "republican" antagonism toward "softness," artifice, and mere wealth-seeking. Many writers fretted over the signs that America was headed toward "the rock on which Rome struck and foundered." Urbanization was the source of corruption, since it produced "crowds" that "assembled without any serious purpose, but solely to pass away the time agreeably." Public amusements were dangerous precisely because they generated crowds. "A crowd is not careful of its conduct, and, above all things, it is not choice in its amusements or disposed to feel itself under the restraints of self-control." Amusements threatened self-hood by removing individuals from intentional communities and inserting them in crowds, within which "choice" could not take place.[16]

Here the conservatives, harking back to a classical republican vision, parted company with the growing ranks of liberals, for whom individual choice was compatible with, and indeed (given urban realities) made possible by, a culture of amusements. "Of course we are not saying that it is any one's positive duty to visit theaters," conceded the *Universalist Review* in 1860. "We should as soon say it is his duty to see the fireworks, or the next regatta. Individual taste must control the action of every one. All that is asked is, that the ban of exclusion shall be removed, that social and ecclesiastical influences shall not interfere, that public sentiment—the sentiment of the intelligent and the pure—shall not operate as a barrier to the gratification of individual preference in the matter." Liberals—secular and religious—thus continued their historic laissez-faire quest to abolish all arbitrary authorities—mercantile controls, church regulations, meta-physical abstractions, kings and queens, and here the moral authority of "public sentiment."[17]

Addressing the international YMCA convention in 1866, the Rev. Marvin Vincent, a Presbyterian minister from Troy, New York, made a rousing statement of the liberal faith.

> We have heard more about keeping unspotted from the world, than of going into *all* the world and preaching the gospel to every creature. . . . And in nothing has this tendency revealed itself more distinctly than in the matter of amusements. For amusement, having the effect to make men feel kindly toward the world, and, more readily than duty, falling in with human inclination, has been regarded as unsafe, and therefore as a thing to be kept at arm's length by the church, and admitted to her folds only under the strictest surveillance, and in gyves and handcuffs.

Vincent noted that the local Troy YMCA had recently taken a stand in the face of active opposition: it added "a large social parlor" with "games of checkers, chess, and dominoes distributed around the room." He "hailed it as a happy omen that the Christianity of our city was beginning to see that the devil had tools which it might use to advantage. . . . But so did not think others who . . . denounced [the Y] *as encouraging gambling*." Vincent was "not without apprehension that the modern reaction in favor of amusements may be carried to an undesirable extreme." But "having taken the ground of individual responsibility in the use of individual liberty, we would leave each man to stand or fall to his own master."[18]

The conflict in Troy over the new social parlor was part of a raging debate over amusements in the Northern churches after the Civil War. The debate had begun in earnest in the late 1850s, perhaps part of the same flurry of religious concern that produced the urban revivals of 1858, and resumed after 1865. In North Adams, Massachusetts, in 1866, the young Congregationalist minister Washington Gladden also campaigned for a game room at the YMCA. But when the rest of the town clergy opposed him, he backed down and made clear that his support for checkers, chess, and backgammon signified no endorsement of the free market in morality preached by liberals such as Vincent. In a widely circulated and very conservative sermon, he zeroed in on "balls and dancing parties," which featured "waltzes and polkas" ("moral abominations") as well as "late hours, gourmandizing, drinking, and promiscuous society." Gladden found no fault with "square dances" in a "private house" where "the company is select." But "round dances," in which couples publicly embraced, led to "abuses too nauseous to be mentioned here." Because of their fruits, such dances were evil in their essence, whatever the dancers' intentions. This is precisely the point at which liberals dissented. Immorality resided only in conscious intentions, they contended, not in actions themselves. For one person, Gladden's liberal reviewer pointed out, a square dance or a ballet would be immoral, since it might "suggest impure thoughts"; another "might waltz and look upon waltzing with innocence." Amusements were sinful only when a person was "consciously receiving detriment"—a standard that shocked conservatives, who had reason to doubt that people mired in temptation could accurately assess their own moral state.[19]

Over the next two decades, while he emerged as a leading Social Gospeller, Washington Gladden's views evolved considerably. By the 1880s he had become a reformer—of amusements as well as other social institutions—and a key formulator of a revised liberal version of the discipline of amusement. Laissez-faire had to go. It was too complacent about social disorganization and too tolerant of moral deviance. But popular amusements could be tolerated since they could be tamed and reshaped by the spiritual forces. Conservatives like Gladden could pass over to liberalism because they became upbeat about the capacity of the "world," with the help of scientifically trained and religiously motivated experts, to embody Christian values.

But their new liberalism subordinated individual liberty and individual responsibility to social management in the sphere of amusement, as elsewhere. The moral issue of amusements was no longer, as it had been for both liberals and conservatives of the previous generation, how to enable individuals to choose the right path through a dense thicket of temptations. The conservatives had believed that true "choice" depended upon the moral guidance—or even the moral control—of the individual by the community. Liberals insisted that traditional communities under-mined individual choice. But for new liberals such as Gladden, the individualist viewpoint was anachronistic. The moral issue was now how to organize leisure so that wholesome influences would predominate in the social environment and as a consequence help to shape individual behav-ior. The social viewpoint took for granted that individuals were no longer independent loci of potency and autonomy, an assumption that earlier conservatives (for all their republican insistence on the communal basis of individual freedom and for all their Calvinist stress on the individual's utter dependency upon God) and liberals had shared. The new liberals sensed that the basic social unit was now the crowd, and they determined to mold the crowd—which conservatives believed to be the antithesis of moral community—into a morally potent force.[20]

The new social liberalism had a distinctive rhetorical embodiment. It was scientific, spare, methodical. Its writings were suffused with light; no mysteries beyond fathoming, no evils too abominable to be mentioned. Late-nineteenth and twentieth century moralists no longer feared evil and no longer quaked at the power of the word. Their language was sterilized, neutral, direct, efficient. They were confident of their power to uncover, name, measure, and re-form social reality, including the "social evil" (prostitution), which was no longer a diabolical, deep-seated, and unmen-tionable communal taint, the inextinguishable product of the evil in individual human nature. It was a dissectible, discussable, and containable (if not erasable) blot on the surface of the social landscape.

Gladden's essay, "Christianity and Popular Amusements," in 1885 rested on the basic liberal conviction that "amusement, like education and religion, is a real need of human beings. . . . It is almost as great a mistake to leave it to take care of itself, and to be furnished mainly by those who wish to make money out of it, as it would be to leave education or religion to be cared for in that way." The vigorous anti-commercialism of his social faith, which historians have routinely admired as "progressive," was joined to an equally insistent anti-individualism: individual members of the crowd could not be left to take care of their own entertainment any more than individual members of the entrepreneurial class could be permitted to earn money entertaining others. It was one thing for "the material interests of men to adjust themselves according to . . . the law of supply and demand." It was quite another for amusement

> to be left to settle itself in this manner, . . . [for] amusement is not one
> of the material interests of men. . . . The business of providing
> amusement for the people ought not to be merely or mainly a

mercenary business; the intelligence, the conscience, and the benevolence of the community ought to recognize this realm of amusement
as belonging to them, and ought to enter in and take possession.

The need for action was especially critical in the theater, which
because of its "flippancy, silliness, sensationalism, and unreality," tended
"to the degradation rather than the elevation of the people." Fortunately
alternatives were emerging. "And inasmuch as an ounce of experience is
worth a pound of theory," Gladden devoted three of his nine pages to a
typically progressive firsthand report from the urban front. The Cleveland Educational Bureau had found a way to beat the commercial
amusement interests at their own game. At the People's Tabernacle, a
"plain but capacious assembly-room" lacking "upholstery" but "brilliantly
lighted by electricity," a crowd of over 4,000 "working people" gathered
on 10 consecutive winter Saturday evenings for "a fourfold intellectual
treat." An opening orchestral concert at 6:45, culminating in a rousing
national hymn, was followed by a "lecture-prelude" of half an hour on
"some scientific or practical subject." Then came the "singing-school," in
which the audience was divided into choirs for antiphonal singing of more
national hymns. Finally, at 8:00 sharp and lasting until 9:30 precisely, the
pièce de résistance: a stereopticon travel lecture or a great debate (Protection
vs. Free Trade, for example, or Women and the Vote). Extra evening
programs were free to the 3,200 season ticket holders (who paid $1.25 for
the entire series): 3,000 women turned out for five cooking classes at which
"whole carcasses of animals were cut into suitable pieces on the platform."
On the evening of his own visit, Gladden sat on the platform and
watched the audience perform. "That it is an extremely well-behaved
audience will be understood when I say that it has abolished encores and
the pandemoniac practice of stamping the feet, and—*ecce signum!*—that it
keeps its seat respectfully until the performance is concluded."
Where, he speculated, would these working-class men and families be
on Saturday night if it weren't for the People's Tabernacle?

> The great majority would be places where their minds would be
> debauched and their morals damaged; where they would find a
> temporary excitement, to be followed by disgust and ennui; where
> they would receive no wholesome impulses and gain no new
> thoughts; and where they would often have their prejudices roused
> and their hearts inflamed against their more prosperous neighbors; for
> the cheap theater is one of the mouth-pieces of the communist and the
> petroleuse.

Social Gospel ministers such as Gladden were devoted to administering a
new regime of "good will" that would bridge the gap between labor and

capital. Their foot-stamping and bomb-throwing working-class, like the avaricious and grasping entrepreneurial class, could be infused with the spirit of fellowship and self-sacrifice.[21]

The increasingly decorous behavior of urban audiences was both cause and consequence of the church's increasing tolerance for theater and other spectacles in the late nineteenth century. Audiences were tamed as more middle-class patrons bought tickets; their presence promoted the peaceful aura that attracted more bourgeois customers. The Cleveland People's Tabernacle, for instance, was made up of "mechanics" and their families, according to Gladden, but he added that about 400 of the 4,000 in attendance were teachers, and there was "a sprinkling of the dwellers on *'Algonquin Avenue'*" in the audience.[22]

By the end of the nineteenth century the mainstream churches had reconciled themselves to the new liberal discipline of amusement—the world was essentially good since despite its flaws it was indeterminately improvable. Christians should concentrate on social, not individual, salvation; amusements were indispensable to modern life, though abuses had to be policed and alternatives administered. The vast literature on amusements kept growing, with an increasingly dominant fact-finding, statistical veneer: nearly all writers in the mainstream Protestant denominations endorsed amusements while urging cleanups of the dirty spots. The theater was the special focus of cleanliness activists. "Few modern plays are clean," as the *Methodist Review* put it in 1907, "and the dirt in them is very dirty dirt."[23]

Yet an occasional voice still sounded a substantive alarm about the theater. Theodore Munger, a leading liberal theologian in New Haven Congregationalism, agreed that amusements were no longer to be opposed as sinful in themselves. But he feared that too many people were making them the stuff of life. In 1908 he mused that "life may be worth living even if it does not provide you with a stunning amusement every 24 hours." Christians need not avoid the theater, but they should be cautious. The threat was not from its immoral excesses, but from its core of unreality. This criticism went back to the Puritans: the theater was morally problematic for Munger "because it is *acting*. . . . On the stage nothing is real; everything from painted scene to costumed actor is fictitious except the bare sentiment of the play, which commonly shares the fate of its medium, and is lost with it at the fall of the curtain."[24]

Acting undermined being: Munger feared the loss of a stable moral standpoint. All commercial entertainments tended to produce "listlessness," since they were "pleasures manufactured and served up for us."[25] They mocked the Calvinist and republican commitment to self-driven work and leisure, to autonomy at the points of production and consumption. But the theater went further: after reducing customers to spectators it then ate away at their understanding of reality. The theater promoted "excitement"—the hunger for novel forms of gratification that all amusements provoked—but it went on to preach the cultivation of a loose, open-ended self in the place of the secure beacon of old. The *New Englander* had asked in 1867, "What exactly is the world? Who shall say? Who shall decide for anyone but himself?" The theater would eventually force people to wonder, "What exactly is the self?"

Like the Reverend Theron Ware, the downward-spiralling hero of Harold Frederick's 1896 novel, *The Damnation of Theron Ware*, those victimized by the theatrical sense would in Munger's view spin weightlessly out of control. But Frederick's novel suggested another possibility. The trying on of a new identity may have wrecked the naive Methodist preacher Theron Ware, but Brother and Sister Soulsby—two actors who toured the rural churches performing hell-fire revivalist sermons for a fee—had built solid selves out of theatrical experimentation. It would be the burden of much popular twentieth century liberal Protestant and secular writing—from Dale Carnegie to Norman Vincent Peale—to validate this open-ended quest to (in Harry Emerson Fosdick's phrase) "become a real person."

The unending hunt for "personality" was not just a cultivating of skills for success in the marketplace of human relations. It was also a lifelong search for warm, organic spirit in a world increasingly perceived as impersonal. In either case the experimental, role-playing talents of the actor came to be seen as pivotal. As conservative Christians had always feared in contemplating the theater, acting was being. Many twentieth century liberals, for whom selfhood became just as reformable as evil had been for Gladden's generation, happily embraced the performing self, the self that created itself continuously in action, especially (given the alienating character of modern labor) in leisure action. Others, from Jane Addams to Martin Luther King, insisted that only older ideals of sacrifice and service could ground selfhood—though even they made fruitful use of theatrical staging in their own self-presentations.

The twentieth century discipline of amusement superficially resembled the mid-nineteenth century laissez-faire liberal discipline in its announced focus on individual selves, its desire to free each individual to choose his or her own way in the world. But we may wonder if twentieth century individuals have not been at a decided disadvantage in comparison with those of the previous century, for whom the moral actor faced grave choices with eternal consequences. Those choices were in many cases exceedingly painful, and countless late-nineteenth century clerical memoirs testify to the psychic suffering they caused. But the sense of living under judgment also bestowed a profound significance upon the individual life, and that substantiality of individual experience has been hard to maintain in an era of secularization (and secularized religion).

In the mid-twentieth century discipline of creation and re-creation, many people tend to construct their selves on a flat spectrum of lifestyle preferences, many of which are commercially packaged and supplied. Mid-twentieth century individualism therefore resembles Gladden's managed crowd as much or more than the individually potent moral choosers of the mid-nineteenth century. But whereas for Gladden social peace depended upon a smoothing over of distinctive identities and unusual urges, upon the creation of a well-behaved and homogeneous audience, liberal Protestant and secular moralists in the twentieth century have discovered that social tranquility is quite compatible with proliferating individual styles in selfhood—styles adopted like new roles in an open drama, and, when original, quickly socialized by the mass media for imitation.

5

BROKERS AND THE NEW CORPORATE, INDUSTRIAL ORDER

William Leach

I think Times Square was developed by the press agents of that era.

Edward L. Bernays (1988)

ETWEEN 1890 and 1929 American society moved decisively into the corporate industrial age.[1] The long march from household production to the consumption of machine-made goods was over. Although the aggregate level of consumption had not changed much in 50 years, the character of consumption and its context had been fundamentally altered.[2] Corporate business took over the production and distribution of goods. Nearly all goods in cities could now be gotten only through acts of pecuniary exchange, where once they might have been bartered or produced largely in self-sufficient settings. Advertising, display and decoration, style, fashion, and service now operated nationally to awaken desire for goods throughout the year. New commercial districts emerged with theaters, stores, restaurants, and hotels, encouraging Americans to discard older moral patterns. Times Square—perhaps the most brilliant symbol of this new consumer order—was created. As the investment banker Paul Mazur put it in 1928, a "staggering machine of desire" had been erected.[3]

A new cultural climate also appeared to propel and sustain this new economic order. Behavior "opened up" to match in some degree the opening up and expansion of the commodity markets. Qualities once seen as subversive and immoral and as existing on the margins of American culture gradually moved to the heart of that culture—carnival color and light, wishing, desiring, dreaming, spending and speculation, theatricality, luxury, and unmitigated pursuit of personal pleasure and gain. These qualities were "consumerist" and are today thought of by many Americans (and by people wanting to come to this country) as the most seductive features of American life and as somehow intrinsic to what it means to be an American.

Between 1890 and 1929 this dimension of American culture was formed and reinforced by a new set of institutions that worked together in an interlocking circuit of relationships. Every culture, if it is to endure, must rest on such a strong institutional circuitry. Before 1895 the institutional circuits that we think of today as crucial to the stability and perpetuation of corporate capitalism were just beginning to emerge. It is therefore a mistake for historians to claim that, somehow, the modern consumer order was already on the scene in 1880. After 1895, however, a full range of institutions—the ones described here and others as well—functioned together in mutually binding patterns to give birth to this new culture and economy.

At the heart of this institutional circuitry was a new group of brokers who facilitated the movement and distribution of images, information, and money central to both economic and cultural formation. Brokers, of course, had always existed—as nonjudgmental go-betweens, bringing people together, arranging deals, negotiating contracts, and, most important, lending money. In the early phases of capitalist development, however, brokers—especially moneylenders—were on the fringes of economic and cultural life. People regarded them with contempt and fear, given their "parasitic" dependence on and willingness to exploit the productive powers of other people. Over time, as the market grew and new kinds of brokers appeared (jobbers, real estate agents, commodity and stock traders, and so forth), such prejudices against brokering began to weaken, although its marginal character persisted.[4]

After 1900 the brokering class took on unprecedented size. It began to fill a place in American life that today seems hardened in stone and which has turned the twentieth century into a century of intermediaries and cities like New York into cities of brokers. The brokering personality—that individual who represses his/her convictions and withholds judgment in the interest of forging profitable relationships between other people—is among the most modern of personalities, occupying a preeminence in today's political and moral economy. Brokers now work in nearly every sphere of activity and have helped to inject a new nonjudgmental "counterculture" into American culture, essentially indifferent to virtue and hospitable to the ongoing expansion of desire.

These new brokers worked largely by selling services or commodities in volume and by trying to maximize the profits of American corporate

The unfinished *New York Times* Building in 1904, seen from Forty-third Street and Broadway. Excavation for the subway can be seen in lower right. Courtesy of The New-York Historical Society, N.Y.C.

Charles Frohman's Empire Theatre at Broadway and Fortieth Street, was still at the northern fringe of the entertainment district in 1898. *The Dramatic Mirror*, next door, was an important theatrical paper. Photograph by Byron, The Theater Collection, Museum of the City of New York.

Entrance to the Times Square subway station, located in front of the Times Building on Forty-second Street, decorated for opening day. Courtesy of The New-York Historical Society, N.Y.C.

A 1909 view of two famous theaters facing on the Square, the Astor and the Gaiety, both associated with George M. Cohan. By the mid-1920s both had been converted to movie houses. Courtesy of The New-York Historical Society, N.Y.C.

Times Square as a public space—crowds on election night watching for returns, November 1916. Courtesy of the United States History, Local History & Genealogy Division, The New York Public Library, Astor, Lenox and Tilden Foundations.

1904

Flat Iron Bldg.   Statue of Liberty   Park Row Bldg.   Brooklyn Bridge

A glossy letter card touting the major tourist shrines. 1904 was too early to have included Times Square, prominent in later cards. Courtesy of Neil Harris.

"Augurio da New Jork." Foreign-language postcards promoted tourism to overseas visitors, circa 1905. Courtesy of Neil Harris.

ELEGANT SUITES
OVER 1000 BED CHAMBERS.
OVER 700 BATHS.

SITUATED IN
HEART OF CITY.

CELEBRATED CUISINE.

HOTEL
TIMES
NEW

The remarkable Hotel Astor! Built in 1904, its luxurious accommodations and facilities served as the social center of theatrical and entertainment life. The Byron Collection, Museum of the City of New York.

ASTOR
SQUARE
YORK

Originally home to Hammerstein's Olympia Theatre, the New York Theatre, circa 1899, was an elaborate entertainment complex. Photograph by Byron, The Theater Collection, 41.420,507, Museum of the City of New York.

An auto show in the Importer's Salon of the Hotel Astor, 1914. Less luxurious trade shows were held in Madison Square Garden. The Byron Collection, Museum of the City of New York.

Civic events and formal gatherings, like this wedding at the Astor, bolstered the city's hotel and restaurant business. The Byron Collection, Museum of the City of New York.

T. Henry French's American Theatre and Roof Garden, 1898, on Forty-second Street, was famous for its then-novel elevator and its nightly musical extravaganzas. Photograph by Byron, The Theater Collection, Museum of the City of New York.

OTHER SHUBERT ATTRACTIONS

THE WINTER GARDEN
Broadway and 50th Street
Tel. 2330 Circle.
Mats. Tues., Thurs., Sat.

THE PASSING SHOW OF 1917

ASTOR THEATRE
Broadway and 45th Street
Tel. 287 Bryant
Matinees Wed. and Sat.

HIS LITTLE WIDOWS
New Musical Play

48th STREET THEATRE
48th St., East of B'way
Matinees Thurs. and Sat.

THE THIRTEENTH CHAIR
By Bayard Veiller

NEW BIJOU THEATRE
45th St., near Broadway
Tel. 430 Bryant.
Matinees Wed. and Sat.

EUGENE WALTER'S Play
THE KNIFE—a Sensation

Maxine Elliott's Theatre
39th Street, near Broadway
Tel. 1476 Bryant
Matinees Wed. and Sat.

ELISABETH MARBURY and LEE SHUBERT
Present
LOVE O' MIKE
Comedy with Music

CASINO THEATRE
B'way and Thirty-ninth St.
Tel. 3846 Greeley.
Matinees Wed. and Sat.

ARTHUR HAMMERSTEIN Presents
YOU'RE IN LOVE

LYRIC THEATRE
42d Street, West of B'way.
Tel. 6216 Bryant.
Matinees Wed. and Sat.

Oscar Strauss' Latest Operetta
MY LADY'S GLOVE

Wm. A. Brady's Playhouse
48th St., 6th & 7th Ave.
Tel. 2628 Bryant.
Matinees Wed. and Sat.

THE MAN WHO CAME BACK

PRINCESS THEATRE
39th St. bet. B'way & 6th Ave.
Tel Greeley 579.
Matinees Wed. and Sat.

F. RAY COMSTOCK'S
NEW MUSICAL PRODUCTION
OH! BOY

JUSTINE JOHNSTONE'S   LITTLE CLUB   in the 44th Street Theatre Building   **ADMISSION FREE**

READ THE NEW YORK REVIEW

EVERY NIGHT at 11—
Who Is She?
Winter Garden Building

THE MASKED HOSTESS (?)
At the **MONTMARTRE**
50th Street and Broadway

A 1917 listing of Shubert attractions from the Lyric's theatrical program. At top, an ad for one of the famous "lobster palaces," the ornate Murray's Roman Gardens. The Shubert Archives.

McBride's Theatre Ticket Agency in the Hotel Cadillac, 1907. A ticket-scalping scandal in 1906 helped to promote such legitimate agencies. The Byron Collection, Museum of the City of New York.

FIRE NOTICE

Look around NOW and choose the nearest Exit to your seat. In case of fire walk (not run) to THAT Exit. Do not try to beat your neighbor to the street.

ROBERT ADAMSON, Fire Commissioner.

WEEK BEGINNING MONDAY MATINEE, MARCH 16, 1914.
Matinee Daily at 2.15.   Evenings at 8.15.

NOTICE—SMOKING WILL NOT BE PERMITTED IN ANY PART OF THE THEATRE DURING THE PROGRESS OF "THE BIRTHDAY PRESENT" OR "THE KID KABARET," AS CHILDREN APPEAR IN EACH ACT.

A   **Palace Orchestra**

Overture—"Our Director" .... Remick
MR. FREDERICK F. DAAB, Conductor.

B   **Eight English Roses**
Dancers.

C   **Ed. Morton**
The Comedian Who Sings.

D   **Cathrine Countiss**
AND HER COMPANY
In The Dramatic Playlet,
"THE BIRTHDAY PRESENT."
Cast.

Gwendolyn .... Cathrine Countiss
Natalie, a maid .... Anita Allen
Billy, a messenger .... James Hyde
Gerald Sturtevant .... John W. Lott
Gerald, his son.. Mac Macomber

E   **Swor and Mack**
Realistic Impressions of Southern Negroes.

"The Original Brinkley Girl,"

F   **Mae Murray**
Assisted by CLIFTON WEBB
(Late of "Purple Road" Company)
With Europe's Society Orchestra.

PROGRAM CONTINUED ON SECOND PAGE FOLLOWING.

The booking formula at work, 1914. A corps of dancers is the opening "dumb" act, followed by a comedian, a dramatic sketch, and a blackface minstrel act. The Theater Collection, Museum of the City of New York.

The entrance and marquee of B.F. Keith's Palace Theatre, the Valhalla of vaudeville, at the heart of the Square on Broadway between Forty-sixth and Forty-seventh streets.
Photograph by Samuel Grierson, The Theater Collection, Museum of the City of New York.

Ziegfeld's *Midnight Frolic*

Ziegfeld's *Midnight Frolic* took place nightly between 1913 and 1927 on the roof of the Amsterdam Theatre on Forty-second Street. Its "see-through" runway allowed patrons an unusual view of the famous chorus line. The Theater Collection, Museum of the City of New York.

The interior of Murray's "lobster palace." Elaborate classical detail distinguished this massive "cabaret for the people." The exterior was French renaissance. The Byron Collection, Museum of the City of New York.

An unlikely pair: David Belasco, producer/director, colorful bon vivant, whose reversed collar earned him the title, "Bishop of Broadway"; and Will A. Hays, former Postmaster General, lobbyist for the film industry (1922-34) and administrator ("censor") after 1934 of the Film Production Code. Photograph by Capital Photo Services, The Theater Collection, 37.399.1750, Museum of the City of New York.

Irene and Vernon Castle, 1914. The premier dance team of their day, they helped promote the ballroom dance craze that swept the country before World War I. Photograph by Dietz, The Theater Collection, 47.253.14, Museum of the City of New York.

Acrobats at Hammerstein's boisterous Victoria Theatre, circa 1909. Acrobats were typical of the "dumb" acts that played while vaudeville patrons were being seated. The Theater Collection, Museum of the City of New York.

Vaudeville nurtured the future stars of legitimate theater and Hollywood—Adele and Fred Astaire, 1906. The Theater Collection, 79.59.2, Museum of the City of New York.

businesses. Among them were the securities dealers whose numbers increased from 250 just before World War I to 6,500 by 1929 (today, the Wall Street "brokerage community" alone contains 230,000 workers, while the total number of security dealers in the country is about 450,000). The number of credit men and bill collectors reproduced themselves at a comparable rate.[5] Among the brokers were the new urban museum curators and art school instructors who taught commercial and industrial "art" to up-and-coming designers. The brokers included the new advertising agents and travel agents; the new business schools and departments attached to universities and colleges; and the people who created the "light and color" for the new commercial districts. These new go-betweens managed the first professional model agencies—such as John Powers Inc. in Manhattan—which brokered female bodies.[6]

Many of these people did what they did merely to make a living. Other men and women, however, were totally Veblenian in outlook: they longed to make a killing (not a living) by plunging into the rapidly widening stream of goods and money. Along with many of the merchants and manufacturers, these people were obsessed with volume turnover, with the movement of goods from producer to consumer, with money and not with goods. For the first time, they studied consumer behavior with great care; they amassed statistics on consumer patterns and organized charts on commodity flows.

This chapter deals in particular with three groups of brokers, all of which helped shape the new economy and culture in significant ways. Each group brokered a different expertise or "commodity" that contributed to the empowerment of corporate business. The first group specialized in creating "images" designed to attract and keep consumer loyalty (here I focus especially on Edward L. Bernays, the public relations man). The second group were "information" brokers, represented here by Herbert Hoover, then secretary of the United States Department of Commerce, and by his appointee Julius Klein, director of the Bureau of Foreign and Domestic Commerce. They dispensed knowledge and ideological support of great strategic consequence to corporate business. I conclude with a discussion of perhaps the most important intermediaries of all—the "capital" brokers, who financed corporate mergers in the consumer sector of the economy and brokered the creation of such places as Times Square. My subjects are Paul Mazur and Waddill Catchings, members respectively of Lehman Brothers and Goldman Sachs, both leading investment banking houses.

This chapter focuses only episodically on Times Square; yet, in the largest sense, it is *all* about Times Square, especially if we think of this region as the quintessential brokered capitalist space. Indeed, the presence of these new brokers constituted a necessary condition for the creation of

Times Square. Had it not been for them and for the large institutional circuits and coalitions they represented, Times Square would have been a much diminished reality on the national scene.

"See what tie-ups can be made with shoes," advised a Gimbel's merchant in New York in 1933. "And why not an expensive evening bag with every evening dress, if you have an assortment on hand. Gimbel's highlights a different bag every few days by calling it 'The Bag of the Hour.'"[7] This kind of sales publicity did not exist in the nineteenth century. There was little methodical "tying-up" of merchandise into pictures or images, although retailers were beginning to arrange furniture into model showrooms and to display artfully some dry goods, mostly women's clothing. Terms like "color-coordination," "accessorizing," "ensembling," and above all, "promotion," all of which were vernacular by the time of the Gimbel's show event, had no currency before 1900 in the sense that we know of them today—as signifying professionalized activities intended to insure the fast turnover of goods.[8]

By the 1920s a variety of merchandise was being ensembled—dishes, beachwear, toilet goods, sporting and kitchen goods, automobile equipment, and so forth. At the same time, a new group of "experts" appeared to advise retailers on how to promote their goods. These people were adept in "sales publicity," in color coordination, and in ensembling; they prided themselves in knowing how to arrange goods into pictures—not only in advertising but in show windows and store interiors. And according to them, individual merchants could no longer be trusted to sell their own merchandise.

Amos Parrish, Tobé Collier Davis, and, most important, Edward L. Bernays were among this group of consultants. Parrish and Davis, both independent fashion consultants, headed syndicates that farmed out fashion ideas and methods to urban retailers. Parrish was "one of the big promotion guys of the '20s," as the fashion designer Elizabeth Hawes put it. He published a popular journal, *Amos Parrish Magazine*, and his *Breath of the Avenue* presented the most "advanced" instruction on "scientific" buying. Parrish or his staff went straight to merchants, sat down in their offices, and talked merchandising. He suggested special features, set sales quotas, and helped plan promotional advertising schemes. In the late twenties he created Amos Parrish Fashion Clinics, because "fashion is on everyone's tongue, on everyone's back, in everyone's home, in everyone's food, in everything everyone owns or hopes to own."[9]

The people eligible to attend Parrish's "clinics" were store owners, merchandising managers, advertising managers, display managers, and buyers—in short, the royalty of merchandising. Twice a year, in clinics around the country, these people congregated to hear Parrish (or his surrogates) expound on "what fashion is" and on how to get it across and make a profit from it. His message was to make everything "new" through fashion. "Things must be new," he said, for without "newness," there is no turnover. "Nothing is going to stop fashion. It wears things out. And industry wants things worn out in order to make more things to build bigger businesses, to pay larger dividends. Things must grow. Fashion is the one thing in the world that will do it. And without Fashion it won't be done. But it will be done." Almost 200 representatives from over 100 stores countrywide packed into Parrish's classes on the Upper East Side in New York City.[10]

Parrish helped erect a corporate merchandising machine to serve the needs of mass corporate manufacturing. So did Tobé Collier Davis, who reproduced many of these same practices in her fashion work. In the late 1920s she created a fashion advisory service and later the Fashion Group Inc., headquartered at Rockefeller Center, which brought together the most ambitious women in merchandising. Behind her stood numerous women in executive positions, including female advertisers, stylists, shopkeepers, and merchandising managers. By 1924, 41 percent of the total 17,493 buyers in the United States were women. Davis's advisory service, broadcasting news daily on fashion trends and on how to make profitable use of them, was the most sought-after service of its kind in the business. "The heads of Federated—Macy's, Gimbel's—all of them counted on her advice and business know-how. . . . She made big money for them—and for herself," remembered Julia Coburn, who in 1938 helped Davis found the Tobé Coburn School of Fashion, which still exists.[11]

The most formidable and ingenious of consulting brokers was Edward L. Bernays, the son of Jewish immigrants from Vienna, nephew of Sigmund Freud, and widely known as the most adroit—if not the most self-conscious—practitioner of the business of public relations.[12] A short, balding, and tireless man, Bernays reminded one of the Wizard in *The Wizard of Oz*. He was a trickster. He spent his life behind the scenes, working pulleys and levers for other people.

At the age of twenty-three in 1913, Bernays got a job as a theatrical press agent for Klaw & Erlanger, the voracious theatrical syndicate operating out of Times Square that monopolized bookings throughout the country. It was a job that he reshaped in a new way, directing it from mere "space grabbing" in the newspapers to producing "public events" to excite interest. "My role," he remembered in his 1962 autobiography, "was not to 'chisel' space in the newspapers" but "to compete with other news, to make my plays or actors so newsworthy that papers would give them attention in their columns."[13]

The job at Klaw & Erlanger's lasted only a year but made a big impression on Bernays "entirely out of proportion to its duration." He loved Broadway. "I hobnobbed with actors and actresses whose names shone on marquees," he later said. "I went backstage whenever I wanted to, had free run of most theaters to catch a glimpse of an act. . . . Life was one thrill after another."[14] Even more important, his press work—along with that of numerous other brokers in the district—helped "create" Times Square into an enticing entertainment spot of national significance, Bernays boasted in a recent interview. "Times Square," he said, "wasn't well established in 1913. Then a very important theater was built around Forty-ninth Street. After that the League of Theaters got to work with publicity. So, I think Times Square was developed by the press agents of that era."[15]

As early as 1917, Bernays had learned skillfully how to make imaginative connections and convey powerful messages and images. In his mid-twenties, he worked for the United States Information Committee on Public Information under George Creel during World War I. This Committee "excelled" in its collaborative work and "opened the eyes of the intelligent few in all departments of life to the possibilities of regimenting the public mind," Bernays said. It was during the war that the full "value of associative processes" in forming taste and determining choice dawned on Bernays.[16]

After the war Bernays joined a swelling number of men and women who were aggressively carving out new independent careers in public relations and who were shaping it to respond to the distributing needs of America's ever-expanding mass-market merchants.[17] Around 1919 Bernays got a firm professional foothold right in the heart of his favorite place—the Times Square district, at 19 East 48th Street—"the center of the universe," as he recently recalled. It was here that he continued to develop and ply his trade.

According to Bernays, the ordinary merchant no longer knew what the public wanted, who the "publics" were, or how to present the most "truthful" image of himself or of his product. A new void, Bernays believed, had opened between the people who manufactured and sold goods and the people who bought them. Something had to be done. Trained "intermediaries" like Bernays had to intervene to interpret reality for the public, to provide "truthful" information, and to connect the various publics back together again into a cohesive whole.[18]

Bernays conceived of public relations as a nonjudgmental technique, similar to psychoanalysis, that could be applied to any institution, person, or commodity needing to have its "image" (ego) bolstered in the public arena. He began by studying his client, although like most psychoanalysts he refused to "treat" pathologically "anti-social" clients (Bernays rejected Hitler, for example, as an impossible client to "treat.") Next, he researched the "mental equipment" of his client's targeted public, hoping to find there the "stereotypes" that might be "tapped" and exploited by his client. Then Bernays interpreted the client's product. He created "associations" between the product and ideas, drawing on his knowledge of the "stereo-types." Finally, he "crystallized" these associations for the public through a coordinated mobilization of largely visual media.[19]

In the spring of 1924 Bernays mounted a "saturation campaign" for "transparent velvet" intended to "titillate the spending emotions of 3½ million women, all potential consumers." His purpose was not only to increase sales but to encourage the manufacturer, Sidney Blumenthal, to adopt new methods of style and fashion. Bernays persuaded Blumenthal to "change his approach to the public." He researched the market and found out that many women carried a "stereotype" of "style and beauty" around in their "heads." He set out to establish connections. He "tied up" velvet with the "sex and glamour" and "sophistication" of New York and Paris. He brought several media together to project a coordinated cluster of images. He sent letters to theatrical agents and movie producers, offering dresses of transparent velvet to the female stars, who took them and, at Bernays's invitation, wore them in public and on stage and screen. At the same time, photographs of velvet gowns were published in fashion magazines and in the photograph sections of newspapers. Bernays and Blumenthal also "worked out a deal" with several chains of movie theaters "in 24 key cities"—including the Paramount and Loew's theaters on Times Square—to present *The Velvet Revue*, a "tabloid musical comedy" as an "adjunct to movie bills." In this advertising "short," all the female performers were dressed in transparent velvet.[20]

Bernays reduced "public relations" to two basic components—"continuous interpretation and dramatization by high-spotting," terms he doubtless picked up from the Broadway stage. "Continuous interpretation," he explained,

> is achieved by trying to control every approach to the public mind in such a manner that the public receives the desired impression, often without being conscious of it. High-spotting, on the other hand, vividly seizes the attention of the public and fixes it upon some detail or aspect that is typical of the entire enterprise.

Bernays was the first well-known architect of what Daniel Boorstin has called "pseudo-events." A finagler of the truth, he staged happenings carrying packaged information for immediate public consumption. His promotions, which marshaled the forces of many different kinds of institutions and media, had the effect of driving out the more significant and "real" events of the times. His image-brokering business belonged to that new array of institutions—the professional consultancies and syndicates—that worked behind the scenes to speed up the flow of corporate-made consumer goods.[21]

In 1929, President Herbert Hoover successfully managed to get the Congress to pass legislation to establish the Census of Distribution—one of the biggest aids to corporate business ever created by government. Sometimes called the "Census of Consumption," it was of immense value to sales personnel and public relations people. The Census showed, according to its promoters, "what kind of goods offered the least resistance to sales promotion." It reported on the local movement of goods through each stage of distribution and marketing, showing where goods were "overdeveloped" and what kinds of goods should be handled by different stores. This Census pointed out "where the consumers were" and "what quantity of goods they would consume." A "master analysis of our distribution system," it was the fullest, most authoritative piece of market research ever undertaken by any country or institution up to this time.[22]

The Census of Distribution was a service of far greater magnitude and importance to business than any service that Edward L. Bernays ever rendered to anybody or for anything. Yet, in principle, the services that Bernays and Hoover delivered added up to precisely the same thing. Both services were meant to connect the people who made and sold goods with the people who bought them. Both were supposed to fill a void between clients and consumers; and both were intended to broker an expertise that business apparently could not obtain on its own. At least this was the argument that Hoover and Bernays presented to the public. But reality was another matter: American corporate business did not need the government to carry the Census. Corporations could have drawn on their own facilities, on advertising firms like J. Walter Thompson, which had sophisticated market research divisions, or on the more "neutral" universities like Harvard or Michigan, which also had the means to perform such services. Corporations, however, chose to accept and welcome the assistance of the federal government. And they still depend (and more heavily) on the government for such aid.[23]

Under Herbert Hoover in the 1920s the federal government committed its resources to brokering and strengthening America's new corporate business economy. As secretary of commerce and as president, Hoover thought there was something terribly wrong with the American system of distribution and marketing. Production was fine, Hoover believed, achieving "maximum efficiency," but people were not receiving or buying the goods fast enough, either because prices were too high, income too low, or markets too glutted. A new complex transportation system, intended to expedite the flow of goods, was actually getting in the way. The rapid shift of populations from urban to suburban centers was muddying an already unclear market picture. So swift were these changes, Commerce officials contended, that businessmen often sold in "blind markets" or had great trouble planning for the future. Where were the markets? Hoover asked. How did merchandise get from one point to another? Surprisingly, no one knew exactly. No one had yet tried to trace the movement of a single commodity from manufacturer to consumer. "We are almost wholly lacking in the basic data of distribution," Hoover told Julius Klein, Director of the Bureau of Foreign and Domestic Commerce, in 1925.[24]

This recognition by Hoover and his Commerce officials of the difficulties inherent in a system of mass distribution and consumption marked a basic reorientation of policy and perspective. It meant that the federal government was no longer looking at America as a "scarcity" society but as a "surplus" and "consumer" one with the brightest prospects for "permanent prosperity" (a term similar to Trotsky's "permanent revolution" coined a few years earlier).

Today, we ordinarily think of our more recent presidents as being "consumer-oriented" or fixated on the movement of goods and capital, but these men have merely followed in Hoover's footsteps. He was perhaps the most pro-consumer and consumption-minded cabinet secretary and president in American history. Much of his mature public life was taken up with problems of distribution and consumption, from his pre–World War I days as a promoter for the 1915 Panama-Pacific Exposition (as a publicity stunt he tried to get the King of England to visit the Fair) to the directorship of the wartime Food Administration. Although he has been depicted as an archaic laissez-faire liberal, Hoover helped institute the eight-hour day and rejected the idea that supply automatically regulated demand. He acclaimed the "great expansion of installment buying of consumable goods" and thought that no relationship whatever existed between poverty and morality.[25]

In 1912 Commerce was a tiny department scarcely a decade old, but by 1931 it was an "octopus," as one ex-Commerce official put it, housed in the biggest office building in the world bestriding three city squares and containing over 3,000 rooms. In the 1920s Hoover had had the entire Commerce Department reorganized by men who had experienced, as he had, the "thrill" of handling large "magnitudes" of labor, money, and commodities during the war.[26] These men believed that consumer demand and desire deserved systematic scrutiny and that businessmen should be encouraged to exploit even more intensely an already dense domestic market, the densest in history. Hoover hired a staff of domestic commercial agents to "investigate domestic, commercial, and industrial problems with particular emphasis on marketing." He instructed them to focus on consumer "wishes and desires" and on "how to discover what the consumer really wants." He published a weekly journal, *Domestic Commerce*, issued "solely to inform its readers of significant development in distribution," which had reached a circulation of over 17,000 businessmen by 1929.[27] Hoover laced the department with countless components, many transferred from older federal agencies. One of the most important was the Bureau of Foreign and Domestic Commerce, which held all the bureaus and divisions assigned specifically to treat distribution and consumption. At the helm of the Bureau he placed the Harvard-trained economist and historian, Julius Klein.[28]

Born on June 27, 1886, in San Jose, California, the son of German Jews, Klein was always moving. He grew up near the San Francisco bay and never forgot the teeming life there, the loading and unloading of exotic cargoes. In 1915 he and his wife drove by car across the country from Boston to Berkeley, a "trip that was a joy to remember," he said. The railroads, the Panama Canal, the Pan American Highway—all stirred his imagination. Klein spent much of his professional life untangling or trying to untangle the problems of movement and commodity circulation. Like the man who hired him, he dreamt of making a seamless economic system without frontiers or boundaries, without conflict, a system of perfect liquidity that would allow for the free passage of ideas, money, people, and commodities.[29]

As a doctoral student at Harvard in the mid-teens, he studied with Dean Edwin Gay of the Business School, who led in directing economic policy away from production toward distribution and consumption.[30] Klein completed a dissertation on the Mesta, a powerful Spanish sheep-grazing and marketing organization which contributed to the economic and political unification of Spain in the late medieval period. In that study, the fruit of two years of original research in Spanish archives, later published by Harvard University Press as *The Mesta*, Klein showed how this fifteenth century organization served as the major circuit for the movement and distribution of goods throughout Spain and paved the way for the brief emergence of a Spanish national market. The book displayed the clear impact of Gay's ideas.[31]

A solid career of scholarship and teaching awaited Klein. But instead he entered the Commerce Department, his own real-life Mesta, where advancement was fast and satisfying. He was ambitious and hard-working. "I stand constantly amazed," wrote an admirer, "at the enormous amount of work you do personally."[32] Klein hammered out two major strategies of the Bureau of Foreign and Domestic Commerce (BFDC), on behalf of business and completely backed by Hoover. He doled out strategic information to businessmen and he propagandized for the corporate "tricks of seduction."

Klein turned the BFDC into a bulging data bank for businessmen to draw on, a policy constituting a major act of governmental intervention, since economists viewed the new "knowledge as a strategically important factor in competition." Access to "sound statistical and economic data," Hoover believed, "was the first step in controlling economic cycles and in bringing consumption in balance with production."[33]

Throughout the twenties, the BFDC convened over two hundred

conferences dealing with different phases of the domestic distribution system. The Bureau published reports (at public expense) filled with data on distribution and consumption so that retailers could solve their most basic problems. In 1924, under Klein's directions and at the request of major trade associations that co-funded them, the first citywide surveys of markets were begun. Soon the reach of the Bureau opened out to "cover the distribution facilities and methods, and the population and purchasing power, and the economic backgrounds of a number of major distributive regions in the United States." "Never before," Klein boasted, "had there been such an arrangement of statistical measures of consumer demand."[34]

In 1926 the BFDC and the Bureau of Census (a bureau of the Department of Commerce) decided together to carry out a Census of Distribution, a study first suggested by Edwin Gay during World War I, when he headed the Central Bureau of Planning and Statistics. In the wake of a major conference on distribution in Washington held by the United States Chamber of Commerce, Hoover induced the Chamber's leadership to sponsor the Census, which effectively started the first stages of the work. Between 1926 and 1928, Klein's staff conducted sample censuses of distribution in eleven cities, with co-funding from the Chamber. Then, in June 1929, Congress approved the Census of Distribution, to be carried out every 10 years with the Decennial Census of the United States.

This gargantuan Census was widely hailed in Europe as a major step in business–government collaboration and a boon for business. Most American businesses also welcomed it, although a few "old-fashioned" ones objected to such "intervention" as "socialistic."

Under Julius Klein, the BFDC did more than disgorge great amounts of useful data to businessmen, however. It also propagandized for business strategies that formed the basis of modern merchandising. Without judging the people who consumed or the practices themselves, BFDC studies and reports endorsed national retail advertising, cooperative advertising, service devices, fashion, style, and display methods of all kinds. Information flowed from the Bureau on how best to deliver goods, widen streets, expand underground transportation, use colored lights, foster store circulation, and show merchandise in "tempting ways."[35]

As Director of the Bureau and later as Assistant Secretary of Commerce between 1928 and 1932, Klein himself went before Congress and the American people, using every available medium to praise and plead the cause of corporate business. He published numerous articles outlining the causes for "American prosperity." America, he wrote in a 1929 *New York Times* article, is "prosperous" because it "is tending toward the realization of desire." The "large corporations," labor output, and absence of labor dissent, the huge domestic market with its "exceptional consuming capacity," and the "spirit of cooperation between government and business" have all worked to promote "prosperity." People know "tomorrow will be better than today—better not simply materially but culturally; yes, and even spiritually."[36]

Klein was perhaps the first American government official to make heavy use of the radio to "speak" to the American people. From 1928 into the early thirties and at the public's own expense, he ballyhooed the nation about American business and its methods in nationwide broadcasts out of Washington. In one 1928 radio show he praised "the independent merchant," while invoking the "large and financially powerful corporations," which really constituted America's new economic bedrock and which—as he said later—were "mounting increasingly to the planes of diversion, entertainment, spiritual enrichment."[37]

In radio show after radio show, Klein talked glowingly about American advertising, merchandising, and industrial design—all the strategies of enticement calculated to excite consumer desire. "Advertising," he said on the air in October 1929, after returning home from attending an advertising convention in Berlin, "is the key to world prosperity." In March 1930 he spoke passionately about the show windows on Fifth Avenue in Manhattan: "American business is proving that an essentially mechanized civilization can nevertheless be majestic—vivid—satisfying—luminous." A year later he gushed over "advances" in industrial design and style, which began to overtake mass production methods at the end of the twenties. "Art as business," he said, "has yielded a profit of 700 percent." Klein reveled over the fact that business was "liberating" Americans from the drab, "utilitarian," and "Puritan" past. Because of business, Americans "live in an everyday world of beauty"; they have "bathroom symphonies, chromatic plumbing," shoes in "color harmonies," pretty dishpans and turnstiles. "Who of us," he asked, "will say that the effect of this new Persian luxury is not delightful?"[38]

"It is imperative," he explained on another broadcast, "for each enterprise to convey to its prospective patrons the most *vivid conception* of the distinctive qualities and merits of the product." "Lure the glance," he told Americans on the air, "fire the imagination by means of brilliant primary colors, unusual composition and mastery of line."[39]

Julius Klein traveled throughout the country and the world as one of the government's main evangelists of business, and it should surprise no one that on October 21, 1929, he ended up in Times Square. He had come to the Square to participate in one of the many tributes honoring the discovery of electrical light that were occurring simultaneously around the country. The biggest tribute was in Dearborn, Michigan, where Herbert Hoover, Henry Ford, and Edward Bernays (who did the public relations for the event) led in singing the praises of Thomas Edison. Klein, however, chose to do his celebrating in Times Square, where he addressed the Broadway Association about the importance of effective lighting in commercial areas. "Light," he explained to the already converted members of this trade association, "increases the advertising value" of interiors and exteriors. The Square excelled in the use of light: its electrical signs with their "infinitely complex and dazzling gyrations" were truly "magnificent" to behold, showing how far American advertising had come from its "simple beginnings in Roman times." Klein spoke almost reverentially of "Broadway with its miles of light and its sunburst centre at Times Square."[40]

Julius Klein was surely among the most ardent zealots of corporate business ever employed by the federal government. A totally uncritical loyalist, he not only brokered huge quantities of information to corporations, he warmly advocated the new cultural perspectives of those corporations as well. Klein did not exceed his authority: he was merely fulfilling the mandate laid out for him by Hoover—to forge the closest "bonds" between the state and business. "Cooperation," he said, in another one of his radio talks, "erects a protective bulwark for our business. It creates a staunch wall of will." Some ex-Commerce Department officials loathed his style. "He gets my goat," one wrote, "he's a man unwaveringly committed to booming expansion . . . who acts like a brisk and talkative press agent." But Hoover thought Klein was a "perfect public servant."[41]

While Julius Klein was erecting a "wall of will" on radio, the Wall Street investment banker Paul Mazur was on a Caribbean yacht putting the finishing touches on the creation of Federated Department Stores, the large merchandising holding company. Mazur was Klein's and Bernays's counterpart in the world of high finance. But Mazur brokered money as well as knowledge. And he was a partner in an institution of great pivotal importance to the consolidation of corporate business and the emergence of the modern mass consumer society.

Investment bankers were among a new group of speculators who came on the scene in the 1890s to service those corporate businesses looking to expand both internally and through the acquisition of other businesses. Here, too, anxiety over "poverty in the midst of abundance" helped hasten the rise of a new brokering class. Many businessmen who wanted to control prices and output through consolidation no longer had enough internal capital to do so. Nevertheless, for the first time in American history, large domestic reserves of capital existed. The only problem was that from the 1850s onward, this capital had been invisibly pooled in the hands of insurance companies and banks. Only the vigilant and already well endowed had access to it. Like the goods, the money was beginning to bunch up, impeding market flow.[42]

To get at and "liberate" this money, therefore, increasing numbers of American businessmen turned to investment bankers for help. The bankers often advised them to "go public," that is, to sell their stocks on the public market and thus reach the abundance of capital that had hitherto eluded them. For high fees, investment bankers brokered this capital by floating securities on the stock exchanges. The bankers also offered financial information, intervened directly to reshape the financial and corporate structures of their clients' firms, and negotiated loans for acquisitions and mergers. By 1900, in fact, investment bankers were the leading promoters of corporate mergers. "Whereas the mergers before 1897 had been initiated by the industrialists themselves," writes historian Alfred Chandler, "many more were now instigated by financiers and speculators."[43]

At first the bankers focused only on manufacturing, processing, and transportation, having little interest in the consumer goods industries. Then, a major shift took place with big implications for the shaping of this country's economy and culture. In 1906 New York bankers decided to finance the expansion of Sears, Roebuck and Company by offering millions of dollars' worth of Sears stock on the public securities market, thus getting for the company the capital it needed to expand. As one historian has written, "Down to 1906, very little of the public money market was open to entrepreneurs in the mass-merchandising field." But the bankers reversed this trend, seeing large financial rewards before them and their clients.[44]

The bankers were Lehman Brothers and Goldman Sachs. Both started out in the nineteenth century as commodity brokerage houses, but now led in the financing of mass market retailers, the light consumer goods industries, and the entertainment business. Besides the Lehman brothers (Philip, Arthur, and Herbert), two other men—Waddill Catchings of Goldman Sachs and Paul Mazur of Lehman Brothers—played equally important roles in directing investment bankers toward the consumer sector.

Catchings was a tall suave Episcopalian born to wealthy parents in Sewanee, Tennessee, in 1879, and Harvard-educated. He was the largest shareholder in Goldman Sachs and its president in the twenties. He seemed personally excited by the financial prospects of the consumer sector. His most notorious venture was the creation of the Goldman Sachs Trading Corporation, an umbrella company consisting of several merged investment trusts. The aim of this company (which collapsed in 1930, wiping out many innocent investors) was to hoodwink people into buying securities whose market value was far in excess of the value of the corporation's assets. Such activity captured the essence of Catchings's career as a promoter.[45]

Paul Mazur, according to Lehman Brothers itself, "made the firm noted for its specialized knowledge of the distribution of consumer goods."

The son of immigrant German Jews, he was born in Boston in 1892 and also attended Harvard. In 1918 he joined the army and was stationed in Tours, France, where, in the middle of the devastation of Europe, a wave of patriotism overtook him. "You just know America is the land of the future," he wrote his close friend, the Boston merchant Louis Kirstein, "the leader by right of progress and example. It is our heritage." At the same time, he also reminded Kirstein that the war would have "two effects on the men's clothing business. The first is closer, tighter lines of the military uniform. The second is a bit more color in the neckties. . .as a reaction against the sameness of O.D. (olive drab). When the men come back there will be tremendous demand."[46]

These two bankers and their firms were among a brokering banking elite in this country who helped create the structure and character of modern American mass consumer society.

The growth of investment banking and the growth of the mass consumption industries were simultaneous and related developments; and both led to the concentration of capital and power in the hands of fewer and fewer men. Mazur and Catchings, in particular, participated in this transformation in a number of important ways. First, they wrote influential books in the twenties urging business and government to take the consumer and consumption seriously; the relationship between consumption and production, they said, could no longer be taken for granted but had to be "managed" and "regulated." They exhorted businesses to take over and merge with other businesses so that they might have greater control over their markets and be better able to insure the steady flow of goods and money throughout the economy. As Mazur said in 1928,

> Mergers must continue because they make available continuous market knowledge of an intensive character. They offer management efficiency, overhead reduction, and the economy of purchasing large volumes. Large scale operations will be most effective not through the building of an unlimited number of new retail units, but through the consolidation of existing stores and chains.[47]

Mazur and Catchings also argued that it was the aim of business not to "make goods" but to "make money." In the manner Thorstein Veblen found so reprehensible, they focused on volume turnover in money and goods, caring little or nothing about goods per se, which were important only for their marketability. Catchings was perhaps more obsessed with money than was Mazur. He was one of the first American economic thinkers to write books on money: he believed it to be the central feature of the modern market, as crucial to the country as blood was to the body. "The mainspring of business is *Profits*," he wrote, in one of the many books he co-authored with William Trufant Foster. "The hope of profits drives the life-sustaining blood to every part of the economic body. The blood is money."[48]

Both bankers, moreover, saw in the expansion of a "culture of desire" one of the keys to continual economic growth and profits. In the true brokering vein, in the vein of Bernays and Klein, they believed that it was not the business of business to judge other people's desires. Rather, business succeeded (and people got jobs) only when business responded to desire, manipulated it, and even labored to extend its frontiers and to deepen its intensity. The proof, Catchings said, was already obvious in all the "cigarettes and cars" that business was making, in "response to orders from consumers. . . . The function of our economic organization is not to determine what the people *ought* to want, but to make the machinery as productive as possible of what they *do* want."[49]

American capitalism, Mazur assured his readers, was compelled to take this route due to the "stupendous" nature of its success. Business had transformed the economy from a "needs" to a "desires" economy, he claimed. The economy was, in fact, overproducing, fostering a grounds for economic crisis. One solution to this problem, which both Mazur and Catchings espoused, was to increase wages and salaries, thereby expanding spending power. Another crucial method was to develop the strategies of enticement further. After all, Americans had invented the "machine of desire" (Mazur's words), so they should continue to abide by its commands and rules. "The machinery which has developed consumer demands," he wrote for *Harvard Business Review* in 1925, in an article that brought him national recognition, "has become so completely accepted that we forget our *duty* to it. We are apt to forget the benefits of the system and find fault with apparent burdens. And yet the safety of the industrial superstructure depends upon the strength of the marketing foundation, just as the foundation would have no value without the industrial structure." "A staggering machine has been built," Mazur said two years later, "to satisfy consumer demand and even the consumer's whispered interests. The machine is here. It now has an appetite of its own which must be satisfied."[50]

Beyond preaching the expansion and consolidation of the mass consumer sector of the economy, bankers like Mazur and Catchings also supplied businesses with the capital that brought the sector into being. Both men were among the many so-called financial specialists who initiated, even pushed, for merger transactions, thus acting as the unseen financial goads to the consolidation of consumer businesses. Their money helped create the circuit of chain stores and chain theaters that knit the country together for the first time into a national consumer market. Without the money and leadership they provided, mergers of any consequence would have been impossible to achieve.[51]

Mazur personally went before his clients to plead for consolidation and centralization, even in the face of protests from the big retailers themselves. In 1929 he traveled the East Coast, arguing on behalf of a merger of major department stores, such as Filene's, Abraham and Straus, F. and R. Lazarus, among others, into a retailing chain. "At the time," he later wrote of his work in financing what became Federated Department Stores, the most important department store merger in American history, "I was the common denominator of that situation."[52]

Meanwhile, Catchings saw a "tremendous" future in the chain movie theater business and did much to promote the expansion and consolidation of that business. According to one film historian, Catchings believed in the economic future of sound films before other people did and urged Warner Brothers to get an exclusive license to the sound process. Catchings floated stocks for Warners, making them and himself instantly very rich. Drawing on the combined capital of six banks, he also supplied Warner Brothers with a multimillion-dollar loan, which allowed them to achieve corporate solvency and to buy out Vitagraph, one of the country's founding film companies. As a result of this buy-out, Warners acquired a nationwide distribution system overnight, which Catchings expanded further by purchasing ten more new theaters in crucial markets (including in Times Square). Over a 5-year period, from 1925 to 1930, the value of Warner's assets rose from $5 to $230 million.[53]

Lehman Brothers and Goldman Sachs helped intensify the "merger-mania" that contributed to the expansion and centralization of America's core mass consumer institutions. Between 1925 and 1929 nearly 40 percent of all chain store expansion was due to acquisition and merger, expedited by investment bankers.[54] Catchings and Mazur were at the center of this activity, participating in the financing of six major department store chains (Macy's, Gimbel's, Allied, Federated, Interstate, and May); several limited-price variety chains and many grocery food chains; and such corporations as General Foods, Studebaker, Phoenix Hosiery, General Cigar, and Welch's Grape Juice. They also financed the creation of one of the biggest "amusement organizations" ever created in the United States—RKO (Radio-Victor-Keith Orpheum), which merged booking organizations, theaters, and RCA into one corporation, "centering under one control almost everything available in the line of amusement."[55]

Mazur and Catchings, then, were among a new group of bankers who not only advocated mergers but helped structure them as well. But their influence reached even beyond these activities to the creation of what we might call America's new "desire centers," those places calculated to speed up the turnover of corporate-made goods and of money in the greatest conceivable volumes. From their downtown haunts on Wall Street, Mazur and Catchings helped to construct such uptown districts as Times Square. Indeed, Times Square as a desire center appeared at the very time that the national corporations and large-scale investment banking houses appeared, because it was the very fruit of these institutions.

The capital provided by investment banks to the movie industry ended up concretized in the palatial flagship theaters that dominated the Times Square district. Investment money was also channeled into the building of electrical signboard monopolies that served corporate business in Times Square, making it prohibitive for small enterprising firms to advertise there. (In November 1929, Warner Brothers, the Catchings-financed movie company, erected at Broadway and Fifty-second Street what was reputed to be the largest electrical sign advertisement in the world, 80 feet high and weighing 115 tons.[56])

Capital brokers also participated in the creation of ever-larger real estate corporations that bought and sold Times Square properties at astronomical prices. One of these companies was the David A. Schulte Company, which combined a nationwide chain of tobacco stores with an extensive real estate operation. Banker capital made it possible for Schulte to speculate in huge blocks of property. In 1925 he bought the Aeolian Building on West Forty-second Street. Soon thereafter, he purchased the Longacre Building site, a half block of land and buildings on Forty-second Street and Broadway, in a highly publicized real estate coup. The Longacre property was the last property in the district owned by Vincent Astor, located at the "busiest traffic corner in the world." Schulte either built tobacco stores on his Times Square properties, held them for "further investments," or sold them almost immediately at enormous profits. He sold the Aeolian Building three months after purchase at a million dollar profit. He had, he said, "great confidence in the real estate values of the midtown section."[57]

If before 1920 any uncertainty still existed regarding Times Square as a viable economic or cultural property, after this date all such doubt dissolved into thin air. After 1920 the district flowered as a central capitalist space, as a national center brokered into existence by an unassailable alliance of investment capital and corporate business. Finance capital, in particular, transformed the region into a showcase for national corporations, chain stores, and theater chains. Such capital helped shape the region into a pecuniary space par excellence, whose raison d'etre was profit or the rapid volume turnover of goods and money. And, perhaps most important of all in cultural terms, capital helped validate Times Square as an amoral space, as a "liberated" realm of fantasy wherein everything was possible, and no limits were placed on what could be bought or sold. By 1925 money had erected an invisible wall around Times Square, protecting it from "moral crusaders" and insuring its continued existence as a linchpin site, as a desire site, in the national circuit of consumer markets.

The role that investment bankers like Mazur and Catchings played in the formation of modern consumer society is of central importance since from the moment that they intervened as major architects of corporate expansion, the whole character of the productive process was transformed. Pecuniary value rather than intrinsic value, mass appeal rather than individual utility—all now emerged as primary factors in producing goods for the market. The broker (or the person who produced nothing) now took the spotlight with the originator, the inventor, the producer, and the entrepreneur. Investment capital, in other words, helped construct the parameters of modern mass consumer culture. It also contributed further to the demise of traditional competitive free enterprise; and it hastened the pooling of wealth, constituting as it did one of the great clandestine sources of power and influence that only a few alert merchants with good advice and the ability to peer around corners could command. "The large organization that is adequately financed," wrote one merchandising expert, "can take advantage of many opportunities that the small business man cannot even consider." Or, as the banker Henry Morgenthau told Lincoln and Edward Filene who were on the verge in 1909 of relying on investment bankers to help finance the building of their new store, "there is no chance of failure, if you have plenty of capital."[58]

The activities of investment bankers, along with the work of the federal government and the new consultancies and public relations firms, were indicative of those major institutions that helped bring to life America's new amoral corporate consumer economy and culture. Herbert Hoover said again and again that he despised centralized interventionist government, but his information-brokering and ideological support of the corporate business expansion amounted to just such intervention. The new order was also propelled by the new image brokers, behind whom stood the far more powerful capital brokers who directed huge sums of money into the hands of mass market retailers.

No other contemporary culture or economy received so much institutional help as this one did. This fact may seem obvious given the supposed overall business character of modern American society. But the matter is a little more troubling once many of the major institutions that have contributed to its creation have been assembled together into one portrait. A business culture, yes, but an overweening and invasive one with the power to color and warp every aspect of everyday life.

ENTERTAINMENT AND COMMERCE

INTRODUCTORY ESSAY

Margaret Knapp

F OR MOST of its history, Times Square has played host to a kaleido-scopic mixture of residential and commercial tenants, but in this century it has been most closely identified with the entertainment business. From the Olympia Theatre, which opened on Broadway in 1895 in what was then considered a dangerous "thieves' lair," to the lavishly renovated Forty-second Street theaters scheduled to reopen in the 1990s as a cure for the street crime that has plagued the area in recent years, mass entertainment in all its forms has been the decisive influence on the image of Times Square for New Yorkers, for the nation, and for the world.

The preceding chapters in this volume have explored a number of factors that led to the development of Times Square: the extent and location of new forms of mass transit; the lure of huge real estate profits; the focal role of the new brokering figures in American commercial life; the protection of certain districts by restrictive zoning ordinances; and the growth of tourism. All of these factors contributed importantly to the desirability of the Times Square area as a commercial precinct. And, as Richard Fox has argued, the growth of theater was abetted by a new tolerance for mass entertainment on the part of some liberal Protestant denominations. But the combination of transportation, finance, politics, and religious acceptance could only create a series of favorable conditions; it was the entertainment industry itself, and most especially the efforts of a number of shrewd (and sometimes visionary) entrepreneurs, that were decisive in the creation and subsequent re-creation of the so-called theater district. As individuals, partnerships, syndicates, or corporations, these entrepreneurs demonstrated an extraordinary ability to anticipate, indeed to create, public demand for new forms of entertainment. From Oscar Hammerstein I and his son Willie scouring the news for new vaudeville "freak acts," to Arthur Mayer converting the Rialto Theatre into a mecca for "men's films," to Billy Rose attracting a whole new class of nightclub patrons to his Diamond Horseshoe, and to Irving Berlin's and Damon Runyon's mining of the area for the local slang in song and story—the successful businessmen of Times Square have always combined financial shrewdness with a remarkable sensitivity to new markets and changing public tastes.

Oscar Hammerstein I, who built the Olympia Theatre on Broadway between Forty-fourth and Forty-fifth streets in 1895, is generally given the title "The Father of Times Square," but his move northward into Longacre Square (as it was known until 1904) was not as great a gamble as it might seem. Other theater builders had been flirting with the Longacre Square vicinity for several years. Rudolph Aronson had opened the Casino Theatre on Broadway and Thirty-ninth Street in 1882; the following year the Metropolitan Opera House was erected on Broadway between Thirty-ninth and Fortieth streets; in 1888 the Broadway Theatre was opened on the southwest corner of Broadway and Forty-first Street; and in 1893 the American Theatre opened on Eighth Avenue between Forty-first and Forty-second streets. With electrification rapidly transforming dark and dangerous streets into safer, more attractive locations for legitimate amusement, the northward movement of theaters into Longacre Square was seemingly inevitable.

The transformation of Times Square into the city's main amusement district coincided with, and was driven by, the fundamental changes in the nature of public entertainment that occurred at the turn of the century. Because of these changes, theater became a potentially lucrative investment, at least for those who could anticipate the public's tastes. In the days before film, radio, and television, live performance (that is, legitimate drama and vaudeville) was the dominant form of public entertainment. And live performance was a profit-making activity. When the first British theater companies arrived in the colonies in the 1750s they brought with them a system of theatrical organization that depended on box office receipts for its existence (unlike opera, the ballet, and the symphony, which followed the Continental practice of at least partial government or private subsidy). With rare exceptions, the legitimate theater continued operating as a capitalist enterprise throughout the nineteenth century. In his chapter in this section Peter Davis explains how the evolution in patterns of theater financing reflected changes in the capitalization of other turn-of-the-century businesses.

By the time Longacre Square was developing into an amusement area at the turn of the century, New York had become the starting point for a vast, nationwide entertainment network known as "the road." This complex theater operation had its beginnings in the 1860s when the traditional method of running a theater, the stock system, was challenged by the growing popularity of touring "combination" shows. In contrast to the stock system, in which a theater manager engaged a company of actors for a season and presented them in a variety of plays, the combination system consisted of a company of actors appearing in a single show which toured from city to city, providing its own scenery, costumes, and sometimes musical accompaniment. Helped by the expansion of the nation's railroads after the Civil War, the combination system eventually killed off the majority of stock companies. By 1904 some 400 combination companies were touring through thousands of theaters in cities and towns across the country.

Of crucial importance to the operation of the combination system was a single location where shows could be cast, rehearsed, tried out on audiences, and then booked for cross-country tours. Since New York was already regarded as the most important theater city in America, it is not surprising that it became the headquarters for the combination system. In addition to the many theaters needed for an initial Broadway production for the shows before they went on tour, New York's theater district encompassed rehearsal halls; the headquarters of scenery, costume, lighting, and makeup companies; offices of theatrical agents and producers; theatrical printers and newspapers; and other auxiliary enterprises. Close to the theater district were boardinghouses catering to the hundreds of performers who came to New York in the hope of being hired for a touring show or a Broadway production.

As Robert Snyder explains in his chapter, vaudeville, which had also grown enormously in popularity at the end of the nineteenth century, had a similar organizational structure. Theaters across the country belonged to different circuits which were labeled as "big time," "small time," or "family time." A group of acts would be booked in New York and then sent out, sometimes for years, to tour a circuit. Many of the auxiliary theatrical enterprises that clustered in New York, such as costumiers and publicists, served both the legitimate stage and vaudeville.

A successful theatrical entrepreneur needed to have a sense of what would "go over" in New York and still be a hit in other parts of the country. That sense was usually developed over a period of apprenticeship, either in out-of-town theaters, or as an assistant to a veteran theatrical manager/ producer. Fortunately for the budding entrepreneur, the theater, which has always been a labor-intensive industry, benefited from the relatively low wages paid in the days before the rise of theatrical unions. This meant that theaters could be constructed at a relatively low cost: Oscar Hammerstein built the Victoria in 1899 for $50,000, and even the elaborate 1,500-seat art nouveau New Amsterdam Theatre, complete with office building, roof theater, and generous helpings of European statuary, was reported to have cost $1,500,000 when it was built in 1903.

In the early years of the decade, land was still relatively cheap and easily leased in the Longacre Square area, so potential theater owners invested comparatively little money in the initial construction of a playhouse. Producing a play was also a fairly inexpensive undertaking. In the days before Actors' Equity became a power to be reckoned with, actors were not paid during the weeks when a show was being rehearsed, and the materials and labor required for constructing scenery and costumes were not costly. Once the show opened, weekly operating expenses were minimal, since low wages enabled producers to hire large casts and stage crews of up to 200 people without straining their budgets. Although ticket prices were low, most theaters had large capacities, which enabled producers to keep even mediocre shows afloat. And even if a show failed in New York there was always the possibility of making money on the road, where audiences might be gullible enough to believe the billboards and posters that read "Smash Hit in New York."

If a theater owner or manager experienced financial reversals, bankruptcy was an acceptable way to emerge from his difficulties. T. Henry French, the manager of the American Theatre, suffered financial losses in the Panic of 1893, which forced him to give up control of his theater (even his father, Samuel French, the founder of the play publishing house that still bears his name, took him to court). More typical was the case of Oscar Hammerstein I, who suffered a financial fiasco with his Olympia Theatre, but was able to rid himself of his debts and open a new theater, the Victoria, in 1899.

So lucrative was the theater at the turn of the century that it was perhaps inevitable that some individual or group would consider coordinating the national theater booking business, thereby cornering the theatrical market, just as the "robber barons" had done with oil, steel, and railroads. And so, in 1896, six theater owners and producers got together to form the "Theatrical Syndicate," whose ostensible purpose was to bring order to the chaotic booking system. Between them, the members of the Syndicate controlled a number of theaters in key towns and cities across America. Since a profitable tour required that combination companies be able to perform at frequent intervals without long and expensive railroad trips between engagements, theaters in small towns along the railroad routes were just as important as playhouses in the major cities. By controlling those theaters the Syndicate could force managers of touring productions to book exclusively in Syndicate houses, both in the small, one-theater towns and in the larger cities where there was a choice of playhouses. Once the theatrical producers were forced (at higher fees) to book exclusively through Syndicate houses, it was possible to force theater managers across the country to accept (at higher fees) only Syndicate-produced shows. The result was a monopoly as effective as any in the Age of Trusts. Opposition was immediate and vocal, but for several years, relatively ineffective. At one time or another producers such as David Belasco and Oscar Hammerstein I, as well as actor-managers such as Richard Mansfield and Minnie Maddern Fiske, declared their enmity to the Syndicate. But with the exception of Mrs. Fiske, whose husband published the anti-Syndicate newspaper, the *New York Dramatic Mirror*, all of the opposition either surrendered or gave up producing legitimate drama. A similar trust was created in vaudeville, under the aegis of the partners B. F. Keith and E. F. Albee.

One result of the war between the Syndicate and the independents was a spate of theater construction, both in New York and in towns and cities across the country. Forced out of Syndicate-owned theaters, independent producers either built playhouses of their own or played in less desirable venues, including roller-skating rinks and circus tents. Theater building proliferated after the Shubert brothers, Sam S., J. J., and Lee, arrived in New York from Syracuse with the aim of challenging the Syndicate. At first the Shuberts managed theaters owned by others, but they were soon building playhouses of their own. In the 1899–1900 season, Manhattan had 22 theaters, only one of which was in Longacre Square. Ten years later there were 34 theaters in Manhattan, most of them new, and most of them in Times Square. By the time the Syndicate and the Shuberts had declared a truce in 1907, New York had more theaters than it really needed, but the pattern had been set, and for the next two decades, new theaters would be constructed at a dizzying rate: by the 1919–20 season 50 playhouses were operating in New York, and by the 1929–30 season there were 71 in use. The expansion in New York was mirrored in theater districts throughout the United States.

At first, the few theaters that were built in Longacre Square blended into a district that harbored a number of different businesses, as well as single-family homes and small apartment houses. The existence of schools, libraries, and churches in the district at the turn of the century attests to the fundamentally residential character of the area. As Timothy Gilfoyle has documented, taverns and houses of prostitution existed in the Longacre Square area even before the theaters arrived, but they avoided the kind of blatant self-advertisement that would lead to a permanent crackdown. The first theaters to be built in Times Square soon attracted both theater-related businesses and other enterprises that catered to both native and visiting pleasure-seekers. Vaudeville quickly followed the legitimate stage into the Times Square area; the first major vaudeville house, Hammer-stein's Victoria, opened as a legitimate theater in 1899, but switched to vaudeville in 1904 after Hammerstein found it impossible to compete with the Syndicate in booking legitimate theatrical productions. And, as Lewis Erenberg demonstrates in his chapter, the restaurants and nightclubs that appeared in Times Square during the early years of the century were frequently as theatrical, in both decor and clientele, as the theaters that surrounded them.

The legitimate theater that moved into Times Square can best be described as the television of its day. Dozens of plays and musicals were produced each year to keep up with the demand of a growing theatergoing public in New York as well as on the road. To appeal to the widest possible audience, shows followed tried-and-true formulas, avoiding themes and ideas that were difficult or controversial. Most plays were adapted from British or Continental successes, and even new musicals tended to hew to the well-worn formulas of European operetta, comic opera, and opéra bouffe. Although a group of young American dramatists emerged in the first decade of the century, they were hemmed in by the demands of Broadway and the road for conventionally moralistic treatments of titillating subjects, such as the hard fate of fallen women or the downfall of greedy tycoons. Many plays were adapted from popular novels and stories, such as *Sherlock Holmes*, *Becky Sharp* (from Thackeray's novel *Vanity Fair*), and *Quo Vadis*. In addition to new productions, Broadway still hosted great stars, both American and European, in limited engagements. For the most part, the stars played for a few weeks in New York before leaving on, or after returning from, national tours.

It is fruitless to argue that any given year marked the high point in the development of Times Square, but there are certain periods that seem to have been transitional for the area. In a chapter in this section, Brooks McNamara focuses on the theatrical season of 1938–39 to give us a vivid sense of the many kinds of entertainment provided by Times Square impresarios in the late Depression era. As a contrast, it is perhaps worthwhile to recall the spring of 1915, when Times Square most closely resembled in reality what it has subsequently become in legend and fantasy: a glamorous, exciting, quintessentially New York amusement district. Although the 1914–15 season was generally considered a disastrous one for the Broadway stage, a total of 133 productions were mounted in 42 theaters. Europe was at war, but America was feeling few of the effects, save for an increased economic prosperity founded on the manufacture and sale of arms and materiel to the allied armies. Denizens of the theater district had the war brought home to them when Charles Frohman, one of the most distinguished theatrical producers and a founder of the Theatrical Syndicate, perished on the *Lusitania*.

At the same time, younger entrepreneurs were appearing on the scene. Florenz Ziegfeld, who had begun his series of *Follies* in 1907 and had moved it to more lavish quarters at the New Amsterdam in 1913, now added a new show, called the *Midnight Frolics*, in the New Amsterdam's roof theater. There he was able to try out new performers, such as Will Rogers, before using them in the *Follies*. And so, in the spring of 1915 a well-heeled theatergoer could see a gorgeously mounted production of the *Ziegfeld Follies*, starring W. C. Fields, Ed Wynn, Ina Claire, and Bert Williams, and then take the elevator upstairs to the roof to view a smaller, but no less elaborate, revue in a cabaret setting.

The ballroom dance craze showed no signs of abating, and Vernon and Irene Castle, the high priest and priestess of the fox trot, hurried each night from vaudeville or legitimate stage appearances to dance at their own cabaret, "Castles in the Air," before winding up at the Club Castle in the basement of the Forty-fourth Street Theatre.

Film, which had endured a great deal of scorn during its primitive beginnings, moved from a novelty to an art form with the New York

125

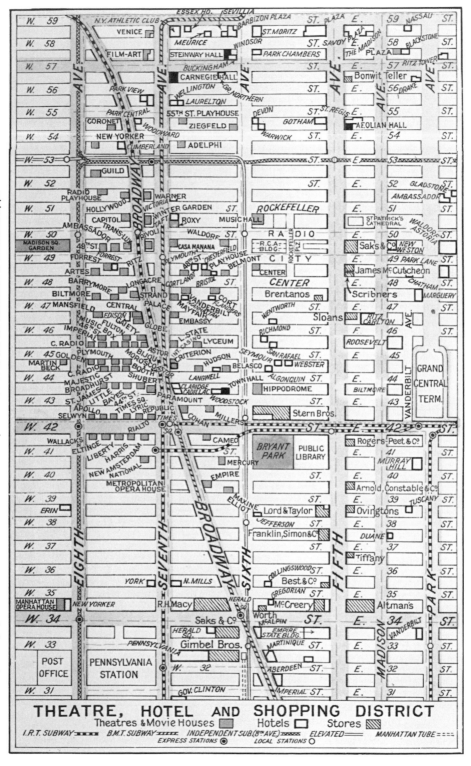

From Rand McNally's Geographical Atlas of Greater New York © 1938, R.L. 91-5-119. From the collection of Charles Knapp.

premiere of D. W. Griffith's *The Birth of a Nation* at Forty-second Street's Liberty Theatre in the spring of 1915. The success of Griffith's film led to more full-length "photoplays," which in the years to come would provide strong competition for live theater. In the 1920s many Broadway theaters followed the Liberty's lead in showing silent films when no live theatrical offerings were available. Eventually, the Depression forced many theater owners to permanently convert their legitimate theaters to movie houses.

In 1915 the future of American drama could be discerned by the thoughtful, not in the theaters in Times Square, but in tiny playhouses in Greenwich Village or on the East Side, for in that year the Neighborhood Playhouse opened as an adjunct of the Henry Street Settlement, and the Washington Square Players gave their first season of performances at the Bandbox Theatre. Both companies presented theatrical fare that was innovative by Broadway standards. The Washington Square Players specialized in the new drama of Europe (Ibsen, Chekhov, Maeterlinck, and the like) while the Neighborhood Playhouse brought modern dance, Asian theater forms, and lesser-known British and European plays to their audiences. And in Provincetown, Massachusetts, during the summer of 1915, a group called the Provincetown Players was formed. The following year they began producing plays in New York, most notably the early work of Eugene O'Neill. Eventually, the Times Square theaters would be forced to take notice of these developments, but in 1915 it remained business as usual on Broadway, as producers still turned to a stable of veteran writers of farce and melodrama for their plays.

Vaudeville was thriving in the spring of 1915, but one event proved to be prophetic of its demise. Oscar Hammerstein I, who had built the Victoria Theatre and, with the help of his son Willie, had turned it into the most important vaudeville house in America, was forced to sell it after Willie's untimely death; the spring of 1915 marked its last season. The loss of the Victoria meant that the Palace, built farther north on Broadway in 1913, would now become the city's premiere vaudeville house, the symbol of success for a generation of vaudevillians. Over the summer of 1915 the Victoria was demolished to make room for the Rialto Theatre, an early movie palace and the first built without a stage. Under the leadership of a new entrepreneur who would be an important name in Times Square, S. F. Rothafel (later known as "Roxy"), the Rialto was committed to film and film alone, shown in a luxurious setting with proper orchestral accompaniment. The movie theater, originally a store-front nickelodeon, was to become the new symbol of Times Square glamor in the 1920s and 1930s, as a succession of great "palaces" was constructed on or near Broadway: the Rivoli, the Capitol, Loew's State, the Embassy, the Paramount, and finally the 5,920-seat Roxy Theatre, the "Cathedral of the Motion Picture," which opened on Seventh Avenue slightly north of Times Square in 1927. The size and popularity of the great movie palaces made them the dominant institutions on Broadway; by the 1920s most new legitimate theaters were constructed on the side streets between Broadway and Eighth Avenue, their marquees barely visible from the Times Square crossroads.

By 1915, as Philip Furia has pointed out, Irving Berlin, working from an office at 1571 Broadway in the heart of Tin Pan Alley, had already developed the generic Broadway song which was to characterize all forms of musical entertainment for the next half century. Damon Runyon, as William Taylor indicates in his study of Broadway slang, was beginning his explorations of local argots in order to evolve the genre of colorful sports reporting that was to characterize the work of a generation of writers from Runyon and Hecht to Ring Lardner.

The Times Square of 1915 thus experienced a season of endings and beginnings. Despite a number of expensive flops, the legitimate stage was thriving, as were cabaret, vaudeville, and film. From that point until the end of the 1920s, entertainment activity intensified in Times Square, with additional theaters opening at a giddy pace. The first playhouses to be built in Times Square at the turn of the century had followed the traditional configurations of nineteenth century European theaters: large rectangles with the stage at one of the narrow ends faced by orchestra seating, boxes, and two or more balconies. As Times Square real estate became scarce and prohibitively expensive, the typical theater design featured a wider, fan-shaped orchestra seating area, fewer boxes, and one or two low-ceilinged balconies extending farther out over the orchestra. Spectators were thus brought closer to the stage, and more seats could be fitted into a smaller area, but the spaciousness of the earlier theaters was now gone. The large lobbies, smoking rooms, retiring rooms, and other amenities of the earlier playhouses were minimized or eliminated as theaters were constructed on ever smaller plots of million-dollar real estate.

The upward spiral of the stock market during the 1920s brought newly minted Wall Street tycoons into the theater business. Constructing theaters or owning long-term leases on them involved little financial risk, since owners and managers had the legal right to evict any production that was not bringing in a substantial profit. Only the theatrical producer who leased a playhouse for one show or for a season might lose money if the show was forced to close before turning a profit. But a producer with some record of success usually had little trouble raising money, since an ever-increasing choir of Broadway "angels" was eager to invest its Wall Street or bootlegging profits in the theater. The staggering number of shows produced in the 1920s, averaging over 200 a season, was thus a sign that the Broadway theater was vastly overextended rather than an indication of its artistic vitality. But as long as the Bull Market continued, little notice was taken of this dangerous overinflation.

While the legitimate theater was burgeoning, a new entertainment business moved into Times Square. "Tin Pan Alley," as the popular music industry was known, relocated from the area around Twenty-eighth Street into the northern part of Times Square in the early 1920s, a time when, as Philip Furia notes in his chapter on Irving Berlin, radio and sound film were about to expand the business far beyond its traditional markets of sheet music and recordings.

Further changes came to Times Square as Prohibition, which went into effect in 1921, forced the well-known restaurants and cabarets to close their doors, while smaller and more discreet speakeasies tucked themselves away in the side streets. New conditions called for new types of entrepreneurs, as Lewis Erenberg explains in his chapter on New York nightlife.

Thus, by the late 1920s, the theater district offered far more than legitimate theatrical productions to those seeking entertainment. The great Times Square movie palaces symbolized the importance of New York to the California-based film industry; glamorous and well-publicized New York premieres were deemed as necessary to a film's success as an elaborate Hollywood first night. The Palace Theatre was still the top vaudeville house in the country. And the composers and lyricists of Tin Pan Alley turned out the songs that were heard in Broadway musicals, in Hollywood films, in the Palace's musical acts, and in the raucous floor shows at the speakeasies.

The stock market Crash of 1929 and the resulting Depression would severely curtail Times Square's dominance of mass entertainment. At first the legitimate theater seemed immune to the worst effects of the Crash, but as theater owners and producers saw their fortunes wiped out, playhouses began to close and production was severely curtailed. In the late twenties there had been several plans to pull down older theaters, especially those on Forty-second Street, and replace them with office buildings and hotels. The Depression put an end to those schemes, and most of the theaters in Times Square remained standing, though many were wired for sound films, the only growth industry in the entertainment field. Vaudeville was even harder hit under the twin onslaughts of radio and sound film, and several vaudeville theaters bowed to the inevitable by featuring vaudeville acts in between film showings. Some just gave up and went completely to films.

Times Square had always attracted a spectrum of pleasure-seekers from all economic classes. The legitimate theaters offered gallery seats for as little as 25 cents at the turn of the century, and the stately restaurants were complemented by lunch counters, family restaurants, and "chop suey parlors." Patrons could see "small time" or "family time" vaudeville in Times Square in addition to the "big time" offerings of the Victoria and the Palace. There were even some modest movie houses, such as the Bryant on Forty-second Street, which presented films and family-time vaudeville for a small admission fee. But the real democratization of Times Square occurred in the Depression years, when a new group of entrepreneurs created and satisfied new tastes in amusement. Among them were the Minsky brothers, who took over the Republic Theatre on Forty-second Street and offered ever more daring burlesque shows, until they were put out of business by the license commissioner; Arthur B. Mayer, the "Merchant of Menace," who served up second-run movie double bills of murder, mayhem, and adventure at the Rialto Theatre; and Billy Rose, who, as Erenberg demonstrates, retooled the swank nightclub into a high-volume, low-price evening out. With the repeal of Prohibition in 1933, small bars began to proliferate in the theater district as well.

Ironically, despite the new kinds of amusement to be found in Times Square, the old image remained practically intact. In a series of backstage films directed by Busby Berkeley, Hollywood defined for the rest of America what Broadway was all about: production numbers of dazzling, almost surreal beauty created by plucky, upbeat youngsters who refused to buckle under to the miseries of the Depression. In an era of sharply reduced production activity on Broadway itself, the Hollywood musical kept alive the aura of the Times Square theater district as an enchanted place where talent and hard work could lead to undreamed-of success.

Those entrepreneurs, both new and old, who survived the worst years of the Depression were rewarded with renewed prosperity during the period of World War II. Much of the activity described by Brooks McNamara as occurring in 1938–39 continued into the 1940s, but it intensified to meet the increasing number of military personnel who were looking for entertainment as they passed through New York on their way overseas. The theater participated by sponsoring the Stage Door Canteen, where soldiers and sailors could mix with theatrical luminaries, and eat or dance before going overseas. And the recruitment booth in a Times Square traffic mall took advantage of the area's reputation for enormous volumes of pedestrian traffic by being the most conspicuous place to "sign up."

Despite optimistic predictions, wartime prosperity did not outlast the war. Developers concentrated on the East Side, where the demolition of elevated subway lines transformed undesirable neighborhoods into attractive investments. The owners and managers of the Broadway playhouses maintained their aging theaters and hoped for better days. Once more, new kinds of entrepreneurs moved into Times Square, this time offering forms of entertainment that existed on the edge of community standards of acceptability. Purveyors of "adult entertainment" and drugs joined prostitutes in challenging the boundaries of what was legal and "respectable" in Times Square, as Laurence Senelick has shown (see Chapter 16). These entrepreneurs preferred to keep their names out of the news, allowing their cadres of lawyers to defend them in their constant legal battles. Increased street crime in the area concerned merchants, theater owners, and investors; throughout the 1960s and 1970s plans were announced for the renewal of the area, particularly Forty-second Street between Seventh and Eighth avenues, widely considered to be the most dangerous block in New York. The city's fiscal crisis in the mid-1970s put a temporary halt to government plans for improvement, but once the city revived, the calls for government intervention began anew. For the first time, state and municipal agencies began to decide what kind of entrepreneurial activity should be permitted in Times Square. Massage parlors and other sex-related businesses were closed down, primarily through zealous enforcement of the building and health codes.

Many of the plans to improve the area revolved around the need to change the public's perception of Times Square, to overcome fears about a neighborhood that had once again become a "thieves' lair" in the minds of both New Yorkers and potential out-of-town visitors. The entertainment industry was central to these efforts. The glamorous days of the past were dusted off and exhibited to the public, as the New York City Landmarks Preservation Commission, the Municipal Art Society, and several other organizations sponsored hearings, exhibitions, symposia, walking tours, and other activities designed to raise awareness of Times Square's glorious theatrical past. The demolition of two Broadway playhouses, the Helen Hayes and the Morosco, lent greater urgency to these calls for theatrical preservation.

In the 1980s the future of Times Square seemed to lie in the combined effects of several market forces: the pornography business took a severe downturn with the proliferation of VCRs, which made it possible for customers to rent or buy videos for viewing at home rather than at a Times Square movie house or porno bookstore. Developers shifted their attention to the West Side, and a number of new hotels began to rise in Times Square, returning it to its former status as one of the city's important hotel districts. But several of the new West Side development projects were large office towers, leading many observers to fear that a massive concentration of office space would alter forever the unique character of the theater district, as Ada Louise Huxtable argues in the Afterword.

The most ambitious project slated for the Times Square neighborhood is the 42nd Street Development Project. Under the aegis of the state's Urban Development Corporation and the city's Public Development Corporation, the 42nd Street Development Project calls for the construction of four office towers and a merchandise mart on Forty-second Street. In return for certain concessions from the city, the developers will contribute to the restoration of seven legitimate theaters on the block.

The original plans for the redevelopment of Forty-second Street merely provided for the renovation of the theaters; the assumption was that existing theatrical concerns would gladly buy or lease them once they had reopened. Over the past few years, the UDC's thinking on theater usage has altered substantially. Realizing that the long-term success of the renovated theaters requires the involvement of imaginative and committed entrepreneurs, the UDC has requested bids from both nonprofit and commercial organizations encompassing a broad spectrum of live entertainment, from theater to dance to rock concerts to circus. A separate entity, called the Forty-second Street Entertainment Corporation, has been established to choose the initial tenants of the theaters and to oversee subsequent operations. At the same time, more theater-related usage is being encouraged for other spaces on the block, including rehearsal halls, office space for performing arts organizations, and restaurants and stores with theatrical themes. One plan involves a glassed-in restaurant that will attempt to duplicate the atmosphere of an old-fashioned Times Square roof garden.

Those opposed to the 42nd Street Development Project argue that it is unnecessary, since the large number of private development projects that have been announced and/or completed in Times Square recently will automatically reduce street crime, as "good" uses (offices, restaurants, hotels, theaters) will drive out "bad" (drug trafficking, prostitution, and other assorted crimes and misdeameanors). But the future of Times Square as an *entertainment* district requires more than the elimination of "undesirable" individuals and businesses. If the past is any indication, Times Square will remain the city's, and the nation's, theater district only if its combination of glamorous past and promising future can inspire a new generation of astute and creative "entrepreneurs of entertainment."

6

VAUDEVILLE AND THE TRANSFORMATION OF POPULAR CULTURE

Robert W. Snyder

A N ARCHAEOLOGICAL dig in Times Square would unearth some of the treasures of American popular culture. Starting from 1991, investigators would find remnants of the videotapes that have transformed public spectacles to private living-room entertainment. A little further down, they would find popcorn boxes, relics of the days when movies were presented in vast, palatial theaters. Deeper, they would find ticket stubs—admissions to an early form of musical theater, the Ziegfeld Follies. At the bottom of the dig, they would reach programs to a vaudeville theater called The Palace, and at that point they would be at the very beginnings of modern American popular culture.

Vaudeville touched virtually every expression of twentieth century American popular culture—films, the music industry, radio, and television. Its influence reached from its personnel, who often graduated to radio or film, to its format, which was adopted by early television variety shows. But vaudeville's most important contribution to the development of American popular culture was to erode the local orientation of nineteenth century audiences, and knit them, despite their diversity, into a modern audience of national proportions. Vaudeville accomplished this feat with appeals to audiences that were direct and intimate, by means of a centralized and bureaucratic industrial organization whose offices and foremost theater were located on Times Square.

Popular culture is defined by broad audiences. But by the middle of the nineteenth century, the conditions under which popular culture was produced and enjoyed were changing. Until then, American popular

133

culture was deeply influenced by custom, tradition, and public festivity. It was usually rooted in a place, like the Bowery of New York City, with its saloons and cheap theaters. Local likes and dislikes exercised a profound influence over shows; artists and audiences responded to each other so directly that audiences sometimes seemed like coproducers of the show.

In the twentieth century, popular culture came to be defined by film, radio, recordings, and television—the products of a centralized entertainment business, which disseminates standardized products from coast to coast and feeds international audiences. And they have undermined the local bases of culture.

Vaudeville arose in the middle of this transition and accelerated it: it marked a watershed in the history of popular culture, especially with regard to the conditions under which it was produced and enjoyed.

Vaudevillians reached audiences with acts that were lively, immediate, and inviting—audiences felt that each show was being invented just for them. But the nationwide organization of the vaudeville industry, with its booking offices and circuits, propelled the industry toward cultural centralization. Even though individual vaudevillians recognized diversity, the thrust of the vaudeville industry was toward a mass audience where much of this diversity would be submerged.

Vaudeville first appeared in the 1880s. Composed of separate acts strung together to make a complete bill, it was the direct descendant of mid-nineteenth century variety theater, which had often catered to carousing middle- and working-class men in saloons and music halls. To attract these men's wives and families, creating a wider and more lucrative audience, entrepreneurs banned liquor from their houses. They censored some of their bawdy acts—or at least promised to. They jettisoned the older name of variety, with its stigma of vice and alcohol, and adopted the classier sounding name of vaudeville.

The most famous and influential of the showmen who engineered this transformation were B. F. Keith and E. F. Albee, two New England showmen best known for their shows' wholesome reputations. But they also applied their energies to industrial reorganization. Backstage, they took the chaotic, informal booking procedures that characterized much of nineteenth century variety theater and put them on a bureaucratic basis, centralized in New York City. By the end of the first decade of the twentieth century, vaudeville entrepreneurs had organized their theaters into nationwide chains, called circuits, which radiated out from New York City in the East and Chicago in the West. Performers toured along the circuits, bringing their acts to the entire country. Critics likened the system to an octopus, with a brain in Times Square and tentacles reaching far into the country.

Times Square was not the first neighborhood of New York City to harbor vaudeville theaters. In the 1880s and early 1890s, the early vaudeville theaters clustered around Union Square, then the theatrical center of New York City. But the one constant of the theatrical district in nineteenth century New York was that it kept moving uptown, staying just ahead of the northward movement of Manhattan's central business district. By the middle of the 1890s, it became apparent that the city's next major theatrical neighborhood would be located many blocks to the north, at the intersection of Broadway and Forty-second Street, then known as Longacre Square.

In November 1895, theatre entrepreneur Oscar Hammerstein opened the mammoth Olympia Theatre on Broadway between Forty-fourth and Forty-fifth streets. At the Olympia, a fifty cent ticket bought admission to a lavishly decorated pleasure palace incorporating a music hall, a theater, a concert hall, bowling alleys, a billiard hall, a two-story rathskeller, lounges, smoking rooms, and a Turkish bath, all capped by a roof garden.[1]

But behind this bold facade was Hammerstein's flawed business management. The Olympia failed to turn a profit, and in 1898 the building was mortgaged away. But Hammerstein's decision to build, and other entrepreneurs' willingness to follow him, showed that Longacre Square was becoming a vaudeville center.[2]

The biggest boost for the area's theatrical fortunes came in 1904, when New York City opened its first subway line. The new Interborough subway line proceeded north from the Brooklyn Bridge along Manhattan's East Side, then headed west on Forty-second Street before turning north at Broadway to continue uptown. When the *New York Times* opened a new office building at the spot where the subway turned north, the intersection acquired a new name: Times Square. Mass transit brought millions to the Square, and in less than 10 years it was Manhattan's new center of theater and entertainment.[3]

By 1913, the bright lights of Times Square illuminated vaudeville houses—Hammerstein's Victoria at Forty-second Street and Seventh Avenue, Loew's American at Eighth Avenue and Forty-second Street, and the Palace at Broadway and Forty-seventh Street (technically Seventh Avenue, but because the theater was at the cross of Seventh Avenue and Broadway, Broadway was used to establish the address).[4]

Times Square, like the districts that preceded it, encompassed different levels of vaudeville; it served both middle class and working class, native and immigrant, male and female audiences—sometimes under one roof, sometimes in different theaters. "In New York, . . . " Andre Charlot wrote in *Variety* in 1914, "Hammerstein's and the Palace are only a stone's throw from one another and the atmosphere of both is absolutely different."[5] The Palace was the embodiment of Keith and Albee's refined vaudeville, Hammerstein's Victoria recalled the Barnum Museum of the mid-nineteenth century.

Proprietor Willie Hammerstein's methods of attracting crowds in hot weather were vintage humbug. In the lobby he placed a thermometer which purported to indicate the temperature inside. The thermometer actually rested on an exposed cake of ice. A blackboard behind it recorded seventy degrees on the hottest days, and a message urged skeptics to look at the thermometer if they didn't believe the blackboard. Hammerstein also heated the elevator that carried customers to his theater's roof garden. When sweltering sufferers reached the roof, they could only conclude that it really was cooler there.[6]

Newsmakers appeared regularly at the Victoria: participants in sexual scandals, prizefighters, wrestlers, bicycle racers, runners, sharpshooters, and suffragists. Hammerstein presented Jack Johnson, the black heavy-weight champion whose affairs with white women were as famous as his pugilism. When chorus girls Lillian Graham and Ethel Conrad were released on bail after shooting Graham's wealthy lover W. E. D. Stokes, the Victoria put them onstage as "The Shooting Stars." They packed the house.[7]

The Victoria's shows also encouraged the rowdy audience participation of the old variety theater. The Cherry Sisters, billed as "America's Worst Act," performed behind a net: it protected them when the audience threw vegetables and eggs. A sketch called "Hanged" climaxed with the warden refusing to spring the trap because he opposed capital punishment. A volunteer was then called from the audience to do the job. "Hanged" evolved into "Electrocution," in which an audience member pulled a switch that sent sparks flying from a simulated electric chair.[8]

The Palace, in contrast, was a different kind of vaudeville theater. It opened in 1913 under the ownership of Martin Beck, head of the Orpheum Circuit, which dominated vaudeville west of Chicago. But it was quickly taken over by Keith and Albee, who disliked seeing a rival so established in the heart of New York City. The Palace, Keith and Albee's flagship theater, was their house for what one observer called "the silk stocking trade." Palace decor was lavish; richly decorated box seats rested beneath sculpted wall ornaments, and its proscenium arch was outlined in bas-relief designs. Palace patrons were said to mirror the theater's design—smart, elegant, and sophisticated.

The Palace was the one theater that all performers wanted to play, the house where a successful appearance meant that they had reached the top of the "big time." It became the center of the vaudevillians' section of New York City. They hung out at coffee shops around the corner, or they milled about on the sidewalks in front of the theater, looking for work.

The Palace was the focal point of Times Square vaudeville (the Victoria closed in 1915, partly the victim of competition from the Palace).[9] But the vaudeville audience was too diverse to be satisfied with just the Palace, however prestigious it might be. So Times Square succeeded because it offered vaudeville and related entertainments in a variety of settings: the rowdy Victoria, the low-priced Loew's American, the massive Hippodrome, and houses where star graduates of vaudeville appeared in revues like the Ziegfeld Follies, or the legitimate theaters. The "vast, floating population"[10] that filled Times Square found something for everyone.

On the circuits that radiated out from Times Square, the vaudeville moguls faced two tasks: to distribute vaudeville nationwide, and to entertain widely different audiences profitably. The key to the distribution of vaudeville was the vaudeville circuit system, headquartered at Times Square in the Keith-Albee booking offices.

The Keith vaudeville empire was based on booking. Although it owned its own circuit of theaters, it controlled many more by becoming the middlemen who charged a fee for bringing together performers and theater managers. Keith's operation had been incorporated in Maine in 1906 as the United Booking Office of America. In subsequent years, despite name changes and structural reorganizations, its basic operations changed little. Other booking systems challenged it, some with a degree of success, but none ever supplanted it. Through such organizations, as theater analyst M. B. Leavitt noted, vaudeville moguls "had things systematized in a manner not surpassed by a national bank."[11]

The U.B.O. was a switching house that linked managers and performers and directed acts around the circuits. Its operations generally followed a basic pattern. Although managers sometimes bid for well-known acts without advance viewing, the steps in booking a big-time act typically began with a tryout, usually for small pay, in an obscure theater where a failure would not attract attention. (Acts sometimes used false names to dodge bad reviews.)[12]

An act might play four or five weeks in tryout houses before attempting a big-time booking.[13] Then, the agent went to the Keith booking system on the sixth floor of the Palace Theatre building.

Within wooden walls topped by a metal grille, the agent found an open trading floor holding some 20 desks of booking managers, or bookers. Each represented specific theaters: a cluster of houses in New York City, for example, or New England. The bookers drew up the bills for each show at their respective theaters.[14]

To an outsider, the sequence of acts looked as random as the scenes glimpsed from a trolley car on a busy city street. Their selections were actually based on established principles of vaudeville. Bookers weighed each act's appeal, cost, and staging requirements, and then judged how it would fit into a complete bill that would satisfy the audience. In 1916, George Gottlieb, who booked shows for the Palace, described his techniques in the book *Writing for Vaudeville*.[15]

First: a "dumb act," possibly dancers or trick animals, to make a good impression that "will not be spoiled by the late arrivals seeking their seats."

Second: anything more interesting than the first act; perhaps a man and woman singing, to "settle" the audience and prepare it for the show.

Third: something to wake up the audience, perhaps a comic dramatic sketch that builds to a "laughter-climax," or any act distinct from the preceding turn, to keep the audience "wondering what is to come next."

Fourth: an act to "strike home," ideally a name performer who will rouse the audience to expect better things from the show.

Fifth: another big name, something the audience will talk about during the intermission.

Sixth: the first act after intermission and a difficult slot to fill, because it had to sustain audience interest without overshadowing the remaining acts. A famous mime comedian to get the audience seated with few interruptions of stage action might work well. But most of all, Gottlieb noted, the sixth act had to begin a build-up that was "infinitely" faster than that of the first half, one that would quickly put the audience in a "delighted-expectant attitude."

Seventh: an act stronger than the sixth to set up the eighth act. Usually a full-stage number like a short comic play, or, if the performers were good enough to warrant it, a serious dramatic piece.

Eighth: the star that the crowd was waiting for, typically a solitary man or woman.

Ninth: the closing act, preferably a visual number—trick animals or trapeze artists—that sent the audience home pleased.[16]

This basic format conformed to the likes and dislikes of each theater's audience. An act might be too refined for a house whose patrons had rough-edged tastes, too dependent on topical political jokes for a placid municipality. Bookers and theater managers tried to pick acts that would be popular with their own particular audience, mindful that what was successful in one theater might not work in another. In a 1907 report on singer Bessie Wynne, theatre manager H. A. Daniels noted that she was a hit in New York but a comparative flop in Cleveland. "Personally, I like her work immensely," he wrote. "She is dainty, clever, and artistic. But as I do not pay to see the show, its not good policy to force my likes and dislikes on the Clevelandites."[17]

As attentive to local preferences as these principles might be, they were applied in a setting that had much in common with a brokerage office. With money and jobs at stake, and bookers and agents in full swing, the booking office vibrated with arguments, excited gestures, and haggling—

"You will find yourself wondering what the panic is about," one writer noted.[18] The agents tried to get their acts "top dollar" and a good touring route, one that touched many theaters without traveling long distances between them. The bookers tried to bargain the salaries down and, at the same time, construct solid shows.

If the agent and booker agreed on salary, the booker arranged for a contract to be signed by all parties. Contracts were signed for one theater at a time, and each house paid the salaries for the performances it presented. In at least some cases—exactly how often it is impossible to determine— the bargaining over salaries was a charade because the bookers met to fix them.[19]

Sometimes, acts that rejected a salary offer were blacklisted from the Keith circuit, and thus banned from virtually all of big-time vaudeville. They might also be banned from Keith theaters and booking facilities if they appeared for Keith competitors, failed to book through the Keith offices, or refused to play without fee at benefits for Keith's company union. Such measures were used to thwart vaudevillians' union efforts in 1910–11 and again in 1916–17, but even when the sanctions were not invoked, they remained a sword over performers' heads.[20]

Once an act was booked, the Keith exchange made deductions which paid the cost of the booking system—and more. Given Keith's dominance of the market, performers were actually paying for the right to work. And, multiplied by the number of acts the Keith exchange booked—7,917 in 1917–18, for example—the sum reveals the lucrative nature of Keith's middleman position.[21]

Assume, for example, that an act was being paid $250 a week, exactly what Fred and Adele Astaire received in 1917–18.[22] Before they received their check from a theater, 5 percent, or $12.50, would be deducted to pay for the services of the United Booking Office. An additional 5 percent would be deducted to compensate the Astaires' agent for his services—a total of $25 in deductions. This deduction was processed by the Vaudeville Collection Agency, a Keith firm, which collected half of the agent's fee for this service (2½ percent of the act's salary). Keith's justification for the Vaudeville Collection Agency was twofold: it prevented agents from charging the performers more than the 5 percent commission allowed by law, and it guaranteed that the agents would receive their fee from the actors, minus the Vaudeville Collection Agency's own deductions. To offset this loss, the agents sometimes charged actors for additional ser- vices—real or imagined. The performer's paycheck suffered an even deeper cut.[23]

The contracts used by the Keith system were as calculated as the commission system. A typical agreement, signed in 1909, limited the theater's obligations to the performer and made the most of the performer's obligations to the theater. It also compelled the performer to book through

Keith's United Booking Office and allowed management to censor or cancel the act at will.[24]

Such arrangements had their attractions for theater owners. In a letter written around 1907, Keith representative Jule Delmar attempted to sell the Keith system to the operator of an upstate New York amusement park vaudeville house. He listed the following benefits: through the commission system, the acts paid for the bookings, not the theaters; theaters gained the drawing power of the Keith name; publicity and advertising were handled in advance by the Keith office; acts were booked on a route and were virtually guaranteed to appear (no small consideration, given managers' concern that acts would break contracts to pursue more lucrative offers), because cancelling one engagement meant cancelling all of them; and finally, acts were forbidden to reduce their novelty by appearing near Keith-booked theaters because "we virtually control the booking field and the various acts would not play other places than ours if we so directed."[25]

Yet the system was not foolproof. From the manager's perspective, both the booking office and the performers posed problems. The bookers might sign acts whose salary or style of performing were inappropriate for a theater, as the manager of Keith's Union Square complained in 1907.

> I think a few people ought to come down from the office and look at some of these acts and they would be convinced that a good genuine variety show with plenty of comedy and good acts is a 100% better than four or five of these tremendous big acts that do not seem to please the audience, and makes the show cost about $2500 when I can do just as well with a $1800 or $2000 show.[26]

And a manager's problems went beyond financial worries. Performers, with their complicated schedules, professional jealousies, and contract demands, confronted managers with many difficulties. This 1909 report from a Boston theater manager on the Keith circuit describes the potential for chaos in the organization of just one vaudeville show. For starters, there was the need to coordinate acts' arrival.

> This proved to be our fifth successive "tempestuous" Monday. This time it is the Pissiutis who are in trouble. Through the stupidity or negligence of the people in the Pennsylvania baggage room in Philadelphia, combined with ignorance and a seeming desire to save a few dollars on the part of Pissiuti, his baggage was too late to make the steamer from New York last night. However, the Pennsylvania people on this end, made arrangements to have the stuff put on the 1 o'clock limited from New York so that it will be here in ample time for the evening show. Under this stress of circumstances we pressed

into service the Sutcliffe Troupe, who played here last week and are
to sail for Europe in the morning.

Then there were unreliable performers.

To add to our troubles one of the young ladies of the Pianophiends
went strolling around the streets looking in the shop windows and
finally showed up at the stage door at the time the act was scheduled
to go on. Fortunately Miss Bergere was ready and we were able to go
along without any wait.

And rivalries and contract disputes.

Outside of these few mishaps everything was lovely until after the
Hawaiian Trio had been on, when "Toots" sent for me and said that
her guitar player and she had had trouble and they couldn't get along.
While she was making her explanation, he came on the scene with his
guitar and grip, saying she had fired him. I finally straightened this
matter out by fixing it so they are both going to work the week out as
a favor to me,—so they said, although I think they have done the same
stunt in other houses. Hence, I do not feel all swelled up on my
prowess as a diplomat. I trust Pat Casey will be able to use the salve so
that they will lay out the rest of their contracts. The guitar player is a
hit and knows it, while "Toots" is jealous of his success, thinking her
Hula dance should be the big feature. Here endeth the story of my
troubles.[27]

From the manager's point of view, the Keith system provided an
element of stability in a volatile industry. It also facilitated both the control
of act content and the evaluation of acts' popularity. Part of the motivation,
following Keith and Albee's reputation for wholesomeness, was the
censorship of ribald or socially controversial performances.[28] But records
of popularity were an incentive for performers to be consistently successful. An anonymous vaudevillian's letter printed in *The Morning Telegraph* in
1915 complained of this rating system.

This vaudeville has gotten to be too hard a game. Every Monday you
go on trial. Every week a report goes in and you wonder what it says.
You have stood the test of every kind of audience and yet you must
constantly show your wares all over again.[29]

And the U.B.O. didn't squeeze just performers—it also squeezed
managers. As "An Old Timer" wrote anonymously in a 1918 letter to

F.T.C. investigators examining whether the U.B.O. violated the Sherman Anti-Trust Act, the U.B.O. had "a double-edged sword. Against the theatre owner it cuts by refusing him the best and the vitally necessary acts if he does not give it the exclusive booking privilege, and against the act it cuts by refusing them work in the best and vitally necessary theatres."[30]

The Keith-Albee interests used access to their booking exchange and grants of regional booking monopolies to encourage or dissuade theater development. Around 1905, Bernard A. Myers was building a theater in Bayonne, a town on the New Jersey side of New York Harbor, when he sought a franchise to book acts through the U.B.O. The theater was to be a low-priced house, with ticket prices ranging from 15–50 cents. The U.B.O. refused him a franchise because it feared competition with its existing Jersey City theater eight miles from Bayonne. Unable to present U.B.O. acts, Myers instead offered dramatic shows. In 1918, he again applied for a U.B.O. franchise. Albee replied that since he had survived so far without U.B.O. vaudeville, he ought to be able to continue on his own.[31]

Vaudevillians were understandably suspicious of moguls who could make such deals. The performers, united in a union called the White Rats, struck in 1901 when Keith-Albee and associated vaudeville managers sought to establish a monopoly over vaudeville bookings that would enable them to collect a commission each time an act signed up to perform. The artists won a hollow victory, one they were unable to enforce, and the commission system remained in force.[32]

A revived and improved version of the White Rats staged another strike from December 1916–January 1917, primarily fighting to establish a union shop. The managers, who coordinated their actions using a blacklist and a company union, beat down this second challenge and destroyed the union for good.[33] Without the White Rats, the vaudeville moguls, especially Albee, dominated vaudevillians' working conditions in a style that was paternalistic at best and coercive at worst.

The Keith system became the dominant business force in big-time American vaudeville. By the early 1920s, Keith and Orpheum theaters covered the entire United States. Keith-Albee interests owned, leased, or operated 5 small-time theaters in New York City, and their subsidiaries controlled 12 theaters in New York and its suburbs. Their system booked as many as 300 theaters east of Chicago. Orpheum covered Chicago and points west. Albee exercised his power through the Keith-Albee organization, which combined with the Orpheum circuit to rule eastern and western vaudeville respectively before the two consolidated in 1928.

Rival circuits of varying size and profitability—Pantages, Fox, Fally Markus, Shubert, and especially Loew at the small-time level—provided a degree of opposition to Keith and Orpheum. The Federal Trade Commission investigated charges that the U.B.O., V.M.P.A., and N.V.A. were guilty of blacklisting and other offenses, but concluded that they had not violated federal regulations. The efforts of rival businessmen and the federal government were not strong enough to destroy the house that Keith and Albee built.[34]

But however powerful the managers were backstage, their efforts at control were complicated by an inescapable reality; although the Keith-Albee regime could deal severely with performers and managers, their organization thrived only by enticing people into vaudeville houses. They had to make sure that their shows, however centrally organized, never lacked for a human and intimate touch. Part of that responsibility fell to the booker, who always gauged the taste levels of his audiences before he signed on an act. But the greatest part of the burden fell to the performer.

In 1922, in the *New Republic*, Mary Cass Canfield wrote about the "unforced and happy communion" between artists and audiences in the vaudeville houses. The vaudevillian, she wrote, was

> an apparent, if not always an actual improviser. He jokes with the orchestra leader, he tells his hearers fabricated confidential tales about the management, the other actors, the whole entrancing world behind the scenes; he addresses planted confederates in the third row, or the gallery and proceeds to make fools of them to the joy of all present. He beseeches his genial, gum-chewing listeners to join in the chorus of his song; they obey with a zestful roar. The audience becomes a part of the show and enjoys it. And there is community art for you. A vaudeville comedian in America is as close to the audience as Harlequin and Punchinello were to the Italian publics of the eighteenth century.[35]

More than its other theatrical contemporaries, vaudeville consistently reached out to make the people in the seats feel like part of the show. Drama and opera could be enthralling, but essentially they created their own reality which people witnessed from their seats; burlesque and early musical comedy reached out to audiences, but their appeal was narrower than that of vaudeville.[36] The performers' goal, in their own words, was to put the act over. As George Jessel recalled of his vaudeville years, "You lived by the reaction of the audience."[37]

Above all, it was a heterogeneous audience. As vaudevillians worked the circuits, they toured across New York City and ultimately the entire country. They encountered crowds of middle- and working-class, immigrant and native-born.

As journalist Marian Spitzer noted in 1924, legitimate theater audiences were generally alike. Jokes usually went over equally well in one house after another. "But vaudeville audiences are different all the time," she wrote. "It's almost impossible to set a performance and then play it that way forever. Each town seems to be different; every neighborhood in the city needs different handling. So a vaudevillian has to be forever on the alert, to feel out his audience and work accordingly."[38]

Vaudevillians learned to establish a fine-tuned rapport by presenting a standard act that was customized for the audience at hand. Even though they performed the same routine for weeks and even years on end, they had to sound fresh and original. The demands were apparent even to a legitimate theater star who toured in vaudeville, Ethel Barrymore. "The vaudeville public is an exacting one," she wrote, "and nothing must ever be slurred for them—perfect in the afternoon and perfect at night, over and over again for weeks and weeks."[39]

There was nothing rote or routine in their craft. In a book published in 1914, Caroline Caffin recognized "that genial familiarity, that confiding smile which seems to break out so spontaneously, the casual entrance and glance round the audience—all have been nicely calculated and their effect registered, but with the artist's sympathy which informs each with the spirit of the occasion and robs it of the mechanical artifice."[40]

Performers learned to tailor their presentations to the crowd before them. A young Eddie Cantor flopped when he presented an English language act in a theater where most of the patrons spoke Yiddish. He translated the act into their language and scored a hit.

> We had simply talked to them in the wrong language, . . . and this in a way is every actor's problem in adapting himself to his audience. Drifting as I did into every conceivable type of crowd, I trained myself to the fact that "the audience is never wrong," and if a performance failed to go across it was either the fault of the material or the manner of presentation. By carefully correcting the one or the other or both with an eye to the peculiarities of the audience I could never fail a second time. I proved this to myself on many occasions later on, when in the same night I'd perform at the Vanderbilt home and then rush down to Loew's Avenue B and be a hit in both places.[41]

Sometimes vaudevillians used references to local geography. "I went from bad to worse, from Jersey City to Hoboken," said a character in a 1912 sketch. The script explicitly noted that two different localities could be inserted outside the New York area. As vaudevillian Frank Rowan observed, "If you're playing Bushwick, you make fun of Flatbush, if you're playing Flatbush, you make fun of Bushwick. That's an old, old game."[42]

Local appeal sometimes involved appreciation of language. Jewish comedian Billy Glason explained that if he played Loew's Avenue B Theatre on the Lower East Side, he would give his act a "hamish," or homey, Jewish quality, perhaps by using Yiddish expressions, to make the audiences feel like "family." If he played a top Times Square theater like The Palace, he would not emphasize Jewish themes, but would use more complicated, sophisticated material.[43]

Yet the vaudevillian's ultimate goal was always to make it to the Palace, and to become a nationwide star. Audiences may have been sitting in Bushwick, but their eyes were on Times Square. The big time was the standard by which all vaudeville was judged. A Palace booking was used as proof of an act's quality, and it opened doors to bookings around the country.

Acts always worked to balance intimacy and a national appeal. Jokes and sketches became trademarks of popular acts, and were performed from one end of the country to the other. Part of vaudeville's appeal was built on the acts' broad familiarity. For many performers, the old lines evoked laughter and recognition. "I luff you Meyer" meant Weber and Fields; "Is everything copacetic?" meant dancer Bill "Bojangles" Robinson. Smith and Dale first performed "Dr. Kronkhite" around 1906 and presented it successfully for decades.

Such performers became the stars of vaudeville. And for audience members, it was the stars and the big-time theaters they played in that became the most compelling face of vaudeville. In interviews I conducted in the middle of the 1980s, elderly fans who remembered New York vaudeville from 1915 on focused on the big acts they saw, like big-game hunters recounting their trophies. The human experience of the shows and their vitality were important also, but they expressed this through their appreciation for well-known routines.[44] As vaudeville fan Murray Schwartz said of the stars, "They were out of this world, they were out of our world."[45]

Theaters routinely promised the stars, but there weren't nearly enough stars to go around for even all the vaudeville theaters in New York City. The solution lay partly in small-timers imitating name performers, and partly in theater managers trading on the U.B.O. reputation for high-class vaudeville. The Keith-Albee seal of approval became a passport to success, and the booking office became a metropolitan arbiter of taste.

In 1911, the Sewell brothers of Staten Island, real estate brokers, announced plans for a vaudeville house in Port Richmond on the north shore of the island. Their theater was unlikely to become a top house like the Palace, but nevertheless they proclaimed their connection to big-time vaudeville. "All of the vaudeville artists who are to appear will be booked through the United Booking Offices," they asserted, "which, as every theatre-goer knows, furnishes the highest class talent to all the exclusive vaudeville theatres in the United States and Canada."[46]

Vaudeville took people out of their neighborhoods and moved them into a world of stars and fans. It foreshadowed the day when people would relate to television and movie stars as if they were intimate friends. As ludicrous as it might be for people to treat television characters as real persons, in vaudeville they at least had the satisfaction of a live person performing before them.

Being vaudeville fans did not make otherwise different people the same. It did, however, give them vaudeville in common, despite all their other differences. And vaudeville did that with a generous, human touch.

In a letter written many decades after she attended vaudeville shows, Florence Sinow captured the attractions.

> I loved it—I miss it—neither film nor tv has the warmth, the excitement, or the life of vaudeville—it moved you with an emotion quite missing in other entertainment—it reached and touched *you*, individually. And also caught you up in a communal happening—a sharing together of a common wonderful experience. Nothing has taken its place. It moved fast, had a wide range that kept you always absorbed—no one act was on long enough so that you lost interest— the evening shifted from excitement to excitement, but on different levels—high comedy, sophistication, slapstick, dancing, singing— sentimental—jazz—acrobats—animals—a panorama that was gorgeous, funny, tearful, each in turn—a kind of entertainment audiences could lose themselves in, individually and collectively.[47]

Vaudeville, and the bright lights of Times Square, represented the best and worst of American popular culture in the twentieth century. The grasping entrepreneurs who created the circuits set too many nasty precedents; the entertainment corporations they founded came to exercise too tight a hold on our culture. But the vigor and energy of vaudeville, and its Times Square setting, were undeniably attractive. Vaudeville, with its human, intimate touch respected human diversity. And it was far more open and generous than most cultural institutions that people encountered at the turn of the century. That was why they loved it, gave their allegiance to it, and became members of a national audience of unprecedented proportions.

7

THE SYNDICATE/SHUBERT WAR

Peter A. Davis

T HE DECLINE of Times Square as the principal center of the American entertainment industry in the twentieth century is a well-documented and much discussed issue in theatre history.[1] Jack Poggi, A. Nicholas Vardac, and others have published accounts both statistical and humanistic for the area's slide from the theatrical pinnacle in the 1920s to its current state as a poor third behind television and film.[2] Even within the context of so-called legitimate theater, Times Square and its economic extension commonly known as Broadway must now compete with a burgeoning regional industry that is equally influential. Most of the blame (and consequently most of the attention) has fallen on the art itself. With the arrival of film, the stage could no longer compete. The best writers, directors, performers, and designers were swept away by the more lucrative and alluring business of film and with them went the audience. At least that is the standard argument—offered convincingly by countless doomsayers and theatrical critics since the mid-1950s.[3] And the New York-based theater industry has done its best to bolster this perception of an art drained by the financial allure of a culturally inferior Hollywood.[4]

Although empirical evidence abounds to document Broadway's steady decline relative to the other entertainment media, most scholarly work has focused on narrative history. Theater scholars and their readers appear more interested in the personal or performance side of the art rather than the economic issues which have driven the theater to the brink of cultural extinction. Exceptions to this rule are rare. Bernheim's classic study, funded by the WPA in 1932, comes the closest to effectively blending economics and history.[5] But the work is now over fifty years old and hardly relevant to the current state of the art. Even Poggi's book (1968), which is rife with facts and numbers, lacks any significant explanation of the reasons why change occurred in Broadway's status, presenting instead a largely chronological summary of events to augment the Hollywood-as-cultural-vampire perception.[6]

147

Overlooked in these studies is the developing role of the theatrical producer, which has changed radically over the last century. Like directing, it is a relatively new aspect of theater, but an essential one. In most respects the commercial theater today has become a producer's art, a fact that is nowhere more apparent than on Broadway. Sadly, the canon of literature on theatrical producing is limited to chatty autobiographies and amateur histories.[7] The difficulty comes in trying to separate the tabloid-like personality studies from the factual material. Part of the problem may be the producers themselves, who remain a relatively reclusive lot in a business not known for its modesty. Because these producers (and their historians) have preferred to focus on the personal side of theater rather than on the business aspects, histories of Broadway—and consequently Times Square—lack any viable information on theatrical producing. Furthermore, from the very beginning of the entertainment industry in America, producing has been controlled by only a handful of monopolistic individuals.[8] Since the turn of the century, the history of theatrical producing can be essentially reduced to the story of two dominant organizations: the Theatrical Syndicate and the Shubert Brothers. It may seem that there is little to say about producing theater on Broadway, apart from a chronological/biographical overview of the leading personalities and their major productions—a view typified by Mary Henderson in her picture book, *Theatre in America.*

This is not true. The history of Broadway producers is a rich field for legitimate research which can shed a tremendous amount of light on American theater. When viewed in the context of business history particularly, studies of the major producers can reveal much about the commodification of aesthetics and the nature of American entertainment values. Although this chapter focuses on the pivotal conflict between the Syndicate and the Shuberts during the first two decades of this century, I will not deal with personalities or productions, but rather with how the internal structure, financing, and management in both organizations were crucial to their survival—and instrumental in their conflict. Other studies that have addressed this conflict have not done so within the framework of business history. Although some have inferred its relevance to the current state of the American theater, no one has offered a cogent explanation from an economic standpoint.[9] Yet it is clear that the present state of Times Square as an entertainment mecca and Broadway as an industry are largely the result of this monumental moment in the history of theatrical producing and the changes it brought about in the financing, management, and organization of the American theater.

It is not unreasonable for theater historians to consider the perennial issue of the Theatrical Syndicate's sudden decline and the Shubert

Brothers' concurrent rise to preeminence as merely another mundane demonstration of economic evolution at work. The story has all the makings of a classic corporate American "survival of the fittest" battle. The linear structure of hegemonic transfer as well as the defeat of an extinction-bound beast at the hands of a better adapted rival are destined to be viewed as corporate Darwinism at its best. But the story holds a greater significance because this particular situation is unique in the history of American business. In no other instance is the evolution of corporate America so readily apparent. Because of the well-known Supreme Court decision of 1907, which upheld the Syndicate's right to exist by declaring the theater industry not subject to the provisions of the Sherman Antitrust Act, the subsequent corporate struggle affords a unique opportunity to study the only instance in American history where two companies in the same business clashed head-on in a confrontation that pitted an outmoded remnant of a monopolistic past against its twentieth century corporate successor.[10] The Syndicate and its rival Shubert organization represent the corporate manifestation of Santayana's struggle between the old and the new—a generational battle between a classic oligopoly and a modern capitalized corporation.[11]

Monroe Lippman wrote what must be considered the reigning view among theater historians of the Syndicate/Shubert conflict. His 1980 article in the first edition of *Theatre Survey* describes succinctly (albeit without documentation) the salient and ready-known facts for a general readership.[12] Lippman benignly summarizes the conflict, citing various events between 1900 and 1916, to justify the theatrical industry's slipping from the control of one monopoly into the hands of another. Lacking any substantial challenge, Lippman's explanations have been widely accepted as the final word on the subject. Yet Belasco's and Fiske's outspoken opposition, the subsequent actors' revolt, and the aborted joint venture into vaudeville with the United States Amusement Company are insufficient for understanding the collapse of an apparently inviolable oligopoly. Putting Sam Shubert's "great personal charm" aside (a thesis popular among the gossip historians),[13] the question still remains how an upstart organization like the Shuberts' could challenge and eventually crush the seemly impervious Syndicate. Lippman mistakes symptoms for causes—failing to explore beyond the immediate realm of the theatrical art.

Much the same can be said for Dorothy Gilliam Baker's 1962 dissertation, "Monopoly in the American Theater," which attempts to trace the cultural antecedents of the Syndicate and Shuberts.[14] Baker discusses the business aspects of each organization but stops short of making the essential connections between corporate organization and the Syndicate/Shubert conflict. She even goes so far as to point out the two companies' decisive differences in financing methods, but does not indicate how or why these differences affected the conflict.[15]

A proper diagnosis must take into account the nature of business in the theatrical industry and requires examination of divergent and changing management techniques, the competitors' respective corporate structures and developmental strategies, prefaced by an historical overview of American commerce at the turn of the century as a foundation for understanding the competitive struggle that would permanently alter the entertainment industry in the United States.

The chain of events leading to the Syndicate/Shubert battle is deeply rooted in the monopolistic drive toward industrial consolidation at the end of the nineteenth century. It began with the rush of corporate restructuring and organizational innovation following the financial collapse of 1873.[16] American business was unprepared to cope with the fallout of what was then the worst financial crisis to hit the country. Aggressive research and development in the latest technologies were one way out of the sluggish post-crash economy for those companies who managed to survive the initial crisis. Railroads, oil, and the new inventions stemming from electricity provided a technological explosion ripe for exploitation by any entrepreneur with enough foresight and capital to corner a market.[17] But new technology alone was not enough to guarantee insulation from another financial collapse. That could be achieved, according to the wisdom of the time, only through unrestricted expansion with the ultimate purpose of controlling a single, indispensable technology.[18]

Initially, monopolistic domination was achieved through horizontal integration—owning or controlling as many companies as possible which produce or manufacture an identical technology.[19] This was the method followed by the first great monopoly, J. D. Rockefeller's Standard Oil Company, between 1867 and 1882. It soon became apparent, however, that domination of a manufactured technology was susceptible to fluctuations in both the availability of raw material and market demand. Starting in the 1890s, the more successful corporations (e.g., Standard Oil, the National Biscuit Company, American Sugar Refining, and American Tobacco) began to expand through vertical integration as well—the owning or controlling of all the stages of manufacturing the product from the raw material to the final sale.[20] Soon, a wave of merger mania swept the nation as companies sought to ensure financial stability through horizontal and vertical integration. But only the wealthiest and most efficient organizations succeeded. And common to all was an ability to maintain a rapid cash flow—a quick turnaround of profits to be reinvested in expansion.[21] When the funds were not readily available, corporations turned to pooling, in which the profits from several major independent investors would be combined to create an immediate source of capital. Pooling was an effective method for entrepreneurs without substantial capital to gain sizable leverage for creating monopolies through verbal or written agreements among former competitors. By agreeing to restrict commerce to only those members of the pool, investors were able to dominate a product without having to risk all of their capital or their market share just to become an entrepreneurial corporate baron like Rockefeller.[22]

Within a short time, cartels, combinations, pools, and trusts (all variations on the same type) came to dominate the corporate structure of late-nineteenth century America. Despite, or perhaps because of, the anticorruption efforts of Grover Cleveland's first administration, the monopolizing of American business continued unchecked. Cleveland's attempts to correct abuses in the civil service directed the government's attention away from abuses in the corporate sector.[23] By 1890 the situation had grown completely out of control, prompting the passage of the Sherman Antitrust Act—a vain attempt to break the monopolies. Unfortunately, its failure to define key terms such as "combination," "trust," and "restraint of trade," plus the lack of any commission to enforce the legislation (meaning violations could be tried only through individual civil action), left the Act virtually powerless.[24] Benjamin Harrison's subsequent Republican administration (1889–1893) was more than willing to look the other way while Big Business exploited enormous loopholes, including massive expansions through vertical integration, which were far less likely to attract attention under the provisions of the Act. In a few years, such organizational restructuring became a standard part of corporate America, so that the Panic of 1893 actually accelerated the growth of monopolies by creating conditions more conducive yet to restructuring and innovation.[25]

The passage in 1890 of the short-lived yet infamous Sherman Silver Purchase Act and the subsequent McKinley Tariff Bill, in addition to Cleveland's unprecedented reelection in 1892, contributed to the devaluation of silver currency and the resulting shortage of ready capital during the Panic of 1893.[26] Companies required to meet increasing financial obligations, particularly loans due, were forced to find other means of capitalization or face bankruptcy. Many companies failed, and a major worldwide depression resulted before alternate ways of corporate capitalizing emerged. Following the monumental Supreme Court decision in the case of *United States* v. *E. C. Knight Co.* (commonly known as the "Sugar Trust Case of 1895"), which substantially weakened an already anemic Antitrust Act, American business was once again caught up in a new and even more vigorous merger frenzy that lasted until 1904.[27]

The significance of this second wave of mergers cannot be overestimated. Some of the most important changes in the history of commerce developed between 1895 and 1904, prompting business historians Ratner, Soltow, and Sylla to pronounce this era of corporate revolution "the most significant . . . in the organization of economic decision making since the development of market orientation and capitalist institutions in the Middle Ages."[28] Paramount among the changes was the trend toward separation of ownership and management—the critical distinction between the organizational structure of the Theatrical Syndicate and the Shuberts.[29]

Up until the early 1890s, venture capital was raised either from the personal wealth of a single entrepreneur or from the pooling of wealth among several investors. In both instances the principal investors were also their corporations' chief executive officers. Management was relatively simple, if unsophisticated, relying entirely upon the wisdom, personality, and skill of the individual entrepreneur or the collective efficacy of each pool member in a given company. But after the Panic of 1893 and the subsequent decline in the currency markets, corporations turned to what was then only a handful of venture capitalists who were eager to sink enormous sums into potentially profitable organizations through negotiable securities, a method of raising capital that had lost much of its appeal just after the Civil War, due to the fraudulent manipulations of Jay Gould, Jim Fiske, and others.[30] This insulated venture capitalists from the day-to-day rigors of running a company and allowed them to spread their financial investments over a wider range of corporations, diversifying holdings while increasing stability and security. Corporate executives, on the other hand, now had a much greater source of ready capital required for the growing trend toward mergers and takeovers (and in some cases essential for survival alone). The new arrangement had severe repercussions for both sides. Investors gave up direct control of companies, turning over management to professional executives responsible for making a reasonable return on investors' money. If the executives failed, they might well lose their jobs.[31]

The aggressive, gifted entrepreneur of only a few years earlier faded from the scene as combinations, pools, and trusts lost their competitive advantage to the more efficient and better organized corporations. Successful firms adopted more rational bureaucratic structures led by integrated groups of specialized managers. Unification of management structures allowed for greater efficiency in coordinating operations and allocating resources. Through an executive committee of departmental heads governed by a chief executive officer, a company's internal effectiveness could be more easily managed, allowing development of long-range growth and strategy for the first time. The modern American corporation was born. Unlike earlier businesses, the new corporations were not dependent upon the enlightened benevolence of a single entrepreneur/owner nor wholly reliant upon continued product innovation. Success could now be enhanced, and even determined, by innovations in management and corporate structure; strategies could be mapped out through a coordinated board of directors; capitalization could be ensured through outside passive investment; cash flow could be increased through internal efficiency. No longer was commercial viability primarily contingent upon inventing a better mousetrap; streamlining the company was just as important.[32]

It was in this great age of mergers and organizational restructuring that both the Syndicate and the Shuberts evolved, though each took distinctly different paths. The greatest difference between them was their internal corporate structures. And the greatest single error the Syndicate ever made was their initial decision in the summer of 1896 to ignore the new forms of corporate restructuring by organizing themselves into an out-moded pool or combination. Why they chose such an obsolete design for their new venture is unclear, though it is apparent that they were reticent to restructure their existing independent firms and felt little need to do so.[33] The members of the Syndicate (Charles Frohman, Al Hayman, Marc Klaw, Abraham Erlanger, Samuel Nixon, and J. Fred Zimmerman) either were ignorant of the subversive subtleties of pooling or they chose to ignore them. It soon became apparent that their chosen corporate arrangement was fraught with difficulties and overwhelming encumbrances in the face of competition.

The principal problem lay in the fact that pools were typically viewed as informal or "friendly" agreements to cooperate, relying entirely upon the trust of the individual members, making even written and signed contracts unenforceable. Any pooling agreement was at best an unstable arrangement, and without legal backing the convenant could be broken at any time.[34] Even the Syndicate's contract contains just such an admission. The ninth and final article states:

> It is expressly understood and agreed by all of the parties hereto, that nothing contained herein shall be construed to disturb or change the control which the respective parties hereto now have in the theatres and places of amusement specifically mentioned and described in Article Second hereof.[35]

And indeed the Syndicate did at various times break ranks to make separate deals without the full knowledge or explicit consent of the other members. Frohman, for example, spent much of his efforts between 1898 and 1910 trying to establish a permanent repertory theatre in London, while Klaw and Erlanger fought a running battle with the Shuberts for control of booking in New York.[36] Although it is impossible to state what effect the Syndicate's factious nature had on the eventual decline of the organization, it certainly could not have enhanced managerial focus or resource distribution.

Another problem with pooling is the misconception that profits are pooled. Although Article Four of the Syndicate's contract expressly discussed the pooling of profits, the result of such an agreement inevitably meant the pooling of debts. Since the pool ensured each agent's sovereignty over their respective properties and investments and provided no facility for the actual pooling of funds, the profits were actually held in each agent's respective company. The Syndicate's agreement provided only for the separation of profits not the actual pooling. As stated in Article Six:

> Each of the parties hereto bind themselves that they will respectively keep just and true books of account receipts from each of said theatres in which there shall be entered all the receipts from each of the said theatres and places of amusement mentioned, as well as all expenses of every kind and nature which may be incurred in their management, and true vouchers of all and every such expense shall be kept, which books and vouchers shall at all times be accessible to either and all parties hereto.[37]

Such a division in corporate accounting would make for awkward cash flow and would accumulate debt obligations rather than expendable profits. Financially, the organization could not operate as a unit: it had to rely instead upon its separate entities to conduct its day-to-day business. Profits or losses were accounted through the individual firms, impeding any unified action on the corporate level. If the individual firms were solvent, the organization would succeed. Thus, the managerial emphasis was on the peripheral firms rather than on the central corporation. Understandably, the separate firms would have been apt to ignore the welfare of the corporation in favor of their own survival during lean periods. This kind of decentralization was typically unstable and inevitably disastrous.[38]

Finally, the pool arrangement as defined by the Syndicate provided for only minimal organizational management and almost no unified growth projection or planning. With each partner managing individually, there was no practical facility for developing long-range goals or even short-term corporate focus. The pool continued to grow outward in all directions, away from the center and away from any cohesive management structure.[39] What is most important is that this structure limited a corporation's ability to react swiftly to changes in the market or challenges from competition.[40] Lacking unified management, clear focus, and ready cash flow, the Theatrical Syndicate as a pool was unable to compete with the vastly more efficient corporate structure of the Shubert Brothers.

Beginning as early as 1894, with funding from Syracuse clothier J. W. Jacobs and factory owner Jesse Oberdorfer, the Shuberts relied on outside, sometimes shady, sources for investment capital. Using little of their own money initially, the Shuberts allowed silent partners to finance expansion.[41] While this forced them to share ownership with investors who were not directly involved with the management of the company, it also gave them plentiful and accessible funding necessary for rapid expansion. And the Shuberts formed a corporate structure that allowed for management specialization and long-term planning. Although they eventually created fifty-one separate corporations to handle various aspects of their expanding empire, the internal management structure always remained the same, with Sam as president (succeeded by Lee in 1905), with Lee or J.J. as vice-president, and a small collection of their most trusted investors as the board of directors.[42] In the fall of 1905, when the Shuberts filed their initial papers of incorporation, they cited a capital stock of $1.4 million and a board of directors that included Lee and Jacob Shubert, J. W. Jacobs, Charles A. Bird, Sol Manheimer, and William Klein.[43] The Syndicate, on the other hand, did not incorporate until 1907, and only in the vain effort to stem the growth of the Shuberts by joining with them in the ill-fated United States Amusement Company (USAC). Even so, the incorporated body was merely a small subdivision of their overall combination, rather than the total corporate entity as was the case with the Shuberts.[44]

With this organizational advantage the Shuberts easily outgrew the Syndicate by 1910, although the Syndicate was well aware of the Brothers' phenomenal expansion rate as early as 1900.[45] Because they were more efficient, the Shuberts were much less susceptible to the event that marked the beginning of the end for the Syndicate: the Crash of 1907. Beginning in 1908, interest rates began to rise sharply under the pressure of increased speculation and the rush of new investment following the brief Depression of 1903–4. With the rapid expansion of trust companies into the banking industry, the financial community was unprepared to handle the sudden price declines in securities and commodities. The panic hit its peak in October 1907 when the Knickerbocker Trust Company of New York collapsed, followed by the Westinghouse Electric and Manufacturing Company. By the end of 1907, business and industry had slumped into a new Depression, failure rates were up, and financial resources were low.[46] Companies with efficient cash flow and ready access to capital fared the best, while those reliant upon extended income from internal sources were hardest hit. This may explain the Syndicate's willingness to join the Shuberts in forming the short-lived USAC (1907), created for the express purpose of expanding into the lucrative vaudeville market already dominated by the leading members of what would become the United Booking Office.[47] The Syndicate had had difficulty filling their houses during the panic year and the prospect of a 51 percent share in the new company's $50 million capitalization must have seemed the perfect remedy for shrinking profits, even if it did mean cooperating with the Shuberts. Faced with the

Panic of 1907, however, the venture ran into immediate trouble, and by January 1908 the rival UBO arranged to buy the failing company for $250,000. While the Shuberts showed little effect from their failed venture (they merely used investment capital to convert their USAC theaters back to their own circuit), the Syndicate went into a steady decline, prompted by the subsequent depression and their irregular cash flow.[48]

Investment strategies also played a part in each company's fate. Initially, the Syndicate was founded on a simple strategy of horizontal integration, merely taking over most of the available booking operations across the country.[49] This made for a relatively simple corporate focus with minimal management. As they adopted vertical integration in the attempt to control all aspects of their product from start to finish, the Syndicate expanded amorphously, spreading the management network beyond capacity and eliminating any clear focus.[50] With broadly diverse income sources and debts, and cash flow encumbered by the inherent qualities of pooling, the Syndicate found themselves falling further behind the Shuberts. In attempting to beat the Shuberts at their own acquisition game, the Syndicate found they were poorly equipped to compete.

While the Shuberts grew along similar lines, starting through horizontal integration with their chain of theaters in upstate New York, they were greatly facilitated in their move to vertical integration by their restructured organization. With a stable capitalization base and efficient management, the Shuberts had quicker access to funds, a greater cushion against market fluctuations, and a more nimble operating style in the face of competition—all of this amply demonstrated in the wake of the 1907 Crash.[51]

Theater historians' assessment of the Syndicate/Shubert war is misconceived in several respects. Describing it as a takeover of an industry by one monopoly from another monopoly reduces the issue to almost incomprehensible simplicity and ignores a fundamental aspect of American business history; namely, that monopolies are not all the same. The Syndicate failed because it was unable to compete effectively with the Shuberts' more efficient corporation. The Shuberts were not able to overcome the Syndicate's domination because they treated actors better or offered a higher class of theatrical entertainment, but because they were able to take advantage of recently developed corporate techniques in capitalization, management, and strategy. The Shuberts' organization was so successful that it dominated theater and maintained healthy profits throughout its battle with the Syndicate and the rise of cinema in the 1920s, and might still be preeminent in the legitimate theater if the government had not broken up the monopoly in 1956.[52]

In the long run, however, the Shuberts' success was the cause of their eventual downfall and ultimately the decline of live theater in the United States. It may seem overly harsh to make such a sweeping accusation, but there is little doubt that the Shubert monopoly had a debilitating effect on the American theater. Beginning in the 1920s, film and radio (supplanted later by television) benefited greatly from the Shuberts' restrictive production practices and conservative aesthetics. Unencumbered by monopolistic restraints, the film industry and the broadcast media flourished in the competitive environment, often absorbing the excess talent that the Shuberts were unable to accommodate. Expanding exponentially in the thirties and forties, film and the broadcast media soon overwhelmed the theater, establishing a permanent dominance. Much of this situation was the result of the mass media's technical and economic efficiency, unrelated to corporate structure. The decline of theater as represented by Broadway and Times Square was inevitable, but the repercussions of the Syndicate/Shubert war certainly accelerated the process, leaving an indelible mark on the business and art of the American theater.

IMPRESARIOS
OF BROADWAY NIGHTLIFE

Lewis Erenberg

D ESCRIBING New York nightlife in early 1937, *New York Times* entertainment reporter Bosley Crowther found business booming, "as has
not been enjoyed hereabouts since the whoopee wild days of the late
twenties." Crowther attributed this development to the return of economic
health and the public's response to Prohibition and Repeal. Prohibition, he
declared, made nightlife sneaky and illegal. Few places could operate
without secrecy and high cover charges. "Night clubs thus became in the
popular mind the exclusive resorts of wealthy revelers and perennial
playboys." Repeal, however, gave nightlife the opportunity to shed its
disreputable past, to charge more moderate prices, and to enter American
culture as more than an outlaw.[1]

Essential to this development were the Broadway entrepreneurs.
Neither "captains of consciousness" nor paragons of social responsibility,
nightlife impresarios were "merchants of leisure" and "cultural brokers"
who, from the 1890s through the 1930s, sought to attract heterogeneous
audiences interested in alternatives to traditional Victorian values. Restaurant, cabaret, and nightclub impresarios provided a free-spending,
wealthy, and theatrical clientele with new urban spaces and enticing
novelties. In large-scale settings of luxury, consumption, and sensuality,
they helped create a new world of personal transformation, risk, and
adventure.[2] They also contributed to making New York City, according to
historian Donald Meyer, the capital of "dangerous love" by promising
romance coupled with the risk of fatal attractions, disturbing lures, and sex
across forbidden barriers.[3]

Nightlife entrepreneurs did not impose this new regime on the public
easily. In fact, they faced intense social and cultural opposition. Theirs
was a culture embedded in contention, not in hegemony.[4] As they

challenged a genteel culture based on self-denial, sexual restraint, and class and gender segregation, they met intense opposition from religious, moral, and political opponents who perceived them as contributors to the decline of the American family and the American civilization. Much of the social and moral resistance culminated in Prohibition, which drove nightlife underground and ushered in the era of the criminal promoter. This evolution reinforced the belief that nightlife was an outlaw in the United States and that New York was not America.

This story of nightlife is more or less known. What is not known is how New York nightlife entrepreneurs legitimized the nightclub and a modern urban culture in the 1930s. As Bosley Crowther suggested, Repeal was essential, for it allowed reputable Broadway showmen to enter the café field and to challenge the primacy of the gangsters and the whole nightlife apparatus that had grown up under Prohibition. With Repeal behind them, café promoters of the 1930s helped make nightlife a more integrated part of American life and culture.[5]

Nightlife promoters were by no means a homogeneous group; their ranks included restaurant operators, theatrical leaders, gangsters, and legitimate showmen. Almost all were immigrants or children of immigrants—outsiders to respectable culture. From French, Swiss, Irish, and then heavily Jewish backgrounds, these "new men" were less products of a new corporate culture, and more challengers to genteel conceptions of proper social life. Moreover, rather than imposing their inventions on manipulated audiences, they found themselves in highly competitive businesses where turnover was rapid and the need to attract audiences great. As Jimmy Durante noted in 1931, "The customers are boss, and you have to please them, no matter how it hurts."[6]

The first group of entrepreneurs, the restaurateurs, followed the theater district northward, starting in the 1890s. These early promoters built restaurants (named for themselves) to cater to New York's rich carriage trade. Men and women of both old and new moneyed backgrounds were fascinated by their accessibility to theater, fine food, and urban celebrities previously associated with aristocratic pleasures. Rector's, Healy's, Shanley's, Bustanoby's, Reisenweber's, Maxim's, Churchill's, and Murray's Roman Gardens vied with each other to present elaborate meals, spectacular decor, and prominent celebrities to theatergoers.

The restaurateurs offered a wider urban public many of the amenities previously enjoyed by the wealthy in private. Indeed, the restaurant owners prided themselves on their European gastronomic backgrounds, the wealthy gourmets who frequented their establishments, and the recipes for which they became known. The Rectors, for example, were

Americans, but their son George studied gastronomy and wines in France. As a result, Rector's became nationally famous for its refined French cooking. As George noted, "It was the ambition of each (Sherry's, Rector's, Delmonico's) to outdo his rivals in rare and toothsome viands."[7] Other owners were Irish and German, and had had experience running oyster saloons, beer gardens, and restaurants in more "cosmopolitan" sections of the city.[8] Often, they had French restaurant backgrounds, in an era when an appreciation for "Continental" food marked one as a person of style. Jacques Bustanoby, son of a cook in Pau, France, followed his brothers to the United States in 1897, worked in several famous restaurants, and then opened the Cafe des Beaux Arts.

The Shanley Brothers and Julius Keller had different roots but similar experiences. Thomas Shanley emigrated from Ireland and worked in restaurants throughout the city, while Keller arrived from Switzerland at the age of ten, worked as a waiter, moved to the Hotel Brunswick, and then transferred to Delmonico's. At the latter two establishments he met society men and learned the art of cuisine, "the epicurean kind."[9] With his knowledge and social connections, he eventually opened Maxim's, at Thirty-eighth Street and Broadway, in 1908.

Most of the restaurateurs started humbly and then became successful, taking obvious pleasure in their acquaintance with prominent men and women.[10] But equally important to their success were their theatrical connections. Thomas Shanley had a modest restaurant on Twenty-third Street, in the heart of the old theater district, across from Daly's Theatre and other playhouses. He drew stars of the American theater, including many Irish stars who were reaching prominence at the turn of the century. Charles Rector had begun by directing a Pullman dining car. He then opened a seafood restaurant in Chicago patronized by the theatrical trade who spread his fame to New York, where he moved in 1899 to tap the already established market. As a result of these contacts, Rector's and Shanley's set the standard for theatrical restaurants where the stars and the beauties of the chorus dined, drank, and socialized. Rector's thus became one of the first places to rely on the importance of celebrities to draw patronage.

This new form of urban sociability proved extremely attractive to the wealthy clientele of these restaurants. Unlike the more sedate Fifth Avenue dining spots such as Delmonico's, Broadway restaurants were stage sets for displaying and acting out dramas of wealth comparable to those in Broadway's gilded theaters. In fact, restaurateurs realized that Broadway dining establishments had to be showplaces for a clientele bent on creating a sensual culture that distinguished them from a more restrained Protestant past.

The model was usually aristocratic France. George Rector bragged, "I brought Paris to New York and improved it by the transplanting. When

Broadway grew jaded and lost its appetite I pampered it with the provender of the gods, simmering in the sauces of Olympus."[11] The stage set for personal transformation went beyond food. Keller declared, "The public eats with its eyes as well as its mouth, and the restaurant which displays the best showmanship catches the crowd." He also carried through on a "spicy" French theme to differentiate his place from more genteel Fifth Avenue venues. The lines from a popular song, "We're going to Maxim's, where fun and pleasure beams," were inscribed on the restaurant's chinaware. Waiters, doormen, and pages dressed in Louis XIV livery—cutaway coats, ruffled shirts, satin knee breeches, silk stockings, silver buckled pumps, and powdered wigs. The orchestra's uniforms—long black pants and red tuxedo coats—"wasn't necessarily Louis XIV, but was fantastic anyway." Authenticity was not the point. Keller was selling a new identity embodied in the color, romance, and the fantasy "of having been transported from the noise of a big city to the peace and quiet of an exotic paradise." String orchestras and rosy lighting helped to complete the romantic aura.[12]

As showmen, restaurateurs invested large sums in building, renovating, and decorating exotic and foreign establishments. Rector's cost $500,000 to build in 1899, while Cafe dell' Opera (1910) cost $2 million. To attract fashionables, declared a dining guide, "the establishment itself must therefore first attract the eye."[13] Each entrepreneur sought to outdo his rivals with aristocratic and regal decor. Shanley's, for example, featured "an Empire Room, a rich combination of mahogany, gold and mirrors."[14] But it was John L. Murray's Roman Gardens (1908), on Forty-second Street, that best exemplified the trend. Modeled on a French castle, the interior copied "the decorative features of the homes of one of the most lavishly luxurious of the world's ancient peoples—the Romans of the Caesarean period . . . at the period of the Imperial city's greatest opulence." Here a wealthy and "cultured" diner could "feast his eyes on an artistic and authentically exact reproduction of the most beautiful features of Rome's most ornate homes, of the palaces, villas and pleasure resorts of her wealthiest and cultured citizens."[15] In Roman gardens and Egyptian and Pompeian rooms, the well-to-do were "translated at once from our prosaic, twentieth century surroundings to the romantic elegance of luxurious Rome."[16] Lavish mirrors heightened the spectacle. In the midst of public dining rooms New Yorkers and out-of-towners could see and be seen.

Although normal restaurant hours were devoted to elaborate dinners, a glamorous theatrical ambiance reigned late at night when wealthy society, sporting, and club men consorted with actresses, actors, and show girls over champagne and lobster suppers. "Lobster palaces" became places for actresses to meet with wealthy sports; for chorus girls, newspaper publicity and an opportunity to build audience interest; for working-class girls, the good life offered by wealthy sports—all attracted to the subculture of sensuality that the theater represented. But actual sexuality remained covert rather than overt. While owners maintained outward gentility (including prohibitions on women smoking in public), they permitted trysts and male gambling parties in the restaurants' private dining rooms. As men of the world, the restaurateurs endorsed these activities as "Continental" freedoms, so long as they did not hurt profits. Indeed, the fact that the lobster palaces were aimed at wealthy playboys and playgirls conveyed to visitors "that they had been transplanted to a 'naughty but nice' environment," where gentility and restraint were open to question.[17]

The Broadway cabaret, an intimate entertainment, emerged almost spontaneously along with the new restaurants and quickly adapted to the lobster palace ambiance. Jesse Lasky, a vaudeville impresario, introduced the idea of the cabaret to Broadway when he combined a number of intimate variety acts and a full stage show at his theater-restaurant, the Folies Bergère, in 1911. His experiment of adding café entertainment and a stage show failed to draw audiences, but the idea caught on among the restaurant men who, in a competitive building spree from 1908 to 1911, desperately sought attractive novelties that would give them an edge over their competitors. As Keller noted, "The slightest indication that [patrons] were growing weary of what we had to offer was the signal for us to call upon our imaginations for a change of scene."[18] Consequently, Shanley's, Reisenweber's, Bustanoby's, and Martin's adapted floor performers and novelty acts to their own establishments. Having built their reputations on Parisian ambiance, the lobster palace builders did not have to extend themselves greatly to adapt new public desires.[19]

The ragtime dance craze of 1912–1916 brought Irene and Vernon Castle, Maurice Mouvet and Florence Walton, and others to prominence, demonstrating the restaurateur's willingness to meet new audience demands. The large restaurants made room for dance and performance space without major renovations by placing the cabaret in special rooms designated for that purpose. George Rector noted the change: "All they wanted to do was dance, and we accommodated them with a dance floor that measured thirty feet by twenty." Grateful for the business, the owners watched elegant dining gradually decline. "Nobody went into Rector's to dine," declared George Rector. "We had a kitchen, but the chefs were all out on the dance floor with the customers."[20] The restaurateurs pioneered sites for public dancing for people of means, and in the process, severed public dancing's connection with vice and the working-class dance hall. As the New York World declared, "The average New York man and woman get no chance to dance except in rooms given over to that purpose by public restaurants."[21]

Much of the demand came from affluent women, wanting to pursue the freedoms that men had long enjoyed, especially the freedom to experiment with their bodies. In attempting to meet women's demands, entrepreneurs opened cafés for women where they might drink in public unmolested. They also offered afternoon *thé dansants* which catered to women out shopping or attending theater matinees. From 3 to 5 P.M., women might dance and drink in public and even indulge in "a booze dansant" where "the cocktails were served in fragile Dresden china teacups," as George Rector put it.[22] Café owners also supplied dance instructions for the uninitiated and dance partners for the unescorted. Otherwise known as gigolos, the partners were well-dressed young men of Italian or Jewish background hired to keep women "occupied" during the afternoon. Rector's motives were clear. The afternoon events were quite profitable, averaging $1,000 per weekday afternoon and more on Saturdays, when suburban college girls were in attendance.[23]

The entertainment provided by impresarios demonstrated their role as cultural mediators. They drew their performers and generic entertainment from the working class and sometimes even from red-light districts and placed them in a setting redolent of aristocratic and luxurious imagery. In such a setting men and women might experiment with new cultural values without losing caste. The "animal" dance steps of the bunny hug, turkey trot, texas tommy, and one-step, for example, derived from black culture, emphasized greater body movement (hugging, jerking, swaying), and brought couples into much closer embrace. Unlike college administrators who banned the new dances, or settlement house progressives who attacked them, entrepreneurs profited by placing fewer restrictions on the types of dances their patrons might do. Starting in the 1910s, they presented black and white jazz bands and Sophie Tucker's "coon shouting." Ethnic entertainers transformed Broadway cafés into complex and exciting social spaces where upper-class glamour and lower-class bravado intermingled. Concretely embodied in the expensive environments and with formally attired waiters and aristocratic decor, the new cultural styles challenged but did not overturn entirely traditional social values.

Cabaret operators also encouraged audience participation and provided new arenas for the expansion of both theatricality and personality. Discouraged by the courts from using big stages, restaurants put their novel acts on the floor amidst the diners. As a result, performers and patrons could interact together in the "sacred" areas of performance. Artists meanwhile sat at the tables or entertained there. In all, the cabaret offered audiences opportunities to express their personalities along with the performers. The table-floor setting was marked by a new urban flux and flow, stimulating patrons to "act" and take risks.

In expanding the space open to public dancing, the restaurant cabarets encouraged a host of competitors. Almost from the start of the dance craze, theater owners and promoters turned their roof gardens into large dance emporiums. William Morris opened Wonderland atop the New York Theatre Roof in 1913 as an indoor Coney Island featuring carnival acts, later renaming it the Jardin de Danse. It soon became the largest dance cabaret in the city, inspiring the Shuberts to turn their roof garden on top of the Winter Garden Theatre into the famous Palais de Danse. Equipped with bigger spaces, the dance gardens could afford to charge less and soon captured much of the audience for public dancing.[24]

As purveyors of newer forms of urban adventure, café impresarios were also middlemen between audiences and critics. To get around curfew laws, for example, café men created the private nightclub. When moralists and progressives objected to suggestive dancing, they hired floorwalkers to prevent obvious abuses. Sometimes, political connections helped alleviate threats of police action. Yet there were times when little could be done. In 1915, fears over "tango pirates" and rich girls created a "moral" scare that threatened to put cabaret operators out of business. Establishments like Morris's Jardin lost their fashionable clientele. New legislation mandating a $500 theater license to present variety acts also hurt the roof gardens. As smaller venues, however, the restaurants remained profitable.[25]

In this uncertain climate, cafés searched desperately for new attractions. Morris tried Greco-Roman wrestlers, others, vaudeville; Florenz Ziegfeld created the Midnight Frolic on the roof of his New Amsterdam Theatre in 1915 which "glorified the American girl." Equipped with a full theater and license, a dance floor, and chorus girls and top acts from the Follies, the Frolic set a new mark for café entertainment with an array of stars no cabaret could match. In a lush and exotic "garden paradise" designed by the Follies' Joseph Urban, great stars such as W. C. Fields, Will Rogers, Fanny Brice, and Bert Williams performed within touch of the patrons. Chorus girls, dressed in playful and glamorous attire, added to the appeal, boldly presenting themselves as consumer objects, as symbols of adornment and success, advertising the body as a locus of desire and personal transformation. Every Broadway café soon followed suit, focusing on the eroticized female body as the centerpiece of the cabaret business. As cafés assumed central roles in the amusement world, impresarios became part of an extremely faddish, consumer-oriented business.

The new urban culture associated with nightclubs spread during the 1920s, encouraged by prosperity, by the growth of youth culture, and by the desire for personal escape and liberation. Consumer capitalism was in the ascendant. Yet, while nightlife expanded, it did so as an ironic comment on Prohibition, which governed nightlife by placing it outside the domain of acceptable middle-class mores. The war against alcohol expressed hostility toward big cities, but it focused on New York as the capital of the new social mores. Besides drink, moralists attacked the movies, jazz, cigarette smoking by women, and the saloons as un-American emanations of a mongrelized culture. Prohibition thus represented an attempt by urban, rural, and small-town Protestants to establish the hegemony of their familial values over the expansive values associated with a more cosmopolitan urban life.[26]

Such moral opposition changed the face of nightlife by pushing out the older owners. "Eating places pay, of course," Tom Shanley explained, but they were "not what I call a restaurant, where a man or a woman can get the best of food and the best of wines, a cocktail and a liqueur." He declared, "We can't go on at a profit on soft drinks. We obey the law and lose money, and we can't afford that." Those who continued selling liquor were padlocked, fined, and lost considerable income. Many sold out to dance-hall or Chinese restaurant promoters, and in 1922 even Ziegfeld folded his Frolic so as not to lose his larger theatrical profits.[27]

Prohibition did not succeed in ending nightlife, but it did manage to change its character by driving it underground. In fact, the number of nightclubs grew greatly during the 1920s; so too did the ethnic origins of promoters drawn to this sector of commercial culture. As demand continued, bootleggers opened speakeasies to avail themselves of the huge profits to be made on untaxed liquor sales. By 1925, when New York City, protected by Tammany and Mayor Jimmy Walker, ceased its local enforcement of the Volstead Act, criminals dominated the nightclub business, a fact that *Variety* confirmed. For urbanites at a variety of social levels, criminals provided consumer services connected with alcohol, entertainment, and prostitution.[28]

Most bootleggers came from "the bottom up," out of the city's gangs and ethnic communities. For them, Broadway represented a splashy entrance onto a larger American stage. Welsh-born Owney Madden, former leader of the largely Irish Hell's Kitchen Gopher Gang, left prison in 1923 to run the Phoenix Cereal Beverage Company, which supplied beer to clubs on the West Side up to Harlem. With several partners, including "Big Frenchy" DeMange and Herman Stark, Madden owned numerous clubs, including Harlem's Cotton Club and Broadway's Silver Slipper. His competitors included the Irishman Larry Fay, who owned the club Napoleon, the El Fey Club, the Del Fay, and others with entertainer Texas Guinan. Italians also ran speakeasies and clubs in Greenwich Village. Jews played a larger role. Gambler Arnold Rothstein loaned venture capital to bootleggers, owned pieces of numerous Broadway and Harlem clubs, and considered Broadway his turf. Gambler Connie Immerman ran Connie's Inn in Harlem; Lou Schwartz ran spots with Harry Richman. Legs Diamond, an Irishman, and Hymie Cohen owned the Hotsy Totsy Club. Tommy Guinan's Playground, the Club Rendezvous, Les Ambassadeurs, Frivolity, Fifty Fifty, Parody, and the Plantation also had gangster ownership.

As liquor dealers and gamblers, the new owners were less attuned than the restaurant men to "civility" and more to primal audience demands: under the direction of the bootleggers, for instance, nightclubs became exclusively drinking environments, and food was of minor interest. People came to drink and be entertained, and illegal liquor and a $2–$5 cover charge provided the profits.[29] Prohibition brought other changes too. The danger of raids made expensive decorations unwise, and many clubs sought the relative anonymity of cellars, basements, and back rooms in the brownstones of the Forties and Fifties. Nils Granlund noted that Larry Fay and Texas Guinan pioneered the intimate clubs in the Broadway area, including the seductive Club Intime. Other criminals followed suit, and "it was impossible to avoid contact with them." El Fay's on Forty-sixth Street, east of Broadway, for example, was on the second floor above a big restaurant, and seated 80. Customers climbed up a narrow stairway to a door with a peephole. Everything was portable. "Membership" cards, peepholes, silk on walls, and a tentlike effect over the dance floor made the nightclub into what Jimmy Durante called "more like an intimate party." Liquor meant profits. Clubs were supposed to supply setups only, but Durante estimated that 90 percent of the clubs sold illegal alcohol. The owner's function was to guarantee protection from local and federal law. Removed from the public eye, people pursued the right to drink as a personal freedom in a more private atmosphere. Gangster owners were tolerated because they challenged restrictions on personal choice.[30]

Many club owners were gamblers. Damon Runyon's romanticized *Guys and Dolls* contains a grain of truth in its linking of gamblers and Broadway nightclubs. Rothstein, patron and backer of clubs, was the most famous gambler in New York, known for having "fixed" the World's Series of 1919. He controlled betting at the tracks, operated bucket shops, and ran high-stakes card games in the Broadway area.[31] Madden played the horses, while Dutch Schultz, the Bronx beer distributor and frequenter of uptown clubs, ran the Harlem numbers racket. Connie Immerman, of Connie's Inn, was another gambler who later managed casinos in Havana. Frankie Marlowe, a Silver Slipper partner, was a high-stakes gambler, prizefight manager, and racetrack owner.

Part of an ethnic gambling and sporting subculture, the new owners viewed life from a rough male perspective. They sought "action" outside established social hierarchies and operated between social worlds. The next card was important, not the past. And as gamblers, they mixed with people from all walks of life. During the 1920s they created and inhabited clubs because Prohibition offered great opportunities for quick cash, and nightclubs provided places to be seen. They welcomed other bootleggers, athletes, gamblers, and entertainers because they were big spenders who lacked firm social connections to any given community. As Durante noted, "the stick-up man or the book-maker makes a bigger flash with his coin than the swankiest member of the four hundred." Club owner Billy Rose concurred. "All dressed up, he (the bootlegger) needed a place to glow. And the only place where he was welcome was Broadway."[32] Concerned more about spending than making money, the sports set the tone for many of the clubs, along with the buyers and other out-of-town businessmen. In the nightclub, money became the symbol of individual freedom, and what it bought was action and risk.

In the highly rivalrous nightclub world of the 1920s, the "boys" often relied on muscle. The Cotton Club's owners, for example, bombed a rival club, The Plantation, and gunned down its promoter. Usually, however, gangsters turned to the "muscling in" tactics that Rose encountered at his Backstage Club. Rothstein's bodyguards offered "protection" for 25 percent of the take. Although many patrons enjoyed the risk of being close to mobsters, there were dangers, and many operators, such as Rose, and entertainment directors, especially Granlund, would have preferred to work without them.[33]

Gangsters also competed through entertainment, and in doing so heightened the role of variety entertainment in the nightclub. Granlund claimed he had a free hand to decorate, refurbish, and put on shows.[34] The Irish and Jewish bootleggers and owners welcomed lower-class entertainers and gave them freer rein than had the more formal restaurateurs. In the smaller, more intimate clubs, they featured a line of girls and innovative "friendly entertainers" who engaged in lively exchanges with patrons, and who were rougher in tone and "more popular" than prewar entertainers. Led by such stars as Ted Lewis at the Parody, Clayton, Jackson, and Durante at the Silver Slipper, Helen Morgan in the House of Morgan, Sophie Tucker at her Playground, Harry Richman in his own spot, and Texas Guinan in several clubs, the nightclub merged people of varying status to create a new vernacular culture. And in that culture, spending and consumption seemed to expand the realm of the personal, promising to free people from authority, hierarchy, and the demands of social position. As a well-known resister to Prohibition, mob-backed Guinan glorified the new personal freedom as part of the public's private rights.

Unregulated by law and protected by the "machine," club owners of the 1920s responded to a wider range of audience demands and expanded the nightclub clientele. As investigations made clear, unscrupulous club owners operated "clip" joints barely a step above whorehouses. These "closed door" spots relied heavily on out-of-town buyers and cheating husbands seeking to "blow off steam," as Durante put it. Often run by low-level criminals, they paid cabdrivers and waiters at other clubs to steer unsuspecting customers to their spots. These club owners were also not above changing the sums on the checks of drunk patrons or using "knock-out" drops to facilitate a robbery.[35]

While the clip joints appear to have been on the lookout for out-of-town businessmen, other clubs expanded the space available for hetero-sexual enjoyment. Around Broadway and on the East Side, Schwartz and Richman's Club Richman, Charlie Journal's Montmartre, Will Oakland's Terrace, Don Dickerman's Villa Vallee, and Madden's Silver Slipper or Cotton Club appealed to younger audiences. The *New Yorker's* female nightlife columnist, "Lipstick," often focused on clubs where young daters could find "Tables for Two" suitable for romance. Public nightlife offered the young a greater range of dances, drinks, and friends without the direct interference of parents, as well as a privacy that their own homes and the more genteel ballrooms could not.[36]

The increased emphasis on personal impulses contributed to the development of exotic activities outside the theatrical zone of amusement. During the 1920s adventurous pleasure seekers could travel downtown to "bohemian" Greenwich Village to spots like Don Dickerman's Pirate's Den or Barney Gallant's Greenwich Village Inn, which merchandised the atmosphere of New York's Latin Quarter. Village entrepreneurs, bohemi-ans originally, now commercialized the "free love" and homosexual aura of the area to appeal to uptown tourists. Nightclubbers also went to Harlem, where criminal promoters played a central role. Owney Madden and the Immerman brothers followed black gambler Baron Wilkins, who ran the Exclusive Club, in exploiting Harlem as a white entertainment center merchandising late night fantasy where "natural primitivism" reigned untouched by civilization.[37]

Blacks ran numerous clubs in "Jungle Alley" (133rd Street), but white bootleggers controlled the alcohol. The two biggest clubs, Madden's Cotton Club and Immerman's Connie's Inn, managed to create a cosmo-politan entertainment world with links to Broadway and society. Geared to downtown whites, the bigger clubs welcomed ethnically mixed Broad-way entertainers and the wealthy, thus mediating the mixing of rich Broadway and society whites and black culture in a sensual but safe environment. The sensual was supplied by the African decor and the primitive themes, while safety emerged from the segregation of blacks from the audience and the overlay of plantation settings. With liquor money at their disposal, the owners assembled the greatest talents avail-able, including Harold Arlen and Ted Koehler, Jimmy McHugh and Dorothy Fields, Ethel Waters, Lena Horne, Buck and Bubbles, and chorus girls chosen for their near-white beauty. They offered their customers the experience of "safely" experiencing the uninhibited quality of black life and of living on the edge.

Jazz bands heightened the exotic image that owners tried to create. The bigger white-owned clubs paid the highest salaries to the best bands, offering national exposure over the radio wires that emanated from the club floors. Duke Ellington, Jimmy Lunceford, Cab Calloway, and Louis Armstrong crossed over to white audiences. Moreover, black musicians gained Broadway show music experience, while Broadway composers, such as Harold Arlen, Jimmy McHugh, and Dorothy Fields, created hits with black-inspired material. As these black bands became household names, Harlem clubs became the pinnacle of black musical hopes. Club owners, moreover, often supplied the money to bring black revues, such as *Connie's Hot Chocolates*, to Broadway. Given the segregated nature of the experience, however, the bands were merchandised as "foreign" and sensual, suitable for the night and Harlem but problematic for the day. As he watched whites dancing at a Harlem cabaret, James Weldon Johnson was amazed how they tried to "throw off the crusts and layers of inhibitions laid on by sophisticated civilization." He was struck by whites striving to "recapture a state of primitive joy in life and living . . . in a word, doing their best to pass for colored."[38] Despite the segregation, club owners had provided a space where jazz could become an essential, if privatized, part of American culture. By the 1930s, a different breed of white club owner would challenge these restrictions.

This nighttime culture, devoted to moral experimentation and consumer spending, was shaped and colored by Prohibition, by criminal ownership, and by the speakeasy. An added component was jazz, an exotic music symbolic of an illegal and perhaps un-American sensuality. Outsiders considered this mixture to be symptomatic of a mongrelized culture, made up of the disreputable wealthy, Jews, Catholics, and blacks. Altogether, an aura of deviance and decadence hung over the nightclub during Prohibition. A new type of urban culture was forged during the 1920s, but the fact that it was condemned by moralists and the state rendered it suspect. Urbanites continued to pursue their activities, but as personal rights outside the official values of the community.

The Crash and the Depression temporarily devastated the nightclub world. By 1932, Broadway from Times Square to Fifty-seventh Street resembled a frontier town with its honky tonks, dance halls, and cheap bars. The once "gayest, white wayest and most expensive nite life street in the world" had turned "cut-rate."[39] The nightclub's association with gangsters and illegal alcohol did not help. Only hoodlums could afford to patronize the remaining clubs, and criminal warfare intensified over diminishing revenues. Films of the early 1930s deepened this negative portrait. Many movies equated art deco speakeasies, gangsters, and socialites with decadent modern life. As a result, the reputations of Harlem and Broadway clubs worsened, and patronage in the former zone dropped off drastically.[40]

By 1936, however, nightclubs were revitalized, aided by New Deal measures that stimulated the economy, and, above all, by the repeal of Prohibition. The end to Prohibition, which took effect in December 1933, helped quiet the moral issues that had divided city from country, and offered the positive inducement of legal alcohol profits to nightclub, hotel, and ballroom operators.[41] For a suffering Broadway, Repeal was a godsend, which energized a renewed optimism along Broadway.[42] As *Variety* declared, "there are more niteries, pubs, taverns, roadside inns, large and small cafes, hotels and nite spots offering entertainment today than there were speakeasies during the Great Drought."[43]

Throughout the decade, however, Broadway promoters struggled with the problem of dwindling audiences brought on by the Depression. Still connected to criminals and deprived of its Tammany protection with the downfall of Mayor Jimmy Walker, Broadway owners faced stiff competition from a vibrant East Side club scene associated with "café society." Now that alcohol was legal, men of wealthy families invested in expensive nightclubs east of Broadway. John D. Rockefeller, Jr., scion of a family that had been a financial mainstay of Prohibition, opened the Rainbow Room atop Rockefeller Center, while Vincent Astor and Jack Vanderbilt opened even more exclusive clubs, among them the Iridium Room, in their East Side hotels. An Oklahoman of Protestant background, Sherman Billingsley, ran the Stork Club. John Perona, of Northern Italian background, achieved world fame as the operator of El Morocco, while an Austrian Jew, Jack Kriendler, together with Protestant Charlie Berns, was responsible for 21. With Repeal, East Side clubs could attract increased society and business audiences to legitimate venues. Moreover, the society zone and its largely non-Jewish ownership offered a more socially exclusive appeal (with anti-Semitic overtones) as a conscious contrast to the more raucous, Jewish, and socially mixed Broadway nightclub. Broadway club owners had other problems with the youth market. Younger jazz lovers now turned to the legal Fifty-second Street jazz bars to listen to black music imported from Harlem, or to the newly important hotel café-ballrooms aimed specifically at the swing-oriented youth market.

Hotels, which entered the business for the first time after Repeal, also provided stiff competition for the Broadway nightclub. In the 1920s, hotels like the Biltmore had offered public and private dance rooms. Prohibition, however, placed severe constraints on how much entertainment they could offer, and as a result, hotels shied away from the café field. After Repeal, however, hotels embarked on dramatic renovation campaigns to provide more glamorous drinking and entertainment spots. Repeal gave them new profit opportunities by encouraging them to switch from their conservative residential patronage to the more lucrative transient trade.[44] Hence, the Sert and Wedgewood rooms of the Waldorf-Astoria and the Persian Room of the Plaza marked a new trend. While these elegant hostelries went after "café society," more modest Times Square business-class hotels, such as the Pennsylvania, the New Yorker, the Lincoln, the Commodore, and the Edison, pursued the youth market by building special rooms designed for the big bands.[45]

Given the new competition, Broadway nightclub promoters sought to use Repeal to create a legitimate café industry aimed at a mass-middle-class audience. The operators who came to the fore after Repeal had been active during the 1920s and, by necessity, had worked for or with criminals. But Repeal gave them the opportunity to break from their former associations and to establish a more reputable Broadway, one more firmly part of American traditions and public culture. A key task lay in jettisoning the cabaret's criminal image. By removing the bootlegger's exclusive supply of liquor, Repeal stimulated legitimate entrepreneurs to enter the café business and to challenge the primacy of gangsters. Still active in the early 1930s, criminals nevertheless faced opposition, led locally by Mayor La Guardia and District Attorney Thomas Dewey, and nationally by the FBI. Although mobsters remained a presence, they were pushed to the background. They might invest money in clubs, but increasingly they had to compete with showmen such as Granlund, Billy Rose, Joe Moss, and Clifford Fischer who, having been forced into association with gangsters during the 1920s, now sought to operate legally. With alcohol legal, the French Casino's Clifford Fischer appealed successfully to Mayor La Guardia for protection. Similarly, Rose used his FBI contacts to prevent his former associates from trying to take over his operations.[46] As a sign that the central role of gangsters had passed, Owney Madden voluntarily entered prison in 1932 for parole technicalities, and a year later he left New York and retired. Larry Fay died from gunshot wounds outside his Club Napoleon, and Texas Guinan fled New York.

Broadway nightclubs also attempted to attract new customers, with Granlund leading the way. Granlund alerted Broadway to a new nightclub formula. In 1929 he foresaw that Prohibition's high cover and liquor charges could not last. Tiring of his gang partners, he went after a more sober moderate class of clientele who might spend less, but endure as a stable source of revenue. His angle was volume. To lure large numbers of moderate spenders he abandoned the objectionable features of the café business of the 1920s—the high cover charges, fancy headwaiters, and extravagant prices. For a modest minimum ($1.50), patrons of his Hollywood Restaurant enjoyed dinner, dancing, and a show. Operating before Repeal, Granlund sold no alcohol in order to discourage mob participation, and instead relied on mass-produced meals for revenue. The outcome was a profitable formula that survived the Crash. In 1930 he inaugurated a similar policy at the Paradise Restaurant across Times Square, attracting eight hundred people with spectacular, scantily clad showgirl revues.[47] *Variety* called the new development the "mass audience," while Granlund declared that the "family man" nightclub had arrived.[48]

Granlund's volume business idea was developed to its logical conclusions by Billy Rose's Casino de Paree (1934), Music Hall (1934), Casa Manana (1937), and The Diamond Horseshoe (1938); Joe Moss's International Casino (1936); and Clifford Fischer's French Casino (1935). Rose created the theater-restaurants, which put cabaret revues, entertainment, and dining service into converted theaters. He became "the key figure of the new Broadway." A champion stenographer who had worked for Bernard Baruch at the War Industries Board, Rose early associated with wealthy men who inspired his quest for success and fed his hunger for a life of "plenty" to compensate for his early poverty. His poverty, Jewish descent, and small stature drove him to prove himself to the world. He pursued his ambitions through songwriting, the musical stage, spectacular exhibitions, and elaborate Broadway nightclubs.[49]

All of the new men on Broadway except for Granlund were Jews, and it was entrepreneurs of Jewish descent who saw the possibilities of the café as a mass show business entertainment during the Depression. Repeal eliminated much of the Irish influence related to alcohol sales, and it allowed new entrepreneurs to develop the mass entertainment side of the business. Rose was explicit about his vision. Cafés could present something for everyone. As he explained, "My experience in the theatre and nightclub field leads me to believe that mass entertainment spectacularly presented has great box-office possibilities."[50] Jewish promoters were in a good position to exploit the new style. Oriented toward vernacular culture pursuits by the Yiddish renaissance, they quickly learned to merchandise the desires of the larger host culture. In the United States, there was a tremendous push in Jewish life to enter mainstream American life. Mass culture became a bridge to assimilation, spanning ethnic and class barriers. Moreover, all these men had long experience in the consumer and show businesses. When it came to selling something for everyone—vaudeville, girls, circus, theater—Rose, Moss, and Fischer excelled.

The new entrepreneurs were able to operate because of the circumstances of Depression and Repeal. Many theaters lay bankrupt and empty, awaiting promoters who would refurbish and redesign them. Rose was one of the first to turn them into theater-restaurants. "Scarcely six months after repeal," he converted the Gallo Theatre on West Fifty-fourth Street near Broadway into the Casino de Paree. Next, he created his Music Hall at a nearby theater. Alcohol revenues helped make such investments possible, and soon the theater-restaurant concept became the "salvation" of depression-torn Broadway, and was quickly imitated, "the rep of the Manhattan spot having so thoroughly saturated nite clubbers' consciousness in the hinterland."[51] In 1938 the Casa Manana, in the old Earl Carroll Theatre, and the Diamond Horseshoe, installed in the basement of the Paramount Hotel, were the two most successful theater-restaurants on Broadway.[52]

To attract large audiences at moderate prices Rose tried to free the

nightclub from its illegal, free-spending past. He and his cohorts emphasized solid "value." The clubs stopped gypping tactics and made "every
effort to protect the rare customer with a bankroll and enlist him as a steady
patron." The big Broadway spots eliminated the detested cover charge,
lowered the price of alcohol, and made it possible to have dinner, dancing,
and a show at a reasonable price. Rose even displayed cards on every table
promising honest value for the money. "I'm not sure that I know what
people like in a nightclub," Rose exclaimed in an ad for the Casa Manana,
"but I think I know what they DON'T like. With a few exceptions, the
Broadway password has always been, 'NEVER GIVE A SUCKER AN
EVEN BREAK.' I DON'T LIKE IT." Rose further claimed the Casa was
dedicated to the interests of "Mr. Forgotten Man (the guy who pays the
check)." At the Casino and the Music Hall minimum prices were $1.00.
Later in the decade prices increased to $2.50. For this, a couple received a
drink, a dinner, and a spectacular show. Rose perfected this policy at the
Diamond Horseshoe, which drew 7,500 customers a week in 1943, and
grossed nearly a million dollars a year.[53]

In seeking to lure audiences, Broadway promoters also redesigned
theaters to place the nightclub more firmly within American culture. As
they refurbished theaters that had failed because of the Depression, the
entrepreneurs worked a design revolution. Architects stripped away the
aristocratic excess, luxury, class distinctions, and exoticism that many
thought had produced the Depression crisis that left theaters dark. They
abandoned the eclecticism of theatrical and lobster palace architecture,
modeled after European aristocratic castles. The decorative motifs of art
deco were criticized as well, designer Raymond Loewy calling them too
"modernistic," unworthy of "the lowliest speakeasy."[54] Instead, Joe
Moss's International Casino, Ben Marden's Riviera (across the George
Washington Bridge in New Jersey), and Rose's Casa Manana featured
streamlined moderne, a style that emphasized clean lines and a smooth
exterior untouched by any hint of dirt or decadance. The new style also
balanced luxurious consumption with attention to values of production.
Long horizontal axes rather than the vertical sight lines oriented patrons
toward the stage so that everyone had unobstructed views. Parabolic
rooms, best expressed by the ubiquitous terrace design of the tables, made
this possible. As part of the process, balconies were removed. To increase
intimacy within the crowd, separate staircases were replaced by long,
curving ones. Art moderne linked itself to the machine and technology and
provided a style appropriate to the amusements of the modern industrial
world.[55]

By removing the facades and excesses of the architecture associated
with decline, the moderne theater-restaurants offered a vision in miniature
of a perfectly working future and suggested the outlines of a more stable
consumer culture. American technology, embodied in the chrome, steel,

glass, and curvilinear electrical motifs, now dominated nightclub design. Moss's International Casino best exemplified the trend. Smoothly working technology, miracle stages, seamless scenery changes, greeted the audience. In these streamlined pleasure palaces patrons inhabited nightclubs that emphasized the imagery of speed, transportation, and movement. Popular culture now reaffirmed progress.

At the same time, nightclub impresarios adopted traditional styles with the same goal—to domesticate the nightclub, to free it from the stigma of deviance and decadent consumerism. Rose explicitly linked his Diamond Horseshoe to the nation's past. The Diamond Horseshoe, which opened in 1938, conveyed Rose's version of the "Gay 90s." He presented his chorus girls in Gay 90s attire, with an array of vaudeville stars and small-timers who had spent years touring the hinterland. The Silver Dollar Bar had a Western motif, with silver dollars embedded in the bar and Western memorabilia hung on the walls. Nostalgia served as a staple in every Rose product, as did presentations of precision dancers or swimmers. By linking the nightclub to this version of the past, he integrated it into Americana. No longer alien, the nightclub, under Rose's tutelage, became an American institution.[56]

The new entrepreneurs presented spectacular shows with something for every taste, which competed successfully with regular theater attractions. Using such stars as Milton Berle, Rudy Vallee, the Ritz Brothers, and others, plus large numbers of chorus girls, the theater-restaurants banked on presenting a safe depiction of a nightclub rather than the intimate urban experience that had been its past hallmark. By placing the show on the stage, removing it from the audience, and emphasizing its theatrical nature, the nightclubs diminished the action and excitement, which made them less morally threatening to tourists and out-of-towners. The emphasis was on spectacle. And while the show was based on "girls," Rose declared, "I glorify wholesomeness."[57] Broadway's French Casino, according to one observer, "hand(s) out flashy entertainments plus food and liquors, with two dance bands, for what is normally the price of theater admissions."[58] Large two-hour semitheatrical revues divided into nine or ten specialized scenes, along with two bands for dancing and upward of thirty chorus girls, became the norm. When the International Casino opened in Times Square, critic Jack Foster exclaimed: "There was never such a conglomeration of acts paraded before the wide-eyed diners." Dog acts, circus routines, pantomime and trapeze performers, plus close to one hundred chorus girls, put the Casino on the map. Rose's clubs, moreover, divided the proceedings into scenes and acts, thereby linking the nightclub to the theater. In order to make profits from a mass audience, the Broadway nightclub became an assembly line, the forerunner of the Las Vegas show, with the patrons more an audience than participants.[59]

In essence, the entrepreneurs of the 1930s made their nightclubs into spectacular tourist attractions that depicted but did not provide the intense excitement of the big city. Indeed, their greatest aim was to make their clubs spectacular tourist attractions. As *Women's Wear Daily* put it, the International Casino was the "Statue of Liberty of Nightclubs—if you really want to see New York you can't miss it!" The experience of the nightclub had changed dramatically on Broadway. *New York Times* entertainment reporter H. I. Brock noted, "control is the word" on Broadway, "no longer abandon." Under the impact of Depression and Repeal, "Broadway," commented one observer, "is business-like, exact, whereas the old Broadway was carefree, what the hell."[60]

As legitimate showmen, Broadway nightclub promoters had greater opportunities to integrate their enterprises into public culture. First, they could now more fully exploit advertising, using newspapers, billboards, and radio wires to promote their names. Huge billboards, for example, advertised restaurants as public attractions. In 1937, Moss's International Casino put up a huge sign (250 feet long with 7-foot-high letters) flanked by a running electric script. No one in Times Square could miss it, or Billy Rose's large billboard nearby which asked, "How Many Times Have You Been to the Diamond Horseshoe?" As *Billboard* noted in 1938, such strategies set this era off from the earlier one, when nightclubs were little more than hideaways. Moreover, as part of their promotional efforts to attract steady patronage, New York nightclubs pioneered the use of professional photographers who took candid photos of guests and then distributed them to such national picture magazines as *Life* and *Look*, and even to hometown newspapers. New York clubs also had access to the syndicated gossip columns of Walter Winchell and other nightclub reporters, whose job it was to provide snapshot portraits of nightlife doings. Reporters like Winchell, Ed Sullivan, and Louis Sobol promoted the image of Broadway and New York nightlife as the most exciting place on earth. Smaller cities and smaller towns ran their syndicated columns.[61]

Rose was probably the most aggressive in pursuing a high turnover policy consciously aimed at a national audience. *Fortune* noted that at the Diamond Horseshoe, the most profitable pre–Las Vegas nightclub in American history, Rose divided his personnel into show and restaurant staffs, overseen by a C.P.A. Equally important, his promotion department used the listings of city gatherings put out by the New York Convention and Visitors Bureau of the Merchants Association to offer each convention special cut rates and benefits. These included tours of the backstage area for representatives of the associations, and if desired, introductions to "any dancer or show girl in the place." On any night except Friday and Saturday, this method brought in 20 percent of bookings. It also created a gold mine.[62] As he sought an explicitly national and moderate spending clientele, Rose commercialized the Broadway nightclub into an institution more palatable to larger audiences. The creation of a legal nightclub industry set the stage for the early 1940s when New York nightclubs achieved their greatest prosperity.

The Depression and Repeal also opened a space for the first nightclub to challenge the prevailing model of consumer culture. At the end of 1938 Barney Josephson opened Cafe Society at 2 Sheridan Square in Greenwich Village. About two years later he opened a branch of the café on the Upper East Side. Repeal made it possible for this political progressive to venture into the nightclub business, but it was the radical politics of the period that provided the audience that such an innovative impresario might tap. In this sense, Josephson created the first political nightclub in the United States.

Josephson was part of the Popular Front effort to challenge segregation in American entertainment. As a buyer for his family's shoe business, he had been taken to the Cotton Club. He was delighted by the music and entertainment but appalled by the segregation that the performers were forced to endure. He was not alone. Bandleader Benny Goodman, committed to breaking the color line in music, invested $5,000 in Cafe Society, as did band booker Willard Alexander. The primary figure, however, was John Hammond, the wealthy talent scout and impresario who fought for the recognition of black musical talent and integration of the music industry. A committed leftist, Hammond also wanted a racially integrated nightclub where he might entertain his black friends—among them singer Paul Robeson and actor Canada Lee—without incident. As unofficial music director of Cafe Society, moreover, Hammond was able to place many of the acts he brought to New York for his "Spirituals to Swing Concerts" in 1938 and 1939, and thus advance his firm belief that jazz and blues were the authentic representations of American culture.

As a result of these efforts, Cafe Society became the first white-owned integrated nightclub in New York City. Blacks were permitted in the audience as well as on the stage, and they were presented with dignity. Josephson insisted that no plantation or jungle imagery mar the proceedings, and he discouraged demeaning racial stereotypes. Lena Horne, for instance, was persuaded to stop performing "When It's Sleepy Time Down South," while Carol Channing was fired for her racial caricatures. Josephson created an environment where white intellectuals and black performers could mingle. It was at Cafe Society where already-famous Billie Holiday became a favorite with intellectuals. Among the latter was Lewis Allen, a Communist songwriter who induced "Lady Day" to sing his "Strange Fruit," a devastating account of lynchings in the South and the song that became her signature. The club also featured integrated bands—Teddy Wilson, Edmond Hall, and Frankie Newton—and authentic blues acts. Among the latter were boogie-woogie pianists Albert Ammons, Meade "Lux" Lewis, and Pete Johnson, who crossed over to a white audience searching for the folk roots of American culture.

Josephson created a club that radiated political criticism of the status quo. The decor was dominated by several murals that satirized the wealthy uptown Cafe Society set. The ads for the club, meanwhile, claimed it was "The Right Place for the Wrong People," and the place for "Celebs, Debs and Plebs." The entertainment could be socially pointed as well. MC Jack Gilford spoofed current movies while comedian Zero Mostel lampooned Southern racism, segregation, anti-Semitism, and antiunionism in his portrayal of Southern Senator Phineas T. Pellagra. During the 1940s, Josephson presented folk singers and other black performers. By staking out a small but significant leftist audience, Josephson made it possible for future impresarios like Max Gordon at the Village Vanguard and Art D'Lugoff at the Village Gate to offer intelligent and politically pointed humor and entertainment.[63]

By the time of Barney Josephson and Billy Rose, the nightclub had undergone a long evolution. By 1940, a full range of nightclubs and their impresarios stood ready to tap the demands of different types of audiences. The big city culture represented by the nightclub had emerged in New York City from the 1890s through the 1920s. Broadway restaurant, cabaret, and nightclub promoters had created institutions that challenged genteel restraints on sensuality and self-expression. Yet they found it difficult to impose their concepts of American life on American society. Indeed, the shifts in nightclub impresarios suggest that contention, not hegemony, dominated the first several decades of the nightclub story. The culture they helped foster was considered foreign and un-American, an impression amplified by Prohibition and its gangster infiltrations. Ironically, it was during the Depression that nightclub owners who formerly had operated outside the law now modified the nightclub to bring it into American life as a legitimate part of urban commercial culture. In this form, the Broadway nightclub, with its cosmopolitan ethnic groups, temptations of the body, and images of streamlined plenty, solidified its national appeal. It was also in the era of legality that political impresarios could create nightclubs that challenged the dominant conception of the nightclub and of American culture.[64]

THE ENTERTAINMENT DISTRICT AT THE END OF THE 1930S

Brooks McNamara

I N OUR FANTASIES, Broadway is a kind of nostalgic generalization. Old movies, casual journalism, and popular fiction assure us that George M. Cohan and Florenz Ziegfeld dine endlessly at Sardi's on some sort of perpetual opening night. Outside, Runyonesque characters loiter in Shubert Alley, beneath a forest of neon signs advertising the *Follies* of nineteen-something-or-other. But the unromantic truth is that the theater district is a specialized commercial neighborhood. The neighborhood has always had a distinctive character, but that character has changed radically over the years.

In Chapter 1 of this book, David Hammack remarks that "specialized land-use districts are as old as cities." He points out that in "nineteenth and twentieth century cities in Western Europe and the United States, of course, the commercial and industrial districts expanded out of all proportion to the rest of the city, and developed finer and more complex internal differentiations."[1] The Times Square entertainment district is one among the many examples of specialized commercial districts in New York City—the nearby Garment District, the Flower District on Sixth Avenue in the Twenties, the Diamond District around Forty-seventh Street near Sixth Avenue. What I propose to do in this chapter is examine some of the "complex internal diffentiations" that marked the Times Square entertainment district ("Broadway") at the end of the thirties. After offering some background on the changes that took place in the neighborhood during that decade, I will concentrate on its identity fifty years ago, during the winter of 1938–39. This examination, I hope, will suggest some comparisons and contrasts with present-day Broadway.

The boundaries of the Times Square area have been defined somewhat differently by different writers. Mary Henderson's history of New York's

178

theater districts, for example, speaks of an area bounded by Thirty-eighth Street, Fifty-ninth Street, Sixth Avenue, and Eighth Avenue.[2] The 1939 Works Progress Administration guide to New York defines the entertainment district as running from Thirty-ninth to Fifty-seventh Street, between Fifth and Eighth Avenue.[3] A 1948 guidebook to the city defines the boundaries as Forty-second Street, Fifty-ninth Street, Fifth Avenue, and Eighth Avenue.[4] Whatever the differences, it is clear that in the late 1930s the heart of the district lay in Times Square itself and in the blocks directly around the square, northward from Forty-second to Fifty-second Street. Here was to be found the greatest concentration of legitimate and motion picture theaters and nightclubs as well as the bulk of related businesses.

In the early years of this century, as Brooks Atkinson points out, Forty-second Street between Seventh and Eighth Avenue, then New York's theater center, "was one of the finest [blocks] in the city and a splendid part of the theater district. People treated the block with considerable respect."[5] But it was not to continue. The Depression— among other developments—would change the old theater street in many important ways.

By 1933, as Margaret Knapp has said, "half of the ten remaining legitimate theaters on the block had given up live production." Two of them had become burlesque houses, and since the motion picture theaters found it impossible to get important new movies, they had to show second-run films. By the fall of the following year, only the New Amsterdam was still attempting to present legitimate shows, and the house was dark much of the time. "Property owners and merchants had begun to complain about the tawdry burlesque houses with their suggestive sidewalk displays, their barkers, and 'steerers.' "[6] The title song of the famous 1933 Warner Brothers film would characterize the block as "naughty, bawdy, gaudy, sporty, Forty-second Street."

But the changes involved more than just Forty-second Street. By the 1930s the whole Times Square area was no longer primarily a legitimate theater district; it had evolved into a much more broadly based entertainment center and, in the process, into a far less genteel area. The change was not so dramatically played out in the blocks above Forty-second Street, but the whole Times Square area was clearly in the process of transformation, due to changes in the theater and motion picture industries, the Depression, Prohibition, and real estate developments.

The peak of Broadway theatrical activity had come during the season of 1927–28 (traditionally, theater seasons run from mid-June to mid-June), when 264 shows opened in the district. From that point on, fewer and fewer shows were produced each season. In 1928–29, for example, the number was already down to 225, and over the next decade it would plummet.[7] Among the reasons for the decline given by Alfred Bernheim in 1929 were bad shows, the increasing costs of production, poor ticket distribution, the decline of the road, and competing forms of entertainment, especially motion pictures.[8] In addition, of course, the long-term effects of the Depression were devastating to producers and theater owners.

As a result, theaters, which had been built to accommodate the Broadway boom of the teens and twenties, were now in oversupply, and an increasing number of them stood dark much or all of the time. As early as 1929, during the holiday season, *Variety* reported that one out of every five Broadway houses was not in use.[9] The number would soon increase sharply. No new theater buildings were built during the thirties, and some of the existing houses were torn down. A number of those that remained became burlesque houses, motion picture theaters, or radio studios.[10]

It is important to note, however, that the beleaguered legitimate theaters did not leave the Times Square area as they had left the vicinity of Union Square some 40 years earlier. There was now nowhere for the Broadway theater district to move. In any case, there was no need for a new theater district and, after the Depression, no money to create one. The theaters remained, as did such traditional theater support businesses as costume houses, scenery shops, and manufacturers of properties. Theatergoing would continue as the "signature" activity of Broadway, but it was fading as the pivotal social and economic activity in the area. Other forms of entertainment had begun to assume more prominent roles in the district's mix of amusements. Chief among these was the movies. The motion pictures have often been blamed for the decline of the Times Square district. In fact, the burgeoning movie business, as we shall see, merely took over a number of the functions of the live theater in the area.

Meanwhile, the Depression, along with the cumulative effects of Prohibition, had robbed the area of many of its first-class cabarets. As Lewis Erenberg has pointed out in Chapter 8, many of the more expensive clubs were now to be found on the East Side, and Broadway nightclub promoters increasingly "aimed at a mass middle-class and middle-aged audience." The thrust—as Erenberg has suggested about one successful nightclub promoter—was now volume.[11] Times Square area restaurants and hotels were rethinking the market as well. The area had, for many years, been the chief hotel district in the city. In 1934, in fact, the Times Square area contained more hotels, many of them first class, and more hotel rooms than any other similar land area in Manhattan.[12] But throughout the thirties a number of these hotels went out of business or were forced to lower their rates to attract patrons. Much the same situation obtained with restaurants in the neighborhood. In 1934 the Broadway Association, a merchants' organization, complained that important restaurants were leaving the area and were being replaced by cheap lunch counters.[13]

Part of the reason for the decline was because many people believed that the Times Square neighborhood had grown unsafe. The reputation of the area as a center for drug dealing and prostitution seems not to have developed until the forties, but, with the coming of the Depression, street crime was perceived to be on the increase. In 1934, Father McCaffrey, a local parish priest, complained of "a hoodlum element that was frightening people off the street," and noted that "weak laws and lenient judges" were hampering the effectiveness of the police. Shortly, the Broadway Association called for a police crackdown.[14]

Whether crime was seriously on the rise or not, everyone agreed that the area had become raffish and down-at-the-heels. The district had always been colorful and uninhibited. But observers were dismayed by the physical changes that had taken place during the thirties, and most of them described the "new" Times Square area in virtually the same unflattering terms. In *The Night Club Era*, for example, published in 1933, Stanley Walker pointed to a rather hard and tarnished Broadway. "Once a street of comparatively modest tastes, of some show of decorum, it has degenerated into something resembling the main drag of a frontier town. Once there were lobster palaces and cabarets; now it is cut rate." Walker noted seventeen cheap dance halls between Forty-second and Fifty-seventh streets, countless street pitchmen selling reducing belts, dubious Southern real estate, "Ten Recitations for Ten Cents," and "100 per cent pure whiskey candies—three for five cents." Broadway, he concluded "has become a bargain basement counter. It has places where one may go, with no cover charge, and gorge on cheap food while watching a ridiculous floor show. . . . There are chow-meineries, peep shows for men only, flea circuses, lectures on what killed Rudolph Valentino, jitney ballrooms and a farrago of other attractions which would have sickened the heart of the Broadwayite of even ten years ago."[15]

Ward Morehouse, a longtime Broadway critic, compared Forty-second Street in the thirties to Coney Island, noting that

> Broadway itself, once the street of Rector's and Churchill's and Stanley's, was now cheapened and nightmarish. It was offering palm readings and photos while-U-wait, live turtles and tropical fruit drinks, sheet music, nut fudge, jumbo malteds, hot waffles, ham and eggs, hot dogs, and hamburgers. A screeching amusement park bedlam that was somehow without a ferris wheel and a roller coaster, but that presented shooting galleries, bowling alleys, guess-your-weight stands, gypsy tea rooms, rug auctions, electric shoeshines,

dance halls—fifty beautiful girls—chop suey, beer on draught, wines
and liquors, oyster bars, bus-barkers, and right there at the curb was
the man with the giant telescope, ready to show you the craters of the
moon for a dime.[16]

The amusement park imagery perhaps gives some insight into the
Times Square of the thirties. The area was not simply in decline but in the
process of redefinition. It is clear that the entertainment district was now
increasingly aimed at a broad, popular audience, and that its appeal
seemed to lie in many of the same elements that characterized Coney Island
and other amusement parks of the period. In a sense, the Times Square
described by Walker and Morehouse had *become* an amusement park—a
chaotic, jarring, slightly sinister entertainment environment in its own
right.[17]

In reconstructing the web of institutions and activities that made up
the Times Square entertainment district at the end of the thirties, I have
made two choices. First, I chose as my center of focus the period between
Christmas and New Year's of 1938–39, because of that week's intense
activity and the resulting news stories and advertising in newspapers and
trade publications. Second, I have looked at the very complex activity in
the district in terms of "overlays." I have discussed the district's institutions in terms of four quite distinct but intimately related categories. Much
of the emphasis has been placed on those institutions that *provided* entertainment. But I will also consider briefly those institutions that *supported*
the entertainment business, those that *supplied* the entertainment business,
and those district institutions that *administered* entertainment, either locally
or nationally or both.

In the winter of 1938–39, some of the most important entertainment
venues consisted of the square itself, legitimate theaters, and motion
picture theaters, a number of which also presented vaudeville or revues or
big bands. There were nightclubs, radio studios open to the public, taxi
dance halls, dime museums, and burlesque theaters masquerading as
something other than burlesque theaters. Within a few blocks of the
district's center core visitors could also find sporting events at Madison
Square Garden, opera at the Metropolitan, lectures and concerts at Town
Hall, and concerts at Carnegie Hall and Steinway Hall.

Visitors to the Times Square area at the holiday season found that it
had retained its carnivalesque quality. The WPA *Guide to New York City*,
published in 1939, noted that an

outer shell of bars and restaurants, electric signs, movie palaces, taxi
dance halls, cabarets, chop suey places, and side shows of every

description cover the central streets. . . . Adjoining elaborate hotel and theater entrances and wide-windowed clothing shops are scores of typical midway enterprises: fruit juice stands garlanded with artificial palm leaves, theater ticket offices, cheap lunch counters, cut-rate haberdasheries, burlesque houses, and novelty concessions.[18]

The beginning of the season was marked in the square by the lighting of two Christmas trees in the shape of the trylon and perisphere, the symbols of the World's Fair, which was to open in April in Flushing. Grover Whalen officiated at the ceremony, which was attended by 2,000 spectators, a number of Broadway stars, and theater producer John Golden, the chairman of the fair's entertainment committee.[19] It was predicted that the fair would be a boon to the Broadway theater business, which was starting to emerge from the worst throes of the Depression. In fact, it was not, and theater publications would later come to see the fair as the enemy. As anthologist Burns Mantle wrote in an essay about the 1938–39 theatre season, producers "belatedly, and a little sadly, discovered that history's greatest show, in its early stages at least, offered competition that could not possibly be met."[20]

But that bad news lay in the future. In the meantime, the fortunes of the Broadway theater business had declined precipitously since the late twenties. Everyone connected with the theater business had been badly hurt, including the supposedly indestructible Shuberts, the wealthiest and most important producers and theater owners in the district. By the winter of 1938–39, however, they, along with other producers and owners, had begun to recover somewhat from the worst effects of the Crash. Of great importance in restoring the Shuberts' fortunes was a runaway hit show which had come to Broadway at the beginning of the 1938–39 theater season. That show, an eccentric revue called *Hellzapoppin*, featured two obscure vaudevillians, Ole Olsen and Chic Johnson, and opened to devastatingly bad reviews. Walter Winchell, however, took up the show's cause and turned it into one of the great Broadway hits of all time. Just before Christmas, *Variety* would note with wonder that "*Hellzapoppin*, the strongest musical bell-ringer Broadway has had in years, has piled up an advance sale of $115,000 at the Winter Garden." The writer concluded that the advance represented a new record, and added that the show was the only one "not affected to some degree by the pre-holiday slump."[21]

In 1927–28 there had been 76 theaters operating in the district, many of them belonging to the Shuberts. No new theaters, however, had been built in the area since the Depression.[22] In the winter of 1938–39, most of the theaters still existed, but a large number of them had been turned over to motion pictures or had become radio studios. Many were simply dark. There were now no theaters being used for legitimate shows (straight plays, musicals, or revues) on Forty-second Street and very few on Broadway itself; the majority were to be found on the side streets around the square. Of these, Forty-fourth and Forty-fifth streets between Times Square and Eighth Avenue (the so-called Shubert streets) were then, as now, the heart of theater activity in the district. Theaters near these two streets or on Broadway were generally felt to be the most desirable by producers. During Christmas week 33 houses in the district were showing live attractions.[23]

A number of the shows were fairly memorable, although the total number of productions was far below that of earlier seasons. Among the straight plays were Robert Sherwood's *Abe Lincoln in Illinois*, Lillian Hellman's *The Little Foxes*, Clifford Odets' *Rocket to the Moon*, S. N. Behrman's *No Time for Comedy*, and Philip Barry's *The Philadelphia Story*. Important musicals and revues included, in addition to Olsen and Johnson's *Hellzapoppin*, Harold Rome and Charles Friedman's *Sing Out the News*, Maxwell Anderson and Kurt Weill's *Knickerbocker Holiday*, George Abbott, Lorenz Hart, and Richard Rodgers's *The Boys from Syracuse*, and two swing versions of *The Mikado*.[24]

Political and social issues seemed especially important on the Broadway stage during the post-Depression 1938–39 season. Burns Mantle pointed to both *Abe Lincoln in Illinois* and *Knickerbocker Holiday* as examples of the trend, along with Elmer Rice's *American Landscape* and Kaufman and Hart's *The American Way*. "All these plays," Mantle wrote, "or the inspiration from which they stem, can be traced, I think, to the political discussions and national problems that have arisen within the last few years to plague and confound the voting citizens."[25]

Thirty-three shows were playing in the week between Christmas and New Year's. Ten had premiered, with high hopes, during this traditionally prestigious week. Virtually none of them, however, is remembered today, except for Thornton Wilder's *The Merchant of Yonkers*. No shows sold preview tickets during Christmas week, since tryouts in this period took place out of town. Straight plays outnumbered musical productions by three to one. Off-Broadway, which was to have a great influence on the course of the commercial theatre, was still a thing of the future. But a number of noncommercial companies, including the Group Theatre, the Mercury Theatre, the Federal Theatre Project (an arm of the WPA), and the Labor Stage (an ILGWU project), were all using Broadway houses during the season.

The Federal Theatre was shortly out of business, on Broadway and everywhere else in America, because of political pressures. On December 21, *Variety* noted that Actors' Equity had protested the F.T.P.'s "lagging production this season" in New York City.[26] A week later, *Variety* forecast the end in a news item which announced that the New York project was required to lay off a thousand people by January 16. "In some quarters," the article pointed out, "it's said that the heavy slicing of the theatre project is attributed to alleged radicals in the various departments. Lists of those dropped will be watched carefully for any possible 'discrimination' against 'radicals.' "[27]

Federal Theatre Director Hallie Flanagan later wrote that the 1938–39 F.T.P. Christmas show, a children's theatre production of *Pinocchio*, had been a particularly important one "because it is a visualization of what we have been able to do in rehabilitating professional theatre people and retraining them in new techniques." The production used "fifty vaudeville people who were at one time headliners and who, through no fault of their own, suddenly found themselves without a market. Now they are artists in a new field."[28]

In fact, vaudeville was now virtually gone from the neighborhood— and from the nation. It was generally believed by show people that the chief villain was the movies, in particular the talking pictures, which had arrived at the end of the twenties. Whatever the cause, there were only a few minor holdouts on Broadway in the winter of 1938–39. At the Shuberts' Majestic a kind of vaudeville-revue, with Molly Picon and "Fats" Waller, called *Vaudeville Marches On*, opened during Christmas week. But there were no houses still playing traditional "straight" vaudeville on Broadway; the famed Palace, for example, was showing motion pictures.[29] Such vaudeville acts as had survived were to be seen in area nightclubs and in the neighborhood's so-called presentation houses—the large movie theaters that featured live stage shows between their films. In April 1939, *Billboard*, the entertainment trade magazine, surveyed a number of theater critics about the form's potential for survival. The consensus was summed up by Brooks Atkinson. "On the whole," he said, "there is nothing wrong with vaudeville except that it is dead."[30]

Burlesque's symptoms were equally serious at the end of the thirties. Throughout the decade, burlesque operators had taken over a number of theaters on Forty-second Street and elsewhere in the Times Square district. In the mid-thirties, in fact, when other forms of live entertainment were suffering, the burlesque business had been excellent. But in May 1937, Paul Moss, the License Commissioner of New York, bowing to pressure from clergymen and moralists, had banned burlesque in the city. The shows' operators fought back in the courts and gained a series of partial reprieves. But basically it was all over.[31]

By 1938 there were only five burlesque shows—then known as "Follies"—in the entire city. By 1939 there were just three shows left, and many strippers fled to the World's Fair, where they could find employment in the Amusement Area. As H. M. Alexander noted in 1938 in his *Strip Tease: The Vanished Art of Burlesque*,

For the present the strip tease and burlesque are through in New York. It's true that the reformers have temporized a little, allowing some of the theatres to reopen. But the operators can't use the tease; the off-color blackouts are forbidden; the word "burlesque" is taboo. The Minskys aren't even allowed to put their own names on the marquee. The jerks pass the theatres by. The one or two houses that remain open are in the red.[32]

In 1942, Commissioner Moss refused to grant any license renewals to burlesque theaters, officially eliminating traditional burlesque in New York. Throughout the late thirties, however, as Irving Zeidman points out in *The American Burlesque Show*, there was a kind of underground burlesque operating on Broadway. These were the

> strip clip-joint nightclubs on 52nd Street which succeeded the burlesque houses. They survived for several years only because they were, in the main, unadvertised, unpublicized, and generally unknown—in exact antithesis of the exploitation that brought about the downfall of the burlesque houses. After a while, they became noticed and noticeable. They had moved from storefronts near Sixth Avenue to gaudy bagnios near Broadway. So they were closed down also. And all that remained were the belly dancers.[33]

The belly dancers were to be seen in cheap sideshow-style presentations connected with the penny arcades and dime museums in the area. The classic dime museum was Hubert's on Forty-second Street, which had been in the area for some years and would continue to operate into the sixties. In the thirties, Hubert's offered visitors freaks and Professor Heckler's popular flea circus.[34] The belly dancers were presumably there, too; a later visitor to Hubert's noted "a tiny stand-up theater in which two United Nations Dancing Girls periodically gyrate modestly to the strains of a horrendous Greek rock-and-roll phonograph record." An interesting symbolism is suggested by the December 1938 news story that a more up-to-date dime museum, Robert Ripley's Believe-It-Or-Not "Odditorium," would soon replace the old George M. Cohan Theatre.[35]

The garish "grinders" surfaced in much the same way. As the 1939 WPA guide noted, on "Forty-second Street west of Broadway, once the show place of the district, famous theaters have been converted to movie 'grind' houses devoted to continuous double feature programs."[36] As huge, elaborate movie palaces like the Paramount and the Roxy arose on Broadway and Seventh Avenue, the old Forty-second Street houses could no longer compete and were forced to lengthen their hours and lower both their prices and their artistic sights. The frankly pornographic films of later years had not yet arrived on Forty-second Street, but by 1939 male-oriented second-run films and ancient comedies were now the staple of the old theater block.

A few blocks to the north, the motion picture business was being played out on a very different scale. The Roxy, Strand, Paramount, Radio City Music Hall, and the other large and important houses were generally doing a considerable volume business during the 1938–39 season. Grosses had been down just before Christmas's week, but that was not uncommon, and the major Broadway movie houses were featuring an appealing list of first-run films. Big bands had become an important attraction and were featured in several of their stage shows. During Christmas week, the Astor was offering *Pygmalion* and the Capitol, *Sweethearts*. The Criterion was presenting *Blondie*, the Globe, *The Lady Vanishes*, and the Music Hall, *A Christmas Carol*. The Paramount was showing *Artists and Models Abroad*, and the Rialto, *Heart of the North*. The Roxy featured *Kentucky*, and the Strand, *Dawn Patrol*.[37]

Some of the old vaudevillians not employed by the Federal Theatre Project were seen in stage shows in the neighborhood's big movie theaters, most of which were "presentation houses" offering patrons live entertainment between films. But there were problems. The American Federation of Actors (the variety artists' union) met with the owners of film theaters which ran stage shows to protest the working conditions of the performers in the shows. The union met first with the management of the Roxy, since, according to *Variety*, "conditions there are worse than in any of the Main Stem houses." The big issue was the fact that chorus members from the shows—the so-called line girls—were underpaid.[38]

Line girls did have a few other options during the winter of 1938–39. Among them were the big new nightclubs that had come into being since Repeal, clubs that specialized in "big revues with elaborate settings" and which catered "to big audiences."[39] Most nightclub operators in the neighborhood were emphatically committed to a cut-rate formula and volume business; and at the end of 1938, they were concerned about their holiday crowds. Just before Christmas, *Billboard* noted that nightclub business was down and that club owners were intentionally keeping their minimums and cover charges low during the holidays. Owners were especially worried that a 3:00 A.M. curfew would seriously hurt their New Year's Eve business.[40] There were labor problems in the clubs as well as in the presentation houses; nightclub waiters were insisting on a $3 per week raise, although they had worked out a compromise with two of the biggest clubs in the district, the International Casino, and Billy Rose's Casa Manana.[41]

Rose, who refined the "volume" concept to an art form during the middle and late thirties, did not have much to worry about, however. In 1938, as Lewis Erenberg has said, Rose's two clubs, "Casa Manana, in the old Earl Carroll Theatre, and the Diamond Horseshoe, installed in the basement of the Paramount Hotel, were the two most successful theater-restaurants on Broadway."[42] The new Diamond Horseshoe, which opened with considerable fanfare on Christmas night, 1938, illustrated Rose's especially creative cut-rate formula, which, as Stephen Nelson says, included "low prices, and exciting pace, familiar old-time material, and an overall feeling of continuous festivity."[43]

Rose's show that night, *The Turn of the Century*, featured an evening in the life of Diamond Jim Brady and Lillian Russell, and portions of it were set in Rector's and Delmonico's. The stars were Fritzi Scheff and a number of other Broadway old-timers who exploited the kind of canned nostalgia for so-called Gay Nineties Broadway (a barber-shop quartet sang during intermissions) also seen in movies and musicals of the period. As Rose himself characterized the essence of the show: "You have to keep in mind that 700 people are wrestling with a five course dinner. The goal is a down to earth show with obvious audience appeal . . . no subtlety allowed."[44]

The result of Rose's efforts, as *Variety* noted, was a palpable Christmas week hit.[45] The press was lavish in its praise and patrons turned up in droves. *The Turn of the Century*, which cost $33,000 to stage, ran for seventeen months and grossed $982,000 in its first year. Not surprisingly, a decade later, Rose—who perhaps understood popular entertainment better than anyone else in his time—was still using the same formula. When the club closed in 1951, it was said that four million people had come to Rose's lucky Diamond Horseshoe and that the club had grossed $20 million.

This brief survey of Times Square entertainment venues during Christmas week of 1938–39 suggests some of the quality of the area at the end of the thirties. But it tells only a small part of the story. In his book on the nineteenth century Union Square theatrical district, John Frick points out that Union Square cannot be explained solely by describing such venues. He believes that the neighborhood was defined quite as much by its concentration of related industries: "by the offices of theatrical agents; by hotels, bars, and restaurants that catered to actors and theatre-goers alike; by costume houses, scenery shops, manufacturers of stage proper-ties, theatrical printers, stage photographers, trade newspapers, and shops that sold the latest foreign and domestic scripts."[46] So it was with Broadway at the end of the thirties. The area contained hundreds of institutions which were connected in some way to its theaters, its movie houses, its nightclubs, and all of its other entertainment venues. Many of these institutions *supported* the entertainment industry (and were sup-ported by it). There were theatrical clubs, such as the Lambs and the Twelfth Night Club, and several churches for actors, like Saint Malachy's and the Union Methodist Episcopal Church. The offices of the Broadway trade papers, *Variety* and *Billboard*, operated in the neighborhood, as did a number of boardinghouses, restaurants, and small hotels like the Schuyler, which catered specifically to performers.[47]

The Astor and Sardi's were among the important hotels and restaurants aimed at visitors who had chosen the area because it was an entertainment center. Unfortunately, in 1939, the first-class hotel and restaurant businesses were in decline. The famous old Knickerbocker Hotel, for example, had recently become an office building. World's Fair tourists would come increasingly to choose East Side hotels in preference to those in the entertainment area because of the area's growing reputation for crime.[48] But quality support institutions were simply being replaced by those directed at a new, broader audience.

There were also those institutions that *supplied* the specialized entertainment industry in the neighborhood, and, to a considerable extent, nationwide. If the theaters remained in the neighborhood after the Depression, so did many of the businesses that provided them with costumes, scripts, makeup, lighting equipment, and the most necessary element, personnel—actors, musicians, dancers, directors, designers, technicians. Many of the same companies also supplied nightclubs, motion picture theaters, and related entertainment venues in the area.

A number of the old companies had gone out of business after the Crash, but trade papers and magazines from the late thirties were still crammed with advertisements for the crafts associated with entertainment. Marcus Loew's old booking agency on Forty-sixth Street was still advertising in *Variety*.[49] Dazian, a theatrical fabric supplier which had come to the neighborhood at the turn of the century, was still doing business there in 1939. An important costumer, Brooks Costume Company, had recently moved to larger quarters in the neighborhood because of World's Fair contracts and, as they said in their advertisements, their "ever increasing clientele."[50] Brooks, like many other entertainment-related industries in the area, was just then emerging from the worst of the Depression.

Related to these support institutions and suppliers was a third category of Times Square institution. I suggested earlier that the neighborhood in 1939 was also center for the *administration* of entertainment, both locally and nationally. It was the hub for performing arts unions and guilds, for the offices of the major theater owners and producers, for the Eastern offices of motion picture companies, the headquarters of carnival entrepreneurs, and popular music publishers. The offices of Actors' Equity and the American Federation of Actors, for example, were to be found in the area, along with the executive offices of Paramount, Loew's, and many other film-related companies. The Brill Building was the headquarters of

America's popular music industry, and the Shuberts still operated their somewhat battered empire out of offices that overlooked their private street, Shubert Alley, the center of the entertainment universe.

Many of these institutions continued to exist in the neighborhood well beyond the winter of 1938–39. As Stuart Little and Arthur Cantor suggested in 1971, "Over the years the directory listing in lobbies may change, but the parochial quality of the district remains. . . . In the theater district theater people work, eat, and transact business with their own kind in their own inbred enclave." Yet, by the late sixties, as Little and Cantor also suggest, the "tendency to congregate in the old rabbit warrens around Times Square" was clearly breaking down.[51] Theaters were disappearing, traditional entertainment-related businesses were leaving the neighborhood, and new—and often undesirable—businesses were swiftly taking their places.

Times Square is clearly not the same specialized commercial district that it was 50 years ago. The entertainment business has changed radically. There are far fewer legitimate theaters in the area and far fewer Broadway shows being produced, although those that manage to survive are often extremely profitable. Motion picture houses are closing, and the various support businesses associated with the entertainment industry have virtually disappeared from the neighborhood. Nevertheless, real estate in the area is extremely valuable, and Broadway is becoming lined with office buildings.

Some people prophesy that the traditional Times Square entertainment district will be dead in another decade. Others claim that the area is already dead, soon to be replaced by an uptown Wall Street in the making. It has also been suggested that the neighborhood is merely undergoing another change, this time into a new kind of entertainment district suited for the twenty-first century. But that is another story, and one that remains to be told.

10

IRVING BERLIN: TROUBADOUR OF TIN PAN ALLEY

Philip Furia

Irving Berlin has no "place" in American music; Irving Berlin IS
American music.

Jerome Kern

J EROME KERN'S equation of Irving Berlin with American music may
seem like theatrical hyperbole, but during the first half of the twentieth century "American music" was largely the product of the industry
known as Tin Pan Alley, and nobody epitomizes the Alley or its music
better than Irving Berlin.

Tin Pan Alley started out in the 1880s as a cluster of sheet music
publishing houses in the Bowery, moved up to Union Square in the 1890s
to be closer to vaudeville, then followed the movement of theaters and
nightlife northward. By 1910 most publishers had moved up to West
Twenty-eighth Street between Broadway and Sixth Avenue, where the
din of pianos concocting, polishing, and demonstrating songs sounded to
songwriter Monroe Rosenfeld like a cacophony of clashing tin pans and
inspired his sobriquet, "Tin Pan Alley." By 1920 Tin Pan Alley had
followed the crowds up to Times Square, with T. B. Harms anchored at
Forty-second and Broadway and other publishers setting up shop along
Broadway to Fifty-sixth Street. In 1931 the new Brill Building at 1619
Broadway became the center of an industry which, by then, reached into
the Broadway theater, Hollywood sound stage, and radio and recording
studios.

More successfully than any other songwriter, Irving Berlin, who

191

owned his own publishing firm, filled every channel of this vast network with his songs. Like all Tin Pan Alley songs, Berlin's were built upon formulas so simple and rigid that, as Charles Hamm notes,

> Songs written by Irving Berlin in 1915 are essentially the same as those written thirty years later; continuity of musical style is one of the most striking features of the Tin Pan Alley era. . . . The style of Tin Pan Alley songs was constant throughout the creative life of Irving Berlin . . . [thus] there is no way to tell, from listening to a song by Irving Berlin or any of his contemporaries, whether it was written for vaudeville, musical comedy, the movies, or simply composed for radio play and possibly recording. . . . The 1910s, 20s, and 30s saw a large number of extremely talented songwriters exploiting a song style that had not yet grown old, that still seemed to them to be perfectly suitable to express what they wanted to express, that could still be modified in its details enough for each of them to carve out a somewhat distinctive profile.[1]

It was with this formulaic product that Tin Pan Alley—and Irving Berlin—monopolized American music for half a century.

From the very start, the publishers of Tin Pan Alley knew that popular songs are *made*, not born, and they marketed their wares through an extensive system of "plugging." In the early days of the sheet music industry, plugging began with staff pianists who relentlessly demonstrated their firm's new songs to the public and to performers seeking new material. But it ranged much farther afield as pluggers were sent out to stores like Woolworth's, which prominently displayed the colorful sheet music on its counters, to busy streetcorners, even out to Coney Island—anywhere a crowd was gathered. At night the pluggers boomed their firm's latest songs in saloons, lobster palaces, and nickelodeon movie houses. One of these early publishers, Edward Marks, recalled that the odyssey of plugging began in the Bowery.

> If a publisher knew his business, he always launched a sales campaign by impressing his song on the happily befogged consciousness of the gang in the saloons and beer halls . . . with its initial break in the beer hall, a song might work up to the smaller variety houses, and finally to Tony Pastor's, on Fourteenth Street . . . whence some British singer might carry it home to London. If it scored there, it might come back here as a society sensation.[2]

Yet no one realized how fruitful such plugging could be until 1892, when one song, Charles K. Harris's "After the Ball," sold 5 million copies of sheet music and galvanized the fledgling industry.

It seems only fitting that Irving Berlin should have arrived in America in the wake of Tin Pan Alley's first million-seller. He was only four years old then, and his name was Israel Baline, the youngest child of Russian Jews fleeing a pogrom in their Siberian village of Temun. The Balines settled in the tenements of the Lower East Side, where Moses Baline, who had been a cantor in Russia, now had to work in a kosher meat factory, give Hebrew lessons, and still struggle to support his family.

When his father died, eight-year-old "Izzy" quit school to sell newspapers in the Bowery. From the street, he could hear the hits of the day drift through the doors of saloons and restaurants, and he soon found that if he sang the songs himself while he sold papers, people tossed coins to him. To his mother one night he confessed his life's ambition—to become a singing waiter in a saloon. This—from the son of a cantor! When his mother objected, Israel ran away from home—to Tin Pan Alley. He started at the very bottom—in the Bowery saloon world described by Timothy Gilfoyle (see Chapter 14). As one of many roving buskers, he serenaded sports and prostitutes with "The Mansion of Aching Hearts" and other paeans to motherhood, home, childhood, fidelity, and fallen virtue, in the hopes of having more coins tossed his way.

In 1902 he applied for a job at Harry Von Tilzer's publishing house, which had already moved up to West Twenty-eighth Street. The composer of "The Mansion of Aching Hearts," as well as such other Victoriana as "I Want a Girl Just Like the Girl That Married Dear Old Dad" and "A Bird in a Gilded Cage," Von Tilzer put young Berlin to work at Tony Pastor's vaudeville house on Fourteenth Street. Back in 1865 Pastor had opened an "Opera House" in the rowdy-world of Bowery variety, but in 1881 he moved up to Union Square, dubbed his entertainment with the more refined term "vaudeville," and, "catering to polite tastes," proffered entertainment suitable for ladies, indeed entire families.

Like other Alley publishers, Von Tilzer recognized vaudeville, with its vast national network described by Robert Snyder (see Chapter 6), as the prime target for making a song nationally popular. To insure maximum plugging for songs, publishers not only palmed their wares off on the performers (sometimes with the added inducement of a bribe) but they planted pluggers in the audience to applaud the numbers wildly and even leap up, as if spontaneously carried away by the song's charm, to lead the audience in chorus after chorus. It was as such a "boomer" or "singing stooge" that Israel was hired, plugging songs for a family act, the Keatons, which featured young Buster.

When the Keatons moved on, Berlin went back to busking, but eventually landed the job of his dreams, as a singing waiter in the Pelham Café in Chinatown. It was not much of a step up from the Bowery, since Chinatown was rife with opium dens and prostitution, and the Pelham "Café" itself was primarily a saloon with a brothel upstairs run by

"Chinatown Gertie." Still, Irving had a job, plus all the coins tossed to him for singing the latest hits and the even more numerous coins for his specialty—risqué parodies of such hits. One day, the owner, a swarthy Russian nicknamed "Nigger Mike" Salter, approached "Izzy" and the café's piano player and ordered them to write a song. Two waiters at a rival café had just written a hit novelty song, "My Mariuccia Take a Steamboat," and he thought that his waiters could produce a far better number.

Berlin wrote a lyric chock full of the worst clichés,

> My heart just yearns for you!

tortured inversions,

> Please come out and I shall happy be!

and strained poeticisms:

> 'neath the window I'm waiting

Still, there were touches, here and there, of the real language of the streets:

> Please don't be so aggravating

The song was called "Marie from Sunny Italy," and the royalties from the sheet music sales netted Israel Baline thirty-seven cents. But the sheet music brought an unexpected bonus: the name Irving Berlin. The typesetter, so the story goes, mistakenly had listed the lyricist as I. Berlin, but Izzy Baline found the misprint fortuitous: it had *class*. To give it even more class, he made the "I" stand for Irving.

He also moved up to a classier café, Jimmy Kelley's on Union Square, where most vaudeville theaters and Alley publishers still held court. Here Berlin devoted more of his efforts to songwriting, not just lyrics but attempts to create some of his own music as well. He picked out tunes on the café piano after closing and picked up a few compositional tips from the piano player. He never would learn to play on much more than the black keys but soon would acquire a transposing piano with a lever that enabled him to hear how his tunes sounded in any other key. The songs he sold to Union Square publishers were usually ones that conformed to Tin Pan Alley formulas of the day—comical immigrant songs that drew on stereotypical caricatures of Italians, Irish, and Jews, or topical songs that celebrated some current event. Sometimes, Berlin would combine the modes, as in "Dorando," where an Italian barber laments his huge bet on a famed marathon runner who lost in the 1908 Olympics. Similarly, "Sadie Salome Go Home" was inspired by the Committee of Fourteen's ban of the

Metropolitan Opera House's production of *Salome* for its "Dance of the Seven Veils." In Berlin's takeoff, stripper Sadie Cohen performs her own version to the chagrin of her boyfriend Mose. Delivered with a thick Yiddish accent, that song earned Fanny Brice a starring spot in Ziegfeld's early *Follies* and moved Berlin up from singing waiter to staff lyricist for the new Union Square publishing house of Waterson and Snyder.

On a salary of $25 a week, Berlin devoted himself full-time to the craft of songwriting and in particular to a formula that most Tin Pan Alley publishers regarded as passé. Ragtime had been a craze of the late 1890s to which Tin Pan Alley responded with "coon" songs—syncopated (sometimes barely so) melodies and lyrics in a confected black dialect. Most ragtime hits, such as "Hello, Ma Baby" (1899) and "Bill Bailey, Won't You Please Come Home" (1902), were written by whites and proffered racist caricatures of blacks. Although the ragtime "coon" songs were a passing fad, such songs altered the general run of popular songs in several ways. With the emphasis upon rhythmic music, a lyricist could not spin out the lachrymose narratives typical of ballads in the 1890s but had to confect brief lyrical pleas, laments, and ejaculations in vernacular phrases, usually laced with slang. Although it began in racial slur and dialect, the ragtime "coon" song, as Max Morath has argued, gradually had "licensed the use of slang and colloquialism" in all popular song.[3]

Berlin doggedly worked to revive the formulas of ragtime with a string of songs from "That Opera Rag" to "Whistling Rag," and even sought to combine it with the formulaic immigrant song in numbers such as "Yiddle on Your Fiddle Play Some Ragtime." But it was in 1911, when he put lyrics to a ragtime instrumental he had composed the previous year, that Berlin created the biggest hit Tin Pan Alley had yet seen and gave ragtime new life.

It has been pointed out countless times that "Alexander's Ragtime Band" is not really ragtime, since it contains barely a hint of syncopation, but no one has noted how skillfully "ragged" the lyric is. What ragtime did for song lyrics generally during the early years of Tin Pan Alley it did for Berlin as well. It licensed the vernacular as a lyrical idiom and forced the lyricist to construct a lyric out of short, juxtaposed phrases marked by internal rhymes and jagged syntactical breaks:

> Ain't you goin',
> ain't you goin',
> to the leader man,
> ragged meter man?
> Grand stand,
> brass band,
> ain't you comin' along?

The "ragged meter man" here is not only Alexander—a code name, going back to "Alexander, Don't You Love Your Baby No More" (1904), which stamps this as a "coon" song—but Berlin himself, who fits slang contractions and telegraphic exclamations to the uneven, bugle-call snatches of his musical meters. Just as he juxtaposed off-rhymes like *leader* and *meter*, Berlin ragged the normal accent of "natural" for an "unnatural" rhyme with "call":

> They can play a bugle *call*
> like you never heard before
> So natur*al*
> that you want to go to war

Years later, in the 1960s, Berlin would change this last line to the less martial "so natural that you want to hear some more," but he still kept ragging his rhymes with *natu*ral and th*at you*.

Because he wrote both words and music, Berlin could keep repeating, yet subtly varying, a series of short, parallel phrases, both musical and lyrical, to build a sense of urgency and excitement:

> Come on along, come on along,
> let me take you by the hand,
> up to the man, up to the man,

The image, like the language, here evokes a revival camp meeting, but we never do get to meet the maker of the music. At the end of the chorus Berlin deftly ducks away from climax with a long subordinate clause—"if you care to hear the Swanee River played in ragtime"—but that sonorous lyrical line is brassily interrupted by a syncopated stop before "played." The final "Come on and hear" thus comes off as casual invitation rather than fervid plea.

The success of "Alexander's Ragtime Band" moved Berlin another notch up on Tin Pan Alley, for he was made a partner in the firm, now called Waterson, Berlin, and Snyder and located at 112 West 38th Street. Immediately, Berlin began cranking out ragtime songs to fuel the national dance craze sparked by "Alexander's Ragtime Band." The turkey trot, the bunny hug, the lame duck, and other exuberantly erotic dances alarmed such guardians of public morality as the New York Commission on Amusements and Vacation Resources for Working Girls, which also cast a suspicious eye on Berlin's firm for the questionable lyrics of "Everybody's Doing It." The dance craze was soon moderated by Irene and Vernon Castle, who toned down the aggressive sexuality of the new dances and made them respectably stylish, teaching the public how to do so as well from their dance school on Forty-sixth Street.

196

By 1914 the Castles had so legitimized the new dances that producer Charles Dillingham decided to showcase their talents in a spectacular revue at the New Amsterdam Theatre, commissioning Irving Berlin to supply all the songs. Although he had placed songs in other Broadway productions, *Watch Your Step* was his first complete score, and its songs radiated the musical and lyrical sophistication that Alley wares acquired when they emanated from the theater. Ragtime had quickly come to signify modernism, and Berlin caught the cultural struggle between Victorian gentility and the purveyors of liberation, indulgence, and leisure in "Play a Simple Melody." This was the first of his famous "double" songs in which two different melodies and lyrics are counterpointed against one another. The first melody is fitted to a nostalgic call for a song "like my mother sang to me," but that genteel request is juxtaposed against a brassily vernacular demand:

> Won't you play me some rag?
> Just change that classical nag
> to some sweet beautiful drag

Such an intricately woven clash of music and lyric pushed the principle of ragging to a larger structural level.

The extraordinary success of *Watch Your Step* catapulted Berlin from Tin Pan Alley onto Broadway. *Variety* praised Berlin as standing out in the theatrical world "like the Times building does in the Square." Berlin himself observed that the show marked "the first time Tin Pan Alley got into the legitimate theater."[4] It was also the year when Broadway got into Tin Pan Alley. Long dominated by European operetta, where songs were so integral to the dramatic context that they were seldom detached to become independently popular, Broadway had begun to turn toward the newer form of musical comedy, with its modern settings, streamlined plots, and songs that were modeled on Alley formulas. Indeed, some songs were written without any regard to the "book" of a musical and were simply interpolated into one show or another in the hopes of becoming popular. In 1914, for example, a subtly sophisticated song by Jerome Kern and Michael Rourke, "They Didn't Believe Me," was interpolated into *The Girl from Utah* and became the biggest hit Tin Pan Alley had seen since "Alexander's Ragtime Band." The fact that 1914 was also the year ASCAP was formed further entrenched the formulas of Tin Pan Alley as the standard for all popular songs.

Once Berlin reached this two-way street, which figuratively connected Tin Pan Alley with Shubert Alley, he set up another office at 1571 Broadway to handle all of his songs written for Broadway shows, while the Thirty-eighth Street office continued to publish songs written for Tin Pan Alley's traditional plugging network. Ironically, in the year between

"Alexander's Ragtime Band" and "Play a Simple Melody," Berlin had experimented with the kind of sentimental ballad that ragtime had displaced. After the sudden death of his wife in 1912, only five months after their marriage, Berlin poured out his grief in "When I Lost You." The song sold well, yet its lyrics are nearly as poetically strained as "Ah! Sweet Mystery of Life":

> The sunshine had fled,
> the roses were dead,
> Sweetheart, when I lost you

Clearly, Berlin still saw the slang of ragtime as an inappropriate idiom for serious romantic expression; not until the 1920s would he adapt its colloquial idiom for love songs.

How much fresher the language of his comical ragtime love song of 1915, "I Love a Piano," with its clever ragging of words against music, such as crushing "pian" into one syllable for "upon a *pian*-o," then drawing it out properly for "a grand pi-a-no," giving back to "grand" some of its original currency. In this song, too, Berlin, almost as if he had been reading the new "imagist" poetry that was appearing in *Poetry* magazine, develops an extended metaphor that implicitly compares the piano to a woman. The cliché "a fine way to treat a lady" turns into "I know a fine way to treat a Steinway," and the various parts of the instrument are transformed into erogenous zones by the singer's exuberant passion:

> and with the pedal
> I love to meddle

or

> I love to run my fingers o'er the keys,
> the ivories

Here the poetic "o'er" is quickly redeemed— and rhymed—by its slangy gloss, the "iv*ories*." At the climax of the song the very letters that name the beloved object elicit a lingering ejaculation:

> Give me a P-I-A-N-Oh, Oh, Oh

Behind the piano-as-woman metaphor Berlin again counterpoints genteel and modern sensibilities as the "upright" and "high-toned" piano is exuberantly and irreverently fondled as a "baby" grand.

In 1918 such witty imagery enabled Private Irving Berlin to invoke the slang he must have heard in his barracks at Camp Upton, New York. The hit of his all-soldier revue, *Yip, Yip, Yaphank*, was "Oh! How I Hate to Get Up in the Morning," which, along with "Over There," was one of the few patriotic Alley songs to survive World War I. In place of Cohan's thumping jingoism, Berlin substitutes the ordinary soldier's perspective on the drudgery of army life. He develops the song from the helpless lament of the title through other slang formulas like "ya gotta get up" and the vernacular threat:

> Someday I'm going to murder the bugler;
> someday they're going to find him dead

Berlin then uses a bizarre image to suggest, however tangentially, the sort of threat a real soldier would make:

> I'll amputate his reveille
> and step upon it heavily

The Latinate "amputate" softens the soldier's pithier "I'll cut off his . . . ," and the French "reveille" merely hints at the instrument the soldier might threaten to sever in pure, but unprintable, Anglo-Saxon.

Flushed with the success of his wartime show, Berlin returned to civilian life and moved his theatrical publishing company to 1607 Broadway. Decorated in a lavish style, the offices attracted an audience of visitors that seemed, to one, like "a crowd in front of a baseball scoreboard, a mob scene, perhaps in a William A. Brady melodrama."[5] He also turned to the creation of a different kind of popular song. Until now, most of his songs were in the Alley formulas of topical numbers, ragtime, songs, and paeans to Dixie ("When the Midnight Choo-Choo Leaves for Alabam' "), Hawaii ("That Hula-Hula"), or pastoral life ("I Want to Go Back to Michigan—Down on the Farm"). Amid all of this staggering output, however, one finds few love songs; when love is the subject, it is usually handled comically, as in "If That's You're Idea of a Wonderful Time, Take Me Home" or "Keep Away from the Fellow Who Owns an Automobile." Berlin had broken into the Alley just as the ballad was being revived, but it was not until after the war that he devoted himself to fashioning romantic laments, pleas, and effusions to the by-then standard framework of the 32-bar AABA chorus. He also laced those lyrics with idioms, catchphrases, and newly minted slang from what H. L. Mencken in 1919 had dubbed *The American Language*, the "slanguage" which, as William Taylor describes, also became the vehicle for Damon Runyon, Walter Winchell, and other New York newspaper writers (see Chapter 11).

A key song in this transition to colloquial ballads was "A Pretty Girl Is Like a Melody," written for Ziegfeld's *Follies of 1919* and staged on Joseph Urban's unique staircase. The lyric is equally innovative, elaborating a single, extended simile in casually colloquial terms: a pretty girl is like an insistent melody that at first "haunts," then starts a ghostly "marathon" that gives you the "runaround," and finally produces both musical and athletic "strain," as her fleeting image reverses itself and imprisons its pursuer. At the end, you "can't escape" because, paradoxically, "she's in your memory." Berlin's "pretty girl" is not so much flesh and blood but a tantalizing mental image:

> She will leave you
> and then
> come back
> again

By breaking up the lyrical phrase to match the musical pauses, Berlin captures the elusive play of fantasy; little wonder that the song became the theme for Ziegfeld's revues, some of which supplied patrons with balloons for playing "catch" with the coyly elusive chorus girls or lariats to "rope" them.

Berlin established himself more firmly in the theater district when he opened his own theater, the Music Box, on Forty-fifth Street. Like Raymond Hitchcock, George White, and other rivals of Ziegfeld, Berlin and his partner, Sam Harris, built the Music Box to stage sumptuous annual revues, featuring Berlin's songs, lovely girls, and witty skits. In his search for such skits, Berlin was drawn into the orbit of wits who regularly lunched around the famed Round Table at the Algonquin Hotel on West Forty-fourth Street. After listening to Robert Benchley deliver a hilarious monolog at an Algonquinite gathering, Berlin and Harris persuaded him to perform the piece in a Music Box Revue. George S. Kaufman also contributed skits for Music Box revues, and later, in 1925, collaborated with Berlin on *The Cocoanuts*, a vehicle for the Marx Brothers, who were also part of the charmed (or some would say vicious) circle of Round Tablers. At times Berlin found the cynical sophistication of the group could sting—as when Kaufman dismissed Berlin's sentimental "Always" with the acerbic suggestion that the first line be changed to, "I'll be loving you—Thursday." But Alexander Woollcott, the self-proclaimed leader of the group, was so taken with Berlin that he wrote a glowing biography of the songwriter in 1925, when his subject was still only 36 years old.

In turn, Berlin's songs reflected the casual urbanity of his new circle of friends. In 1924 he composed the wistfully wry lament, "What'll I Do?" at a champagne birthday party thrown by Dorothy Parker at Neysa McMein's studio salon on Fifty-seventh Street, where the Algonquinites frequently gathered in the evenings. Yet even before he fell in with this group, Berlin was aware that urbane elegance was to be stylish in the 1920s; the song he composed for the opening of his first Music Box Revue, "Say It With Music," reflects, musically and lyrically, the classical lines of

the theater's elegant new facade. Giving yet another twist to the meta-
phoric equation between romance and music, Berlin took an advertising
formula and elaborated it with nonchalant turns of American talk:

> Somehow they'd rather be kissed
> to the strains of Chopin or Liszt

Even though he had abandoned ragtime songs, Berlin found he could still
adapt the technique of ragging words against music. Using parallel whole
notes to stretch out the first syllables of "beautiful" and "music," for
example, gave him a subtle but sonorous rhyme. The triple "el" rhyme that
runs through "melody mellow played on the cello" sets up a quiet fourth
rhyme when "Helps" is drawn out by another whole note.

Such distortions were the lyrical equivalents of the "syncopation"
which Berlin theorized freely about in the 1920s. Syncopation, he af-
firmed, was the characteristic style of modern American music; its "broken
harmonies" and "ragged time" set a "new rhythm," a "new method of
movement" that brought modern music in tune with the age of the
"automobile."[6] Much of the lyrical artfulness of Berlin's "sob-ballads," as
he called them, stems from his subtle fragmentation and juxtaposition of
words *against* music.

The newspapers, however, interpreted such hits as "Always" (1924)
and "Remember" (1925) in the light of Berlin's courtship of socialite Ellin
Mackay. It was a fairy-tale romance that was covered by all the New York
papers, most melodramatically by Hearst's *New York Mirror*, and even
inspired such Tin Pan Alley numbers as "When a Kid Who Came from the
East Side (Found a Sweet Society Rose)." Berlin insisted, however, that
the only song he ever wrote out of personal experience was "When I Lost
You"; the "sob ballads" were merely his new line of wares for a public that
now, in the 1920s, "would rather buy tears than smiles."

While he continued to write novelty and topical songs for revues in the
1920s, his popular hits—those written strictly for sheet music sales—were
almost all romantic laments. In the best of these ballads there is an easy
"syncopation" of vernacular phrases. One of the earliest of them, "All By
Myself" (1921), takes the simple catch phrase of the title and lifts it out of its
ordinary context as a child's boast ("I did it all by myself") into a literal
scene, as barren and simplified as the language that describes it:

> I sit alone
> with a ta-
> ble and a chair
> so un-
> happy there
> play-
> ing solitaire

By breaking up the verbal phrases in this way, Berlin's "ragging" produces fragments that rhyme in unusual ways, the first syllables of "*ta*ble" and "pl*ay*ing," then an off-rhyme between the second syllable of "al*one* and "*so* *un*happy."

Berlin was reworking the traditional figure of the forlorn lover, placing him in a room as empty as a prison cell, and, three years later, with "All Alone," he injected some humor into the uncluttered scene:

> waiting
> for a ring,
> a ting,
> a ling

The repetitive rhymes capture the obsessive sensibility of such a prisoner of love, and Berlin's insistent folding of sound fragment around sound fragment tightens the psychological chains. Even the catch phrase title, "*all al*one," is a readymade instance of faceted, repetitive sound fragments. Still another raggedly repetitive pattern closes the song, as Berlin at first matches three musically parallel phrases with two lyrically parallel ones:

> wond'ring where you are,
> and how you are,

But then, as Gerald Mast observes, the third lyrical phrase is a "syntactic surprise,"[7] which leaves the thought dangling,

> and if you are

only to be completed by the standard return to the title: "all alone, too."

Significantly, "All Alone" was first heard not on the stage but over the radio, sung by Frances Alda in a broadcast honoring Irving Berlin. Not only was it introduced over a new medium for plugging, it was one of Berlin's first songs whose million-record sales equaled its sheet music sales. Like many publishers, Berlin was suspicious of these new developments, but as long as the recording companies relied upon Alley publishers for their songs and as long as ASCAP collected hefty fees from radio stations that played Tin Pan Alley music, radio and recordings were not a threat.

Berlin even saw that radio and records invited a subtle modulation of the ballad into a more intimate and solitary song such as "All By Myself" and "All Alone." Such ballads also responded to the trend of American mass culture in the 1920s, as analyzed by Lewis Erenberg, toward a preoccupation with private experience.[8] Traditional balladeers sang stories to audiences, and the early Alley songs were similarly geared for either the stage audience or for the group sing around a parlor piano piled high with sheet music. Berlin's ballads of the twenties, however, imply a solitary listener, at the phonograph or radio, and his technique of folding the tiniest rhyming fragments over and over one another creates a lyrical "space"—self-enclosed, repetitive, faceted—that is designed for the self-absorbed, plaintive singer who inhabits it. The solitary consumer of "sob ballads," in turn, inhabits the same space, the space that T. S. Eliot described so bleakly in *The Waste Land*:

> When lovely woman stoops to folly and
> Paces about her room again, alone,
> She smooths her hair with automatic hand,
> And puts a record on the gramophone.

The bare room, right down to the gramophone, is the same one sketched in Berlin's ballads; the song Eliot's typist listens to could easily be "All By Myself."

Probably no song better illustrates the adaptability of the ballad formula better than Berlin's "Blue Skies." Originally written as a free-standing popular number, it was interpolated into Rodgers and Hart's 1927 musical, *Betsy*, and, that same year, was sung by Al Jolson in *The Jazz Singer*. With the development of sound films, Tin Pan Alley forged a deeper alliance with Hollywood studios: not only did Tin Pan Alley feed the new appetite with "theme" songs for virtually every new movie, it made its songs the staple of the evolving film musical. Hollywood producers were adamant about not having characters in film suddenly burst into—and out of—song, so the rule was that songs in film had to be done as "performances" by actors playing the parts of nightclub singers, neighborhood kids "putting on a show," or, most commonly, Broadway "babies" seeing that the show must go on. Hence the plethora of "back-stage" musical films, such as *Broadway Melody* and *Forty-second Street*, reflecting "hot-shot, ace-high, lowdown, dirty, crazy New York" and its "gritty vernacular ambience"[9] in songs that sounded—and were meant to sound—as if they had come hot off Tin Pan Alley's assembly line.

With the Depression, big studios, such as Warner Brothers, bought out T. B. Harms and other old-line publishing firms, and even transported songwriters to the West Coast. But the adage that Hollywood "killed" Tin Pan Alley is an overstatement. The same formulas were used for song production on both coasts, and some publishers opened branch offices in Hollywood, while major Hollywood studios had offices in Times Square. New publishers also moved into Tin Pan Alley: Chappell, for example, set up shop in the RKO Building in 1934 and specialized in songs from Broadway shows (eventually buying back the Harms catalog from Warner Brothers). Berlin, always astride every new development, opened yet another office—in Hollywood.

He also wrote some of his finest songs for early film musicals such as *Puttin' on the Ritz*. The title song carries the principle of lyrical ragging to the furthest possible extreme, so distorting verbal accents against musical ones that the lyric, when sung, comes out as Gertrude Steinese or a jazzy idiom that might be called Berlintz:

> *Come* let's *mix*
> where *Rock-e-fell-*
> ers *walk* with *sticks*
> or *um*-ber-*el-*
> as *in* their *mitts*,
> *put*-tin on the *ritz*!

Here the musical accents break down sentence, phrase, and word into tiny cubistic fragments fitted "mosaically" to musical shards. The sharp rhymes only highlight the discordant levels of diction—"ritz" and "Rock-efellers" clashing with "mitts" and "puttin," and the elegant walking stick reduced to the prosaic "walk with sticks," while the ordinary umbrella is elevated by enunciated elongation.

Such a lyric realizes the possibilities of "ragging" that opened at the turn of the century with such "coon songs" as "Under the Bamboo Tree," and Berlin must have had those origins in mind for, in one of the sets of lyrics he provided for "Puttin' on the Ritz," he celebrated not the "well-to-do" on "Park Avenue" but blacks parading on "Lenox Avenue" where "Harlem sits":

> *spang*led *gowns*
> up*on* a *bevy*
> *of* high *browns*
> up*on* the *levee—*
> *all* mis-*fits*,
> *put*tin on the *ritz*!

What the lyric describes—Harlem blacks in elegant finery—it also enacts in its own linguistic "mix" of slang and refined diction and allusion, its clever "misfits" of rhythmic and verbal accents.

It is ironic that "Puttin' on the Ritz," one of Berlin's best lyrics, was written during a period when he began to fear his creative powers were waning. The very titles of his recent—and perhaps, he thought, last—hits, "The Song Is Ended" and "Where Is the Song of Songs for Me?" seemed to express the fear that he could write no more. Although Berlin's dejection was largely personal, it is significant that it should come at another turning point in the history of popular music. The simple, repetitive musical style of the 1920s was giving way to more sophisticated adaptations of jazz and blues styles by composers like Gershwin and Arlen. The ante was upped for lyrics too. In the hands of Lorenz Hart and Ira Gershwin, songs began to radiate sophisticated sentiments and witty rhymes. It is significant that when Berlin found himself unable to meet his commitment to write songs for the show *Fifty Million Frenchmen* in 1929, the task went to a relative newcomer, Cole Porter, whose lyrics, even more than Hart's or Gershwin's, prefigured the insouciance, the urbanity, the antiromantic stance of the height of the golden age.

A number of lyricists who flourished during the 1920s saw their seemingly endless supply of hit songs dry up after 1928, and for a time, it seemed, Irving Berlin would fade away as well. He had already begun to sound like an elder statesman, railing against "swing" music and "sophisticated" lyrics, yet in 1933 he made a spectacular comeback on Broadway with *As Thousands Cheer*, the longest running show of the year. Like the Gershwins' Pulitzer-prize-winning *Of Thee I Sing* (which played at Berlin's own Music Box Theatre), Berlin's show was sophisticated and satirical, but where the Gershwins had carefully integrated their songs into a well-wrought "book" show, Berlin relied upon the traditional looseness of the revue. Yet he dressed that old form up by basing its format on the newspaper—an early instance of the self-reflexive relations between theater and newspapers analyzed by William Taylor (see Chapter 11). Each segment of the revue took up a different section of a newspaper. The "weather report," for example, featured Ethel Waters doing a saucy "Heat Wave," with such uncharacteristically naughty lines as "she started the heat wave by letting her seat wave" that give a Porterish overtone to the "heat" of the title. In the "news" section Berlin gave Waters "Supper Time," a Southern black woman's lament for her lynched husband, a song that showed that Berlin, too, like Gershwin and Arlen, could adapt the idiom of the blues into popular song. The big hit of the show, however, was the "fashion report" song, a throwback to the good old days. The music for "Easter Parade" had been written in 1917 for a song called "Smile and Show Your Dimple," but it was a flop then, and Berlin had judiciously filed it away. In the 1930s, he updated it with a new lyric, one that evokes a bygone era with "the quaint image of the rotogravure," which, as Timothy Scheurer notes, gives the song "a feeling of being bathed in sepia tones."[10]

Berlin stayed on Broadway only long enough to establish himself as definitely *back*; for most of the decade, he wrote in Hollywood, which by then was rivaling both Broadway and the radio as an outlet for popular song. While Broadway songs were becoming increasingly sophisticated, the movies still wanted simpler fare and offered him the perfect opportunity to ply his artful artlessness. Once again Berlin displayed his uncanny foresight by working with RKO, a small studio that had just pulled itself out of bankruptcy and was staking its fortunes on Fred Astaire, teaming him with Ginger Rogers in Cole Porter's *The Gay Divorcee*. For the next Astaire-Rogers film, RKO commissioned Berlin to write the songs. Writing for Astaire required subtle adjustments in the standard musical and lyrical formulas: melodies had to be kept within Astaire's limited vocal range; rhythmically, the music had to showcase his extraordinary dancing; and lyrically, the song had to express his elegantly casual style in language.

Berlin responded with numbers such as "Cheek to Cheek," which stretched the thirty-bar chorus to seventy-two measures with subtle shifts from major to minor, with a chatty lyric that opened with an offhanded "Heaven—I'm in heaven." The title song, "Top Hat, White Tie, and Tails," is another extreme instance of musical accents ragging verbal ones, though the distortions are not so intricate as they are in "Puttin' on the Ritz." They mostly occur in the verse, where the misplaced accents give a lilt to the words that reflects the buoyancy of the singer:

> *I* just *got* an *invita-*
> tion *through* the *mails*

then the staggered, fragmented lines of the formal invitation itself:

> your *presence*
> re*ques*ted
> this *eve*ning
> it's *for*mal

The chorus continues to fragment words against music but lingers over initial syllables of participles to bring out the *i*-rhymes: "T*y*-in' up my wh*i*te t*ie*."

In the release, yet another rhythm rags the long formal phrase into short units,

> I'm steppin' *out*
> my *dear*
> to breathe an *at-*
> mos*phere*

which then are followed by an abrupt shift to street slang:

> that simply *reeks* with *class*

Berlin clashes the same high and low diction in the next pair of phrases, the elegant "I trust that you'll" jammed against the slangy "excuse my dust when I step on the gas." As in "Puttin' on the Ritz," the rhythmic distortion of formal diction is reflected in the subject of the song: at the

206

end, the singer gleefully looks forward to "Puttin' down my top hat" and "Mussin' up my white tie." The final line, "Dancin' in my tails," is a good description of how Berlin has made the formal language dance against the music and the jostling intrusions of street slang.

In a different but still thoroughly Astaire vein was "Change Partners," which lent itself perfectly to his seductive nonchalance. "*Must* you dance—*every* dance—with the same—fortunate man," Astaire asks in elegant exasperation, exasperation underscored by buried rhymes in d*a*nce and m*a*n. Berlin also reaches back to his 1920s ballads for similar rhymes and imagery in the release, but here they serve Astaire's coy sophistication:

> Ask him to sit this one out
> and while you're alone,
> I'll *tell* the waiter *tell* him
> he's wanted on the *tel*ephone

Equally urbane is Astaire's understated final plea—"change partners and then—you may never want to change partners again."

Berlin continued to write film songs and hits throughout the 1930s and found Hollywood a haven. In 1940, however, he returned to Broadway with *Louisiana Purchase*, which presaged, in its regional emphasis, *Oklahoma!* Returning to the theater must have made Berlin feel a little like Rip Van Winkle: just as Rip had slept through the American Revolution, Berlin had waited out the golden age of Manhattan urbanity in the California sunshine. Where Rip returned to find everything utterly changed, however, Berlin found the new style in popular songs much as it had been twenty years earlier. Topical songs had returned with the war, and Berlin's first popular songs were as made to order as they had been in World War I: "A Little Old Church in England" and "Any Bonds Today?" Back again were songs about the South and places like Vermont and Capistrano, Kalamazoo and Kansas City. Once more there were lyrics about trains and airplanes, cowboys and soldiers; even birds were back— skylarks, bluebirds, swallows—birds that hadn't been seen in the Alley for over a decade.

Back, too, were simplicity and sincerity: a sentimental song of 1931, "As Time Goes By," was revived from oblivion and became a tear-jerking hit in *Casablanca*. Going, if not gone, were insouciance, cynicism, and sophistication, along with some of their purveyors, such as Lorenz Hart, dead in 1943—the man who sniffed in congealing love the "faint aroma of performing seals" replaced by a cock-eyed optimist who even loved the whiskers on kittens. Berlin himself pronounced the era's epitaph, noting that nothing is "so corny as last year's sophistication," adding, "I mean corny lyrics . . . there's no such thing as a corny tune."[11] A decade that had begun with Ira Gershwin's flippant post-Crash patriotism in "Of Thee

I Sing—Baby" (1931) closed with Berlin's solemn look at impending war in "God Bless America" (1938). Berlin had his big Broadway success in 1942 when he reincarnated *Yip Yip Yaphank* as *This Is the Army*, replete with new-old songs, and, symbolizing the unchanging changes, Berlin appeared in his World War I uniform (which still fit) to sing "Oh! How I Hate to Get Up in the Morning."

In other ways, however, the popular music industry was changing profoundly. By 1940 records had finally displaced sheet music as the major product of the industry, and radio corporations like RCA and Columbia began buying up recording companies. Still, they relied upon Tin Pan Alley for their songs, and in 1942 Berlin used that reliance to create the biggest selling record of all time in "White Christmas," which Bing Crosby crooned in *Holiday Inn*. Even as its sales mounted, however, developments had already taken place that would eventually undo Tin Pan Alley's monopoly on "American music." In 1940 ASCAP had demanded that radio stations pay twice as much in royalties for the right to play its music. The stations refused and formed their own organization, Broadcast Music Incorporated (BMI) in Chicago and sought out non-ASCAP songwriters and their products.

> Those who benefitted immediately were the hillbillies, who by now had their own well-established network of local country radio shows, and the black musicians, who for years had been recorded for little or no financial reward. The ASCAP monopoly was broken and the absolute domination of Tin Pan Alley came to an end.[12]

But radio stations and ASCAP came to an agreement in 1941 and Tin Pan Alley's songs returned to the air. Yet, by the middle of the next decade the fusion of black and country music would create radically new formulas which not even Irving Berlin would be able to adapt.

In 1943, however, Broadway, too, was changing, largely as a result of the enormous success of Rodgers and Hammerstein's *Oklahoma!* and the equally successful sales of its original cast recording—the first such recording ever produced. Songs for Broadway musicals assumed a character that they have maintained ever since. No more the "interpolated" song of twenties and thirties musicals, which had so little relevance to the plot or to the characters of the libretto that it could be freely shunted from one show to another. Theater songs after *Oklahoma!* had to be "integrated" into character and dramatic context, and sometimes even had to advance the plot.

That Irving Berlin, nearly sixty, was able to write any theater songs in the new style is impressive; that he was able to write one of the greatest "integrated" musicals is remarkable; that he was able to write it in the space of a few weeks is astounding. *Annie Get Your Gun* was produced by Rodgers and Hammerstein in 1946. They had commissioned Dorothy and Herbert

208

Fields to write the book and Jerome Kern to do the music. When Kern died suddenly, they turned to Berlin. According to Martin Gottfried, Berlin

> didn't quite believe the producers' excuse that they were "too busy with another project" to write this one themselves. Rodgers, he thought, can write anything, so Berlin concluded that Hammerstein considered *Annie Get Your Gun* too superficial an entertainment for the team. Berlin was also uncertain that he could write lyrics for the rural characters in *Annie Get Your Gun*. Hammerstein assured him, "All you have to do is drop the 'g's. Instead of 'thinking' write 'thinkin'."[13]

Although Berlin felt uncomfortable writing what he termed a "hillbilly" musical, he soon saw the confluence between the "wild west" and the New York theater world (see Chapter 11) and realized that it was "a musical about show business."[14] In the next few hectic weeks he wrote a string of superb songs—"Anything You Can Do," "You Can't Get a Man With a Gun," "I Got the Sun in the Morning," "I Got Lost in His Arms." The most famous song from *Annie Get Your Gun*, "There's No Business Like Show Business," was nearly dropped from the show. When Berlin played it for Rodgers and Hammerstein, the two men just sat there, too awed to speak. Mistaking their silence for disapproval, Berlin simply tossed the song aside and promised to come up with something better.

Berlin's songs from *Annie Get Your Gun* looked both backwards and forwards in American musical theater history. They nearly all became independently popular (*Annie Get Your Gun*, affirms Gerald Mast, "contained more individual hit songs than any musical ever, before or since"[15]), a throwback to the days when a musical had a book that merely served as a clothesline for Tin Pan Alley songs. But those songs were also "integrated" in the style of the new musical play inaugurated by *Oklahoma!*: they expressed dramatic situations, rendered conflict, and delineated character.

In writing such integrated lyrics Berlin displays a whole new range of writing techniques with apparent effortlessness. He can open a song quietly, with a deadpan irony whose colloquial ease belies its naughty joke: "Oh, my mother was frightened by a shotgun, they say; that's why I'm such a wonderful shot." In the space of a few bars he can build short phrases to an outraged climax:

> If I went to battle
> with someone's herd of cattle,
> you'd have steak when the job was done,
> but if I shot the herder,
> they'd holler bloody murder,
> and you can't shoot a male
> in the tail,
> like a quail,

then suddenly twist it off with the helpless rage of "Oh, you can't get a man with a gun."

The same Annie who sings that aggressive lament still guards her feelings in a love song with "They say," the same phrase she used to recollect her mother's shotgun wedding, turned now to a protective hedge:

> They say that falling in love is wonderful,
> it's wonderful (so they say)

Here, too, Berlin recasts the "wonderful" from the braggadocio of "I'm such a wonderful shot" to underscore hesitant innocence.

Berlin went on to write other musicals in the fifties, such as *Call Me Madam*, and to produce hits in record time. He loved to write for the brassily elegant Ethel Merman ("she makes sure you can hear my lyrics in the back row of the balcony"), whose voice at once embodied the barbaric yawp of the West and the hip, hooray, and ballyhoo of Broadway. When Merman suggested the second act needed a little more punch, Berlin stayed up all night and turned out another of his complex double-songs, the kind he had written for the Castles in his first Broadway score back in 1914. "You're Just in Love" pits the sweet romantic strain of "I hear singing and there's no one there" against Merman's bristling street talk:

> you don't need analyzing,
> it is not so surprising . . .
> there is nothing you can take
> to relieve that pleasant ache;
> you're not sick—you're just in love!

and spiced with elegantly erotic touches:

> Put your head on my shoulder,
> you need someone who's older,
> a rub-down with a velvet glove

Using the musical emphasis to reverse the verbal accent here (not "*rub*-down" but "rub*down*"), Irving Berlin was still the ragged meter man of Tin Pan Alley.

Berlin eased into retirement as Tin Pan Alley's monopoly was crumbling under the onslaught of a new kind of music. Small, independent recording companies sprang up across the country and the Tin Pan Alley publishers, from the bastion in the Brill Building, tried to assimilate the new musical formulas as well as palm off their traditional ones to the new performers. Unable or unwilling to adapt yet one more time, Berlin doggedly continued to write songs for new shows, new songs for revivals of old shows, and then, finally, songs for himself alone. His death in 1989, at the age of 101, marked a century since enterprising sheet music publishers set up shop on West Twenty-eighth Street. The "American music" produced by Tin Pan Alley for most of that century was created by many talented composers and lyricists, but Irving Berlin proved, time and again, that anything they could do he could do better.

11

BROADWAY: THE PLACE THAT WORDS BUILT

William R. Taylor

Lobster Alley is the theatrical section of New York as it has grown under the patronage and guidance of the weekly newspaper *Variety*, and its inspired editor, Sime Silverman.[1]

Hiram Motherwell, *The Bookman*, 1930

Every phase of our complex civilization, and every class have contributed something to what is becoming a national slanguage. The bootleggers with their "hooch," "drums," "tail," "frontiers," "fixers"; the underworld with its jargon, almost unintelligible to an outsider; the outdoor show game with its "rag front," "pitch," "ballyhoo," "grift," "rolldowns," and "shills" and hundreds of other words; horse racing with its "front runners," "morning glories," "stoomers," "workouts," "pencil men," "wind suckers," "chumps." . . . It is not beyond the range of possibility that an entire new language will evolve and that some pioneer will write an entire book in it without recourse to what we now know as pure English. And why not?[2]

Jack Conway, *Variety*, 1926

I took one little section of New York and made half a million dollars writing about it.[3]

Damon Runyon, 1941

L ATE IN 1933 W. J. Funk, the lexicographer, circulated a list containing the names of the most prolific makers of American slang. The list was sent to a number of leading newspapers for comment. Most of the ten names, strikingly, were identifiable figures on the Broadway scene. The list included Sime Silverman, editor of *Variety;* cartoonists Thomas Aloysius (Tad) Dorgan and Reuben (Rube) Goldberg; Eugene Edward

(Gene) Buck, songwriter and principal librettist for Ziegfeld; Damon Runyon, by then famous as a writer of Broadway stories as well as a sportswriter and humorist; Walter Winchell, gossip columnist on McFadden's *Graphic* (and later the Hearst *Mirror*); Indiana humorist George Ade; sports writer, humorist and playwright Ring Lardner; Gelett (Frank) Burgess, coiner of "bromide," "the goops," and "blurb"; and H. L. Mencken of the *Baltimore Sun* and the *Smart Set*, published just east of Times Square.[4]

A copy sent to Mencken reached him as he was preparing a fourth and enlarged edition of *The American Language*. This list, with Mencken's commentary, was included in the reorganized chapter on American slang. Mencken went on to document the coinages and inventions of the figures on the list and then added additional figures: Jack Conway of *Variety*; playwright James Gleason, whose 1925 *Is Zat So?* had been a comic sensation; Milton Gross, who had introduced readers to the tenement-dwelling Feitlebaums and his "Yidgin English" in his 1926 *Nize Baby*; playwright Wilson Mizner; Johnny Stanley; and songwriter ("Melancholy Baby") Johnny Lyman.[5]

How Funk and Mencken arrived at their particular choices is not known, but the provenance of the figures they chose was scarcely surprising: Winchell had had an almost identical list six years before. Funk and Wagnalls was a Brooklyn house, and Funk, the son of the founder and originator of the dictionary, was something of a sport and probably knew the Broadway world firsthand. Mencken was an active if part-time New Yorker. When his work on the *Smart Set* brought him to the city, he stayed at the Algonquin on Fourty-fourth Street near the magazine's offices.

By the early thirties, word that the Times Square area was a productive site for the coinage of language had traveled far. Eric Partridge, a young New Zealander lecturing at Manchester and London universities, was caught up in the vogue for Runyonese that swept England after the publication of the Broadway stories. He turned his attention from the study of Shakespearean English to the contemporary development of slang. The first edition of his *Dictionary of Slang and Unconventional English* was published only a few years later in 1937. After several periods of American study he published his *Dictionary of the Underworld, British and American* in 1940. This work, with its lengthy verbatim transcriptions from American prisons, stands as a monument to the then-current belief that there was a special kind of vitality and creativity in the speech of criminals and their sporting associates in the underworld.[6]

World fame had come abruptly to an area that a decade earlier was still something of a novelty, even to sophisticated New Yorkers. In November 1927 Walter Winchell had published a revealing article in Condé Nast's *Vanity Fair*, which prided itself on scooping entertainment news in the city and tracking recreational fashions. The title of Winchell's article, "A

Primer of Broadway Slang: An Initiate Reveals Some of the Mysteries of the Much Quoted Theatrical Idiom," tells part of the story. In the article, Winchell proclaimed Broadway "the slang capital of the world," adding that "it is difficult to imagine any other spot on the globe where the citizenry take so readily to slang." He left no doubt, furthermore, that he was inducting his readers into a linguistically coded world. "Most of the argot Broadway invents," he concluded, "is relished and rolled on the lips of 'Main Drag' tongues, but little of it is comprehensive [sic] west of the Hudson and north of Harlem."[7]

It is worth noting that the slang that Winchell cited as localisms in 1927 was in common usage a decade later and is commonplace today, some of it scarcely detectable as slang, so rapidly and so expansively did the circle of usage and acceptance spread. He included such words as click, hit, fan, flop, wow 'em, up-stage, bimbo, baloney, push-over, cinch, pay off, gate, turkey, the last word, phoney, racket, bump off, plug, take for a ride, squawk, squeal, a flame, a rat, a heel, burned up, all wet, gyp, crash the gate, wash-out, belly laugh, laugh off, and ball and chain (wife). Winchell also included enough locutions, such as Tad Dorgan's "Yes, we have no bananas" and Texas Guinan's "Hello, sucker" and "A big butter and egg man," to suggest that he was referring to a manner of speaking and not simply some fresh new words.[8]

In this and similar compilations that appeared over the next decade, what was referred to as Broadway slang included a great deal more than Winchell's "theatrical idiom." *All* the occupational groups of the area contributed. These contributions included many types of lingo: what was once 'trade' cant, a kind of intentional Babel; fan talk; and journalistic coinages like those of Winchell, designed to upstage fellow journalists, as in his description of Broadway as "the hardened artery," and of divorces as "Reno-vations." For Winchell the key to all this inventiveness was provided by the volatile spirit of Sime Silverman's *Variety*, which he joined others in calling "the Bible of the theatrical profession."[9]

A more satisfactory explanation for the composite character of the language in these lists, as well as for some of its remarkable vitality, probably lies in the human chemistry of Times Square. By the mid-thirties the area in the vicinity of Times Square could be divided into roughly three overlapping sectors. In ascending order moving north from Forty-second Street were the newspaper, theater, and sporting/nightlife zones. The southernmost sector, extending from Forty-first to Forty-fifth streets and radiating out from the *Times* building at the south end of the square, contained a significant new concentration of newspaper and magazine offices. This concentration represented a significant relocation of newspaper and journalistic publishing into the midtown area. As late as 1920, for example, key publications, like Hearst's *American*, which printed Runyon, Baer, and Fowler, were located downtown on South Street, and McFadden's *Graphic*, which first carried Winchell's column and Dorgan's cartoons, was located near Park Row not far from Pulitzer's *World*. By contrast, Hearst's *Mirror*, which picked up Winchell and Runyon along with other Broadway "scribes" such as Lardner, was located, starting in 1924, far east on Forty-fifth Street, and the *Daily News*, beginning in 1929, on Forty-second Street, three blocks to the south.

In the immediate vicinity of the *Times* and the *Times* Annex around the corner on Forty-third Street was the *Herald Tribune* on Forty-first Street west of Seventh Avenue. Symbolic of the sector as a kind of beacon of journalistic metropolitanism was the out-of-town newsstand at the northern tip of the *Times* building. The principal magazines specializing in urban sophistication, *Vanity Fair*, the *Smart Set*, and *The New Yorker* were clustered by the mid-twenties on Forty-third and Forty-fourth streets east of Sixth Avenue, along with the hostelries and hangouts that "the magazine crowd" preferred, such as the Algonquin and Royalton hotels. Farthest north were the offices of *Variety*, just west of Broadway on Forty-sixth Street, appropriately situated within the sector that contained the largest concentration of theaters and paratheatrical institutions.

This sector probably lay between Broadway and Eighth Avenue and Forty-fourth and Forty-seventh streets, the area radiating out from Shubert Alley. Theatrical life in the more general sense, including major theaters along Broadway north of Forty-seventh Street, however, was dispersed throughout a much wider area stretching from the Metropolitan Opera at Broadway and Thirty-ninth into the Fifties.

This theater zone also contained an astonishing array of support institutions and facilities. The locus of legitimate theater shifted northward after 1920 as theatrical productions along Forty-second Street dwindled. What gave the mid-Forties further centrality was the presence there of key institutions such as *Variety*. On Seventh Avenue near its junction with Broadway below Forty-seventh Street was the monumental Palace and next door the American Federation of Actors, whose membership consisted mostly of variety entertainers. Central to the theater world were the Astor Hotel, on Broadway just east of Shubert Alley, and the Lambs Club on Forty-fourth Street. The Lambs Club served the vaudeville and musical theater crowds as a social organization in much the same way as the Friars Club four blocks north on Forty-eighth Street catered to theatrical promoters and publicity men.

Scattered over these blocks were hangouts that especially catered to different parts of the theatrical world. Sardi's on Forty-fourth Street west of Shubert Alley, the Blue Ribbon, a German rathskeller on Forty-fourth Street east of Broadway, Ye Eat Shoppe on Eighth Avenue between Forty-fifth and Forty-sixth streets, were favorite hangouts for groups within the entertainment community. Around the corner from the Palace on West Forty-seventh Street, once known as "Dream Street," the sidewalk in front of the offices of *Billboard* was a meeting place for carnival managers and owners. Actors' Equity was just down the street on the east side of Sixth Avenue.

By the twenties, Tin Pan Alley, like the newspaper and theater worlds, had moved north and was dispersed over the area above Forty-fifth Street east and west of Broadway, but its focus and social center after 1931 was probably the Brill Building to the north, on the southwest corner of Broadway and Forty-ninth Street—a building that had a warren of small gyms and the offices of fight promoters and commission agents, in addition to demonstration rooms for vocalists, songwriters, pluggers, and other personnel of this unlikely combination.[10]

The Brill Building was located in a sector that had become dominated by nightlife, developing into an important meeting ground for the sporting crowd and the underworld. The ground floor of the Brill Building housed the Turf, an important musical hangout, and Jack Dempsey's Cafe, an important sporting hangout. One of Irving Berlin's offices was at 1607 Broadway, a block to the south. Dave's Blue Room on Seventh Avenue north of Fifty-first Street was a key place where the music crowd and the sporting world mixed.

It is easy to see why this northernmost sector of the area became prime Runyon country. Its flagship institution, completed in 1925, was the second Madison Square Garden on Eighth Avenue between Forty-ninth and Fiftieth streets. The Garden drew huge crowds to its sporting events, prizefights, rodeos, circuses, and other spectacles. It also drew its camp followers of ticket scalpers, gamblers, bookies, racing buffs, and minor hoods and knockabouts. It was, because of the rodeos, the locus where the cowboy entered the Broadway scene.

The sidewalk in front was one of the locations of "Jacobs' Beach," named after fight promoter and impresario Mike Jacobs. Jacobs' Beach was the hangout for the sporting and racing crowds and their hangers-on. For many years it was located between Forty-ninth and Fiftieth streets on Broadway, a block to the east in front of Lindy's restaurant. Lindy's, named for its owner and manager Leo Lindemann, was Runyon's "Mindy's," and this location was a popular late night (and early morning) social center.

This northern sector was preeminently the center of nightlife. Most of the famous cabarets and speakeasies were concentrated here, a majority along its upper fringe. Some of the most famous were located in the low Fifties to the east beyond Fifth Avenue, but the immediate area was well represented. The Hollywood Club on Broadway above Forty-eighth Street, built by the Granlund Syndicate in 1928, was a huge cabaret, which was designed to make up in volume what it lost by not selling liquor. For a decade the Hollywood featured big bands, famous acts, and the Ziegfeld girls who moonlighted in its revues. The Silver Slipper, around the corner west on Forty-eighth Street, was probably Broadway's best known night spot and catered to a mixed crowd from the stage, high society, and the underworld ("gangland"). Earl Carroll's Vanities— "Through These Doors Pass the Most Beautiful Girls in the World"—was located two blocks north on the southeast corner of Fiftieth Street.

The lower Fifties were known as speakeasy streets. The various establishments of the colorful Texas Guinan were in this vicinity (along with Runyon's fictional 300 Club, operated by his character Missouri Martin). One of the most famous, Club Napoleon, was located in a townhouse, once the Woolworth mansion, at 33 West 56th Street. Leon and Eddie's was on Fifty-second Street between Sixth and Seventh avenues. Jack Kriendler and Charlie Berns ran "The Puncheon Grotto" at 42 West 49th Steet until after the Crash. They moved to 21 West 52nd Street on New Year's Day in 1930, and it became known as the 21 Club. El Morocco and Sherman Billingsley's Stork Club, where Winchell occupied table #50 for many years, were further east.

Other haunts, residential and recreational, were crucial to establishing the character of the area. The Garden Cabaret at Fiftieth Street and Eighth Avenue, Roth's Grill on Seventh Avenue above Forty-eighth Street, and Jack Dempsey's two restaurants, on Broadway and on Eighth Avenue, were important hangouts for the sporting crowd. Jack Doyle's billiard parlor at Forty-second Street and Broadway was the headquarters for Runyon's H.B.E. (hardboiled egg) Club and a hangout for minor hoods and the press, which Runyon, among others, frequented in the twenties. For reporters on the crime beat, the 18th Precinct Station far west on Forty-seventh Street and the "Fly-beat" across the street were important places. The Fly-beat ("Ask for Hickie") was a 24-hour office maintained for the press. After Runyon had finished with the scene, one could have said, "Through these doors pass the most famous hoods in the world."

Billy La Hiff's Tavern on Forty-eighth Street west of Seventh Avenue was for a time a key show business hangout popular with the press. The two floors above the restaurant functioned as a kind of Broadway dormitory for married men like Runyon and Winchell who seldom went home. Winchell lived there after his divorce and Runyon stayed there "more than somewhat," to steal a favorite phrase. At one point, Runyon, Sherman Billingsley, Jack Dempsey, and Bugs Baer all occupied the rooms simultaneously. For a long time in the twenties, Runyon lived in the Forrest Hotel on Forty-ninth Street between Broadway and Eighth Avenue, next door to the Forrest Theatre and halfway between the Garden and the Brill Building, astride the experiential worlds of his fiction.[11]

In retrospect, it is difficult to determine what it was that fused all these elements into the Broadway subject and created such enormous receptivity for almost any version of it. Proximity and adjacency do not explain it. Lower Manhattan with its rabbit warren of occupational and ethnic worlds from Wall Street, Chinatown, and the Lower East Side was never linguistically fused in such a way, despite the concentration of newspapers along Park Row and the presence of talented journalists who might have exploited such an opportunity.

It is tempting to conclude that Broadway, as an idea, was the creation of the circuity of a particular historical moment as much as it was the product of a place or location. This complex circuitry of special languages and working journalists, in turn, appears to have inspired a unique combination of adoption and invention. Writing of Broadway at the end of the thirties, Mencken concluded that

> it is from this quarter that most American slang comes, a large part of it invented by gag-writers, newspaper columnists and press agents, and the rest borrowed from the vocabularies of criminals, prostitutes and the lower orders of showfolk. There was a time when it was chiefly propagated by vaudeville performers, but now that vaudeville is in eclipse the torch has been taken over by the harlequins of movie and radio.[12]

To the journalists working the area, the *way* people talked *was* the story. It was their discovery that for a time language was itself something you could take off and run with. "Without slang," Jack Conway once remarked, "I know a lot of guys who would be doing pantomime. On Broadway it was the pay-off. For we all speak and think it. I never knew it could be peddled until I fell into a job at *Variety* and found a home. On this sheet where they use the dictionary for a doorstop, I can rip and tear— and I have."[13] If the language of the press became a performance medium for the writers, it became a kind of theater for its readers.

This historical moment—when slang crystallized as language theater—was comparatively brief, twenty years at the most. The fully fleshed-out Broadway of myth was available only in the barest outline to Fitzgerald in 1925 when he wrote *The Great Gatsby*, as evoked in the Broadway character of Meyer Wolfsheim. As early as the mid-thirties, the creative energy that had fired the myth had begun to dissipate, and the versions of Broadway produced by Hollywood and by wordsmiths elsewhere were becoming formulaic and repetitive.

For writers and others who were tracking it, Broadway was always a moving target that required quick responses, as Mencken implies in his reference to the switch from vaudeville to film and radio as the source of slang. One important factor in keeping *Variety*, which had started publication in 1905, at the center of the Broadway scene was Silverman's shrewd sense of the direction in which show business was moving. Founded when vaudeville and variety entertainment were near their peak, *Variety* moved quickly to cover developments in the film industry and in radio. By the thirties, these new media were prominent in the area. Every major Hollywood studio occupied space on Broadway, from the offices of Paramount and Fox on West Forty-fourth Street to the offices of Universal, RKO, and Goldwyn on Sixth Avenue between Forty-ninth and Fifty-first streets on either side of Rockefeller Center and behind the new RCA building.

Journalists like Runyon, Ring Lardner, and Jack Conway of *Variety* were quick to exploit the earthy energy of these languages in forging new journalistic styles for themselves. They were in the vanguard of the creation of an American slang that rapidly spread through the local then national press, magazines like the *Saturday Evening Post*, which published Runyon's Broadway stories, and finally, during the thirties, through national network radio and through Hollywood films to the rest of the country. A whole cast of Broadway characters out of *Guys and Dolls* with their colorful monikers and vivid speech had found a place in some national dramatis personae. The authority challenged by his soft-hearted gangsters and gamblers was less the law than the formalities of written English and Emily Post. One revolution that Times Square had helped to bring off was a revolution in vernacular speech, a revolution that a sometime habitué of the area, H. L. Mencken, had been trying to track in the various editions of *The American Language*.

Meanwhile, an important transition was taking place in Times Square, as press replaced theater as the voice of the area, a transfer of energy, one might say, from stage to page. Fundamental to such a shift was the century-long history of variety entertainment in New York, which possessed a vitality that no technological changes seemed capable of dampening. So powerful was its influence that the format of the burgeoning tabloid press soon imbibed its qualities.

Variety entertainment, developed around the enticements of what was known as "naked dancing," was basically a theater of pastiche—swift shifts in substance and tempo to match the expectations of impatient and knowing urban publics. *Variety*, the bible of variety theater, was quick to mimic its moods and pace. By the twenties, *Variety*, intended as the medium for communicating within the Broadway world, itself became the message. The distinction between press and theater, in fact, soon became almost meaningless as crossover figures from one area to the other proliferated, until finally the slanguage of the press became the best show in town. Winchell, who began his career in the song-and-dance team of Winchell and Green, was only one of the figures to make the transition into the new era and medium of performance. Reporters like Runyon and

Winchell, who were sent uptown as emissaries to cover the entertainment world in midtown, eventually became its stars, dragging the press, so to speak, after them.[14]

A surprising number of journalists, like Runyon, Lardner, and Hecht, wrote plays. Runyon collaborated with Howard Lindsay in *A Slight Case of Murder* (1931), and Hecht and Charles MacArthur jointly produced the immensely successful *Front Page* (1928). With Broadway's enthusiastic reception of plays about the press, one could say that it had completely turned the tables. The press was now the subject and Broadway theater had become the reporter. The story the press covered in the ensuing years was the sporting life of Broadway, its lingo, its antics, its dirt, and its colorful repertoire of anecdote.

Contributing to the creation of the Broadway subject were the traditions within American journalism that possessed something of the same kind of performative energy as variety entertainment. One of these was the convention of the whimsical, informal essay, highly personal in point of view, which had evolved alongside hard news by midcentury. The first such essays appeared in Western papers. This tradition drew on an even older tradition of colloquial, Western humor going back to newspaper writing by Bret Harte and Mark Twain in the 1860s. Edgar Watson Howe of the *Atchison* (Kansas) *Daily Globe*, who began such a whimsical column in the late 1870s, was an early practitioner whose influence outran the circulation of his paper. Donald Robert Taylor of the *Chicago Tribune*, Finley Peter Dunne of the *Chicago Post*, and Don Marquis of the *New York Evening Sun* were writing in this vein before the 1920s. Franklin Pierce Adams (F.P.A.) writing "The Conning Tower" in Pulitzer's *World* and Hecht's essays for the *Chicago Daily News* carried this tradition into the twenties. These essayists created distinctive personas, and some of them, like Dunne, were beginning to experiment with dialect.

There is considerable evidence to suggest that the conventions of theater criticism and sportswriting that were developed during the twenties grew out of this tradition of informal, highly personal, sometimes whimsical or humorous commentary. Humorist Robert Benchley, after a brief career as a feature writer for the *World*, became the drama critic for the old *Life*, and, after its founding, for *The New Yorker*. Alexander Woollcott served as drama critic for the *New York Times* for almost ten years before 1922. During the twenties, Heywood Broun wrote an influential theater column significantly entitled, "It Seems to Me," for the *World*. In 1927 Woollcott took it over. It was out of this tradition that figures like Ring Lardner launched such successful careers. Lardner began as a writer for South Bend, Indiana, papers in 1905 and wrote a successful sports column for the *Chicago Tribune* until he moved to New York in 1919. So far had conventions in sportswriting moved from other kinds of reporting, however, that most sportswriters of 1920 were advertised as "humorists" ten years later. The columns that Runyon wrote under the heading of "My Wife Ethel" and under the byline "A. Mugg" took him into the mainstream of journalistic humor, far from the ring, the stadium, and the racetrack.[15]

This tradition makes the Western origins of Broadway's principal architects a little less puzzling. The extraordinary fecundity and inventiveness of New York journalism during the twenties and thirties owe much of their vitality to the traditions of Western journalism by means of the flow of talent into New York from San Francisco, Denver, Chicago, and Des Moines. Runyon, who had the ear of Arthur Brisbane and sometimes Hearst himself, brought young journalists he admired from other cities, as he brought Gene Fowler from the Denver paper he himself had left. The *Denver Post* and the *San Francisco Chronicle* in this period were the most abundant sources of journalistic talent, in effect, the "farm teams" for Hearst sports reporting and graphic art.

New York papers with their large circulation and huge advertising revenues were pots of gold to provincial journalists. Coming to Hearst's *American* or the *Mirror* in those years must have been a little like playing the Palace. The cartoonist Rube Goldberg was earning $150,000 a year from Hearst and national syndication only a few years after he moved to New York from San Francisco.

Coming out of Western journalism, most of them had already tapped the mainstream of American newspaper humor before they arrived in New York. This mainstream of humor in 1920 was defined as much by Will Rogers as by any one figure. Rogers, who galloped into New York as part of a Wild West show that debuted in the Garden in 1905, had become a Ziegfeld star by 1916, just playing his "natchell self." By the twenties he had branched off into journalism and was writing a syndicated column, profoundly conservative, in which he poked fun at anything new or unconventional as well as anything old or new that appeared to him fake or stodgy or phony. Together, he and Runyon covered the Republican national convention in 1924.

Meanwhile, the kinds of feature writing that were included, especially in Sunday editions of the tabloid press, mushroomed as such writing became a key factor in expanding circulation. Hearst and other publishers paid the highest salaries to attract such talent, sometimes more than they paid to their editors.

No one, not even Winchell, had a larger hand in exploiting the linguistic wealth of the Broadway subject and what was then the New Journalism than did Damon Runyon, who came to New York in 1910 as a seasoned journalist from the West. He was born, ironically, in Manhattan, Kansas, the son of a heavy-drinking itinerant newspaperman. He came to personify Broadway, yet he was over thirty and a seasoned journalist when he arrived in New York and took his first job on Hearst's *American* in 1911.[16] His relationship to New York, to the Broadway beat he covered, was unique.

For journalists like Runyon, Times Square was a crossroad where special languages—dialects, cants, argots—hitherto confined to ethnic or occupational groups, converged in a kind of linguistic funnel to create a new national slang with a pronouncedly New York accent. The sporting world, the underworld, the worlds of vaudeville, theater, and carnival, had all developed rich and expressive argots by the beginning of the twenties. This extraordinarily creative period in American journalism was over in less than twenty years.

By the end of the thirties Runyon had virtually left New York and was dividing his time between Florida and Hollywood. He thus joined the significant westward migration of Broadway talent. Several of his Broadway stories, written in the early 1930s for national magazines, were made into successful films, bringing the mythos of Broadway to movie audiences across the country at just the moment when the Broadway world that he knew was on the point of disappearing.

Runyon's contributions to the Broadway mythos were distinctive and set him off from all the other figures who haunted the area and wrote about it during the twenties and thirties. More than anyone else, he was the creator of "slanguage," as *Variety* dubbed it. Slanguage reflected, among other sources, the richness of Jewish humor and the Yiddish theater. The linguistic product that emerged during the twenties and thirties was more than a slang vocabulary. It was less imitation than similacrum. It more closely resembled a distinctive manner of speech, in effect an amalgam of languages highly expressive of the historical moment: jokes, an inventive punning and toying with words reminiscent of vaudeville, new ways of representing speech in dialect, a distinctive syntax and temporal mode (i.e., Runyon's historical present tense), a repertoire of characters unmatched since the early days of Western humor, a colorful array of "monikers" to designate them, and anecdotal lore and narrative configurations that sealed the locality in myth.

Runyon did not write dialect like Gleason, Milt Gross, and other contemporaries. Nothing was further from his style than the gossipy, breathless staccato columns with their showy neologisms like "Chicagorilla" that brought Winchell fame and national recognition as the personification of Broadway by the end of the twenties. In 1931 Winchell appeared on the cover of *Time*, and little wonder, since what he had achieved stylistically was closely akin to the Timestyle being manufactured simultaneously a few blocks to the east. Winchell's column was a difficult target for parody since it approached self-parody almost by nature, but Lardner managed to do it by mocking his breezy delivery:

> A Lincoln and Gen. McClellan are on the verge . . .
> Jimmy Madison and Dolly Payne are THAT WAY . . .
> Aleck Hamilton and Aaron Burr have phfft . . .

Finally, Runyon differed in both style and focus from the writers who created the snappy, slangy, highly elided language of *Variety*. *Variety* was devoted to the world of show business and was probably best known outside its inner circle for its brief, jazzy, comically compressed headlines, such as "Stix Nix Hix Pix" for "movies about farm life play poorly in small towns." Runyon had, moreover, little sustained interest in the theatrical world as such, only in the bright aura with which it surrounded the Broadway scene. It was the Broadway sporting, gaming, and nightlife world that consumed his attention as a writer. His career, therefore, remained close to the conventions of the sporting writer, as the genre was then called, unlike Winchell or the writers identified with *Variety* or theatrical writing.

Soon after he arrived in New York and began covering sports for the *American*, he fell into the routines as journalist that were to guide the early part of his career. He arose at noon and set off for one of his Broadway haunts, Jack Dunston's restaurant near the old Hippodrome, or later, the Garden cabaret where the sporting crowd gathered, and he could listen to baseball or boxing anecdotes and pick up racing tips. After 1913 he left the city for several months each year, spending time with baseball teams during their spring training. In 1914 he traveled to Paris with the Giants and White Sox and covered their tour through Europe, sending home comic accounts of such incidents as the presentation of McGraw and Comiskey to George V.

For the rest of his career, he divided his energies between what amounted to feature writing, more and more humorous, about sports, and straight reporting, which fascinated and repelled him simultaneously. In this sense, his writing reflected contrary tendencies that had been present in American journalism for much of the century.

A writer for *American Speech* in 1927 described this dialectical process of the press with such precision that his comments, though long, seem worth quoting in full. The article, entitled "Color Stuff," begins with a series of complaints about the deterioration and dullness of news reporting, which the author ascribes to a "standardization of the news" imposed by the business office and advertising departments. The writer then pays tribute to "sporting writers" as

> the sole survivors of that golden age in journalism when color made the news article as intriguing and fascinating as the brightest of short stories.

But the sports writer—facts to him are incidental. He molds his stories, often grotesque, usually colorful, and always unfettered by the restrictions which hem in the boys in the city room, out of less tangible substances.

He is a freebooter. He goes into the street for his slang. He invents words when his dictionary fails him. He writes what is in his head, how and as he wishes. The general reporter may not do this even if he could—and generally he couldn't.

Why is this so? For one reason, the sporting writer serves a clientele which is not so much concerned with facts as with good, rollicking tales of the diamond, the mat, the gridiron, and the boxing ring. . . .

Of all the sporting writers, he who pictures the stirring battle of the ring is the breeziest. He knows no restraint. Slang, he uses in full measure, and his readers like it and the slangier he is, the higher is he held in their esteem. It is he who invents such spicy phrases as: "honeyed kisses and brotherly love stuff"; "took two more reeffs in his wampum belt"; "speared him on the whiskers"; "knocking them bowlegged"; ". . . kid himself into the throne room."

After several paragraphs of further examples, the writer concludes with some general observations.

A fertile imagination coupled with a flair for invention is the sporting writer's greatest asset. Writing stories averaging a column in length six and sometimes seven times a week, and injecting into each of these fresh expressions or phrases, calls for more than ordinary ingenuity. As I have mentioned previously, it is his privilege either to pick up his material in the street or to invent it. Some, possibly many, of the expressions which he has conceived while extolling a fighter have become a living part of the American slang. I do not believe that all the boxing slang which we hear in conversation and later see in the newspapers travelled from the spoken word into print. The contrary is also true.[17]

During much of his career Runyon had clearly internalized some such dialectic of city desk versus sports desk. He wrote straight news accounts of the Chicago trial of his friend Capone in 1931 without hinting at their personal relationship. At the same time he was composing humorous, informal feature articles about a range of subjects for almost every Sunday edition of the *American*. He seems, over the course of his newspaper career, to have been fascinated by the drama of court proceedings. He actively sought out notorious trials like that of Bruno Hauptmann in the Lindbergh case. But as a correspondent in France in 1918, he appears to have seen himself principally as a feature writer concerned with the experience of individual soldiers, and he therefore played to the Sunday editions, which in this period emphasized such human interest topics. Still, he continued to do straight sports reporting, as when he chose to do a serialized biography of his friend Jack Dempsey for King Features in 1919.

When he began writing and publishing his so-called Broadway stories in 1929, therefore, he was clearly embarked on a new phase of his career, one that carried him psychologically away from newspaper work altogether and, for much of his subsequent career, from New York itself. Between 1929 and the end of the thirties Runyon wrote some eighty of these stories. Most of them were completed by 1935 when the third collection of them was published. They appeared in *Colliers, Cosmopolitan, Liberty, The Saturday Evening Post*, all of which had large, middle-class readerships. The stories were an instant success and, almost at once, were in great demand. Magazines estimated a Runyon story to be worth 60,000 subscriptions.[18]

Magazine stories are no longer a staple, and it is therefore a little difficult to gauge the qualities that made these stories so instantly appealing. The appeal, moreover, did not wear off with their first publication. Many of these stories were later republished by the Hearst papers, and several of them were made into successful Hollywood films, "Madame La Gimp" became a film of the same name, starring Shirley Temple, and "Little Pink" became *When Irish Eyes Are Smiling*. Much later, *Guys and Dolls* played on Broadway as a hit musical.

Such success is incredible in a novice story writer entering the competitive field of magazine fiction at the end of the twenties. For Runyon to succeed he would have to compete with the likes of F. Scott Fitzgerald. Yet in a sense this is what he did. Runyon, it is true, had written a few stories about Western town life before he left Denver in 1910, and some of his feature writing, such as his column, "My Wife Ethel," were whimsical fictions, but the Broadway stories still seem to have come out of the blue.

These stories have by now received an inordinate amount of academic study from literary scholars, including a book-length critical study by Jean Wagner, entitled *Runyonese*. Another scholar has succeeded in locating 750 slang expressions in a group of stories, and has determined that almost half of these expressions derive from the underworld Runyon came to know so well. Still another study has placed Runyon as the last of the Local Colorists. None of these studies, however, seems to have addressed the problem that is most interesting today, though they offer some interesting clues.[19]

To read Runyon's Broadway stories today is to enter a special narrative world, a world that is almost entirely voice. The plot, settings, and the characters with their colorful "monikers" change from story to story. Less than half of the Broadway stories actually take place on Broadway. Some are set at various racetracks across the country, in college stadiums, even in faraway places like the island of St. Pierre off the coast of Labrador. The plots of these stories seem formulaic. The rescue of a damsel in distress is a common theme, though all of Runyon's damsels don't make it, as in his story, "Little Miss Marker," in which the child dies as her hood friends stand weeping at her hospital bedside. Rich, obnoxious society people "get" it in one story after another just as tough hoods frequently reveal hearts of gold.

If plots were the essence of Runyon's fiction, his success would be unintelligible. There is almost nothing in his fiction, moreover, that would qualify today as "local color." There is little description of any kind: there is comparatively little dialogue. So much for the appeal that these stories might once have had for those longing for a fictional glimpse of the Broadway scene. Although there is slang in abundance, it is not used in the way that Winchell or *Variety* writers deployed it. It is fused into the narrative voice and, while important, is not an element in and of itself. Even the famous "monikers" are ultimately a function of voice, for it is the narrator who designates the characters in the stories, just as it is the narrator who in the course of the stories relabels the human goods of the Broadway world. The narrator, of course, is immediately identifiable as a Broadway guy, sometimes named, sometimes not. But it is this Broadway voice, or what we come readily to accept as a Broadway voice, that must have given this fiction its authentic appeal. It is this voice that has survived, as far as anything has, during the fifty years since the last of these stories was written.

"One morning about four bells," the "Bloodhounds of Broadway" begins, "I am standing in front of Mindy's restaurant with a guy by the name of Regret." A bit further into the story, we read

> this Marvin Clay is a very prominent society guy. . . . and he has plenty of scratch which comes down to him from his old man, who makes it out of railroads and one thing and another. But Marvin Clay is a most obnoxious character.[20]

In the story, Marvin Clay is soon dead, "plugged" by an indignant hood for his abusive treatment of a young female friend.

Taken together, the Broadway stories are timeless fables recounted by a voice that is at once socially accepting and morally firm. This voice appears to know that his Broadway friends cut a comic figure at a Park Avenue party, but their very awkwardness is portrayed as a virtue that places them above the mannered world that is discomfiting them. They are redeemed by their candor and their innocence. They are, in Runyon's description, "citizens" or "peasants." They belong to what becomes a small familiar world, what amounts to a village in the center of New York. Rough parallels to Runyon's fictional world can be found in the other fictions of small-town America where narrative voices structure the community, as in Sherwood Anderson's *Winesburg, Ohio* or Thornton Wilder's *Our Town*. In Runyon's stories Broadway becomes a small town, very like the towns that figure in Runyon's early Western stories, where everyone knows everyone by name. This aspect of Runyon's stories clearly had the effect of giving his readers, who must have felt they were looking for something new, something that was at the same time familiar to them.

But there is one important dimension to Runyon's Broadway scene which makes these comparisons to other stories comically inept, accurate though they may be in some generic sense. Runyon's world is a manic world, in some ways closer to that of the Marx Brothers or Tad Dorgan's comic strip, "Boob McNutt," than to that of any literary parallel. In Runyon's fiction, when someone throws a ham, the narrator comments:

> Well, this ham hits poor old Bodeeker ker-bowie smack dab on the noggin. The doc does not fall down, but he commences staggering around with his legs bending under him like he is drunk.[21]

In general, Runyon composes highly visual fiction, but it is a visual fiction that is very dependent on voice. In this world of mayhem, it is the function of the narrative voice to exercise a slightly distant controlling influence. The historical present tense in which he addresses us is a measure of his narrative control. It is, in a sense, the voice of Runyon, the reporter, speaking from location: "I am standing in front of Mindy's . . ." The success of these stories is also, I suspect, heavily dependent on the even greater popularity of radio drama. It is no coincidence that they appeared at just the moment when radio plays, broadcast over national network radio, had saturated the air waves, adding still further authenticity to these New York narrators as on-the-spot reporters. They reached a wide national audience, moreover, which was attuned to drama arriving by voice.

Jean Wagner and most later students of Runyon have exaggerated certain similarities between the careers and story lines of Runyon and Alfred Henry Smith, an earlier (1858–1914) writer who, like Runyon, was born in Kansas, and also, like Runyon, wrote Western stories of saloons, cattle thieves, and gamblers in stories focusing on a fictional town. Smith then came East, working on newspapers, and then wrote a series of stories about the New York underworld, collected in 1912 under the title, *The Apaches of New York*.

The coincidence is striking, but one look at Smith's stories is enough to dispel the idea that Runyon's fiction was in any important sense derived from that of Smith. Smith's stories are recounted by a third-person genteel narrator, like those employed by William Sydney Porter (O. Henry) a generation earlier. Porter was another New York writer whose Western origins and preoccupation with petty criminals parallel those of Runyon. It seems less likely that Runyon read these other writers than that all these writers drew from a common tradition of Western storytelling.

This tradition may help to account for still another and striking feature of Runyon's fiction, one that it shares with other verbal lore of Broadway. Runyon's world is preeminently a world of men. Women figure in it as obsessions, as hostages, as prizes. They are "dolls" or "molls" or "gams" but never "citizens" or "peasants" or anyone important. In the transformation from the West to Broadway, one is tempted to view them as replacing the cattle in these earlier fictions. They are stolen or hustled. They provoke violence in men and they seldom talk. In the slanguage of Broadway they are characteristically the butts of jokes. They are dumbbells, dumb blondes, if they are not the eel's hips or the cat's whiskers. Dumb wives who outsmart their husbands, as in Runyon's column, "My Wife Ethel," were a standard feature of variety entertainment from Runyon to the Honeymooners.

The jokes that convulsed readers in the twenties would make any modern woman "pull in her ears," as in "Bugs" Baer's quip that paying alimony "was like feeding oats to a dead horse." Homoerotic bonding was at the very heart of Runyon's fiction as, one suspects, of his life. Homoerotic bonding remained equally a regular feature of what might be called "the West of memory." As incorporated into Runyon's fiction this version of the West acquired a New York accent.

Runyon may, partly for these reasons, turn out to be the most important of the Broadway writers, even though his Broadway stories now seem dated and mechanical. He was an odd kind of New Yorker, almost fiercely involved with anything touching on Broadway. Gene Fowler remembered being startled in 1917 when he arrived in New York and heard Runyon, six years after his arrival, talking as though he had invented the place, as in a sense he had. Another friend noted two years later, when Runyon was serving in France, that he latched onto any snippet of information or any New Yorker with Broadway ties "like a miner jumping a claim."

Yet by the mid-thirties, Runyon had left New York and was dividing his time between his house on Hibiscus Island near Miami (and that of his friend Capone) and a house in Beverly Hills, where he was by then earning a sizable income as author, scriptwriter, and, finally, producer.

He had become so ambivalent about New York at the end of his life that he hesitated when making his funeral arrangements as to whether to have his ashes scattered over Miami or over Broadway. In the end, he opted for Broadway, thereby enhancing the myth; and his friend Eddie Rickenbacker performed the task as he requested. Yet, unlike many of his journalist contemporaries, who had left reporting once they had established themselves as writers, Runyon continued to practice straight news reporting from time to time, reporting proudly and impartially for Hearst on trials or disasters, and conducting interviews, including one with Hearst himself in 1941. During the last weeks of his life, as he was dying of throat cancer and literally speechless, he spent the hours when he wasn't at Winchell's table at the Stork Club, riding around the city answering police calls in Winchell's car.

His life, one could say, encapsulated a central contradiction in the journalism of his time. Reporting was clearly in his blood and a fundamental part of his identity. As the son of an itinerant, quasi-failure of a newspaperman, whose migratory lifestyle and hard-drinking ways Runyon began by imitating, he also prided himself on being a reporter. Yet, despite his attachment to reporting, his best and most important work— the Broadway stories that he began in 1929—were in clear reaction to the restrictiveness of journalism and were published, as he published nothing else, not in newspapers but in large circulation national magazines like *Cosmopolitan* and *Liberty*.

In his personal life, too, he seems to have been equally enigmatic and contradictory. Although he surrounded himself with talkative, even garrulous friends with whom he spent the better part of every day, and his stories contain endless accounts of conviviality and partying, he himself was reticent, even taciturn and, in the eyes of many of his friends, inscrutable. Many of his stories revolve around themes of loyalty and undying affection, yet in his personal relationships he appears to have been aloof, even cold. He shamelessly neglected his first wife and his children by her, with tragic results. Although he imbued his portrayals of nightlife with a manic gaiety and wrote with comic nonchalance about dolls and chorines, speakeasies and bootleggers, he remained personally prudish, most of his life a teetotaler, and was apparently always shocked by accounts of sexual immorality.

Finally, although a passion for egalitarian justice and a distrust of wealth and privilege characterize the whole body of his stories, he himself carefully withheld any political criticisms he may have had and avoided any but comic commentary on the events of the day. To the end he remained loyal to and uncritical of Hearst. His bitterest attack upon the morals of his time appeared, characteristically, on the editorial page of Hearst's *American* in 1921, when he compared the crowds on Broadway to so many hogs grunting and pushing. Commenting on a description of pigs running free on Broadway almost a century earlier in Charles Dickens's *American Notes*, he wrote:

> Since Mr. Dickens' time, the pigs of Broadway have changed in form
> only, having taken on the semblance of humans. You can see them

today in streetcars and subway trains, pushing and grunting their way to seats while women stand clinging to straps. You can see them wandering along Broadway, old hogs familiar with every sty in the city, and young porkers just learning the ways of swine, their little eyes eagerly regarding every passing skirt.

Of an evening they gather in cabarets, wallowing in illicit liquor and shouting their conversational garbage made up of oaths and filthy stories and scandal. A pig is a pig even when it wears evening clothes.[22]

Over and over he repeated his credo to other reporters who criticized his determination to remain emotionally and politically aloof: "Never bite the hand that feeds you," and "Go for the money!" Yet friends who felt they understood him hesitated to call him either a cynic or a hack. He always struck them as in the grip of some slightly elusive and mysterious passion.

He seems to have been by nature a listener, always withholding a bit of himself from what he did and said. In some sense, of course, these contradictions may be less personal to Runyon than an embodiment of some more general ideal he had internalized and nourished of the newspaper writer. In the end, his life and career may have been defined less by the personal and the enigmatic than by the model he had chosen. What he left behind may prove to be more a measure of the newspaper culture in which he worked than of personal idiosyncracy.

His success and the wide popularity of his stories about gangsters may, in fact, have been the result of the degree to which his work embodies a tension between respectability and prurience that was central to his time. In portraying petty criminals and hoods as sympathetically and engagingly as he did, he was catering to what Winchell once described as society's "underworld complex," a middle-class love affair with the underworld that began during Prohibition. In striking out at the ruthlessness of wealth and privilege as he did, he may simply have been inverting the class spectrum, leaving its pieties intact.

To reach such a conclusion about Runyon is to raise certain larger questions about the meaning of the Broadway mythos and about what we have been calling commercial culture. One is tempted to ask some fifty years later what the consequences of this seemingly liberating moment in our history have been. It is sobering to recall that this moment occurred during economic good times and faded during the system failure of the Great Depression. Certainly, the vitality and energy that went into transforming everyday speech and the language of the press have left a permanent stamp on our culture, but we may have lost the passion for city life and the excitement about other subcultures that informed this linguistic transformation.

The most important question concerns our use of the concept of commercial culture. Much that we have written about it in this book assumes that the era of commercial culture represents an historical moment before the intervention of mass culture when cultural production still reflected in some way the interactions of the city as a community. We have inferred that cultural exchange and monetary exchange were for a time closely and generatively interrelated in the urban setting of New York City. One product of this interrelationship was the stimulation given to linguistic invention across the whole spectrum of urban occupational life: songwriters, gag-writers, publicity men, sportswriters, playwrights, copywriters, poets, socialists—during these years all were engaged in some kind of intensified linguistic invention. In this sense, the twenties and thirties were a fecund moment in the history of American cultures. The coming of mass culture appears to have brought this creativity to an end. If this is so, it is ironic that the very circuitry of press, radio, and film that delivered Broadway slang and all the other freshly minted lingoes to the nation, at the same moment deprived us of the vital communal impulses that made Broadway itself possible. One wonders in retrospect, in tandem with Runyon, whether the ashes of Broadway should be dropped on Times Square or on Hollywood.

COMMERCIAL
AESTHETICS

INTRODUCTORY ESSAY

William Leach

V ISITING PARIS in 1912 the novelist Edith Wharton was upset to find
that the French had adopted commercial floodlighting, which she
identified with America. Once, she wrote, "the great buildings, statues,
and fountains" along the Champs-Elysées were "withdrawn at dusk into
silence and secrecy." Now, they are "being torn from their mystery by the
vulgar intrusion of floodlighting." About the same time, Wharton's friend,
Henry James, was lamenting the spread in America "of towers of glass,"
the business buildings full of newly installed commercial windows. These
windows had nothing to do with "formal beauty," James said; they had
nothing in common with older kinds of windows, with stained glass
church windows, for instance, which were the "loveliest of images." No,
these windows "spoke loudest for the economic idea." They were "invid-
ious presences" intended to "bring in money—and was not money the only
thing a self-respecting structure could be thought of as bringing in?" They
were "window upon window, at any cost," each with a "light having a
superlative value as an aid to the transaction of business and the conclusion
of sharp bargains."[1]

Wharton and James were reacting to a new kind of aesthetic in
America which increasingly marked urban life and which we might
call—loosely—a commercial aesthetic. By 1920 this aesthetic was remaking or deeply affecting the way Americans experienced everyday reality.
Its purpose was to move and market goods, to produce a pecuniary climate,
and to excite the spirit of acquisition and appropriation. At the same time,
it was intended or had the possible effect of "thrilling" onlookers and of
conveying a sense of wonder and awe. As one enthusiast of urban light put
it in 1923, the advertising spectacle of New York's "white light district" is
"the only New York possessing a thrill. It is . . . the carnival supernal."[2]

This commercial aesthetic was already visible in the urban streets and
centers of America in the late nineteenth century. But its greatest advance
occurred after 1895, with the rapid rise of corporate business and the
appearance of new technologies and materials. Growth came with the
invention of new artificial commercial colors—bright colors, brighter than

234

anything in nature; growth came with the introduction and production of window glass and plate glass (before 1885 Americans imported almost all their plate glass from France; by 1915 Americans were consuming one-half the plate-glass in the world); and, above all, it arrived with the invention of improved incandescent electrical lights, which facilitated the "transformation of night into day." Growth came at the world's fairs, where Americans were first exposed to floodlighting, spotlighting, and outline lighting, in both white and colored forms. And it took a leap forward with the creation of more effective merchandising and advertising for mass urban markets.[3]

Between 1895 and 1930, American business decisively took control over the new color, light, and glass materials primarily to stimulate the movement and sale of goods and money. New kinds of show windows were constructed in New York and elsewhere, effectively focusing and orchestrating color and light to attract consumer attention. The outdoor advertising business had emerged, at first serving only the patent medicine business, but soon snaking out to include large corporate enterprises, small manufacturers, national political parties, and even the federal government during World War I.[4] A crucial sideline of this business—electrical outdoor advertising—had also begun to take shape. By the turn of the century, several electrical advertising firms were competing for business and devising new electrical styles. In the mid-1890s, merchants were beginning to employ the first (albeit primitive) "spectacular" electrical displays, mounted on skeletal steel frames with flashing devices.[5]

Among the entrepreneurs—the brokers of commercial light—was O. J. Gude, who first coined the phrase "The Great White Way." Known as the "Napoleon of publicity," Gude was a shrewd confidence man who saw opportunities perceived by few others. He upgraded the traditional bill posting business into a substantial national corporate enterprise that invested millions of dollars in new sign technologies. He invented the permanent signboard for painted advertising (rather than for paper printing) and contributed more signs, electrical signs and painted billboards, to the business than any signboard advertiser before 1920.[6] By the end of his career, three kinds of electrical advertising, in particular, had been developed—electric signs studded with lamps, illuminated signboards, and the floodlighting and outlining of exteriors. Electricians had also redesigned the marquees of theaters, hotels, department stores, and other businesses, putting the names of people, companies, and productions "up in lights" for the first time in reliable ways. The first "talking" signs were chattering in American cities and resort towns, followed after 1912 with "panoramic" and "moving" signs, the "sky signs" that allowed merchants to change reading matter every day and to move it rapidly along the boards from right to left.[7]

Gude claimed that his work actually integrated art and business. It helped, he said, to lift the aesthetic standards of Americans, and brought more "aesthetic pleasure" to people than any other medium did. "Outdoor advertising has . . . felt and shown the effects of the artistic spirit of the people in this country," he said—it is "beautiful," rather than "brutally dominant." But what really pleased Gude was the way electrical signs *forced* people to read them, whether they wanted to or not. Gude liked the *power* of this advertising. Electrical signboard advertising, he wrote,

> literally forces its announcement on the vision of the uninterested as well as the interested passerby. . . . Signboards are so placed that everybody must read them, and absorb them, and absorb the advertiser's lesson willingly or unwillingly. . . . The constant reading of "Buy Blank's Biscuits" . . . makes the name part of one's sub-conscious knowledge.[8]

The rise of the commercial aesthetic at the world's fairs and in American advertising and merchandising, then, greatly contributed to its growth. But it was the formation of commercial districts like Times Square, where commercial light and color were gathered into one spot to an unusual degree, that pushed the commercial aesthetic to the visual forefront of American urban life. It was this concentration of light in commercial districts that often drew tourists from around America and the world, tourists who filled the sightseeing coaches to see what O. J. Gude called "the phantasmagoria of the lights and electric signs."[9]

When Wharton and James were writing, Times Square was still on its way to being born and had not yet achieved any kind of "aesthetic" dominance. The centers of commercial light and color in Manhattan—to the extent that they existed at all—were further downtown along Broadway. For some time, the Great White Way was not even identified with Times Square. Then, in the wake of the opening of the Times Square subway station in 1904, the area started to assume its connection with spectacular light (and then colored light) that it still retains. More and more people traveled to the district. There was an upsurge of entertainment and commercial activity. Bigger crowds came, streaming through the district at close range to one another—captured audiences, as it were—waiting to be courted by the electrical advertising business. In 1916 a zoning law permitted full-scale building of giant billboards. In a few more years, one promoter bragged, "more people were passing through [the district] than any other spot, creating a concentrated purchasing power of potential customers."[10]

By 1920 New York City's commercial aesthetic had found its most potent ally in Times Square. "Hundreds of thousands of people," wrote one contemporary, "are now thinking of New York in terms of the 'whiter light district' . . . centering around Times Square. To them this is the spirit of New York."[11] Outdoor advertising by local businesses and by national advertisers was booming by 1922, expenditures having increased sixfold over the previous three years.[12] On any one day or night in February of that year, passersby might see electrical signs advertising actress Marion Davies in *Buried Treasure*, Macy's department store, the Fisk Tire Company, the Paramount Theatre, Chalmers Underwear, or Ivory Soap ("It Floats"). By 1924 the national corporations, in particular, the automobile companies, the gasoline firms, the cigarette and soda businesses, were swamping the area, eating up the advertising leases to such a degree that many of the local businesses (with the obvious exception of the heavily capitalized movie house chains) could not compete. Outdoor advertising monopolies, which reflected the consolidation taking place in mass manufacturing, also came on the scene to broker the advertising for any business that could pay the price. The area was now the most densely packed and most expensive advertising space in the world.[13] In such a primal battleground, only the most opportunistic, ruthless, and rich survived. "Advertising magnates battle like Vikings for strategic locations," said an observer, "sometimes paying for a location and not using it simply to keep others out."[14]

Two features of the signage in Times Square in this decade, which established later patterns, are worth noting—its spectacular character and its gradual reliance on colored rather than white light. First, the signage was "spectacular" (an industry term), and the most spectacular of all was the signage of the local movie theaters and of the national corporations. These signs jumped and wiggled and flashed to attract attention; they visually "shook" (as well as covered) the facades of buildings or the air space above buildings. By the mid-twenties, the movie ads were "sensational," forming an almost organic part of the whole experience of "going to the movies." "What a magnificent spectacle," wrote one English critic, G. K. Chesterton, after he first saw these signs on Broadway, ". . . for a man who cannot read."[15]

In February 1925 the Criterion Theatre at Broadway and Forty-fourth Street advertised Cecil B. DeMille's "The Ten Commandments" in a typical 40-foot-high display covering the entire front of the building. The ad depicted 600 chariots led by the Pharoah in a "tumultuous scene" filled with many black horses, all metal cut figures seeming to leap "madly toward the spectators." A giant Moses, holding his tablet with the Ten Commandments, looked grimly down on the street. Every few minutes, the theater released 100,000 volts of energy in the form of a "streak of lightning that flashed across the sky in a bluish flame," hitting the Commandments in a huge "crack" of light. From night to night, an electrical device floodlighted the advertisement in a different color.[16]

As early as 1917, a national corporation, Wrigley Spearmint Gum, had erected what was soon billed as the biggest electric sign "in the world," occupying a space for the next seven years at the heart of the Square.

Eighty feet high and 200 feet long, it contained 17,500 lamps and showed a little animated group of electrified "brownies" standing next to the words "Wrigley Spearmint Gum," "jabbing" the night, in off-and-on flashes of light, with their little spears. Later in the decade, the O. J. Gude Company built the "Twins of Power" on Fifty-fourth Street and Eighth Avenue, a flashing sign meant to advertise the gas and oil products of Purol and Tilene. The first flash revealed a huge bull's eye being suddenly pierced by a flash of lightning, followed by the flashing on of "Twins of Power" in giant letters, then by the words "Purol," then by "Gasoline," and "Pure Oil Company," and so forth, in rapid and repeated sequence.[17]

A three-story bottle of Cliquot Ginger Ale towered over the Square in the summer of 1924. This Gude sign pictured the bottle in a giant sleigh driven by a smiling Eskimo boy in white furs. In flashing sequences, the boy snapped a six-foot-whip, which, in turn, activated three other Eskimo boys who ran rapidly on their "little legs" pulling the ginger ale. Another whip-crack set the name "Cliquot" flashing in the sky, followed by "Ginger Ale," all the while the little boys "running bravely in the night to bring that precious bottle of Ginger Ale into camp," as one account described it. In the spring of 1925, 5,000 lights radiated from a 100-foot-wide General Motors sign, which stood 82 feet above the General Motors Building at Fifty-seventh Street, facing Times Square. The words, "General Motors," along with the motto, "A car for every purse and purpose," burned continuously in the night. Flashing alternately on and off were the names of the GM products, Chevrolet, Oldsmobile, Buick, Cadillac, Oakland, and GM trucks, along with the message that every car has a "body by Fisher."[18]

Year by year, the signs got bigger and bigger. In 1928 the automobile manufacturer, Dodge Brothers, hoisted onto the top of the Strand Theatre on Forty-eighth Street "the largest electrical sign in structural dimensions on Broadway," according to the broker Edward Bernays, who did the publicity work for Dodge in the twenties. The sign's upper part held the Dodge Brothers' name, the bottom part a ribbon motograph announcing the "Variety Six and other Dodge cars." This "moving sign," said Bernays, who could see it from his office window, "was half a city block in length" and "can be viewed by a million people passing through Times Square in a day."[19]

An increasing adoption of color added to the ballyhoo of this scene. In the early twenties most of the signs lacked color, although advertisers often floodlighted in colors (as the "Ten Commandments" ad illustrates) and sometimes even relied on color-coated incandescent lights (but these were mostly unreliable). The invention of neon light by the Frenchman Georges Claude around 1915 changed all this; and by the end of the next decade, white light was the least favored and least common light in Times Square. "The ruling color is not white" on Times Square, the *New York Times* reported in 1929, "for the white lights celebrated in song and legend are now almost obliterated by the reds, greens, and orange-yellows" (the *Times* might have said the "blues" as well) "made possible by the luminous gas arrangement."[20]

According to contemporary accounts, neon light marked the biggest advance in advertising light since the invention of Edison's incandescent filaments. It was a cheap cold light, wasting little energy and requiring little electrical current. It was a powerful light that, given the peculiar properties of its rays, could not be absorbed by sunlight. It was a light that seemed to glow in intensity from a distance; most importantly, it could be seen in the day, at night, through fog and rain. Luminous gas light (and it came in many gas forms besides neon) not only provided businesses with colors, it made selling "in light" possible "all the time."[21]

Luminous signs first threaded regularly through the district by the mid-twenties or soon after a huge factory was built on Amsterdam Avenue and 132nd Street, financed by real estate developers and city wholesalers, to supply the district with a steady stream of such signs. In a few years, as the *Times* reported, luminous colors were visible at Times Square from every direction on the compass. "Looking to the east," the *Times* said, "deep red is easily the favorite."

> At the northern end is the most prominent advertising spot in the Gay White Way, which alone illustrates the color riot that Broadway's outdoor decorators have concocted. At the very top is an electric sign in deep yellow advertising a brand of coffee. Below this is a white sign on a blue background dotted with yellow lights, calling attention to a brand of automobile. Further down, one's eyes are assailed by a large square sign advertising a toothpaste, which first flashes a message in orange-yellow, switching to red and finally to green. Underneath this is a cigarette advertised in white letters on a large red background.[22]

In no other city in the world did the commercial aesthetic unfold to the degree it did in New York City. Paris and Berlin, to be sure, were known as "cities of light." Paris's fame for light extended as far back as the seventeenth century when Louis XIV had lanterns lit by tallow dips installed along many of the streets. At the turn of the twentieth century, the Champs-Elysées and surrounding boulevards were the most completely illuminated arteries in the world, flanked by thousands of gas and electrical lights burning night and day. By the time of Edith Wharton's visit to Paris in 1912, however, a new commercial pattern of lighting was apparent; and in the mid-1920s, nearly 6,000 neon advertising signs were crowding the nighttime horizon. These "alluring advertisements written in the dark by thousand-candle power," one German visitor wrote in 1929, "reach to the high, retreating sky. A big green drop drips into a gigantic champagne goblet. Immense glass tubes glow with red fire, or gleam with condensed sunshine." In Berlin, too, people were seeing commercial neon lights for the first time. "When I arrived in Berlin . . . in the mid-twenties," writes Christopher Isherwood, "the first thing I saw there were two enormous cinemas, the Ufa Palast and Gloria Palast with neon lights." Berliners themselves were impressed by "glimmering reflections of advertising that gave the boulevard an intimate feel."[23]

Still, during these years at least, the Germans and the French slapped legal restrictions over the spread of such "spectacular" advertising. In June 1929 a Paris law, which the Prefect of the Seine imposed on the city following further signage expansion, ordered the removal of "all electric signs that did not advertise goods actually sold on the premises." Advertising by non-locally based national businesses, in other words, was forbidden. The law sent shock waves through cigarette and automobile companies on Broadway, but it pleased many of the French. As one said, "Paris is proud to be known as the City of Light, but she wants it to be intellectual rather than electric."[24]

In New York there was some attempt made to control and rationalize electrical advertising—indeed, the commercial aesthetic itself—but not in this French way. The American way was to concentrate or confine such activity to a limited space, while at the same time *liberating* it to an unparalleled degree (today, television advertising is a good illustration of the American way). Throughout the twenties, a battle was waged in Manhattan between rival trade associations over signage restrictions. On one side was the Broadway Association, which wanted no controls whatsoever placed on signage; on the other side was the grandiose and aggressive Fifth Avenue Association, which fought for control from 1916 onward, insisting that all "projecting and illuminated signs" be banned on Fifth Avenue from Washington Square to 110th Street. In 1922 the Fifth Avenue group persuaded the city's Board of Aldermen to pass a sign ordinance that not only legalized the ban but extended it to include parts of Madison Avenue and Thirty-fourth Street. Fearful of the snowball effect, the Broadway and Forty-second Street associations launched a counterassault, but they actually had little to fear, for the Fifth Avenue Association had no intention of advocating the banning of signage in Times Square. The O. J. Gude Company and Macy's and Gimbel's (both stores were Times Square advertisers) were actually members of that Association! The merchants on Fifth Avenue, moreover, *wanted* the patronage of the tourists who were attracted to New York by the lights of Times Square; and they certainly had nothing against commercial light and color, as their hundreds of show windows demonstrated. What the Fifth Avenue Association did not want, however, was a "carnival spectacle" that might bring an influx of the "wrong kind of people" into the Avenue on a daily basis, an influx that might jeopardize real estate values and undermine the control these merchants had over *their* property.[25]

The sign ordinance stuck and richly rewarded both business groups, further clarifying and rationalizing areas of market domination. Signage may have been banned on Fifth Avenue and in other places, but it was to have a carnival field day on Times Square. The ordinance, in fact, triggered even greater growth in a more concentrated space. In this space, businessmen did what they wanted with the commercial aesthetic. Here commodity fetishes—the disembodied icons of national corporations and chain theaters—could float freely in a glittering nocturnal void.

The overall visual outcome was a provocative and sometimes suffocating effusion of light and color that came to dominate the culture (and still dominates it, not only through places like Times Square but through the movies and television). It was a bottom-line aesthetic that manipulated color, glass, and light in the hopes of speeding up the distribution and circulation of money and goods in the biggest conceivable volumes; it was never a subtle aesthetic but a bright and carnivalesque one, employing only a prescribed palette of colors designed to milk mass markets. Such an aesthetic inspired many people, who thought it expressed the very "promise" of America. It excited—of all people—the poet Ezra Pound, when he visited New York shortly before World War I. Is "New York," he asked, "the most beautiful city in the world? It is not far from it. . . . Electricity has made for [people] the seeing of visions superfluous. . . . Squares upon squares of flames, set and cut into one another. Here is our poetry, for we have pulled down the stars to our will." The aesthetic also inspired Stewart Culin, one of America's foremost folklorists. It is a "great achievement in the newest and most amazing medium for artistic expression," he said in 1928 of the Dodge Brothers' sign in Times Square. "This sign is prophetic, not only of man's uninterrupted activities through all the hours driving night away, but of the coming of masters who will create with light as the painters of old did with pigment."[26]

Over the years, these same thoughts would be repeated again and again by people who believed that the color and light of commercial districts were somehow related or intrinsic to the "greatness" of modern capitalism. Scott Fitzgerald expressed these ideals in his novels, as did Ernst Lubitsch, later, in his film *Ninotchka*, in which Garbo, drably dressed as a Soviet functionary in Paris, looks down from her hotel room at the brilliant city lights spread out before her; or, as did Paul Mazursky, even later, in his worshipping neopropagandistic film, *Moscow-on-the-Hudson*, which opens in an almost liturgical way with the colors and lights of Times Square.

There were some people at the time, however, who were deeply repelled by this commercial aesthetic. In his *Absentee Ownership*, written in

1923, Thorstein Veblen blasted America's "sales publicity" for enlisting all the devices and strategies of religion on behalf of the marketing and sale of goods. Outdoor advertising in particular, Veblen said in a powerful indictment, is being exploited in such a way as to reproduce and even displace the older Christian "Propaganda of the Faith." Veblen loathed the cheap replication of the classic Christian strategy—the promise of "the Kingdom of Heaven" that could not be delivered. "Spectacular displays," Veblen wrote, have been marshaled in a "dim religious light" to make fraudulent promises to Americans. With their signs and symbols, colors and lights, and "gestures," sign advertisers have promised "the Kingdom of Heaven" and saturated their goods with "sacred" meanings that ultimately mean nothing and go nowhere. "The wriggly gestures with which certain spear-headed manikins stab the nightly firmament over Times Square," Veblen said, in reference to the Wrigley Gum sign, "may be eloquent and graceful but they are not the goods listed in the doctrinal pronouncements." They are "not the effectual delivery of chewing-gum. Bona-fide delivery of the listed goods would have to be a tangible performance of quite another complexion, inasmuch as the specifications call for Hell fire and the Kingdom of Heaven."[27]

America's new commercial aesthetic was exemplified most powerfully in Times Square's outdoor advertising and signage, but we can also find it "inside" the consumer and entertainment institutions in and around the Square. The chapters that follow focus on some of these institutions and on some of the people who designed them. Woody Register analyzes the work and career of Frederic Thompson, who operated the New York Hippodrome and Luna Park in Coney Island and was one of America's most successful exploiters of commercial aesthetic. And then Gregory Gilmartin examines the career of one of America's most influential decorative architects who, before 1930, designed the interiors and exteriors of many of New York's most important restaurants, stores, and theaters. Joseph Urban managed to integrate two different aesthetics—one aristocratic and the other commercial—into one pecuniary aesthetic that appealed to many Americans.

12

NEW YORK'S GIGANTIC TOY

William Wood Register, Jr.

I N DECEMBER 1904 a recent innovation in electrical billboard advertising called the "talking sign," high above Brooklyn's most crowded shopping district, heralded the arrival of a new era in theatrical entertainment. With successive flashes of incandescent typescript, the sign exclaimed, "NEW YORK HIPPODROME . . . ENTERTAINMENT FOR THE MASSES . . . MANAGEMENT THOMPSON & DUNDY . . . NOW BUILDING OPEN JAN 1905." Using a novelty to advertise a novelty was typical of the promotional style of Frederic Thompson, the showman who, with his partner Elmer S. "Skip" Dundy, had opened Coney Island's most famous amusement park, Luna Park, in 1903. In 1904 and 1905 they laid claim to building the world's largest theater, the New York Hippodrome, along the full length of Sixth Avenue between Forty-third and Forty-fourth streets in Manhattan. Thompson was literally the architect of both enterprises. He designed the Hippodrome as a great showplace for the same millions of New Yorkers who filled Thompson & Dundy's coffers with dimes at Luna Park, but who had thus far been priced out of the legitimate Broadway theaters. But the Hippodrome was to be more than a very large "people's theater." Thompson sought through its spectacular productions to bring adult play to the center of the metropolis, using the modern technologies of electricity, hydraulics, and illumination, and the systematic organization of the factory to expand the reach of his marketplace of play from Coney to Manhattan island. Thompson fashioned his Hippodrome as a plaything for the masses, a "gigantic toy" for the overworked, play-starved men and women of the twentieth century.[1]

This vocabulary of toys, novelty, childhood, and play was at the center of Thompson's project for the Hippodrome during the short period of fourteen months that the partnership of Thompson & Dundy was its proprietor. Between 1902 and 1912 Thompson proclaimed himself the "toymaker of New York," but the playthings he built were aimed specifically at adult consumers, not children. He had opened the sensational Luna Park in May 1903 as a spectacularly enlarged children's playground in order to exploit what he believed was the universal desire of grown men and women to return imaginatively to their childhoods. Thompson took the diagnostic position that turn-of-the-century Americans needlessly suffered from excessive work and too little play. He organized the Hippodrome's eclectic concoction of spectacle, pantomime, vaudeville, circus, and musical comedy as a commercial remedy—in effect, a toy—for this condition.[2]

Thompson's version of play had little to do with the rage at the end of the nineteenth century for the so-called "strenuous life." His play was to be consumed in an active state of imaginative, not physical, engagement. The showman wanted the men and women in his audience to be transformed by a theatrical fairy tale of lights, color, movement, and music, which would temporarily release them from the responsibilities of everyday life by transporting them back to the world of the child at play. As such, the Hippodrome was more than a marginal enterprise responding to a new demand for the commodities of leisure and amusement. It was a powerful expression and promoter of a new range of meanings for twentieth century Americans participating in a modern consumer economy. Its version of the good life, presented in Thompson's radiant spectacles, *A Yankee Circus on Mars* and *A Society Circus*, rejected the time-honored model of the thrifty, industrious, property-owning, male citizen-producer. Thompson encouraged men and women to become children again, to play, spend money, and enjoy themselves in his festive marketplaces of pleasure and desire. He offered his own life and accomplishments as evidence of the propitiousness of adult play and as a new behavioral model for success in American life and business. To his contemporaries the showman appeared to be a child-man whose achievements resulted less from his self-possession and self-control than from a preternatural access to his own innate child spirit. He seemed the very embodiment of the spirit of play, a magical Peter Pan whose life and marvelous amusement projects exemplified the imaginative and liberating power of play and childhood.[3]

Frederic Thompson was not the first American showman to propose building a gigantic hippodrome. A recent and successful predecessor was P. T. Barnum, who had imported spectacles from England and Europe in 1874 for his Roman hippodrome, built between Twenty-sixth and Twenty-seventh streets in Manhattan. The arena seated 8,000 spectators before extravaganzas which, according to Neil Harris, "mingled peril with magnificence" and heraldic opulence with the thrill of chariot races and Wild Western violence. But Barnum's hippodrome stayed with the circus format of an elongated oval performance space surrounded by a grandstand arrangement of seating and relied on tested European productions for the entertainment.[4]

Even Barnum's grandiose spectacles paled in comparison with Steele MacKaye's messianic designs for the Spectatorium, a permanent theater seating 10,000, which MacKaye planned to erect for the 1893 Columbian International Exposition in Chicago. MacKaye was born in 1842 and his career as playwright, acting instructor, and stage designer culminated in his effort to fulfill the "divine duty" of building a great national theater and school of drama reflecting his religious devotion to Art and his radical ideas for redefining drama. He did not plan to break completely from the entertainment basis of Barnum's productions but to leaven the content of the amusement, "whose aim," he contended, "should be to uplift as much as to amuse." Like his successor, Thompson, MacKaye envisioned an art for the masses and diagnosed many of the same social evils on which the designer of Luna Park would later base his amusement enterprises. MacKaye convinced leading Chicago industrialists and financiers to invest in an American Bayreuth on the shores of Lake Michigan, which would offer spiritual sustenance to an impoverished age "benumbed by over-work, calloused by coarse occupations, stricken by great sorrows, or deadened by the poisonous sweets of luxury." The problem that confronted him was in making "the lofty and the refined popular" without diminishing its Olympian stature. MacKaye would never realize his theatrical dream of "subsidizing the genius of the whole world, for the education and inspiration of the masses, while affording them, at moderate prices, an entertainment as irresistibly fascinating as it was ennobling." The construction of the Spectatorium progressed no farther than its steel skeleton when the Panic of 1893 frightened away investors.[5]

Thompson was living in Chicago in 1893, working at the exposition as a demonstrator in an industrial machinery exhibit, and undoubtedly was aware of MacKaye's project. His own background, however, was in neither art nor entertainment but in the industrializing economy of the American Midwest after the Civil War. His father, "Casey" Thompson, was a steel and iron manufacturer who, for the first sixteen years of his son's life, moved his family to a succession of towns and cities in the East and Midwest before settling permanently in Nashville, Tennessee, in the late 1880s. Born in 1873 in Ironton, Ohio, Frederic displayed a precocious attraction as a youth to machinery and a remarkable acuity at turning fortuitous opportunities into income. By his own admission he preferred "pottering around the mill" to attending school. His only formal training amounted to several years of architectural study under his uncle, a prominent architect in Nashville, for whom Thompson worked sporadically between 1890 and 1897. Thompson's informal education was as important for his later career as his architectural apprenticeship. By the time he moved to New York in 1899 to study art, he had also tried other occupations, including steel and iron working, hydraulic machinery, furniture design, journalism and illustration, brokering construction materials, art school, mining engineering, and designing world's fair midway amusements.[6]

He left Nashville in 1893 for Chicago and the Columbian exposition. Afterward he was involved with every American world's fair through Buffalo's Pan-American exposition in 1901. His investment in commercial midway amusements, unintentional at first, grew progressively with each fair. Thompson won an architectural medal for his design of the Negro Building at the Tennessee Centennial in 1897, but his more meaningful contributions in terms of his later career were the midway attractions which he and a partner designed and built for various showmen. At Nashville and later at Omaha's fair, he was forced to take over amusements in lieu of payment from showmen who went bankrupt while still owing him money. Thompson adroitly resuscitated the commercial fortunes of these shows by injecting narrative action, movement, and mild sexual titillation to otherwise passively educational and self-consciously artistic spectacles. By the close of the Omaha exposition in 1898, Thompson had not only demonstrated his instincts for show business; he also had become, in his words, "a kind of exposition fiend," involuntarily drawn to the festivity and "throngs" of a great world's fair.[7]

Thompson's transformation into an "exposition fiend" was reflected in his plans for the 1901 Buffalo fair. He teamed with a rival showman, "Skip" Dundy, to form Thompson & Dundy. In later years the two men claimed that they formed a perfectly symbiotic partnership in which Dundy managed the money and his partner dreamed up the amusement projects. Thompson & Dundy followed its lucrative successes at Buffalo with Luna Park and the Hippodrome, and had begun producing Broadway plays when Dundy died in 1907.

Thompson approached the Pan-American as an amusement entrepreneur, introducing his most famous midway illusion, "A Trip to the Moon," which later formed the cornerstone of his Coney Island amusement park. "A Trip to the Moon" was a participatory fairy tale for adults which used theatrical scenery and lighting to give its customers the sensation of flying in a winged ship from earth to the Kingdom of the Man in the Moon. Upon their lunar arrival, the passengers did not merely observe the landscape or listen to an educational lecture; they shopped in the lunar marketplace, viewed the monstrous "Moon Calf," sampled green cheese offered by the indigenous midget population, and viewed a musical vaudeville show in the palace of the Man in the Moon. Many of the major themes which Thompson & Dundy would incorporate in their future ventures were contained within "A Trip to the Moon." Thompson wove together the modern industrial technologies of electricity, illumination, and hydraulics with theatrical spectacle, illusion, and participatory drama to create a narrative tale of transport from earthly darkness to a luminous fairyland.[8]

Thompson & Dundy used this amusement formula when they transformed the run-down Sea Lion Park, which covered some twenty-two acres on Coney Island, into Luna Park in the fall and winter of 1902–03. With the Pan-American exposition in mind, Thompson designed the park as a unified, enclosed amusement city. It featured the regular amusement fare of world's fair midways, including "A Trip to the Moon," reproduction native villages, free circus performances, a ballroom, and numerous rides. In addition, Thompson introduced a new architecture of amusement which converted the Beaux-Arts classicism of the great exposition cities into "palaces of amusement." Amusement architecture, according to Thompson, had to affirm human desires and encourage release, freedom, and spending instead of admonishing people to deny themselves pleasure and to restrict their desires. Above all, the amusement park had to manufacture the carnival spirit by insuring energetic movement instead of rest and stasis in the park's attractions as well as in its architecture. At night tens of thousands of electric lights traced the edges of Luna's buildings, creating an incandescent spectacle which was visible for miles out to sea and inland toward Brooklyn and Sheepshead Bay. Thompson claimed that his combination of Oriental and fantastic architecture and electrical lighting transformed the monumentality of the world's fairs into a liberating celebration of the power of adult play. Luna's popularity was established overnight. The *Brooklyn Eagle* estimated that 60,000 filled Luna the first night and an attendance record of 245,000 was set on the Fourth of July weekend. Thompson & Dundy boasted that they paid off their entire indebtedness of one million dollars after the first summer.[9]

The idea of building a hippodrome in the heart of Manhattan apparently occurred to Thompson after the Pan-American and before he and Dundy decided to build Luna Park. New York and especially Manhattan appealed to the showman because of their concentrated "throngs" of comparatively affluent middle-class men and women and the city's highly developed and integrated urban transportation system. When Thompson moved to New York from Buffalo in 1901, he found that the city's legitimate theaters had hardly altered the appeal of their entertainments or expanded the foundation of their audience over the last decade of the nineteenth century. The theaters still catered to the carriage trade to the exclusion of the mass middle-class audience which had grown up around them. "I was astounded at the conditions as they existed," Thompson explained in July 1904, shortly after construction had begun on the Hippodrome. "Here was a city with millions of people in its confines, and not one amusement resort which appealed to more than 25 per cent. of them at the very outside." Thompson claimed that he and Dundy tried as early as 1901 to put a hippodrome at Seventh Avenue and Thirty-ninth Street in Manhattan but had to back down because of opposition from neighborhood residents. In the alternative they concentrated on Coney Island, but the gist of what Thompson was trying to accomplish was the same, whether at Luna or the Hippodrome.[10]

"We are coming to the age of the department store in theatricals," Thompson declared in September 1904. "The masses are ready to welcome it." The concept of the department store provided Thompson with an organizational model for his theater as well as a democratic vocabulary of public service. As a number of historians have shown, urban retailing was increasingly dominated at the turn of the century by huge retail establishments, often housed in extravagantly palatial buildings where a diverse array of goods, previously sold in separate stores, was offered to consumers. In small as well as large cities like Philadelphia, Chicago, and especially New York, these stores catered to a densely populated urban region by concentrating on high volume and high turnover sales of lower-priced items for their profits rather than on high markup on individual items. Stores like John Wanamaker in Philadelphia and later in New York developed innovative advertising and merchandising schemes as well as a host of free services available to all customers regardless of their ability to buy—to attract the consuming millions and to promote shopping as an important activity, particularly for middle-class women. Retail entrepreneurs located their stores at the confluence of major urban transportation systems. Service became the pervasive slogan of urban retailing, and, as a recent historian has noted, a "certain heady democracy" reigned in the store where the city's wealthiest and humblest walked the same aisles even if they could not buy the same goods.[11]

With the Hippodrome Thompson sought both to expand the potential audience for theatrical productions and to redefine the ethos of theatrical entertainment in the progressive, public-spirited vocabulary of the modern department store. He would cater through the Hippodrome's expanded seating capacity, low ticket prices, and varied showbill to the millions who could not afford what he pilloried as the high-priced entertainments of the exclusive legitimate theaters on Broadway. Thompson counted as many as three million New Yorkers who never attended the cheaper vaudeville or the fashionable Broadway theaters.

> They are nice, respectable, intelligent people, but cannot afford to pay $2 for an orchestra seat in a fancy Broadway theatre among a lot of overdressed people. They feel as though their clothes were not good enough, and so they stay at home. They have too much self respect to

go up in the gallery and too much intelligence to go to the cheap theatres. Those are the patrons we are after, the masses, and our motto will be to give them the best possible show for the least possible money.

Hippodrome tickets ranged from twenty-five cents to a dollar.[12]

Thompson claimed that the Hippodrome had democratized theater-going in the same way that department stores had democratized shopping; the rich as well as the humble mingled at the Hippodrome as they could at no other Broadway theater. In truth, Thompson wanted to tap the urban constituency of middle-class consumers which daily filled the city department stores and which, after 1915, would fuel the proliferation of motion picture houses in American cities. The world's fairs and especially Luna Park had shown Thompson and his partner Dundy that great fortunes could be made from collecting millions of dimes and nickels. The Hippodrome, to duplicate this formula, demanded unrelenting full houses attracted by its inexpensive tickets to offset the enormous price of producing theatrical luxury for what *Broadway* magazine called "the great outstanding masses."[13]

To attract these throngs Thompson had not only to make the tickets affordable but also, like the department stores, to fashion a dramatic representation of abundance and pleasure, an entertainment of unstinting luxury that was more affirming than proscriptive. As he explained in 1907, the aim of "lighter forms of amusement" was not to challenge or instruct the audience with the intellectual fare of "the higher forms of the drama." The attitude of the viewer seeking "lighter" entertainment, according to Thompson, "is one that says:

'We are young, and being young we want to be made to laugh, no matter how foolish is the method by which you do it; we are young and we believe everything, therefore do the most impossible things and we will pretend to believe them and applaud; we are poor, . . . make us forget that there are luxuries and perhaps necessities beyond our means—stir us so that we will remember the hours that we are spending with you for months to come; we are tired and weary and overworked—don't add to our burdens, lighten them by your most fantastic and foolish endeavors.' "[14]

According to this strategy, then, the Hippodrome's therapy was not a numbing anodyne administered by a managerial elite. Like the original midway illusion, it relied on the audience's voluntary and conscious credulity and participation in its implausible plots and cheerful mixture of incongruous attractions, which replicated Luna Park's marketplace of adult play. The effect was to construct a theatrical amusement park, a commercial dreamworld of pleasure, abundance, insouciant youth, fluid-ity, fantasy, and magic, accessible to a mass audience for the small price of admission.

Predictably equating his own personal benefit with that of the com-munity, Thompson assured the Broadway theatrical establishment that the Hippodrome was good not only for the people but also for the theatrical world in general. He forecast that his Hippodrome would "impart the theater habit" to millions with "slim purses" who either had lost interest in drama because of the high prices or never had had it. Thompson & Dundy's Hippodrome was creating a new audience for theater which would spread into rival houses much as the partners claimed responsibility for expanding the patronage and leavening the moral quality of all of Coney Island's amusements. The press generally praised the partners for this progressive innovation. "This great building fills a long-felt want," *Broadway* reported. "Its prices are for the public. Its vast proportions make its appeal for patronage thoroughly sincere and honest. The plan of amusement is of that human sort that makes the whole world kin." Another magazine, linking the Hippodrome to progressive politics and slogans, called it a "square deal" in safety, comfort, price, and value. "And not least of its attractions are the civility and courtesy which replace the usual contemptuous and boorish treatment the theatre-goer encounters in other places of amusement." Simply stated by Thompson & Dundy's publicity department, the Hippodrome offered "A revel of recreation at rational rates."[15]

As the Hippodrome was an unprecedented venture in popular amuse-ments, it was unclear who its competitors were. Broadway impresarios were neither impressed nor reassured by Thompson's generous promises, especially since the Hippodrome, with 5,200 seats and matinee and evening performances six days a week, would be seeking a potential audience in excess of 60,000 weekly. Oscar Hammerstein, who was planning his Manhattan Opera House at the same time, condescendingly equated the Hippodrome with the annual visits of the circus. "The theatres will suffer immensely . . . for at least the first six weeks," he predicted. "The enormous crowds that will naturally be attracted by the novelty of this establishment must come from somewhere, and they will be drawn from the regular theatres." The damage will be temporary, he added, as it was when the Barnum & Bailey Circus came to New York. Nevertheless, Hammerstein announced fictional plans to surpass Thompson & Dundy with an even larger theater of his own. More serious, however, were the alleged efforts of Abraham Erlanger and Marc Klaw of the Theatre Syndicate, who were suspected at the time of waging sub rosa warfare through the city Building Department to delay Thompson & Dundy's project. Numerous roadblocks were brought by building inspectors with challenges to the Hippodrome's construction features. The allegations against the Syndicate are not surprising, inasmuch as the firm, which held a near monopoly on theatrical productions in America, was generally despised during a time of antitrust sentiments. In addition, one of Klaw & Erlanger's contributions to American theatrical life was the importation of spectacular London pantomimes, with which presumably the Hippodrome would have directly competed. However, a recent student of the controversy has found no decisive evidence of "actual collusion" between Klaw & Erlanger and the city Building Department. In any event, the Syndicate responded to Thompson's populism by announcing a drop in ticket prices at its New York Theatre to one dollar. Another "prominent manager" predicted a decline in ticket prices all over the city to $1.50 from $2.[16]

Rumors were also published of a pending "circus war" between Thompson & Dundy and the Barnum & Bailey Circus. Thompson, who had skillfully used the publicity generated by conflicts with clergymen and business and civic leaders to promote his world's fair ventures, "boomed" the impending war with the "Circus Trust." "We have procured all the billboard space available in New York," he proclaimed in January 1905, "and are prepared to wage a merry war on our three ringed opponents. There will be fur flying before this conflict is over." James Bailey of the circus dismissed Thompson's challenge but added superciliously that "if a fight comes we will give them all they want. We are not Coney Island showmen." There was actual substance to this rivalry beyond Thompson's immediate challenge to the circus hegemony of Barnum & Bailey. Thompson & Dundy had raided American circuses, including Barnum & Bailey, for arena acts. According to one newspaper account, Bailey responded by arranging a non-competition agreement with Ringling Brothers Circus in exchange for which Ringling broke its agreement to provide acts to the Hippodrome. Barnum & Bailey further waged war over their famous clown, Frank "Slivers" Oakley, whom Thompson & Dundy hired for the Hippodrome. In January of 1905, Barnum & Bailey announced it would inaugurate the longest circus season in New York's history during the coming spring. Both Barnum & Bailey and the Hippodrome managed to survive the 1905 season, but the conflict with the circus as well as with the legitimate theaters indicates that Thompson had conceived of an amusement that challenged both elite and popular forms of entertainment, to a degree dissolving the boundaries between them.[17]

Nor were the residents of the Sixth Avenue area certain of the meaning of the Hippodrome. The carnivalesque and popular appeal of the theater's presumed entertainments intruded rudely on a neighborhood ordinarily insulated from the commercial and theatrical nightlife of Forty-second Street and Broadway by a broad city block and the Sixth Avenue elevated track. Shortly after construction began in late June of 1904 the *New York Times* reported that news of the Hippodrome had "come as a great surprise" to the staid residents of Forty-fourth Street between Fifth and Sixth avenues, the formidably exclusive domain of the Harvard, Yale, and New York Yacht clubs known in tourist vernacular as "Rubberneck Row." The concept of a permanent circus hippodrome struck some of the residents as unpleasantly demotic, even before Thompson had advertised his plans to make the theater a popularly priced house. After all, said the displeased secretary of the City Club, "A circus is a circus, no matter how artistic the buildings." A real estate agent in the neighborhood claimed nothing good could possibly come from the project. "No theatre, not excepting the Metropolitan Opera House, is any good for business except to restaurants and saloons."[18]

Thompson designed the Hippodrome as more than just a very large, popularly priced theater. The Hippodrome also was a machine which systematically organized an unprecedented collection of human labor power and electrical and hydraulic technology to manufacture fantastic entertainments. As such, its meaning extended beyond the immediate theatrical community of Broadway. Expansively detailed and laudatory accounts of the Hippodrome's construction and stage effects appeared in many of the technical magazines on engineering, illumination, electricity, and architecture. These articles, as well as those appearing in middle-class magazines and daily newspapers, presented lavishly detailed descriptions of the building, from how many bricks covered the theater (six million) to how many feet of copper wiring (110,000) were used in connecting the Hippodrome's 25,000 incandescent lights. It was an age fascinated, as William R. Taylor has shown, with human and technological quantification. In the case of the Hippodrome, however, the seemingly endless listings of measurements emphasized the designers' ability to marshal hundreds to hundreds of thousands of minute parts, details, and people into a methodical system which responded efficiently and willingly to their commands. The Hippodrome was not just big, but controlled and organized bigness at the service of amusing the great middle class.[19]

Thompson & Dundy advertised the total price of the Hippodrome, the Sixth Avenue property, and its stage entertainment as $3,500.000. Luna Park had been a munificent benefactor during its first two seasons, but hardly to the extent necessary to finance a project of this size. John W. "Bet-a-Million" Gates emerged as the big money behind Thompson & Dundy, both at Luna Park and at the Hippodrome. Gates was a notorious gambler and speculator who had made a fortune in barbed wire, oil, and steel manufacturing. The United States Realty Company, of which Gates was a principal, owned the Sixth Avenue property where the Hippodrome was built and for all intents and purposes the theater itself. In mid-September Thompson & Dundy borrowed $900,000 from the New York

Security and Trust Company—an institution closely tied to U.S. Realty —and shortly afterward it was announced that Gates would be president of the Hippodrome Company. Aside from Dundy, all of the company's directors also were on the board of U.S. Realty: Harry S. Black, who was president of the realty company, Richard G. Babbage, Robert E. Dowling, and Gates. Black was a Canadian who had married the daughter of George A. Fuller, one of the leading American builders of skyscrapers and major public buildings. The Fuller Construction Company was later absorbed by U.S. Realty, creating a formidable alliance which, as it turned out, provided the real estate, financing, and contractors to build the Hippodrome. From the beginning, then, Thompson & Dundy's hold on the Hippodrome was tenuous and subordinate to the investment interests of their backers who were powerful businessmen and financiers, not impresarios of pleasure and play. Having comparatively little capital themselves, Thompson & Dundy triumphed by convincing these businessmen of the viability of their own unique formula of amusement as a money-making investment. With Luna Park as evidence, the success of the Hippodrome must have seemed certain.[20]

The size of the Hippodrome stage and the magnitude of the productions he had planned presented Thompson with problems of coordination of movement, color, perspective, mechanics, actors, and animals which were unprecedented in the American theater. His most immediate predecessors were the brothers Kiralfy who had staged the massive outdoor spectacles at several American world's fairs. As he had ransacked Europe and the United States for circus acts and theatrical novelties, Thompson combed both continents for theatrical "experts"—one writer called them "broker[s] in beauty"—to translate his extravagant ideas into material form on the Hippodrome stage. Thompson's lieutenants did not fit easily into rigid definitions of high and low culture, but tended to move in both spheres. The result was unusually eclectic. The Hippodrome's productions mixed popular songs and circus and vaudeville acts with opulent stage settings, avant-garde ballet, and Luna Park lighting and mechanical effects.[21]

The Hippodrome's ballet master, Vincenzo Romeo, had choreographed the ballets in spectacles imported from Europe like *Bluebeard* and *Ali Baba*. The composer Manuel Klein, who had at least one Broadway musical to his credit, was selected as the principal conductor and composer and promised the Hippodrome would have an orchestra, not a circus band: "People like blare all right, but they like something else, too. They like light and shade and delicate effects." The stage manager Edward Temple had directed grand opera for the Grau-Savage Grand Opera Company as well as productions for Klaw & Erlanger. Luna Park's Hugh Thomas and Edward Carrigan built the lighting and stage properties. Claude Hagen, who had invented the stage effects for the chariot race in *Ben-Hur*, was

253

hired to design the stage, although he and Thompson & Dundy fell out before the project was completed. Hagen had directed Luna Park's outdoor disaster spectacle, "Fire and Flames," in 1903 and would go on to design the haughty New Theatre's revolving stage as well as to direct and manage other Coney Island summer shows. The Hippodrome's equestrian corps was supervised by the veteran circus trainer Frank Melville.[22]

The two most important figures emerging from Thompson's world-wide search were the Hippodrome's costume designer Alfredo Edel and the scenic designer Arthur Voegtlin. Thompson reportedly had seen Edel's work when in Paris, although it is possible that he had witnessed the Kiralfy spectacle, *America*, in 1893 at the Columbian Exposition; this had been Edel's only prior costume work in the United States. The *New York Times* credited Edel with creating the costumes for more than 300 spectacles, operas, and burlesques. His work had appeared in Verdi's later operas, *Otello* and *Simon Boccanegra*, in Massenet's *Hérodiade*, and in productions at the Comédie Française. The divas Melba and Eames had worn his gowns. "In his line no man in Europe has a higher reputation or more successes to his credit," according to the *Times*. His specialty was "stage beauty en masse," coordinating the color and texture of a stage tableau composed of hundreds of chorus girls. "Of course," he said, "my work takes me most into that realm of theatric art where the stage is crowded with people, especially with pretty girls in many-colored, brilliant garments of various sorts and designs." In terms of size, the Hippodrome premiere was "one of the largest undertakings" of his exemplary career. "I am designing costumes for a stage that will hold 400 people at a time," he told the *Times*. "I am in the position of the artist who has to paint a big picture with a small brush. The result will be impressionistic." Edel's affiliation with the Hippodrome outlasted Thompson & Dundy's, as he continued to design costumes for the Shubert brothers when they assumed control of the theater from Thompson & Dundy in the early summer of 1906.[23]

As scenic designer, Thompson chose Arthur Voegtlin, who had been reared in the atmosphere of nineteenth century spectacle theater and artistic realism. Like Thompson, Voegtlin was portrayed in the press as a visionary artist and inspired dreamer. He always claimed that he had never visited any of the exotic settings which he duplicated on a vast scale of realism on the Hippodrome and other stages; these visions came to him almost magically during inspired reverie. His father, William Voegtlin, had been a leading scenic designer of the late nineteenth century, known for his work presented in the spectacles at Booth's Theatre and Niblo's Garden. Unlike the father, the son wanted most to be an artist. "Art stung me very badly early in life; in fact, I never quite recovered," he revealed in a 1912 interview. "I wanted to paint pictures, and nothing could stop me, even the admonition of my eminent father." After studying landscape painting for several years, poverty forced him into an apprenticeship with his father. He later undertook an independent career, gaining a reputation for staging lavishly detailed realistic scenery. When the Madison Square Garden arena was transformed into a circuit of piazzas and canals for "Venice in New York" in 1903, Voegtlin designed and managed the reconstruction of the Italian city. Thompson employed his services for outdoor dramas at Luna Park, including "The Great Train Robbery," for which Voegtlin wrote the script and designed the scenery. "These pictures simply come to me," Voegtlin explained to the *New York Times*, which summarized his creative process:

> He plans his spectacles from the sweep of a skyline to the scarf on a native's shoulder, apparently out of nothing. He goes into the dark, by preference the dark of night as it approaches the day spring, carrying with him a plenitude of cigarettes and a free and unfettered imagination. He opens his eyes for the vision, and it comes. And perhaps the most astounding of all the aspects of this curious mode of creation is the fact that the vision comes timed to a minute, spaced to an inch, and colored to an overtone.

Voegtlin's visual imagination and his gift for adjusting these dream pictures to the dimensions of the Hippodrome made him an ideal "broker in beauty" for Thompson and a culture increasingly attuned to brokered images. After his career at the Hippodrome, he expanded the application of his stage pictures to the elaborate fashion and commercial spectacles of the late 1910s and early 1920s. Not surprisingly, he finished his career in Hollywood.[24]

The Hippodrome itself seemed to appear almost magically, rising from a cleared lot behind the Sixth Avenue elevated railroad between Forty-third and Forty-fourth streets to its completed form in a matter of ten months. Construction had not begun until June of 1904. Thompson promised that round-the-clock labor would guarantee a Christmas opening some six months later. Numerous delays were encountered along the way—Sabbatarian protests against Sunday construction and the difficulties brought by the city Building Department—so the Hippodrome did not open until April 12, 1905, which still was a remarkable feat considering the size of the project and its cost.[25]

Its construction mixed illusion with innovative technology to create a final product of unprecedented size and scale. The brick facade with terra cotta trimmings and decoration hid the steel framework of the actual building. Steel wall columns supported massive roof trusses, which spanned the breadth of the theater and were reportedly the biggest ever used in the United States. The actual building was a hollow box, seventy-two feet tall in the front and about two hundred feet long and wide, squatting stolidly along a full block of one of the city's principal north-south thoroughfares. Commentators had difficulty citing its architectural roots; some called it "free" or "Spanish Renaissance," others, "Moorish." But the critics generally were complimentary. The *New York Herald* anonymously quoted "one of the foremost architects of New York," who called the theater "a marvel as a public building, as an architectural effort, as a triumph of artistic endeavor." The *American Architect*, apparently amazed at the accomplishment of two Coney Island showmen, praised the design as "unusually successful in all that concerns provisions for the comfort and safety of the audience" and the interior decorations in light red, antique gold, and ivory as "unusually simple and quiet."[26]

Thompson had eccentrically mixed classical styles with Thompsonian fancy in designing the building. In front, tall Corinthian porticos with fluted columns flanked a central Roman arch with an impressive elephant-head keystone. Towers mounted the front corners, each cradling skeletal orbs, some ten feet in diameter and outlined with incandescent lights. Inside, the auditorium seating took the form of three steps ascending from the orchestra pit, with most of the seating in the balcony and gallery. This tiered effect left the auditorium, for the most part, open, thus accentuating its vastness. The ceiling appeared to be an expansive dome, manifesting no means of support except for four pillars at each corner. In fact, the dome was an illusion. The ceiling was actually dropped from the roof trusses, which were hidden from view, and the pillars merely decorative. The stage was divided into two parts. The main stage was fifty feet deep and two hundred feet wide and located behind the proscenium arch. A second, semicircular stage, or "apron," extended sixty feet beyond the proscenium into the auditorium. A water tank, fourteen feet deep, was hidden beneath it and unveiled by lowering the apron floor.[27]

The Hippodrome, observed the *New York Clipper*, was "a place of magnificent distances." But Thompson's theater was not big solely for the sake of being the largest theater in the world. One of the showman's favorite amusement tricks at Luna Park was the antic alteration of scale and perspective which momentarily disturbed the viewer's sense of his own size and identity. Thompson acutely comprehended the psychological effect of a shifting architectural environment. Architecture, in his opinion, affected its inhabitant's sense of self even more readily than the theatrical entertainments which were offered on its stage. The effect of the Hippodrome's size was not just to shock the spectator with its hugeness but to impress heavily upon the viewer his own relative smallness. A number of commentators noted the effect of entering the vast auditorium and gazing out into that distance for the first time. Looking into the audience, *Billboard*'s correspondent recalled, "you tremble and shrink before a mountain-wave of human faces that threatens to overwhe[l]m you. It is a vision that awes." The *New York Herald* reported the bewilderment of a well-known comedian upon his introduction to the Hippodrome's stage. "Why, I'd be lost here," he protested. "It would be like trying to act in a ten acre lot." For the producer, recalled R. H. Burnside, who directed many Hippodrome shows in the 1910s, "the fact he had always upper-most in his mind was its immensity. He *had* to think on such a scale." According to Burnside, the Hippodrome's elephants "never ceased to be a wonder to the audience" because they "emphasized the immense proportions of the stage." Even the elephants were awed by the scale of the Hippodrome.[28]

These structural facilities, however, were only backdrops for Thompson's more dramatic use of electricity, machine technology, and human labor power to translate a theatrical fairy-tale world of amusement to the Hippodrome stage. Thompson's stage director, Edward Temple, promised no mere circus performances at his theater. "To my mind the modern circus is the perfection of monotony," he commented smugly, citing Thompson's formula for popular amusements: "We have sought for constant change, unceasing action, never-halting movement."[29]

Electricity was the animating spirit of the Hippodrome, providing the power for the menial as well as the spectacular effects. "Give me dynamos," Thompson boasted, "and I can make dividends." The most obvious use of electrical current appeared in the Hippodrome's advertising, illumination, and stage effects. Thompson & Dundy pointed the way to their theater with an electrical billboard at Broadway and Thirty-fourth Street. Likewise, the block-long facade of the theater itself was electrified as a signboard. Thompson & Dundy traced the name of the production in lights, outlined the edges of the building, and, most impressively, ignited the skeletal balls surmounting each corner with thousands of lights. On opening night, the effect was a blinding incandescent advertisement which, according to the theater critic Alan Dale, "threw a fire and glare of electric illumination for miles." As the elevated train approached the theater, "a tumult of sudden light hit you on the eyeballs . . . you couldn't possibly pass it by unnoticed." Thompson had brought electrical ballyhoo to the heart of theatrical New York.[30]

The lights on the interior of the Hippodrome were not derived so directly or glaringly from Luna Park. The lighting of the main auditorium, according to the critic from the *Illuminating Engineer*, was "worked out with consummate skill." Thompson clustered unfrosted lamps of varying intensity in a radiating sunburst at the peak of the domed ceiling. Lines of smaller and dimmer bulbs spanned the ribs that spread from the sunburst and red and white bulbs alternated along the auditorium's arches. When lit at once, the lights equaled the illumination of 12,000 sixteen-candle-power lamps.[31]

The same equivalency of brilliance was used in the stage lighting.

257

Electricians devised an unusual switching system to cope with the orchestration of many different circuits. It allowed thousands of lights to be simultaneously extinguished then relit in a new configuration, producing wondrous lighting effects with the unequaled use of electrical power for stage illusions. New York Edison provided the bulk of the current, some 13,000 amperes, practically all of which was used in the production of *The Court of the Golden Fountains* during the Hippodrome's second season. "There are over 4,000 central station[s] in the United States," the *Illuminating Engineer* reported, and "the maximum output of a majority of these stations is less than the amount of current used on the Hippodrome stage." All of which led the magazine to conclude, "Without the electric light what would the Hippodrome be?" Electricity also warmed the grease paint and curling irons for the hundreds of chorus girls; wardrobe used electric irons to press costumes; electric carriage calls operated at either side of the theater; carpenters heated their glue with electricity; chefs used electric ovens for cooking and electric machines for washing dishes, not to mention the electrification of the fire extinguishing system, heating and cooling thermostats, water pumps, exhaust, ceiling, and cooling fans, and "no end of telephones and electric signals and all sorts of things."[32]

Electricity also powered the hydraulic elevators and mechanical hoists that produced the Hippodrome's stage effects. As the illumination magazines praised the Hippodrome's lighting, the *Engineering Record* extolled Thompson's theater as "a mechanical triumph of high order" employing "a series of mechanical effects of a variety and extent never before attempted for amusement purposes. . . . The undertaking is in all respects one of the boldest ever attempted along mechanical lines." Powerful hydraulic lifts stationed beneath the main stage could raise a large section of the floor as high as eight feet. Additional lifts located beneath the arena floor could lower it by fourteen feet. Thompson used these machines to produce marvelous stage illusions. The arena floor, when lowered, revealed the water tank below, thus creating a river or lake on the stage. The stage lift, on the other hand, could enact a levitation in the midst of a scene, as it did during *The Court of the Golden Fountains*, when much of the cast was raised eight feet above the rest of the stage.[33]

Instead of lowering and raising stage sets from a gridwork above the stage, the Hippodrome was forced, by virtue of the enormous size and weight of its stage scenery, to employ a system of concentric runways which surrounded the stage like a horseshoe. Scenery was stored in "pockets" behind the wall of the balcony boxes away from the view of the audience, then hauled onto the stage and back by electrically powered hoists which ran on rubber wheels along a rail, cushioned with oak strips to prevent noise, high above the stage floor. Thompson installed an indirect heating and cooling system, using massive exhaust fans to fill the vast auditorium with fresh cooled or warmed air by drawing foul air out through the ceiling.[34]

The showman also designed the Hippodrome for the rapid, friction-less movement of people, animals, and stage properties. The theater's mass transportation system consisted of broad semicircular passageways, running roughly parallel on each of the building's five levels. In the auditorium, the principal seating areas emptied in the rear onto wide, crescent-shaped thoroughfares leading to exits at either side of the building. In the basement, a horseshoe-shaped runway began at either side of the apron stage and descended beneath the orchestra seats to connect stage-right with stage-left out of the view of the audience. Arranged along the sides of this broad highway were horse and elephant stables and storage areas for stage equipment. The arrangement allowed immediate access to animals and properties which then swiftly flowed on and off the stage. The passageway also facilitated creating the illusion of an infinite profusion of animals and actors. For instance, a cavalry charge leading from stage-right to left would circle beneath the audience and reemerge at stage-right, appearing as an unceasing flow.[35]

The organizational imperative also extended into the front office. To administer "so complicated a human mechanism as the Hippodrome," one observer noted, Thompson employed a hierarchical arrangement of departments—engineering, carpentry, stage management, choreography, costumes, illumination, electricity, scene design, music—each governed by one "broker in beauty," answerable only to Thompson. As he described it, the Hippodrome was a consanguineous machine. "We have no friction," he said. "We work together like a big family."[36]

The systematic organization which governed movement off the stage was also dramatically represented in front of the audience. Edward P. Temple, the Hippodrome's stage manager, was in charge of the "discipline" onstage and the presentation of Thompson's grandly imagined stage picture. Critics marveled at the synchronized order of the choruses and ballets, which frequently numbered as many as 400 young women, as in this odd description mixing mechanistic and naturalistic images: "The lines of advancing figures look something like the busy threads of a shuttle which are being woven into some fanciful design, sometimes like the filaments of a spider's thread, sometimes like the ripples on the shore as the waves advance and retreat."[37]

The Hippodrome initiated a novel form of scenery changing between scenes: The actual mechanics and system of moving the stage materiel were enacted as part of the performance. In *A Yankee Circus*, "a smooth-faced boy in a velveteen suit and top boots" barked commands to his troop of stagehands, costumed in white and conventionally referred to as the "Hippodrome scene shifting army." These men, operating with the exactness and discipline of a military tattoo, marched properties off and on stage in view of the audience. "It was a show in itself to see the way the white uniformed army . . . flew at their task and whisked things out of the way," the *New York Sun* reported. Thompson further filled in the gaps between scenes with circus performances, eliminating any pause in action or movement, insuring that each scene flowed seamlessly into the next.[38]

A number of writers expanded the organizational metaphor from the structure and layout of the theater to the actual composition of the audience. The Hippodrome, by virtue of its size and economical prices, seemed a microcosmic representation of the community at large. "The Hippodrome is a city in itself," reported the *New York World*. The *Sun* and the *Times* offered the theater as a unique example of an American consumer's democracy, packing in everyone from "millionaire to gamin." "There were millionaires in it," reported the *Sun*. "There were ragged fellows who possibly had come by the quarter which let them into the top gallery by questionable methods. There were men of every walk of life—and there were women of every variety of age, beauty and costume." The Hippodrome, it seemed, truly was America's national theater, serving regally luxurious entertainments to a harmonious and democratic audience.[39]

Overall, then, the Hippodrome was a beehive arrangement of circles and semicircles housed within the boxlike structure of the theater. Thompson conceived of his theater as an orchestration of different fluids, whether in terms of the audience, the performance, or the production of stage effects. The Hippodrome was a metaphor of organized, efficient transportation within an urban mass society and, as such, paralleled other significant developments in modern mass transportation during the first decade of the twentieth century, including Pennsylvania and Grand Central stations in Manhattan. More importantly, Thompson's creation of a fluid theatrical environment of incessant, frictionless movement enacted what William Leach has described as the obsession of turn-of-the-century entrepreneurs of consumption "to make urban space and time completely amenable to the circulation of commodities." The founder of the Hippodrome simply channeled his compulsive preoccupation with commodity flow into the manufacturing and distribution of fantasy and illusion for the "great outstanding masses." As one visitor to the Hippodrome observed, the "[m]ost surprising fact of all . . . is the perfect system, the quiet that reigns here" behind the stage. A columnist writing in 1910 noted, without irony, the importance of rational organization to the production of the Hippodrome's stage fantasies: "The fact is that what mortal man has accomplished behind the Hippodrome scenes, by drill and system, is as wonderful as anything that the most fanciful dreamers of fiction have imagined."[40]

The organized hyperbole, steadily manufactured since Thompson

Sheet music envelope, circa 1910, featuring the young Berlin, published before his move to the Times Square office in 1918. The Theater Collection, 65665.102, Museum of the City of New York.

Irving Berlin's office at 1571 Broadway was located on the second floor of the Strand Theatre. Built in 1914, the Strand was one of the area's first great movie "palaces." Photograph by Byron, The Theater Collection, 41.420,400, Museum of the City of New York.

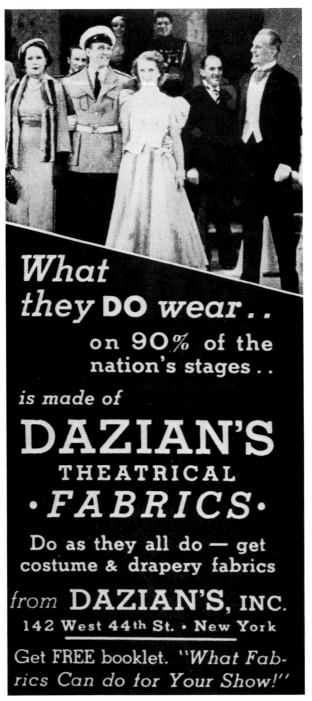

An ad for Dazian's, the most prominent firm dealing in theatrical fabrics, located on Forty-fourth Street off the Square. The departure of such paratheatrical businesses underscored the decline of theater in the area. The Shubert Archives.

Impresario Billy Rose's Casa Manana cabaret, established in 1938 at Fiftieth Street and Broadway, featured statuesque chorus girls ("Junos") like the figure on this 1939 program. The Theater Collection, 48.210.21-53, Museum of the City of New York.

The second Madison Square Garden opened in 1925 on Eighth Avenue between Forty-ninth and Fiftieth streets and provided a large arena for rodeos, circuses, and sporting events. United States History, Local History & Genealogy Division, The New York Public Library, Astor, Lenox and Tilden Foundations.

Samuel "Roxy" Rothafel (center), the entrepreneur behind Radio City Music Hall and other movie palaces, directing the first coast-to-coast radio broadcast from Rockefeller Center on November 14, 1932. Wladimir Padue is playing the piano. New York Daily News Photo.

Damon Runyon (center) with his wife-to-be, the dancer Patrice Gridier, at a favorite haunt, Miami's Hialeah race track, near his home on Hibiscus Island. Billy Rose Theatre Collection, The New York Public Library for the Performing Arts, Astor, Lenox and Tilden Foundations.

The New York Hippodrome, Thompson & Dundy's "department store in theatricals,"
covered the entire block between Forty-third and Forty-fourth streets along Sixth Avenue.
It opened its doors in 1905. The Wurts Collection, Museum of The City of New York.

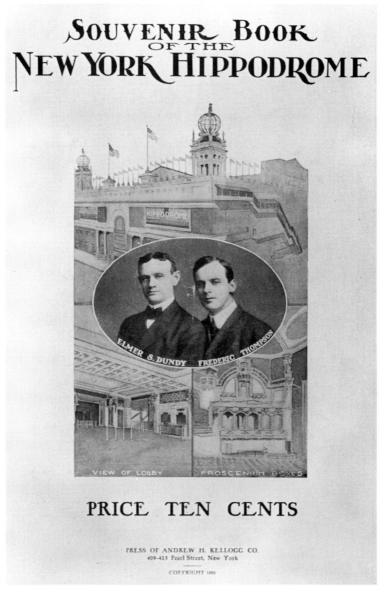

Elmer S. "Skip" Dundy and Frederic Thompson (inset), creators of the
Hippodrome and Coney Island's Luna Park, were partners until Dundy's
death in 1907. The Theater Collection, Museum of the City of New York.

"The Court of the Golden Fountain" was a characteristic Hippodrome spectacular, featuring stage illumination on an unprecedented scale—some 13,000 amperes. Photograph by White, The Theater Collection, Museum of the City of New York.

The stylized facade of the Ziegfeld Theatre illustrates architect/designer Joseph Urban's elegant blend of European modernism and American commercial design. Museum of the City of New York.

The St. Regis Hotel's Roof Garden, designed by Urban in 1927. Joseph Urban Papers, Rare Books and Manuscript Library, Columbia University.

Joseph Urban (foreground) and the technical staff of a 1915 production of Edward Sheldon's "The Garden of Paradise," Urban's Broadway debut. Billy Rose Theatre Collection, The New York Public Library for the Performing Arts, Astor, Lenox and Tilden Foundations.

A Tenderloin "street dancer," pictured here in stylish dress typical of turn-of-the-century prostitutes. (Respectable women would not have appeared on the street alone.) Courtesy of The New-York Historical Society, N.Y.C.

The Knights of Columbus "welcome hut" in the middle of the Square, circa 1918, was a precursor of the USO clubs of World War II. Museum of the City of New York.

Presbyterian clergyman Charles H. Parkhurst established the Society for the Prevention of Vice in 1892 to rid the city of prostitution. Courtesy of Timothy J. Gilfoyle.

REV. CHARLES H. PARKHURST, D.D.

PASTOR MADISON SQUARE PRESBYTERIAN CHURCH

PRESIDENT SOCIETY FOR PREVENTION OF CRIME

The Republic at 207 W. 42nd Street was one of three legitimate theaters converted during the 1930s to burlesque houses by Billy Minsky. The Republic's shows, theater critic Brooks Atkinson observed, "were the bawdiest this neighborhood has seen in years." Courtesy of The New-York Historical Society, N.Y.C.

Times Square today: The Rivoli, one of the great movie palaces of the 1920s, became a venue for "adult" films. © 1991 Cervin Robinson.

The Solomon Equities building at 1585 Broadway triumphs over adjacent architectural and redevelopment mediocrity. © 1991 Nathaniel Lieberman.

announced his project the summer before, reached a climax the week of the opening, as the theater's hacks blanketed the metropolitan area with advertisements, news stories, and circus-style posters. "Doubtless there never was in the history of the world a place of amusement or attraction that was so thoroughly, systematically, and consistently advertised," *Billboard* reported. The week before the Wednesday opening, a full-page anouncement appeared in the *New York Times* headlining "The National Theatre." More than an advertisement, it was a messianic manifesto proclaiming a new age of democratic amusement in America:

New York's permanent new amusement institution, the Hippo-drome, is the largest, safest, costliest playhouse in the world and first, single and independent of its kind. America's only real representative amusement institution. Representing a triumphant alliance of capital, experience and genius and an outlay of $3,500,000. Its equal nowhere in the world. Ushering in a glorious new era in amusement history and framed for the tastes and pleasure of the whole people.

Thompson & Dundy proclaimed a superhuman break with history, "Dispossessing the by-gone old age of theatrical routine and circus monotony with stirring progress and rousing reform, breaking free in method, style and price of performance and different and distinct from every other playhouse in construction, equipment and conduct."[41]

After a delay of several months, the Hippodrome opened April 12, 1905, with two productions, *A Yankee Circus on Mars* and *Andersonville, A Story of Wilson's Raiders*. Several of the city's newspapers treated the opening as sensational news with exclamatory headlines. "Bigness was in the air," one paper reported. "Men told each other that this was the biggest hippodrome in the world. 'Big' men sat in the boxes." The *New York Herald* concluded that the Hippodrome had "satisfied the national craving for something that shall be the biggest and most imposing in its dimensions." Everything this opening night, it added, "was to be on Brobdignagian [sic] proportions."[42]

More than just big, the Hippodrome from its opening was associated with play. This massive citadel out of the Arabian Nights with its Corinthian porticos and blinding incandescent billboards was, in the words of a number of newspapers, a big "toy." "The subway's nose is out of joint," noted one New York paper, "the town has a newer toy." Variously, writers called the theater a "playground," a "pleasure palace." The Hippodrome was Thompson & Dundy's "new, gigantic toy. It was also New York's new toy. And New York was hugely pleased," another paper reported. This association with an adult version of childhood, play, and playthings became an indelible and central facet of the theater's identity until it was torn down in 1939.[43]

Thompson opened his great theater with a sermon on play and its precarious status in American culture. In part, *A Yankee Circus on Mars* expanded on the winning formula of his original amusement fantasy, "A Trip to the Moon." As in the case of the world's fair illusion, Thompson began with movement or transport, from this world to another. "I've made so many trips to the moon at Luna Park," he explained shortly before the premier, "that a trip to Mars seemed the most natural thing in the world, or, rather, out of it. The only thing that bothered me was finding an excuse for taking a circus there." The answer to this minor problem was suggested in a newspaper report that the debt-ridden Forepaugh & Sells Brothers' circus was going to be auctioned off.[44]

The significance of this piece of news undoubtedly was not lost on Thompson. *A Yankee Circus on Mars*, with its spectacle of dancing girls and automobile-driving elephants, disclosed Thompson's view of the world. On opening night as many as 6,000 New Yorkers saw this original production about the extraterrestrial rescue of a bankrupt New England circus by the pleasure-loving King Borealis of Mars, an updated version of the children's fairy tale of Santa Claus as the guardian of play and toys. Whisked away in a flying ship from benighted Yankee land and its hostility toward pleasure, the troupe journeys to Mars and discovers there that "work" is "play," and that the planet's strange citizens possess a childlike zest for festive entertainment. The Hippodrome audience was treated to a plenitude of circus acts, Martian choruses and dancers, and as a finale, 150 young women performing the "Dance of the Hours" from Ponchielli's *La Gioconda*, dressed in Edel's costumes representing morning, day, evening, and night, with different lighting effects for each hour. "It was breathless," the *Sun* recounted, "the shifting tender beauty of it; it was unearthly." The ballet and final chorus "fairly made the crowd go mad with the intoxication of sound and sight."[45]

An intermission followed the finale, giving the audience a restful pause before the Civil War romance, *Andersonville*, which revealed for the first time the Hippodrome's water tank. At the conclusion of this production, the tank became the setting for the battle at Rocky Ford, with Union and Confederate cavalry and infantry charging across the stage river. But the hit of the evening was Thompson's dramatic presentation of an adult world of play, freed from the earthbound culture of work and transported to a distant pleasure-loving planet. Thompson had translated a fantasy ordinarily associated with children into an adult fairy tale showcasing the delights of twentieth century life—abundance, happiness, pleasure, play, and escape from care.[46]

To a degree, this was not a unique accomplishment. *A Yankee Circus on Mars* had been preceded by numerous adult versions of children's literature, including the pantomime spectacles, *Mother Goose* and *Humpty Dumpty*, imported from London in 1903 and 1904 by Klaw & Erlanger. The most important domestic productions of children's literature were the popular stage musical of L. Frank Baum's *Wizard of Oz* and its spin-off, *Babes in Toyland*, featuring the music of Victor Herbert. Running at the same time as Thompson's *Society Circus* at the Hippodrome was J. M. Barrie's *Peter Pan*, starring the famed actor of child-man parts, Maude Adams. *A Yankee Circus on Mars*, in other words, was a particularly noteworthy early example of the general adaptation of the literature and fantasies of American children to the domestic stage during the first three decades of the twentieth century, with *Peter Pan* an important contribution from London. Childhood, as impresarios quickly discerned with the success of the stage version of the *Wizard*, presented a profitable new source of stage material, although it had to be updated significantly for adult consumption. Thompson did not need these precedents to convince him of the charm of commercialized and dramatized play, although the general success of such shows on Broadway probably eased his ability to attract financial backing. The Hippodrome represented an expansion and development of the ideology behind Luna Park, both in terms of its uses of industrial technologies to produce amusement and its celebration and advocacy of play and recaptured childhood.[47]

As in all of his previous amusement ventures, Thompson wove incandescent lighting into the fabric of his Hippodrome plots. On one hand, he designed the productions to showcase the marvelous effects which the theater's unmatched lighting equipment could create. Lighting, as Thompson employed it, became enlightenment, a transformative and uplifting power enacted as part of the performance itself. Illumination literally moved the plot of *A Yankee Circus*. The transportation from the deteriorating commonwealth to the festive kingdom of Mars involved Thompson's favorite theme of ascending movement from the darkness of a work-bound Earth to King Borealis's incomparable Queen of the Stars, which, as the national anthem informed the audience, "lights other worlds with it's [sic] sheen." On Mars, the comical entanglement and waltzing romance of the king and the "saucy soubrette" of the circus were enacted against the shimmering background of an artificial aurora borealis. The production concluded with the ballet of the transient phases of light in the "Dance of the Hours."[48]

The success of Thompson's incandescent fairy tale of play led him to design even more spectacular uses of lighting and electricity for his second season of Hippodrome productions, *A Society Circus* and its glimmering finale, an incandescent and aquatic tableau vivant called *The Court of the Golden Fountains*. The first part of the bill followed the formula of *A Yankee*

Circus with the pleasureless land transferred from Vermont to Bohemia; gypsies instead of Martians played the pleasure-loving natives. The thin plot examines the troubles of Lady Volumnia, whose unbounded wealth gives her no pleasure until she meets an itinerant gypsy who brings gaiety to her barren life by suggesting that she sponsor a circus performance with her misbegotten fortune. At the end of the production Lady Volumnia and the gypsy are married, followed by *The Golden Fountains*, which fittingly honors the union of abundance and pleasure.[49]

For this scene Thompson marshaled almost all of the electrical and illuminating power of the Hippodrome as well as the entire main stage and water tank. "When this curtain revealed the climax," the *New York Times* reported, "the audience sat hushed for a moment, and then burst into applause that made what had been given before seem tame." As the curtain rose, the entire stage lighting capacity of the Hippodrome began dimly to illuminate the scene, gradually ascending to full power, directing 10,000 amperes of electrical current at the stage. The tableau thus revealed presented Thompson's stage-picture of a new golden age of abundance and pleasure, an incandescent phantasmagoria. In the background spreading the full width of the stage, costumed wedding guests and gilded extras were arranged on terraces which ascended as high as the proscenium arch. In the midst of the seven-minute revelation of the fountains, the hydraulic plungers beneath the main stage snapped into action, magically lifting the terraces and the cast eight feet above stage level. In the foreground, a large golden ship outlined with small lights and populated with tiers of costumed chorus girls lay moored in the Hippodrome lake. Luminous and feminine aquatic life was scattered about the pool. Gigantic sea shells encrusted with incandescent lights sheltered chorus girls holding strings of glowing pearls—actually circuits of round incandescent lamps. As the curtain rose, illuminated mussels parted to reveal the feminine mollusc within, her face lit by concealed lamps. Thrones composed of electrical bullrushes surrounded the golden boat, each holding a chorus girl in a bower of cattails whose tips were formed by elongated incandescent lamps dyed with the "desired color tone."[50]

A pair of gilded electrical fountains on either side of the golden vessel "spouted forth what looked like liquid flames in all colors of the rainbow." Chorus girl caryatids appeared to hold up the fountains, as underwater lamps focused shimmering light on them. Two brilliant searchlights—one in and one above each of the fountains—produced the rainbow effects with multicolored light. Women clutching illuminated wreaths surmounted dolphins whose eyes glowed with green lamps. Another 1,700 lamps studded the background scenery. Live swans navigated among incandescent lilypads and other aquatic electrification, and a cloud of white doves descended from the peak of the auditorium's dome.[51]

264

Intoxicated with the success of his two amusement ventures, Luna Park and the Hippodrome, Thompson planned to outdo his depiction of the new golden age of abundance and pleasure the following season with "a *ballet* spectacle as the world has never seen." The showman's description reveals the messianic zeal at the heart of his enterprise: "It's to be the biggest thing of all, the Creation. But I don't call it that. I call it 'The Birth of the Elements.'" Beyond the hyperbolic pretense of producing his personal version of Genesis, "The Birth of the Elements" demonstrates the way in which Thompson employed illumination as a medium for manufacturing as well as for giving meaning to stage fantasy. It should come as no surprise that the production was to begin "with darkness."

> The different groups of dancers, as they come on, will suggest the first development of life on the earth—the vegetables, and flowers, and animals. The stage will keep growing lighter and more brilliant; the scenery will change, until finally we have man and woman, the light floods the stage, the people crowd into the picture, the scene changes into the most brilliant stage spectacle you ever saw, the chorus bursts out, . . . and then, at the climax, a hundred white doves are released up in the dome of the auditorium and they swoop down with a rush and perch on the stage as the curtain falls.[52]

By the time this account of his plans was published in July 1906, Thompson & Dundy had lost the Hippodrome to Gates and his fellow powers at the U.S. Realty Company. The initial sensation of the Hippodrome had appeared to confirm Thompson & Dundy's exaggerated claims for their own unique foresight and genius. A string of mighty Hippodromes in major American cities, fed by productions emanating from the Sixth Avenue theater, seemed a certainty after the first season. *A Yankee Circus* went on tour in Chicago, Philadelphia, and Boston, the only cities where Thompson & Dundy could find a stage remotely large enough for their extravaganza. Thompson returned from abroad in February 1906 and announced the imminent construction of a London version of the New York Hippodrome. All of these plans, however, proved illusory. Shocked by an unexpected decline in attendance during the run of *A Society Circus* and alarmed by Thompson's production extravagance, Gates and the Hippodrome's other backers battled with the producers to raise ticket prices. *Variety* reported that Thompson had further infuriated his investors with plans for an amusement park on Manhattan island, which Gates saw as a competitor with the Hippodrome. U.S. Realty tendered the theater to more experienced and businesslike promoters. Lee and J. J. Shubert took over the Hippodrome early in the summer of 1906 as Thompson & Dundy were ushered out the door. The "triumphant alliance of capital, experience and genius" had withered scarcely a year after it had coalesced.[53]

Although the partners controlled the theater for only fourteen months, Thompson & Dundy's proprietorship of the Hippodrome fixed their places in contemporary American culture. More than mere showmen, Thompson and Dundy, but especially Thompson, because of his youth, energy, and flare for self-promotion, were performers who advertised themselves as representative figures of twentieth century America, living embodiments of modernity and progress. "It is true that they had attracted much attention with their colossal undertaking at Luna Park," observed Robert Grau, an astute contemporary writer on the theater, "but it was the Hippodrome that caused these mere boys to be regarded with open wonder. When inaugurated, the entire enterprise was so wholly beyond anything New Yorkers had ever known, that it really took a year to reach a gait." The theatrical daily, *The Sunday Telegraph*, hailed Thompson as a paragon of his age, "a wonder—a type of young man not possible in any age but this, nor in any country but this, where energy has no limit and success follows fast on the heels of endeavor. Maybe it is the pace that kills, but what a glorious funeral a man may have!"[54]

In the interviews of the two partners, Dundy invariably referred writers to Thompson as the creative genius of the partnership. The magic of finance, which was Dundy's occupation, attracted far less attention in the popular press than the enchantment which Thompson conjured. Older by a decade and recognizable by the ridiculous toupee he wore, Dundy played the role of the practical straight man burdened with finding the money to pay for the wizard's extravagances.[55]

With the announcement of the Hippodrome, Thompson's personality emerged as a preeminent aspect of Thompson & Dundy amusements, so much so that Thompson became a performance in himself, virtually indistinguishable from the content of his Coney Island and theatrical productions. He seemed to represent modernity itself, acting out its most frenetic characteristics—youth, energy, dreams, gaiety, speed, move-ment, and play. According to the Chicago theater trade magazine *Show World*, he was the "ideal promoter of the Twentieth Century—a man who dreams things and then goes ahead and brings them into realization." Or, as one newspaper pegged him, he was "Frederic Thompson, capitalist, amusement inventor and perennial small boy."[56]

Thompson had not reached his thirty-first birthday when he inaugu-rated the construction of the Hippodrome. But the source of his status as a "boy-wonder" of New York extended beyond his numerical age. The development of Thompson's imagination, as contemporary observers figured it, had been prematurely arrested, leaving him in a magical middle ground where he was neither child nor man but a marvelous combination of the two. In the articles later published under his name, Thompson never claimed outright to be a child-man, although he contributed directly to this construction by promoting himself as a toymaker and his amusements as antidotes to the culture-wide illness of lost childhood. But the chroniclers of his accomplishments unquestioningly accepted this reading of his personality and attributed his extraordinary success to his magical boyishness. Those who know Thompson, according to one newspaper writer, "are familiar with a peculiarly faraway infantile smile which comes over him sometimes when he is sitting alone. Mr. Dundy, who finances Mr. Thompson's dreams, has said that he is always made nervous by that smile." Other writers noted his "boyish way" of laughing, or his "soft voiced, pink cheeked, lazy moving" collegiate youthfulness and insouciance. The audacity to build the Hippodrome seemed to flow from the unconsciousness of youth. "Only a young man, and ahead of his time at that, could have conceived and carried out such an enterprise," observed the circus veteran, W. W. Cole. To the popular novelist Samuel Merwin, who was the most determined student of Thompson's career, the showman's life seemed scripted out of Barrie's stage play, *Peter Pan:*

> For he is a boy who has never grown up. He is a sort of everyday Peter Pan who has lived to carry out absolutely his boyish dreams. No grown man could conceivably have done what he has done, for your grown man would have known at the start that it was impossible. His executive ability and physical and mental stamina are those of maturity; his dreams and his courage are wholly the dreams and the courage of youth. The combined result is one of the rarest and one of the finest things in the world. Apparently the only danger in his path is the danger that some day he may suddenly grow up. If this should happen, he will be lost. It is sheer, sublime boldness that has carried him thus far; it is sheer boldness that must carry him through.[57]

Thompson seemed to combine the rationality of the mature capitalist with the instinct, generosity, imagination, and audacity of the child. During the winter and spring of 1906 New York had two Peter Pans, one played by Maude Adams in Barrie's enormously popular play and the other in the brilliant figure of Frederic Thompson. Both seemed to respond to a longing among urban Americans to return to a lost Never-Never-Land of childhood. Contemporaries pointed to Thompson as the exemplar of a new kind of creative, energetic individualism which was needed to revitalize American life and to realize the delights of the new century. Thompson prototypically captured the youthful spirit of vitality and "high-level consumption" which, as Lary May has shown, were celebrated in the screen and private lives of Douglas Fairbanks and Mary Pickford in the late 1910s and 1920s.[58]

As an "everyday Peter Pan," Thompson seemed also to possess the primitive's nonrational access to the imaginative material of his dream consciousness. Thompson, his contemporaries maintained, did not generate his ideas or plans in words or through rational thought process or in the numbers of an accountant's ledger weighing costs against revenues. Instead, he thought in nonconceptual dream pictures or visions which occurred to him during moments of inspirational reverie. As Merwin noted, "the man has a curious and extremely interesting habit of thinking in symbols. He glimpses his big idea shining through a nebula of artistic detail, and at once he soars to meet it and lay hold on it." Mere mortals, contended Merwin, cannot hope to achieve such flights into "the land of daydreams in which his subconscious mind seems to dwell." Thompson passed on his dreams to his more pragmatically minded lieutenants or "broker[s] in beauty" in the form of crude, childlike, almost primitive sketches, which Merwin characterized as "singularly meaningless drawings" augmented with a "torrent of enthusiastic description." Words seemed "almost too clumsy a medium for the flow of his ideas," according to Merwin. "His enthusiasm is irresistible. He sweeps you out of yourself. He makes you see visions. With him you ignore the tremendous difficulties in the way of molding men and women and materials into dream-pictures." Thompson's visual imagination was particularly suited to a commercial culture which increasingly used display techniques to arouse the consumer's appetite and which was simultaneously expanding the use of mechanically reproduced images in advertising, magazines, newspapers, and soon, moving pictures as a means of attracting the consumer. Thompson thought in gorgeous pictures which he then duplicated not on canvas, as he had aspired to do during his art school years, but on a stage as large as the Hippodrome or Luna Park before an audience of millions.[59]

As a primitive or child, Thompson had little sense of history. He was constantly making over himself as well as the world around him, claiming to defy all precedents, limitations, qualifications, and doubts. The world, in his mind, was a plastic medium full of possibilities for his powerful imagination, oblivious to all obstacles, physical, financial, or otherwise. Thompson "never stops to think whether a thing can be done or not," the *Sun* observed. "The moment his imagination shapes a plan, in that moment is the practicability of the plan settled. . . . Nobody ever did such a thing before? . . . So much the better; originality pays."[60]

To the journalists of the time, the showman seemed the highest human expression of energy, movement, and speed, exhibiting the same qualities of modern life that his stage and amusement park productions celebrated in dramatic form. A writer for the *New York Herald*, after enumerating the many uses of electricity at the Hippodrome, declared Thompson "something of a human dynamo himself . . . [who] radiates energy and good humor at a high voltage." Merwin marveled that the showman "doesn't burn up" with the heat of his thinking. The magazine *Human Life* claimed "His brain is always seething like a freshly charged electric battery." Innumerable publications referred to his nervous habit of clinking silver quarters in one hand while holding a cigar in the other. Thompson, it seemed, was never at rest.[61]

Like his productions, Thompson seemed to thrive on incessant movement, an obsession which he indulged with the purchase and exploitation of the new technologies of speed and communication. He reportedly established new records for intercontinental travel as he ransacked Europe and northern Africa for circus acts. He and Dundy kept three cars in a garage beneath their Luna Park office because, he explained, "when we need one we need it as a man needs a pistol in Texas." The riches gleaned from Luna Park and his other ventures enabled Thompson to purchase or lease the era's ultimate adult toys, pleasure and racing yachts and, after 1910, aeroplanes. Yachts and oceangoing liners, with their alluring speed and luxury, were a favorite melodramatic plot device in many of Thompson's stage and amusement park productions.[62]

Much as he merchandised and acted out his fascination with speed, communications, and movement, Thompson sold the commodities of good cheer, joy, and gaiety—the emotions widely ascribed to childhood—at his various amusement marketplaces and demonstrated their efficacy in the conduct of his daily life. Asked how to "succeed as a showman," Thompson responded that the sure way was "to be cheerful. Nobody can succeed with a 'grouch.' Good spirits and success go hand in hand."[63]

In building his image, Thompson publicized his well-meaning prodigality, not only in his purchase of amusement technologies for his own enjoyment, but also in his theatrical and Coney Island productions. "It has been demonstrated . . . ," Thompson stated after the opening of the Hippodrome, "that we consider our audiences first and our check books afterward, and this will always be our rule in giving to New York the very best entertainment it is possible to provide." The showman came to be portrayed as a public-spirited spendthrift, distributing the commodities of play and happiness instead of hoarding away his money. "He doesn't care for money itself," Thompson's assistant, Harry Kline, told the *Cleveland Leader*. "It is just made to be spent in doing something else." As Merwin observed of Thompson's Hippodrome, "There is no spirit, in this house, of an employer who is merely working against the day when he shall have money enough to withdraw to his yacht. In spite of his driving executive ability, Thompson seems to have very little money sense." Thompson's self-promotion was indistinguishable from his generosity. He feted his employees, hosted both newspaper delivery boys and metropolitan newspaper executives at Luna Park, and organized an abundant succession of circus parades to announce the opening of his various productions. An endless advertiser and self-promoter, he nevertheless demonstrated almost no desire to store away his income; he displayed instead a decidedly irrational desire to be known as the Santa Claus of New York.[64]

As the Santa Claus of New York and the proprietor of the city's biggest toy, Thompson translated the childworld of playthings and fantasy literature into the new commodity forms of a mass consumer culture. Thompson & Dundy seemed to have fulfilled their incandescent promise of luxurious "Entertainment For The Masses" by marshaling the modern technologies of industrial production and the systematic organization of scientific management to the service of the imagination. *A Yankee Circus on Mars* and *The Court of the Golden Fountains* were not simply spectacles or hodgepodge collections of variety entertainments, but theatrical myth-making which suggested that the promise of American life extended beyond the utilitarian sphere of work and self-denial to encompass the realm of desire and pleasure. In future years moralistic critics would acidulously condemn Thompson's creations for promoting a misleading, false religion with escapist fantasy—what Lewis Mumford would deride in 1925 as "architectural anaesthesia" and "the malady of the unreal." The thrust of these criticisms was that, in Mumford's words, such "architectural hocus-pocus" gives the false illusion of spiritual fulfillment by escaping modernity, whether in the form of overcrowded cities, exploitative working conditions, or disabling poverty. The "Architecture of Escape" evades social reality instead of confronting it. Thompson was a masterful merchandiser of escape, but he offered the Hippodrome not so much as an evasion of modernity as its possible fulfillment, the delightful abundance of the American consumer economy—play, color, speed, luxury, lights, energy—brought together by youthful entrepreneurs and fashioned as marvelous, dreamlike entertainments for a democratic audience of millions. The Hippodrome promised to transport its audience away from the benighted city of work to luminous worlds of play. As with Thompson's original amusement sensation, "A Trip to the Moon," it was an imaginary journey that was emancipating even as it was concocted out of canvas, colored lights, and paint.[65]

13

JOSEPH URBAN

Gregory F. Gilmartin

ARL MARIA Georg Joseph Urban—his friends would call him Pepi or Dickus (Fatty)—was born in Vienna in 1872 into a bourgeois Catholic family.[1] His father was director of the city school system, a noted educational reformer. It was against his father's wishes—at first, without even his knowledge—that Urban studied architecture at the Technische Hochschule and the Academy of Fine Arts. He became a protégé of Karl Freiherr von Hasenauer, the director of the Academy's architecture section and the last of the great eclectic Ringstrasse architects, and after graduating in 1893, Urban worked in Hasenauer's office. He also organized the Siebener Club, a group of former classmates and young artists that included the architects Joseph Maria Olbrich and Josef Hoffmann and the painters Koloman Moser and Max Kurzweil, figures who would soon become prominent in the Secession. The Siebener Club fostered an active collaboration of artists and architects, foreshadowing the Secession's concern with a visual *Gesamtkunstwerk*, and it was there that the international art nouveau movement—first encountered by the Club in the pages of *The Studio*—began to evolve into the Viennese *Jugendstil*.[2]

Urban, however, grew estranged from the Siebener Club over a series of personal, political, and philosophical disputes, and when the Secession was formed in 1897 he was not a member. He formed instead a partnership with the artist Heinrich Lefler, his future brother-in-law, and the two eventually led a second secession from the Künstlerhaus, forming the Hagenbund in 1899. The Hagenbund was an association of progressive architects and artists, both *Jugendstil* and impressionist. In 1902 it acquired its own gallery, a heady *Jugendstil* design by Urban, and it enjoyed aristocratic and government support.[3]

Urban and Lefler, in the meantime, enjoyed a diverse practice. They collaborated on book illustrations (Lefler rendering the human figures, Urban the decorative borders and architectural backgrounds),[4] paintings (their *Mask of the Red Death* won the *Kaiserpreis* in 1899), postage stamps, furniture, exhibits at the Hagenbund and at foreign expositions (including the interiors of the Austrian Art Pavilion at St. Louis in 1904), a hunting lodge in Hungary for Count Carl Esterhazy, and villas in the Viennese suburbs and the resort town of Semmering. Their work also extended to the theater. From 1900 to 1903 Lefler was Gustav Mahler's director of productions at the Vienna Court Opera[5], Urban, Lefler, and the painter Alexander Goltz later collaborated on *Faust* and Schnitzler's *Der Junge Medardus* at the Hofburg Theater; and the Hagenbund itself instituted a sort of protocabaret, with programs ranging from modern dance to short plays and Urban's own performances of *fiaker lieder*.

Urban's career in Vienna climaxed, and ended, when the Hagenbund was placed in charge of the Imperial Jubilee of 1908. Urban's casualness with government funds erupted in scandal, and in 1909 the Emperor revoked the Hagenbund's imperial favor. Urban resigned from the group in order to save it and abandoned Vienna for a second career, this time as a designer and director on the international opera circuit.[6]

Between 1909 and 1914 Urban wandered between the stages of London, Paris, Berlin, Budapest, and a slew of provincial German theaters. His most regular position was as director of productions at the Boston Opera, a post obtained with the help of Claude Debussy, who admired his production of *Pelléas et Mélisande*.[7] The war bankrupted the Boston Opera, however, and Urban's Broadway debut, a 1915 production of Edward Sheldon's *The Garden of Paradise*, left him insolvent and stranded. It led to his engagement, however, by Florenz Ziegfeld, an association that lasted until Ziegfeld's death in 1932.

From 1915 to 1925, Urban was active almost exclusively as a stage designer, and his life revolved around three patrons. For Ziegfeld he designed musicals and the annual editions of *The Midnight Frolic* and *The Follies*; for Otto Kahn, dozens of productions at the Metropolitan Opera; for William Randolph Hearst, art direction for the Cosmopolitan Film Studios, an organization intended to make Hearst's lover, the former Ziegfeld girl Marion Davies, into the nation's leading movie star.

In 1926, however, Urban resumed his architectural practice. Ziegfeld's Palm Beach social circle commissioned a series of houses and clubs in a lavish, "Mediterranean" style, inaugurating the most productive phase of his career, with designs for theaters, nightclubs, and hotels. He became a leading figure in the evolution of art deco, drawing on expressionist and modernist vocabularies to create a complex synthesis that came to characterize the style in America.

Urban's role in America was that of a bridge linking the forms and techniques of European modernism with American commercial art, which, whether theatrical or architectural, is so dominated by concerns of marketability that it has difficulty innovating from within. Commercial art can be cannibalistic, falling back on successful formulas that are eventually designated "conventions," and thus it tends towards standardization. But since this provokes its own crisis of marketing, commercial art looks to high, or at least higher, culture; it seeks a new generation of aesthetic themes that it can adapt to its own ends. Urban proved an especially valuable property in this regard, for his entire career was devoted to digesting the reigning modernism of the given moment.

We know that Urban's favorite opera was *Die Meistersinger*.[8] That he was a Wagnerite was typical of his generation, but what was unusual was for him to lay such stress on this particular opera. His very first act, when he embarked on an independent career in 1895, was to head for Nuremberg, and his drawings of the town were his first published works.[9]

Die Meistersinger provided him with an aesthetic and a social model. It was designed to be a popular opera, and the drama itself celebrates a reconciliation of traditional song and the "music of the future," of the volk and the avant-garde. In the process, however, innovation is tempered: Hans Sachs lectures Walter von Stolzing on the need to discipline his feverish abandon with rules that shape but do not bind his art, the arias and ensembles of grand opera return to Wagner's oeuvre, and the chromaticism of Walter's Act I Trial Song yields to a diatonic C-major in Act III. It concludes with a resolution of social and aesthetic tensions. A revolutionary aesthetic becomes an evolutionary one, and a rebellious individual aligns himself with the interests of an existing social order.

One can hear the echo of Hans Sachs in the Hagenbund's program. In answer to the motto carved on Olbrich's Secession Building—"To the age its art, to art its freedom"—the Hagenbund published a conspicuously qualified manifesto:

> We recognize tradition, cherish and love it, but do not cling to it.
> We admire progress, strive for forceful expression, but shun sensationalism.
> We stand by youth and will remain young because of it. To youth—Eternity.[10]

This emphasis on youth came to mean a devotion to modernity rather than modernism. In the 1890s, Urban assimilated the art nouveau; in the 1900s, both Hoffmann's *Secessionstil* and the monumental *Junge Klassizität* of Berlin; in the 1920s, he incorporated German Expressionism into his repertoire; and by 1930, the machined vocabulary of the International Style. His aim was always to "express our modern life" or create "an expression of modern trends,"[11] to celebrate the present moment rather than reform it. He was brilliantly facile with each permutation of style, and buoyantly optimistic: what Schoenberg saw as a "death dance of principles,"[12] Urban saw as the march of fashion.

In the twentieth century the Hagenbund's manifesto will no longer pass for a ringing polemic, but it did provide a kind of blueprint for Urban's career. In Vienna he hewed to the nineteenth century model of the artist serving the needs of both the bourgeoisie and the state. His particular talent, however, was to manipulate aesthetic progressivism to represent the totality and stability of Austrian culture. He was not part of the Vienna of "fragmented critical energies."[13] His stylistic innovations, rather than social or political reforms, were presented as evidence that the empire was not moribund.

Many of his early works, though not all, appear to be as stylistically radical as those of the Secession, but their iconography invariably stresses themes of social and historical continuity that contrast vividly with the oedipal imagery associated with the Secession. Alfred Roller's 1898 illustration for the first issue of *Ver Sacrum* depicted a box tree whose roots burst their container; in the same year Urban collaborated with Lefler and the Hagenbund painter Alexander Goltz on the decor of the Rathauskeller. Their murals depicted, for instance, the merchant class of Vienna bowing in homage to the Hapsburg throne.[14] The style was conciliatory as well, as much medieval as art nouveau. In 1899, the year the Secession exhibited Arthur Strasser's *Mark Antony*, an image of the idle aristocrat as a besotted, obese despot, Urban designed a hunting lodge for Count Carl Esterhazy.[15] In its plan and massing the building is a baroque chateau, but one that has burst to life with art nouveau ornament. The interiors are dominated by images of warfare, the hunt, and sexual conquest as the origins and prerogatives of the aristocracy. In 1902 he designed the Hagenbund galleries, modeled on Olbrich's facade for the Ernst Ludwig Haus in Darmstadt. Olbrich inscribed over his door the words of Hermann Bahr: "The artist will show his world, which never was, nor ever will be." Urban's facade was marked by its social imagery, with an image of Pallas Athena—not the artist—as mother of the arts.[16]

In America Urban found a surrogate for the centralized state in the notion of commercial culture. Here, modernity was presented as evidence that capitalism was leading society's evolution toward more progressive and democratic forms. Urban shifted his political allegiances in the United States: references to the "decaying aristocracy of Europe" crop up repeatedly in his writing,[17] and historical eclecticism is presented as a style that must be superseded because it is so tainted by allusions to tyranny and conservatism. His design for the Metropolitan Opera House, it was explained, was not a monumental urban set piece in the European manner, nor was it clad in baroque pomp, because "American society is too democratic and American business is too progressive" to allow for aristocratic grandeur.[18]

274

Urban's willingness to let contemporary society determine the content and shape of his art was controversial throughout his career; it flew in the face of artistic idealism. In the 1890s it had been the source of his rift with Olbrich; in the 1910s it caused consternation among the contributors to *Theatre Arts*; in the 1920s it aroused the ire of Lewis Mumford. Mumford accused him of representing "the aesthetic collywobbles of the pusher, the advertiser, the booster." Kenneth Macgowan lamented the promiscuity with which he accepted work in the theater rather than "waiting for the one play a year" worthy of him, while Sheldon Cheney accused him of a "selfish exploitation of his own talent."[19]

Urban, then, was almost destined to succeed on Broadway. He brought to the *Ziegfeld Follies* "Sensations, intuitions of contemporary life, the spectacle in which we are a part, the Present, in which we feel the surging of our own passions, the Modern."[20] Before Urban arrived in New York the *Follies* was much like any other revue, distinguished only by a somewhat more beautiful chorus line, a more harmonious sense of color and costume, and a bit more taste in the handling of nudity. Urban contributed the "New Stagecraft" that he had first brought to Boston and this, more than any other factor, ensured that Ziegfeld is remembered more than fifty years after his death.

The Boston productions were of great significance for the American theater. They marked perhaps the first break with romantic naturalism on a professional American stage, the first declaration that scene painting was an art form, and the first blow against the scenic studios. True, this occurred in the relative obscurity of the Boston Opera House, but his audience included the aesthetes of Harvard and the circle of students attracted to George Pierce Baker's drama class, figures such as Kenneth Macgowan, Robert Edmond Jones, Lee Simonson, Deems Taylor, Sheldon Cheney, and Edward Sheldon.[21]

Urban arrived in Boston with the reputation of being "a leader but not a revolutionary" in the German theater,[22] and this was apt. His sets often showed the influence of Reinhardt's productions in Berlin and especially of the designs of Alfred Roller, Ernst Stern, and Emil Orlik. In form they were simple and architectural, abandoning false perspective and painted wings. They used changes in level to control the scale of the playing area and achieve dramatic compositions of actors. They abandoned footlights for spotlights; falling from above, the light accentuated the plasticity of both the stage architecture and the actors. Light was also used for psychological effect: in the set for *Monna Vanna*, for instance, the disposition of light and shadow enhances the sense of the stage's depth, focuses attention on the principal actors at the rear, and lends a menacing character to the silhouetted soldiers left and right.[23]

The most striking aspect of Urban's stage design, however, was his use

275

of color, and this too was a function of light. Urban had picked up color theory from the Hagenbund's impressionists, and a pointillist method of painting. His sets were painted with spots and stipples of contrasting colors and appeared gray in natural light. In colored light, however, his skycloths acquired a sense of atmospheric depth, and even his most realistic designs possessed an unearthly richness of hue. This escape from the literalism of the painted stage was originally an attempt to capture the dreamlike quality that Nietzsche ascribed to the Apollinian "illusions" of Greek theater. It made for stages that were "more than real life . . . gay-er . . . more dramatic . . . an enhancement of life," as Urban put it.[24]

Urban brought to the *Follies* a linear, stylized aesthetic, a talent for bizarre and sometimes discreetly erotic images, and brilliant color. He also employed certain strategies designed to counter the episodic character of the revue (which was exacerbated by the fact that the music was often culled from several composers). Urban's sets were designed before any other part of the production had been fixed. This allowed him to use visual leitmotifs that reappeared through the evening, and to develop a pattern of color sequences. The 1915 *Follies* was known as the "Blue Follies," for instance, and the color scheme was dominated by the sky, "a sky without cloud or star," as John Corbin wrote in the *Times*,

> but the coloring, the lighting of this sky has exhausted the resources of the modern theatre. It is a deep and magic blue; velvety in texture, yet suggesting limitless regions of heaven. It is a symbol, if you wish, of the Mediterranean . . . and it dominates the successive scenes with a sense of imaginative unity only less persuasive, compelling, than that of music.[25]

There was also an architectural strategy at work in the *Follies*, and this had a curious provenance. When Urban published his drawings of the Ziegfeld Theatre and—pointing to its combination of a proscenium, apron stage, and "portals"—described it as "Shakespearean,"[26] few of his readers understood him. Urban was drawing, however, on a tradition of mistaken German attempts to reconstruct the Globe Theatre that began with Lautenschlager's attempt in Munich in 1888 and continued with the theaters of Max Littmann. Some of Reinhardt's productions of Shakespeare used the same model. Lautenschlager had been unwilling to believe that the Globe was entirely unlike the nineteenth century wing theater; he interpreted references to an "inner stage" and a "curtain" to mean that the Globe had possessed a miniature proscenium equipped with illusionistic scenery, that this sat behind an apron, and that the proscenium frame contained doors to the apron.[27]

Urban's cleverness lay in realizing that this stage was useful for certain hybrid genres of theater: the Italian "number" opera, the Broadway musical, and the revue. Since the New Amsterdam Theatre had a pronounced proscenium, the *Follies* sets were a slight compromise. Urban, however, relied on this use of a spatially distinct forestage accessed from the sides—an intimate and shallow playing for comedians, solo vocalists, and transitional scenes. Behind this lay a drop curtain in a second, inner proscenium, and this stage was the province of Urban's spectacular scenic transformations.

The manipulation of this stage provided a sense of architectural rhythm the *Follies* had previously lacked, and the strategy was quickly taken up by other producers. Urban applied it to the musical as well, where it allowed for a kind of rhetorical articulation of the two time scales found in both opera and the Broadway musical. There is real time and there is musical time: events pass on stage in dialogue or recitative in a tempo not too dissimilar from real life, but the aria or song follows the constraints of a musical structure. Action halts or slows as a character gives vent to his or her feelings, and real time is suspended as the singer follows the musical logic of his argument to a rhetorical climax. This is as true of *Showboat* as it is of *Cosi fan tutte*, and in both cases Urban's stage architecture allowed the singer to literally step out of the action, to leave the stage set for the median zone of the forestage and address himself directly to the audience—whether imploring it for sympathy, bubbling over in joy, or merely displaying his virtuosity. In *Showboat* the drop curtain often closed behind the singer during the last reprise (Kern's tunes are mostly composed in an AABA structure) or during an encore (encores were carefully planned as part of the production). This "puts the artist in intimate touch with the audience," Urban wrote. "He is no longer a dim figure, lost in the atmospheric background; he is in the same room with his listeners."[28] These few moments of solo performance allowed the stage-hands time to roll the next set into place. When the applause died down the curtain went up immediately on a new scene, and these rapid changes of scene contributed a sense of dramatic urgency to the production.

Urban's use of the apron stage to engage an audience spatially in the performance stemmed from two sources. One was Urban's own history as a singer in Vienna. He specialized in *fiaker lieder*, singing them first in impromptu performances at the Café Sperl and Zum Blauen Freihaus, later at the Hagenbund's cabaret, in aristocratic salons, and at private dinners for Empress Elizabeth. In all of these situations the spatial relationship between Urban and his audience was of the utmost intimacy and allowed for a certain reciprocity between the two.[29]

The second influence was Max Reinhardt, whose work Urban knew since at least 1906. They were acquainted by 1910, and Urban summered with Reinhardt's circle on the Lido in the 1920s.

Urban's unbuilt theaters—the projects for the Metropolitan Opera and the Reinhardt Theatre, the speculative Music Center and Jewish Art Theatre—were published by *Theatre Arts* in 1929, and were all concerned with an attempt to break down the rigid spatial division of the proscenium theatre.[30] At the opera house, ancillary stages, screened by colonnades, would have flanked the proscenium. When used in concert the three playing areas would have enveloped a portion of the audiences, and the coffered proscenium could, as in Urban's perspective, function as part of the stage set itself.

The Music Center—Roxy's inspiration for Radio City Music Hall—develops the same theme, but Urban added a color organ controlling bands of concealed light in the auditorium ceiling. The color and intensity of light would have been integrated with the performance, as in Scriabin's tone poems—and in silent movie theaters.

The most subtle of Urban's designs, however, was for the Reinhardt Theatre, commissioned as part of Otto Kahn's effort to convince the director to establish a New York base. Here the apron stage is actually an oval surrounding the orchestra level seating. The musicians were placed in a gallery at the top of the auditorium. The actors could approach the stage up a flight of stairs where the orchestra pit was usually placed; for those sitting in the orchestra level, the actors would seem to rise out of the ranks of the audience itself. All of these strategies were meant to envelop the audience, spatially and acoustically, and thus make of it a silent chorus participating in the action.

Had any of these projects been built it might have helped correct the public image of Urban. As it was, a "myth of Urban" developed, as Kenneth Macgowan complained, a myth of "gargantuan swaths of color; stairs, platforms, pyramids of carpentry; pearls and pillars in the amber moonlight; rivers of roses; Wanamaker's entire drapery department on parade, all in the endless stream of pictures turned out by the scenic trust to interfere with the tunes of Irving Berlin."[31]

This myth made Urban famous and paid for a lavish household. Yet there was a curious frustration to his first decade in America, the period of his heyday as a stage designer. He had become a household name, there was a fad for "Urban blue" and "Urban curtains," yet his career was at a standstill. He made no secret about being an architect, but the crowds who gasped at his stage sets had no wish to build an Urban home to match their curtains. His commissions were pitifully few: some minor work at the Ziegfeld estate, a renovation of Reisenweber's in 1919, the St. Regis Roof Garden in 1922. He opened the Wiener Werkstätte of America in 1922, in a suite of *Secessionstil* rooms he had designed, and promptly lost his investment. He designed a few *Secessionstil* film sets for Hearst—*Young Diana* and *Enchantment*—but was forced to give it up. Such works "do not appeal to conservative people of established taste and fashion," William Laurel Harris wrote in *Good Furniture*, "but rather to progressive leaders in present-day ideas who feel that in our times there must be progress and perpetual change in decorative arts as there is in all the arts and sciences."[32]

These leaders had at first but few followers. When Urban resumed his architectural practice in the mid-1920s, it was because clients admired his historical sets for Hearst's ponderous costume dramas. Mar-a-Lago, the stupendously vulgar Post-Hutton house in Palm Beach, then home to the Trumps, was closely related to the film *Zandar the Great*.

The Follies had been successful because they were modern, but Urban's dilemma was that in the 1910s and early 1920s Americans seemed determined to keep modernity safely contained behind a row of footlights. Even on Broadway, as Oliver Sayler observed, the public hailed "novelty, experiment, in the revue, while shying skittishly from it" in vaudeville or serious drama.[33] Modernity was thought of as the province of *Follies*, *Vanities*, and *Scandals*, or as the Shuberts' revue put it, *The Passing Show*. That last title (borrowed from an earlier revue, just as the Shuberts' stage designers often parroted Urban) was especially apt: it implied a stationary observer, a witness to change who remains fundamentally untouched by it.

The mid-1920s saw that invisible barrier begin to break down, and modernity become a driving force in American architecture. There were a variety of reasons for this: the 1916 zoning law undermined classical canons; the influx of borrowed money in real estate development required an acceleration of the construction process, achieved by replacing handicraft with industrial techniques; America's failure to participate in the 1925 Exposition des Arts Décoratifs played upon the nation's cultural insecurity; the opulent historicism of the new movie theaters and middle-class lunchrooms led to the desire for a new "high" style; the propaganda of the business community, stressing the progressive nature of capitalism, prompted a demand for an equally progressive architectural style.

Modernity was also discovered to be a valuable marketing tool. A progressive architectural design was sufficiently traditional if its connections to the past were recognizable to a broad public—the building was not threateningly strange nor likely to be misread—yet it was novel enough to be presented as "new and improved." In many ways the boom did convey genuine benefits to the public—the offices and apartments of the 1920s were significant improvements—but Urban's contributions were again confined to the realm of representation.

In 1926, when Urban anonymously told the *Times* of his plans for a skyscraper opera house for the Metropolitan, his argument for this solution was basically pictorial: "There is only one style of architecture that would do for a new opera house in New York, and that is the modern New York style. It should be representative of New York, a skyscraper with towers and terraces in the revised Babylonian style of New York."[34]

It would have been truer to New York to point out that rents from commercial space would provide a subsidy for the opera company, and to design a building that would produce as much rental income as possible. Urban's first inclination, however, was to translate a European conception of architectural parlance to a city of skyscrapers. The drum-shaped mass of his office building was an attempt to magnify the form of a Roman amphitheater, and this overriding concern for pregnant imagery led Urban to a solution that was illegal and impractical, closer to *Metropolis* than to New York.

I mention this to clarify Urban's position in the art deco insurgency. By the late 1920s, Urban, Raymond Hood, Ely Jacques, and Ralph Walker had become New York's most prominent architectural celebrities. They had succeeded in wresting control of architectural culture from the gentleman architects of the previous generation; they had made their reputations with commercial rather than domestic or monumental commissions; they were all identified with a progressive aesthetic and agreed that this was the proper style for a dynamic commercial culture (and they all met at Mori's Restaurant on Friday afternoons to drink frothy cocktails concocted by Urban).[35] Urban, however, never truly shared the pragmatism of his American colleagues and never pictured himself as a businessman-architect whose first task was to maximize the return on a client's investment. He lacked their desire for reform as well. While Raymond Hood sought to rationalize the urbanism of the skyscraper city by calling for a city of freestanding towers, Urban merely demanded a richer palette of "new surfaces . . . flashing enamels, colored glass, metal trim [and] all the new methods of illumination—from panels of frosted glass . . . to tubes of vapor light."[36]

It was on this level that Urban contributed to the art deco. He was unique among his colleagues in that he had been a progressive stylist for thirty years. He encouraged Hood's use of polychromy and is said to have suggested the black and gold color scheme of the American Radiator Building.[37] Urban's adoption of expressionist crystalline geometries and his use of intricately scaled murals to dissolve wall surfaces, as at the Ziegfeld Theatre and the St. Regis Roof Garden, influenced Walker's interiors. Urban also helped place Viennese draftsmen from the Hoffmann school in Kahn's office.[38]

Urban's energies were concentrated on developing the carnival aspects of the city. His description of the Reinhardt Theatre project in the *Times* was headlined "Wedding Theatre Beauty to Ballyhoo." Parts of the article are based on Harvey Wiley Corbett's 1924 meditation on Hood's American Radiator Building, a marriage of architecture and advertising, but the tone is different. Corbett was careful to justify Hood's commercialism:

> Commercialism in its present significance spells gradual freedom and liberty for the average man. . . . Our modern civilization, in contrast with that of the Pharaohs, is formed upon the idea of service to the many. The mainspring of that service is advertising . . . the animating agency behind the commercial age. It would be strange indeed if architecture were not affected by this spirit.[39]

Urban distilled this into a far balder message:

> Architecture and advertising—the two great practical arts of America—were bound to collide. At their highest there is indeed a natural affinity between the two. A beautiful building is indeed the sandwich board of its owner.[40]

Urban was willing to apply this last proposition literally. The facade of the Ziegfeld Theatre was originally meant to seem like an architectural poster. The bowed mock proscenium, equipped with its own "footlights," was to have been rendered in white marble, while the rest of the building would have been a simpler box of glossy, blue-black glazed brick. At night the building would have faded into the darkness save for the brilliantly reflective marble. Ziegfeld—or Hearst, who financed the building—insisted on more dignity, and made the unfortunate decision to clad the entire building in limestone. The ironic quality of Urban's conception gave way to something more ponderous, resembling the UFA Kinos built in Berlin in the early 1920s.

The contrast between the Ziegfeld and Reinhardt theater facades marks an enormous advance. If the Ziegfeld and the International Magazine Building resembled German designs transplanted to New York and adapted to the new world with only partial success, the Reinhardt reflects a more complex approach. Urban took his cues from the vernacular cityscape: the fire escapes (which foreigners often find as characteristic of New York as skyscrapers); the competition among billboards, marquees, and electric signs; and the reduction of buildings to mere facades in a city of party-wall buildings. Most American architects treated these as unavoidable complications. Urban viewed them with the objective eye of a foreigner, and sought to extend the *Gesamtkunstwerk* to the visual hurly-burly of the theater district.

More than any other building type, however, restaurants and bars most heavily rely on architecture as a marketing device, and it was in the decor of nightspots that Urban came to specialize. The St. Regis Roof Garden, operated as a club by A. J. Drexel Biddle, a friend of Ziegfeld, was conceived as a precious variation on its competitors: the "garden," neither real nor papier-mâché, was a continuous mural over the walls and vaults.[41] Biddle also served as a front for underworld money at the Central Park Casino, another nightspot, he explained, intended for "gentlemen." Urban designed an eclectic set of vividly contrasting interiors, as well as a private suite upstairs for Jimmy Walker.

The Casino, it was said, was a place where Walker could "display his private life" in front of the public—some of the public.[42] It was a place, also, where fur coats were showered on chorus girls, and patrons were known to leave $1,000 tips. And as Urban designed more nightspots, they became ever more attuned to this culture of status. The St. Regis Roof had been refined and elegant; the last series of nightclubs was designed for narcissists. They were so extensively mirrored that one suspects the basic point was to allow patrons to see themselves within the decor and within the crowd: both actors and spectators in a comedy of fashion and consumption. At the Park Avenue Club on East Fifty-eighth Street, designed in 1931, the effect was kaleidoscopic: the circular chrome bar was set in a mirrored niche that fractured reflections into a cubist vision of simultaneity.[43] (Built for Tom Guinan, the club was padlocked three times before Treasury agents took sledgehammers to it. It was the prototype for The House of Morgan, designed in 1936 by Urban's former employees, Scott & Teegan.[44]) At the Persian Room in the Plaza Hotel, completed in 1933 after Urban's death, a different sort of spatial ambiguity came into play: mirrors created the illusion of a vast hypostyle hall, its edges defined by the real and reflected images of Lillian Langseth-Christensen's murals, inspired by Persian miniatures.[45] At the Supper Room in the Congress Hotel in Chicago the gridded, mirrored walls stretched the room towards infinity.[46]

These last works mark Urban's adoption of the machined vocabulary—but not the syntax—of the International Style, and the point at which he lost his position on the cutting edge of American design. Philip Johnson mocked the New School for Social Research building in 1931, describing it as "the illusion of a building in the International Style rather than a building resulting from a genuine application of the new principles."[47]

The International Style challenged the basic tenets of Urban's architecture. It abandoned the principles of classical composition that had held together the disparate threads of his work, and it pointed an accusing finger at the gulf between scientific rationalism and the tissue of sentiments, customs, and traditions that persisted in everyday life.

Urban had begun his career by rebelling against historicism, an architecture of invocation in which the forms of the past were recreated as challenges to contemporary life. When he died in 1933 architecture was turning towards a movement that claimed to discern the future form of building and of society. And between these two orthodoxies, Urban had sought a more modest goal, making theater of the present moment.

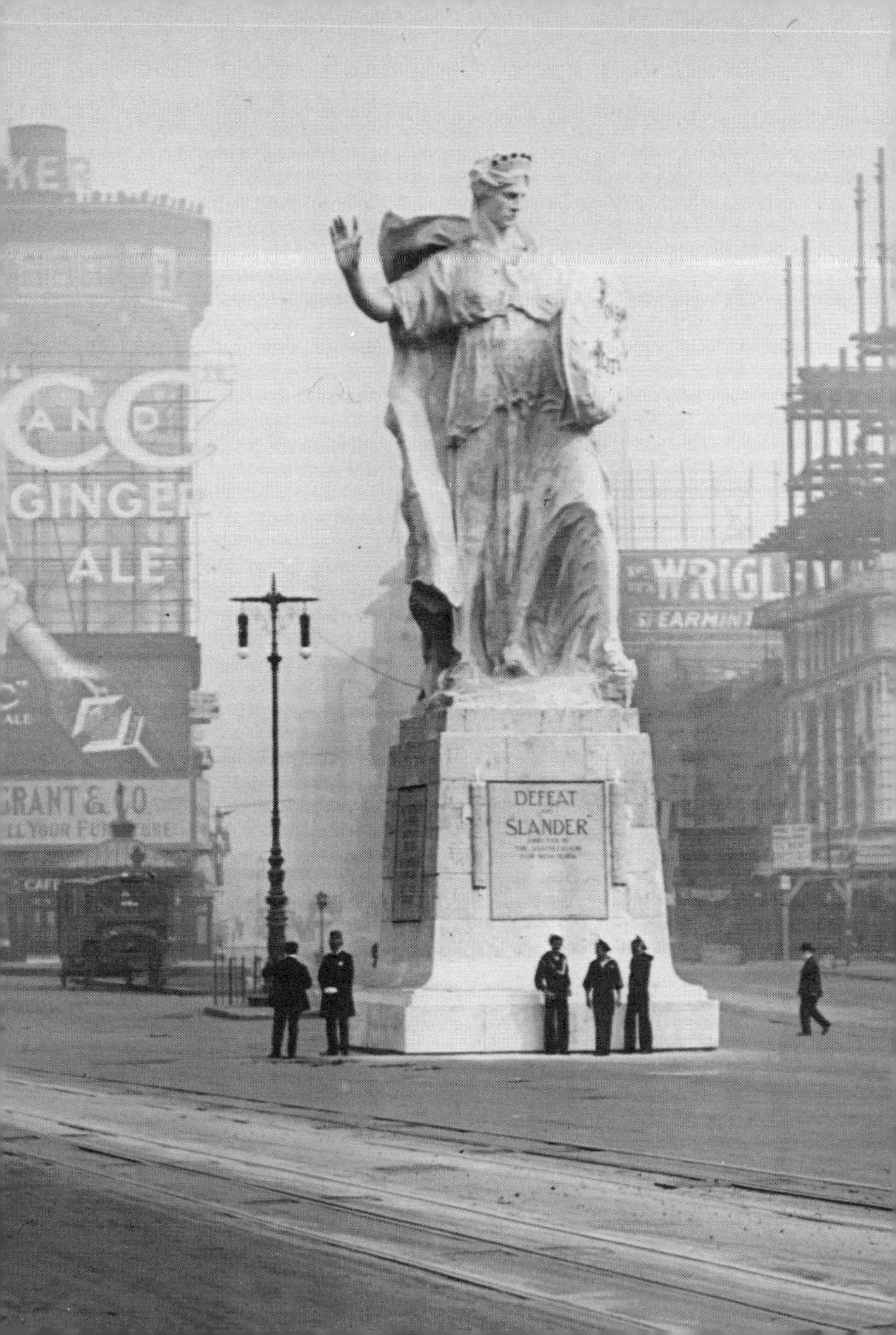

GINGER
ALE
WRIGL
EARMINT
GRANT & CO
DEFEAT
SLANDER

IV

BOUNDARIES OF RESPECTABILITY

INTRODUCTORY ESSAY

Peter G. Buckley

T HE FOLLOWING three chapters survey a range of "transactions," cultural and sexual, not usually remembered in connection with Times Square's Golden Age. Timothy Gilfoyle explores the presence of prostitution in advance of the theatrical development of the area. George Chauncey describes the various strategies developed by gay men to find space for their recreational and sexual life in commercial establishments and public places. Finally, Laurence Senelick details what might be termed the *long durée* of connection between the entertainment and sex industries on Times Square.

As Senelick notes, illicit sexual activity is, to a large extent, boundless and timeless. Prostitution especially has had a deep historical and geographical connection with commercial theater in Western societies. Even in early New York's most legitimate house, the Park, *femmes du pave* were a regular feature of the third tier, or balcony, until 1848. Yet, as the last date suggests, "smut," "prurience," and "respectability" are subject to historical articulation. The prostitutes at the Park Theatre were removed to make way for the so-called "family circle" and they retreated to the street, where they still remain. Any culture establishes "boundaries"—legal, moral, or geographical—to their practice and expression; or, to employ another metaphor, there never has been a free market in sexual activity: as in other areas of the economy, the state regulates certain transactions by imposing external costs.

For the historian, this raises the question whether the placement of such boundaries and costs shifted substantially at Times Square between 1900 and 1930. Much of the recent scholarship on the more conventional forms of "performance" culture has stressed the greater freedom in sexual expressiveness, especially for women, in and through the mythical Jazz Age. According to Lewis Erenberg, the expansion in commercial culture witnessed nothing less than a "transformation" in urban life, from Victorian rigidities to a vibrant amusement economy, tolerating, indeed celebrating, new vistas of sexual expressiveness and cosmopolitanism. The constellation of amusement activities in central zones, from cheap dance halls to pricey theaters, witnessed a coalescence of the classes, sexes, and races in an ever-increasing frequency of cultural exchange. Journalists,

photographers, and advertising personnel, sometimes on the periphery
but mainly as participants, fashioned from these transactions a new image
of the city characterized by an open, sophisticated nightlife. The boundaries to respectability were redrawn in ever-increasing radii, or so
breached as to be viewed only as temporary barricades on the road to new
expressive freedoms.[1]

Though the three chapters reveal a depth and diversity of sexual
practice certainly unrecorded by conventional historians of New York's
amusement, they differ somewhat in their estimates of the effectiveness
and timing of police intervention and moralistic suppression. Gilfoyle,
following closely the reports of the Committee of Fifteen, finds enough
evidence to believe that commercial prostitution fell under the pressure of
more effective enforcement between 1900 and the Depression; indeed,
Times Square, or its image, was then "sexually austere." Towards the end
of the same period, Chauncey finds gay men remembering the area as
something of a haven; homosexuals could construct spaces for their
differing cultures in the interstices of an amusement landscape packed with
bars, hotels, cinemas, and theaters. And Senelick, though recording the
periodic attempts to enforce "morality," basically charts the "age old
symbiosis" between illicit sex and the stage.

A careful look at the dates, the sources, and the kinds of illegal activity
examined by the authors would no doubt bring these chapters into
alignment. However, it seems to me a more useful task to step back from
the details of the sexual economy in order to look again at how notions of
"respectability" were applied and policed in the more general field of
amusement. Any key to the uniqueness of Times Square within the
oscillations of expression and control has to be found in the smaller
compass of politics; that is, in the relations between the audience or
customers and the legal authority of the state.

Tim Gilfoyle's chapter provides a useful approach when he notes that
Times Square emerged at the northern edge of the Tenderloin District,
indeed it effaced Longacre Square and its previous associations with many
forms of horseplay. The Tenderloin was a reasonably well known geographical district, running from Twenty-fourth to Fortieth streets on
either side of Sixth Avenue, but it more certainly referred to a way of doing
business in the popular amusement industry. The Tenderloin catered
mainly to a male clientele, composed of sports of many classes, from
slumming gentlemen to sailors. Its central institution was the Concert
Saloon, which offered a mixture of cheap performance along with liberal
access to prostitution and gambling. As Gilfoyle observes, this semipublic
economy of vice and amusement possessed its own forms of taxation
extracted by politicians and controlled, or serviced, by a police force
remarkably discretionary in their modes of operation.

The police interfered with houses of ill-fame and concert saloons only when there were direct complaints from local residents. With the rise of the political machine after the Civil War such discretionary practices became a steady source of personal and party funds. The various attempts by reform administrations to clean up New York, most notably under Abram Hewitt's mayoralty, led most immediately to an increase in fees for carrying on business as usual and only infrequently to closure. As Frank Moss cynically observed in 1895, "raids," often staged by the police before an audience of journalists, simply increased corruption and were seen as an institutionalized method of increasing returns. Commissioners were removed, mayors came and went, yet the flurries of reform did little to change the autonomies of police captains and the ranks below who had more enduring alliances with local businessmen and ward bosses.

Certainly there was no shortage of laws and regulations on the books. After midcentury, in the fallout from the Astor Place Riot, the municipality and state had firmly exercised their "right" to control many aspects of popular performance, especially the audience itself, through the municipal codes. The state also enacted additional statutes to handle elements of the general population who were seen to be particularly at risk, such as the 1859 law banning the presence of unaccompanied children in places of performance. The rise of the Concert Saloon in the 1860s led to further restrictions that attempted to separate any performance from either the consumption of alcohol or the presence of single women, and in 1875 a municipal code targeted the abolition of suggestive dancing after the advent of the can-can. By 1900, when the first book on American theater law was compiled, it was assumed that the law could identify a polite audience whose rights had to be protected from those who might behave otherwise: "The manager has the full right to insist that his patrons behave in an orderly manner and not in such a way as to interfere with the comfort and enjoyment of others."

Yet however much these state laws and municipal codes testify to a reformist desire to check promiscuous mixing or erect barriers between audience and stage, the actual enforcement of policy fell far short of the mark. The procedures for theater regulation were remarkably byzantine compared to London, for instance, where since the days of the old Lord Chancellor's office the authorities at least tended to speak in a single voice. In New York, however, practical control of the popular theater and amusement was distributed between the managers, the state, local police and politicians, as well as private reform agencies such as The Society for the Reformation of Juvenile Delinquents, to whom all license fees were given after 1823.

In response to such police inactivity and political graft there arose what George Frederickson has called the lineaments of a private state in various agencies which successfully secured their own police powers of arrest and enforcement directly from Albany, bypassing local jurisdictions. The

Tenderloin after 1873 was regularly "swept" by reformers such as Comstock's Society for the Prevention of Vice, in search of salacious pictures and prurient tableaux, or Bergh of the SPCA, for animals abused in variety amusements and menageries, or the SPCC, for underage children on stage. Yet these sweeps were hardly sweeping in their effect. They do not testify to any fits of Victorianism within the population as a whole but rather are tied to the fortunes of Tammany Hall and the periodic reform insurgences. The cycles of prurience and respectability in the history of New York amusement from 1850 to 1890 may simply mirror the better-known political oscillations of Bossism and Reform.

If this proves to be the case, there are interesting links to be made between the advent of Times Square as a central amusement zone after 1895 and that body of reform movements known in the general literature as Progressivism. The Lexow Commission of 1894, which unearthed the workings of police graft in the Tenderloin, may not have immediately eradicated those practices though it marks the beginnings of a period in which such investigations were institutionalized into the fabric of city government. As Gilfoyle suggests, the Committees of 14 and 15 are notable for both their longevity and close ties to effective enforcement. Nevertheless, perhaps "Progressive" deserves to stand in quotation marks, since recent histories of urban reform have cast doubt on the originality of its ideological positions, finding in men such as Frederick Law Olmsted, Washington Gladden, or Charles Loring Brace a strand in liberal Protestantism that displays no decisive break at the turn of the century.

Progressive reform was novel, however, in the way it considered amusements central to the reconstruction of public life for cities, in the way it harnessed the power of state agencies, and in its accommodation with the managers of refined amusement. The constituency and personnel of urban progressivism were very different from the older Protestant reform. The hallmark of Progressive activity in New York lies in its highly articulated structure, bringing together in ever-shifting alliances the clergy, academics, womens' groups, neighborhood associations, and new immigrant reformers. Notions of disinterested and therefore nondenominational social science proved successful in harnessing German-Jewish philanthropy. Without the intellectual energies of the Seligmans or the deep pockets of the Strauss family, the scale of the investigations into popular culture would have been considerably reduced. In addition, this new ethic of research offered more attractive employment for educated young women than the older purity departments of the W.C.T.U.

Another marked change from previous versions of urban reform was the importance accorded to the "recreation side of life." Notable social activists, such as John Collier, R. A. Seligman, Hutchins Hapgood, and Jane Addams (even E. A. Ross), who had done innovative work in matters industrial, residential, and hygienic before 1900, decided to hammer the

289

problem of commercial amusements into "American consciousness." They wished, according to Michael Davis, Jr., author of *The Exploitation of Pleasure* (1911), "to create a public problem instead of merely a series of countless individual ones." The timing of this wholesale shift in Progressive attention might be explained by the dramatic rise in the volume of commercial amusement sites and by the introduction of novel forms, such as the dance hall, vaudeville, and the motion picture. Certainly many articles in *The Survey* opened with such observations, often claiming that "universal patronage" of recreation was the next great change in American society after the granting of universal male suffrage. In order to prove this, at least 15 city reports were prepared between 1908 and 1915 showing that the weekly attendance at some form of show in every large U.S. city more than exceeded that city's population.

But Progressive interest and activism were more than direct responses to the novel conditions of an expanding amusement industry. As Progressives turned to social psychology rather than to the Bible, they dispensed with notions of direct visual contagion; audiences did not simply become what they beheld, and it was assumed that the population "at risk" from commercial culture could be identified with great accuracy. Adults, whether immigrant, working class, or "leisured," possessed a structured mental life that served as a buffer to the power of representation. For that reason, the vogue for "problem" plays dealing with sexual infidelity, white slavery, and venereal disease were tacitly supported by Progressives against clerical and moralistic attack. Social psychology also made "folk" culture legitimate, indeed necessary, since it was deeply rooted in immigrant life and thus served as a barrier to the blandishments of the market.

Progressives introduced a theoretical latitude into the policing of leisure perhaps because of its new social significance. If indeed "joy" was "power," then in modern cities joy encountered congestion. The human demand for self-expression found only artificial spaces for its articulation. The cramped urban home could no longer be the site of social education and amusement, thus people, especially children, had to find pleasure in a commercial city run for profit. As amusement left what was nicely termed "home society" it entered public life and became, for the first time, a zone for the state to actively reconstruct. They carefully took aim at the nineteenth century: "laissez-faire, in recreation as in industry, can no longer be the policy of the state."

They were clear, however, that the state could not choose the methods of control worked out by the church, Comstock, or older machine politics. Legislation would ideally come second to "reconstruction." John Collier and Charles Smith, working with the People's Institute, sketched out a highly articulated counter public sphere of amusement, in line with Olmsted's early thoughts on parks, yet breaking with his aesthetic priorities. The street would be transformed through processions and parades that expressed the "authentic folk life of the immigrant"; pocket parks would provide spaces for childrens' games and socialization. High schools should become cultural community centers offering music, lectures, and plays free of charge. So expansive was Smith's vision that he imagined a series of People's Halls located throughout the city. These would provide dramatic performances, lectures, gymnasia, and assembly rooms of such superior quality that all social classes of all ages would be drawn together. The stakes were high; without such halls the people's movement would be like

> a great soul searching for a body, and there is no work for the future of America that we can do equal to that of giving it such a body. He who builds a worthy people's hall will set an example to all other centres of population. Halls like this will be the home of a new sane democracy, founded not on the class struggle but on the union of all for the welfare of all.[2]

Since such halls never materialized, The People's Institute was forced into an uneasy though novel alliance with the best elements of their enemies in commercial culture. In 1905 they approached thirteen managers of mid-town theatres with the idea that they would distribute reduced priced tickets for "approved" plays to working-class New Yorkers. In 1907, as many as 60,000 people attended plays at one-third of their original admission price. In order to establish which plays were without "moral blemish," the Institute established a "Department of Music and Drama" which, over the next decade, undertook systematic inspections of theaters, categorizing both the nature of the audience and performance, and issuing lists of approved plays at the ticket distribution centers.[3]

In these reports, Times Square, with its preponderance of what was termed "standard" houses, did not serve as a focus for Progressive concern. As a newly developed area it was thankfully free of penny arcades, dime museums, and other forms of "recessive" working class amusement. According to their own statistics, standard theaters drew only 18 percent of the estimated total weekly audience for staged performance (860,000) and only 5½ percent of their most impressionable and vulnerable category, children. Nevertheless, the very complexity of legitimate theater patronage proved too enticing for the Progressive rage for categorization. Investigators were therefore sent to 14 centrally located theaters in the spring of 1910 to determine the audience composition.

Having little use for the term "middle class," investigators reported that standard theaters contained a dominance of leisured class folk (51 percent), while the clerical or business class composed 47 percent of the total. The working class, found in the galleries, took only 2 percent. This contrasted strikingly with an accounting of 36 Manhattan vaudeville houses where the hierarchy was reversed (working, 60 percent; clerical, 36 percent; vagrant, gamin, and leisured (!), 4 percent). Yet since they were relying mainly on visual clues for class recognition, reporters broke away from occupation and income categories in their detailed statements, returning to older notions of "types" and "sets." Here, the list becomes predicable in that the terms had been deployed widely since the 1870s onward: the fashionable, the literary, the professional, the out-of-towners and, most problematic of all, the sporting:

> The theatre provides the sporty man with a place whither to take women, see women, and seek prey; and fills in his life the same part that the dance hall does for his brother without a dress suit.

Apart from the small sporting component, for whom no percentages were provided, standard theaters were not viewed as sites for promiscuous mixing (like dance halls and cheap vaudeville), so attention shifted to "the kind of influence" exerted by the plays themselves. Three theater "experts," not connected with the profession or with newspapers, were asked to grade plays according to their social influence, and they were instructed in the elaborate color-coded grading procedures that had been worked out by the committee to examine vaudeville: "P" for positive; "Q," not objectionable; "R," lowering; "S," demoralizing; and "T" for vicious. In keeping with the newer understanding of socially determined tastes, these values were seen as relative "to the best ideals of the social groups chiefly composing that audience":

> A melodrama may preach an important moral lesson at the New Star Theatre, while the same message would be too elementary to serve, even to interest, the usual patrons of the Empire.

Not surprisingly, under those criteria, the moral grade scores of legitimate theater were as dismal as those achieved by that ogre, vaudeville: "high priced theatre rises higher, and also sinks lower, than the popular priced." The "low" character of commercial theater was especially evident in successful, long-run productions catering, it was presumed, to "the out-of-towner and hotel dweller:" "Rhythmic girly froth, well launched, can run for some time without exhausting this clientele." After much beating about the statistical bush the investigators decided that the standard theaters presented only a case of missed opportunities, rather than of danger to the denizens of the city of whatever social class. Even the new vogue for "frank" sex, in the problem play, was not seen as pernicious in its influence "because it reaches few save of an already sophisticated group:" the notion of an "adult" audience formed in lockstep with "child culture."

Thus, the People's Institute seldom intervened on Times Square stages. It advocated a "positive censorship" in which lists of approved educational plays would be distributed through the public high schools and discount ticket outlets, and in these efforts it received the whole-hearted support of the city administration. Such efforts dovetailed with Tammany boss Charles Murphy's understanding of "positive" govern-mental action to uplift and improve immigrant life.[4] Progressive social reformers did however advocate the idea of "citizens juries" which could be convened to pass judgment on a play should they encounter opposition. In a most obvious contrast to nineteenth century practice, managers em-braced the notion of citizens' juries in their attempt to head off the vestiges of Comstockery and clerical morality. The modest success of their efforts to informally control the market for commercial theater encouraged the People's Institute's next move into the regulation of "cheap amusements," especially the nickelodeon. Their founding of the National Film Board of Review in 1908, along with the producers' desire for uptown markets, successfully suppressed the racy Mutoscope subjects which had been the mainstay of Bowery and Coney Island arcades. As with the experiment for "standard" theaters, "advisory" warnings were issued, branding films as suitable or unsuitable for children. Such Progressive innovation still continues today.[5]

Entrepreneurs of amusement matched the reformers in their love of associational activity, banding together to support or head off legislation affecting the regulation of performance. After the Lexow Commission, managers preferred to submit themselves before a reformed administration rather than run the gamut of the agencies of a private state. In 1895, for instance, twenty managers met to support passage of a bill shifting responsibility for the oversight of child acting from the A.S.P.C.C. to the mayor's office.

Why managers might have been willing to accommodate progressive plans for community review makes sense only within the changing structure of the industry itself and the new relationship to property and "location" that the aggregation of popular amusement in Times Square brought about. Even that ogre, "vaudeville," was transforming in ways that echoed progressive desires for elevation. In the early 1890s variety entertainment became vaudeville, a shift in terms that indicated few changes in the content or structure of the performance on stage but definite changes in the management of the business and its presumed audience. Through the nineteenth century, "variety," an unstructured collection of acts ranging from dance to comic routines, drew mainly working-class males and was the primary fare in the notorious Concert Saloon in the Tenderloin. Though something less than "respectable," imaginative entre-preneurs, such as Barnum and Tony Pastor, devised ways to distance their own variety productions from alcohol and prostitution in the hope of drawing the mythic family audience. Direct prohibition of alcohol and unaccompanied women were probably not as successful for the long-term incorporation of variety into respectable entertainment as shifts in the location and scale of the amusement offering. The conventional bench-mark year in New York for variety's uptown, and therefore upmarket, move is Tony Pastor's relocation to the Tammany Society Building on Fourteenth Street, in close proximity to the commercial emporia on Ladies' Mile (Sixth Avenue) and the existing respectable Rialto in Union Square.

Together, Barnum and Pastor appear to have worked out almost all of the enduring strategies for the management of popular audiences: polite ushers, allocated seating, continuous performances, displayed rules of conduct, in addition to the careful, backstage supervision of scripts and talent. Yet however innovative they may appear to be in retrospect in establishing a new behavioral landscape for American popular amuse-ment, they were only operators of single sites whose uniqueness is evident against a backcloth of Tenderloin business as usual.

At Times Square the innovations of Barnum and Pastor were incorpo-rated into the very fabric of the buildings. After the Depression of 1892, variety operators, hoping to attract a broad clientele resistant to the higher price of legitimate theater, either took over existing refined houses or built new structures full of the amenities of politeness. In New York the new notion of a "Pleasure Palace," stuffed with all forms of public rooms and including more than one kind of performance, first appeared in Proctor's (Fifty-eighth Street and Third Avenue) in 1895, though it was soon overshadowed in its appointments by Hammerstein's Olympia. These two theaters set a standard for Times Square which had been exceptional before the 1892 Depression.

Popular variety performance, then, was reassembled on a respectable terrain in which an audience might be molded by the social tone of the house; spectators left their occupational and geographical origins behind them as they settled into a "palatial" staging of leisure. As Erenberg has shown, the new range of cabarets, supper clubs, and dance halls also specialized in the architectural and aesthetic structuring of pleasure, allowing "drink" and "sex" to return yet again to performance spaces. Certainly, the sensuality and nudity of revues, follies, and nightclubs were far more visually suggestive than anything offered in the old Tenderloin, yet the female form was presented in a new landscape of "sophistication," in which the audience was safely voyeuristic rather than being raucous participants. Beginning in 1907, Ziegfeld's Follies, and a host of imitators, including the Shuberts and George White, carefully removed from feminine sexual spectacle all markers of its previous working-class and "downtown" associations. The performers were unusually svelte by the standards of the time, indeed they became almost mere models for the ten

costume changes that Ziegfeld lavished upon them during a single performance. Even when the women began to appear nude from the waist up by
the mid-1920s, the continuing presence of a mixed, fashionable audience
served as a buffer to religious and "purity" protest. If such "outrage"
became a matter of press concern, as in the Shuberts' "Review of 1923,"
there was always the "jury" system to which to defer.[6]

The use of innovative strategies by Times Square impresarios to
encase their shows in visual splendor is even more notable when compared
to the fortunes of "burlesque." From one perspective, the arrival of the
brothers Minsky at Times Square in 1931 may appear to conform to a
trajectory of ever greater demand for nudity and voyeuristic performance.
Yet striptease had its origin elsewhere. As burlesque attempted to differentiate itself as a separate and sustainable genre from vaudeville, it turned
to ever greater displays of female flesh. The Minskys became pioneers in
this movement when they acquired the National Winter Garden Theatre
on the Bowery in 1913. They experimented with stock vaudeville and film
before discovering that the employment of "cooch" dancers, on a runway
extending into the audience, offered the surest returns.[7]

Throughout the teens and twenties, the operations of the Minskys
attracted the attention of purity crusaders, including the Society for the
Suppression of Vice, which initiated the famous raid of April 1925. But in
this period, burlesque was confined to the traditional "downtown" locations for prurience, and as a result few judges used the full extent of the
criminal statutes against performances "likely to be a corrupting influence
on minors and others" (Section 1140a). The advent of the Minskys in
Times Square occurs only within the context of the Depression and the
collapse of legitimate theater. In 1931, Billy Minsky bought the Republic
Theatre on Forty-second Street, and within two years four other continuous performance, "grind" houses occupied the block between Seventh
and Eighth avenues.

Only then did "burlesque" receive the full attention of the authorities,
and the complainant on this occasion was the 42nd Street Property
Owners Association rather than the Society for the Suppression of Vice.
The Association first attempted to have the shows branded "obscene"
under section 1140a, but without success. It next turned decisively to
political rather than judicial measures, using the mayor's office to block the
renewal of licenses. In late April 1932 the Association conducted a
remarkable parade of witnesses before the Commissioners of Licenses, a
parade that encompassed dozens of concerned parties, ranging from
Cardinal Hayes to the Women's Municipal League. The burlesque managers countered with testimony from old female dressers who stated that
prolonged contact with the burlesque business had not subverted their
moral character. Yet such a defense missed the point. The primary concern of the Association was no longer just the obscenity of the perfor-

295

mances, but rather the physical presence of the theaters themselves and the barkers who were changing the social tone of the locale. Land value came before moral value. As the *Times* noted, "The alleged obscenity of the burlesque shows is exceeded by their external frowsiness. The neighborhood of such theatres takes on the character of a slum."[8]

Though Minsky's Republic closed for just a month, it was only the beginning of a concerted campaign against burlesque and strip joints that lasted over the next four years. It was left to La Guardia and his activist commissioner Paul Moss to refine the tactic of license renewal, now limited to ninety-day terms, in an overall strategy "against the incorporation of filth." And, as George Chauncey's chapter makes clear, the State Liquor Authority, at the same moment, also became a strong arm of enforcement against bars frequented by homosexuals. Both forms of licensing hardly eliminated appetites and behavior then considered "unseemly." Given the complexity and layered nature of the district, with its many bars, cafés, hotels, theaters, and its multiple audiences, it proved impossible to suppress all forms of cultural and sexual commerce. Yet, as George Chauncey's chapter shows, the various "strategies" for survival and personal pleasure were shaped by the politics of public space. Licensing laws, curfews, fire regulations, and "juries" proved successful in reestablishing geographical parameters to the public expression of sexuality and in drawing "new boundaries between the acceptable and the unacceptable."

Thus, two strands of rather conventional history, the formation of integrated businesses or trusts and the rise of Progressive reform, need to be woven into the cultural story of Times Square. The luxurious encasing of shows by managers established new claims for normative behavior, so that, as Philip Fisher says of Dreiser's novels, "places supplanted manners." In this connection, it seems unnecessary to hypothesize "a new middle class" which drives commercial amusement in the direction of calm, receptive audiences. The need by managers of extended enterprises for the broadest markets and assured spaces matched the Progressive interest in a revival of civic spirit. Producers of movies, vaudeville, and theaters saw that notions of community review through citizens' juries would be less costly than their forebears' dances with Comstockery and the police in the Tenderloin. Whatever manifest changes in behavior and desire can be detected at the local level, a cultural history of Times Square also requires the frame of a political narrative that runs from the Lexow Commission of 1894 to La Guardia's innovative use of regulatory agencies in the late 1930s.

14

POLICING OF SEXUALITY

Timothy J. Gilfoyle

OR MOST OF the nineteenth century, prostitution was an integral part of New York's thriving leisure economy. Brothels and theaters, concert saloons and dime museums, even restaurants and cigar stores introduced, protected, and profited from commercialized erotic activity. Sexual pleasure for men of elite, middle- and working-class backgrounds was frequently treated as a commodity, bought and sold in the urban entertainment marketplace. Distinct subcultures of prostitutes, "sporting men," and underworld entrepreneurs were conspicuous elements of city life. During the final quarter of the century, entertainment districts like the Tenderloin in midtown, the Rialto in Union Square, and the Bowery in the Lower East Side were nationally known centers for these activities.

At the turn of the twentieth century, a variety of public and private authorities criticized and finally waged war on this "underground" economy, particularly against the most visible institutions of commercial sex. By 1910, Times Square was a cultural battleground for competing forms of leisure, entertainment, and sexuality. In time, sporting male culture was criminalized, prostitution became clandestine, theaters treated sexuality in more masked and moralizing forms, and censorship became standard in mass leisure industries like movies. While the discourse on sexuality grew more pronounced and popular, commercial and promiscuous expressions were increasingly forbidden. The salacious Tenderloin was supplanted by a more sexually regulated Times Square.[1]

The early history of the Times Square neighborhood could not have predicted its rise as New York's premier sex district. Led by Clement Clarke Moore and William B. Astor, real estate entrepreneurs between 1830 and 1860 developed the west side north of Fourteenth Street into an elite suburban community. Astor alone built approximately 200 brownstone houses northwest of Longacre Square (Times Square after 1904) from West Forty-fourth to Forty-seventh streets. By 1860, magnificent row houses lined the area, inducing one observer to describe the neighborhood as having "a superior class of residents than those on the East Side of town."[2]

After the Civil War, however, the quiet residential atmosphere of this area was upset by the forces of commerce and industry. Beginning with the Academy of Music's opening on Union Square in 1854, leading theaters migrated north along Broadway. Many moved into the one-time elite, row-house neighborhoods of Chelsea and Madison Square. By 1870, Twenty-third Street, with the Grand Opera House, Booth's Theater, Koster and Bial's, and Madison Square Garden, was the major theater district. And the concurrent opening of elevated railroad lines encouraged New York's leading entertainment institutions to abandon their older downtown surroundings. By 1885, Herald Square and Thirty-fourth Street became a nightlife district. "Crowds throng the sidewalks," wrote James McCabe. The "lights of the omnibuses and carriages dart to and fro along the roadway like myriads of fire-flies; the great hotels, the theatres and restaurants, send out their blaze of gas-lamps, and are alive with visitors. . . . All sorts of people are out, and the scene is enlivening beyond description." One police officer remembered that "the Tenderloin drew to its streets most of the visitors and the best people in the city."[3]

Furthermore, industrialization in lower Manhattan forced prostitution, along with entertainment, residential, and other less profitable land uses, uptown. After 1865, for example, the cast iron factories designed by Griffith Thomas, Henry Fernbach, and James Duckworth rapidly replaced the brothels along Mercer, Wooster, Greene, and Crosby streets (Soho today). Real estate in this mid-nineteenth century sex district doubled and tripled in value between 1850 and 1880, hastening the conversion from residential to industrial use. A sanitary inspector making his rounds in the neighborhood concluded that the "large number of houses of prostitution . . . for which this district was . . . so notorious . . . [were] rapidly disappearing from this section of the city, . . . being soon crowded out by the encroachments of mercantile business." Similarly, George Ellington admitted in 1869 that Mercer Street property was so expensive that "warehouses of immense proportions [were] taking the places of the houses where scenes of revelry were once enacted."[4]

The most commercialized forms of prostitution quickly followed the uptown migration of leisure institutions. As entertainment and commerce made the neighborhood undesirable, wealthy New Yorkers abandoned their well-built brownstones for newer ones uptown. Landlords who were unable to attract middle-class residents had two choices: subdivide the houses into multiple family dwellings for working-class tenants, or lease to agents who in turn rented to prostitutes who could afford the higher rents. The plentiful neighborhood theaters made the latter option the most profitable. Thus, the former domiciles of middle-class respectability were transformed into brothels. "[H]ouses of prostitution," remembered one Tenderloin police officer, soon "lined up in an unbroken row of brown-stone fronts."[5]

After 1880, no single block was preeminent in Tenderloin prostitution. West Thirty-first and West Thirty-second streets, for example, were populated with at least 19 brothels apiece in the 1880s and had a minimum of 10 each during the following decade. The honky-tonk atmosphere around Longacre Square to the north earned it the nickname of "Thieves Lair." And just south of the Square, a string of more than a dozen brothels lined West Thirty-ninth and West Fortieth streets. Beginning in 1883 with the opening of the Metropolitan Opera House, these nearby brothels thrived. Patrons consistently complained about the streetwalkers soliciting men entering and exiting the establishment. West Thirty-ninth Street, in particular, drew attention for its French-run bordellos. Dubbed "Soubrette Row" during the 1880s, these houses were so famous that they, according to one observer, "were known all over the country."[6]

The movement of hotels and theaters up Broadway into the Longacre Square neighborhood continued after the opening of the Metropolitan Opera. In 1888, for example, the Broadway Theatre premiered on Forty-first Street. Within five years, the Empire and Knickerbocker theatres were running on Fortieth and Thirty-eighth streets, respectively. In 1895, Oscar Hammerstein opened his magnificent, 6000-seat Olympia Theatre on Broadway between Forty-fourth and Forty-fifth streets. And from 1903 to 1907, no less than 9 theaters were constructed in the vicinity, many along Forty-second Street. When the new subway line opened in 1904, the *New York Times* moved to Longacre Square and convinced the city to rename it Times Square.[7]

The uptown movement of elite leisure institutions precipitated an expansion of New York's Tenderloin, pushing its northern border to West Forty-second Street. "As everyone knows," former police chief William McAdoo aptly concluded in 1906, "the city is being rebuilt, and vice moves ahead of business." Indeed, by 1901, Committee of Fifteen investigators identified at least 132 different addresses with prostitutes in the immediate 33 blocks of the neighborhood (see map). At least 63 row houses, many of them the old, Astor-built brownstones, functioned as brothels and "parlor houses." On Saturday and Sunday nights, lines of eager young men formed outside the most popular. At the same time, thick numbers of streetwalkers prowled West Forty-second Street (between Sixth and Ninth avenues), with many others on Broadway, Sixth, Seventh, and Eighth avenues. Many lived and worked in the 61 tenements and 8 apartments that investigators found filled with prostitutes.[8]

Commercial sex seemed to define the midtown area. The Rev. Adam Clayton Powell, Sr., for example, contended that his West Fortieth Street

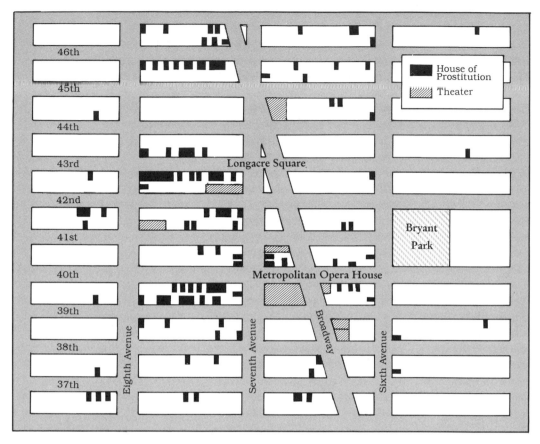

Houses of Prostitution in Longacre Square: 1901

church was in "the most notorious red-light district in New York City." There "harlots would stand across the street on Sunday evenings in unbuttoned Mother Hubbards soliciting men as they left our service." A block away, Tammany Hall's Archibald Hadden ran the popular and prostitute-filled German Village and Denver Hotel. By 1901, the sobriquet of "Soubrette Row" had moved to West Forty-third Street, a block where almost every house was a brothel and directly across from the future site of the *New York Times*. Observers insisted that Broadway from West Twenty-seventh to Sixty-eighth streets was a two-mile parade of prurient commerce, "ten to twenty prostitutes . . . seen nightly on every block." Such pedestrian activity convinced even the *Times* that "the glittering splendor of 'the Great White Way' does not symbolize the best spirit of the people of New York."[9]

More so than any other phenomenon, these neighborhoods and their socially defined "illegitimate" activities embodied what critics labeled the "negative vitality" of the city.[10] By the onset of the twentieth century, commercial sex in the Forty-second Street neighborhood, like other parts of New York, was organized around three distinct subcultures. Prostitutes themselves formed the most visible and controversial element, usually subjected to the most severe penalties by law enforcement agencies. Second, a "sporting male" culture celebrating male heterosexual sexual activity grew more public. Not only was this behavior tolerated by many municipal authorities, but it was an increasingly prominent form of masculinity and male identification. Finally, the high demand for sexual services induced numerous entrepreneurs to systematically organize various leisure institutions, thereby controlling significant portions of this underground economy.

By 1885, prostitutes were a prominent and visible part of the Forty-second Street community. In 1888, for example, a Fortieth Street resident complained that prostitutes dominated certain blocks of the neighborhood. One house sold liquor without a license and was, he lamented, "a place in which 'fast women' [were] allowed to prey upon humanity at will." Most importantly, "children of tender years have to pass up and down the stairs and consequently pass the door of this pest house coninuely [sic]." Two blocks south, another neighbor charged that the brothels sponsored "disgusting magic lantern exhibitions . . . given for the benefit of the neighbors on the opposite side of the street." Retired carpenter George Stone decried this state of affairs.

> It is a public scandal that the police should have permitted people of the class which now occupy many of the houses in the neighborhood to get in here, and I don't wonder that the respectable people who still live here have at last been brought to see the importance of taking some decisive action to rid themselves of these objectionable neighbors.

Stone claimed that ten years earlier, the neighborhood was free of prostitutes. Now, they were virtually everywhere. And after buying a residence on West Thirty-ninth Street in 1892, Dean Osgood was surprised to learn that his neighbors comprised numerous prostitutes. Out of his rear window, women in a Thirty-eighth Street brothel "used to dance naked; the shades . . . up and all such performances" in full view.[11]

Before 1900, the subculture of prostitutes was fluid and revolved around the brothel. The most successful madams remained in business for significant periods of time. May Livingston, for instance, ran two houses on West Fortieth Street and another on West Forty-fifth Street for many years. Similarly, Annie Grey ran three houses, all on West Forty-sixth

Street, including one that remained open for three decades. Most women, however, rarely remained in any one establishment longer than several months. Prostitutes like C. A. Lawrence were typical. Most times she streetwalked along Broadway between Times and Herald squares. But when business was slow, she moved uptown and worked in Harlem.[12]

Inside, brothel prostitutes performed at seemingly fantastic rates. According to account books in one fifty-cent house, one prostitute copulated with 273 men in two weeks, an average of 19 per day (her high was 28 in a day), earning $136.50 for the house. She managed to keep $68.25 from which she paid board and expenses. Two other prostitutes in the same house saw an average of 120 and 185 men each week, respectively, one seeing as many as 49 in one day. The surprising volume was contingent upon each woman's willingness to work sixteen hours daily. In other examples, Madge Williams made $58 one evening in 1909, and "French Viola," $25 per week, usually after accommodating 180 clients. Incongruously, she admitted "drift[ing] into the business because of the easy time."[13]

By the twentieth century, the prostitute subculture in the Tenderloin had a high proportion of immigrants. For example, of the 464 women found in Tenderloin hotels in one Committee of Fourteen survey, 30 percent were French, 20 percent Jewish, and 6 percent German. Of those remaining, at least 38 percent were American-born, including 18 percent Irish-American and 7 percent African-American. Similarly, when investigators counted 187 women in 32 boardinghouses and brothels in the Tenderloin, only 13 percent were American-born. Over half (51 percent) were Jewish, with more than a third (36 percent) French.[14]

Race and ethnicity divided the subculture of prostitutes. African-Americans, for instance, remained segregated to the periphery of Times Square. The streets from West Thirty-seventh to Forty-third, west of Seventh Avenue, were known for their large numbers of black prostitutes. One observer noted in 1913 that "every night, from seven o'clock to about four in the morning they [the prostitutes] stand and sit outside of their houses very irrespectably dressed, and speak to all men who pass, especially white men, and take them up to their flats."[15] "To make men follow them," remembered Adam Clayton Powell, Sr., "prostitutes would snatch their hats and run into hallways." On other occasions, they were downright intimidating. "Numerous colored women walk up and down the street," wrote one citizen, "blocking the passage of white men and boys, and in some cases force them into the gutter, in order for them to get clear of them." In his opinion, the women were "increasing and becoming bolder all the time."[16]

Just as white and black prostitutes little associated with one another, in most cases neither did women from different ethnic origins. This was most noticable with the French. One investigator concluded this was due to more than just language. "The French girls in these houses," he wrote, "resort to unnatural practices and as a result the other girls will not associate or eat with them. This is the general reputation of French girls: that they will resort to lower practices than any other class."[17]

The popularity of prostitution also produced a distinct subculture for males that often cut across class divisions. For approximately four decades, "sporting men" in the Tenderloin and elsewhere celebrated personal autonomy, promiscuity, extramarital sex, and physical isolation from the nation's strict Victorian mores. "Sporting men" admired and rewarded displays of "rough masculinity"—prizefighting and pugilism, street gangs and heavy drinking, verbal bravado and sexual aggression.[18] The emphasis on physical prowess combined with the increasing commercialization of leisure produced a distinct male world with its own set of sexual norms. Since sex was something to buy for many men, a variety of erotic behaviors were consistently available for purchase in the urban marketplace.

Sporting male culture was never homogeneous. Yet its popularity among males of educated and middle-class status generated considerable attention by the end of the nineteenth century. Howard Crosby of the Society for the Prevention of Crime, for example, lamented that "the vilest haunts" in New York were frequented by "sons of our best-esteemed citizens—merchants' and bankers' clerks, book-keepers, and tellers of banks, employees of insurance offices, city, county, and State office-holders." Popular Bowery concert saloons were populated, wrote another, with "reverend judges and juvenile delinquents, pious and devout hypocrites, bankers, merchants, and libertines." Leading Tenderloin brothels "were frequented by all classes, 'silk hat' roisterers, college boys visiting the city for 'a time,' businessmen out for a night of gayety, clerks and working men." Even the female physician Elizabeth Blackwell complained that the sporting male lifestyle was so popular that "young women of the middle and upper classes . . . are brought by these customs of society, into direct competition with prostitutes."[19]

This pattern of male sexual license grew more pronounced by the turn of the century. When questioned about the widespread prostitution in New York, for example, Mayor Robert A. Van Wyck defended it. "I think those boys do now what I did when I was a boy," he asserted. Similarly, the Society for the Suppression of Vice complained of the sexual displays in theaters and "low play houses." "Matters which were formerly relegated to disorderly houses," concluded one report, "received the patronage of so-called decent society." Observing a row of brothels two blocks from Times Square in 1905, another investigator counted over 550 males visiting the various houses on a weekend evening, one house entertaining over 100 in less than three hours. The frequency of these stories convinced Helen Campbell that many of the clients of Tenderloin brothels were "stockbrokers from Wall Street, great importers, merchants, and representatives from every wealthy class in the city." An undercover investigation even learned that the famed banker J. Pierpont Morgan routinely employed prostitutes, "conveying his kept women to an apartment he maintained in Westchester County."[20]

At the turn of the century, sporting men were more willing than ever to admit their sexual activities. For example, during the Mazet Committee investigations of municipal corruption in 1899, testimony revealed that nearly 200 men complained to the police of being robbed by prostitutes during an encounter. Nearly two-thirds of the clients (64 percent) lived in the city, more than a quarter (28 percent) in the same ward as the prostitute. Philandering was so tolerated that many felt no compulsion to conceal their behavior. When George Kneeland concluded that the daily clientele of New York's prostitutes exceeded 150,000 by 1913, he claimed that

> There are thousands of these men in New York. No home ties restrain them; no home associations fill their time or thought. Their rooms are fit only to sleep in; close friends they have are few or none. You can watch them on the streets any evening. Hour after hour they gaze at the passing throng; at length they fling themselves into the current— no longer silent or alone.

Prostitution was such "an accepted fact of city life," concluded one police officer, that "there seemed little that could be done to check it."[21]

Finally, Tenderloin prostitution was among the best organized parts of Gotham's underground economy. "Startling as is the assertion," claimed police captain Thomas Byrnes in 1886, "it is nevertheless true, that the traffic in female virtue is as much a regular business, systematically carried on for gain, in the city of New York, as is the trade in boots and shoes, dry goods and groceries." By the twentieth century, the organization of commercial sex impressed even the most critical. "It is surely no exaggeration to maintain," concluded George Kneeland in 1913, "that prostitution in New York City is widely and openly exploited as a business enterprise."[22]

Reform investigations increasingly identified entrepreneurs of the Tenderloin economy with foreign elements. For example, in one investigation, reformer Frances Kellor noted that many of the Jewish vice organizers from the Lower East Side, especially the Independent Benevolent Association, had moved into the Times Square area. In addition, examinations of the Tenderloin by the Committee of Fourteen in 1910 and 1912 found over 50 French-operated houses and resorts, more than double those identified as Jewish or black. More so than Jewish pimps, a French syndicate actively recruited French prostitutes abroad, many entering as wives, relatives, or maids of their pimp or recruiter.[23]

The French syndicate included numerous proprietors of French restaurants and was headquartered in the Tenderloin. Restaurant owner Maurice Chevalier, for example, was known for his close associations with this syndicate. Frances Kellor concluded that the French syndicate received less attention because of their experience in more tolerant French cities, allowing them to run "their business as nearly compatible with the rules laid down by the police department." Their compliance with local politicians and police convinced the Women's Municipal League and the City Club that such activity "could not exist without the connivance or acquiescence of the party in power," and blamed Tammany Hall.[24] "As far as the business end of this trade is concerned," concluded Kellor in 1907, "one might safely leave out all other nations." In another investigation two years later, antiprostitution reformer Hattie Ross complained that "syndicate" establishments dominated West Forty-first Street "where they never were before."[25]

Even after 1900, when the brothel was declining in popularity, profits remained substantial. George Kneeland's 1913 survey of 30 one-dollar brothels in the Tenderloin found that the average monthly profit was $2,069, almost $25,000 annually. Similarly, 8 five-dollar houses averaged $1,415, or nearly $17,000 annually. Frances Kellor discovered even higher profits in 1907, figuring that landlords of Tenderloin brothels made about as much as $800 per week in profit, a rate that brought their annual lucre to $41,600.[26]

Despite these profits, brothels were not the most lucrative form of commercial sex after 1900. Hotels rapidly became the most profitable habitats of prostitutes. Moving north along Broadway, the Delavan at Fortieth Street, a favorite of "sporting men and race track toughs," was run by Tom O'Rourke and filled with 50 "cadets" and 30 prostitutes of all nationalities. Similarly, the Garrick, Valko, and Metropole hotels at the confluence of Forty-second Street, Seventh Avenue, and Broadway each housed 16 to 20 such ladies. The Churchill Hotel, on the southwest corner of Forty-sixth Street, was a 5-story, 130-room structure operated by a former police sergeant, where approximately 20 frustrated actresses, chorus girls, and shop girls worked as prostitutes. The popularity of these and Raines Law hotels prompted brothel madams to refer to them resentfully as "charity places."[27]

Adjoining cross streets were filled with similar enterprises. For example, the Hotel Plymouth on West Thirty-eighth Street was inhabited almost entirely by prostitutes, the permanent guests being "used as a cloak for the carrying on of a disorderly house business," according to one investigator. Similarly, when registering at the King Edward Hotel on West Forty-seventh Street, bell boys routinely inquired if guests wanted "a woman introduced into their apartment." And in the Hotel Lyceum on West Forty-fifth Street, "women leaned half naked out of windows trying to attract attention of men in adjoining houses."[28]

In the heyday of the Tenderloin, therefore, various "underworld" institutions interacted with elite institutions of culture. The Metropolitan Opera House, Broadway theaters, and exclusive restaurants were neighbors to rows of public brothels and Raines Law hotels. The "robber barons" and parvenus who built the Opera House shared its front sidewalk with streetwalkers. As an entertainment district, the Tenderloin was never homogeneous in its patronage and available forms of leisure. In contrast to the prescriptive Victorian literature of the era, social elites shared the streets and institutions of the neighborhood with more ribald elements of New York's sexual underworld.[29]

This did not pass without opposition. But throughout most of the nineteenth century, attacks were sporadic, largely ineffectual, and centered upon "disorderly" brothels, "low dives," and concert saloons. The Ladies Female Moral Reform Society in the 1830s, the Five Points House of Industry in the 1850s, and the mayoral administrations of William R. Grace and Abram S. Hewitt in the 1880s conducted well-publicized anti-prostitution campaigns that proved short-lived and without lasting impact.[30] Beginning with the Rev. Charles Parkhurst in 1892, however, a sustained movement emerged, producing a series of state investigations and purity reform organizations which survived into the Great Depression.

Although he never made it to Longacre Square during his famed nocturnal journey through New York's underworld in 1892, Parkhurst later attacked the rampant Tenderloin prostitution. For example, when Dean Osgood's complaints about West Thirty-ninth Street fell upon deaf ears at the police station, he went to Parkhurst. "The Society [for the Prevention of Crime] went to work there with their detectives," he gratefully proclaimed, "and the doctor himself took a personal hand." After organizing public meetings and media coverage, arrests and brothel closings became more frequent. Parkhurst considered the police so corrupt and ineffectual regarding commercial sex that he instructed his organizations, the Society for the Prevention of Crime (SPC) and the City Vigilance League, to "take the initiative in these matters."[31]

Parkhurst's campaign benefited from already existing but disparate reform organizations. First, the Society for the Prevention of Cruelty to Children (SPCC) in the 1880s, fearing the historic association of the theater with prostitution, engaged in a lengthy campaign to prohibit children from performing in city theaters. Eventually, the SPCC successfully lobbied for a child exhibition law in 1892 that restricted the stage activities of children under 16.[32] Second, some property owners organized and exerted scattered resistance to prostitution. When noise from Nettie Grant's West Thirty-ninth Street brothel grew excessive, for instance, property owners on the block formed a committee to end the problem. The noise ceased after the police allegedly raised "the ante" on Grant. Similarly, by 1897 the Forty-fourth Street Property Owners Association, led by Joshua Sanders, successfully (with the help of the police) closed the Sixth Avenue Hotel, a popular resort for streetwalkers. Still others, like the Clinton Community Association, organized to fight the encroachment of prostitution north of Forty-second Street and west of Broadway.[33]

Parkhurst and his legions also assumed law enforcement powers and bypassed the police, building upon the tradition of earlier antiprostitution and preventive societies. Some criticized this policy. "By granting to private associations the powers that rightfully belong to the police you have destroyed the morale of the force," testified Assemblyman Wauhope Lynn. "You have delegated to the Society for the Prevention of Vice, the S.P.C., the S.P.C.C., and the S.P.C.A. powers that rightfully belong to the police."[34] Most importantly, Parkhurst's campaign did not dissipate as had earlier antiprostitution efforts. For more than a decade after, investigations of the New York underworld remained a fixture in New York politics. Continuing with the Lexow Committee in 1894 and the Mazet Committee five years later, the sexual reform mantle passed to the Committee of Fifteen in 1900 and ultimately to the Committee of Fourteen in 1905.

A "citizens association" allied with the Anti-Saloon League, the Committee of Fourteen captained the most extensive and successful antiprostitution campaign in New York's history. For a quarter-century, the Committee marshaled its many resources in the most concerted effort to eliminate conspicuous displays of sexuality in Times Square, theaters, and cabarets. Initially concerned with streetwalkers and Raines Law hotels, the Committee eventually expanded its definition of "commercialized prostitution" to include certain theatrical performances, cabarets, venereal disease, homosexuality, and burlesque.[35]

Shortly after its birth, the organization lobbied successfully for the Ambler Law of 1905, eliminating the majority of Raines Law hotels.[36] Citywide, the Committee made on-site investigations, presented evidence of violations to the Department of Excise, and pressured brewers supplying saloons, real estate owners, the Tenement House Department, and the police. In Times Square, the Committee closed numerous brothels and hotels on West Fortieth and Forty-first streets. In 1910, the Committee convinced District Attorney Charles Whitman to prosecute remaining "vice resorts" and institute a special grand jury chaired by John D. Rockefeller, Jr. Over the next two decades, Committee investigators visited restaurants, dance halls, cabarets, massage parlors, tenement houses, and any other institution sponsoring some variety of commercial sex. "[C]onstant vigilance is necessary," wrote General Secretary Frederick Whitin, "for a change of police policy might easily be followed by the renewed activity of repressed forms of the evil."[37]

The Committee of Fourteen's success was the product of a constellation of factors and timing. First, they were a critical element of the

Progressive political movement to reform New York's law enforcement system. Appearing at a moment in New York history that saw the adoption of Women's Night Court, probation and parole, juvenile and family court, and the indeterminate sentence, the Committee forced sexual politics and especially commercialized sex to the forefront of the reform agenda. Furthermore, upon contributing to the reorganization of the municipal court system, the district attorney's office, and the police, the Committee focused on some of the larger structural causes of commercial sex.[38]

Second, crime fighting and law enforcement regarding sexuality noticeably changed. Before 1910, New York's police were greatly politicized and often enjoyed arbitrary power on the street. "The individual policeman was respected and feared in the '90's much more than he is to-day [sic]," wrote Cornelius Willemse in 1931. "They were powerful fearless men, mostly of Irish birth, and they dispensed the law with the night-stick, seldom bothering to make arrests." In addition, a majority of officers were members of political clubs affiliated with Tammany Hall. Reformers like Frank Moss considered the police department to be "the most perfect machine ever invented in this city. It knows every prostitute, it knows every house, and no prostitute, no gambler, can live for a moment in any place in the city without being known."[39]

The Committee of Fourteen responded to this municipal cooperation with underworld institutions by assuming some law enforcement responsibilities. When investigating tenement house prostitution, for example, the Committee gave its list of suspect buildings to the Tenement House Department who in turn provided the Committee with the owners of record. Bypassing the police, the Committee contacted owners, informed them of the violations and the consequences of failure to comply with the Tenement House Law of 1901. By World War I, the Committee, not the police, performed undercover investigations of prostitution near military training camps.[40]

In essence, the public regulation of commercial sex was shared with a private body by the second decade of the century. The Committee of Fourteen, in its own words, served as a self-appointed and "necessary adjunct in the broad scheme of law enforcement for the civic welfare." As in other U.S. cities, police policy shifted away from social control to crime fighting. Less concerned with moral issues and more with serious crime, police abdicated the regulation of sexuality to private reform bodies like the Committee.[41]

Such pressure affected the police in unprecedented ways. They stopped arresting and fining prostitutes, subpoenaing them instead. Bail was thus avoided, undermining corrupt bondsmen in cahoots with dishonest police officers.[42] By World War I, police commissioners like Richard E. Enright actively supported the suppression of prostitution and other varieties of commercial sex. And in 1929, the Police Department created a Crime Prevention Bureau to supervise dance halls, nightclubs, and poolrooms, while vigilantly suppressing speakeasies and resorts identified with prostitution.[43]

Third, the Committee of Fourteen departed from earlier antiprostitution groups by attacking the absolute sanctity of private property. Supporter George Kneeland admitted that "any group of citizens which hopes successfully to combat prostitution must study the uses of property, especially real property, in such commerce." Kneeland complained that "so many respectable owners of property seem to have no conception of their legal and moral responsibilities." Similarly, a Committee report concurred that there "can be no prostitution without the use of property for that purpose, and property cannot systematically be so used without the consent or collusion of owners and agents." The most effective method of attacking property owners proved to be the Injunction and Abatement Law of 1914. The legislation, initially introduced by State Senator Robert F. Wagner and later by State Senator Walter T. Herrick, penalized real estate owners for illegal uses of their property by restricting its use for any purpose up to a year. When the district attorney proved reluctant to prosecute offenders, the Committee threatened "to act independently" and enforce it themselves. While the Committee of Fourteen did not question property rights, real estate was nevertheless "subject to the proper exercise of the police power . . . [and] must be used not improperly to cause harm to our neighbor."[44]

A fourth departure from past reform groups was the Committee's efforts to force centralized trade associations to reverse their tolerant attitude of commercial sex. Most notably, brewers supplying disorderly saloons and hotels were compelled to discontinue their support. At the turn of the century, brewers had controlled the retail liquor trade and an estimated 80–90 percent of the city's more than 11,000 saloons through the chattel mortgages they issued. Historically, they tolerated, in some cases encouraged, commercial sex for the sake of profits. But in 1908, the New York Brewers Association agreed to cooperate with the Committee for the first time. Joined by Jacob Ruppert, Jr., and the Brewers Board of Trade, the most powerful breweries severed their ties with illegal saloons and abandoned repeated excise law violators. Likewise, the surety companies that provided bonds and private security for landlords, real estate agents, and saloons similarly retracted their tolerant policies.[45]

Finally, the Committee of Fourteen was not a single-handed agent of change in Times Square. New economic forces also contributed to this new organization of leisure. Most notably, the completion of new transit centers in mid-Manhattan transformed the neighborhood. The Independent Rapid Transit system (1904), Pennsylvania Station (1910), and Grand Central Terminal (1913) stimulated a real estate boom. After 1910, corporations began migrating uptown from Wall Street, relocating in the midtown area. In addition, clusters of hotels appeared near these important transit sites. By 1929, the Forty-second Street Property Owners and Merchants Association recognized that midtown Manhattan was "a vast centralization of business and of pleasure." The new hub of a growing mass transit system, Times Square attracted theaters, hotels, advertisers, tourists, and related industries, remaking the Forty-second Street area into New York's foremost entertainment district by the 1920s. Speaking about the dangers of prostitution to this new economic activity, Chamber of Commerce President Charles Stewart Smith warned not about venereal disease but rather about lost profits. "New York is the most expensive place in the world in which to do business," he proclaimed in 1901, "and business will seek a more favorable atmosphere unless we purge the city."[46]

The Committee of Fourteen was neither isolated nor unique in their efforts to restrict public expressions of sexuality. In 1905, for example, the campaign to repress public prostitution outside theaters moved inside when Anthony Comstock successfully closed George Bernard Shaw's *Mrs. Warren's Profession* after a single performance. Likewise, in 1907, Richard Strauss's *Salome* at the Metropolitan Opera House stopped after one show. A few years later, the Columbia Theatre was attacked for displaying women in flesh-colored tights. Similarly, in 1913, William Hammerstein and two associates were arrested for presenting the "immoral" "Dance of Fortune" at Hammerstein's Victoria Theatre. The Committee on Public Morals of the American Federation of Catholic Societies complained about the shows at the Princess Theatre as "a mass of grewsome [sic] filth." And burlesque house owners like Morton Minsky charged that a "theatrical double standard" tolerated partial nudity in places like Ziegfeld's before World War I but not thereafter.[47]

More so than other reformers, the Committee of Fourteen recognized that efforts to eradicate prostitution and public displays of sex usually fell upon deaf ears. Moral suasion did little to change sexual behavior or thwart the underground economy. The Committee concluded that only by restricting marketplace behavior would such carnal activity decline. Thus, landlords, brewers, bondsmen, and theaters, the very institutions that directly and indirectly profited from and protected prostitution, were singled out for action. Certain underworld entrepreneurial activities once accepted or tolerated—renting to prostitutes, supplying prostitute-filled saloons with liquor and protective bonds, permitting solicitation—were criminalized. For these progressive reformers, laissez-faire in the marketplace did not extend to the nightclub.

Ultimately, these forces produced a new kind of entertainment district in Times Square. By World War I, prostitution in New York was a clandestine, camouflaged activity. As one Bureau of Social Hygiene report concluded: "In 1912, prostitution was open, organized, aggressive and prosperous; in 1916, it is furtive, disorganized, precarious, unsuccessful."[48] Near Times Square, the numerous furnished rooming houses from Thirty-seventh to Forty-second streets between Seventh and Eighth avenues were closed to prostitutes. On the eve of World War I, the Committee of Fourteen insisted that New York had "less open vice than any other of the world's largest cities." Reformer Raymond Fosdick concurred, stating "that for a city of its size . . . [New York] is the cleanest city in the world."[49]

This new kind of entertainment district differed in several ways from the older Tenderloin and its subculture of sporting men, prostitutes, and underworld businessmen. First, sexuality was regulated by centralized, citywide agencies like the Committee of Fourteen. Municipal police and ward politicians, with their decentralized, local control of prostitution, relinquished power to these new authorities. Second, the power of local, ward-based officials ranging from politician to judge to police officer was weakened by centralized law enforcement, a product of Progressive reform. Finally, entertainment institutions that previously encouraged, or at least tolerated, an independent sporting male culture changed. This transformation was epitomized by Jacob Ruppert. As president of the New York Brewers Association, Ruppert broke the longstanding ties between breweries and local saloons, which had given the latter a great deal of independence. Cooperating with the Committee of Fourteen, Ruppert worked to break the association of saloons with commercial sex. He later purchased the New York Yankees, transforming another "sporting male" institution into one with a wider audience.

Theater owner-producers like Oscar Hammerstein, David Belasco, Augustin Daly, Florenz Ziegfeld, and the Schubert brothers, hoping to attract an affluent, middle-class patronage, never opposed efforts to remove commercial sex from the neighborhood. Their new theaters and palaces of amusement, splashed in a sea of electric lights, transformed Broadway into the Great White Way. References to the neighborhood as the Tenderloin declined, replaced by a new name, Times Square. As electricity replaced gas, Forty-second Street emerged as one of the nation's first centers of mass culture and "cosmopolitan" entertainment, available to young and old, male and female, resident and visitor alike. The aggressive, commercialized sexual aura of the Tenderloin gave way to a more sexually pristine Times Square.[50]

The most noticeable impact was on the institutions of commercial sex. Brothels, for example, were replaced by "call houses." During the 1870s, 70 percent of Gotham's prostitution was found in brothels, furnished rooming houses, or "panel" houses. Even by the final decade of the century, approximately 66 percent of New York's prostitutes worked in some kind of parlor house environment. But with the rise of the Raines

Law hotels after 1896, the general movement of prostitutes into hotels in Times Square and other areas and the decline in municipal toleration, brothel prostitution diminished throughout the city. From 1900 to 1910, for instance, only 22 percent of New York's commercial sex was in such establishments. By the following decade, the figure was less than 10 percent. As one report concluded, "disorderly women . . . largely re sorted to flats and cheaper apartment houses to continue their business." Even streetwalkers were less brazen and more hesitant to openly approach men on the street.[51]

These changes transformed the subculture of prostitutes. As brothels vanished, prostitutes had to work on their own, often becoming dependent on pimps. In hotels, restaurants, and cabarets, prostitutes operated the "team way," relying upon bellboys, waiters, taxi drivers, and pimps to recruit customers. Prostitutes in Maurice Chevalier's Restaurant, for example, were introduced to prospective customers only through third parties. One investigator found "an elderly woman and a young girl of about sixteen . . . [who] were mother and daughter; . . . the daughter is soliciting men while the mother acts as a cover to her." Hotels were even required by police to secure the names of male customers with no baggage, as well as prove that the women with them were their wives. Increasingly forced underground, call girls grew more prominent. Throughout the 1920s, Committee of Fourteen investigators filed numerous reports on specific women working via telephone. Other Times Square prostitutes even worked out of taxis. Charging $5 for the sex and $3 for the taxi, increasing numbers of streetwalkers abandoned hotels, furnished rooming houses, and apartments for the automobile. As one hotel clerk declared in 1918, taxis were "nothing but floating whore houses."[52]

This transformation in the prostitute subculture was further related to a profound change in the sexual underworld of Times Square. By 1927, Times Square did not even rank among the leading neighborhoods for sexually related crimes. Whereas only 11 percent of such arrests occurred in Times Square, 20 percent were in Harlem, 16 percent in Washington Heights, 15 percent in the Upper West Side, and 12 percent in the Lower and Middle West Side. In time, reformers remembered 1920 as "the low water mark in prostitution."[53]

More importantly, establishments once supportive of prostitutes publicly altered their ways. For example, Harry Salvin of the Tokio Restaurant and Cabaret agreed to exclude all prostitutes, promising to dismiss doormen, captains, or head waiters who allowed unescorted women to enter or dance. And cabaret performers were no longer permitted to mix with audiences. Likewise, Morton Lein of the Pekin promised to eliminate "objectionable" cabaret performances, using "every endeavor [sic] to prevent prostitutes from frequenting the place, accompanied or unaccompanied." Lein instructed his doormen to prohibit streetwalkers and other "such women" from entering, as well as permitting no men to dance with unescorted women. By 1929, the Committee claimed that their activities against speakeasies with prostitutes "in the Times Square area had driven some of them into the Harlem section."[54]

As prostitution in Times Square became less public after 1920, the Committee widened its scope of concern. Law enforcement investigations soon included speakeasies and homosexual activity. In 1927, for example, investigators learned that the Times Square Building was a "hangout for fairies and go-getters." Sailors in particular were attracted to the locale. A concessionaire in the building claimed "that whenever the fleet comes into town, every sailor . . . comes to the Times Square Building. It seems to be common knowledge among the sailors that the Times Square Building is the place to go if they want to meet any fairies."[55] Finally, the Committee actively lobbied for criminalizing the double standard. Beginning in 1923, the organization supported passage of a "customer amendment," legislation designed to "hold the man who pays a woman for immoral relations equally guilty with the woman who accepts payment for such acts."[56]

"The Tenderloin, enticing its victims of both sexes with its dismal gayety," remarked City Club President Richard S. Childs in 1926, "is only a memory, and the red lights are gone." Red lights indeed gave way to white ones as the neighborhood once equated with prostitution and sporting male culture was transformed into a thriving center of leisure and mass culture. By the 1920s, Harlem, with its white-controlled speakeasies and nightclubs, replaced Times Square as New York's underworld entrepôt. And more than a generation after the Rev. Charles Parkhurst captured the public imagination with his purity crusade, the mantle passed onto Mayor Fiorello La Guardia. From gamblers to striptease queens, the "Little Flower" shared the prudish sensibilities of the Presbyterian minister and his reform heirs. He rejected the sporting male culture that had flourished for decades and went about New York smashing slot machines and closing burlesque houses. La Guardia thus kept alive Parkhurst's mission.

These efforts to carefully structure public expressions of sexuality and eliminate the "rough" aspects of sporting male culture coincided with similar efforts elsewhere in American society. In 1906, for example, President Theodore Roosevelt, horrified over the increasing number of deaths resulting from college football, induced several university presidents to stop the slaughter and organize the National Collegiate Athletic Association. In 1920, major league baseball owners, hoping to clean up the sport in wake of the Black Sox scandal in the 1919 World Series, hired federal judge Kenesaw Mountain Landis as commissioner. Within several years, American steel companies helped organize the local, ill-financed semiprofessional football teams in the steel-belt cities of the North into the National Football League. And Will Hays was appointed to head the Motion Pictures Producers and Distributors Association in 1922, thereafter providing self-regulatory control over the content of American films.[57] Like male sexuality in the Tenderloin, male sport fell under increasing scrutiny and regulation.

These newfound ways of policing male amusement reflected, in part, some of the centralizing trends in American urban life. By the 1920s, power over commercial sex had shifted, allowing larger and better-capitalized institutions like the Committee of Fourteen to exert control over most public displays of sexuality. While prostitution never vanished, it no longer commanded such a visible physical presence in Times Square as it had at the turn of the century. Even new underworld groups promoting commercial sex, such as Lucky Luciano's organized crime network, tended to be clandestine and secretive. By the Great Depression, prostitution in Times Square was a forgotten issue for both the public and the reformer.

15

THE POLICED: GAY MEN'S STRATEGIES OF EVERYDAY RESISTANCE

George Chauncey, Jr.

ORTY-SECOND STREET was *it*, when I was a teenager," recalled Sebastian ("Sy") Risicato, referring to the days in the late 1930s when he still lived with his parents in the Bronx but was beginning to explore New York's gay world. "Forty-second Street then was our stamping ground," he continued:

> Closet queens, gay queens, black, white, whatever, carrying on in men's rooms, and in theaters. There was a Bickford's [cafeteria] there all night, and a big cafeteria right there on 42nd Street, one of those bright cafeterias where johns used to sit looking for the young queens. Lots of queens, everybody was painted and all, but they weren't crazy queens: drugs weren't big then. Forty-second Street was like heaven—not heaven, [but] it was a joy to go there! And the sailors at the Port Authority, and the soldiers, and the bars. . . . During the war all the soldiers and sailors used to go to the "crossroads" and you'd pick them up—Forty-second Street and Times Square—and you'd take them out to the furnished rooms in the neighborhood: furnished rooms, and dumpy little hotels and Eighth Avenue rooms, which you'd rent for the night. There were a lot of gays living in that area, [too,] oh yes, people from out of town, and the boys whose fathers had pushed them out, with the tweezed eyebrows and beards. . . . You'd go down to Forty-second Street and feel like, *here's where I belong*.[1]

Forty-second Street was almost heaven in the 1930s for the self-described "painted queens" and "street fairies" like Sy Risicato who were

315

forced to escape the hostility of their own neighborhoods and families in order to forge a community of their own. The world they built in the furnished rooms, cafeterias, theaters, and streets of Times Square offered them enormous support and guidance in their rejection of the particular forms of masculinity and heterosexuality prescribed by the dominant culture. By the 1930s they had made Times Square one of the most important centers of gay life—particularly white, working-class gay male life—in the city. But the heaven such men created seemed hellish to many of the other people who knew the Square. Risicato's coterie was a notable part of the "undesirable" element regularly implicated in the "decline" of the theater district by more respectable New Yorkers, who mobilized a variety of policing agencies and strategies to eradicate their presence from the Square. They also appalled many other gay men who frequented the theater district, particularly middle-class men more conventional in their behavior, who regarded the "fairies" as undesirable representatives of the homosexual world. These men constructed their own, more carefully hidden gay world in the theater district; but they, too, had to contend with the agencies of moral policing.

Ironically, the world gay men created in the 1920s and 1930s has remained even more invisible to historians than it was to contemporaries; most historians who have bothered to consider the matter have assumed that gay men remained isolated from each other and helplessly subject to the self-hatred preached by the dominant culture. This chapter proposes an alternative view of gay life in these years. It examines the manner in which gay men, like other criminalized and marginalized peoples, constructed spheres of relative cultural autonomy in the interstices of an amusement district governed by hostile powers. It analyzes the stratagems different groups of gay men developed to appropriate certain commercial institutions and public spaces as their own and their complex relationship to the district's commercial entrepreneurs and moral guardians. A battery of laws criminalized gay men's association with each other and their cultural styles as well as their narrowly "sexual" behavior. Their social marginalization gave the police even broader informal authority to harass them and threatened anyone discovered to be homosexual with loss of livelihood and social respect. But the culture of the theater district, the weakness of the policers themselves, and the informal bargains struck between the policers and the policed—often with the mediation of certain commercial entrepreneurs, including those of the criminal underworld—enabled gay men to claim much more space for themselves than those obstacles implied.

Thus, while this chapter surveys the ways in which the agents of the dominant cultural order sought to police the presence of gay men in the Square, it focuses on the informal strategies gay men developed to resist that policing on an everyday basis in the decades before the emergence of a gay political movement. Analyzing the emergence of a gay world in Times Square illuminates the character of urban gay male culture in the interwar years more generally, since gay men visiting the district were forced to draw on the same panoply of survival strategies they had developed in other settings as well. It also illuminates the history of the Square itself, for the changing fortunes of gay men's efforts in the 1920s and 1930s both depended upon and highlighted the changing character of the Square during the transition from the era of jazz and Prohibition to that of Depression and Repeal.

The anonymity of urban amusement districts such as Times Square has often been cited to explain their development as "vice" zones, and, indeed, the relative anonymity enjoyed there by gay tourists from the American heartland—and even from the outer boroughs—was one reason they felt freer there than they would have at home to seek out gay locales and behave openly as homosexuals. To focus, however, on the supposed anonymity of Times Square (a quality that is always more situational and relative than its absolutist formulation suggests) is to imply that gay men remained isolated (or "anonymous") from each other. But Times Square was not so much the site of "anonymous," furtive encounters between strangers (although there were plenty of those) as the site of an organized, multilayered, and self-conscious subculture, or, to use gay men's own term, a "gay world," with its own meeting places, argot, folklore, and norms of behavior. Rather than focusing on the supposed "anonymity" of Times Square, then, it will prove more productive to analyze the ways in which people manipulated the spatial and cultural complexity of the city to constitute the Square as their *neighborhood*, where some of them worked or lived, and many others joined them to build a community.

Indeed, a gay enclave developed in Times Square in part because so many gay men lived and worked in the area. The theater and the district's other amusement industries attracted large numbers of gay workers, who got jobs as waiters and performers in restaurants and clubs, as busboys in hotels, and as chorus boys, actors, stagehands, costume designers, publicity people, and the like in the theater industry proper.[2] Although gay men hardly enjoyed unalloyed acceptance in such work environments, the theatrical milieu offered them more tolerance than most workplaces. As one man who had been a theatrical writer in the mid-teens observed, "the New York theatrical world [of that era was] . . . a sort of special world . . . with its own standards of fellowship [and] sexual morals."[3] Homosexuality, along with other unconventional sexual behavior, was judged by unusually tolerant standards by people who were themselves often marginalized because of the unconventional lives they led as theater workers. Some men could be openly gay among their coworkers, while many others

317

were at least unlikely to suffer serious retribution if their homosexuality were discovered. The eccentricity attributed to theater people and "artistic types" in general provided a cover to many men who adopted widely recognized gay styles in their dress and demeanor.[4]

Moreover, many men working in the amusement district lived there as well, and they were joined by other gay men who appreciated the advantages of the transient housing the district offered. Times Square and, to the west of Eighth Avenue, Hell's Kitchen together comprised one of the major centers of housing for single adults in the city. In many respects the area constituted a prototypical furnished room district, the sort of neighborhood dominated by a nonfamily population in which, as the Chicago sociologists discovered in the 1920s and historians such as Mark Peel and Joanne Meyerowitz have more recently remarked, unconventional sexual behavior was likely to face relatively little community opposition.[5] The district was crowded with rooming houses, theatrical boardinghouses, and small residential and transient hotels serving theater workers, as well as most of the city's elegant bachelor apartments.[6] The housing varied in quality and social status, but most of it shared certain qualities useful to gay men as well as to transient theater workers. Most of the rooms were cheap, they were minimally supervised, and the fact that they were usually furnished and hired by the week made them easy to leave if an occupant got a job on the road—or needed to "disappear" because of legal troubles.

Middle-class men tended to live to the north and east of the Square in the West Forties and Fifties, where many of the city's fashionable apartment hotels designed for affluent bachelors were clustered, and where many of the elegant old row houses between Fifth and Sixth avenues had been converted into rooming houses as the intrusion of commerce resulted in the departure of their original residents. Another, poorer group of men lived to the west of the Square in the tenements of Hell's Kitchen and the large number of cheap hotels and rooming houses to be found west of Seventh Avenue and Broadway. Many gay men, for instance, lived in the Men's Residence Club, a former YMCA hotel at West Fifty-sixth Street and Eighth Avenue; a number of the theatrical boardinghouses in the area housed gay men; and some tenement apartments served as collective homes for the poorest of gay theater workers.[7] Groups of theater and restaurant workers were joined by gay teenagers forced out of their natal homes by hostile parents (as Risicato recalled), gay migrants from small towns and the outer boroughs, hustlers, gay bartenders, and men who had more conventional jobs elsewhere in the city but who valued the privacy, convenience, and tolerance such housing offered. The district also included numerous transient hotels and rooming houses where male (or heterosexual) couples who met in a bar or on the street could rent a room for an hour.[8]

The men who lived and worked in the district formed the core of a social world— or several social worlds, really—in which men who both lived and worked elsewhere could participate. Times Square served as the primary social center for many such nonresidents, the place where they met their friends, built their strongest social ties, "let their hair down" (once a camp expression for being openly gay), and constructed public identities quite different from those they maintained at work and else-where in the straight world. They built a gay world for themselves on the basis of the ties they developed in the commercial institutions which entrepreneurs had developed to serve the needs of the theater workers rooming in the district and the tourists who flocked there.

Gay men mixed unobtrusively with other customers at most of the district's restaurants, but a few places attracted a predominantly gay patronage and developed a muted gay ambiance. Louis' Restaurant on West Forty-ninth Street, for instance, became well known to gay men and lesbians as a rendezvous for several years in the early 1920s, and even came to the attention of private anti-vice investigators in 1925 as a "hangout for fairies and lady lovers [lesbians]." But the people who met there were sufficiently guarded in their behavior—at least in the main public dining rooms—that outsiders were unlikely to suspect they were gay. A sedate 1925 restaurant guide even recommended Louis' to its readers, describing it, clearly without apprehending the full significance of its observation, as "one of the institutions of the neighborhood."[9]

Such restaurants had existed before the 1920s, but, ironically, they proliferated and became more secure during Prohibition. Prohibition had been enacted in part to control public sociability—and in particular to destroy the immigrant, working-class male culture of the saloon, which seemed so threatening to middle-class and rural Americans. But in cities such as New York, Prohibition had resulted instead in the expansion of the sexual underworld and had undermined the ability of the police and anti-vice societies to control it. The economic pressures Prohibition put on the hotel industry by depriving it of liquor-related profits, for instance, led some of the second-class hotels in the West Forties to begin permitting prostitutes and speakeasies to operate out of their premises.[10] More significantly, the popular opposition to enforcement, the proliferation of speakeasies, and the systematic use of payoffs and development of criminal syndicates to protect those speakeasies all served to protect gay clubs as well as straight. It became easier during Prohibition for establishments where gay men gathered, such as Louis', to survive, because they stood out less. All speakeasies—not just gay speakeasies—had to bribe the authori-ties and warn their customers to be prepared to hide what they were doing at a moment's notice.

Prohibition also changed the character of the Square in ways which led to the increased visibility of a group of gay men different from those who patronized Louis'. It drove many of the district's elegant restaurants, cabarets, and roof gardens out of business, and they were replaced by cheap cafeterias and restaurants whose profits depended on a high turn-over rate rather than on a high liquor-based profit margin. Moreover, by the end of the twenties the decline of the district's theater industry, due to the collapse of the national theatrical road circuits as well as the rise of the movies, forced growing numbers of theaters to convert into movie houses, often of the cheaper sort. Both factors combined to transform the Square in the 1920s and early 1930s, in the eyes of many contemporaries, from a distinguished theater district to a "tawdry" amusement district, a develop-ment only hastened by the onset of the Depression.[11]

It was in this context that the flamboyant gay men known as fairies began to play a more prominent role in the culture and reputation of the Square. Part of the attraction of amusement districts such as Times Square, after all, was that they constituted liminal spaces in which visitors were encouraged to disregard some of the social injunctions that normally constrained their behavior, allowing them to observe and vicariously experience forms of behavior which in other settings—particularly their own neighborhoods—they might consider objectionable enough to sup-press. This appeal was only enhanced by the cultural developments of the Prohibition era, for the popular revolt against the moral policing of Prohibition as well as the shifting character of the Square. The culture of the speakeasies themselves encouraged clubgoers to transgress conven-tional social boundaries and experiment with the norms governing accept-able public sociability.

The Square already had something of a reputation for fairies in the early 1920s (one 1924 account bemoaned the number of "impudent sissies that clutter Times Square"). But as the Square became more of a "tawdry" amusement park, visiting it became more of a theatrical experience in itself, and "fairies" increasingly became part of the spectacle of the Square, part of the exotica clubgoers and tourists expected and even hoped to see there. Thus, when *Vanity Fair's* "intimate guide to New York after dark" noted in 1931 that the tourist could see "anything" on Broadway at night, it included "pansies" among the sights along with the more predictable "song writers, college boys, . . . big shots, [and] bootleggers."[12] A New York tabloid added that "The latest gag about 2 A.M. is to have your picture taken with one or two pansies on Times Square. The queens hang out there for the novel racket."

If the highly flamboyant, working-class street fairies who gathered at Bryant Park represented one extreme of gay self-presentation, the highly circumspect middle-class men and women who met at restaurants like Louis' represented another. But the self-described fairies—not the "nor-mal"-looking men at Louis'—constituted the dominant public image of the male homosexual during this period; as a character representing the author in a 1933 gay novel complained, *"we're all,"* to the "normal man, . . . like the street corner 'fairy' of Times Square—rouged, lisping, mincing."[13] This distressed many of the more conventional men, who felt the fairy drew unwanted and unflattering attention to the gay world. Ironically, though, it was the very brilliance of the fairies that diverted attention from those other, more guarded men, and thus helped to keep them safely in the shadows. The presence of the fairies facilitated the process by which such middle-class men constructed their own, more carefully hidden, gay world in the theater district.

Different groups of men, then, adopted different strategies for negotiating their presence in the city, and the divisions within the gay world of Times Square became even more complex as the district continued to reel from the impact of Prohibition, the declining fortunes of the theater industry, and the onset of the Depression. The effect of these changes is best seen in the changing organization of the district's street culture. Indeed, the street life of the Square deserves considerable attention, since it was there that much of gay life occurred. Moreover, the shifting spatial and cultural organization of just one aspect of gay street culture—that of male prostitution—highlights the extent to which the bustle and apparent chaos of the most active street scenes masked a highly organized street culture, whose boundaries and social conventions were well known to the initiated.

The Square, already an important center of female prostitution, became one of the city's most significant centers of male prostitution in the 1920s. Initially, two distinct groups of male prostitutes, whose interactions with customers were construed in entirely different ways, worked the Times Square area. Well-dressed, "mannered," and gay-identified hustlers serving a middle-class, gay-identified clientele generally met their customers as the latter walked home from the theater on the west side of Fifth Avenue from Forty-second to Fifty-ninth streets. Although a regular part of the Times Square scene, neither the hustlers nor their customers attracted much attention since neither conformed to the era's dominant stereotypes of homosexuals. During the 1920s, though, a second group of prostitutes, much more easily recognized by outsiders, came to dominate Forty-second Street itself between Fifth and Eighth avenues: effeminate (but not transvestite) "fairy prostitutes" who sold sexual services to other gay men and to men who identified themselves as "normal," including the Italians and Greeks living to the west of the Square in Hell's Kitchen, as well as tourists from afar. The self-presentation of the prostitutes operating on the two streets thus differed markedly, as did the self-conception of their customers, and their proximity highlights the degree to which Times Square was the site of multiple sexual systems, each with its own cultural dynamics, semiotic codes, and territories.

The transformation of Forty-second Street during the late 1920s and early 1930s had enormous repercussions for the street's gay scene, and resulted in a new group of hustlers coming to dominate it. Forty-second Street was the site of the oldest theaters in the Times Square district, and the city's elite had regarded it as a distinguished address early in the century. By 1931, however, it had effectively become a working-class male domain. The conversion of two prominent theaters into burlesque houses in 1931 had both signified and contributed to the masculinization of the street: not only the strippers inside but the large quasi-pornographic billboards and barkers announcing the shows on the streets outside contributed to the image of the street as a male domain, threatening to women.[14] The masculinization of the street was confirmed by the conversion of the remaining theaters to a "grind" policy of showing male-oriented action films on a continuous basis and the opening of several men's bars and restaurants that catered to the increasing numbers of sailors, servicemen, and unemployed and transient men who frequented the street.

As the gender and class character of Forty-second Street changed, it became a major locus of a new kind of "rough" hustler and of interactions between straight-identified servicemen and homosexuals.[15] As the Depression deepened, growing numbers of young men—many of them migrants from the economically devastated cities of Pennsylvania, Massachusetts, New York, and the industrial South, and some of them servicemen—began to support themselves or supplement their income by hustling. Not gay-identified themselves, many became prostitutes for the same reason some women did: the work was available and supplied a needed income. "In the Depression the Square swarmed with boys," recalled one man who began patronizing their services in 1933. "Poverty put them there." The hustlers, aggressively masculine in their self-presentation and usually called "rough trade" by gay men, took over Forty-second Street between Seventh and Eighth avenues, forcing the "fairy" prostitutes to move east of Sixth Avenue, to Bryant Park. Taking note of the shift, the police began conducting periodic "fairy roundups" in the park in the late 1920s and 1930s, arresting any gay men they found loitering there.

The precise locus of the hustlers' and other gay men's activity on Forty-second Street shifted several times over the course of the 1930s. The details of the shifts are unimportant in themselves, but they reveal something of the social organization of the streets in general, for they resulted largely from the shifting geography of the gay bars and other semipublic sites where men met. The hustler street scene followed the bars from Sixth to Eighth Avenue and from the north to the south side of

Forty-second Street in part because the bars attracted customers and offered shelter from the elements, but also because the streets and bars functioned as extensions of each other. Each site had particular advantages and posed particular dangers in men's constant territorial struggles with policing agents, as the men subject to that policing well knew. The purchase of a beer at a bar legitimized behavior involved in cruising which might have appeared more suspicious on the streets, including a man's simply standing about aimlessly or striking up conversations with strangers. But while the police periodically tried to "clean up" the streets by chasing hustlers and other undesirable loiterers away, they could not permanently close the streets in the way they could close a bar. Moreover, in a heavily trafficked, nonresidential area such as Forty-second Street, no one had the same interest in controlling pedestrians' behavior on behalf of the police that a bar owner who was threatened with the loss of his license had in controlling his customers. Thus, while the police might harass men on the street simply for standing about with no apparent purpose, bars might evict them simply for touching, and plainclothesmen might arrest them for homosexual solicitation in either locale. The relative dangers of either site varied and depended on the momentary concerns of the police, and much of the talk on the streets was necessarily devoted to their shifting tactics. On more than one occasion in the 1930s and 1940s a man noted in his diary that all of the street's hustlers had suddenly disappeared, apparently aware of some danger their customers did not perceive.

The numerous cheap cafeterias, Automats, and lunchrooms that crowded the Times Square district were perhaps the safest commercial spaces available to poorer gay men. The Automats seem to have become even more secure with the onset of the Depression, when they developed a reputation, due to their cheap prices and lack of supervision, for being a refuge for the unemployed and luckless. Four Horn & Hardart Automats stood on Forty-second Street between Madison and Eighth avenues, and during the winter, according to one 1931 account, the Automat across Forty-second Street from Bryant Park became a favorite haunt of the men who gathered in the park during the summer.[16]

Automats were particularly famous for their lack of inhibition, but even the large cafeterias in the Childs chain could become astonishingly open. This was particularly true late in the evening, after the dinner hour, when managers tolerated a wide range of customers and behavior in order to generate trade. Indeed, several cafeterias seem to have premised their late-night operations on the assumption that by allowing homosexuals to gather on their premises they would be able to attract sightseers out to see a late-night "fairy hangout." Gay men seized on the opportunities this portended and quickly spread the word about which restaurants and cafeterias would let them gather without guarding their behavior; moreover, the campy antics of the more flamboyant among them became part of the draw for other customers. One gay man who lived in the city in the late 1920s recalled that the Childs restaurant in the Paramount Building was regularly "taken over" by "hundreds" of gay men after midnight. Even if his recollection exaggerates the situation, it suggests his sense of the extent to which gay men felt comfortable there; in any case, *Vanity Fair's* 1931 guide to New York informed its readers that the Paramount Childs was particularly interesting because it "features a dash of lavender."[17]

Well-established chains such as Childs usually had sufficient clout to prevent police raids, although raids did occasionally occur when either the police or the private anti-vice societies thought gay patrons had become too uproarious, or the management feared that the authorities were about to reach that conclusion. In February 1927, for instance, after gay men had been congregating at the Forty-second Street Liggett's drugstore for some time, the management, perhaps sensing a temporary hardening of police attitudes or simply fearing for its reputation, suddenly called on the police to drive the men from its premises, which led to a raid and the arrest of enough men to fill two police vans.

After the repeal of Prohibition in 1933 gay bars quickly became the most important centers of gay male sociability in the city, but they also became the most sharply contested. The legalization of bars made them more numerous, more accessible, and easier to find—for gay men as well as straight. But it also subjected them to the authority of the newly created State Liquor Authority (SLA), which quickly proved to be a much more effective agent in the enforcement of state regulations than the Prohibition era's Volstead agents had been. From its inception, the SLA threatened to revoke the liquor license of any bar that served homosexuals, whose very presence, it ruled, made a bar "disorderly." In the three decades following Repeal its agents and the police investigated and closed hundreds of bars in New York that served gay men or lesbians, sometimes through adminis-trative action, sometimes through raids that resulted in the arrest of the staff and, in some cases, even the patrons.

Those bars that profited by serving homosexuals—who would pay high prices and were in no position to demand better services—were thus forced to devise a variety of extralegal stratagems to protect themselves, paying off the local patrolmen and negotiating informal limits on the conduct of patrons that were less draconian than those imposed by the law. Most became dependent on the Mafia, the only organization powerful enough to offer them systematic protection. But while police payoffs and Mafia connections served to keep at least some gay bars open, sometimes for years at a time, despite their prohibition, such arrangements were periodically overwhelmed when enforcement agencies were put under special pressure to close the bars by the press or by politicians seeking publicity for their election campaigns.

During such crackdowns, some straight bars in "suspicious" neighborhoods such as Times Square or the Village sought to protect themselves by posting signs over the bar reading "If You Are Gay, Please Stay Away" or "It is Against the Law to Serve Homosexuals—Do Not Ask Us to Break the Law." At other bars, the bartenders were simply instructed to eject anyone who appeared to be gay, or, if they had not suspected them initially, to refuse to serve them any more drinks once they did.

Gay bars that continued to serve gay patrons during crackdowns sought to protect themselves by hiring floormen who made sure that men did not touch each other or engage in campy, or otherwise "obvious," behavior, which might draw the attention of the authorities by marking the bar's patrons as gay. State policies thus had the effect of turning bar managers into agents of SLA policy enforcement. They also exacerbated the class and cultural cleavages already dividing the gay world: since the presence of "obvious" homosexuals or "fairies" in a bar invited the wrath of the SLA and the police, most bars refused to serve them, and other gay men were encouraged in their hostility toward them.

The number of bars serving homosexuals—and particularly those serving *exclusively* homosexuals—proliferated in the 1930s and 1940s, but most of them were short-lived, and gay men were forced to move constantly from place to place, dependent on the gay grapevine to inform them of where the new meeting places were. When the SLA launched a campaign against bars serving homosexuals as part of its effort to "clean up the city" in the months before the 1939 World's Fair opened, it quickly discovered just how effective that grapevine could be. After closing several bars in the area patronized by homosexuals, including the Consolidated Bar and Grill on West Forty-first Street, the Alvin on West Forty-second, and more distant bars that were part of the same circuit, the Authority's investigators discovered that many of the patrons of those bars had simply converged on the Times Square Bar & Grill on West Forty-second Street and turned it into their new rendezvous. In late October an SLA investigator, sent to the bar after a police report that "about thirty . . . fairys [sic] and fags" had been seen there, noted that several of the gay men he had previously seen at the other bars were "now congregating" there, along with a large number of soldiers.[18] The owner himself, who sought to cooperate with the police in ridding his bar of homosexuals once he realized their presence threatened his liquor license, insisted that "we never looked for . . . this kind of business. . . . [The police] close some places; [the fairies] come over here. . . . It was the neighborhood—[the fairies] know what places . . . are [open to them]. The word passes so fast. They knew [when a bar] is a degenerate place."[19]

Although many men continued to go to gay bars despite the risks, some stopped patronizing them during crackdowns for fear of being caught in a raid, which might result in their being arrested or at least being forced to divulge their names and places of employment, which carried the threat of further penalties if the police contacted their landlords or employers. Nonetheless, they found other places to meet their friends and to continue their participation in gay society. Private parties were especially important at such times, but so, too, were commercial establishments not known for their gay patronage. Not only were the police less likely to raid such places, but a man's homosexuality would not necessarily be revealed if he happened to be seen there by a straight associate.[20] Some men of moderate means joined the fairies in the restaurants and cafeterias in the area, which, because they operated without liquor licenses, continued to be relatively safe even after Repeal, but men of greater wealth and social status had access to more secure venues, whose very respectability offered them protection against the dangers of being arrested or recognized as homosexual. Several of the elegant nightclubs that opened to the north and east of the Square in the late twenties and thirties tolerated or even welcomed such men, so long as they remained discreet.

A somewhat more varied group of men frequented the highly respectable businessmen's bars found in many hotels, such as the Oak Room at the Plaza and the King Cole Room at the St. Regis, whose respectability and political clout offered them protection, and where well-dressed men drinking by themselves or with a few male friends would hardly draw attention.

The longest-lived and most famous such bar in the Times Square area (although not the most elegant one) was the Astor Hotel bar at the corner of Seventh Avenue and Forty-fifth Street. Although it had served as a gay meeting place since the 1910s, it became particularly well known during the Second World War, when it developed a national reputation among gay servicemen as a place to meet civilians when passing through New York. Gay men's use of the bar was carefully orchestrated—in both its spatial and cultural dimensions—to protect both their identities and its license. Gay men gathered on only one side of the oval bar, where the management allowed them to congregate so long as they did not become too "obvious." As one man who frequented the Astor during the war recalled, "the management would cut us down a little bit when it felt we were getting a little too obvious. . . . If you got a little too buddy, or too cruisey . . . too aggressive, they'd say cut it out, men, why don't you go somewhere else? You had to be more subtle." Men on the other side of the bar, he added, were allowed to "do anything they wanted; they could put *their* arms around each other, *they* could touch, because it was very obvious that they were butch."[21]

Gay men had to be "subtle" so that the straight men all around them—including the occasional strangers who unknowingly sat down on the gay side of the bar—would not realize they were surrounded by "queers." Gay men used the same codes they had developed in other contexts to alert each other to their identities: wearing certain clothes fashionable among gay men but not stereotypically associated with them, introducing certain topics of conversation, or casually using code words well known within the gay world but unremarkable to those outside it ("gay" itself was such a word in the 1930s and 1940s). Using such codes, men could carry on extensive and highly informative conversations whose real significance would remain unintelligible to the people around them.

Two other examples will illustrate gay men's ability to covertly but surely appropriate public spaces for their own purposes, even in the context of the post–Prohibition clampdown. For, on a much larger scale than at the Astor, gay men regularly gathered en masse at the performances of entertainers who (for reasons beyond the scope of this chapter) assumed special significance in gay culture. Whether or not the other members of the audience noticed them, *they* were aware of their numbers in the audience and often shared in the collective excitement of transforming such a public gathering into a "gay space," no matter how covertly. Judy Garland's concerts would take on this character in later years; Beatrice Lillie's concerts were among the most famous such events within the gay world in the early 1930s. "The Palace was just packed with queers, for weeks at a time, when Lillie performed," remembered one man who had been in the audience; one of her signature songs, "There Are Fairies at the Bottom of My Garden," was a camp classic in the gay world, and twenty years later Lillie noted that she still "always" got requests for it from her audience.[22]

The Metropolitan Opera, on Broadway at Fortieth Street, was another "standard meeting place," according to the same man, and another man whimsically recalled that "since there were no known instances of police raids on [such distinguished] cultural events, all stops were pulled out as far as costume and grooming. The hairdos and outlandish clothes many gays wore were not to be equaled until the punk rock era."[23] The cultural significance of such events had always been determined as much by the audience as by the stage; but as their role in gay culture suggests, such events were the site of multiple audiences and productive of multiple cultural meanings, many of them obscure to the class that nominally dominated them.

Far from being confined to marginalized locales, then, gay men claimed some of the most conventional of cultural spaces as their own. Such were the politics of public space in much of Times Square. Gay men and straight men often used the same sites in entirely different ways, with the latter not suspecting the presence of the "queers" in their midst, in part because the "queers" did not look or behave like the "fairies" they saw at

Bryant Park. Thus the Astor maintained its public reputation as an eminently respectable Times Square rendezvous, while its reputation as a gay rendezvous and pickup bar assumed legendary proportions in the gay world; and on certain nights the Metropolitan Opera became the "biggest bar in town."

Still, gay men's use of the Square was a hard-won and unstable victory, which required them to engage in constant territorial struggles with the agents of the dominant cultural order. Different groups of men adopted different strategies of everyday resistance to the dominant order, different strategies for staking out and defining their worlds, and those differences often brought them into conflict. Nonetheless, even those men who chose to remain most hidden from the dominant culture were not hidden from each other. Gay men became part of the spectacle of Times Square, but they also transformed it into a haven.

16

PRIVATE PARTS IN PUBLIC PLACES

Laurence Senelick

"If you get three Americans in one place, two will get together to reform the morals of the third."

H. L. Mencken[1]

A LONDON MAGAZINE reported recently on the current proliferation of prostitutes in the Earls Court area and commented on a passage of arms between a black transvestite and a "civilian": "This incident occurred not, as you might have expected, on the sidewalk of Times Square but outside the Underground station in Earls Court Road."[2] Violent encounters and flaunted deviancy are taken by the world at large to be "expected" in Times Square: the Great White Way is now a byword for ostentatious flesh-peddling in an open-air meat-rack. How has it come about that Times Square should be perceived as, to use Steven Marcus's term, pornotopia?[3] Is it the condition or the perception of the condition that is novel?

A current sociological study notes that, whereas in 1933 the musical film *Forty-Second Street* portrayed Times Square as a glittering world of show business, John Schlesinger's *Midnight Cowboy* in 1968 characterized it as a squalid subculture of sex-for-hire.[4] This is a popular contrast but a superficial one, promoting the civic myth of a primordial Square that was once an Arcadian playground for all white New Yorkers. The differences between the two films are not so great. Made during the Depression, *Forty-Second Street* actually draws a cynical picture of hungry girls like "Anytime Annie" ("she only said No once, and then she didn't hear the question") who will "put out" for a part in the chorus; they may be loose in the hilts, but are shown as brave, self-reliant, and realistic in a tough time.

The sexual economics of *Midnight Cowboy* are more blatant and, because the prostitute is male in a patriarchal society, allegedly more depraved. Both films offer depictions of microcosms—the closed system of the theater, with untouchable allure projected across the footlights, and the closed system of hustling, with attainable allure flashed on the street corner. But because the former is kept behind its proscenium frame and remains expensively out of reach (especially for a Depression public), it retains glamor, whereas the latter, all too approachable, seems sordid in its potential for realization. Loud protests are raised nowadays about the flamboyant drag queens who "turn tricks" on Eighth Avenue, but no one objected in 1895 when Oscar Hammerstein's Music Hall on Forty-fifth Street and Broadway opened with a female impersonator on its bill.[5] The footlights neutralized and beautified what was unacceptable under the streetlights. Still, what Una Merkel in *Forty-Second Street* purveys to the chorus director behind the scenes and what Jon Voight purveys to closet cases in penny arcades in *Midnight Cowboy* remain the same commodity. Times Square did not gradually change from the Great White Way to the City of Dreadful Night; rather, its veneer rubbed off to reveal the economic realities that had always been present.

Illicit sexual activity in New York has never been limited to any particular neighborhood; certain vicinities gained a reputation for vice simply because gamy goings-on were more conspicuous there than elsewhere. Before the Civil War, moralists and visitors characterized the Bowery and the Five Points as the sinkhole of the city, but by the 1870s and 1880s, as commercial and public life moved uptown and westward, so did what the reformers stigmatized as the Social Evil—prostitution. Satan's Circus, the nickname for the area between Fifth and Seventh avenues and bounded by Twenty-fourth and Fortieth Streets, became the focus of attention for reporters seeking a lurid story or preachers a sensational sermon. It was also at this time that the stretch of westside streets from Fourteenth to Forty-second won the name Tenderloin, allegedly from a venal cop who contrasted the pickings to be had there with those from a rumpsteak area. Less affluent and opulent in its display of vice was Hell's Kitchen, the area north and south of West Thirty-fourth Street and west of Eighth Avenue, which rose to notoriety in the 1890s. Some said it was so called because of the emanations from the many steam vents in the roadway; others, because a veteran police officer had opined that hell was a mild climate compared to it.[6] Only ten blocks from Times Square, its reputation for gang warfare and abject poverty went unchallenged until most of it was demolished for the Lincoln Tunnel and the bus terminal.

From its beginnings, then, the Times Square region was ringed round with red lights. The business districts near West Forty-second Street between Sixth and Seventh avenues and the residential areas near West Fifty-fourth between Fifth and Eighth avenues were honeycombed with parlor houses. After a series of raids made them inoperative, their activities transferred to Raines Law hotels. The Raines Law had been passed to prevent sales of liquor in saloons on Sunday, but it was legal to sell drink in hostelries with no fewer than ten bedrooms. Saloonkeepers opened up hotels in such numbers that over ten thousand new bedrooms were added to Manhattan in short space, most of them occupied by prostitutes. After the crusading citizens' Committee of Fourteen forced cleanups in 1905 and again in 1912, these were converted to male-only residences, but after World War I they reverted to their original use. Most of the side streets leading off Broadway's theater district were occupied exclusively by such hotels, where it was alleged that during an entr'acte you could get anything from a quick "knee-trembler" to an abortion.[7]

In the early days of Times Square, prostitution was carried on openly, but because it was upscale and discreetly conducted (the discretion prompted in part by the ongoing action of the Committee of Fourteen), the public attitude towards it was relaxed, not to say tolerant. Discriminating brothels in the upper Forties and lower Fifties between Broadway and Fifth refused to admit customers if they failed to arrive in cabs or taxis. Broadway was the avenue most favored by streetwalkers, but only of the most expensive kind, and it was *de rigueur* not to solicit. The woman would linger at a shop window and wait for a man to approach her with the formulaic "Anything doing tonight, dearie?" These high-priced hookers received commissions from the managers of the cafés and hotels they patronized, and they could afford to pay graft to the police and protection to their pimps. In turn, the pimps and the cops were in collusion to harass any streetwalker who tried to maintain her independence.[8]

Chorus girls and kept women were entertained at fashionable restaurants, some of which, like their European counterparts, provided *chambres séparées* complete with sofas, to accommodate digestive coition. (Rectitudinous Rector's did not, but limited itself to supplying a gastronomic prelude, thus acting as kind of sexual off-license.) The interclass dalliance promoted by Times Square restaurants was such common knowledge that a line from a Weber and Fields revue became proverbial. A chorus girl is asked if she ever found a pearl in an oyster; she replies, "No, but I got a diamond from a lobster over in Rector's last night." The final curtain line of Eugene Walter's 1909 play about a kept woman, *The Easiest Way*, also turned into a catchphrase; the heroine, abandoned by both her keeper and her lover, proclaims at the end with an insouciance worthy of Scarlett O'Hara, "I'm going to Rector's to make a hit and to hell with the rest."[9] Any Broadway audience of the time would deduce that she meant to pick up a new protector there.

The proximity of restaurants to theaters, which, to pay the increasing rentals, expanded into cabarets and roof gardens, encouraged this reciprocity between the actress's dressing room and the millionaire's boudoir. The murders of Louise Lawson and Dot King, both young actresses kept by well-to-do men and both strangled with their own stockings, and the case of Evelyn Nesbit Thaw, a former chorus girl whose rich husband shot her lover, the architect Stanford White, impressed this intercourse on the public mind.[10]

It was an age-old symbiosis. In 1753 a writer in the London journal *The World* had sarcastically suggested that "at the Play-house, young gentlemen and ladies were instructed by an Etheridge, a Wycherley, a Congreve and a Vanbrugh, in the rudiments of that science which they were to perfect at the Bagnio."[11] In the early nineteenth century, American theaters had stayed solvent because of receipts from their bars and admissions to the third tier, a haunt of prostitutes.[12] Moralists who attacked the theater had powerful ammunition in this economically dictated nexus between sex and stage, and would soon train their gun sights on Times Square.

The rapid sleazification of Times Square was due not to a moral breakdown but to a most moral experiment: the passage of the Volstead Act in 1919. Divested of their liquor sales, the restaurants and roof gardens folded. They were replaced by after-hours, nonalcoholic cabarets which, for a fifty dollar cover charge, provided chorus girls or walk-on actresses for each table: the customer could take it from there.[13] A highly symbolic transfer occurred in 1924 when Murray's restaurant, famous for its revolving dance floor, closed, and its well-located premises, on Forty-second Street between Broadway and Eighth Avenue, were leased to Hubert's Museum. A typical dime museum specializing in freaks, platform acts, and Professor Heckler's Flea Circus, along with a view of the "Hidden Secrets" of sex as displayed by the "French Academy of Medicine, Paris," Hubert's was often cited in the thirties as a sign of the area's decay. But it proved to have great survival potential, and persisted into the 1960s, by which time, despite turning into a pinball arcade, it had become, after the New York Public Library, "the ranking cultural institution" on Forty-second Street.[14]

The reason this shift from posh restaurant to cheap dime museum is symbolic has to do with more than the decline from carriage trade to *hoi polloi*. It signals a transference from participation to, if I may coin a word, spectation. Wining and dining a chorus girl was a sport of the rich or at least the well-heeled; the sexual consummation was a private tête-à-tête (or *corps-à-corps*) behind closed doors. What took place was experienced solely by the parties involved, even though a host of constables, waiters, barmen, cabbies, and florists may have benefited financially from the transaction.

The dime museum, on the other hand, represents a spectacle offered to the eyes of the multitude, a spectacle that promises to unveil the hidden, the forbidden, the secrets of the alcove. In downtown dime museums, the manager would bawl, "In de rear room, gemmen, dere's a exhibition of such a nature dat no ladies an' no boys uner sixteen is allowed. Ten cents admits each an' every sport!"[15] The rear room may have contained nothing more titillating than Indian artefacts and a tame bear, for dime museums sought to avoid scandal, but the claim to enlightening the public was bolstered by displays of wax casts of venereal ailments, deformed genitalia, and graphic depictions of embryo development. Within the dimly lit sanctums of the dime museum, those aspects of human nature normally kept under wraps were solemnly exfoliated. The male viewer—the "sport"—could gaze, but not touch, on the mysteries of generation, ostensibly for his edification, but also for a surreptitious titillation, the sense that here one was admitted, in all safety, to a prohibited pleasure. One might savor the aroma of the fruits of the tree of knowledge without actually biting into them. The joys of the dime museum are passive: the imagination is stimulated without an outlet for physical gratification. But it had to remain a backroom pleasure. As late as 1911, Anthony Comstock, the egregious Dogberry of American morals, had had asexual wax figures removed from the window of a Broadway garment manufacturer because they exhibited their anodyne nudity.[16]

A similar voyeurism is an ingredient of the theatrical spectator's pleasure as well, and as Prohibition-era reformers managed to sweep prostitution off the streets, making it low key and discreet, they trained their attention on the theater. Oddly enough, it may be George Bernard Shaw who pioneered the notion of "adult entertainment" in Times Square. When, in 1904, Arnold Daly sought to stage *Mrs. Warren's Profession*, Shaw's comedy about brothel-keeping as a capitalist enterprise, the playwright inserted a special clause into the contract stipulating that "the Manager shall endeavour as far as may be practicable to apprise the public of the fact that the Play is suitable for representation before serious adult audiences only."[17] Despite Shaw's proviso that his play be X-rated, the 1905 production at the Garrick Theatre was attacked by the newspapers as gangrenous smut-peddling, and, incited by Comstock, the police closed it down. Shaw coined the term "Comstockery" to characterize such officious prudery. A generation later, the prudes were back on the prowl.

In 1923 a magistrate dismissed charges against a downtown burlesque dancer with the observation, "The standard of morals is no higher on the East Side than at Broadway and Forty-second Street."[18] What he meant was that scantily clad but high-toned revues were flourishing on Broadway while cheaper burlesque was relegated primarily to the Lower East Side. Ziegfeld, the Shubert Brothers, George White, and Earl Carroll all featured female nudity as an attraction, the spectrum running from Ziegfeld's refined artiness to Carroll's blatant eroticism.[19] Bernard Sobel complained, without irony, that the morals of burlesque were being ruined by Broadway: strippers were no longer having affairs with company members, but

> employ the gold-digging methods perfected by some Broadway show girls; that is, prostitution so thickly coated with stage glamor and publicity that it escapes this invidious term; systematized prostitution, nevertheless, with consistent holding out, conscious capitulation and definite subsidy.[20]

To the reformers it seemed as if the sex they had swept from the streets had settled on the stage. Throughout the 1920s and well into the 1930s, the revues were raided and the legitimate theaters regularly attacked by John Sumner and the Society for the Suppression of Vice. In 1923 religious organizations declared a ban on a very mixed bag which contained Brieux's anti-syphilis play *Damaged Goods*, Sholem Asch's Yiddish melodrama *The God of Vengeance*, Avery Hopwood's romantic comedy *The Demi-Virgin*, and two musical revues, *Topics of 1923* and *Artists and Models*.[21] A stage censorship bill introduced in Albany failed to win passage, but three years later the district attorney empaneled three hundred citizens to "pass on the moral content of theater productions."[22] He drew up a list of shows he regarded as unacceptable, and when the managers failed to close them, he raided the three he considered most degrading: Edouard Bourdet's neurasthenic lesbian drama *The Captive*, Mae West's lighthearted period piece *Sex*, and William Francis Dugan's *The Virgin Man*. Fines and short jail terms were imposed on the authors and producers.

Although Governor Alfred E. Smith opposed official censorship and New York's bon vivant mayor Jimmy Walker was heard to remark, "Did you ever know a woman who was ruined by a book?"[23] as good Catholics they were pressured into complying with the religious community's onslaught on the drama. In 1927 Smith signed into law the Wales Act, which allowed theaters to be padlocked for a year, with a caution that licenses might not be renewed if the police decided, before its opening, that a play was obscene or if a jury decided, after the opening, that the show on display tended to corrupt minors.[24] This placed the onus on the theater-owner to oust the offending show or else suffer financial loss. The first play so prosecuted was the French drama *Maya*, about a Marseilles prostitute whose customers' fantasies deify her; neither the critics nor the producer Lee Shubert found anything offensive in it, but it was withdrawn after a week.[25] At the same time, the district attorney made no effort to close the melodrama *The Shanghai Gesture*, which the critics had excoriated as flashy sensationalism; a kind of *Mrs. Warren Goes East*, it is set in Mother Goddam's elegant Shanghai bordello, where girls wait in hanging cages to be chosen. Apparently the district attorney believed that exoticism and an unhappy ending defanged vice, while the lowly setting of *Maya* and the equation of whore with earth goddess put public morals in jeopardy. The following year, when the cast of Mae West's *Pleasure Man* was arrested after two performances, the critic Hiram Motherwell pointed out the law's Catch-22:

> The Wales law can only be invoked where the theatre manager or owner refuses to alter or eject a play which the police have adjudged obscene. In an undefendable case like that of *Pleasure Man* no producer or owner is going to defy a clear police order. But in a case like that of *The Captive* it may be the moral right and duty of the producer to protest the irresponsible decision of the police and insist on a fair trial in the courts—in other words, to take exactly the action which would make Wales procedure virtually mandatory.[26]

Note his own offhand assumption that a comedy is unjustifiable, a sexual tragedy justifiable. There was clearly no consensus on what constituted stage obscenity. Who was being protected: sophisticated Broadwayite, visiting hicks, or Mr. Podsnap's "young person"? Despite the Wales Act's patent unconstitutionality, it remained on the statute books for four decades.

Constrained to mute their erotic appeal and sexual frankness when these elements were clearly to the audience's taste, the high-priced theaters succumbed during the Depression to the laws of the marketplace: those that did not convert to cinemas were taken over by entrepreneurs of the bump-and-grind. Three of these five conversions were engineered by the Minskys, who leased the International at Columbus Circle, the Central at Forty-seventh Street, and, most notoriously, the Republic at 207 W. Forty-second Street. Turning his back on earlier attempts to camouflage burlesque as "musical comedy," Billy Minsky trumpeted the vulgarity of his shows to such effect that Brooks Atkinson was compelled to admit that they "were the bawdiest this neighborhood has seen for years."[27] The Minskys' success emboldened other entrepreneurs: the Apollo Theatre, which had housed the sophisticated nudities of *George White's Scandals* for eight years, now sheltered Max Wilner's high-class burlesque; under Max Rudnick, the Eltinge also went the way of all flesh. It was noted that the good fortune of Times Square burlesque depended on low salaries and secondhand scenery, abetted by the curiosity of the man in the street. Outside New York, rising railway fares and the conversion of theaters to movie houses had all but vanquished the circuits or Wheels; burlesque's last stronghold was Forty-second Street and Seventh Avenue.[28] By 1937, chronicler Irving Zeidman reports, "burlesque. . .was threatening to engulf the entire Broadway area,"[29] ever more daring in its advertisement and sumptuousness.

The ensuing protests and opprobrium had, as usual, an economic foundation, and, under the smokescreen of religious outrage, their instigators were theater owners and producers envious of burlesque's takings. Uptown burlesque shows differed in no essential quality from those downtown, which were temporarily left unscathed. It was the "frowsiness" of the facades of those in Times Square and the slumlike environment they seemed to engender that were accused of devaluing neighboring businesses and fostering a clientele unpropitious to other commercial interests. With burlesque's street barkers and gaudy posters, the district had taken on the coloration of a carnival midway, and what had once been discreetly concealed behind elegant facades was now emblazoned in the open.

Even before the invasion of burlesque, Times Square had become the venue of "pickled punk," shows featuring fetuses in alcohol, living statuary which was always unrobed if immobile, and lecturers on restoring virile potency. It housed a Salon des Arts hung with thirty nude paintings, where, as patrons of the finer things looked on, an artist in smock and beret would churn out fresh masterpieces based on the nude model on display.[30]

Some deplored the decline from lobster palaces to chop suey joints, but many, like the painter Reginald Marsh, found the change exhilarating: Minskyville, as *The New Yorker* renamed the district, seethed with life, an Hogarthian lustiness lit by neon and punctuated by the spiels of the pitchmen. As Brooks McNamara has noted (see Chapter 9), the Square was redefining itself as an entertainment district for a broader popular audience.[31] It was a year-long version of the fairground, and, as in Ben Jonson's comedy about *Bartholomew Fair*, there were always plenty of Justice Overdos and puritanical Zeal-of-the-Land Busys eager to see it banned.

A recent sociological study has stated that *"regardless of the level of crime,* little tends to undermine the fabric of a city more than visible street deviance [which] creates an offensive atmosphere, especially for children."[32] This is a relatively modern and remarkably culture-bound attitude: ignoring long traditions of bazaars and public squares, it derives from nineteenth century modes of social control, policing, and city planning, which sought to contain outdoor activity of all sorts within closed, licensed premises. It distrusts social plurality and the interaction of classes and attitudes, while it subjects urban life to stratification or compartmentalization. At present it contributes to the proliferation of surburban malls and the Disneyland style of sterilized amusement park. In its view, the efflorescence of sexuality in plain sight, illicit or not, was and would remain deplorable in Times Square.

The attempts to curtail burlesque in 1933 and 1934, while the Depression still raged, had scant success, since celebrities were willing to attest that it was no dirtier than many profane Broadway hits. Literary figures insisted that the padlocking of Republic burlesque was the thin edge of the wedge that would imperil legitimate theater.[33] Female employees in burlesque houses testified that they had never been attacked or pestered by customers. This suggests that the current ongoing debate as to whether erotic shows incite or defuse the spectator's lust had already been engaged. But in 1937, a number of external factors combined to eliminate burlesque entirely. First, a series of sex crimes had occurred in the city just before licenses were to be renewed, and it was claimed, with no hard evidence, that the moral chaos created by burlesque had bred a climate in which such crimes could flourish; one Brooklyn clergyman declared that a man who had seen such a show came home and assaulted his own daughter.

Nowadays, when burlesque is an object of nostalgia, it is hard to imagine the vehemence of the attack launched on the burley houses of Times Square in 1937. Although the rallying cry was still the preservation of morality, the spearhead of the attack was the 42nd Street Property Owners and Merchants Association, which enlisted the aid of the Society for the Suppression of Vice and the local clergy, but always remained the front man of the legal actions. When enjoying such affectionate recreations as *Sugar Babies*, we should bear in mind that burlesque theaters at that time were branded as "breeders of vice" and "loitering places for men who trade on the shady side of night life," and Forty-second Street as "a cesspool of filth and obscenity." One theater manager complained with some justice, "We've been accused of everything except kidnapping the Lindbergh baby."[34]

Most important to the success of the attack, there was a reform administration in office which had to live up to its billing. After smashing fruit machines with a sledgehammer for the news cameramen in his war against gambling, Mayor La Guardia was eager to be seen as the David who slew the Goliath of what he called "incorporated filth."[35] Licenses were denied to all fourteen existing burlesque houses in New York, and no new ones were issued; by fiat the very word "burlesque" disappeared from the lexicon of show business advertising.[36] Complaints from the American Civil Liberties Union were met with the prudish mayor's insistence that burlesque was just so much sewage and he had the right to abolish it in the interests of public health. So for 20 years, New York and Times Square in particular did without burlesque—with no perceptible improvement in the moral climate of the area. As one historian remarks, burlesque was usually behind the times, sexually speaking, and any evils that might trail in its wake were "symptoms of more basic deficiencies."[37]

337

An incidental effect of La Guardia's ban was that the few remaining Times Square playhouses devoted to live entertainment finally metamorphosed into cinemas or "grinders," cheap continuous showings which made their appeal to an exclusively stag trade.[38] By the late 1930s, Times Square was already notorious for its honky-tonk atmosphere, its once-elegant restaurants replaced by luncheonettes, its cigar stores and lobbies inhabited by a new element of petty hoodlums. Its hotels, avoided by out-of-towners for fear of crime, charged streetwalkers a dollar for the time it took to turn a trick. The Times Square working girls were now regarded as almost the cheapest white prostitutes in the city, hard put to make seventy-five dollars a week.[39] However, this pervasive ambience of lawlessness and squalor was not particularly licentious: off-track betting was a more common misdemeanor than sexual solicitation.

Sex on the hoof really returned to the area with the Second World War. The blowsy blonde runway queens and front-row baldheads in the paintings of Reginald Marsh were superseded by the riotous gobs and gals in the paintings of Paul Cadmus. Servicemen and their adolescent companions flooded into Times Square to kick up their heels on the eve of destruction. The urban tourist described by Neil Harris (see Chapter 3) as a by-product of the commercial city[40] had evolved into the sexual tourist, who could breathe a heady aroma of freedom from small-town mores in Times Square, and, submerged in its crowds, experience a reassuring assumption of anonymity. Anonymity is the privacy of the crowd. It is still an important factor in the sexual tourist's attraction to Times Square. In wartime, it was abetted by the electrical dimout which tempered the carnival atmosphere with one of mystery, when even the MPs were powerless to prevent the fracas that occurred in the subway arcades.

The invasion of servicemen made another feature—men picking up men—more conspicuous. Previously, and from the 1870s, the downtown area adjacent to Broadway and Houston was regarded as the happy hunting ground of male-to-male sexuality, and Greenwich Village took on a reputation it still merits. In the gay nineties, as his memoirs relate, the self-styled "androgyne" Earl Lind cruised for rough trade in Stuyvesant Square and on Mulberry Street between Grand and Broome; male prostitution had moved as far uptown as Fourteenth Street.[41] The Times Square Building became a popular rendezvous in the late twenties, but wartime put the activity back on the streets. By the early 1940s, young Tennessee Williams was making "abrupt and candid overtures" to groups of sailors and GIs on Times Square street corners; when, as often as not, they accepted his solicitation, he would bring them back to his cruising partner's Village "pad" or to his own, closer room at the Y.[42]

The first civic measure taken to curtail such activity appears to be the nightly closing of Bryant Park to the public in 1944, because, according to

338

Mayor La Guardia, "various types of undesirables are gathering there." "Undesirables" became the temporary euphemism, tabloid headlines screamed UNDESIRABLES ARRESTED.[43] Both cruising and its consummation moved into the "grinders" and went on undisturbed in restrooms and movie balconies.

The postwar calls for a cleanup were, as usual, economically founded, as corporations and their taxes moved out of midtown Manhattan and many theaters were left empty. Revisions of the zoning codes in 1947 and 1954 did little to halt what most chroniclers lament as the downward slide of Times Square. One study has wryly noted that the new zoning code unintentionally "encouraged the advent of the Forty-second Street porno bookstore by driving out competitors for space on the street."[44] The prevention of the opening of new penny arcades and similar sucker-bait led to the proliferation of souvenir shops which sold imitation bronze Empire State Buildings over the counter, and photographs of other sorts of erections in the backroom. The ostentation of the arcade, a public space, was replaced by the clandestine "dirty bookshop," a more private space protected by the social assumption that what was invisible did not exist.

The sensational press reported that both streetwalkers and what science had taught it to call homosexuals were more abundant and more conspicuous in their abundance than ever before. Yet there was clearly a division of opinion as to whether Times Square was the Sodom and Gomorrah it was made out to be. Throughout the course of his 25-year tenure at Holy Cross Church, an annual jeremiad from the parish priest Father McCaffrey inveighed against the degeneration of the neighborhood; by 1960 he was insisting that murder and rape were potential at any moment. At the same time, the Police Department stated that out of New York's eighty-one precincts, Times Square would not fall in the top quarter of the list for major crime. It housed no brothels, only one legitimate nightclub, and was responsible for only four drug arrests in 1959. Commentators on these phenomena put them down to the transient nature of the neighborhood and the low incomes of its denizens.[45] Poverty and vagrancy in a nonresidential area were now being cited as deterrents to serious crime.

According to the same commentators, the police considered the major nuisances in 1960 to be chestnut vendors, beggars, intemperate evangelists, and the "fags" on Forty-second Street. In the late forties, a new style of male hustler had emerged, often ex-servicemen or youths openly declaring that their sexual preferences were for rent. Most of the hustler bars were on the East Side, but Forty-second Street between Seventh and Eighth avenues became the weekend Mecca for out-of-town kids.[46] The loitering of young men in open shirts and dungarees became well established, yet most arrests of males in Times Square in the fifties were for brawling. At this unenlightened period, both police and their reporters complained that the boys in what they deemed "Queens County" were "not easy to identify," devoid of tell-tale marks of effeminacy, and solicitation was not so simple to descry as with a female prostitute and her more obvious markings. Distinguishing the female whore from the modern woman was also tougher than in the days when, as one hotel manager remarked, "You used to be able to tell a prostitute by the fact that she let you see her smoking."[47]

What John Rechy was later to melodramatize as the "boiling subterranean" world of the hustler's Times Square[48] remained invisible to the average passerby, who would go his way unperturbed, unaware that sexual synapses were being formed by—to use a Shakespearean word—"oeillades." Eye contact bears great significance in an area where those who are merely passing through keep their eyes modestly downcast or unfocused. In Alan Bowne's recent play *Forty-Deuce*, one underage hustler refers to these unwitting pedestrians as the "goyim" who "just look at you like you wasn't there or like the street was a movie and you was this extra?"[49] On the other hand, knowing linkage of eyes between potential consumer and potential consumable is the complicitous signal of entente. Taking pictures of Hispanic juvenile hustlers, the photographer Larry Clark was fascinated by "kids' eyes, the way a kid looks at a man. . . . It's a look, right? It's an entire attitude. It's a way of seeing things, but it's all polished up. It's a point of sale."[50]

This unobtrusiveness and ocular complicity between hustler and client drove—and still drives—the authorities wild, by evading their measures for control. In 1961 the Wagner administration, urged on by the press, tried to validate its credentials for crime-fighting by sealing "the Hole," an IRT entrance through the Rialto Arcade known to be a pickup point for teenagers; it also prosecuted *louche* bookstores and cinemas. These were token gestures, though, since the police candidly admitted their inability to curb the sexual interest males take in one another.

Father McCaffrey's lament in 1959 that things could not get worse was remarkably shortsighted. The consensus perception is that the increase of Times Square's sexual activity throughout the 1960s had something to do with an enlarged drug trade, but it should be remembered that even in the late thirties, Times Square was, next to Harlem, the city's most open market for cheap reefers.[51] More certain is the fact that the drug culture introduced an element of violence and petty crime hitherto uncommon to sexual solicitation.

The libertarianism of the sixties, informed by new Supreme Court decisions on obscenity, paved the way for the sex industry, as entrepreneurs began purveying allurements to the libido on a grand scale. What had formerly been considered liminal and illicit moved into the forefront of

340

the American consciousness, borne in by all the power of advertising and its media. Times Square had the advantage of being an old-established firm in the sex business; the under-the-counter and hole-in-corner triumphantly bobbed to the surface. Prostitution of all gender affiliations, massage parlors, live sex shows, and bookstores now called "adult" (Shaw would have been amused) burgeoned into the most characteristic features of the area. Over the next two decades not only did erotica shed its plain brown wrappers, but newstands blossomed with such mass-appeal publications as *Screw* and *Hustler*. The traditionally eroticized female body was now joined in the open by its male counterpart: the most prominent billboard in Times Square was rented by Calvin Klein to display models naked from the waist up, their buttocks snugly fitted into his designer jeans. "The tighter they are, the better they sell." was his rationale.[52]

In 1966 the first twenty-five-cent peepshows were introduced amid the comparatively tame wares of Times Square bookshops. Instant success caused overnight conversions of many small businesses back to arcades now featuring explicit magazines and film loops, which, to suit quickening public demand, intensified their content from nude dancers to copulation. Higher profits, which had sent the cost of leases skyward, attracted the attention of the mob which muscled in around 1968; even after paying for protection, peepshow vendors could become millionaires. Their machines proliferated to about a thousand throughout the city, mostly located at first in fetid backrooms and curtained cubicles of porno bookshops. One reporter recalls that "viewing time in the good old days was two minutes for a quarter; inflation would drop this to thirty seconds in just a dozen years."[53]

A major factor in the popularity of peepshows was the introduction of curtains and doors, offering privacy to the customer.[54] This heightened the crucial factor of anomie, for while peepshow sex is a form of public enjoyment, sexual consumption, usually by masturbation, remains private. To quote one researcher, "in the pornographic arcade, the dominant theme of behavior is one of mutual inaccessibility of patrons"[55]; another student of the Times Square sexual community believes that "anonymity" must be *socially created* by rules patrons observe. Hiding behavior functions as a sense of shame or show of apology for 'deviant' behavior."[56] This would suggest that customers for pornography are among the best-behaved, most self-effacing, least lawbreaking one might imagine. The tacit refusal to acknowledge the presence of other clientele keeps the atmosphere muted and innocuous.

Ironically, and despite the plaints of reformers, the new sex industry eventually upgraded the neighborhood. Replacing the turn-the-crank peeps and fleapits, Show World Center, which opened in 1977, was antiseptic, well lit, up-to-date, offering a choice of printed, cinematic, or live pornography; structurally sound, it has defeated assaults on it via the building code. Show World inspired imitators. Hubert's Museum may have discontinued its live freakshows in 1965, but in 1978 Peepland carried on the dime museum tradition of unveiling the arcane by opening a basement exhibition of sex loops featuring donkeys, eels, and German shepherds.[57] Emporia like Show World continue to promote anonymity while reducing guilt, since they are more reminiscent of supermarkets than of old "scumatoriums."

Live peepshows behind glass had begun to filter in in the early 1970s, and by 1978, the glass partitions were removed, so that the customer could touch, feel, taste the far-from-obscure object of his desire, the girls negotiating the price for particular favors. This kind of promiscuity ended in January 1980, when Show World reinstalled its windows, not on account of hygiene or morality, but for purely legal reasons. As the manager said, "Girls were makin' all kinds of deals with the customers—in fact, we were threatened that we'd be shut down for prostitution." They lost money as a result, but even the peeps that retained an open-window policy limited contact to breasts. (The sexual entertainment industry is, by its own standards, cautiously law-abiding, eager to keep its distance from prostitution and drug-pushing and to observe its proscription to minors.[58])

The honor of first showing a live deed of kind in Times Square falls to the Mini-Cine in the Wurlitzer Building, which, in 1970, presented it as part of a so-called "studio tour" of the filming of porno loops. From an ethnographic standpoint, public copulation, either real or simulated, is a time-honored and ancient rite connected with fertility and recalling the union of Heaven and Earth.[59] As a community becomes secularized, the act loses its sacral meaning, although sex is never wholly divested of its occult allure; and when the society is in upheaval or intense transition, such routines, normally confined to brothels, seek a public stage, as was the case in Paris after the fall of the Bastille and in Berlin after World War I. Much of what goes on on the third floor of Show World is simply the logical culmination of what burlesque and even earlier Aristophanic comedy had suggested, with dildos the more graphic embodiment of emblematic slapsticks and harlequin bats. Show World even uses an acting coach to help develop skits which have more than a tinge of Minsky about them: *Going Down* concerns a man and a women stuck in an elevator; *Lois and Clark* shows Lois Lane and Superman in bed together for the first time; and *Love Potion No. 69* deals with a mad scientist and his newly discovered aphrodisiac.[60] Performers are taught timing, to give audiences a chance to anticipate, posing for maximal viewing effect, and similar skills. Any lust thereby incited can be slaked on the premises. It may be objected that the graphic nature of these displays, which leave little or nothing to the imagination, are inferior to the alleged wit or style of the defunct burlesque show; but these are aesthetic, not moral, arguments.

In 1982 a German woman of twenty with a sociology degree sought employment in the New York sex industry. Turning down a position in a live-sex show which paid only ten dollars for twenty minutes' work and eschewed condoms, she took a job in a peepshow on the guarantee of "no contact" and lots of money. In her tiny cubicle, she found a way to conceal a camera and adjust the lighting so that she could photograph her customers as they masturbated in her presence. Consequently, her book of reminiscences, interviews, and pictures cannot be published in this country, and her pseudonym Elisabeth B keeps her safe from lawsuits and extralegal retribution.

Encounters last only forty seconds before the screen comes down and the man must reinsert a quarter token (the normal stint runs to two dollars at most, but regulars can time their orgasms to two forty-second terms: Elisabeth B equates this with the "fast food" phenomenon, and wonders if her clients are equally efficient when actually engaged in coition). Since the woman receives half the money spent, it is to her advantage to prolong the session. Elisabeth B was struck by the absolute mediocrity of her clientele: most of them white and white-collar, between the ages of thirty and forty, with briefcases, shined shoes, and the *New York Times* under their arms, occasionally a grandfatherly type or some 20-year-old in jeans. No blacks, a great many exceedingly polite Asians. No rowdies, revolting monsters of ugliness, or cliché perverts. They generally arrived during their lunch hours or after their offices closed at 5. At least half were habitués who turned up three to five times a week; some seemed to spend all their leisure time there. One was a chauffeur who killed a couple of hours while his passengers were at the theater, an unexpected instance of the theater/sex nexus. As one regular, an investment counselor, put it: "I go with prostitutes too. But here it's cheaper and has exactly the same result."[61]

These men were uninterested in cunning stripteases or Playboy bunny poses: they wanted simply and staidly to study female anatomy in detail, and so Elisabeth B found herself most often taking the same position she would during a gynæcological examination. This aspect was underlined by the manageress periodically calling over the loudspeaker, "We need some hot pussy-inspectors down here."[62] Using the phone in their booth, younger customers asked Elisabeth B to show them where the clitoris is, how far a woman can open up, and similar details. She was touched by what she saw as an initiation rite in a society too puritanical to permit public nudity, topless sunbathing, and compulsory sex education. The peepshow had, *faute de mieux*, become a visual aid in instruction, just as the dime museum had been in the past.

In any prostitutional situation, as we have noted, the preliminary eyeballing is meant to culminate in a commercial transaction in which two or more parties participate. No matter how abstracted the prostitute's

343

participation may be, she or he is required as more than a mere simulacrum. But in the case of the peepshow, the client consumes not a body but the image of a body, under glass. The act of autostimulation uses the proffered image as three-dimensional pornography, a kind of jump start to the libido. No transaction, only reaction, takes place. Is this more or less degrading to the object of the client's lust? Is this more or less dehumanizing to both parties than the flesh-on-flesh commerce?

The received wisdom about such encounters is that they reify women and degrade men, but Elisabeth B's experiences offer some interesting qualifications. There were customers who preferred peepshows to prostitutes because actual physical contact prevented the exercise of the imagination, and as soon as the act was consummated, the woman left. "Whereas the girl behind this glass—she's all for you, whatever you desire in your fantasy. . .and *I'm* the one who leaves and can come back when *I* feel like it."[63] The masculine need for total control is certainly present here, a miserly hoarding of pleasure to one's self, along with the gnawing belief that in an ordinary prostitutional transaction, the customer is, in fact, at the mercy of the prostitute.

While admitting that she was required to become objectified, Elisabeth B also felt that she underwent a mythic metamorphosis into Woman with a capital W, the worshipped mystery of sex. She writes:

> The feeling of being reduced to a sexual object is in everyday encounters with men an annoyance, but here it is precisely the basis of the relationship; . . . in the changing-room I put this role on with the professional undergarments. . . . That I am desirable as an individual I know, but to incite someone wholly as Woman, as twat, as bosom, as legs, without doing anything else, has something reassuring about it.[64]

For her, the performance was a return to the original, sacred roots of prostitution as an act of devotion, an adoration of the fecund goddess, and the expenditure of semen a tribute laid at the source of fertility. The tacky was made transcendental.

With *Variety* tolling the knell for the Square as a theater district and Jerry Minskoff mourning the vacant third of his new office tower, Mayor Lindsay's Times Square Development Council, organized in 1971, debated ways to sanitize midtown, to no avail. A kind of climax came the following year when Gail Sheehy published two long articles in *New York* magazine, exposing the legal shenanigans of what she called "the landlords of Hell's bedroom." Her exposé revealed that the actual owners of the properties most cited as blights on the district were among the most influential, most taxed, and most prominent in the city, including members of the Development Council itself—banks, reformers, up-market developers. (Nothing new about this: in Elizabethan London, whores were known as "Winchester geese" since the brothels in Southwark were under the jurisdiction of the Bishop of Winchester.[65]) Most property owners claimed ignorance of what went on in their buildings, but one, a prominent heart surgeon, used to phone to check receipts at the all-male Eros cinema. The greed of the landlords and the growing public demand for hard-core pornography were too great to be stemmed by police foot patrols and license revocations. Moreover, police crackdowns on prostitution increased crime, since prostitutes having to meet their pimps' daily quotas found it easier to mug their clients than to have sex with them.

Faced with an area high in crime and low in residential population, the mayoral response in 1972 was to create two police "super precincts". Midtown South, dealing with Forty-second Street down to Thirtieth, and Midtown North, responsible for Forty-third to Fifty-ninth streets, Lexington Avenue west to the Hudson River.[66] Its periodic raids of massage parlors, closings of bookstores, mass arrests of prostitutes, always made a big splash in the newspapers but had no enduring effect on the streets. Most of the businesses were in the hands of organized crime, which could easily afford bail, court fees, and elaborate litigation.

Moreover, it turned out that no more than 5 percent of actual crime related to prostitution, and by law the police could deal with prostitution only on a criminal, not a moral, basis. Midtown North objected to the proliferation of prostitutes and pornography primarily because they attracted unspecified "undesirables" to the area along the "Minnesota Strip," fifteen blocks of Eighth Avenue running parallel to Times Square and intersecting it at the Deuce, the argot abbreviation for Forty-second Street. It got its name from the usual answer prostitutes gave desk sergeants when asked where they came from; their statement of origin often proved to be true. The cops who piloted the arrest van, the so-called Pussy Posse, maintained a reasonably friendly contact with their detainees; as for the girls, they were on the job because they could make an annual income four times that of a school teacher or a staff nurse.[67]

After 4 years of this labor-intensive but ineffectual policing, 1976 saw the foundation of the Office of Midtown Enforcement, which has been described as "a twenty-member legal swat team"[68]; it can as easily be seen as a grey flannel vice squad, endowed by the mayor with extraordinary powers. Its goal was not to chastise vice but to return Times Square real estate to "good commercial uses." It may be no coincidence that the same year, 1976, the 42nd Street Development Corporation was born, with a starry-eyed hope of creating a "river-to-river Grand Boulevard that would

345

become a magnet for private investment." The Office of Enforcement enlisted heavy fines, zoning law amendments, and Health Department ordinances in its service, and its successes were many, including the virtual banning of massage parlors, pinball arcades, topless bars, and peepshows. Simultaneously, the Development Corporation took over and reconditioned the proscribed buildings, opening a police substation where a kiddie-porn peepshow had flourished and housing the Mounted Division in what had once been a prostitutes' hangout. Even so, when the time came for the construction of the Marriott Hotel, it was two eminent theaters and none of the buildings housing the sex industry that were razed to make room for it.

The first wave of organized feminism also turned its attention to Times Square, in the belief that sexually explicit words and images were causally linked to sexual violence against women. It demonstrated its anger when some six thousand Women against Pornography marched from Columbus Circle to Times Square on October 20, 1979. Brandishing banners reading TAKE THE HARD-CORE OUT OF THE BIG APPLE, PORN IS RAPE ON PAPER, and DEATH TO PATRIARCHY!, they garnered a great deal of publicity but little else. The vehemence of the rhetoric and the simplistic attribution of social abuses to single sources were reminiscent of the temperance parades at the turn of the century. Of course, the temperance parades made their point: Prohibition was eventually enacted, and we are still living with the results of that noble experiment. One old black man outside a peep show on Forty-second Street had shouted at the passing parade, "They got all those fine young girls inside. How else my gonna get my joint hard, you just tell me that!"[69] Twenty-five-cent peepshows put fantasy sex within the reach of even the poor, and antipornography movements, like most moral crusades, have the immediate effect of denying recreational releases to those of low income.

Women against Pornography then proceeded to organize twice-weekly bus tours of the Bright-light Zone, which, with sureties of safety, conducted gaggles of suburban housewives through the porno parlors: not unlike Mrs. Pardiggle in *Bleak House* descending on the undeserving poor with a handful of tracts, albeit without Mrs. Pardiggle's hands-on involvement. Ostensibly, the purpose was to alert these women to a terrible social evil. I have spoken to some of those taken on such a tour and the lesson worked: they had been shocked and were indignant that these fleshpots were permitted to thrive in the midst of Manhattan. But they were no more enlightened as to the sources of the so-called problem than were visitors to the old freakshows about hormonal imbalance. The denizens of Forty-second Street were displayed to them as Ubangis and pygmies were once shown to gaping yokels in dime museums, exhibited in such a way that the yokels felt most superior to the objects of their gawking.

However well-intentioned these coach tours through the Inferno, they exacerbate the simplistic Manichaeism of *them* and *us*, the street people versus the decent people, which demarcates society's attitudes. They are simply a different form of sexual tourism, a voyeurism one step removed from that of the peepshow customer, the enjoyment resulting from aroused indignation rather than aroused passion. It is worth noting that these tours have been temporarily discontinued, because the sponsoring group is more occupied in organizing a conference on International Trafficking in Women.[70] This implies a realization that the exploitation of actual women may be a more genuine issue than the transmission of women's images.

The feminist position on pornography rapidly diversified, and within the ranks dissent has argued that to attack pornography is a step away from attacking female sexuality.[71] Opinions became even more contradictory over the question of prostitution, for feminist prostitutes' unions promote a liberal view of sex-for-pay as a private commercial transaction, not a public nuisance. Yet the move to decriminalize and license prostitution has been supported by the same feminist groups who argue for greater state interference in the private spheres of conjugal rape and battered wives, which they characterize as sexual exploitation. Logically, once you grant that a whore is an ordinary working woman, you have difficulty maintaining that she is sexually victimized. Those feminists who oppose censorship as a threat to sexual freedom have not favored a laissez-faire market in prostitution any more than the antipornography warriors have heretofore urged a crusade against prostitution.

In the absence of an ideological consensus as to whether prostitutes are empowered vendors of their own persons or exploited victims, their legal status continues to be dictated by concerns over property values and urban development. Campaigns against streetwalking do not therefore alleviate the situation, but simply move the walkers to other streets.[72]

The latest statistics from the Office of Midtown Enforcement give a superficial impression that the angels of light are gaining the upper hand. In 1977 there had been ninety-six sex-related businesses in Times Square; by 1987 they had declined to and stabilized at thirty-five. But the Office itself had to admit that these reductions were due less to its clean-up efforts than to economic factors:

One is the technological advancements in the video industry which have led to the rise in home viewing of pornography tapes rented from neighborhood stores. This phenomenon has led to a decrease in the patronage of the x-rated movie houses and peepshows. Another principal reason is the physical redevelopment of Times Square: in 1986, a number of buildings and sites which had been locations of sex-related businesses came under construction or were being cleared for assemblages.[73] . . . [Another factor is] the value of real estate escalating the dollar value of store rentals beyond what these businesses can support.[74]

In addition, the AIDS epidemic impelled most entrepreneurs to eliminate live-sex displays from their shows.

Whatever its victories over the indoor sex industry, from its inception the Office of Midtown Enforcement was never very successful in uprooting street prostitution. Since streetwalking was only marginally connected with real estate and hence with mob-financed businesses, it was not susceptible to the Office's standard legal harassments. The individual pimp was left relatively unmolested, and the thousands of prostitute arrests were ultimately pointless, particularly since their clientele went unscathed. Obviously, as the local *maisons de passe* and fleabag hotels were converted to other uses, there would be fewer opportunities for casual carnal exchanges. In the meantime, prostitution continued unabated there and elsewhere, transvestites or "knobbers" crowing that they needed only hallways in which to satisfy their patrons efficiently and manually.

Unable to prevent an adult's choice to sell his or her body, the Office of Midtown Enforcement in October 1985 launched a major drive to eliminate juvenile prostitution from Times Square entirely. Uniformed officers patrolled the so-called chicken hawk hangouts in arcades and fast-food outlets; posing as hustlers, young undercover officers ensnared individuals the police reports loosely identify as "pedophiles"; social service workers and groups like Trudee Able-Peterson's "Street Work Project" tried to identify underage prostitutes and offer them alternative lives. The enticing undercover officers made a number of arrests; stiff sentences were handed out to the so-called pedophiles (technically, a pedophile is someone who fancies children between ages six and ten) as well as to the alleged Fagins of juvenile prostitution rings; and word went out that blatant solicitations had decreased in number.

Again, however, the reports make it clear that the standard approach to this improvised problem is not very effective. Intensified police harassment steps up street activity by dispersing and dislocating it.[75] Driven out of Times Square, the chicken and the hawk roost in less policed areas, and even the Port Authority bus station has never ceased its activity. In addition, the report notes "Hustling by a core group of older teenagers, aged 16–19 years old, remains a problem which the task force will continue to evaluate and attempt to resolve by 'outreach' programs."[76]

It is easy to foment outrage about juvenile prostitution, and media coverage tends to distort and sensationalize it. An analogous situation occurred before World War I when New York was barraged with exposés of the White Slave trade: newspapers and magazine articles, short stories, plays, and films made the public believe that any unaccompanied woman was in danger of being abducted and sent to a cathouse in Venezuela. In 1910 the Rockefeller Grand Jury investigation concluded that there was no evidence of organized white slavery in New York.[77] The paranoia had more to do with folk fears about the jeopardy of young women's innocence in the big city than to any actual abuse.

So it is with juvenile prostitution, which is generally discussed in tones of blind alarm, ignoring variations and complexities. The American notion of children's sexuality is fraught with confusion. In part it preserves the Puritan idea of the child as limb of Satan, who must be kept in order by strict monitoring, and in whom any whiff of sex is a sin to be chastised and uprooted. This has been complicated by the contradictory post–Rousseauian concept of the child as innocent whose every perception is to be protected to preserve it from taint by society's abuses. Both concepts are on the alert for signs of contamination. Consequently, we tend to label individuals as children long after they have passed puberty and grant them adult status much later than many societies do. Finally, there is the overlay of Freud that admits sexuality from infancy on, but assigns it developmental phases, so that behavior can be clinically graded as aberrant, precocious, or retarded if it fails to conform to pattern. This mélange of attitudes has either rendered juvenile sexuality inadmissible or hedged it round with taboos and safeguards.[78]

Having sex with one's own children has been a feature of family life since Lot and his daughters, and the mass selling of juveniles for sexual purposes was common in the Eastern Hemisphere from ancient times until very recently. The rise of the modern metropolis revived the practice in the Western world. Pre-revolutionary Paris and Victorian London housed hordes of adolescents hawking their persons in the Palais Royal and the Haymarket. The crusading editor W. T. Stead was jailed for his exposé of the trade in 1885, because, as part of his research, he actually purchased a little girl from a brothelkeeper.[79] Officialdom in New York began to recognize the existence of child prostitution from the 1850s, citing girls between the ages of eight and sixteen. The practice of blackmail was evidently prevalent, which suggests that their clientele came from a respectable stratum of society.[80] One of the causal features may be the high price put on virginity in an age of endemic syphilis, but the corruption of innocence, even ostensible innocence, is, in itself, a powerful motive.

The influx of juvenile prostitution to Times Square seems to be a legacy of the 1960s counterculture: running away from home and joining a tribe was a standard rite of passage. To keep the commune in marijuana and lentils, selling one's body was useful and facile, especially at a time when sexual sharing was part of the creed. For the runaway, there was no real distinction between peddling macramé, pushing grass, or prostitution. Throughout the following decades, the big city went on luring juveniles fleeing unhappy homes and seeking independence and selfhood long after the communal "let-it-be" philosophy had evaporated. The popular subculture of youth, domiciled in the streets, remained the alternative, and from the 1970s on, became more polymorphous, drug ridden, and unscrupulous. What had been primarily situational became habitual; gang members whose older brothers would have beaten up the habitués of gay bars now sell themselves to those habitués with the same amorality.[81] Teenagers who identified themselves as "gay" gravitated to gay areas, their relationships with older men a career move that provided a kind of upward mobility; whereas the adolescent hustlers in a mixed zone like Times Square were, in addition to being economically needy, more troubled and confused about their motives.[82] Hence more prone to crime and violence, they became easy prey for police and social workers.

A reflection of the intricate muddle of motives and responses to juvenile prostitution is to be found in the writing of Father Bruce Ritter, who established Covenant House in Times Square in 1972 as an asylum for homeless boys and girls—the abused, the forlorn, the abandoned, the exploited. In his imploring book, *Sometimes God Has a Kid's Face*, he is urgent and persuasive in describing their degradation by all manner of causes. Still, Father Bruce is candid about his own ambivalence towards his charges: he dwells again and again on their physical beauty, their animal magnetism, the fact that when he walks the streets he is picked out as one in search of sex. He undergoes dark nights of the soul, anatomizing his ambivalent feelings towards pimps who give him money to support his efforts and unredeemed youths who enjoy their lives as objects of lust. Clearly, the ambiguity of these adolescents cannot be summed up on a police blotter. They are the same kind of amoral urchins Caravaggio turned into pagan deities in his paintings and Pasolini rhapsodized over as butch angels of death.

With whose eyes, then, are we to see? The strident upholders of consensus morality, who are more upset by the notion of adolescent sexuality—and especially male-to-male sexuality—than by the ugly family situations that drive these children to the streets; the politicians, who can gain a few points by attacking juvenile prostitution, knowing it has no constituency; the realistic but pressured police, for whom these kids' sexual delinquency is more dangerous as a seedbed for theft, drug-pushing, and viral transmission than in itself; the social workers, who are on the lookout to reclaim and heal those unable to survive in the jungle of cities but who regard experience as a set of problems craving solutions; the developers, who want to extirpate anything that might lower property values and clutter their architects' pristine renderings; the photographer Larry Clark, who is struck by their innocence, or the playwright Alan Bowne, who unjudgmentally registers their toughness and their vulnerability in the face of an uncaring world?

In an appendix to his book, Father Bruce, who served on Attorney General Meese's Commission on Pornography, provides a series of "Observations and Suggestions," which spell out the attitude that often shapes the Samaritan stance. Along with such unexceptionable statements as "Kids should not be bought and sold" are more debatable ones: "Sex was never supposed to be a spectator sport," "Sex isn't love and love isn't sex. It's good and beautiful when it's between married people who love each other and it's private."[83] Dr. Ruth Westheimer is attacked as "the high priestess of hedonism" for blessing premarital sex, although there is a grudging admission that she provides the enlightenment our schools refuse to supply. At bottom, this is the age-old voice of Mother Church imposing ascetic straitjackets on human nature and mourning the loss of her authority as the sole arbiter of social conduct; it sounds exceedingly quixotic howling in the wilderness of the Minnesota Strip. Are St. Augustine's minority views on sexual desire, which have dominated Western thought since the fifth century, of any relevance to the construction of social codes in Times Square?[84] What sort of validity should they be granted when they are used to reinforce the territorial imperatives of real estate developers?

Yet when Father Bruce insists that "there is no ethical or moral or qualitative difference between spending $25 to see *Oh! Calcutta!* for your sophisticated evening at the theater, and spending that 25 cents at the peepshow owned by members of organized crime, or watching the action at a West Side hangout on West Forty-fifth Street . . . or enjoying the entertainment at . . . a sexual supermarket,"[85] he has touched on a truth which applies, even when stripped of his censoriousness. When he points out that a continuum exists between the entertainment industry and the sex industry because they both supply a deeply rooted public demand, he has put his finger on an abiding—not abuse—but fact of life.

The spectation, delectation, and exploitation of private parts in public places exist not because organized crime has inveigled us into some new vice or because conspiracies of perverts are infiltrating an otherwise utopian society. The myriads of customers who frequented and continue to frequent Times Square for these services are not "undesirables" in any other context; they are cognate with the matinee audiences of the theaters. The clienteles of the peepshows are largely respectable office workers and businessmen, releasing their pent-up tensions in an anonymous, efficient manner, the manner taught them by the modus operandi of their business lives; or ordinary adolescents completing their sex educations in a virally safe puberty rite. A great many of the men who pick up youths are fathers of families who have had drummed into their heads from childhood that sex between men is vile; so they explore their sexual identities in the only way available to them, anonymously and with partners who make no emotional demands. The men who solicit female prostitutes and transvestites have been sold the idea that extramarital sexual pleasure is perforce exotic, out of the ordinary, dwelling in a sinful milieu. The women, girls, and boys who cater to these needs are making a living, sometimes the best living available in their circumstances, preferring victimless crime to the other sort. There is no historical example of any urban society that has so managed its economy or its biology as to eliminate this cottage industry. Social mobility and anonymity are the modern determinants of this cultural universal, and, as one scientist has contended, prostitution and pornography are "functional alternatives."

> Both provide for the discharge of what society labels anti-social sex: prostitution provides this via real intercourse with a real sex object, and pornography provides it via masturbatory, imagined intercourse with a fantasy object.[86]

By accepting the stigmata placed on them, the commercial purveyors of sexual services uphold the norms that define nonmarital sexual expression as illegitimate and thus serve as pillars of the very society that stigmatizes them.[87] When sex ceases to be a taboo experience and is freely engaged in by mutual consent, both prostitution and the family are equally threatened.

The spectrum of perception of Times Square's sexual aura, its uses and abuses as a pornographic marketplace, is thus a broad one ranging far beyond mere condemnation. One end of the spectrum: A vice president for planning and design of the New York State Urban Development Corporation declares: "We want to get rid of the pederasts, prostitutes and pimps and bring the bright lights back to the Great White Way."[88] As one of the city's power brokers, she readily subscribes to Durkheim's idea that immorality is identical with social disorder and seeks to remedy disorganization by imposing morality from without. The other end of the spectrum: A member of the dissenting subculture recognizes that morality is situational, created within the everyday experience; what is alleged to be deviant is, in its context, normal. "We bring a lot of tourists to this area," a male prostitute tells a researcher. "If not for us, this town would be dead. How many men would want to come to New York if they couldn't find kids like me? What for—to go to see the Statue of Liberty?"[89] It remains to be seen whether Times Square can accommodate both the bright lights and the night frontier; history's lesson is that when social planning fails to come to terms with the sexual side of human nature, they both end up screwed.

AFTERWORD

RE-INVENTING
TIMES SQUARE: 1990

Ada Louise Huxtable

Times Square became Times Square on April 9, 1904. If it seems as if it has always existed in Manhattan schist and the universal consciousness, it is actually, at this writing, eighty-seven years old. That was the day Mayor George McClellan signed the proclamation that renamed Longacre Square in honor of the new Times Tower. At 375 feet, it was the city's second tallest building, a stolid edifice faced in limestone and cream-colored brick, designed by Eidlitz and MacKenzie for the *New York Times*—a building notable chiefly for its progressively engineered steel frame and pedantically designed details. It was referred to as Giotto's campanile, New York style. The fact that the renaming of the square owed as much to the assiduous promotion of the new underground rail lines and the stunning real estate opportunities they opened as to the structure being celebrated, was quintessential New York style. And if the Times Tower was more of a lumpenskyscraper than Louis Sullivan's ideal of a proud and soaring thing, it was destined for an enduring role.

It is the passage of almost a century that allows us to understand the forces that have turned Times Square into what it is today. Most of these chapters deal with the particular commercial and cultural features that have contributed to its unique character as New York's central entertainment district; this original, provocative research casts new light on the colorful configuration of institutions and practices that brought Times Square to national, and then to international, prominence. Change has been part of its dynamic, as Brooks McNamara has demonstrated. But change has come again to Times Square with relentless speed and aggression and with an unprecedented scale even as we document its history and debate its fate. It is ironic that we should end this investigation, not with new ideas about the future, but with new buildings that virtually foreclose it—immense new buildings already lining and transforming Broadway and Seventh Avenue, with the promise of still larger ones at the historic crossroads, courtesy of a city- and state-sponsored renewal plan, the 42nd Street Development Project, which will bring towers of a bulk and density surpassing anything permitted in the city today.

The destruction and recreation of Times Square is visibly under way. Its physical nature is, as always, an invention and function of New York real estate. The net effect of these new buildings will be to irreversibly tip the area from its traditional image and functions by their sheer bulk, square footage, and conventional commercial uses. In essence, they undermine any other activity in Times Square that does not offer an equivalent financial return. Their land costs and rental scales doom the already weakened network of small businesses and support services essential to the theatrical and entertainment world, which have been the base of the variety, economy, and character of the area. Many have already moved or simply closed shop. Theater is always tenuous; interlocking entertainment and recreation uses are, at best, a chain of weak links depending on talent, trends, and fickle tastes. Acknowledging the situation in a perverse way, the new buildings are required by law to include large illuminated signs as facade elements to recreate the appearance of the Times Square they are driving out. New York puts great skill and effort into its complex absurdities.

The impact of this completed and planned new construction on the life and the look of the place that so many seek, in some way, to preserve, makes discussion problematic, if not moot. However, there is still a Times Square there, at least until the bulldozers move in for the crossroads kill. Technically, Times Square extends from the crossing point of Broadway and Seventh Avenue, marked by the Times Tower at Forty-third Street, to Forty-fifth Street. A second triangle, from Forty-fifth to Forty-seventh streets, Duffy Square, completes the "bowtie" that the world knows as Times Square. Beyond Forty-seventh Street, the boundaries are fluid. The wedge-shaped structure on the undersized triangular island that Arthur Ochs gambled on for his newspaper's headquarters while many of the city's institutions remained downtown survived the *Times's* move to a larger building on Forty-third Street in 1913; it had become anchor and symbol of an extraordinary place. It disappeared briefly in 1984 in models and renderings of the 42nd Street Development Project. The sponsor and his architects had decided that it did not suit their West Side version of Rockefeller Center in paper-doll postmodern dress, and they planned to level the landmark as part of the much-touted "cleanup" of the area.[1] The definition and the aims should have become suspect then. After predictable howls of protest, the Times Tower was restored to the plan.[2]

Like Times Square itself, the building has gone from genteel to tawdry. In 1964, it was stripped to its bare steel bones and reborn as the

Allied Chemical Tower, its stodgy academic credentials replaced by a no-style skin of lavatory white marble with the look of cut cardboard.[3] One could sermonize about the shoddiness and expediency of this kind of quickie curtain-wall aesthetic—that it reflects or expresses a popular culture of fast food, fast takes, and even faster obsolescence—and one would not be too far off the mark. When available techniques are used to produce effects that reflect current societal tastes and norms, it is not coincidence or totally inappropriate. Packaging today is more important than the product, and what is not disposable, looks it. Junk architecture has its place. But the transformation of the building made little difference. To the world it was still the Times Tower. It could probably be made of marzipan and it wouldn't matter. The odd little icon is universally known by the illuminated signs that, in themselves, provide a history of a modern aesthetic of new materials and technology. They have changed from the bulb-lit, bright-white news ribbon of earlier years to the colorful electronic messages of the current computerized displays, from news as advertising to advertising as entertainment. Signs of the times, in every sense.

Like the Times Tower, Times Square has been largely illusion. It has always been theater and stageset for a lively and sometimes problematic assortment of social and urban activities. As part of its consciousness-raising campaign about the problems facing Times Square, the Municipal Art Society, in anticipation of development plans, commissioned the architectural photographer, Cervin Robinson, to take pictures of the Square from a central point with the camera at eye level; he was to record what the visitor sees, or thinks he sees, or, as it turned out, what is really there. The results were a revelation. They are remarkable photographs, and in their artfully cool objectivity they reveal that there has been no architecture there at all. or at least architecture as commonly understood. Immediately surrounding the Square were blockfronts of small, nondescript structures, one- or two-story buildings, faced or surmounted with giant gridlike scaffolding holding the familiar, chaotic mélange of signs and messages. Larger buildings were anonymous and recessive, upstaged and dematerialized by the displays. This was a non-architecture of place, with one of the strongest images of place in the world.

J. B. Jackson, who has written so eloquently of the function of the street, pioneered the identification of the architecture of the commercial strip—that contextless bazaar of goods and services strung out along the highway to lure the passing motorist by catching his eye at high speeds. In *Learning From Las Vegas*, Robert Venturi and Denise Scott Brown describe many of the characteristics of this twentieth century architectural aesthetic of transience and high visibility.[4] Powerful visual symbols and messages—buildings as billboards—announce the means to gratify needs and desires instantly while enjoying largely ersatz and temporary experiences. Design as communication, however, is a universal contemporary aesthetic that is quite independent of the car. The movement that counts in Times Square is on foot, and although it is far from the leisurely pace of an Italian hill town, and it goes well beyond the traditional intimate human scale, this is an unparalleled pedestrian precinct. It is an environment of enormous visual and sensory overload. There is still another form of motion that compounds the experience, characteristic of no other time: the movement of the design elements themselves. It is tempting to treat this brilliant, kinetic environment as a colorful abstraction, but it is not, like so much studio art, a theoretical exercise. Its aims are accessibility, utility, and profit. Its stylistic roots are real; they go deep into our consumer- and communications-oriented culture. The importance of its artifacts is increasingly recognized by the keepers and cataloguers of that culture. Preservationists are fighting for, and achieving the protection of, such familiar symbols as the large Citgo sign in Boston's Kenmore Square, much to the dismay of those who see it as visual pollution. Times Square is the epitome of this dynamic aesthetic of expediency and conspicuous display.

In the early part of the century, legitimate theaters and the great hotels and restaurants established a more substantial image and style for Times Square—part bourgeois, part bohemian, characteristically sybaritic and shocking, extravagantly luxe, heavily Beaux Arts—anchored by the mansarded brick and stone mass of the area's two great turn-of-the-century landmarks, the Astor and Knickerbocker hotels. The Astor, the work of Clinton and Russell in 1904, was a massive "French Renaissance" pile between Forty-fourth and Forty-fifth streets on the west side of Broadway; its elaborate, somewhat *retardataire* facade hardly prepared one for the wildly exuberant catalogue of interior styles. "The lobby floor contained Chinese alcoves, a Flemish smoking room, a Pompeian billiard room [and] . . . an orangerie. . . . The basement included the Old New York Lobby and the American Indian Grill Room." Ballrooms and meeting rooms under the giant mansard roof offered Colonial, Oriental, and Art Nouveau settings. A German Renaissance Hunt Room had "stag horn electroliers and . . . hunting scenes [with] deer in full relief . . . sporting genuine antlers."[5] The Knickerbocker, at Forty-second Street and Broadway, by Trowbridge and Livingston, preceded the Astor in 1902, and while it embraced the same stultifyingly top-heavy mansarded genre, its interiors were somewhat more restrained. Both survived into the 1960s, the Knickerbocker gutted for an office building, the Astor relentlessly and horribly "modernized." Both were demolished by the 1970s.

Traditional standards applied until after World War II, however, as the area continued its pursuit of an exotic eclecticism that flouted conventional rules. The Forty-second Street theaters, in their original state, and the later theaters that followed in the Forties east and west of Broadway, were a romantic sampling of historical allusions, from elegant Adam to all of the Louis of France, in which the audience occupied a stageset as evocative as the production itself. The New Amsterdam brought a superior example of fashionable art nouveau to Broadway. The movie palaces of the 1920s and 1930s turned eclecticism into phantasmagoria: Seville and Araby vied with ponderous superbaroque. With novelty piled on novelty in the search for the new and different, sensation eventually supplanted style. When conventional sources have been wrung dry, the door is opened to no-style and free-style, to increasingly hyped effects, and to the shock value of those things usually considered taboo. Times Square has always dealt in fantasy and fulfillment; it has always been a testing ground of limits. This has been its unique societal and urban role. By the 1950s and 1960s, a similar testing was taking place in society at large. A shorter attention span and an increased appetite for change, due in part to the conditioning of consumerism and the media and fed by a nihilistic rejection of traditional values, led to a need for heightened stimuli and constantly increased levels of sensory response. The outrageous became mainstream culture in all of the arts, far from Times Square.

What changed between the wars, and accelerated after World War II, was more than style. When the theaters turned into grind houses and the sporting life became the solitary gratifications of the porno parlors, class gave way to mass. Because Times Square has habitually catered more to basic appetites than to esoteric experiences, peepshows and exploitation films of sex and violence quickly found their audience. The area's magnetic attraction continued—a combination of promise and threat, of exhilaration and fear—the impersonality and constant flux of the crowds suggesting that almost anything was possible. Size and anonymity make it both a private and a public place, where offbeat or offcolor desires can be openly or secretly satisfied, but where New Yorkers can also gather at moments of crisis or triumph; to celebrate the end of war, to wait for and share important news. The ball still drops on New Year's Eve by popular demand.

In this city, such places do not arise spontaneously or naturally in response to society's needs. Nor do they come into being solely as free market phenomena. Nothing in New York has purely social or moral imperatives. Almost everything that happens here is a product of land values, which are, in turn, the product of decisions about such things as land use, tax policy, and zoning codes. Destiny is profoundly influenced by the city's actions. William Leach's "brokers" are active at every level, and among the most active are the real estate lawyers who have virtually invented a new profession as liaison between the city and its developers, interpreting and manipulating, or "brokering" the rules and regulations by which they build. In New York, politics and real estate have always been closely allied. Substantial donations by developers to political campaigns are the local way of doing business and a political fact of life. Private profit, not public policy, is the bottom line, and there is a fairly straight line from one to the other. It is not without significance that New York's most comprehensive planning effort was the mapping of Manhattan Island into a grid of standardized, easily marketed building lots in 1811.

But the process by which the city is shaped today is neither so clear nor so crass. Betsy Blackmar has shown how morality and development were partnered in the nineteenth century, and how this broke down in places like Times Square, where risk and unconventional mixed uses became economically acceptable. Today, entrepreneurial objectives are glossed by claims of public improvement; jobs are stressed, and amenities such as open space and better circulation are featured, even when sun and light are blotted out by the bulk of the ever-larger and more profitable structures towering above them. The benefits to the city's tax base are publicized rather than the builder's tax breaks. The city's Department of Planning is staffed by some remarkable practitioners whose idealism is tempered by a particular brand of New York superrealism. Skilled professionals, they serve under a City Planning Commission of political appointees. They must reconcile a planning vision manifestly lacking at other levels with the immutable political fact of abuses of massive overbuilding that have not only been permitted but encouraged. Theirs is a balancing act between excesses and the highly inventive "ameliorating" factors they devise. Masters of "mitigation" (in planningspeak), faced with the ongoing destruction of the purpose and intent of zoning, they mount rescue operations through creative zoning amendments and remedial urban design. In the customary scenario, the prize goes to the developer, a consolation prize in the form of some highly touted and often token tradeoff goes to the public, and some very fancy footwork by the planners turns rape into seduction.

Recent city policies have done an enormous amount to destroy Times Square. If the intention had been to deliberately set out to accelerate the damage already under way it could not have been carried out more effectively. By the 1960s, this was an area in deep trouble; social, cultural, and commercial changes had advanced far beyond the city's control.

361

Fashion, taste, the cutting edge of the new and profitable, had moved on, and a mixed bag of limit-stretching, low-end entertainment had moved in, bringing drugs and pornography with it. All this had softened the area's value and utility in purely economic terms. Property was being rented to anyone who could turn a profit and it no longer paid to put money into maintenance or upgrading.

With that kind of disinvestment and deterioration an area becomes vulnerable; places and institutions have a hard time surviving. If the affected area is prime midtown land in one of the most vital cities in the world, it will not simply languish; when it is no longer able to produce what the city and its investors consider appropriate revenue, it becomes a target for rebuilding. If conditions have deteriorated to the point where investors will not take the risk, the city usually helps. The methods devised—subsidies, tax write-offs, land write-downs, city- and state-aided redevelopment plans—are designed to create a package acceptable to conventional real estate practice. One can only conclude that blight was defined as virtually everything that existed in and around Times Square, and that the operation was meant to sanitize the area with the one kind of construction the city's builders understand and are willing to undertake— the usual offices and, since a tourist market still existed, the usual hotels. It was impossible to be unaware of the broad impact of the consequences of such a policy. It is particularly ironic that this bulldozer-style renewal, advertised as the way to get rid of drugs, pornography, and crime, brought development full circle in Times Square, back to a partnership of morality and economics, in the same place where they had parted company.

The city had sought redevelopment of the area unsuccessfully since the 1970s. From 1973 to 1975, an on-again, off-again proposal for a new hotel made by the architect-developer John Portman of Atlanta, promised a full-block bunker and beachhead as well as an infusion of new life and capital. Measured against the multiplying massage parlors, it was seen as a giant step toward salvation.[6] When the hotel was finally opened as the Marriott Marquis in 1985, it had destroyed two theaters, the Alvin and the Helen Hayes, while Portman literally stonewalled the city's planners by insisting on brutal, blank concrete sides at street level.

While Times Square deteriorated, the fashionable midtown East Side was being monstrously overbuilt, with everything from blockbusters to "sliver" buildings forced onto minimal sites with fashionable addresses. In 1982, in response to increasing public alarm, the City Planning Commission devised a Special Midtown Zoning District which was meant to address the excesses of the overheated East Side and the ills of the sluggish West Side.[7] The idea was to damp down East Side construction and encourage new building on the West Side, where developers did not wish to go. To do this, the new rules increased the size of buildings that could be constructed across town, while eliminating the East Side incentives.

Expectations of the greater profitability of the larger buildings promised by the new zoning immediately boosted West Side values. But conditions in Times Square continued to slide; owners held on to their property for the best market value, with even less reason to invest in existing buildings and uses. In 1984, land prices more than doubled from the previous year.[8] However, the new zoning had a "sunset" clause, which meant that the more generous provisions would expire in 1988. To no one's great surprise, there was a rush to file plans and start construction before that date.

In what might be called the second part of a two-pronged attack on Times Square, the city presented the 42nd Street Development Project in November 1984. The 1982 zoning change was seen primarily as a way of reallocating construction incentives; the Development Project was advertised as the way to reclaim Forty-second Street and reverse its sordid spillover into Times Square. Where the zoning incentive was strictly business, the state-city project was to be a "cleanup" operation; it would rescue Times Square from the forces of evil. The project's boundaries are the heart of the area—the Forty-second and Forty-third street blocks surrounding the Times Tower, and the notorious Forty-second Street block from Seventh to Eighth avenues. The project site is under the joint jurisdiction of the New York State Urban Development Corporation and the city's agencies. The use of the state agency makes it possible to condemn and assemble privately owned land by eminent domain and to circumvent some of the city's rules and procedures. In essence, this pivotal part of Times Square has been removed from most regulatory and review requirements. In addition to the write-down of the public purchase and assembly of the land, other subsidies are provided through city tax abatement.

It did not take long for a developer to see the advantageous bottom line of four massive office buildings generously underwritten by the plan, large enough to form their own enclave and environment; Park Tower Realty in conjunction with the Prudential Insurance Company of America signed on as sponsors of the towers that would loom over the Square. Designs were released in which the buildings were dressed to kill by his architects, John Burgee with Philip Johnson, in mansarded postmodern costumes. To stabilize the area at its worst, and western, boundary, the plan called for a merchandise mart and a hotel at the Eighth Avenue end of Forty-second Street, neither of which has materialized. The public tradeoff—retaining a theatrical presence in the face of an overwhelming influx of standardized commercial uses—is the promise of the restoration of some of the historic

Forty-second Street theaters for a mix of profit and not-for-profit entertainment functions, as well as the rebuilding of the more squalid parts of
the Times Square subway.

It is instructive to note that the city's zoning plan, with its combination
of incentives and time limits, worked. Builders reacted with a parade of
blockbusters on Broadway and Seventh Avenue unequaled since the
march down Sixth Avenue twenty years ago. On the other hand, the 42nd
Street Development Project has not worked. To date, nothing at all has
been built. The lumbering state-city machinery inched along, mired in
controversy, from 1984 to the early 1990s, when recession killed the
construction market. No sponsors came forward, even in the boom years,
for the merchandise mart and hotel. There have been equally serious
problems finding adequately funded and operating groups for the theaters.
Unlike the office towers, where the developer is guaranteed an advantageous tax position and competitive advantage well into the future, there are
no future guarantees for the theaters of anything except a precarious and
questionable existence.

From the start, the premises of the Development Project were wrong.
This was a back-from-the-dead example of the thoroughly discredited
bulldozer urban renewal of the 1960s. It was predicated solely on the aims
and principles of private development, even though it was a publicly
sponsored and assisted project which used substantial amounts of public
money. The linkage to public purpose in the preservation of the theaters
was tenuous, and the cleanup was a convenient cover for conventional
development. There were no neighborhood or citywide planning objectives beyond the promotion of new commercial construction, and the full
impact of such construction on existing use patterns and support systems
was never properly evaluated. There was no realistic coupling of incentive
and intent. It is hard to believe that no one understood that the combination of city and state initiatives meant wipeout, rather than salvation, for
Times Square, that the sheer size and bulk of the new office buildings
would turn it into just another big business district. It is easier to believe
that this is exactly what everyone involved really wanted. It is certainly,
eventually, what Times Square will get.

As a late gesture to a so-called Times Square style, there has been a
scene change in the Burgee-Johnson towers, from pseudohistoricism to
jazzy deconstructivism. By any name, this is trendy window dressing, a
kind of slipcover architecture. Since the buildings are wrapped and padded
in financial advantages as well, offering one of the larger potential profit

packages ever handed to a New York developer, they will probably go ahead when market conditions improve. The Deuce, as Forty-second Street is called in the local argot, continues in its wicked ways. The "sleaze" has slithered up Eighth Avenue through the Forties into the Fifties, where all-male movies with "live sex shows" coexist with more conventional heterosexual fare in a smut-zone far greater than the targeted Seventh to Eighth Avenue block. A well-publicized effort to keep interest in the project alive produced a token conversion of one Forty-second Street theater from a blood-and-gore movie house to Shakespearean drama and an amazingly articulate outburst from its habitués, who liked it just the way it was. They turned out not to be derelicts and druggies but connoisseurs of the genre, who inveigh passionately and knowledgeably on the merits of varying degrees of violence, perversion, and horror. At the upper level of this curious coterie, there is even a well-circulated newsletter.[9]

By the late 1980s and early 1990s, a group of New York's most dramatic new skyscrapers had risen just above the project area on Broadway and Seventh Avenue from the mid-Forties to the Fifties. Quite aside from their inevitable impact on Times Square, this spectacular construction makes the stalled Development Project redundant and academic. Unfortunately, it does not make its commitments null and void. But the use of public subsidies when private investment has been pouring into the area becomes outrageous at a time of serious budget deficits and other critical needs. Catastrophic cuts were made in human and city services while these subsidies remained inviolate.

As early as the mid-1980s, at least 8 of 17 possible development sites around Times Square not in the project area were already in planning, design, or construction stages, spurred on by the "sunset" provision of the zoning that would reduce building bulk in 1988. Excavations and hoardings created a new urban landscape from Forty-sixth to Fifty-second streets. The City Planning Commission noted "intense development pressures." The Municipal Art Society exhibited cautionary computer-generated studies of how it all would look. The Department of City Planning carried out an extensive study of the character of Times Square and the changes taking place and recommended a set of amendments to the 1982 Special Midtown District zoning. The objective, in the planners' words, was "to ensure that the unique and valuable sense of place of Times Square will be retained and nurtured as new development occurs."[10] These amendments, dealing with what was called the Theater Subdistrict Core Area, from Forty-third to Fiftieth streets, were passed in 1987. However, because of the peculiar exempt status of the stalled 42d Street Development Project, and the fact that the unbuilt towers almost everyone had learned to hate by then had already been designed (twice) and officially approved, none of the requirements applied to that crucial part of Times Square.

Those 1987 zoning amendments are meant to deal with the negative effects of the new construction. They are written and illustrated as "performance standards," which spell out the final effects that the law requires without specifying the exact formulas for achieving them; how it is done is left to the talent and ingenuity of the architects and designers. They concern the height and setback of street walls as they relate to the traditional, but unconventional, scale of Times Square and to the area's theaters—unique conditions that exist nowhere else in the city. They mandate lively ground floor uses on the street, with full visibility. The most striking provision of all is for the required electric signage on the buildings' setbacks and facades, with specifications as to placement, number, size, and types of illumination and animation. Another, later amendment requires new buildings to include a certain amount of square footage, calculated in relation to building size, for entertainment-related uses that are being lost.

In fairness, one must say that this is an unusually skilled and thoughtful set of urban design rules. More creative, groundbreaking guidelines through innovative zoning have yet to be devised. Never was a barn more splendidly locked after the horse was out. Ironically, this is important legislation because it is on the leading edge of the art of place-making through visual and physical means. New York, as usual, has delivered something special. And it has also demonstrated, once again, its absolute mastery of Catch-22: The zoning defines the characteristics of the area brilliantly and supplies the criteria meant to protect and preserve those characteristics; but because they are being destroyed by the new construction, and because the new construction is also destroying the place that supplied the characteristics, recreating them is an exercise in artifice and futility. They become a kind of splendid wallpaper, or light show for a performance that isn't there.

The source of the fallacy is that the planners' rationale has been limited to maintaining certain recognizable Times Square hallmarks. They state: "The mandating of street walls, transparency, active ground-floor uses and entertainment-related uses provides the critical framework for the life of Times Square."[11] But the framework, and the life, go deeper. They are symbiotic, part of a network in which use, character, and economy are mutually interdependent. It is the activities, mostly affordable, that have created the special scale and ambience, that bring the people who participate in the range of theatrical and other pleasures, and who form the audience for the displays and advertising, who *are* the life of the place. Use and demography create the framework of Times Square; they are intrinsic to, and definitive of, its visual style. If the tenants of the office towers already completed are a harbinger of the future—and there is no reason to doubt it—the population will shift to lawyers, brokers, and accountants, and those carefully specified, visible ground floor shops will be totally predictable chains and franchises—mini-malls instead of arcades. The mandated signs are already proving punishingly expensive to rent or to run, and the office space behind them is proving even harder to rent to establishment business types. Everything seems to be following Murphy's Law.

Stylistically, the new architecture that is being produced is a mind-boggling mix. There has obviously been a tug-of-war between the desire to build enormously impressive and handsome skyscrapers—given the rare opportunity to do so provided by the temporary zoning bonuses of the 1980s—and the city's legal requirements, with their emphasis on fragmentation and flash. One must never underestimate the ingenuity of architects working for developers determined to build status structures for an upscale market. Astute builders will find ways around the rules if they believe the rules adversely affect their calculations. Even in Times Square, visions of Rockefeller Center dance in their heads. In at least one case the mechanism of the mandated signs has been put inside glass panels so that the signs are only visible when lit at night; by day, they are an unseen part of the building's elegant facade.

Curiously, those buildings that go for the glitz are the most disappointing. But in an unexpected side effect, the challenge of the regulations and the effort to create something beyond the usual commercial cookie cutter mold to "suit" Times Square, have opened up the more serious problems of skyscraper design: the definition of scale and style through expressive massing and the exploration of the more exciting aesthetic and technological possibilities of the curtain wall. The result has been some of the city's most innovative and sophisticated new buildings—not in Manhattan's more elegant precincts, as one would expect, but on Seventh Avenue and Broadway—a truly dazzling group in no realistic way related to Times Square, or ever intended to be. In fact, a new skyscraper architecture is appearing here. It has moved from the posturings of postmodernism through a kind of modernism redux to explore new frontiers of design. It goes far beyond the work of the 1970s and 1980s when the much-vaunted postmodern "freedoms" tended to be clumsy and self-limiting as their proponents rushed down dead-ends of historical mimicry and optional trim. It is in the office buildings, rather than the hotels, however, that one finds the most interesting design, in part because the developers were so anxious to circumnavigate the standard ideas of flash for structures that could be marketed as prestige buildings.

The signals being given by the city were as loud and clear as they were anachronistic and unrealistic: the directive was to recreate the gaudy vitality of the area's incremental, ad hoc bricolage in the huge, conventional buildings that would replace it. Some architects, like Alan Lapidus (the son of Morris Lapidus, inventor of the Architecture of Joy in Florida in the 1960s), opted for the more obvious Vegas-Atlantic City hotel image. His design for the Holiday Inn Crowne Plaza Manhattan hotel at Broadway and Forty-ninth Street is earnestly flamboyant and the result is singularly joyless. It is not easy for a 46-story structure faced in burgundy glass and pink granite, shaped like a juke box, with a 100-foot-high arched entrance, an 80-foot-long waterfall, and 12 stories of lights and signs to be dull, but this one succeeds. Inside, it is a far cry from the architecture of "gorgeous." What management calls "exhilarating public spaces" are ill-defined and strangely detached from the traffic through them, which consists chiefly of middle America in sneakers and T-shirts rather than stage or film stars, or thrill seekers on the wild side. The style is straight out of a traditional furniture showroom with updated Deco touches, or something ordered up from Hotel Central Decorating which really needs a different cast of characters. If this is fantasy, how impoverished are our dreams!

There is also some ambiguity and disorientation at the other large new hotel, the Embassy Suites by Fox and Fowle, at the southeast corner of Seventh Avenue and Forty-seventh Street, but the architecture is far more interesting. The interior ambience—a version of the currently fashionable, hard-edged, high-style French hotel-chic made popular by Andrée Putnam and Philippe Starck—offers a setting of trendy fashion light years from middle America or Times Square, but acceptable (if somewhat off-putting) as a mechanism of fantasy or escape. The hotel lobby, on an upper level, is a search-and-find operation, not too clearly signaled. It features aggressive pieces of abstract sculpture and fifties-ish furniture, in a bold red and blue color scheme with a black and white checked floor. Flower arrangements of a matching exotic severity are challenging. One has a feeling that no one there quite understands what it is all about.

The site demanded the utmost ingenuity: the 38-story building is a slender tower, bent around a corner and built over the 5-story Palace Theatre, a city landmark. The tower is carried on huge steel trusses that leave the theater below it free of visible construction; from that point on the material is reinforced concrete. It is an impressive engineering feat. The building's exterior of dark metal and glass, with vertical and horizontal sections divided by a striking red fin, is a complex composition that emits a number of stylistic signals, from basic Bauhaus to Detroit modern with Constructivist overtones. It is saved from cleverness by the expert and rigorous organization of its parts. Lapidus sees the Times Square idiom as pop art and Fox and Fowle see it as Broadway boogie-woogie. Each has invented and rationalized an image according to his own attitude and eye.

The office buildings are the real achievement. Among the city's largest, they represent some of the most advanced and ambitious work of New York's leading architects. Gwathmey Siegel Associates' skyscraper, a 42-story tower at 1585 Broadway, built for Solomon Equities, with Emery Roth and Sons Associated, is a stunning event.[12] It carries the sheer, sleek precision of the modernist curtain wall to new intricacy and richness. This is the building that conceals the required signs within its glass-faced podium, and whether or not they are actually in place or lit is irrelevant to its suave appearance. The podium and a curved setback above it make a transition to the tower which shifts its axis away from the diagonal of Broadway to the city's orthogonal grid. The bulky shaft is scaled and shaped by a precise geometric pattern of blue-green, white, and mirror glass and aluminum and steel panels. These expanded visual and architectural effects are all achieved within the stringent modernist vocabulary of the glass-walled skyscraper. The architects even risk, and get away with, the purely formalist "tipping" of the corners with a flash of brilliant mirror glass. This building's glitter is strictly upscale. The promotional brochure promises "every advantage of prestige, comfort, service and management"; it reaches resolutely east for the attractions of its "local ambience," ranging from "the Whitney Museum and the Museum of Modern Art to Carnegie Hall and Radio City Music Hall." Without blinking, it promises tenants "a haven of convenience, privacy and safety"[13] on Broadway at Forty-fourth Street. Its architects clearly go for the gold medal, not the brass ring.

On the Broadway-Seventh Avenue block bounded by Forty-ninth and Fiftieth streets, Kevin Roche of Kevin Roche John Dinkaloo Associates has created another "signature" building for Solomon Equities at 750 Seventh Avenue, a 35-story tower of stepped sections that appear to spiral around it to a pinnacled top. Here, too, the modernist aesthetic of the taut glass skin has entered a more advanced phase; a palette of grays and silvers in reflective glass within a grid of ceramic-coated glass affords prismatic changes in light and tone. Both 1585 Broadway and 750 Seventh Avenue utilize dramatic developments in glass technology in which the material reacts visibly to changing conditions for a subtler, more elaborate and dynamic aesthetic than previously possible.

The same preoccupation with innovative design marks the building for Eichner Properties, called One Broadway Place, at the center of the Times Square "bow tie" where Broadway and Seventh Avenue cross between Forty-fifth and Forty-sixth streets. No Vegas vulgarity here. David Childs of Skidmore, Owings and Merrill has divided a 44-story tower into office and retail functions, using the program and zoning requirements to create a dynamic relationship of distinctly defined parts, with a dramatic curtain wall of overlapping glass grids that create an abstract pattern with the illusion of depth. This brilliant solution makes one wonder about the miles of "traditional" trim of Childs's recent buildings that only seem to exacerbate the ambiguous problems of skyscraper scale and detail; they display none of the skill and drama demonstrated here.

A planned extension of Rockefeller Center to Seventh Avenue, called Rockefeller Plaza West,[14] will be the connecting link between the East and West sides. The design, by the firm of Kohn, Pederson Fox, marks a critical turning point in the way architecture is understood and practiced today. Here the curtain wall is dealt with as both structure and symbolism, looking back to the historic modernism of the RCA (now GE) Building and out toward Times Square. Also scheduled for the 1990s is 1580 Broadway, by Mayers and Schiff Associates with Schuman, Lichtenstein, Claman, Efron, for developer Jeffrey Katz. This structure will fill the small island at the head of Duffy Square that separates Broadway and Seventh Avenue between Forty-seventh and Forty-eighth streets. Ironically, the new buildings may turn out to be the best show on Broadway. *Pace* Playland.

Clearly, the question "Can Times Square be saved?" is rhetorical and sentimental. The efforts to do so are focused on preserving myths and illusions and some emblematic characteristics divorced from their original functions and meaning—metaphors, of a sort, for Times Square. Times Square cannot be saved in any form resembling what so many want to save; the process of physical and economic conversion is overwhelmingly and irreversibly at work.

What we are talking about is saving an image or a legend. This is not the first change in the area or the last. What is different is that this one is unique in terms of scale and destruction, and the sense that something is being lost rather than gained. Even if the performing arts and the theaters can hold fast, it will be in a context of an overpoweringly standardized commercial culture, and no matter how distinguished the artifacts, this will be another kind of place. Times Square is dead; long live Times Square.

NOTES

PROLOGUE   Times Square: Secularization
and Sacralization

1. The list of such works is large, but I would note in particular: Lary May, *Screening Out the Past: The Birth of Mass Culture and the Motion Picture Industry* (New York: Oxford University Press, 1980); Perry Duis, *The Saloon: Public Drinking in Chicago and Boston, 1880–1920* (Urbana, IL: University of Illinois, 1983); Lewis A. Erenberg, *Steppin' Out: New York Nightlife and the Transformation of American Culture, 1890–1930* (Westport, CT: Greenwood Press, 1981); Roy Rosenzweig, *Eight Hours for What We Will: Workers and Leisure in an Industrial City, 1870–1920* (New York: Cambridge University Press, 1983); John Kasson, *Amusing the Million: Coney Island at the Turn of the Century* (New York: Hill and Wang, 1978); Kathy Peiss, *Cheap Amusements: Working Women and Leisure in Turn-of-the-Century New York* (Philadelphia: Temple University Press, 1986).

2. George Lipsitz, "The Meaning of Memory: Family, Class, and Ethnicity in Early Network Television," in *Time Passages: Collective Memory and American Popular Culture* (Minneapolis: University of Minnesota Press, 1990), 39–75.

3. Richard Wightman Fox, "The Discipline of Amusement." See Chapter 4 in this book.

4. Quoted in Lionel Crocker, *The Rhetorical Theory of Henry Ward Beecher* (Chicago: University of Chicago Press, 1934), 64.

5. Erenberg, *Steppin' Out*, Chap. 4.

6. Anne de Bremont, "Beecher's Histrionic Power," *The Theatre* (London), XVIII (May 1, 1887): 248.

7. Letter of James Steele MacKaye to William R. Alger, November 1, 1872,

Box 7, James Steele MacKaye Collection, Dartmouth College Library, Hanover NH. For more information on MacKaye, see Percy MacKaye, *Epoch: The Life of Steele MacKaye, Genius of the Theatre*, 2 vols. (New York: Boni & Liveright, 1927).

8. Quoted in MacKaye, *Epoch*, Vol. 2, 348.

9. Poster reproduced in Neil Harris, *Humbug: The Art of P. T. Barnum* (Boston: Little, Brown, 1973), 262–263.

10. Steele MacKaye, unidentified lecture, ca. 1877, Box 7, James Steele MacKaye Collection, Dartmouth College Library, Hanover, NH.

11. Simon Nelson Patten, *Product and Climax* (New York: Huebsch, 1909), 45; Daniel M. Fox, *The Discovery of Abundance: Simon N. Patten and the Transformation of Social Theory* (Ithaca, NY: Cornell University Press, 1967), 25.

12. Warren Susman, *Culture as History: The Transformation of American Society in the Twentieth Century* (New York: Pantheon, 1984), Chap. 12.

13. Susman, *Culture as History*, 251.

14. Quoted in Susman, *Culture as History*, 250–251.

15. Susman, *Culture as History*, 250–251.

16. See Lawrence Levine, *Highbrow Lowbrow: The Emergence of Cultural Hierarchy in America* (Cambridge, MA: Harvard University Press, 1988), 85—168.

17. Even Susman asked: "If the culture of abundance *has become* manipulative, coercive, vulgar, and intolerable in all the ways these critics would have it, why did this happen? Did it have to follow? Were there alternatives?" *Culture as History*, xxix (emphasis added). To find a different view of mass culture, one would have to study recent developments in the cultural studies movement.

PART I STRUCTURAL CHANGES
Introductory Essay

1. "From Union Square to 34th Street
the great thoroughfare is ablaze with the
electric light, which illumines it with the
radiance of day. Crowds throng the sidewalks; the lights of the omnibuses and
carriages dart to and fro along the roadway like myriads of fireflies; the great
hotels, the theatres and restaurants, send
out their blaze of gas-lamps, and are alive
with visitors. The crowd is out for pleasure at night, and many and varied are the
forms which the pursuit of it takes.
. . . The throng fills the street until a late
hour of the night. Then the theatres pour
out their audiences to join it, and for an
hour or more the restaurants and cafés are
filled to their utmost capacity. Then as
midnight comes on, the street becomes
quieter and more deserted. The lights in
the buildings are extinguished, and gradually upper Broadway becomes silent and
more deserted. New York has gone to
bed; and Broadway enjoys a rest of a few
hours only to begin at daybreak a repeti-
tion of the scenes of the previous day."
James D. McCabe, Jr., *New York by Sunlight and Gaslight* (Philadelphia: Hubbard,
1882), 153–155. Half a century later Al
Dubin and Harry Warren said much the
same thing in the immortal "Lullaby of
Broadway"!

2. Hideous outdoor billboards already
covered some of the sparsely built, tacky
structures of the Longacre in the 1890s,
advertising Robert Burns Cigars,
"Kremonia 'better than amonia,' " the
Castle Square Opera Co. at the American
Theatre, "Go to Bergen Beach for 5
cents," and so on. The first electric sign,
apart from theater marquees on Broadway, extolled the "ocean breezes" of Coney Island from a building in Madison
Square in 1897. The facade of the Casino
Theatre displayed the Floradora Sextette,
outlined in carbon bulbs, dancing in the
air above Thirty-eighth Street, and Maxine Elliott (1871–1940) is said to have been
the first actress to "see her name in lights
on Broadway." Advertising came early to
the new Times Square, both daytime

outdoor and the increasingly spectacular
electric billboards at night, and it is the
latter for which Times Square became
known before 1920 after early variances
were granted from zoning restrictions and
safety laws affecting supporting structures were "pushed to the limit." The
first of the great illuminated spectacles—
four stories high—was the Wrigley's
Chewing Gum fountain, which confronted Rialto patrons between Forty-
fourth and Forty-fifth streets from 1917
through the early 1920s. See Jill Stone,
Times Square: A Pictorial History (New
York: Macmillan, 1982).

3. When the pennant of "ether advertising" was run up the flagpole after World
War I, hardly anyone rose to salute. Wireless telegraphy, or "radio," in the United
States was supposed to uplift the *Lumpen*
through education, information, and (the
all-accommodating word) culture. The
Secretary of Commerce, Herbert
Hoover, addressing a radio conference in
the nation's capital in 1922, thought it
"incredible that we should allow so great a
possibility for service to be drowned in
advertising chatter." But AT&T decided
otherwise when it announced its New
York City transmitter open for "toll
broadcasting" as "the telephone booth of
the air," which anyone was "free" to
use—at the right price. The First Amendment "Rights" of commercial and political
advertisers were thus preserved for pos-
terity; caveat emptor. National Carbon
Company, maker of "Eveready" batteries
for receiving sets, supported the move
and N. W. Ayer & Son "was quick to
recognize the new opportunity." Ayer
arranged a radio talk for Shur-on Optical
Co. over KDKA Pittsburgh and later in
the year another for E. R. Squibb & Sons
over WEAF in New York City.

4. Paul M. Mazur, *American Prosperity:
Its Causes and Consequences* (London:
Jonathan Cape, 1928), 63, 103–108, 254;
Irving S. Michelman, *Consumer Finance: A
Case History in American Business*, with a
preface by Leon Henderson (New York:
Frederick Fell, 1966).

5. In 1883 the railroad Caesars had divided the country into four parts—stan-

dard time zones—to suit their own rather than the sun's convenience (previously there had been fifty-odd local time belts.) The railroad managers' decision was ratified by the International Meridian Congress in 1884 but not by the elected representatives of the people until 1918. On the importance of western resources to United States prosperity and competitiveness see H. S. Perloff et al., *Regions, Resources, and Economic Growth* (Baltimore, MD: Johns Hopkins Press, 1960), 109–121, 191–221; Eric E. Lampard, "The Evolving System of Cities in the U.S.: Urbanization and Economic Development," in H. S. Perloff and L. Wingo, eds., *Issues in Urban Economics* (Baltimore, MD: Johns Hopkins Press, 1968), 107–139; Eric E. Lampard, "The New York Metropolis in Transformation," in H. J. Ewers et al., eds., *Future of the Metropolis: Economic Aspects* (New York: de Gruyter, 1986), especially 53–72; also, Peter R. Knights, *The Press Association War of 1866–1867* (Austin, TX: Journalism Monograph No. 6, 1967); and R. A. Schwarzlose, *The Nation's Newsbrokers, II, The Rush to Institution from 1865 to 1920* (Evanston, IL: Northwestern University Press, 1990).

6. Sales competition by means of advertising, special promotions, service, or other *non-price* inducement was among the preferred modes of competition adopted after the great corporate merger wave, 1898–1902, and taken up by the new Federal Trade Commission—"friend and counsellor to the business world"—after 1914, when practices resulting in "objectionable price discrimination" were ruled out by the Clayton Antitrust Act. Competition had compelled firms to expand and innovate not only to achieve lower unit costs in the interest of "efficiency" or "profits," but also to secure necessary market share *meanwhile* (without regard to immediate profitability) against like-motivated domestic competitors. Indeed, the dynamics of competitive survival—rather than technological advances in transport and communications or the possibility of mass markets per se—explain the rise of "big business." Competitive price cutting

under conditions of rising fixed cost and highly cyclical fluctuations in demand had led to horizontal mergers whereby six, seven, or a dozen firms held major shares of their respective markets coast to coast. Since businesses themselves were generally unable to maintain "order" in such markets—even under the tutelage of investment bankers—the genie of federal power was invoked by 1890 to curb "unfair," "wasteful," "cutthroat," and other forms of "unbridled" competition in interstate commerce that tended "to monopoly" or other "restraint of trade." Fierce competition for admen's services and sharp agency practice came to a head in 1915 when the Associated Advertising Clubs of the World (*sic*), aided by the trade journal *Printers' Ink* (originally Rowell's house organ), persuaded the FTC to stigmatize "false advertising" as "an unfair method of competition." M. S. Handler, "False and Misleading Advertising," *Yale Law Journal* 39 (November 1929), 22–51; Ralph M. Hower, *History of an Advertising Agency: N. W. Ayer & Son at Work, 1869–1939* (Cambridge, MA: Harvard University Press, 1939); and Daniel A. Pope, *The Making of Modern Advertising* (New York: Basic Books, 1983). Arthur J. Eddy, *The New Competition* (New York: Appleton, 1912) indicated that the retreat from competition was not confined to the oligopolistic markets of big business. He showed how "cooperative competition" by "open price" trade associations had brought stability to many smaller firms through lobbying, advertising, and informational activities and "steady profits," making their business "more steady, dependable, and calculable from year to year."

7. *Atlanta Journal* (May 1, 1886). Coca-Cola Company, *The Chronicle of Coca-Cola Since 1886* (n.p., n.d.), 24, reports people seeking "bottling franchises on the moon" after the success of the Apollo mission. In 1982, after its long and eventful advertising competition with rival beverages, Coca-Cola finally went into the entertainment industry with the purchase of Columbia Pictures Industries: "an exciting area for growth in a consumer market

compatible with the Company's existing main business." Also, Coca-Cola Company, *Opinions, Orders, Injunctions, and Decrees Relating to Unfair Competition and Infringement of Trademark, I, 1886–1923* (Atlanta, GA: Foote & Davis, 1923). On the pioneering use of magazines to promote women's paper dress patterns by New York manufacturers: *Metropolitan Monthly* (E. Butterick) and the tonier *Demorest's Monthly Magazine* (Mme. Demorest), see Margaret Walsh, "Democratization of Fashion: The Emergence of the Women's Dress Pattern Industry," *Journal of American History* 66 (September 1979), 299–313; Hower, *History of an Advertising Agency*, 60–61, 97–100, 274–276. Efforts to measure circulation (audience) go back to G. P. Rowell's *American Newspaper Directory* (1869) and Ayer & Sons' *Manual for Advertisers* (1874), but no systematic measurement was accomplished before the publishers' Audit Bureau of Circulation, 1914. See Volume of Expenditures on Advertising for all media ($ millions) from *Printers' Ink Advertisers' Annual* (New York: P.I. Publications, 1955 ed.); Net National Product and Flows of Goods and Services to Consumers (including government services to consumers—$ billions): S. Kuznets, *Capital in the American Economy: Its Formation and Financing* (New York: National Bureau of Economic Research, 1961). On Engel's law and differences in working-class expenditures between Saxony and the United States see F. Stuart Chapin, *Field Work and Social Research* (New York: Century, 1920), 10–11; and W. F. Ogburn, *Quarterly Publications of the American Statistical Association* 16 (June 1919), 374. Frank Munsey, "Advertising in Some of Its Phases," *Munsey's Magazine* (December 1898), 476–486.

8. William H. Lough, *High-Level Consumption* (New York: McGraw-Hill, 1935); Julius Weinberger, "Economic Aspects of Recreation," *Harvard Business Review* (Summer 1937); J. Frederick Dewhurst et al., *America's Needs and Resources: A New Survey* (New York: Twentieth Century Fund, 1955 ed.), 965–980. On the "agencies of mass impression," especially

the motion picture, M. M. Willey and S. A. Rice, "The Agencies of Communication," *Recent Social Trends*, Vol. 1 (New York: McGraw-Hill, 1933), 208–211.

9. J. F. Steiner, "Recreation and Leisure Time Activities," *Recent Social Trends*, Vol. 2, 912–957, especially "commercial amusements." Hower, *History of an Advertising Agency*, 160–170, "pioneer work in radio advertising." Erik Barnouw, *The Sponsor: Notes on a Modern Potentate* (New York: Oxford University Press, 1978). Randy Cohen, "Songs in the Key of Hype," *More* (July/August 1977), 12.

10. Earnest E. Calkins, *Business the Civilizer* (Boston; Little Brown, 1928), 3, 8, 292; Stuart Chase, *The Tragedy of Waste* (New York: Macmillan, 1925); Stuart Chase and F. J. Schlink, *Your Money's Worth* (New York: Macmillan, 1927). F. J. Schlink, "The Technique of Buying Under Specifications," *Journal of Home Economics* 19 (October 1927), 589–590, was virtually a consumer manifesto. Roger Babson, *The Folly of Installment Buying* (New York: F. A. Stokes, 1938). Earlier Babson was among writers who had attributed part of the improved consumption to the purchasing power released from alcoholic drinking by prohibition, cited by Herman Feldman, *Prohibition: Its Industrial and Economic Aspects* (New York: Appleton, 1927), 381–393. W. T. Foster and W. Catchings, *Business Without a Buyer* (Newton, MA: Pollak Foundation for Economic Research, 1927), 57–76; W. T. Foster and W. Catchings, "Old King Cole in Trouble," *Atlantic Monthly* 138 (July 1926), 94–100; and W. T. Foster and W. Catchings, *Profits* (Newton, MA: Pollak Foundation, 1925), 223–236, on "cash for consumers." Martha L. Olney, "Advertising, Consumer Credit, and the 'Consumer Durables Revolution' of the 1920s," *Journal of Economic History* 47 (June 1987).

11. *Saturday Evening Post* (April 18, 1916); W. H. Grimes, *The Story of Commercial Credit Company* (Baltimore, MD: Commercial Credit Co., 1946), 30.

12. *New York Times* (February 17, 1928), 23; (May 9, 1928), 30; (October 16,

1928), 30. New York's Uniform Small Loan Law was finally passed June 1, 1932. E. R. A. Seligman, *Economics of Installment Selling: A Study in Consumers' Credit* (New York: Harper, 1927); L. H. Seltzer, *Financial History of the American Automobile Industry* (Boston: Houghton Mifflin, 1928). D. M. Kennedy, "Credit and Savings Institutions Other Than Banks," *Banking Studies* (Washington, DC: Federal Reserve, 1941), 141–166: "Personal and installment loans—formerly left almost entirely to sales and personal finance companies—are now also made by banks." Neil H. Jacoby and Raymond Saulnier, *Business Finance and Banking* (New York: National Bureau of Economic Research, 1947), 110–117, 128–130, 160–162, concludes that the growing interest of commercial banks in consumption credit before 1940 was "at least partly substitutive in nature" compensating for loss of production credit business, especially to insurance companies. C. B. Moore, "We Can't Curb Production—So We Are Increasing Consumption," *Printers' Ink* (January 8, 1931), 80–84. R. S. Lynd with Alice C. Hanson, "The People as Consumers," *Recent Social Trends*, Vol. 2, 864, 911: Lynd concluded that the lack of coherent policy regarding the consumer in government bureaus "has its roots in a long tradition of focusing attention upon the productive forces of the nation, of identifying consumer welfare with business prosperity, and of over-dependence upon the rational adequacy of the consumer's unaided choices." Here Lynd reiterated one of the themes of Wesley C. Mitchell's classic "The Backward Art of Spending Money," *American Economic Review* 2 (June 1912), 269–281.

13. Jack N. Poggi, *Theater in America: The Impact on Economic Forces, 1870–1967* (Ithaca, NY: Cornell University Press, 1968).

14. Franklin W. Ryan with Leon Henderson, *Family Finance in the U.S. During 1930 and 1931*, Franklin Plan Economic Bulletin (January 1932).

CHAPTER 1 Developing for Commercial Culture

1. That there would be commercial culture in America is another subject altogether, one to be addressed separately from this chapter. That the United States would have national, state, and municipal governments that were relatively weak by comparison with their counterparts in Continental Europe, and that it would have a more-or-less free market economy,

Short and Intermediate Term Consumer Credit, 1929–1957
($ millions outstanding end of calendar year)

Year	Total	CC per capita ($1947–49)	Percentage Installment	CC as Percent GNP Personal Consumption Exp.
1929	7,116	80	49.5	9.2
1932	4,026	55	41.5	8.3
1935	5,190	70	54.3	9.3
1940	8,338	105	66.1	11.8
1946	8,384	71	49.8	5.8
1947	11,598	84	57.7	7.2
1949	17,364	114	57.6	9.8
1953	31,393	172	73.3	13.6
1955	38,830	205	74.6	15.3
1957	44,970	217	75.3	16.0

SOURCE: Federal Reserve System, *Supplement to Banking and Monetary Statistics,* Section 16, 1929-1955, and monthly F. R. Bulletins. U.S. Department of Commerce, *National Income and Product Accounts of the U.S., 1929-1965.*

are also distinct subjects. On New York City's early centrality, see Allan R. Pred, *Urban Growth and the Circulation of Information: The United States System of Cities, 1790–1840* (Cambridge, MA: Harvard University Press, 1973), 28–42.

2. David C. Hammack, *Power and Society: Greater New York at the Turn of the Century* (New York: Russell Sage Foundation, 1983), 37–38.

3. Census data provide one index that seems relevant to this point. In 1890 New York City had 4.4 percent of all jobs in the United States, but 10.1 percent of all jobs for "authors, editors, and reporters"; in 1910, when the city had 5.6 percent of all jobs, it had 12.6 percent of the writing jobs.

4. Martin Clary, *Mid-Manhattan. The Multimillion Area* (New York: Forty-second Street Property Owners and Merchants Association, 1929), 120–121.

5. Hammack, *Power and Society*, Chap. 8. For another account of rapid transit in New York, see Charles W. Cheape III, *Moving the Masses: Urban Public Transit in New York, Boston, and Philadelphia, 1880–1912* (Cambridge, MA: Harvard University Press, 1981).

6. Jameson W. Doig, *Metropolitan Transportation Politics and the New York Region* (New York: Columbia University Press, 1966), 14.

7. *Mid-Manhattan*, 121–127.

8. Edwin H. Spengler, *Land Values in New York in Relation to Transit Facilities* (New York: Columbia University Press, 1930), 19–24.

9. Hammack, *Power and Society*, 232–234.

10. This refers to a coordinated expansion of the IRT and BMT, approved by the Board of Estimate in 1913.

11. *Mid-Manhattan*, 107–112.

12. *Mid-Manhattan*, 121.

13. M. Dorothy George, *London Life in the Eighteenth Century* (London: Kegan Paul, Trench, Trubner, 1964), 173.

14. Stanislaw J. Makielski, Jr., *The Politics of Zoning: The New York Experience* (New York: Columbia University Press, 1966), 12.

15. For an account of this alliance, see J. Joseph Huthmacher, *Senator Robert F. Wagner and the Rise of Urban Liberalism* (New York: Atheneum, 1971), Chaps. 1–3.

16. Thomas Adams, "The Character, Bulk, and Surroundings of Buildings," Adams et al., *Buildings. Their Uses and the Spaces About Them*, Vol. VI of *The Regional Survey of New York and Its Environs* (New York: Regional Plan of New York and Its Environs, 1931), 82–83.

17. Adams, "The Character, Bulk, and Surroundings," 82–83. A map of "New York's Theaters in the Times Square District," published by the Regional Plan Association in 1931, shows no theaters west of Broadway below Forty-first Street. Thomas Adams, *The Building of the City*, Vol. II of *The Regional Plan of New York and Its Environs* (New York: Regional Plan of New York and Its Environs, 1931), 318.

18. Mary C. Henderson, *The City and the Theater* (Clifton, NJ: James T. White, 1973), 171, 198.

19. Walter Zvonchenko, "A Historical Study of the Relation of Theater and Broadcasting to Land Use in Midtown Manhattan in the Years 1925 Through 1928." Unpublished Ph.D. Diss., City University of New York, 1987, 17.

20. Alfred L. Bernheim, *The Business of the Theater: An Economic History of the American Theater, 1750–1932* (New York: Actors Equity Association, 1932; reprint, New York: Benjamin Blom, 1964), 26; cited by Margaret M. Knapp, "A Historical Study of the Legitimate Playhouses on West Forty-second Street Between Seventh and Eighth Avenues in New York City." Unpublished Ph.D. Diss., City University of New York, 1982, 12.

21. Knapp, "A Historical Study," 13.

22. Brooks Atkinson, *Broadway*, Rev. Ed. (New York: Macmillan, 1974), 11; quoted in Knapp, "A Historical Study," 14.

23. Henderson, *The City and the Theater*, 189–191, asserting that the Syndicate dominated Times Square theaters by 1905; for a more balanced view see Knapp, "A Historical Study," 70, 89, 100, 135, 179.

24. Knapp, "A Historical Study," 220–???

25. Knapp, "A Historical Study," 194, 206, 245.

26. Knapp, "A Historical Study," 245.

27. Jack Poggi, *Theater in America: The Impact of Economic Forces, 1870–1967* (Ithaca, NY: Cornell University Press, 1968), 29–30; cited by Knapp, "A Historical Study," 226.

28. Zvonchenko, "A Historical Study," 13.

29. Zvonchenko, "A Historical Study," 91–93.

30. Edward M. Bassett, *Zoning: The Laws, Administration, and Court Decisions During the First Twenty Years* (New York: Russell Sage Foundation, 1940), 70.

31. Adams, *The Building of the City*, 317. The Regional Plan group was created and controlled by the Russell Sage Foundation and those associated with the foundation (and the Charity Organization Society of New York) in promoting the Zoning Resolution of 1916. These people included Bassett, who drafted the resolution; George McAneny, who as President of the Board of Aldermen between 1914 and 1916 had moved the resolution through to passage; Lawson Purdy, a longtime Commissioner of Taxes and executive of the Charity Organization Society who also served on the Russell Sage board; Lawrence Veiller, the advocate of housing reform through the regulation of building codes; and Robert W. deForest, Veiller's sponsor, President of the Russell Sage Foundation, and key member of the Regional Plan Committee. Indeed, the Regional Plan is striking for its complaint that the Times Square theaters were "too closely packed together in a small area," and its wish that "the cost of remedying the situation" could be "considered as a liability against the theaters rather than against traffic as such." It proposed to relieve pedestrian congestion in mid-Manhattan with a system of arcaded, elevated sidewalks, to be built into the facades of buildings from Penn Station along Thirty-third Street to Madison Avenue, up Madison to Forty-second Street at Grand Central Station, across Forty-second Street to Seventh Avenue, and up to Fifty-second Street. The elevated sidewalks would line both sides of Madison and both sides of Times Square, and include a mid-block connection between Fifth and Sixth avenues from Thirty-third Street to Fifty-seventh Street. Adams, *The Building of the City*, 411–415. Apart from its criticism of congestion in Times Square and this proposal, the Regional Plan has almost nothing to say about the theater district or the entertainment industry. It treated theaters simply as another commercial use, omitting them entirely from a map of "cultural institutions in the City of New York," which included high schools, art schools, libraries, museums, exhibition galleries, and auditoriums. Adams et al., *Buildings*, 45.

32. Bassett, *Zoning*, 91–92.

33. Zvonchenko, "A Historical Study," 98–100.

CHAPTER 2   Uptown Real Estate and the Creation of Times Square

I thank William Leach and William Taylor for their valuable comments on the original paper.

1. *Real Estate Record and Builders Guide* (*RERBG*) (November 3, 1900).

2. *RERBG* (October 31, 1903).

3. *RERBG* (February 14, 1903).

4. "The Stranger's Path," in Ervin Zube, ed., *Landscapes: Selected Writings of J. B. Jackson* (Amherst, MA: University of Massachusetts Press, 1970), 92–106. For the linked promotion of midtown and the city as the "center of amusement" for strangers see *RERBG* (September 19, 1904).

5. Elizabeth Blackmar, *Manhattan for Rent* (Ithaca, NY: Cornell University Press, 1989), Chaps. 4–5.

6. Peter Buckley, "Culture, Class and Place in Antebellum New York City," in John Hull Mollenkopf, *Power, Culture, and Place: Essays on New York City* (New York: Russell Sage Foundation, 1988), 34–35.

7. Christine Boyer, *Manhattan Man-*

ners: Architecture and Style, 1850–1900 (New York: Rizzoli, 1985), 43–120.

8. Betsy Blackmar and Roy Rosenzweig, *The Park and the People: A Social History of Central Park* (Ithaca, NY: forthcoming), Chaps. 1–2.

9. See, for example, *RERBG* (May 30, 1891; January 17, 1891; August 20, 1892).

10. Blackmar and Rosenzweig, *The Park and the People*, Chap. 12.

11. On the development of apartments and their new conveniences for middle-class living, see Elizabeth Cromley, *Alone Together: A History of New York's Early Apartments* (Ithaca, NY: Cornell University Press, 1990).

12. *RERBG* (January 16, 1907); compare proposal to build theater on Central Park West, *RERBG* (February 19, 1906; August 7, 1907).

13. *RERBG* (November 3, 1900; August 24, 1907).

14. Edward Spengler, *Land Values in New York in Relation to Transit Facilities* (New York: Columbia University Press, 1930), 65, concluded "a subway reflects the conditions of the sections through which it passes. . . . It does not cause the increase" in land values. *RERBG* (June 15, 1918), on the other hand, credited rapid transit with transforming the areas around Grand Central into the city's "hub."

15. Margaret M. Knapp, "A Historical Study of the Legitimate Playhouses on West Forty-second Street Between Seventh and Eighth Avenues in New York City." Unpublished Ph.D. diss., City University of New York, 1982.

16. *RERBG* (October 31, 1903; March 17, 1906; December 7, 1907).

17. On residential resistance see *RERBG* (July 2, 1904).

18. See, for example, in the New York Regional Plan, Robert Murray Haig, *Major Economic Forces in Metropolitan Growth and Arrangement*, Vol. 1B, 13–32; Edward Bassett, "Control of Building Heights, Densities, and Use of Zoning," 376–377 and passim; and Thomas Adams, "The Character, Bulk and Surroundings of Buildings," 33–34, 157–58, both in *Buildings: Their Uses and Spaces*

Around Them, Vol. 6 (New York: Regional Plan of New York and Its Environs, 1927–1931). See also, e.g., Homer Hoyt, *One Hundred Years of Land Valves in Chicago* (1933; New York: Arno Press, 1970), 320–367; Arthur Weimar and Homer Hoyt, *Principles of Urban Real Estate* (New York: Ronald Press, 1939), 94–101; Walter Firey, *Land Use In Central Boston* (Cambridge, MA: Harvard University Press, 1947), 224–261.

19. Kristin Miller, "Work and Entertainment: The Radicalization of the Actors' Equity Association, 1913–1924." Unpublished Master's thesis, Columbia University, New York, 1987, 25–26.

20. Walter Zvonchenko, "A Historical Study of the Relation of Theater and Broadcasting to Land Use in Midtown Manhattan in the Years 1925 Through 1928." Unpublished Ph.D. diss., City University of New York, 1987.

CHAPTER 3 Urban Tourism and the Commercial City

1. Dean MacCannell, *The Tourist. A New Theory of the Leisure Class* (New York: Schocken, 1976), 13, 16.

2. American domestic travel in the nineteenth century is treated in a variety of texts. See, among others, the essays and bibliographies in Alf Evers et al., *Resorts of the Catskills* (New York: St. Martin's, 1979); Lesley Dorsey and Janice Devine, *Fare Thee Well: A Backward Look at Two Centuries of Historic American Hostelries* (New York: Crown, 1964); Billy M. Jones, *Health Seekers in the Southwest, 1817–1900* (Norman, OK: University of Oklahoma, 1967); Jeffrey Limerick et al., *America's Grand Resort Hotels* (New York: Pantheon, 1979); Earl Pomeroy, *In Search of the Golden West: The Tourist in Western America* (New York: Knopf, 1957); John F. Sears, *Sacred Places; American Tourist Attractions in the Nineteenth Century* (New York: Oxford University Press, 1989); and Jefferson Williamson, *The American Hotel: An Anecdotal History* (New York: Knopf, 1930). For the later period see especially John A. Jakle, *The Tourist: Travel in Twentieth-Century North America*

(Lincoln, NE: University of Nebraska Press, 1985)

Two interesting essays on the development of European tourism, with parallels and contrasts for this paper, are Jack Simmons, "Railways, Hotels and Tourism in Great Britain, 1839–1914," *Journal of Contemporary History* 19 (April 1984): 201–222; and Robin Lenman, "Art and Tourism in Southern Germany, 1850–1930," Arthur Marwick, ed. *The Arts, Literature, and Society* (London and New York: Routledge, 1990), 163–180.

3. "The Tourism Industry," *Independent* 55 (August 20, 1903):2004–2005. For some statistics on the history of American travel to Europe see *Literary Digest* 101 (June 8, 1929):68–70. The literature on American travel abroad in the nineteenth century is vast. Some places to begin are Paul R. Baker, *The Fortunate Pilgrims. Americans in Italy, 1800–1860* (Cambridge, MA: Harvard University Press, 1964); Allison Lockwood, *Passionate Pilgrims. The American Traveler in Great Britain, 1800–1914* (New York: Cornwall, 1981); and William L. Vance, *America's Rome*, 2 vols. (New Haven, CT: Yale University Press, 1989).

4. For the history of Cook's see John Pudney, *The Thomas Cook Story* (London: Michael Joseph, 1953); and Edmund Swinglehurst, *The Romantic Journey. The Story of Thomas Cook and Victorian Travel* (London: Pica, 1974).

5. Alden Hatch, *American Express. A Century of Service* (Garden City, NY: Doubleday, 1950), reviews the history of this enterprise. See also Hugh De Santis, "The Democratization of Travel: The Travel Agent in American History," *Journal of American Culture* 1 (Spring 1978):1–17.

6. For more on the massive arrangements required for the Columbian Exposition see David F. Burg, *Chicago's White City of 1893* (Lexington, KY: University of Kentucky, 1976), especially Chap. 3; Reid Badger, *The Great American Fair. The World's Columbian Exposition and American Culture* (Chicago, IL: Nelson-Hall, 1979), particularly Part 3; and Robert W. Tydell, *All the World's a Fair. Visions of Empire at American International Expositions, 1876–1916* (Chicago, IL: University of Chicago Press, 1984), Chap. 2.

7. Charles Rollinson Lamb, "Civic Architecture from Its Constructive Side," *Municipal Affairs* 2 (March 1898):67. This entire issue was devoted to municipal art and architecture. For more on the subject of the world's fairs and the City Beautiful movement see William H. Wilson, *The City Beautiful Movement* (Baltimore, MD: Johns Hopkins University Press, 1989), Chap. 3.

8. For the City Beautiful movement in New York see Harvey A. Kantor, "The City Beautiful in New York," *New-York Historical Society Quarterly* 58 (April 1973):149–171. For the deliberate use of European urban models as a spur to action see the exhibition catalogue organized by Deborah Bershad, *Imaginary Cities. European Views from the Collection of the Art Commission* (New York: Hunter College Art Gallery, 1986).

9. Daniel H. Burnham and Edward H. Bennett, *Plan of Chicago* (Chicago, IL: Commercial Club, 1909; New York, NY: Da Capo, 1970), 124. There is a chapter by Walter L. Fisher entitled "Legal Aspects of the Plan of Chicago," which follows the last paragraph in the form of an appendix.

10. For the lengthy campaign to create Grant's Tomb see Neil Harris, "The Battle for Grant's Tomb," *American Heritage* 36 (August/September 1985):70–79.

11. Geo. R. Cromwell, ed., *America. Scenic and Descriptive. From Alaska to the Gulf of Mexico* (New York: James Clarke, 1894).

12. This tradition is examined exhaustively by John W. Reps, *Views and Viewmakers of Urban America* (Columbia, MO: University of Missouri Press, 1984). For New York City see the great work by I. N. Phelps Stokes, *Iconography of Manhattan Island, 1498–1909*, 6 vols. (New York: Dodd, 1915–1928). Peter Conrad's *The Art of the City. Views and Versions of New York* (New York: Oxford University Press, 1984) is a stimulating treatment of the paintings, movies, photographs, prints, as well as many important works

of fiction, poetry, and architecture provoked by New York City.

13. Frank Moss, *The American Metropolis. From Knickerbocker Days to the Present Time*, 3 vols. (New York: Collier, 1897). Moss was an attorney and was counsel to the Society for the Prevention of Crime.

14. *New York Times* (June 18, 1911) Section 5, 4.

15. *New York Tribune* (May 1, 1889): 6.

16. For descriptions see *Harper's Weekly* 36 (October 8, 1892):966–968, and 36 (October 22, 1892):1012–1018; and "The Great Parade," *New York Times* (October 13, 1892): 4.

17. "Grant Day and Business," *New York Times* (April 3, 1897):6.

18. "Dewey Celebration," *New York Times* (September 18, 1899):6.

19. The letter appeared in the *New York Times* on September 19, 1899, page 3; the newspaper's response appeared on September 20, 1899, on page 6.

20. George and Dorothy Miller, *Picture Postcards in the United States, 1893–1918* (New York: Potter, 1976), 11.

21. "No other American city was given half the attention in the magazines that New York received," Frank Luther Mott noted. "Not only was she described by her own periodicals; but those of other cities, recognizing in her picturesqueness a source of 'good copy,' printed occasional articles about her development and the life of her people." Frank Luther Mott, *A History of American Magazines, 1865–1885* (Cambridge, MA: Harvard University Press, 1957), 26. Mott notes that of the periodicals in the hundred-thousand circulation category during any part of the 1865–1885 period, New York was home to two-thirds.

22. The founding in 1875 of the *New York Dramatic News*, and four years later of the *New York Mirror* (whose title changed almost immediately to *New York Dramatic Mirror*), together with the *New York Clipper* gave the city three major dramatic papers. The halftone process made it increasingly possible, in the nineties and thereafter, for general magazines as well as theatrical journals to feature photographs of the stars of the stage.

23. "New York, the Unrivalled Business Centre," *Harper's Weekly* 46 (November 15, 1902):1673.

24. Randall Blackshaw, "The New New York," *Harper's Weekly* 46 (November 15, 1902):1673.

25. John DeWitt Warner, "Matters That Suggest Themselves," *Municipal Affairs* 2 (March 1898):123.

26. For a bibliography of tourist brochures for a slightly later period see Michael Vinson, *Motoring Tourists and the Scenic West, 1903 to 1948* (Dallas, TX: DeGolyer Library, Southern Methodist University, 1989).

27. The history of these efforts was reviewed in "New York Entertains Nearly 200,000 Strangers Daily," *New York Times* (August 18, 1912) Section, 5, 4.

28. Edward W. Townsend, "New York—The Greatest Summer Resort," *Harper's Weekly* 44 (September 1, 1900): 821. See also George Ethelbert Walsh, "New York as a Summer Resort," *Independent* 71 (July 6, 1911):12–16.

29. For more on the city's landscape of pleasure see Lewis A. Erenberg, *Steppin' Out. New York Nightlife and the Transformation of American Culture, 1890–1930* (Westport, CT: Greenwood Press, 1981), especially Chaps. 1–3.

30. Townsend, "New York—The Greatest Summer Resort," 821. For more on the theater area's roof gardens see Stephen Burge Johnson, *The Roof Gardens of Broadway Theatres, 1883–1942* (Ann Arbor, MI: University of Michigan Press, 1985).

31. "Strangers in New York," *Harper's Weekly* 46 (March 1, 1902):266. For more on advertising New York as a summer resort see *New York Times* (April 23, 1911):9.

32. "Strangers in New York," 266.

33. *New York Times* (August 18, 1912) Section 5, 4. For an earlier discussion of New York commuting patterns as well as daily tourist visitors see Richard Barry, "How People Come and Go in New York," *Harper's Weekly* 42 (February 26, 1898):204–207.

34. For local hotel history I have relied

upon the *Hotel Monthly*; Jefferson Williamson, *The American Hotel*; Edward Hungerford, *The Story of the Waldorf-Astoria* (New York: Putnam, 1925); and various biographical encyclopedias. The history and design of many of these establishments is treated by Robert A. M. Stern, Gregory Gilmartin, and John Massengale in *New York 1900. Metropolitan Architecture and Urbanism, 1890–1915* (New York: Rizzoli, 1983).

35. For Statler see Rufus Jarman, *A Bed for the Night* (New York: Harper & Row, 1952). For the midtown hotels see the description in Martin Clary, *Mid-Manhattan. The Multimillion Area* (New York: Forty-second Street Property Owners and Merchants Association, 1929), Chap. 5.

36. There is an extensive literature and bibliography on the building of the two stations. Two volumes by Carl Condit, *The Port of New York: A History of the Rail and Terminal System from the Beginnings to Pennsylvania Station* (Chicago, IL: University of Chicago Press, 1980), and *The Port of New York: A History of the Rail and Terminal System from the Grand Central Electrification to the Present* (Chicago, IL: University of Chicago Press, 1981), offer the best place to start.

37. See *New York Times* (January 30, 1910) Section 6, 10, for an announcement of the proposed Grand Central Palace. Within two years the building was up and holding, among other things, the first Travel and Vacation Exhibition to be held in the United States; see *New York Times* (April 14, 1912):9. Opening the show on May 23, 1912, Chauncey Depew declared that "New York is now the centre of everything. Everybody wants to be seen here"; *New York Times* (May 24, 1912):10.

38. This information comes from the monthly serial *World Convention Dates*, which began publication in 1916.

39. Thaddeus S. Dayton, "Chicago as a Railroad Center," *Harper's Weekly* 56 (December 28, 1912):111–112.

40. For estimates see *New York Times* (December 26, 1926) Section 10, 1–2, and (January 1, 1927):10.

41. George Ethelbert Walsh, "New York as a Summer Resort," *Independent* 71 (July 6, 1911):12–16, gives information about tour and excursion boats and sightseeing automobiles. *The Official Hotel and Red Book Directory* (New York: Official Hotel Red Book and Directory Company, 1912) contains advertisements for some of the tours. See also Ray Brown, "Rubber-Necking in New York," *Everybody's Magazine* 34 (January 1916):105–114; and the reference to the sightseeing coach in Rupert Hughes, *The Real New York* (New York: Smart Set Publishing, 1904), 375.

42. I know of no extensive bibliography of these materials. Ephemeral in form and fragile in substance, examples survive in only limited quantities. Most major libraries (and antiquarian bookstores) do contain pieces put out by stores like Siegel and Cooper, by Macy's, by newspapers, hotels, and various retail establishments. As representatives of this literature see *New York. A Small Book of Facts About a Big City* (New York: Hotel Claridge, n.d.); *Pocket Guide to New York* (New York: Merchants' Association of New York, 1906); and *New York. Metropolis of the World* (New York: John Wanamaker Store, 1916).

43. "The Spectator," *Outlook* 76 (February 6, 1904):305–306.

44. "The Spectator," 306. See also Harrison Rhodes, "What Is a New Yorker?" *Harper's Weekly* 133 (August 1916):321–332.

45. Julian Street, "Lobster Palace Society," *Everybody's Magazine* 72 (May 1910):646–647.

46. Julian Street, *Welcome to Our City* (New York: John Lane, 1913), 19, 57. The title essay in this collection originally appeared in *Collier's*.

47. *Welcome to Our City*, 80–81.

48. Robert Shackleton, *The Book of New York* (Philadelphia, PA: Penn Publishing, 1920), 214–215; see also *New York Times* (November 24, 1912) Section 7, 1.

49. "F. P. A.," " 'It's a Fine Place to Visit, Yes—But I'd Hate to Live There,' " *Everybody's Magazine* 34 (February 1916):181–189.

50. "The Later-Day Audience: Its

Characteristics and Habits," *Harper's Weekly* 46 (May 17, 1902):632.

51. "The City Majestic," *Independent* 69 (September 15, 1910):603.

52. "F. P. A.," " 'It's a Fine Place to Visit.' " 189.

CHAPTER 4 The Discipline of Amusement

1. "——ing Evils in Stage Play" (first word illegible) and "Theatre Heeds Garb Protests," newspaper clippings in Shubert Archives. Penciled on the first clipping is "New York Times, November 28, 1923," and on the second, "New York American, December 5, 1923." A check of the microfilm edition of the *Times* shows no such article in the November 28 issue, so it is unclear where the article appeared. The subcommittee in the audience at the Shubert was only one of many Protestant, Catholic, and Jewish groups who joined the attack on stage "filth" in the fall of 1923. Theater managers rushed to make cosmetic changes in order to head off legal censorship. (I am indebted to Minda Novak for finding these clippings in the Shubert Archives. I also thank Elizabeth Beverly for many conversations about the cultural contours of work, play, and language; her ideas have informed mine at every point. And I am grateful to Jean-Christophe Agnew and William Leach for their critical readings of an earlier draft of this chapter.)

2. Nineteenth century Protestant advocates of worldly amusements often appealed to the Hebraic tradition, within which dancing, for example, was perfectly acceptable. They rarely appealed to Catholic traditions, however. The perceived Catholic threat to republican virtue and middle-class propriety was still too tangible.

3. Baptist minister John Roach Straton's "Will New York Be Destroyed If It Does Not Repent?" *The Watchman-Examiner* 6 (July 25, 1918):953–954, is a good example of the doomsaying rhetoric that continues to the present day in the conservative denominations. "Is it not a disgrace," he asks, "that our churches are empty, while the playhouses night after

night and Sunday too are packed to suffocation?" (p. 954). As the recent flap over Martin Scorcese's *Last Temptation of Christ* (1988) also suggests, conservative Christians depend upon various kinds of "wickedness" as tangible proofs of the world's depravity—not to mention needling to exploit them for recruitment purposes. Unlike liberals, they seek not to eradicate moral turpitude but to heighten consciousness of it.

4. "To Keep a Clean Stage," [700,000 daily theatergoers], clipping in Shubert Archives marked "New York Herald, November 3, 1923"; Mary C. Henderson, *The City and the Theater* (Clifton, NJ: James T. White, 1973), 188 [80 theaters], 194 [the estimate of visitors from outside New York City in 1923].

5. William Prynne quoted in Edmund S. Morgan, "Puritan Hostility to the Theatre," *Proceedings of the American Philosophical Society* 110 (October 1966): 342. See also A. F. Findlay, "Amusements," in James Hastings, ed., *Encyclopedia of Religion and Ethics*, Vol. 1 (New York: Scribner's, 1908), 400–404.

6. Henry Ward Beecher, "Popular Amusements," *Twelve Lectures to Young Men on Various Important Subjects*, 2nd ed. (New York: George H. Doran, 1879), 162, 164, 167, 169, 173, 176–177. "Popular Amusements" was delivered as a lecture in 1844 and first published in *Seven Lectures to Young Men* in 1845. Among the many straightforward antebellum restatements of the Puritan view—pro-"recreation" and anti-"amusement"—see "Amusements," *The New Englander* 9 (August 1851):345–359.

7. "Recreation," *Christian Examiner* 8 (May 1830):205, 209. By the 1820s the term "liberal" was in common use to describe the anti-Calvinist position in theology and ethics; the corresponding noun was usually "liberality," not "liberalism."

8. "Amusements," *Christian Examiner* 45 (September 1848):157–158, 160–161.

9. "Public Amusements and Public Morality," *Christian Examiner* 63 (July 1857):49, 58–59, 64; "Amusements," *Monthly Religious Magazine* 21 (January 1859):33–34.

10. "Public Amusements and Public Morality," 52–54. "The question of amusements has become a great social question," wrote the Congregationalist *American Church Monthly* in 1857. "An entirely new phenomenon has lately appeared in connection with it. It is that certain members of the so-called liberal portion of the religious world are taking the popular side of the question." "City Amusements," *American Church Monthly* (August 1857):129. Unitarians (who in 1855 numbered only about 14,000) and Universalists (about 100,000) had taken the liberal side for a generation and thereby distinguished themselves from the (in their view) stodgy Congregationalists. What was new in the 1850s was the dawning of a liberal view among Congregationalists, who in 1855 numbered about 200,000, and other mainstream groups such as the Northern Baptists (about 400,000). Membership estimates from Timothy L. Smith, *Revivalism and Social Reform* (New York, Harper & Row, 1965 [1957]), 20–21.

11. "The Test of Legitimate Amusements," *Universalist Review* 17 (October 1860):389–391, 400.

12. Edwin Holt Hughes, "Our Mistaken Legislation on Amusements," *Methodist Review* 106 (September 1923):720. Membership figure from Smith, *Revivalism and Social Reform*, 20.

13. "Places of Public Amusement," *Putnam's Monthly Magazine* 3 (February 1854):143, 147.

14. "City Amusements," 137.

15. "City Amusements," 129, 140.

16. "Some of Our Popular Amusements," *Mercersburg Quarterly Review* 6 (July 1854):410; "City Amusements," 132–133.

17. "The Test of Legitimate Amusements," *Universalist Review* 17 (October 1860):400.

18. Marvin Vincent, *Religion and Amusement* (Troy, NY: W. H. Young, 1866), quoted in "Amusements," *The New Englander* 100 (July 1867):401, 407, 423–424.

19. Washington Gladden, *Amusements: Their Uses and Abuses* (N. Adams, MA:

James T. Robinson, 1866), quoted in "Amusements," *New Englander*, 408, 413, Jacob H. Dorn, *Washington Gladden: Prophet of the Social Gospel* (Columbus: OH, Ohio State University Press, 1967), 46–47. On the urban revivals of 1858 see Smith, *Revivalism and Social Reform*.

20. "Amusements," *New Englander*, 417.

21. Washington Gladden, "Christianity and Popular Amusements," *The Century* 29 (January 1885):388–392. On the Social Gospel in general, and Gladden's part in it, the best source is still Henry May, *Protestant Churches and Industrial America* (New York: Harper & Row, 1967 [1949]), especially 170–181.

22. Gladden, "Christianity and Popular Amusements," 391.

23. "Amusements," *Methodist Review* 89 (November 1907): 879.

24. Theodore Munger, *On the Threshold*, rev. ed. (Boston: Houghton Mifflin, 1908), 195, 201.

25. Munger, *On the Threshold*, 203, 206.

CHAPTER 5   Brokers and the New Corporate, Industrial Order

1. I would like to thank Elizabeth Blackmar, Elizabeth Cromley, and Eric Lampard for giving me useful criticisms of the various drafts of this chapter.

2. Harold G. Vatter and Robert L. Thompson, "Consumer Asset Formation and Economic Growth—The United States Case," *Economic Journal* 76 (June 1966): 312–327; United States Board of Governors of the Federal Reserve System, "Growth and Import," *Consumer Instalment Credit*, Vol. I, Part I (Washington, DC, 1957). I would like to thank Eric Lampard for directing me to these sources.

3. Paul Mazur, quoted in *Retail Ledger* (second February issue, 1927):1. On the continuation of bartering in the country districts see Susan Strasser, *Satisfaction Guaranteed. The Making of the American Mass Market* (New York: Pantheon, 1989), 73–74.

4. For recent discussion of this evolution see Ann Fabian, *Card Sharps, Dream*

Books, and Bucket Shops: Gambling in 19th Century America (Ithaca, NY: Cornell University Press, 1990).

5. On the increased number of securities dealers in the twenties see Ron Chernow, *The House of Morgan* (New York: Atlantic Monthly Press, 1990), 303; on credit men see *The Philadelphia Retail Ledger* (January 17, 1923):12. For the latest figures on securities dealers and brokers see Grace Toto, ed., *The Security Industry of the '80s*, SIA Fact Book (New York: Securities Industry Association, 1990), 6.

6. John Robert Powers, *The Power Girls. The Story of Models and Modeling* (New York: Dutton, 1941); Jay Cantor, "Art and Industry: Reflections on the Role of the American Museum in Encouraging Innovation in the Decorative Arts," in Ian M. G. Quinby and Polly A. Earl, eds., *Technological Innovation and the Decorative Arts* (Winterthur Report, 1972), 332–354; L. C. Marshall, "The American Collegiate School of Business," in L. C. Marshall, ed., *The Collegiate School of Business, Its Status at the Close of the First Quarter of the Twentieth Century* (Chicago: University of Chicago Press, 1928), 4–44; Daniel Boorstin, *The Image, a Guide to Pseudo-Events in America* (travel agencies) (New York: Atheneum, 1971); and Stephen Fox, *The Mirror-Makers. A History of American Advertising and Its Creators* (New York: Morrow, 1984).

7. *The Philadelphia Retail Ledger* 28, (April 1933): 4, 10.

8. On the genesis of "accessorize" and "accessory" as American merchandising terms see *The Supplement to the Oxford English Dictionary* Vol. 1 (1972), 11; and *American Speech* Vol. 4 (1939), 36. My reading of many trade journals, published over a thirty-year period from 1890 to 1929, confirms the claim of these dictionaries regarding all of these terms (including promotion, color coordination, and ensembling). See also Roland Marchand, *Advertising the American Dream, Making Way for Modernity, 1920–1940* (Berkeley, CA: University of California Press, 1985), 122–149.

9. *Amos Parrish Magazine* (June 1928): 11; (April 1925):1; (January 1926):13;

(June 1928):6; *Women's Wear Daily* (February 8, 1928); Elizabeth Hawes, *Fashion Is Spinach* (New York: Random House, 1938), 113; *The Merchants' Record and Show Window*, Vol. 49 (December 1931):37.

10. *Amos Parrish Magazine* (August 28, 1928):8–9; (February 1929):11.

11. Julia Coburn, oral interview conducted by Mid Semple (April 30, 1984): 11, transcript in possession of author; Estelle Hamburger, *It's a Woman's Business* (New York: Vanguard Press, 1939), 211; *Women's Wear Daily* (December 6, 1927):1; *The Merchants' Record and Show Window*, Vol. 75 (February 1935):30; *Sheldon's Retail Trade in the United States* (New York: Phelon, Sheldon, and Marsar, 1924), 1–9. The statistics on buyers were taken from the Sheldon volume, which is still the standard directory in the country on retail buyers.

12. For a history of public relations see Alan R. Raucher, *Public Relations and Business, 1900–1929* (Baltimore, MD: Johns Hopkins Press, 1968). Raucher makes clear that Bernays—in spite of Bernays's own claims to the contrary—did not create public relations methods but simply carried them as far as they could go.

13. Edward L. Bernays, *Biography of an Idea: Memoirs of Public Relations Counsel Edward L. Bernays* (New York: Simon and Schuster, 1962), 77.

14. Bernays, *Biography of an Idea*, 75, 78.

15. Interview with author, June 21, 1988, Cambridge, MA.

16. Edward L. Bernays, *Propaganda* (New York: Boni & Liveright, 1928), 27, 58; and Bernays, *Biography of an Idea*, 155–172.

17. On these new public relations people see Raucher, *Public Relations and Business*, 93–113.

18. Edward L. Bernays, *Crystallizing Public Opinion* (New York: Boni & Liveright, 1925), 14, 34, 125–126, 173; Bernays, *Biography of an Idea*, 287–300; and interview with author, June 21, 1988, Cambridge, MA.

19. Bernays, *Crystallizing Public Opinion*, 61–63, 95, 162.

20. Bernays, *Biography of an Idea*, 316 318.

21. Bernays, *Biography of an Idea*, 240; Daniel Boorstin, *The Image, A Guide to Pseudo-Events in America*.

22. Robert P. Lamont, Secretary of Commerce, radio address (December 1, 1929), General Files 024, Census (1930); "Philadelphia and the Census of Distribution," General Files 024, Census (May 3, 1930), 1–4; "What the Census of Distribution Is," General Files 024, Census (1933–1934), 1–2 (Washington, DC: National Archives).

23. This Census, its history and its importance for business is one of the great "unstudied" documents of American economic history. On market research facilities offered by advertising agencies and universities before 1925 see Stephen Fox, *The Mirror-Makers. A History of American Advertising and Its Creators* (New York: Morrow, 1984), 84–85; and Melvin Copeland, *And Mark the Era, the Story of the Harvard Business School* (Boston: Harvard University Press, 1958), 16–25, 214–216, 431.

24. Herbert Hoover to Julius Klein (May 23, 1925), Papers of the Bureau of Foreign and Domestic Commerce (BFDC), Record Group (RG) 151, 402.1, General Files 024 (Washington, DC: National Archives); Frank Surface, Assistant Director of Domestic Commerce, *Domestic Commerce* 2 (February 3, 1928), 4; "Report on the Census of Distribution," BFDC, RG 151, General Files 024 (1933–1934). This report summarizes the major themes governing Commerce policy throughout the 1920s.

25. Daniel Fox, *The Discovery of Abundance, Simon Patten and the Transformation of Social Theory* (Ithaca, NY: Cornell University Press, 1967), 164; David Burner, *Herbert Hoover, A Public Life* (New York: Oxford University Press, 1979), 158–159, 173–175, 203; Craig Lloyd, *Aggressive Introvert. A Study of Herbert Hoover and Public Relations Management, 1912–1932* (Columbus, OH: Ohio State University Press, 1972), 158–160. On the impact of a new economic theory on Hoover see Joseph Dorfman, *The Economic Mind in American Civilization*, Vol. 4 (New York: Viking, 1959), 349–352, 360–377; Allan G. Gruchy, *Contemporary Economic Thought, The Contribution of Neo-Institutional Economics* (Clifton, NJ: A. M. Kelley, 1972), 45–52; Ellis Hawley, "Herbert Hoover and Economic Stabilization," in Ellis Hawley, ed., *Herbert Hoover as Secretary of Commerce: Studies in New Era Thought and Practice* (Iowa City, IA: University of Iowa Press), 43–70; Carolyn Grin, "The Unemployment Conference of 1921: An Experiment in National Cooperative Planning," *Mid-America, An Historical Review* 55 (April 1973): 83–107.

26. Wesley Clair Mitchell, "The Prospects in Economics," in Rexford Tugwell, ed., *The Trend in Economics* (New York: Crofts, 1930 [1924]), 24–26.

27. S. L. Kedsierski, Costs and Operations Analysis, Merchandising Research Division, to Max Kelley (November 28, 1930), BFDC, RG 151, entry 1 NE–27, General Records 402.301, Retail, Consumers; Dr. Frank Surface, Assistant Director of BFDC, quoted in *Domestic Commerce* 3 (January 30, 1931), 27; Julius Klein, *Frontiers of Trade* (New York: The Century Co., 1929), 120, 141.

28. Robert Seidel, "Progressive Pan Americanism: Development and United States Policy Abroad Toward South America, 1906–1931." Unpublished Ph.D diss., Cornell University, Ithaca, NY, 1977, 138–139; *New York Times* (June 16, 1961). On the Commerce building see R. L. Duffus, "A New National Symbol in Stone," *New York Times* (May 15, 1932), Section 5, 10–11, 15.

29. Seidel, "Progressive Pan Americanism," 169, 185, 278; Julius Klein to Edwin Gay (June 24, 1915), Edwin Gay Papers, Baker Library, Harvard University Business School, Cambridge, MA.

30. Melvin Copeland, *And Mark the Era*, 16–25, 214–216, 431; Edwin Gay, quoted in Herbert Heaton, *A Scholar in Action, Edwin F. Gay* (Cambridge, MA: Harvard University Press, 1952), 18, 38–49, 62–70, 80, 98–99.

31. Julius Klein, *The Mesta. A Study in Spanish Economic History, 1273–1836*

(Cambridge, MA: Harvard University Press, 1920), vii–xi, 9–22, 28–42, 52; Julius Klein to Edwin Gay (September 7, 1917), Edwin Gay Papers.

32. Franklin Johnston to Julius Klein (August 8, 1928), BFDC, RG 151, Criticism; Julius Klein, biographical sketch in *Who's Who in Government*, Vol. 1 (New York: Houghton Mifflin, 1930), 312.

33. Wesley Clair Mitchell, "Economic Resources and Their Employment," in *Studies in Economics and Industrial Relations* (Philadelphia: Houghton Mifflin, 1941), 2; Willford I. King, "Trade Cycles and Factory Production," in Warren Persons et al., eds., *The Problems of Business Forecasting* (Boston: Houghton Mifflin, 1924), 13–16, 27, 35; Francis Walker, "New Data Needed for Forecasting," in Persons et al., eds., *The Problems of Business Forecasting*, 85–91.

34. Julius Klein to Congresswoman Edith Rogers (October 16, 1928), BFDC, RG 151, 402.10, New England General, National Archives; A Heath Onthank to the Chamber of Commerce, Cleveland, OH (May 6, 1925), General Files 402.1; "The Retailer and the Consumer in New England," *Trade Information Bulletin* 575, (Washington, DC: U.S. Government Printing Office, October 1925): 1–3; and Irving Paull to Jon Rink (N. Y. Ayer & Sons, August 22, 1923), RG 151, 402.4.7.

35. For a sample of BFDC publications see "Retail Store Planning," *Trade Information Bulletin* 291 (1924): 2–3; "Cooperative Retail Advertising," *Trade Information Bulletin* 302 (January 1925); "Measuring a Retail Market," *Trade Information Bulletin* 272 (October 13, 1924); "Planning Salesman's Territories," *Trade Information Bulletin* 214 (1924); and "Retail Store Problems," *Domestic Commerce Series* 8 (1926).

36. Julius Klein, "Fundamental Basis of Our Prosperity," *New York Times*, 11 (December 15, 1929): 3, 20.

37. Klein, report on CBS radio show, *New York Times* (January 20, 1930): 9.

38. For Klein's radio show on industrial design, see "Beauty as a Business Builder," in *The Merchants' Record and Show Window* 66 (June 1930): 7–9; on show windows see "Art in Industry Pays Dividends," *Merchants' Record* 66 (March 1930): 4, 13–7; and *Domestic Commerce* 5 (March 1930): 9, 98; on advertising see *New York Times* (October 14, 1929): 41.

39. *New York Times* (October 14, 1929): 41.

40. *New York Times*, editorial (October 22, 1929): 28; Bernays, *Biography of an Idea*, 445–459.

41. Herbert Hoover, *The Memoirs of Herbert Hoover, the Cabinet and the Presidency, 1920–33*, Vol. 2 (New York: Macmillan, 1952), 79; Donald Breed to O. P. Hopkins (April 25, 1932), BFDC Papers, RG 151, 101.1, Criticism; Julius Klein, radio address (November 25, 1929).

42. On the concept of capital "pooling" see Marshall Sahlins, *Stone Age Economics* (Chicago: Aldine-Atherton, 1972); Douglas North, "Capital Accumulation in Life Insurance Between the Civil War and the Investigation of 1905," in *Men in Business. Essays on the Historical Role of the Entrepreneur* (New York: Harper Torchbooks, 1962), 238–354; Alexander Dana Noyes (financial editor of the *New York Times*), *The Market Place, Reminiscences of a Financial Editor* (Boston: Little, Brown, 1938), 179; and Alfred D. Chandler, *The Visible Hand: The Managerial Revolution in American Business* (Cambridge, MA: Harvard University Press, 1977), 315–344.

43. Chandler, *The Visible Hand*, 333. The best general history of American investment banking is Vincent Carosso's *Investment Banking in America. A History* (Cambridge, MA: Harvard University Press, 1970). See also Ralph Nelson, *Merger Movements in American Industry, 1895–1956* (Princeton, NJ: Princeton University Press, 1959; Thomas Nevin and Marion Sears, "The Rise of the Market in Securities," *The Business History Review* 29 (June 1955): 2, 105–139.

44. Allan Nevins, *Herbert Lehman and His Era* (New York: Scribner's, 1963), 49.

45. John Kenneth Galbraith, *The Great Crash 1929* (Boston: Houghton Mifflin, 1961), 48–70. On Catchings see Joseph Dorfman, *The Economic Mind in American Civilization*, Vol. 4 (New York: Viking,

1959), 339–341; *New York Times*, obituary, (January 1, 1968): 15.

46. Paul Mazur to Louis Kirstein (May 12, 1921), Louis Kirstein Papers, Baker Library, Harvard University Business School, Cambridge, MA. On Mazur's place at Lehman's see Lehman Brothers, *A Centennial, Lehman Brothers, 1850–1950* (New York: Lehman Brothers, 1950), 46.

47. Paul Mazur, quoted in *Women's Wear Daily* (March 17, 1928): 1.

48. Waddill Catchings and William Trufant Foster, *Progress and Plenty, Two-Minute Talks on the Economics of Prosperity* (Boston: Houghton Mifflin, 1930), 45. This book is a compendium of articles Catchings and Foster wrote in the late twenties.

49. Waddill Catchings and William Trufant Foster, *The Road to Plenty* (Boston: Houghton Mifflin, 1928), 173; and *Progress and Plenty*, 18.

50. Paul Mazur, quoted in *The Philadelphia Retail Ledger* (second February issue, 1927): 1; Paul Mazur, "Is the Cost of Distribution Too High?" *Harvard Business Review* 4 (October 1925): 1, 5–6. See also Paul Mazur, *American Prosperity* (New York: Viking, 1928), 24–25, 92–95; and "Future Development in Retailing," *Harvard Business Review* 3 (July 1924): 4, 5–6.

51. John Allen Murphy, *Merchandising Through Mergers* (New York: Harper, 1930), 4–5.

52. Paul Mazur, oral interview by Edward Edwin (January 14, 1965), Oral History Project, Columbia University, 57. The objection to Mazur's role in fostering this merger came from A. Lincoln Filene, who believed that if a merger had to come at all, it should come from the merchants themselves (Filene's, F. and R. Lazarus, Bloomingdale's, etc.), not from some "meddling investment banker." See Paul Mazur, "Memorandum on Retail Research Consolidation" (May 1, 1925), Kirstein Papers.

53. Neal Gabler, *An Empire of Their Own. How the Jews Invented Hollywood* (New York: Crown, 1988), 132–138; Douglas Gomery, "The Coming of Sound: Technological Change in the American Film Industry," in Tino Balio,

ed., *The American Film Industry* (Madison, WI: University of Wisconsin Press, 1985), 248; Waddill Catchings, "25th Anniversary Report, Harvard Class of 1901" (Boston: Harvard University Alumni Records), 124–126.

54. United States Federal Trade Commission, *Chain Stores*, Part 4 (Washington, DC: U.S. Government Printing Office, 1935), 1–67. On the Goldman Sachs Trading Corporation see John Kenneth Galbraith, *The Great Crash 1929*, 48–70.

55. Murphy, *Merchandising Through Mergers*, 19–20. On the merger work of these firms see Carosso, *Investment Banking in America*, 19–20, 82–85; Boris Emmet and John E. Jeuck, *Catalogues and Counters, A History of Sears and Roebuck, and Company* (Chicago: University of Chicago Press, 1950), 55–58; Anna Rochester, *Rulers in America, A Study in Finance Capital* (New York: 1936), 81–82, 186, 246; Lehman Brothers, *A Centennial*, 31–46.

56. On the Warner Brothers sign see *New York Times* (November 11, 1929): 55.

57. David Schulte, quoted in the *New York Times* (April 30, 1925): 1. See also "How Schulte, Tobacco Man, Won Success," *New York Times* (May 10, 1925), Section 9, 4; obituary (July 30, 1949): 15; and Murphy, *Merchandising Through Mergers*, 55–57.

58. Henry Morgenthau to Lincoln Filene, recorded in Lincoln Filene, "Notes on Meeting on Basis of Capitalization" (October 1909), accompanied by cover note to Louis Kirstein (November 1, 1909), folder "New Stores," No. 62, Kirstein Papers, and Murphy, *Merchandising Through Mergers*, 56.

CHAPTER 6 Vaudeville and the Transformation of Popular Culture

NOTE: This chapter originally appeared in a different form in Robert W. Snyder, *The Voice of the City: Vaudeville and Popular Culture in New York City* (New York: Oxford University Press, 1989), and appears here with the permission of Oxford University Press. It contains information cited from the *Federal Trade Commission versus Vaudeville Managers' Protective Asso-*

ciation et al., Docket No. 128, housed in the Washington National Records Center at Suitland, Maryland, hereafter referred to as FTC 128; and information cited from the Keith/Albee Collection, Special Collections Department, University of Iowa Libraries, Iowa City, Iowa, hereafter referred to as Iowa Collection.

1. On Hammerstein's role in developing Times Square and the Olympia see William Morrison, "Oscar Hammerstein I: The Man Who Invented Times Square," *Marquee* 15 (first quarter, 1983):7–9; on the interiors and décor see William Harvey Birkmire, *The Planning and Construction of American Theatres* (New York: Wiley, 1896), 41–46.

2. See Morrison, "Oscar Hammerstein I," 7–9.

3. On the subway and the development of Times Square as a theater district see Brian J. Cudahy, *Under the Sidewalks of New York: The Story of the Greatest Subway System in the World* (Brattleboro, VT: Stephen Greene Press, 1979), 14; on the Square as a center of theater and entertainment see Stephen Jenkins, *The Greatest Street in the World: The Story of Broadway, Old and New, from the Bowling Green to Albany* (New York: Putnam, 1911), 256, 270.

4. On marquees see Edward Renton, *The Vaudeville Theatre: Building, Operation, Management* (New York: Gotham Press, 1918), 51.

5. "Music Hall Audiences," *Variety* (December 25, 1914):44.

6. Abel Green and Joe Laurie, Jr., *Show Biz from Vaude to Video* (New York: Henry Holt, 1951).

7. Green and Laurie, *Show Biz*, 18, 20, 22.

8. Green and Laurie, *Show Biz*, 17–20, 155. The Cherry Sisters, who hailed from an Iowa farm family, are said to have thought that the missiles were directed at them out of jealousy. See Avery Hales's article in *Coronet* (September 1944): 92–96, reprinted in Anthony Slide, ed., *Selected Vaudeville Criticism* (Metuchen, NJ: Scarecrow Press, 1988), 45–50, especially 47–48. Also see the sisters' biography in Anthony Slide, *The Vaudevillians:*

A Dictionary of Vaudeville Performers (Westport, CT: Arlington House, 1981), 25.

9. Marian Spitzer, *The Palace* (New York: Atheneum, 1969), 131.

10. Walter Richard Eaton, "The Wizards of Vaudeville," *McClure's Magazine* 55 (September 1918):48.

11. On the number of vaudeville circuits see Alfred L. Bernheim, "The Facts of Vaudeville," *Equity* 8 (November 1923):39; on the significance of booking in controlling vaudeville see Robert Grau, *The Business Man in the Amusement World* (New York: Broadway Publishing, 1910), 1–2; Hartley Davis, "The Business Side of Vaudeville," *Everybody's Magazine* 17 (October 1907); Bernheim, "The Facts of Vaudeville" (September 1923):9–10, 32; and Charles Grapewine, FTC 128 (October 14, 1919), Box 72, 2550. For the Leavitt quote see M. B. Leavitt, *Fifty Years in Theatrical Management* (New York: Broadway Publishing, 1912), 190.

12. Marian Spitzer, "The Business of Vaudeville," *Saturday Evening Post* (May 24, 1924):18–19; Bernheim, "The Facts of Vaudeville" (December 1923):20, 34; Billy Glason in Bill Smith, *The Vaudevillians* (New York: Macmillan, 1976), 34; also Smith, "In Vaudeville," 138.

13. Spitzer, "The Business of Vaudeville," 18–19.

14. For a description of the office see Spitzer, "The Business of Vaudeville," 19; on drawing up the shows see Pat Casey, FTC 128 (February 4, 1919), Box 70, 181; Maurice Goodman, FTC 128 (February 17, 1920), Box 72, 3358.

15. On the importance of the order of the show see Samuel Hodgdon entry, Report Book for September 21, 1903, to March 17, 1904, 74, Iowa Collection. For elaboration on this point see the words of George Gottlieb, who booked shows for the Palace, in Brett Page, *Writing for Vaudeville* (Springfield, MA: Home Correspondence School, 1915), 7–10.

16. See Gottlieb in Page, *Writing for Vaudeville*, 7–8.

17. For the evaluation of Bessie Wynee see Report Book 6, 169; for similar entries gauging the popularity of an act with a particular audience see entry from

Charles Barnes on a February 4, 1907, show in Philadelphia, Report Book 6, 4; entry on the December 25, 1905, show at Keith's Union Square Theatre, Report Book 4, 134; entry on a December 3, 1906, show in Cleveland, Report Book 5, 185; and entries on two shows in Union Hill, New Jersey: an April 4, 1910, show, Report Book 10, 200, and a December 12, 1910, show, Report Book 11, 166. All report books in the Iowa Collection.

18. Spitzer, "The Business of Vaudeville," 19; also Casey, FTC 128, Box 70, 172. For the "panic" quote see Smith, "In Vaudeville," 138.

19. On signing with each theater see Spitzer, "The Business of Vaudeville," 19. On salary fixing see Bernheim, "The Facts of Vaudeville" (December 1923): 34–35; also the testimony of John A. Collins, *Max Hart versus B. F. Keith Vaudeville Exchange et al.*, Federal Court, Southern District, New York (January 4, 1926), 264, 270, 273, 277.

20. On the blacklist see "More Blacklisting," *The Player* (April 15, 1910):1; "Albee and Blacklist to Go," *The Player* (April 8, 1910):1; "Joe Woods Blacklisted," *The Player* (December 7, 1909):1; "Artist Canceled Because Name Is on Blacklist," *The Player* (January 13, 1911):1, and "Blacklist Abolished," *The Player* (March 17, 1911):1. On pressuring acts see Bernheim, "The Facts of Vaudeville," *Equity* 9 (March 1924):20.

21. On the number of acts booked by the Keith exchange see Samuel Hodgdon, FTC 128 (February 6, 1919), Box 71, 604.

22. FTC 128, Exhibit 130 (received November 5, 1919), Box 73.

23. On these points see Spitzer, "The Business of Vaudeville," 129; on the U.B.O. rationale for its deductions see Casey, FTC 128 (February 3, 1919), Box 70, 71–72, 421.

24. See contract of August 27, 1909, signed through United Booking Offices between Fonda, Johnstown, and Gloversville Railroad Company; and Jordan, Braubeck, and Chilita in vaudeville file, Warshaw Collection, NMAH.

25. See February 1, Jule Delmar letter, vaudeville file, Warshaw Collection,

NMAH. For an example of a cancellation and its consequences see May 4, 1903, report from Keith's Boston theater by M. J. Keating (n.d.) unnumbered Report Book, 258, Iowa Collection.

26. Report from Keith's Union Square Theatre, week of August 12, 1907, Report Book 6, 199, Iowa Collection.

27. Report from Carl D. Lothrop, Keith's Boston theater, week of May 17, 1909, Report Book 9, 140, Iowa Collection.

28. On booking office records of censorship see Sophie Tucker, in collaboration with Dorothy Giles, *Some of These Days: The Autobiography of Sophie Tucker* (Garden City, NY: Doubleday, 1945), 149; Marian Spitzer, "Morals in the Two a Day," *The American Mercury* 3 (September 1924), 38; and Spitzer, "The Business of Vaudeville," 133. On censorship directed from the central office see clippings, "No Jibes at 'Y' Allowed on Keith Circuit" (n. p., April 28, 1919), NYPL-LC, and "Keith Artists Ordered to Eliminate References to Prohibition," Toledo *Blade* (August 18, 1922), both in the Keith clipping file, NYPL-LC.

29. See "News and Gossip of the Vaudeville World," *The Morning Telegraph* (October 24, 1915), Section 4, 2.

30. "An Old Timer," FTC 128 (August 16, 1918), File 128-A-14, Box 73.

31. See Bernard A. Myers's testimony, FTC 128 (February 16, 1919), Box 71, 492–496.

32. Bernheim, "The Facts of Vaudeville" (September 1923):11.

33. Joe Laurie, *Vaudeville, from the Honky-Tonks to the Palace* (reprint, Port Washington, NY: Kennikat, 1972), 313. On blacklisting, which was invoked to prevent actors from both unionizing and from playing for circuits competing with Keith/Albee, see Casey, FTC 128 testimony, Box 70, 115–121; John Walsh, FTC 128 (February 16, 1920), Box 72, 3337; and Martin W. Littleton, in *Max Hart versus B. F. Keith et al.*, U.S. District Court, Southern District, New York (January 24, 1924), 47–49; on the founding of the Vaudeville Managers' Protective Association see Goodman, FTC 128

(February 17, 1920), Box 72, 3401–3405; on the founding of the National Vaudeville Artists see Spitzer, "The Business of Vaudeville," 130.

34. Bernheim, "The Facts of Vaudeville," (November 1923):33–40. On the findings of the Federal Trade Commission see resolution of Case 128 in *Federal Trade Commission Decisions: Findings and Orders of the Federal Trade Commission, July 1, 1919, to June 30, 1920*, Vol. II (Washington, DC: Government Printing Office, 1920), 464.

35. Mary Cass Canfield, "The Great American Art," *New Republic* 32 (November 22, 1922):335.

36. On the appeal to the audience that was characteristic of vaudeville, burlesque, minstrelsy, the circus, and Harrigan and Hart productions see Garff B. Wilson, *A History of American Acting* (Bloomington, IN: Indiana University Press, 1976), 179–184. For a magazine writer's analysis of vaudeville's appeal to the audience see Harvey Denton, "The Technique of Vaudeville," *The Green Book Album* 1 (May 1909):1068–1074.

37. George Jessel quoted in Smith, *The Vaudevillians*, 29.

38. Marian Spitzer, "The People of Vaudeville," *Saturday Evening Post* (May 24, 1924):6.

39. Ethel Barrymore, *Memories* (New York: Harper, 1955), 177.

40. Caroline Caffin, *Vaudeville* (New York: Mitchell Kennerly, 1914), 216–217.

41. Eddie Cantor, *My Life Is in Your Hands* (New York: Harper, 1928), 76.

42. See Page, *Writing for Vaudeville*, 489; also author's interview with Frank Rowan in Englewood, New Jersey, February 7, 1984.

43. Author's interview with Billy Glason in New York City, January 18, 1984.

44. See author's interviews with Harold Applebaum, Jack Gross, Murray Schwartz, Arthur Kline, Harold Applebaum, and Howard Basler, all conducted in New York City, 1983–1984.

45. Following the points in John F. Kasson, *Amusing the Million: Coney Island at the Turn of the Century* (New York: Hill

and Wang, 1978), 39–40. Also Schwartz interview.

46. "For New Theatre," *Staten Islander* (October 7, 1911):1.

47. Florence Sinow, written communication with author, 1984.

CHAPTER 7 The Syndicate/Shubert War

1. A version of this chapter was presented at the 1988 meeting of the American Society for Theatre Research at Columbus, Ohio.

2. Jack N. Poggi, *Theater in America: The Impact of Economic Forces, 1870–1967* (Ithaca, NY: Cornell University Press, 1968); A. Nicholas Vardac, *Stage to Screen: Theatrical Origins of Early Film, David Garrick to D. W. Griffith* (New York: Da Capo Press, 1987); see also the last two chapters in Garff B. Wilson, *Three Hundred Years of American Drama and Theatre*, 2nd ed. (Englewood Cliffs, NJ: Prentice-Hall, 1982), 278–322.

3. For example, see Bernard Hewitt, *Theatre USA, 1665 to 1957* (New York: 1959), 482–487.

4. For the most comprehensive collection of statistical data, see *Variety's* annual June edition, which reviews the box office receipts from the previous year. An overview of *Variety* since 1973 indicates that ticket sales and attendance reached a peak in the 1981/1982 season and have steadily declined since. In the ten years before the 1981/1982 season, ticket sales climbed from 16 million dollars to 223 million dollars, whereas attendance rose from 5.7 million to 10.1 million. Since 1982, sales have leveled off at about 209 million dollars and attendance has fallen below 9 million.

5. Alfred L. Bernheim, *The Business of the Theatre. An Economic History of the American Theater, 1750–1932* (New York: Actors Equity Association, 1932; reprint New York: Benjamin Blam, 1964). Far more typical are the traditional narrative histories. See Hewitt, *Theatre USA*, and Glenn Hughes, *A History of the American Theatre, 1700–1950* (New York: 1951). For a cross between the traditional narrative and popular gossip history see Mary Caroline Crawford, *Romance of the Ameri-*

can Stage (New York: 1940); Mary C. Henderson, *Theater in America* (New York: Harry N. Abrams, 1986).

6. See Poggi, *Theater in America*, 245–275.

7. Among the better-known examples are Cheryl Crawford, *One Naked Individual* (New York: Macmillan, 1977); Jean Dalrymple, *From the Last Row* (Clifton, NJ: 1975); Daniel Frohman, *Daniel Frohman Presents* (New York: 1935); Stephen Langley, ed., *Producers on Producing* (New York: 1976); Stuart Little, *Enter Joseph Papp* (New York: 1974); Harvey Sabinson, *Darling, You Were Wonderful* (Chicago: 1977); Jerry Stagg, *The Brothers Shubert* (New York: 1968). There are also a handful of articles that fall into the same category; for example, see Hollis Alpert, "Broadway's Abominable Snowman," *Esquire* (January 1960); John E. Booth, "Producer's Changing Role," *New York Times* (December 13, 1959); Samuel Freedman, "Last of the Red Hot Producers," *New York Times Magazine* (June 2, 1985); Michiko Kakutani, "The Public and Private Joe Papp," *New York Times Magazine* (June 23, 1985); Herman Levin, "The Producer's Lot," *Theatre Arts* (October 1958).

8. America's earliest theatrical entrepreneurs are surveyed in James S. Bost, *Monarchs of the Mimic World* (Orono, ME: University of Maine Press, 1977). There are also fine essays on Stephen Price and Edwin Booth by Bernard Hewitt and Charles H. Shattuck, respectively, in Joseph W. Donohue, ed., *The Theatrical Manager in England and America* (Princeton, NJ: Princeton University Press, 1971).

9. Steve Travis, "The Rise and Fall of the Theatrical Syndicate," *Educational Theatre Journal* 10 (March 1958):35–40; Bernheim, *Business of Theater*, 85. See also Poggi, *Theater in America*, and Vardac, *Stage to Screen*.

10. Poggi, *Theater in America*, 17–18. For a transcript of Judge Rosalsky's decision see *The Billboard* (June 29, 1907):18.

11. George Santayana, "The Genteel Tradition in American Philosophy," in Douglas L. Wilson, ed., *The Genteel Tra-

dition: Nine Essays by George Santayana* (Cambridge, MA: 1967), 37–61.

12. Monroe Lippman, "Death of the Salesman's Monopoly," *Theatre Survey* 1 (1960):65–81. See also Monroe Lippman, "The Effect of the Theatrical Syndicate on Theatrical Art," *Quarterly Journal of Speech* 26 (April 1941):275–282.

13. Stagg, *The Brothers Shubert*, Chaps. 1–2.

14. Dorothy G. Baker, "Monopoly in the American Theatre: A Study of the Cultural Conflicts Culminating in the Syndicate and Its Successors, the Shuberts." Unpublished Ph.D. diss., New York University, 1962.

15. Baker, "Monopoly in American Theatre," 499.

16. Naomi R. Lamoreaux, *Merger Movement in American Business, 1895–1904* (New York: Cambridge University Press, 1985). See also David D. Martin, *Mergers and the Clayton Act* (Berkeley, CA: 1959); Ralph L. Nelson, *Merger Movements in American Industry, 1895–1956* (Princeton, NJ: 1959); Hans B. Thorelli, *The Federal Antitrust Policy: Origination of an American Tradition* (Baltimore, MD: 1955); Alfred D. Chandler, *The Visible Hand: The Managerial Revolution in American Business* (Cambridge, MA: Harvard University Press, 1977).

17. Arthur C. Bining, *The Rise of American Economic Life* (New York, 1943), 356–357; Robert Higgs, *The Transformation of the American Economy, 1865–1914* (New York, 1971), 13–14, 45–47; Sidney Ratner, James H. Soltow, and Richard Sylla, *The Evolution of the American Economy: Growth, Welfare and Decision Making* (New York: Basic Books, 1979), 371–394.

18. The two seminal works promoting this thesis are Kenneth E. Boulding, *The Organizational Revolution: A Study in the Ethics of Economic Organization* (New York, 1953) and Elvin F. Donaldson, *Business Organization and Procedure* (New York, 1938).

19. Harry N. Scheiber, Harold G. Vatter and Harold U. Faulkner, *American Economic History* (New York: 1976), 231–232.

20. Lamoreaux, *Merger Movement*,

29–30, 91–93, 153–157; Scheiber et al., *American Economic*, 234–238; Ratner et al., *Evolution*, 288–289.

21. Alfred D. Chandler, Jr., has termed this phenomenon "economies of speed." See Chandler, *The Visible Hand*, 281–282 and Lamoreaux, "*Merger Movement*," 32–33.

22. Richard Norman Owens, *Business Organization and Combination* (New York: 1951), 296–312; Alfred S. Eichner, "The Megacorp as a Social Institution and Business History," in Paul Uselding, ed., *Business and Economic History* (Urbana, IL: 1975), 56; Ratner et al., *Evolution*, 286–288.

23. Bining, *Rise of American Economic Life*, 364–365, 386.

24. Bining, *Rise of American Economic Life*, 381–382.

25. Donaldson, *Business Organization*, 513–516.

26. Bining, *Rise of American Economic Life*, 450–451; Charles Hoffman, *The Depression in the Nineties: An Economic History* (Westport, CT: 1970), 65.

27. A. F. Burns and W. C. Mitchell, *Measuring Business Cycles* (New York, 1946), Chap. 12.

28. Ratner et al., *Evolution*, 296.

29. Baker, "Monopoly in American Theatre," 499.

30. Lamoreaux, *Merger Movement*, 62; see also Thomas R. Navin and Marian V. Sears, "The Rise of a Market for Industrial Securities," *Business History Review* 29 (1955), 106–115; and Fritz Redlich, *The Molding of American Banking: Men and Ideas* (New York: 1972), 381–396.

31. Ratner et al., *Evolution*, 295–296.

32. Bining, *Rise of American Economic Life*, 352–353; Thomas C. Cochrane, *200 Years of American Business* (New York: 1977), 161–166, 168–169.

33. Their decision to utilize a pooling arrangement in the aftermath of the Sherman Antitrust Act is indicative of the contempt most held for the Act's efficacy as well as the Syndicate members' confidence in their business's inviolability—a position that would be validated by the Supreme Court ruling of 1907. Nonetheless, the members of the Syndicate were reluctant to announce their new arrangement. It would be at least a month before the theater industry discovered the Syndicate's existence. Baker, "Monopoly in American Theatre," 162–164.

34. For a succinct discussion of pools, trusts, and monopolies see Scheiber et al., *American Economic History*, 231–234; see also Owens, *Business Organization*, Chap. 19. One of the best studies of trusts and monopolies remains Edward J. Nolan, *Combinations, Trusts and Monopolies* (New York: 1904).

35. *New York Dramatic Mirror* (March 26, 1898):3–4.

36. Bernheim, *Business of Theater*, 65; see also *The Sun* (July 15, 1905):2. For a history of Frohman, typical of the popular theatrical biographies that dominate this field, see Isaac F. Marcosson and Daniel Frohman, *Charles Frohman: Manager and Man* (New York: 1916).

37. *New York Dramatic Mirror* (March 26, 1898):3–4.

38. Owens, *Business Organization*, 310–312.

39. Donaldson, *Business Organization*, 419–430. One of the first proponents of the disintegration model of pools was W. Z. Ripley in *Trusts, Pools and Corporations* (Boston: 1916), Chaps. 1–5.

40. Owens, *Business Organization*, 311.

41. Bernheim, *Business of Theater*, 64–66; Stagg Brothers, 14.

42. Bernheim, *Business of Theater*, 66.

43. *Dramatic Mirror* 54 (September 9, 1905):17.

44. Bernheim, *Business of Theater*, 68.

45. *Dramatic Mirror* 44 (November 17, 1900):15.

46. Bining, 526–527; Scheiber et al., *American Economic History*, 308–309.

47. The United Booking Office was established in September 1907 by an association of vaudeville producers that included Albee and Keith, Martin Beck, B. S. Moss, F. F. Proctor, and Percy Williams. Lippman, "Effect of Theatrical Syndicate," 72; see also Bernheim, *Business of Theater*, 68.

48. Bernheim, *Business of Theater*, 68.

49. Bernheim, *Business of Theater*, 50–54.

50. Bernheim, *Business of Theater*, 55–63.

51. Bernheim, *Business of Theater*, 64–67.

52. The Shubert Organization's divestment began with the House Judiciary Committee's investigation in the late 1940s and culminated with the Supreme Court decision of February 18, 1956, forcing the sale of a dozen theaters and the United Booking Office in order to comply with antitrust regulations. See Stagg, 365–367, 386–388.

CHAPTER 8 Impresarios of Broadway Nightlife

1. Bosley Crowther, "Hi-De-Ho! The Night Clubs Turn 'Em Away," *New York Times Magazine* (March 21, 1937):14–15.

2. On the transformative nature of early urban consumer culture see William R. Leach, "Transformations in a Culture of Consumption: Women and Department Stores, 1890–1925," *Journal of American History* 71 (September 1984):319–342.

3. Donald B. Meyer, *Sex and Power* (Middletown, CT: Wesleyan University Press, 1987), 346–347; Peter Conrad, *The Art of the City, Views and Versions of New York* (New York: Oxford University Press, 1984), 193–206.

4. For hegemonic captains of consciousness see Stuart Ewen, *Captains of Consciousness: Advertising and the Social Roots of the Consumer Culture* (New York: McGraw-Hill, 1976); and the more nuanced Stuart Ewen and Elizabeth Ewen, *Channels of Desire: Mass Images and the Shaping of American Culture* (New York: McGraw-Hill, 1982), which attempts to show how mass culture draws on real mass discontents, but still channels these to false answers. The "merchants of leisure" was pioneered by Gareth S. Jones, "Class Expression Versus Social Control? A Critique of Recent Trends in the Social History of Leisure," *History Workshop* 4 (Autumn 1977): 163. Frank Couvares, "The Triumph of Commerce: Class Culture and Mass Culture in Pittsburgh," in Michael Frisch and Daniel J. Walkowitz,

Working-Class America (Urbana, IL: University of Illinois Press, 1983), 123–152, and Kathy Peiss, *Cheap Amusements* (Philadelphia, PA: Temple University Press, 1986) use this approach. I would characterize my approach as an experiential one—that is, I want to know what consumers get out of a particular amusement, why they put so much energy into it. This may or may not have an effect on the working class.

5. Lewis A. Erenberg, *Steppin' Out: New York Nightlife and the Transformation of American Culture, 1890–1930* (Chicago: University of Chicago Press, 1985, orig. 1981); and Lary May, *Screening Out the Past: The Birth of Mass Culture and the Motion Picture Industry* (Chicago: University of Chicago Press, 1984) analyze two important elements of modern commercial culture from the 1890s through the 1920s.

6. Jimmy Durante and Jack Kofoed, *Nightclubs* (New York: Alfred A. Knopf, 1931), 126.

7. George Rector, *The Girl from Rector's* (New York: 1927), 44–49.

8. Perry Duis, *The Saloon* (Urbana, IL: University of Illinois Press, 1983), 143–157, notes that in Boston and Chicago most of the saloons in central areas were run by the two immigrant groups that were most familiar with American culture.

9. Julius Keller, *Inns and Outs* (New York: G.B. Putnam's Sons, 1939), 33.

10. George Rector, obituary, *New York Herald Tribune* (November 27, 1947), Rector File, Lincoln Center; Louis Sobol, "Bustanoby, Papa of Cafe Society," *American Weekly* (May 5, 1952):4; Keller, *Inns and Outs*, 52–53.

11. Keller, *Inns and Outs*, 51.

12. Rector, obituary, 3; Keller, *Inns and Outs*, 115–116, 136.

13. *Where and How to Dine in New York: the Principal Hotels, Restaurants and Cafes of Various Kinds and Nationalities Which Have Added to the Gastronomic Fame of New York and Its Suburbs* (New York: 1903), 14.

14. Julian Street, "Lobster Palace Society," *Everybody's Magazine* 22 (May 1910): 648; *Where and How to Dine*, 61.

15. *New York Plaisance* 1 (1908): 34.

16. *Plaisance*, 53.

17. Lois Banner, *American Beauty* (New York: Knopf, 1983), 175–201, has an extended discussion on the importance of lobster palace society and the actresses' role in it. Keller, *Inns and Outs*, 119; for more on lobster palaces see Erenberg, *Steppin' Out*, 40–59; only Churchill's, run by a former police captain, prohibited these "bachelor" apartments and private rooms.

18. Keller, *Inns and Outs*, 142; for the Folies Bergère see Jesse Lasky with Don Weldon, *I Blow My Own Horn* (New York: Doubleday, 1957), 81–84.

19. See George Rector, *The Girl from Rector's*, 204, for the dance craze.

20. Rector, *Girl from Rector's*, 204, 205.

21. *New York World* (April 3, 1913):2.

22. Rector, *Girl from Rector's*, 212.

23. Rector, *Girl from Rector's*, 213. The tango teas were soon at the center of many scandals and drew the fire of many progressives concerned about the chastity and safety of young girls.

24. Stephen B. Johnson, *The Roof Gardens of Broadway Theatres, 1883–1942* (Ann Arbor, MI: UMI Research Press, 1985), 137–144, shows the evolution of the rooftop dance cabarets, the entrance of theater promoters into the cabaret business, and the search for audience attractions.

25. Johnson, *Roof Gardens*, 145.

26. For general information on Prohibition and the cultural war of the 1920s see Paul Carter, *The Twenties in America* (New York: 1968), 67–98; and Andrew Sinclair, *Era of Excess: A Social History of the Prohibition Movement* (New York: 1964). See Donald S. Kirschner, *City and Country* (Westport, CT: Greenwood, 1970), for a discussion of how these issues continued through the 1920s in Iowa and Illinois, where the target was big bad Chicago. For the war against jazz see Neil Leonard, *Jazz and the White Americans* (Chicago: University of Chicago Press, 1961), 29–46; and Macdonald Smith Moore, *Yankee Blues: Musical Culture and American Identity* (Bloomington, IN: University of Indiana Press, 1985), 82–108.

27. Thomas Shanley, obituary, *New York Times* (October 3, 1932), New York Restaurants Vertical File, Local Division, New York Public Library; see also *Variety* (March 17, 1922):4 and (July 14, 1922): 30; and Durante and Kofoed, *Nightclubs*, 192, for cabarets trying to survive under Prohibition, and for their selling out to dance halls in the early 1920s.

28. *Variety* (December 30, 1925):11. Durante and Kofoed, *Nightclubs*, 206, estimate that 90 percent of clubs in the golden age (1924–1928) sold liquor.

29. Nils T. Granlund, *Blondes, Brunettes and Bullets* (New York: McKay, 1957), 127; Stanley Walker, *The Nightclub Era* (New York: 1933), 86–125, 246–249; and Robert Sylvester, *No Cover Charge. A Backward Look at Nightclubs* (New York: Dial Press, 1956), 3–25, discuss the role of criminals in nightclubs in the 1920s. *Variety* (December 30, 1925): 11, and Ronald Morris, *Jazz and the Underworld* (Bowling Green, OH: Bowling Green University Popular Press, 1976), also note the importance of bootleggers. Durante and Kofoed, *Nightclubs*, 177, note that patrons were often too drunk to care about good food service.

30. Granlund, *Blondes*, 124, 137–138. On Madden see Edward Jablonski, *Harold Arlen, Happy with the Blues* (New York: 1961), 53. On the importance of personal choice in the 1920s among college students see Paula Fass, *The Damned and the Beautiful* (New York: Oxford University Press, 1979), 291–361.

31. Fass, *The Damned*, 170–171. Mark Haller, "Policy Gambling, Entertainment, and the Emergence of Black Politics: Chicago from 1900 to 1940," (unpublished, 1987), has alerted me to the importance of gamblers in the entertainment world.

32. Durante and Kofoed, *Nightclubs*, 136. Billy Rose, *Wine, Women and Words* (New York: Simon & Schuster, 1947), 85.

33. N.T.G. claimed that his bosses never mistreated him or any entertainers. Other performers, however, such as Lena Horne, testified to the contrary. Certainly the mob presence could be dangerous, as Billy Rose noted when he saw

Waxey Gordon smash in a drunk's face for no reason

34. Granlund, *Blondes*, 147–149.

35. Durante and Kofoed, *Nightclubs*, 157–160, discuss the investigations by the Committee of Fourteen into the clip joints.

36. Ellin Mackay, "Why We Go to Cabarets, a Post-Debutante Explains," *New Yorker* (November 28, 1925):7–8, notes the preference of the wealthy young for public nightlife.

37. See Nathan I. Huggins, *Harlem Renaissance* (New York: Oxford University Press, 1971), 84–136, for Harlem nightlife, as well as Erenberg, *Steppin' Out*, 245–248.

38. James W. Johnson, *Along This Way* (New York: Viking, 1968), 328.

39. "Times Square Goes Still Cheaper," *Variety* (January 17, 1933):1.

40. On general show business decline see *Variety* (December 29, 1931):3; (December 31, 1930); Robert Sklar, *Movie-Made America: A Cultural History of American Movies* (New York: Random House, 1976), 162; Lary May, "Making the American Way: Moderne Theatres, Audiences and the Film Industry During the Great Depression," *Prospects* 12 (1987): 89–124; and Andrew Bergman, *We're in the Money* (New York: New York University Press, 1971), xix–xxii. On clubs see *Variety* (January 7, 1931): 9; (December 13, 1932): 38; and (February 7, 1933): 57. On speakeasies see *Variety* (January 9, 1934): 1/51 and (December 13, 1932): 46, for national nightclub trends. Howard Mandelbaum and Eric Myers discuss art deco, nightclubs, and decadence in *Screen Deco* (New York, 1985). For the criticism of consumer values see Lawrence Levine, "American Culture and the Great Depression," *Yale Review* 74 (Winter 1985): 209–212. For the decline of jazz in the early thirties see Lewis A. Erenberg, "Things to Come: Swing Bands, Bebop and the Rise of a Postwar Jazz Scene," in Lary May, *Recasting America: New Perspectives on the Post-War World* (Chicago: University of Chicago Press, 1988). *Blonde Venus* (1932) associates dangerous female sexuality with sleazy cabarets, black jazz,

and "hot voodoo." When Marlene Dietrich dresses up in a gorilla suit to sing "Hot voodoo makes me bad," all the elements come together.

41. David E. Kyvig, *Repealing National Prohibition* (Chicago: University of Chicago Press, 1979), analyzes the movement for Repeal.

42. *Variety* (June 26, 1934):48/59, notes Billy Rose's optimism. Rose was not alone in his optimism about the New Deal. Hollywood studios, often with Warner Brothers in the lead, produced entertaining shorts for the NRA. Among them are *New Deal Rhythm*, and *The Road Is Open Again* (in my possession). The former equates optimism with Repeal and big city culture as representatives from state after state sing about their desire for alcohol, hootchy-kootch, and fun. At the climax, Broadway Babies dance a Busby Berkeley-style salute to the New Deal.

43. *Variety* (December 11, 1934):47; Abel Green, "Nighteries on Road Back," *Variety* (January 6, 1937):195; H. I. Brock, "Now Our Nightlife Glows Again," *New York Times* (February 11, 1934), Section 6, 10/19; (February 18, 1934), Section 6, 11/20. Arnold Shaw, *52nd St., The Street of Jazz* (New York: Da Capo Press, 1977). "Manhattan Nightlife," *Fortune Magazine* 13 (March 1936):94–105.

44. Abel Green and Joe Laurie, Jr., *Show Biz from Vaude to Video* (New York: Henry Holt, 1951), 440–446.

45. Malcolm Johnson, "Cafe Life in New York," *New York Sun* (October 24, 1939), in Artie Shaw Vertical File, Library of the Performing Arts, Lincoln Center (hereafter LPA,LC).

46. "Manhattan Nightlife," *Fortune Magazine* 13 (March 1936):101; Billy Rose, *Wine, Women*; Granlund, *Blondes, Brunettes, and Bullets*.

47. Crowther, "Hi-De-Ho!" Granlund, *Blondes*, 203–205, 225–226. For material on nightclub practices in the 1920s see Texas Guinan Scrapbooks, LPA,LC; Edmund Wilson, "Night Clubs," *New Republic* (September 1925):71.

48. Green and Laurie, *Show Biz*, 439; Mark Hellinger, "All in a Day," *New York*

City Mirror (June 5, 1933), LC; H. I. Brock, "Night Life," *New York Times* (March 2, 1930), Section 5, 9. Gilbert Seldes, "From Chicken Shack to Casino," *Esquire* (March 1938), LC; Granlund, *Blondes*, 222, on "family man."

19. "The Effendi Billy Rose," *Literary Digest* (July 7, 1934):19. "Girls, Girls, Girls," *Fortune Magazine* (July 1939):120. For details of Rose's life, see Polly Gottlieb, *The 9 Lives of Billy Rose* (New York: 1968), 15–100; Gottlieb was his sister. See also Rose, *Wine, Women*.

50. Stephen Nelson, *"Only a Paper Moon": The Theatre of Billy Rose* (Ann Arbor, MI: UMI Research Press, 1987), 81, quotes Rose.

51. Green and Laurie, *Show Biz*; Rose, *Wine, Women*; "Manhattan Nightlife," 105.

52. "Manhattan Nightlife," 120. Quote from *New York Evening Post* (July 26, 1934), in Billy Rose Scrapbooks (BR hereafter), LPA,LC.

53. *Variety* (December 31, 1930):32. Programs, cards, and scripts from Rose's Music Hall and the Diamond Horseshoe, BR, LPA,LC. "Diamond Horseshoe," *Life Magazine* 15 (July 26, 1943):75. Sucker policy advertisement, Billy Rose Collection, as in Nelson, *"Only a Paper Moon,"* 83.

54. Lowey quoted in Jeffrey Meikle, *Twentieth Century Limited* (Philadelphia, PA: Temple University Press, 1979), 136.

55. Pictures of the designs can be found in the International Casino Scrapbooks, LPA,LC. The best analytical accounts of the new architecture are Meikle, *Twentieth Century Limited*, and May, "Making the American Way," 89–124, which examine streamlined moderne as it applies to movie theaters.

56. For descriptions of Diamond Horseshoe see BR, LC, and Nelson, 87–94.

57. *New Brunswick Home News* (January 10, 1938), as in Nelson, 83.

58. *Variety* (August 28, 1936): 1–17.

59. Jack Foster, "Neon Nights," *The Oklahoma News* (January 6, 1938), LPA,LC.

60. *Women's Wear Daily* (January 14, 1937), LPA,LC; Brock, "Now Our Nightlife Glows Again."

61. See *Variety* (March 20, 1934):45, and (January 8, 1935), on advertising. International Casino billboard in *New York Tribune* (January 5, 1930), LPA, LC, Jill Stone, *Times Square*, cover of Diamond Horseshoe billboard; *Billboard* (January 5, 1938), LPA, LC. Stories about Broadway clubs appeared in newspapers from Oklahoma to Maine during the 1930s and 1940s, suggesting that Rose and his competitors were consciously using "planted" stories as national advertising.

62. "Girls, Girls, Girls," 180.

63. For a good account of Cafe Society, boogie-woogie, and its audience see Peter J. Silvester, *A Left Hand Like God* (New York: DaCapo, 1989), 137–160, and my interview with Josephson, September 1971, tape and transcript in my possession.

64. For the idea of New York culture expanding nationally during the Depression see William R. Taylor, "Toward the Launching of a Commercial Culture: New York City, 1860–1939," paper delivered at New York Working Group Conference, sponsored by the Social Science Research Council, March 16–19, 1984; Lewis A. Erenberg, "From New York to Middletown: Repeal and the Legitimization of Nightlife in the Great Depression," *American Quarterly* 38 (Winter 1986):761–778.

CHAPTER 9 The Entertainment District at the End of the 1930s

1. David C. Hammack, "Developing Times Square for Commercial Culture: Infrastructures of Power." Conference paper, "Inventing Times Square: Commerce and Culture at the Crossroads of the World, 1880–1990," New York Institute for the Humanities (October 28, 1988), 13.

2. Mary C. Henderson, *The City and the Theatre* (Clifton, NJ: James T. White, 1973), 198.

3. Works Progress Administration, *The WPA Guide to New York City* [1939] (Re-

print, New York: Pantheon Books, 1982), 170.

4. The Editors of *Look*, *New York City* (Boston, MA: Houghton Mifflin, 1948), 123–124.

5. Brooks Atkinson, *Broadway* (New York: Macmillan, 1970), 11–12.

6. Margaret M. Knapp, "A Historical Study of the Legitimate Playhouses on West Forty-second Street Between Seventh and Eighth Avenues in New York City." Unpublished Ph.D. diss., City University of New York, 1982, 371. Knapp treats the decline of Forty-second Street in considerable detail; see especially 370–413.

7. Jack Poggi, *Theater in America: The Impact of Economic Forces, 1870–1967* (Ithaca, NY: Cornell University Press, 1968), 47.

8. Alfred Bernheim, "The Theater: A Depressed Industry," *New Republic* (February 13, 1929):341. For an extended discussion of the causes of the decline, see Poggi, *Theater in America*, 65–96.

9. Quoted in Bernheim, "The Theater," 341.

10. Compare Henderson, *City and Theater*, 196–197.

11. Lewis A. Erenberg, "Along the Great White Way: Impresarios of Broadway Nightlife, 1893–1940." Conference paper, "Inventing Times Square: Commerce and Culture at the Crossroads of the World, 1880–1990," New York Institute for the Humanities (November 17, 1988), 24.

12. New York City Housing Authority, *Real Property Inventory, City of New York, 1934* (Non-Residential Report), Tracts 119, 125, 131, 137.

13. "West 42nd Street: The Bright Light Zone." Report, Graduate School and University Center, CUNY, (1978), 67.

14. "West 42nd Street," 68.

15. Stanley Walker, *The Nightclub Era* (New York: Frederick Stokes, 1933), 201–203.

16. Ward Morehouse, *Matinee Tomorrow* (New York: McGraw-Hill, 1949), 260.

17. For a discussion of the concept of entertainment environments see Brooks McNamara, "The Scenography of Popular Entertainment," *Drama Review* T-61 (March 1974): 23–24.

18. *WPA Guide to New York City*, 167–170.

19. *New York Times* (December 21, 1938).

20. Burns Mantle, ed., *The Best Plays of 1938–39* (New York: Dodd, Mead, 1939), 3.

21. *Variety* (December 21, 1938).

22. Poggi, *Theater in America*, 47–48.

23. *New York Times* (December 21, 1938).

24. Mantle, *Best Plays*, lists all shows that opened during the season.

25. Mantle, *Best Plays*, 3.

26. *Variety* (December 21, 1938).

27. *Variety* (December 28, 1938).

28. Hallie Flanagan, *Arena* [1940] (Reprint, New York: Limelight Editions, 1985), 346.

29. *Variety* (December 21, 1938).

30. *Billboard* (April 8, 1938).

31. For a discussion of the decline of burlesque in New York City see Irving Zeidman, *The American Burlesque Show* (New York: Hawthorn Books, 1967), 219–235.

32. H. M. Alexander, *Strip Tease* (New York: Knight Publishers, 1938), 117.

33. Zeidman, *American Burlesque*, 173–174.

34. Helen Worden, *The Real New York* (Indianapolis, IN: Bobbs-Merrill, 1932), 26.

35. Bill Ballantine, *Wild Tigers and Tame Fleas* (New York: Rinehart, 1958), 231; *Variety* (December 28, 1938).

36. *WPA Guide*, 175.

37. *Variety* (December 21, 1938).

38. *Variety* (December 21, 1938).

39. *New York Times* (December 21, 1938).

40. *Billboard* (December 31, 1938).

41. Ibid.

42. Erenberg, "Along the Great White Way," 31.

43. Stephen Nelson, *"Only a Paper Moon": The Theatre of Billy Rose* (Ann Arbor, MI: UMI Research Press, 1987), 90.

44. Nelson, *"Only a Paper Moon,"* 94.

45. *Variety* (December 28, 1938).

46. John Frick, *New York's First Theatrical Center: The Rialto at Union Square* (Ann Arbor, MI: UMI Research Press, 1985), 2–3.

47. *Variety* (December 21, 1938). Many of the institutions mentioned here may be located in the *WPA Guide*.

48. "West 42nd Street," 67.

49. *Variety* (December 21, 1938).

50. *Billboard* (December 31, 1938).

51. Stuart W. Little and Arthur Cantor, *The Playmakers* (New York: Dutton, 1971), 18–19.

CHAPTER 10 Irving Berlin: Troubador of Tin Pan Alley

1. Charles Hamm, *Yesterdays: Popular Song in America* (New York: Harper & Row, 1976), 338–339.

2. Edward Marks, *They All Sang* (New York: Viking, 1935), 3.

3. Max Morath, "Introduction," in Robert A. Fremont, ed., *Favorite Songs of the Nineties* (New York: Dover, 1973), ix.

4. Laurence Bergreen, *As Thousands Cheer: The Life of Irving Berlin* (New York: Viking, 1990), 101, 110. I am indebted to Mr. Bergreen's biography for much of the information about Berlin's life.

5. Bergreen, *As Thousands Cheer*, 166.

6. Michael Freedland, *Irving Berlin* (New York: Stein & Day, 1974), 69.

7. Gerald Mast, *Can't Help Singin': The American Musical on Stage and Screen* (Woodstock, NY: Overlook Press, 1987), 45.

8. Lewis A. Erenberg, *Steppin' Out: New York Nightlife and the Transformation of American Culture, 1890–1930* (Westport, CT: Greenwood Press, 1981), 242.

9. Ethan Mordden, *The Hollywood Musical* (New York: St. Martin's, 1981), 44.

10. Timothy Scheurer, "Irving Berlin." Paper delivered at the American Popular Culture Conference, Atlanta, April 6, 1986.

11. Freedland, *Irving Berlin*, 129.

12. Tony Palmer, *All You Need Is Love: The Story of Popular Music* (New York: Grossman, 1976), 112.

13. Martin Gottfried, *Broadway Musicals* (New York: Abradale Press, 1984), 240.

14. Bergreen, *As Thousands Cheer*, 451.

15. Mast, *Can't Help Singin'*, 41.

Irving Berlin lyrics:

CHAPTER 11   Broadway: The Place That Words Built

1. "The Language of Lobster Alley," *The Bookman* (1930): 72, 396.

2. "Why I Write Slang," *Variety* (December 29, 1926).

3. John O. Rees, "The Last Local Colorist," *Kansas Magazine* (1968): 73–81.

4. H. L. Mencken, *The American Language*, 4th ed. (New York: Alfred Knopf, 1938), 560.

5. Mencken, *American Language*.

6. Eric Partridge, *In His Own Words* (London: Andre Deutsch, 1980); *A Dictionary of Slang and Unconventional English, Including Language of the Underworld* (London: Macmillan, 1937).

7. Walter Winchell, "A Primer of Broadway Slang," *Vanity Fair* (November 1927): 67.

8. Winchell, "A Primer."

9. Winchell, "A Primer."

10. Stanley Walker, *The Night Club Era* (New York: Frederick A. Stokes, 1933); Jack Lait and Lee Mortimer, *New York Confidential* (New York: Crown Publishers, 1948).

11. The best accounts of the layout of the Broadway locale are to be found in Lait and Mortimer, *New York Confidential*, Walker, *Night Club Era*, and in Lewis A. Erenberg, *Steppin' Out: New York Nightlife and the Transformation of American Culture* (Westport, CT: Greenwood Press, 1981).

12. Mencken, *American Language*, 646.

13. "Why I Write Slang," 5, 7.

14. Herman Klurfeld, *Winchell. His Life and Times* (New York: Prager, 1976).

15. J. Willard Ridings, "Use of Slang in Newspaper Sports Writing," *Journalism Quarterly* VII (December 1934): 348–360.

16. Standard biographical sources on Runyon's life are: Edwin P. Hoyt, *A Gentleman of Broadway* (Boston: Little, Brown, 1964); Jean Wagner, *Runyonese, The Mind and Craft of Damon Runyon* (Paris:

Stechert-Hafner, 1965). No fully satisfactory biographical study of Runyon exists. Jimmy Breslin is said to be completing a new biography at the present time.

17. "Color Stuff," *American Speech* III (October 1927): 28–36.

18. Hoyt, *A Gentleman of Broadway*, Chap. 15.

19. Wagner, *Runyonese*.

20. Damon Runyon, *The Bloodhounds of Broadway & Other Stories* (New York: Morrow, 1981), 124–125.

21. "A Very Honorable Guy," 86.

22. Lait and Mortimer, *New York Confidential*, 125.

PART III   COMMERCIAL AESTHETICS
Introductory Essay

1. Henry James, *The American Scene* (Bloomington, IN: Indiana University Press, 1969), 94–95; and Edith Wharton, *A Backward Glance* (New York: Appleton, 1934), 320.

2. J. George Fredericks, *Adventuring in New York* (New York: Nicholas Brown, 1923), 38.

3. On developments at the fairs see W. D'A. Ryan, "Building Exteriors, Exposition, and Pageant Lighting," in Charles Steinmetz, ed., *Illuminating Engineering Practice* (New York: McGraw-Hill, 1917), 547–556; and Matthew Luckiesh, *Light and Color in Advertising and Merchandising* (New York: Nostrand, 1923), 150–151. On American plate-glass consumption by 1915 see Warren Scoville, *Revolution in Glassmaking* (Cambridge, MA: Harvard University Press, 1948), 259.

4. Thorstein Veblen, *Absentee Ownership and Business Enterprise in Recent Times, The Case of America* (New York: Huebsch, 1923), 315.

5. Veblen, *Absentee Ownership*, 315–316; and *Signs of the Times* (December 1912).

6. On importance of Gude see Robert Grau, *The Business Man and the Amusement World* (New York: Broadway Publishing, 1910), 247–248; and *WPA Guide to New York City*, with an introduction by William H. Whyte (New York: Pan-

theon, 1982; originally published in 1939), 170.

7. *Signs of the Times* (August 1912): 9, and (October 1912): 246–247; and Leonard G. Shepard, "Sign Lighting," in *Illuminating Engineering Practice*, 544.

8. O. J. Gude, "Art and Advertising Joined by Electricity," *Signs of the Times* (November 1912): 3; and Gude, "10 Minute Talk on Outdoor Advertising," *Signs of the Times* (June 1912): 77.

9. O. J. Gude, "Art and Advertising Joined by Electricity," 3.

10. *Signs of the Times* (March 1927): 60. On the zoning laws see Jerome Charyn, *Metropolis, New York as Myth, Marketplace, and Magical Land* (New York: Avon Books, 1985), 43–44.

11. Fredericks, *Adventuring in New York*, 38.

12. Veblen, *Absentee Ownership*, 315.

13. For an ordinary advertising day in the district in 1922 see *Signs of the Times* (February 1922): 11; and for 1924 see (February 1924): 35. According to the *Signs of the Times*, automobile advertising began to dominate district advertising by 1924; see "Automobile Advertising Leads Survey of Electric Signs Being Used," (February 1924): 35. See also *WPA Guide*.

14. Fredericks, *Adventuring in New York*, 38.

15. Quoted in Joseph Urban, "Wedding Theatre Beauty to Ballyhoo," *New York Times* (August 19, 1928), Section 4, 10.

16. *Signs of the Times* (February 1925): 48.

17. *Signs of the Times* (January 1923): 45, and (September 1920): 1.

18. *Signs of the Times* (April 1925): 48, and (August 1924): 27.

19. Edward L. Bernays to Stewart Culin, January 26, 1928, Stewart Culin Papers, Manuscripts Division, Textile Collection, Brooklyn Museum, Brooklyn, NY. Edward L. Bernays, *Biography of an Idea: Memoirs of a Public Relations Counsel* (New York: Simon & Schuster, 1962), 403–418; and *New York Times* (February 2, 1928): 5.

20. "Broadway's Colors," *New York Times* (June 23, 1929), Section 5, 21; and on Georges Claude see *Signs of the Times* (March 1927): 60.

21. On the all-day advertising advantages of neon see *Signs of the Times* (March 1927): 60, and "Luminous Tube Signs Rapidly Developing in Popularity," *Signs* (May 1926): 52.

22. "Broadway's Colors," 21. On the Hupmobile see *Signs of the Times* (September 1928): 18; on the Watson Stabilator see *Signs* (March 1929): 62; and on the Lucky Strike ad see *Signs* (March 1927): 60.

23. Christopher Isherwood, quoted in Alex de Jonge, *The Weimar Chronicle, Prelude to Hitler* (New York: Paddington Press, 1972), 125; Friedrich Sieburg, quoted in Elisabeth Finley Thomas, ed., and trans., *The Paris We Remember*, with an introduction by Elliot Paul (New York: Appleton, 1942), 117–118; Henry Haynie, *Paris Past and Present*, Vol. I (New York: Frederick Stokes, 1902), 339–341; and, on the 6,000 neon signs in Paris see *Signs of the Times* (March 1927): 60.

24. *New York Times* editorial (June 18, 1928): 18. "What consternation would greet that order," said the *Times*, "if Mayor Walker were to promulgate it here? . . . Cigarette and motorcar advertisements would have to go, along with Tex Rickard's electric pointer."

25. On the "battle" between the Fifth Avenue and Broadway associations see *Signs of the Times* (April 1922): 54; (June 1922): 38; (July 1922): 48; and the *New York Times* (February 12, 1928), Section 2, 5. On the Gude company's membership in the Fifth Avenue Association see *The Annual Report of the Fifth Avenue Association* (New York: Fifth Avenue Association, 1919), 33.

26. Stewart Culin to Edward Bernays, January 26, 1928, Culin Papers; and Ezra Pound, *Patria Mia* (Chicago: Ralph Fletcher, 1950 [but written around 1913], 32–33.

27. Veblen, *Absentee Ownership*, 321–322.

CHAPTER 12   New York's Gigantic Toy

1. "General Advertising by Means of Electric Signs," *Brooklyn Edison* 3 (January 1905): 36–38; "gigantic toy" quotation comes from clipping of "Opening of Hippodrome," *New York Tribune* (April 13, 1905), in Hippodrome Scrapbook No. 9872, in the Billy Rose Theatre Collection, New York Public Library at Lincoln Center, Astor, Lenox, and Tilden Foundations (hereafter cited as TCNYPL). The "talking sign" was manufactured by the Mason Monogram Company of New York and exhibited at the Pan-American International Exposition in Buffalo in 1901. Thompson and Dundy were partners in amusements on the exhibition's Midway and undoubtedly witnessed the "talking sign" in operation at the fair. See J. A. Goldberg, "The Development of Motion Effects in Electrical Signs," *Illuminating Engineer* 2 (February 1908):852; "The 'Talking' Electric Sign," *Brooklyn Edison* 1 (June 1903):82–83. Earlier and later versions of moving electrical signs are discussed in David E. Nye, *Electrifying America: Social Meanings of a New Technology, 1880–1940* (Cambridge, MA: MIT Press, 1990), 50–57.

2. "Frederic Thompson's Tribute to Toys," *Playthings* 7 (July 1909):115. The best statement of Thompson's amusement strategy and psychology appears in Frederic Thompson, "Amusing People," *Metropolitan* 32 (August 1910):601–610, and Fred Thompson, "Fooling the Public," *Delineator* 69 (February 1907):264–266.

3. George M. Fredrickson, *The Inner Civil War: Northern Intellectuals and the Crisis of the Union* (New York: Harper & Row, 1965), 166–180. On Thompson as Peter Pan, see Samuel Merwin, "Thompson and His Hippodrome," *Success* 9 (July 1906):528. In general I have been influenced by Warren Susman, *Culture as History: The Transformation of American Society in the Twentieth Century* (New York: Pantheon, 1984), especially xix–xxx, 271–285.

4. Neil Harris, *Humbug: The Art of P. T. Barnum* (Boston: Little, Brown, 1973), 243–246, 260.

5. Percy MacKaye, *Epoch; The Life of Steele MacKaye, Genius of the Theatre*, II (New York: Boni & Liveright, 1927), 311, 347–348. MacKaye attempted to solve the difficulty of translating the lofty into the popular through a "new art form" that replaced dialogue with poetic choruses and extravagant visual symbolism, a faintly Dionysian form of theater without the sensuality of Nietzsche's celebration of pre-Apollonian theater in *The Birth of Tragedy*. Actors did not speak; "they were enlarged to giant human personalities." MacKaye's plans to eliminate the egoism of the individual actor went so far as to envision seven different actors—one of them himself—portraying the lead role in his dramatic biography of Christopher Columbus, *The World Finder*. MacKaye believed his orchestration of innovative scenic techniques and lighting equipment with his new art of acting would resolve the aesthetic division of nature and art that had bedeviled Western intellectuals in the nineteenth century. See MacKaye, *Epoch*, 353; and Friedrich Nietzsche, *The Birth of Tragedy and The Genealogy of Morals*, Francis Golffing, trans. (Garden City, NY: Doubleday, 1956), 1–146.

6. The best biographical account of Thompson's life appears in "Frederic Thompson, The Proof of Youth," *New York Sunday Telegraph* (April 2, 1905):7. Clipping contained in the Hippodrome Scrapbook, R. H. Burnside Collection, TCNYPL (hereafter cited as Burnside Scrapbook, TCNYPL).

7. "Frederic Thompson, The Proof of Youth."

8. The best account of "A Trip to the Moon" appears in Richard H. Barry, *Snap Shots on the Midway of the Pan-American Exposition* (Buffalo, NY: Robert Allen Reid, 1901). For a more instructive and less participatory version of an imaginary visit to the moon, see the description of the "illustrated lecture" called "A Trip to the Moon" provided in Albert A. Hopkins, *Magic Stage Illusions and Scientific Diversions* (New York: Munn, 1901),

348–351. The lecture antedated Thompson's illusion by several years and used "trigonometric mensuration of the shadows, and application of their values by perspective . . . to represent the general features of the [lunar] landscape with fidelity." Thompson's amusement was also closely related to H. G. Wells's science fiction story, "The First Men in the Moon," which had been published in serial form in the United States during the months preceding the Buffalo fair; on the latter see *Cosmopolitan* 30 (November, December 1900; January, February, March, April 1901):65–80, 195–206, 310–323, 415–429, 521–534, 643–656. Even if Thompson did not originate the idea of "A Trip to the Moon," he uniquely staged it as a dramatic, participatory fairy tale and expanded its audience beyond the exclusive readership of *Cosmopolitan* and the audience of scientific lectures.

9. Thompson, "Fooling the Public," 266; "Luna Park Is Opened; 60,000 People There," *Brooklyn Daily Eagle* (May 17, 1903):6; "Big Crush at Coney; Crowd Record Eclipsed," *Brooklyn Daily Eagle* (July 6, 1903):5.

10. See clipping of "Frederic Thompson, The Proof of Youth"; and "Zoo, Circus, Spectacle, All in One . . ." *New York Times* (July 3, 1904):21.

11. Clipping of " 'Big Store' Idea to Give Masses Entertainment," *New York Morning Telegraph* (September 26, 1904), Burnside Scrapbook, TCNYPL. For discussion of department stores see William R. Leach, "Transformations in a Culture of Consumption: Women and Department Stores, 1890–1925," *Journal of American History* 71 (September 1984):319–342; Susan Porter Benson, *Counter Cultures; Saleswomen, Managers, and Customers in American Department Stores, 1890–1940* (Urbana, IL: University of Illinois Press, 1986), especially 12–30; quotation appears on page 20.

12. Clipping of " 'Big Store' Idea"; " 'Fred' Thompson Tells of the Trials and Joys of a Showman's Life and Says That to Be Successful, Be Cheerful," *New York Herald* (January 1, 1905), Section 3, 9. On

ticket prices see page advertisement in *New York Times* (April 9, 1905).

13. The theater "had to be kept filled to make real money," said R. H. Burnside, who directed the Hippodrome's productions for many of the years between 1900 and 1923. "To raise seat prices was to drive away a large part of the audience . . ." See R. H. Burnside, typescript of "Secrets of the Hippodrome" (March 15, 1932):20, TCNYPL. On motion picture audiences see Lary May, *Screening Out the Past; The Birth of Mass Culture and the Motion Picture Industry* (Chicago: University of Chicago Press, 1983), 147–166; Harold Ackerman, "The New York Hippodrome," *Broadway* (April 1905), in Hippodrome Scrapbook No. 6453, TCNYPL.

14. Thompson, "Fooling the Public," 264.

15. See the following clippings in Burnside Scrapbook, TCNYPL: " 'Big Store' Idea"; untitled clipping from the *Chattanooga Times* (January 29, 1905); "Record Breaking Hippodrome Sale," *New York Herald* (April 11, 1905); untitled clipping from the *New York Inquirer* (March 4, 1905); clipping of Ackerman, "The New York Hippodrome"; clipping of "The Elephants, the Lions and Maeterlinck," *Life* (November 2, 1905); Hippodrome Scrapbook No. 9872, TCNYPL; unidentified clipping (November 12, 1904), Burnside Scrapbook, TCNYPL.

16. Vincent Sheean, *Oscar Hammerstein I: The Life and Exploits of an Impresario* (New York: Simon & Schuster, 1956), 118–119; also see the following untitled clippings, Burnside Scrapbook, TCNYPL; *New Haven Register* (December 4, 1904), and clipping of "The Usher" (n.d.); Milton Epstein, "The New York Hippodrome—From Luna Park to Sixth Avenue," unpublished Master's thesis, New York University, 1982, 18–20; clipping of "New York Theatre Seats, $1" (December 12, ca. 1904), in Burnside Scrapbook, TCNYPL. After losing control of the Hippodrome in the late spring and early summer of 1906, Thompson & Dundy joined the Syndicate alliance.

17. See the following clippings in the Burnside Scrapbook, TCNYPL: "Circus War Is Soon to Begin," *New York Herald* (January 23, 1905); "Hippodrome and the Circus," *New York Morning Telegraph* (February 25, 1905); "Barnum & Bailey Enjoin Their Clown," *New York American* (April 7, 1905); "Will There Be a Circus War?" *New York Dramatic News* (January 28, 1905).

18. The *Times* listed the following impressive institutions on "Rubberneck Row": the restaurants Sherry's and Delmonico's, the Harvard, Yale, New York Yacht, and City clubs, the Century Association, Mrs. Osborn's Theatre, the American and the Mechanics' institutes, the Little Home of the Four Doctors, the Bar Association clubhouse, the Royalton and Algonquin hotels, and the New York Academy of Medicine. See "Don't Want Circus in 'Rubberneck Row,' " *New York Times* (July 2, 1904):7.

19. In addition to the technical magazines examined below see, for example, the detailed descriptions in "Wonders of the Hippodrome," *New York Sun* (April 9, 1905):10, and "Frederick [sic] Thompson Explains How Electricity Has Revolutionized Mechanics Behind the Scenes, Exemplified in New York's New Hippodrome," *New York Herald* (February 12, 1905), Section 3, 10. William R. Taylor, "The Evolution of Public Space in New York City: The Commercial Showcase of America," in Simon Bronner, ed., *Consuming Visions; Accumulation and Display of Goods in America 1880–1920* (New York: Norton, 1989), 294–296. Other figures offered to the public included 10,000 dynamite blasts to clear the construction site and 35,000 truckloads of dirt to build the foundation. Cited by Norman Clarke, *The Mighty Hippodrome* (New York: Barnes, 1968), 13. The most general statement relating the values of organized bigness and efficiency to contemporary political and social changes is Robert H. Wiebe, *The Search for Order, 1877–1920* (New York: Hill & Wang, 1980), especially 111–223.

20. "Opening of the Hippodrome and New Plays of the Week," *New York Herald* (April 9, 1905), Section 3, 9. See the following clippings in the Burnside Scrapbook, TCNYPL: "Saunterings," *Town Topic* (March 9, 1905); "Gates President of Hippodrome Co.," *New York Commercial* (September 30, 1904); "Long Time Loan for New Hippodrome Co.," *New York Wall Street Summary* (September 17, 1904); Clarke, *The Mighty Hippodrome*, 21–22; "Black Faction Wins in U.S. Realty Fight," *New York Times* (January 16, 1904):16. The *Annual Report of the Superintendent of Banks, Relative to Savings Banks, Trust Companies, Safe Deposit Companies, and Miscellaneous Corporations for the Year 1904* (Albany, NY: Brandow Printing, 1905), 526, lists the directors of the New York Security and Trust Company, several of whom also were on the board of U.S. Realty when the Hippodrome deal was sealed, including James Stillman, who was identified as a principal backer of the Hippodrome. In an interview published in the *New York Times* (July 3, 1904), Thompson portrayed the selection of the Sixth Avenue site as though it were chosen irrespective of its connection with Gates and the realty company. Thompson claimed he turned down an alliance with a beer brewery, insisting that the theater "would be all hippodrome and all Thompson & Dundy." This story made it appear that Thompson & Dundy was the principal owner of the enterprise, a fiction that was belied by the company's election of directors the following September; see "Zoo, Circus, Spectacle." On Gates see Lloyd Wendt and Herman Kogan, *Bet a Million! The Story of John W. Gates* (Indianapolis, IN: Bobbs-Merrill, 1948).

21. On the Kiralfy brothers see Barbara M. Baker, ed., *Bolossy Kiralfy, Creator of Great Musical Spectacles: An Autobiography* (Ann Arbor, MI: UMI Research Press, 1988); Samuel Merwin refers to the "broker[s] in beauty" in "Thompson and His Hippodrome," 467.

22. On Romeo see Epstein, "The New York Hippodrome," 25–26. On Temple see untitled clippings in the Edward P. Temple envelope, TCNYPL; "The New

Hippodrome Ballet Under Rehearsal," *New York Sun* (January 29, 1905), Part 2, 3; and Charles Darnton, "The Man Who Staged the Biggest Show on Earth," *New York Evening World* (April 15, 1905):9. On Carrigan and Thomas see Merwin, "Thompson and His Hippodrome," 467. On Hagen see Robert Grau, *The Business Man in the Amusement World; A Volume of Progress in the Field of the Theatre* (New York: Broadway Publishing, 1910), 168–169; "Not Much Balm for Hagan [sic]," *New York Morning Telegraph* (December 16, 1904), Burnside Scrapbook, TCNYPL; and Claude Hagen, letters to Lee Shubert (October 7 and 16, 1908, and August 15, 1908), General Correspondence 1908–1910, Shubert Archive. Klein's previous composition was *Mr. Pickwick*, produced in January 1903. See Burns Mantle and Garrison P. Sherwood, eds., *The Best Plays of 1899–1909 and the Year Book of the Drama in America* (New York: Dodd, Mead, 1944), 427. On Melville see "Death of Frank J. Melville," *New York Morning Telegraph* (December 5, 1908):2.

23. "American Woman Charms Famous European Costumer," *New York Times* (December 18, 1904), Part 3, 7.

24. Colgate Baker, "Arthur Voegtlin, The Genius of the Hippodrome," *New York Review* (July 13, 1912), in Voegtlin clipping file, TCNYPL; clipping of "Big Things Conceived for New Hippodrome," *New York Commercial* (March 6, 1905), in Burnside Scrapbook, TCNYPL; "How Arthur Voegtlin Dreams His Big Spectacles," *New York Times* (September 8, 1912), Part 5, 12; Dana Gatlin, "Arthur Voegtlin," *American* 76 (August 1913):38–39; Arthur Voegtlin, "Paint's Part in Successful Play," *Pittsburgh Leader* (November 25, 1910), in Locke Collection envelope No. 2439, TCNYPL; Arthur Voegtlin, *The Great Train Robbery, a Realistic Drama Spectacle in Three Scenes* (ca. 1905), Harris Collection of American Poetry and Plays, John Hay Library, Brown University, Providence, RI. On "Venice in New York" see "Duss's 'Venice' on View," *New York Times* (June 1, 1903):7. For a peculiarly arch view of Voegtlin and his work see Djuna Barnes's "Interviewing Arthur Voegtlin Is Something Like Having a Nightmare," in her *Interviews* (Washington, DC: Sun and Moon Press, 1985). On post-Hippodrome career see "The National Merchandise Fair," *Dry Goods Economist* 77 (July 7, 1923):15–21; "Merchandise Fair Opens in 3 Buildings," *New York Times* (July 2, 1923):14; "Arthur Voegtlin, Stage Producer, 90," *New York Times* (January 20, 1948):23. On "brokered images" see William Leach, "Brokers, and the New Corporate, Industrial Order," Chapter 5 in this volume.

25. Clarke, *The Mighty Hippodrome*, 14–16.

26. "The New York Hippodrome," *Scientific American* 92 (March 25, 1905):242. The Fuller Construction Company invented a colossal movable wooden crane, 109 feet tall, to lift the trusses after they were assembled on the ground and put them in place; this innovation accelerated the pace of construction by eliminating the need to construct elaborate falsework to support the building of the trusses at the roof level. See "The Erection of the New York Hippodrome Roof Trusses," *Engineering Record* 51 (March 18, 1905):334–335. "Opening of the Hippodrome"; "Zoo, Circus, Spectacle"; "New York Hippodrome Opens in a Blaze of Glory," *Billboard* 17 (April 22, 1905):20; "Greatest of Hippodromes Is Opened with Splendor," *New York Herald* (April 13, 1905):1; "Illustrations," *American Architect and Building News* 87 (May 13, 1905):156.

27. "Wonders of the Hippodrome," *New York Sun* (April 9, 1905):10; "Steel Work in the New York Hippodrome," *Engineering Record* 51 (March 25, 1905):352–353; "The New York Hippodrome," *Architects' and Builders'* 6 (August 1905):490–498.

28. *Clipper* quoted in Clarke, *The Mighty Hippodrome*, 26; "The Hippodrome," *Billboard* 17 (April 29, 1905):10; "Frederic Thompson Explains"; Burnside, "Secrets of the Hippodrome," 19. The best statement of Thompson's ideas about architecture appears in Frederic

Thompson, "Amusement Architecture," *Architectural Review* 16 (July 1909):85–89.

29. Darnton, "The Man Who Staged the Biggest Show."

30. "Frederic Thompson Explains"; "Electricity at the New York Hippodrome," *Electrical World* 47 (May 5, 1906):916; "The Illumination of the New York Hippodrome," *Illuminating Engineer* 1 (April 1906):75; clipping of untitled article by Alan Dale (ca. April 13, 1905), in Hippodrome Scrapbook No. 9872, TCNYPL.

31. The best description and photographs of the Hippodrome lighting appear in "Electricity at the New York Hippodrome," 911–916, and "The Illumination of the New York Hippodrome," 72–73.

32. "Electricity at the New York Hippodrome," 913–914, 916; "The Illumination of the New York Hippodrome," 74–75, 77; "Frederic Thompson Explains."

33. "Mechanical Plant of the New York Hippodrome," *Engineering Record* 52 (August 26, 1905):229–230.

34. "Mechanical Plant of the New York Hippodrome," 233–234. "A 'Society Circus' is Vastest of Spectacles," *New York Times* (December 14, 1907):7.

35. Comments on the design of the Hippodrome are taken from the plans of the Hippodrome published in *The American Architect and Building News* 87 (May 13 and 20, 1905), international edition. For further efficiency, another narrower horseshoe passageway followed immediately inside the inner wall of the basement runway. This was used for animals, such as jungle cats, which had to be kept separate from the horses, elephants, and people, yet within easy reach of the stage. This runway was further connected by two auxiliary passageways to glass cages on the rear wall of the promenade behind the orchestra seats, where patrons could observe them during intermissions.

36. Merwin, "Thompson and His Hippodrome," 467.

37. "The New Hippodrome Ballet Under Rehearsal," 3.

38. Zoe Anderson Norris, "One Woman's Impressions of the 'Hippo's' Opening," *New York Times* (April 16, 1905), Part 4, 6; "The New Hippodrome Opens," *New York Sun* (April 13, 1905):5; see also description in Clarke, *The Mighty Hippodrome*, 28, 31.

39. Roy L. McCardell, "Hats Off to the Hippodrome! The World's Greatest Amusement Palace," *New York World* (April 16, 1905), Metropolitan Section, 1; Norris, "One Woman's Impressions"; "The New Hippodrome Opens."

40. William Leach, "Strategists of Display and the Production of Desire," in Simon Bronner, ed., *Consuming Visions*, 100–101; "Behind the Scenes at the Hippodrome," *New York Sun* (April 30, 1905), Section 2, 3; Lorraine B. Diehl, *The Late, Great Pennsylvania Station* (New York: American Heritage, 1985); Colgate Baker, "Through the Hippodrome Wonderland," *New York Review* (October 15, 1910), in R. H. Burnside clipping file, TCNYPL.

41. "New York Hippodrome Opens in a Blaze of Glory"; advertisement in *New York Times* (April 9, 1905).

42. "Opening of Hippodrome," *New York Tribune*; "Greatest of Hippodromes Is Opened with Splendor." According to *The Best Plays of 1899–1909*, 489, *A Yankee Circus on Mars* was performed 120 times at the New York Hippodrome, including daily matinees, arranged by Frederic Thompson, with book by George V. Hobart, lyrics by Harry Williams, music by Manuel Klein and Jean Schwartz, produced by Thompson & Dundy (April 12, 1905); *Andersonville, or The Raiders* was arranged by Frederic Thompson, with book by Carroll Fleming and music by Manuel Klein.

43. See "Opening of Hippodrome," *New York Tribune*, and various untitled clippings in Hippodrome Scrapbook No. 9872, TCNYPL (all ca. April 13, 1905); also "New York's Mammoth Pleasure Palace," *New York Daily News* (February 19, 1905), Burnside Scrapbook; and "Theatrical Incidents and News Notes," *New York Daily Tribune* (April 16, 1905):9.

44. Charles Darnton, "A Peep at the Hippodrome," *New York Evening World*

(April 8, 1905):9. Neither *A Yankee Circus on Mars* nor *Andersonville* was part of the production originally planned for the Hippodrome, although both resemble what was described in Thompson's announcement of the theater. The productions he initially promised were more closely related to Luna Park's scenic offerings, in particular, the Indian Durbar Thompson built at the park for the 1904 summer season. The first part of the show was organized around "the triumphal entry of a mighty monarch of Biblical days—some individual, his personality has not been decided upon yet, whose love of feasting and fêtes is well known"— and the impressive circus performed for his entertainment. The second half of the bill was *The Boys of '40*, a Wild West adventure that included a shootout with one hundred genuine Sioux Indians in and around the Hippodrome's stage lake. Thompson also originally planned to show moving pictures during intermissions and major scene changes to occupy the audience's attention; these plans were not followed through once the theater opened. See "Zoo, Circus, Spectacle."

45. For an account of the production see typescript of *The Yankee Circus in Mars*, [sic] Script Collection, Shubert Archive; Norris, "One Woman's Impressions"; Clarke, *The Mighty Hippodrome*, 26–37; and "The New Hippodrome Opens."

46. Clarke, *The Mighty Hippodrome*, 34–36, 41. *Andersonville* was later replaced by *The Romance of the Hindoo Princess*, which featured the Hippodrome's elephants sliding down a stage mountain into the lake.

47. Both *The Wizard of Oz* and *Babes in Toyland* originated in Chicago, not New York, and were produced by the team of Fred R. Hamlin and Julian Mitchell. The *Wizard of Oz*, with book and lyrics by L. Frank Baum and music by Paul Tietjens and A. Baldwin Sloane, opened in Chicago in 1902 and toured the eastern and southern United States before it played 293 performances at the Majestic Theatre, beginning January 21, 1903; it returned a year later for 48 additional performances. *Babes in Toyland*, with libretto

by Glen MacDonough and music by Victor Herbert, after a hit opening in Chicago in the summer of 1903, played 192 performances at the Majestic Theatre, New York, beginning October 13, 1903. J. M. Barrie's *Peter Pan* opened November 6, 1905, at the Empire Theatre in New York for 223 performances, Charles Frohman, producer; it reopened a year later for another 40 performances. *A Society Circus* was performed 596 times at the New York Hippodrome, beginning December 13, 1905, with book by Sydney Rosenfeld, lyrics by Rosenfeld and Manuel Klein, music by Klein and Gustav Luders, produced by Thompson & Dundy. See *The Best Plays of 1899–1909*, 427, 440, 500, 503.

48. Typescript of *The Yankee Circus in Mars*, Scene 2, 2–4.

49. See the script for *A Society Circus* in Script Collection, Shubert Archive.

50. "A 'Society Circus' Is Vastest of Spectacles"; "Electricity at the New York Hippodrome," 915–916.

51. "A 'Society Circus' Is Vastest of Spectacles"; "Electricity at the New York Hippodrome," 915–916.

52. Merwin, "Thompson and His Hippodrome," 528.

53. Untitled clipping, *Engineering News* (September 15, 1904), and "Hippodrome for Chicago," *Billboard* (March 11, 1905), both in Burnside Scrapbook, TCNYPL; "Hippodrome for London Next," *New York Morning Telegraph* (February 14, 1906), Thompson clipping envelope, TCNYPL; "New Hippodrome Scheme," *New York Times* (January 12, 1905?), Burnside Scrapbook, TCNYPL; "Thompson & Dundy Leave the Hippodrome," *Variety* 3 (June 16, 1906):4; "Thompson & Dundy Quit the Hippodrome," *New York Times* (June 9, 1906):9. The Shuberts were not publicly named the new managers of the Hippodrome until July; see "Hippodrome Leased to the Shuberts," *New York Times* (July 8, 1906):1.

54. Grau, *The Businessman in the Amusement World*, 328; "Frederic Thompson, the Proof of Youth."

55. Clarke, *The Mighty Hippodrome*, 20.

56. "Frederic Thompson to Make New Productions," *Show World* 1 (July 20, 1907):28; "Coney Island Opened Up," *New York Sun* (March 14, 1905):7.

57. Clipping from *Spotlight* (October 27, 1906), in Thompson clipping envelope, TCNYPL; "Ballet Girls Put on Horseback and Elephants Put into Autos," *New York Sun* (January 8, 1905), Part 2, 10; Darnton, "A Peep at the Hippodrome"; "The Hippodrome's Birthday," *New York Sun* (April 14, 1906):5; McCardell, "Hats Off to the Hippodrome!"; Merwin, "Thompson and His Hippodrome," 528. Merwin followed Thompson closely one summer and used the showman as the model for a character in the novel Merwin and Henry K. Webster wrote, *Comrade John* (New York: Macmillan, 1907). See "Thompson as a Book Hero," *New York Morning Telegraph* (November 8, 1907), clipping in Thompson & Dundy clipping envelope, TCNYPL.

58. May, *Screening Out the Past*, 96–146.

59. Merwin, "Thompson and His Hippodrome," 467, 528. Also see Jean Christophe Agnew, "The Consuming Vision of Henry James," in Richard Wightman Fox and T. J. Jackson Lears, eds., *The Culture of Consumption; Critical Essays in American History, 1880–1980* (New York: Pantheon, 1983), 65–100.

60. "Ballet Girls Put on Horseback and Elephants Put Into Autos."

61. "Frederic Thompson Explains"; Merwin, "Thompson and His Hippodrome," 467; "Creator of Enormous Amusement Enterprises," *Human Life* 2 (November 1905):8, 26.

62. "Frederic Thompson, the Proof of Youth." Stage ships appeared in Thompson's productions of *Brewster's Millions, Via Wireless, Little Nemo, The Court of the Golden Fountains*, and *A Fool There Was*. At Luna Park, ships or yachts were used in "The Wreck of the Corsair," "Saved by Wireless," "The Merrimack and the Monitor," not to mention rides such as the "Chutes," "Witching Waves," and "A Trip to the Moon." See also the following clippings in Thompson & Dundy clipping envelope, TCNYPL: "Thompson and Barr Collaborate," *New York Morning Telegraph* (June 25, 1908); "Thompson Yacht Likes the Going," *New York Morning Telegraph* (June 6, 1907); "Elephant Laughs When Yacht . . ." *New York Morning Telegraph* (July 8, 1908); "Thompson and the Sea," *Thompson's Mile-a-Minute Specials* (September 4, 1908).

63. " 'Fred' Thompson Tells of the Trials and Joys of a Showman's Life."

64. "Behind Scenes at Hippodrome with 450 Actors," *New York Herald* (April 13, 1905):4; "Fred Thompson, the Wizard," *Cleveland Leader* (n.d.), in Thompson & Dundy clipping envelope, TCNYPL; Merwin, "Thompson and His Hippodrome," 468; "The Hippodrome's Birthday"; untitled clipping from *New York Globe*, in Thompson & Dundy clipping envelope, TCNYPL; "Sunday Benefits Realize $17,000," source unknown, (May 30, 1906); "Well What's This? . . ." *New York World* (May 17, 1908), Robinson Locke Collection, Vol. 448, 94, TCNYPL.

65. The most frequently quoted critics of Luna Park and the rest of Coney Island are James G. Huneker, "Coney Island," in *New Cosmopolis* (New York; Scribner's, 1915), 149–177; Maxim Gorky, "Boredom," *Independent* 63 (August 1907): 309–317; and Lewis Mumford, "The Architecture of Escape," *New Republic* 43 (August 12, 1925): 321–322.

CHAPTER 13   Joseph Urban

1. Most of Urban's surviving papers and drawings are in the Joseph Urban Collection, Butler Library, Columbia University. Scattered through the collection are typescripts of unpublished interviews with a number of his Viennese contemporaries. These were conducted by Gretl Urban, his daughter, as research for an unfinished biography, and they provide important information on Urban's early years. During his lifetime Urban was the subject of many articles in theater and architecture magazines, but the most extensive treatment was a memorial issue of *Architecture*, 69 (May

1934), with articles by Deems Taylor, Ralph Walker, and Otto Teegan. For more personal viewpoints see Lillian Langseth-Christensen's memoir, *A Design for Living* (New York: Viking, 1987), and William Muschenheim's reminiscences in the Oral History Collection at Columbia University.

2. "Karl Schuster," typescript in the Joseph Urban Collection, Butler Library.

3. "Karl Schuster," "Hofrat Rudolf Mitterer," "Karl Ritter von Wiener," and "Alexander Goltz," Joseph Urban Collection, Butler Library; Nicholas Powell, *The Sacred Spring: The Arts in Vienna, 1898–1918* (Greenwich, CT: New York Graphic Society, 1974), 128–129.

4. Giovanni Fanelli, *La Linea Viennese: Grafica Art Nouveau* (Florence, Italy: Cantini, 1989), 109–112.

5. Wolfgang Greisenegger, "Set Designs and Costumes," in Andrea Seebohm, ed., *The Vienna Opera* (New York: Rizzoli, 1987), 190–194.

6. "Karl Stemolak," Joseph Urban Collection, Butler Library.

7. See Debussy's letter to Jacques Durand, January 1912, reprinted in François Lesure and Roger Nichols, eds., *Debussy Letters* (Cambridge, MA: Harvard University Press, 1987), 255.

8. Kenneth Macgowan, "The New Stagecraft in America," *Century* 87 (January 1914):416–421.

9. "Biographical Notes," Joseph Urban Collection, Butler Library.

10. See the collection of Hagenbund Exhibition catalogues in the Joseph Urban Collection, Butler Library.

11. Joseph Urban, *Theatres* (New York: Theatre Arts, 1929).

12. The title of one movement of an unfinished symphony by Schoenberg. Carl E. Schorske, *Fin-de-Siècle Vienna: Politics and Culture* (New York: Vintage Books, 1981), 358–359.

13. The phrase is Michael Steinberg's, from his "Jewish Identity and Intellectuality in Fin-de-Siècle Austria: Suggestions for a Historical Discourse," *New German Critique* 43 (Winter 1988):10.

14. Photographs and drawings in the Joseph Urban Collection, Butler Library. Some of the interior is still intact.

15. The presentation drawings are in the Joseph Urban Collection, Butler Library; see also "Schloss Esterhazy in St. Abraham bei Dioszegh," *Der Architekt* 6 (1900):3, 35, plate 7, *Das Interieur* 1 (1900):47, 52–53, plates 1, 47; Franco Borsi and Ezio Godoli, *Vienna 1900: Architecture and Design* (New York: Rizzoli, 1986), 285, 287.

16. For the Ernst Ludwig Haus see Ian Latham, *Joseph Maria Olbrich* (New York: Rizzoli, 1980), 52–57. For The Hagenbund Galleries see photographs in the Joseph Urban Collection, Butler Library, and Borsi and Godoli, *Vienna 1900*, 287–288.

17. Urban, *Theatres*.

18. Urban, *Theatres*.

19. Lewis Mumford, "Notes on Modern Architecture," *New Republic* 66 (March 18, 1931): 119–122; Kenneth Macgowan, "The Myth of Urban," *Theatre Arts* 1 (May 1917):98–109; and Macgowan "Profile: Caprice Viennois," *New Yorker* 3 (June 25, 1927):21–23.

20. Willis Steel, "The Art of Joseph Urban," *The Theatre* 22 (September 1915):124–125, 141.

21. Sheldon first brought Urban to New York to design *The Garden of Paradise*; Jones designed the costumes for Urban's 1916 production of Percy MacKaye's *Caliban*; Macgowan became the most perceptive critic of Urban's stage designs; Cheney publicized his theater designs; Taylor's two operas were first mounted by Urban, and the composer waged a campaign on behalf of Urban's designs for the new Metropolitan Opera House; Simonson borrowed from Urban's sets while disparaging him in print. O'Neill ignored him.

22. Louis V. De Foe, "A New Experiment with the Fairy Play," *Green Book* (February 1915):267–278.

23. Deems Taylor, "The Scenic Art of Joseph Urban: His Protean Work in the Theatre," *Architecture* 69 (May 1934): 275–290.

24. Urban, *Theatres*.

25. John Corbin, quoted in Taylor, "The Scenic Art of Joseph Urban," 275.

26. "The Ziegfeld Theatre, New York," *Architectural Forum* 46 (May 1927), 414–421.

27. Gunter Schone, "Karl Lautenschlager, Reformer of Stage Scenery," in Francis Hodge, ed., *Innovations in Stage and Theatre Designs* (New York: American Society for Theatre Research, 1972), 60–77.

28. "The Ziegfeld Theatre, New York," *Architectural Forum* 414. For a detailed reconstruction of a scene from the Follies see Barbara Naomi Cohen Stratyner, "Welcome to 'Laceland' "; An Analysis of a Chorus Number from *The Ziegfeld Follies* of 1922, as Staged by Ned Wayburn," in Glenn Loney, ed., *Musical Theatre in America: Papers and Proceedings of the Conference on the Musical Theatre in America*, 1981 (Westport, CT: Greenwood Press, 1984), 315–321.

29. "Urban" and "Alexander Goltz," typescripts in the Joseph Urban Collection, Butler Library.

30. Urban, *Theatres*.

31. Kenneth Macgowan, "The Myth of Urban," *Theatre Arts* 1 (May 1917):98.

32. William Laurel Harris, "Back to Duncan Phyfe—or Forward to Art Nouveau?" *Good Furniture* 19 (December 1922):257–259.

33. Oliver Sayler, *Our American Theatre* (New York: Brentano's Publishers, 1923), 247.

34. "Kahn Awaits Voice of Public on Opera," *New York Times* (January 16, 1926):1.

35. Walter Kilham, Jr., *Raymond Hood, Architect: Form Through Function in the American Skyscraper* (New York: Architectural Book Publishing, 1973), 81.

36. Urban, "Wedding Theatre Beauty to Ballyhoo," *New York Times* Magazine (August 19, 1928): 11.

37. Walter Littlefield Creese, "American Architecture from 1918–1933." Unpublished Ph.D. diss., Harvard University, Cambridge, MA, 1949, 1, 7–8.

38. See Robert A. M. Stern, Gregory Gilmartin, and Thomas Mellins, *New York 1930* (New York: Rizzoli, 1987), 55–85.

39. Harvey Wiley Corbett, "The American Radiator Building, New York City, Raymond Hood Architect," *Architectural Record* 55 (May 1924):473–477.

40. Urban, "Wedding Theatre Beauty to Ballyhoo," 10.

41. Otto Teegan, "Joseph Urban's Philosophy of Color," *Architecture* 69 (May 1934):257–271.

42. Lloyd Morris, *Incredible New York* (New York: Random House, 1951), 339; "Central Park Casino," *Architectural Record* 66 (August 1929):97–108.

43. Otto Teegan, "Joseph Urban's Philosophy of Color," 270.

44. "The House of Morgan," *American Architect* 148 (February 1936):41–43.

45. "Persian Room and Bar, Hotel Plaza, New York," *Architectural Forum* 61 (July 1934):45–48.

46. William Muschenheim, "Restaurant Design," *Architectural Record* 81 (January 1937):23–32.

47. Philip Johnson, "The Architecture of the New School," *Arts* 17 (March 1931):393–398; reprinted in Peter Eisenman and Robert A. M. Stern, eds., *Philip Johnson: Writings* (New York: Oxford University Press, 1979), 32–36.

PART IV BOUNDARIES OF RESPECTABILITY
Introductory Essay

1. As, for instance, Lewis Erenberg's *Steppin' Out: New York Nightlife and the Transformation of American Culture, 1890–1930* (Chicago: University of Chicago Press, 1985), though his argument is considerably more sophisticated than the one offered above. Indeed, the novelty of Erenberg's approach is to take apart the notion of the jazz age and to locate changes in appetite and behavior within specific urban environments before the mythic 1920s.

2. Charles Smith, "A Theatre for the People and the Public Schools," *Charities* (February 4, 1905).

3. *The People's Institute Annual Report*,

1907, 17; and "New York City's Censorship of Plays," *Theatre Magazine* (May 1908).

4. Though progressive reformers still supported the sundry Fusion candidates at the ballot box, Tammany, under Charles Murphy's leadership (1902–1924), began to abandon the practices of laissez-faire politics in the hope of broadening its appeal to non-Catholic immigrant voters. Thus "Times Square" developed in a period when there was a measure of bipartisan support for municipal services and regulation. The best account of Tammany politics in the period remains Nancy Weiss, *Charles Francis Murphy, 1858–1924: Respectability and Responsibility in Tammany Politics* (Northampton, MA: Smith College Press, 1986).

5. See Robert C. Allen's *Vaudeville and Film 1895–1915: A Study in Media Interaction* (New York: Arno Press, 1980).

6. Ziegfeld's innovations in the display of feminine sexuality are well discussed in Erenberg's *Steppin' Out*, 206–221.

7. The most vivid account of the "discovery" of the strip is Morton Minsky and Milt Machlin, *Minsky's Burlesque* (New York: Arbor House, 1986); see also Robert Allen's *Horrible Prettiness* (Chapel Hill, NC: University of North Carolina Press, 1991), Chap. 8.

8. *Times* (May 17, 1933):15.

CHAPTER 14 Policing of Sexuality

1. On the development of "nightlife" in New York see Lewis A. Erenberg, *Steppin' Out: New York Nightlife and the Transformation of American Culture, 1890–1930* (Chicago: University of Chicago Press, 1981). In this essay the Times Square and Forty-second Street area is defined as the ten blocks from West Thirty-seventh Street to West Forty-seventh Street, between Sixth and Eighth avenues.

2. Charles Lockwood, *Manhattan Moves Uptown* (Boston: Little Brown, 1976), 250–252. On Clement Clarke Moore see Elliot Willensky and Norval White, *A.I.A. Guide to New York City* (New York: Macmillan, 1978), 104.

3. Cornelius Willemse, *Beyond the Green Lights* (New York: Knopf, 1931), 83–84; James D. McCabe, Jr., *New York by Sunlight and Gaslight* (Philadelphia: Hubbard Brothers, 1882), 153, 250–252. On theaters see Michael Brown, "Times Square," *Preservation* 1 (January 1982): 5–6; Robert A. M. Stern, Gregory Gilmartin, and John Massengale, *New York 1900: Metropolitan Architecture and Urbanism, 1890–1915* (New York, Rizzoli, 1983), 303–308.

4. George Ellington, *The Women of New York, or the Under-World of the Great City* (Burlington, IA: Root and Smith, 1869), 232; Citizens Association of New York, *Sanitary Condition of the City, Report of the Council of Hygiene and Public Health* (New York: D. Appleton, 1866), 24–26.

5. Willemse, *Green Lights*, 80–85; George J. Kneeland, *Commercialized Prostitution in New York City* (New York, 1917), 4–5.

6. The brothels were between Seventh and Eighth avenues. See Affidavits for 311 West Forty-fourth Street, March 1901, Box 24; Clippings, August 30, 1901, Box 45, both in Committee of Fifteen Papers, New York Public Library (hereafter C15P). On the French houses at 245, 247, and 249 West Thirty-ninth Street see Investigator's Report (1905?), Box 91, Lillian Wald Papers, Columbia University. On Times Square see Robert A. M. Stern, Gregory Gilmartin, Thomas Mellins, *New York 1930: Architecture and Urbanism Between the Two World Wars* (New York: Rizzoli, 1987), 87–88, 229; Stern et al., *New York 1900*, 203–208. On the Metropolitan see Paul E. Eisler, *The Metropolitan Opera: The First Twenty-Five Years, 1883–1908* (Croton-on-Hudson, NY: North River Press, 1984), 1–19; John Frederick Cone, *First Rival of the Metropolitan Opera* (New York: Columbia University Press, 1983), 1–5, 29. A "soubrette" was a coquettish young woman or actress in stage comedies. By the early twentieth century, soubrettes were equated with burlesque and the youngest featured women on the program. See Morton Minsky and Milt Machlin, *Minsky's Burlesque: A Fast and Funny Look at America's Bawdiest Era* (New York, Arbor House, 1986), 7.

7. Willemse, *Green Lights*, 83–84. On Charles Frohman as "the most active and enterprising entrepreneur" in the United States see *The Independent* 55 (1903): 1984.

8. William McAdoo, *Guarding a Great City* (New York, 1906), 91. The addresses were in C15P and were traced in George S. Bromley, *The Atlas of the City of New York* (New York: G. W. Bromley, 1899). On streetwalkers see Affidavits for 311 West Forty-fourth Street, March 1901, Box 24, C15P. On popular brothels see the Investigators Reports for 208, 210, 212, 228 West Forty-fourth Street, 1905(?), Box 91, Wald Papers.

9. *Times* (July 21, 1907); Adam Clayton Powell, Sr., *Against the Tide: An Autobiography* (New York: R. R. Smith, 1938), 49. On theaters and prostitution before 1870 see Timothy J. Gilfoyle, *City of Eros: New York City, Prostitution, and the Commercialization of Sex, 1790–1920* (New York: W. W. Norton, 1992), part 1. Streetwalkers usually charged $1.00 per customer. The more expensive brothels in the late nineteenth century charged between $5.00 and $10.00 per customer. The Denver Hotel, 209 West Fortieth Street, and the German Village, 147 West Fortieth Street, were operated by Hadden, who escaped punishment after at least three unsuccessful prosecutions. He was represented by George H. Engel, special counsel to Thomas Foley, Second District Tammany leader and New York County Sheriff. See Confidential Bulletin, December 19, 1913, Box 3; Reports, 1913, Box 28, both in Committee of Fourteen Papers, New York Public Library (hereafter C14P); Police Commissioner to Woods, February 11, 1914, Mayors' Papers, New York City Municipal Archives and Records Center (hereafter MP), Box MJP-17; Confidential Bulletin, September 9, 1914, THC-Prostitution Folder, Box 168, Community Service Society Papers, Columbia University (hereafter CSS); Theodore A. Bingham, "The Organized Criminals of New York," *McClure's* 34 (1909): 66. On 563 Seventh Avenue (tenement), see Affidavits for Seventh Avenue and Broadway, 1901, Box 21, C15P. On police arresting prosti-

tutes along Seventh Avenue see Police Commissioner to Gaynor, December 3, 1910, MP GWJ-18. On West Thirty-ninth and Fortieth Street brothels see letters to Mayors Hewitt and Grant in MP 87-HAS-28, 87-HAS-32, 87-HAS-33, 87-HAS-39, 87-HAS-40; letters to Inspector Byrnes in MP 89-GTF-14; letters to Mayor Gaynor in MP GWJ-17, GWJ-35, GWJ-36, GWJ-37, GWJ-56; Investigators' Reports, 1905(?), Box 91, Wald Papers; Cases for 1911, Box 13, CSS.

10. Lewis Mumford, *The Culture of Cities* (New York: Harcourt Brace, 1938), 271.

11. Stone lived at 202 West Fortieth Street. See Murphy to Murray, September 30, 1888, *Evening World* clipping, September 1888, MP 87-HAS-33; "A Resident of Fortieth Street" to Hewitt, April 15, 1888, MP 87-HAS-32 ("fast women"); "Neighbor" to Hewitt, July 1888, MP 87-HAS-33 ("lantern exhibitions"). The brothels were at 203 and 205 West Thirty-eighth Street. For other complaints of prostitution between West Thirty-seventh and Forty-second streets prior to 1890 see "Resident" to Hewitt, July 12, 1888, MP 87-HAS-33; "An Honest Citizen" to Hewitt, May 29, 1887, MP 87-HAS-38. Osgood owned 270–272 West Thirty-ninth Street. See New York State Assembly, *Special Committee Appointed to Investigate Public Officers and Departments of the City of New York* (Albany: James B. Lyon, 1900) (hereafter *Mazet Committee*), 1551–1555.

12. Typed Information, Houses and Resorts of Prostitution, Arranged According to Street, 1910, and February 1, 1912, Box 28, C14P. Livingston ran 210, 214 West Fortieth Street, and 150 West Forty-fifth Street. Grey operated 114, 206, and 214 West Forty-sixth Street, the latter for thirty years. On Lawrence, see Handwritten Report, July 6, 1913, Box 28, C14P.

13. On the fifty-cent houses see Booth, *The White Slave Traffic*, Supplement, in Box 2 Chute Papers. On Williams see Typed Information, Houses and Resorts of Prostitution, Arranged According to

Street, 1910, Report for 138 West Thirty-second Street. On French Viola, see Undated Report on 144 West Thirty-second Street, Box 91, Wald Papers.

14. Compiled from Undated Raines Law Hotel Reports and Undated Boarding House and Parlor House Reports, Box 91, Wald Papers.

15. Acting Police Commissioner to Gaynor, July 22, 1913, MP GWJ-74; Fahey to Police Commissioner, October 25, 1910, MP GWJ-17; Police Commissioner to Mitchel, March 11, 1914, MP MJP-18. On clubs and cafés see Typed List of Houses, Arranged According to Streets, 1910; Report of Mrs. A. M. White, April 2, 1910; Report of William Pogue, April 6, 1911; Anonymous Report, March 17, 1910, all in Box 28, C14P.

16. Powell, *Against the Tide*, 49; Letter of "A Citizen" attached to Police Commissioner to Gaynor ("gutter"), July 26, 1913, MP GWJ-73; Investigator Reports (Marshall's), 1910, Box 28, C14P. On West Fifty-third Street see Jervis Anderson, *This Was Harlem: A Cultural Portrait, 1900–1950* (New York: Farrar, Straus & Giroux, 1981), 30–32.

17. On French houses on West Thirty-ninth Street see Investigator's Report; Frances Kellor Report, October 17, 1907, quotes pp. 1, 6, 9, all in Box 91, Wald Papers.

18. For the antebellum origins of this see Gilfoyle, *City of Eros*, Chap. 6; Elliot J. Gorn, " 'Good-Bye Boys, I Die a True American': Homicide, Nativism, and Working-Class Culture in Antebellum New York City," *Journal of American History* 74 (1987): 388–410: Elliot J. Gorn, *The Manly Art: Bare-Knuckle Prize Fighting in America* (Ithaca, NY: Cornell University Press, 1986).

19. Society for the Prevention of Crime, *Third Report* (New York, 1879), 20–21; Elizabeth Blackwell, *Counsel to Parents on the Moral Education of Their Children* (New York: Brentano's, 1881), 72–73, 50–51; Willemse, *Green Lights*, 68–69 ("roisterers"); *National Police Gazette* (August 28, 1880) (Bowery).

20. *Mazet Committee*, 941 (Van Wyck); Society for the Suppression of Vice, *Twenty-third Annual Report* (New York, 1897), 13; Handwritten Report on Avenel Hotel, July 8, 1913, Box 28, C14P (Morgan); Helen Campbell, *Darkness and Daylight; or Lights and Shadows of New York Life* (Hartford, CT: Hartford Publishing Co., 1893), 209; Report for November 1905, and Report on 140 West Twenty-fourth Street, Box 91, Wald Papers (550 males).

21. Kneeland, *Commercialized Prostitution*, 109–111; Willemse, *Green Lights*, 69 ("accepted fact"); *Mazet Committee*, 2461–2479, 2504–2517.

22. Thomas Byrnes, *1886—Professional Criminals of America* (New York: Cassell & Co., 1886), xxi; Kneeland, *Commercialized Prostitution*, 50–51.

23. Report of Hattie Ross, 1909, Folder 150, Harriet Laidlaw Papers, Schlesinger Library, Harvard University; U.S. Senate Immigrant Commission, *Importing Women for Immoral Purposes*, Sixty-first Congress, Second Session, Document No. 196 (Washington, DC: 1909), 14–19; Typed Information, Houses and Resorts of Prostitution, Arranged According to Street, 1910, and February 1, 1912, Box 28, C14P. The Committee found that fifty-three houses were French-run or housed primarily French women, twenty-five were Jewish, twenty-five African-American, seven Italian, two Greek, two Chinese, two Swedish and one Irish.

24. The French syndicate was headquartered at 124 West Twenty-ninth Street and at the Franco-American Democratic Club at 117 West Twenty-eighth Street. See Kellor Manuscript, quotes pp. 1, 6, 9; Statement of the Women's Municipal League, 1909, Box 91, Wald Papers; Clippings for October 24, 1901, Box 47, C15P. Judging from federal court convictions, some Italians were similarly engaged in trafficking women across the Atlantic. And Irish groups like the "Sullivan men" and "McCarren men" were allegedly involved in promoting prostitution. See Bingham, "Organized Criminals," 62, and the list of federal court convictions for white slavery in Anonymous, *Political Protection of the White Slave*

Trade (?, 1910), 6–8, in Box 91, Wald Papers. Chevalier's restaurant was at 133 West Forty-fifth Street. See Reports of J. S., 1, September 5, 1915; August 29 and 31, 1919, Box 34, C14P. A third alleged syndicate was the "O.S. Club," but I have no descriptive information on it. See *Political Protection*, 12.

25. Kellor Manuscript, pages 1–3, Box 91, Wald Papers; Ross Report, Folder 150, Harriet Laidlaw Papers. On Ross, "a colored missionary," see McAdoo, *Guarding a Great City*, 100. On the I.B.A. and Jewish prostitution in Times Square see Edward J. Bristow, *Prostitution and Prejudice: The Jewish Fight Against White Slavery, 1870–1939* (New York: Schocken, 1983), 165–173, 275–276. On Jewish leadership in commercialized entertainment in New York at the turn of the century, see Lary May, *Screening Out the Past* (New York: Oxford University Press, 1980); Robert Sklar, *Movie-Made America: A Cultural History of American Movies* (New York: Random House, 1975), 30–32, 41–47. Only with the daytime murder of former pimp and gambler Herman Rosenthal in front of the Metropole Hotel in 1912 did reformers and others concern themselves with "syndicate" prostitution and commercial sex. On the impact of the Rosenthal murder see *Outlook* (December 1917), in Box 96, C14P; Jenna Weismann Joselit, *Our Gang: Jewish Crime and the New York Jewish Community, 1900–1940* (Bloomington, IN: Indiana University Press, 1983), 75–84; Arthur A. Goren, *New York Jews and the Quest for Community: The Kehillah Experiment, 1908–1922* (New York: Columbia University Press, 1970), 148–158; Kneeland, *Commercialized Prostitution*, 155.

26. Kneeland estimated that the city-wide annual profits were about $2 million. See Kneeland, *Commercialized Prostitution*, 128–130; Kellor Manuscript, p. 9, Box 91, Wald Papers.

27. Undated Reports for 245–249 West Thirty-ninth Street; The National, 3 Irving Place; Metropolitan Hotel and Winter Garden, 278 Third Avenue; and Wundling's Hotel, 39 Third Avenue, all in Box 91, Wald Papers ("charity");

Kneeland, *Commercialized Prostitution*, 39–40. "Cadets" were usually young males who recruited, seduced, or sometimes even forced young women into prostitution. Many functioned as pimps for the prostitutes in the hotels. See Raines Law Hotel Reports, 1905(?); Raines Law II Folder; Raines Law III Folder, all in Box 91, Wald Papers. Authored by State Senator John Raines and passed by the state in 1896, the "Raines Law": (1) raised excise license fees to $1,200, (2) put excise licenses under state control, (3) required a $1,800 bond from all saloon keepers that would be forfeited upon any violation of the law, and (4) restricted Sunday liquor sales to hotels with ten or more beds. Unexpectedly, saloons divided rear and upstairs space into small "rooms" and took out hotel licenses, thereby converting saloons into houses of prostitution.

28. Woods to Mitchel, July 13, 1915, MP MJP-41 (Hotel Plymouth); Police Commissioner to Woods, February 27, 1914, MP MJP-18 (King Edward Hotel). Hotel Lyceum was a five-story elevator apartment hotel at 139 West Forty-fifth Street. See Police Commissioner to Gaynor, September 6, 1911, MP GWJ-36. For prostitution in other hotels see Sanders to Police Commissioner, July 22, 1897, MP 90-SWI-45. For streets with multiple houses of prostitution after 1900 see Police Commissioner to Gaynor, January 26, 1911, MP GWJ-33; Report of May 12, 1913, Box 13, Society for the Prevention of Crime Papers, Columbia University (hereafter SPC Papers); Baker to Gaynor, October 12, 1910; Fahey to Police Commissioner, October 25, 1910, both in MP GWJ-17; Police Commissioner to Mitchel, March 11, 1914, MP MJP-18; Anonymous letter attached to Acting Police Commissioner to Gaynor, July 22, 1913, MP GWJ-74 (all West Thirty-seventh Street); *Mazet Committee*, 1551–1555; C15P, Box 22 (West Thirty-ninth Street); Powell, *Against the Tide*, 49; Boxes 15 and 22, C15P; Police Commissioner to Gaynor, October 28, 1910, MP GWJ-17; Police Commissioner to Gaynor, December 3, 1910, MP GWJ-18; and

Committee of Fourteen, *Annual Report* (New York, 1914), 11–12; "A Citizen" to Gaynor, July 1913, MP GWJ-73; Report of May 12, 1913, Box 13, SPC Papers; Undated Reports, Box 91, Wald Papers (all West Fortieth Street); Affidavits for 311 West Forty-fourth Street, March 1901, Box 24; Affidavits on Forty-second Street, Box 21; Clipping for August 30, 1910, Box 45, all in C15P; New York City Police Department, *Annual Report for 1919* (New York, 1920), 37–38; Police Commissioner to Gaynor, October 28, 1910, MP GWJ-17 (West Forty-second to Forty-seventh Street).

29. In this manner New York mirrored other eighteenth and nineteenth century Western cities that frequently integrated the business of leisure and entertainment with that of sex. At the Palais Royal in Paris, Vauxhall Gardens and the Mall of St. James's Park in London, the Prater in Vienna, and the Paseo in Mexico City, female prostitutes publicly mingled with the affluent. See Mark Girouard, *Cities and People: A Social and Architectural History* (New Haven, CT: Yale University Press, 1982), 186–188, 192–193, 203–204, 237. For more on Paris see Orest Ranum, *Paris in the Age of Absolutism* (New York: Wiley, 1968), 12; and Jill Harsin, *The Policing of Prostitution in Nineteenth-Century Paris* (Princeton, NJ: Princeton University Press, 1985), 141, 163.

30. On these antiprostitution campaigns see Carroll Smith-Rosenberg, "Beauty, the Beast, and the Militant Woman," *American Quarterly* 23 (1971):562–584; Gilfoyle, *City of Eros*, Chap. 9.

31. Parkhurst to Police Commissioners, January 16, 1894, MP 89-GTF-14; *City Vigilant* (October 1894); Parkhurst to Capt. James Price, January 16, 1894, MP 89-GTF-14 ("attitudinizing"). On Parkhurst see Charles W. Gardner, *The Doctor and the Devil: A Startling Exposé of Municipal Corruption* (New York: Gardner & Co., 1894). On Osgood see *Mazet Committee*, 1551–1555.

32. For examples see the correspondence between the SPCC and various mayors, 1892, MP 88-GHJ-49; 1893–94, MP 89-GTF-16; 1895–97, MP 90-SWI-49. Mayor Gilroy frequently rejected the SPCC's opposition and gave permission for the children to perform. The law prohibited rope walking, gymnastics, wrestling, contortionists, acrobatics, begging, soliciting alms, singing or dancing in a wandering exhibition, an immoral or indecent exhibition, and presenting a deformity or unnatural physical formation by any child under age 16. The mayor retained power to permit singing and dancing at concerts. See *Laws of 1892*, Chap. 309, penal code 292. For more on the SPCC see Timothy J. Gilfoyle, "The Moral Origins of Political Surveillance: The Preventive Society in New York City, 1867–1918," *American Quarterly* 38 (1986):637–652.

33. Sanders to Police Commissioner, July 22, 1897, MP 90-SWI-45. On Smith see Clipping of November 28–29, 1901, Box 31, C15P. On Grant see New York State Senate, *Investigation of the Police Department of New York*, II (Albany: James B. Lyon, 1895) (hereafter *Lexow Committee*), 2286. On Clinton see Committee of Fourteen, *Annual Report* (New York, 1912), 27. Real estate broker and resident Edward Gallon remarked that high-handed, if not excessive, methods were often necessary, requiring "some clubbing once in a while to educate [newcomers] to the New York mode of living." See Gallon to Hewitt, August 9, 1888, MP 87-HAS-35. Gallon's real estate office was at 257 West Forty-second Street and residence at 305 West Forty-first from 1862 to 1888.

34. Clipping of February 6, 1901, Box 34, C15P. The S.P.C.A. was the Society for the Prevention of Cruelty to Animals.

35. On the Committee and venereal disease see Committee of Fourteen, *Annual Report for 1923* (New York, 1924), 4–6. On broadening the definition of "commercialized prostitution" see *Annual Report for 1924* (New York, 1925), 10–12.

36. The Ambler Law required hotels built after 1891 and over 35 feet high to be fireproof with walls 3 inches thick, rooms at least 30 square feet, and doors opening onto hallways, thus eliminating most

Raines Law hotels. See clippings from 1905 in Box 96, C14P.

37. Frederick H. Whitin, "Obstacles to Vice Repression," *Social Hygiene* 2 (1916):146–150. On Rockefeller's support see Whitin to Hinman, January 11, 1911, Box 1, C14P; *American* (May 26, 1910); and *Evening World* (May 20, 1910), both in Box 96, C14P. On violations in the Times Square area see "Violations and Protest Lists," 1905–1918, Box 44, C14P. The original members and affiliations of the Committee of Fourteen included: Reverend John Peters, Rector, St. Michael's Episcopal Church; Thomas Reed, Secretary, Anti-Saloon League; Rev. William Daly, Paulist Fathers; Rabbi Bernard Drachman, Zichron Ephraim Congregation; Rev. Lee Beattie, Madison Square Church House; George Haven Putnam, publisher; Professor Francis Burdick, Columbia University; Mary Simkhovitch, Greenwich House; Rabbi Pereira Mendes, Shearith Israel Congregation; Lawrence Veiller, Secretary, City Club; William Bennett, Counsel, Anti-Saloon League; Reverend Howard Russell, Superintendent, Anti-Saloon League; Edward J. McGuire, lawyer; Isaac Seligman, banker; Frederick Whitin.

38. Committee of Fourteen, *Annual Report for 1923*, 13–15. On Progressive reform see David J. Rothman, *Conscience and Convenience: The Asylum and Its Alternatives in Progressive America* (Boston: Little, Brown, 1980). The onset of World War I precipitated a rebirth of overt, public sexuality in Times Square. For examples see J.A.S. Report on "Street Conditions," 1918; Report of D.O., May 5, 1919, both in Box 33, C14P.

39. *Lexow Committee*, IV, 4495–4498; Willemse, *Green Lights*, 20. For similar descriptions of the police see McAdoo, *Guarding a Great City*, 17–69, 185–192, 328–349. Theodore Roosevelt ordered all policemen, upon being named police commissioners, to resign from political clubs as required by law. See *Herald* (May 17, 1895), in Theodore Roosevelt Papers, Library of Congress, Reel 454, Series 15.

40. *Evening Post* (March 11, 1918);

World (March 12, 1918), in Box 96, C14P. On tenements see the correspondence among the Committee of Fourteen, the Tenement House Department, and the various landlords from 1914 to 1928, Box 23, C14P.

41. Committee of Fourteen, *Annual Report for 1925*, 8; *Annual Report for 1926*, 21; *Annual Report for 1930* (New York, 1931), 20–31. For one example of this trend after 1920 see Eugene J. Watts, "Police Response to Crime and Disorder in Twentieth-Century St. Louis," *Journal of American History* 70 (1983), 341–356. Although the Committee of Fourteen stressed its willingness to cooperate with police officials in its annual reports (see *Annual Report for 1925*, 14–19), private papers indicate numerous disagreements between investigators' findings and weak law enforcement by the police.

42. *Evening Sun* (November 26, 1906), in Box 96, C14P. On changing police policy see Committee of Fourteen, *Annual Report for 1924*, 8–9; *Annual Report for 1929* (New York, 1930), 32.

43. Committee of Fourteen, *Annual Report for 1929* (New York, 1930), 10–11. Enright was police commissioner from 1917 to 1925. See Committee of Fourteen, *Annual Report for 1925*, 14–17.

44. George Kneeland, "Commercialized Prostitution and the Use of Property," *Social Hygiene* 2 (1916): 561, 566–570; Committee of Fourteen, *Annual Report* (New York, 1916), 18, 28; *Annual Report* (New York, 1914), 23–24.

45. Committee of Fourteen, *Annual Report* (New York, 1916), 12. On the liquor industry see George Kneeland, "Commercialized Vice and the Liquor Traffic," *Social Hygiene* 2 (1916): 69–90; *The Standard* (May 15, 1909); *Collier's* (n.d.); *World* (March 15, 1908); *Tribune* (March 15, 1908); and clipping, August 24, 1909, all in Box 96, C14P. See also the voluminous correspondence between the Committee and individual brewers supplying "disorderly saloons" from 1910 to 1918 in Boxes 2, 3, and 17, C14P.

46. Martin Clary, *Mid-Manhattan. The Multimillion Area* (New York: Forty-second Street Property Owners and Mer-

NOTES FOR PAGES 310–312

chants Association, 1929), 22–23, 27. On Smith see clipping of November 28–29, 1901, Box 31, C15P.

47. Minsky and Machlin, *Minsky's Burlesque*, 26, 43, 60, 80, 139, 145. On sexual themes at the Princess see clipping from *Brooklyn Eagle* (September 28, 1913); Police Commissioner to Kline, October 14, 1913, MP GWJ-76. The Princess was located at Thirty-ninth Street and Sixth Avenue. On outrage over "Aphrodite" and the depiction of courtesans and the "promiscuous intermingling of semi-nude negroes and half-naked women" at the Century Theater, see *New York Journal* (December 2, 1919), Box 33, C14P. On I. B. Seney's complaints of the Columbia see Police Commissioner to Mayor, February 24, 1911, MP GWJ-33. The Columbia Theater was at Forty-seventh Street and Broadway. The police did not consider this play immoral. On Hammerstein see Police Commissioner to Gaynor, February 26, 1913, MP GWJ-13. During these years the federal government attempted to forbid Maxim Gorky's entrance into the United States, and the New York Public Library moved to restrict some of George Bernard Shaw's writings. In 1906 Comstock raided the Art Students League and the Herman Knoedler Gallery for painting and displaying nudes. And in 1914 Margaret Sanger was compelled to flee New York and the United States to avoid prosecution for her militant advocacy of birth control. See Hal Sears, *The Sex Radicals: Free Love in High Victorian America* (Lawrence, KS: Regents Press of Kansas, 1977), 264–265.

48. *Outlook* (December 1917), in Box 96, C14P.

49. Raymond B. Fosdick, "Prostitution and the Police," *Social Hygiene* 2 (1916): 16; Committee of Fourteen, *Annual Report* (New York, 1922), 10; and *Annual Report* (New York, 1925), 7–8.

50. For an example of the declining reference of "Tenderloin" see Kneeland, *Commercialized Prostitution*, 37, which refers to it only once. On censorship as a vehicle to protect youths, women, and the

poor from "threatening" sexual images see Walter Kendrick, *The Secret Museum: Pornography in Modern Culture* (New York: Viking, 1987).

51. Report on "Street Conditions," Seventh Avenue, Thirty-fourth to Forty-second streets, February 6 and 19, 1918, Box 33, C14P. The percentage distribution of the various institutional forms of prostitution was based on compiling all reported addresses from 1870 to 1920. For a specific breakdown and list of sources see Gilfoyle, *City of Eros*, Chap. 10, Note 3; Chap. 11, Note 2.

52. On Chevalier and other French and Belgian proprietors see Committee of Fourteen to Chief Inspector John Daly, November 27, 1918, Box 17, C14P; Report of J.S., September 1–5, 1915, August 29–31, 1919, Box 34, C14P. For more on decline of prostitution, see Gilfoyle, *City of Eros*, Chap. 14. The most conspicuous prostitution moved north of Fiftieth Street. See Investigators' Reports, 1900–1918, Box 17, C14P. On furnished-room houses and hotels see Report on "Street Conditions," Seventh Avenue, Thirty-fourth to Forty-second streets, February 6 and 19, 1918, Box 33, C14P. The suppression of streetwalkers and brothels in Times Square increased nearby tenement prostitution, but most of this remained underground and secret. See Madge Headley, Secretary of Tenement House Committee of Charity Organization Society to Bailey Burret, June 24, 1914, File 60, Box 23, CSS. For arrests see Committee of Fourteen Folder, 1920, Box 109, CSS; and THC-Prostitution Folder, January 29, 1914, Box 168, CSS. From 1927 to 1929, Committee of Fourteen investigators only found thirty-two addresses with prostitution. See Investigators' Reports, 1927–1929, Box 36, C14P. On call girls, see Investigators Reports, 1927–1928, Box 36, C14P. The first example of a "call girl" I found was at 48 East Twenty-ninth Street in 1901. See Affidavit for 203 West Forty-eighth Street, March 4, 1901, C15P.

53. Committee of Fourteen, *Annual Re-*

port for 1929 (New York, 1930), 35. On the decline see *Annual Report for 1927* (New York, 1928), 41–42.

54. Committee of Fourteen, *Annual Report for 1929* (New York, 1930), 57; Lein to Committee of Fourteen, September 21, 1918, Box 17, C14P. Salvin to Committee, September 23, 1918, Box 17, C14P. The Tokio was at 141–143 West Forty-fifth Street. Other reports show that the Tokio still allowed prostitutes. See Investigator's Report, January 11, 1919, Box 17; J.A.S. Report, 1918; Charles Briggs Report, 1918; Report of D.O., May 5, 1919, all in Box 33, C14P. For similar letters see Gaillard W. Boag of the Moulin Rouge to Committee of Fourteen, September 30, 1918; and Abram Bernheim, saloon at 681 Eighth Avenue, September 25, 1913, both in Box 17, C14P.

55. Miscellaneous Report, March 2, 1927, Box 36, C14P. The Committee of Fourteen expressed its concern over homosexuality for the first time publicly in 1929, noting that of the 392 nightclubs and speakeasies investigated more than once, 13 catered to homosexuals. See *Annual Report for 1928* (New York, 1929), 12. On speakeasy investigations see Investigators Reports, 1927–1928, Box 36, C14P.

56. Committee of Fourteen, *Annual Report for 1925* (New York, 1926), 20–26; *Annual Report for 1923* (New York, 1924), 3–8; *Annual Report for 1924* (New York, 1925), 15–35; *Annual Report for 1926* (New York, 1927), 24–25, 36; *Annual Report for 1927* (New York, 1928), 7. Interestingly, the "customer amendment" was opposed by Lawrence Veiller of the Charity Organization Society, Police Commissioner Richard Enright, and the Society for the Prevention of Crime because of the difficulties it presented in prosecuting prostitutes and potential for police abuse. See *Annual Report for 1925*, 21.

57. Benjamin G. Rader, *American Sports: From the Age of Folk Games to the Age of Spectators* (Englewood Cliffs, NJ: Prentice Hall, 1983); Sklar, *Movie-Made America*, 82–85; Eliot Asinof, *Eight Men Out: The Black Sox and the 1919 World Series*

(New York: Holt, Rinehart & Winston, 1963).

CHAPTER 15 The Policed: Gay Men's Strategies of Everyday Resistance

1. Sebastian Risicato, interviewed by the author August 28, 1988. At the request of the editors I have kept the footnotes to a minimum in this paper, but full documentation will appear in my forthcoming *Gay New York: Urban Culture and the Making of a Gay Male World, 1890–1940*. Major sources include the records of the police, private moral reform organizations, and the governmental agencies which investigated bars suspected of serving homosexuals, several diaries, newspaper articles, and my interviews with approximately seventy gay men who lived during the era.

2. It is impossible to trace the involvement of gay men in any industry with precision, of course, given the absence of the census records historians normally use for such purposes, and I offer no estimates of the rate of their participation. My claim is not that gay workers predominated in the theater, hotel, or restaurant industries, but simply that disproportionate numbers of gay men worked in them, and that many of them enjoyed greater tolerance in them than they would have elsewhere. This assertion is based primarily on the accounts provided in my interviews with men who worked in the industry or were otherwise familiar with it, including Max Adams, interviewed January 11, 15, and 27, 1988; Harry Hay, interviewed October 6, 1988; and Martin Goodkin, interviewed November 21, 1987; as well as some documentation from the period itself.

3. Harold E. Stearns, *The Street I Know* (New York: Lee Fuerman, 1935), 92.

4. On this point see my article, "Long-Haired Men and Short-Haired Women: Building a Gay World in the Heart of Village Bohemia," in Leslie Berlowitz and Rick Beard, eds., *The Village of New York* (New Brunswick, NJ: Rutgers University Press, 1992).

5. For general accounts of the culture of lodging and furnished-room houses, and the character of the districts in which they predominated, see Albert Benedict Wolfe, *The Lodging House Problem in Boston* (Boston: Houghton Mifflin, 1906); Harvey Warren Zorbaugh, *The Gold Coast and the Slum: A Sociological Study of Chicago's Near North Side* (Chicago: University of Chicago Press, 1929), 69–86; Mark Peel, "In the Margins: Lodgers and Boarders in Boston, 1860–1900," *Journal of American History* 72 (1986):813–834; and Joanne J. Meyerowitz, *Women Adrift: Independent Wage Earners in Chicago, 1880–1930* (Chicago: University of Chicago Press, 1988).

6. James Ford, *Slums and Housing: With Special Reference to New York City: History, Conditions, Policy* (Cambridge, MA: Harvard University Press, 1936), 341–344; Robert A. M. Stern, Gregory Gilmartin, and John Montague Massengale, *New York 1900: Metropolitan Architecture and Urbanism, 1890–1915* (New York: Rizzoli, 1983), 275–278; Charles Lockwood, *Bricks and Brownstone: The New York Row House, 1783–1929* (New York: Abbeville, 1972).

7. Daniel O'L., for instance, reported that he and a gay friend took a room in a theatrical boardinghouse when they moved to New York from Boston around 1931, as recorded in George W. Henry, *Sex Variants* (New York: Paul Hoeber, 1941), 431–432. C. A. Tripp, who observed New York's gay scene in the 1930s, has written that "in New York during the depression of the early 1930's, young homosexuals (especially those aspiring to the theater) often lived in groups, saving rent by sharing a single large apartment" (*The Homosexual Matrix* [New York: McGraw-Hill, 1975], 184–185). See also my interview with Donald Vining, January 25, 1986; *WPA Guide to New York City* (New York: Random House, 1939), 170, 179.

8. Remarkably little has been written about the theater district as a residential district, but two pieces of evidence generated by police actions indicate its residential significance. The three chorus girls arrested when the police raided a burlesque show at the Gaiety Theater in 1935 all lived in hotels and rooms in the upper Forties between Sixth and Eighth avenues ("Burlesque Dancers Held," *New York Times,* April 5, 1935). Similarly, all of the men arrested for homosexual solicitation by plainclothes members of the vice squad who were investigating a Forty-second Street bar in 1938 lived in the area or made use of its transient hotels. Several of them invited the plainclothesmen home to their apartments or furnished rooms in the West Forties and Fifties between Seventh and Ninth avenues. Others, whose homes were more distant or unavailable for homosexual trysts, or who had no homes at all, hired rooms in the area for prices ranging from sixty cents to two dollars: at the Hotel Fulton on West Forty-sixth Street between Seventh and Eighth avenues, another hotel on Eighth Avenue and Fortieth Street, and a rooming house on Eighth Avenue at Forty-fourth Street. See *Times Square Garden & Grill, Inc., v. Bruckman, et al.*, Nathan Kirschenbaum report to the SLA, November 30, 1938, contained in Record on Proceeding to Review, 24–28; Memo, Commanding Officer, 3rd Division [vice squad], to Police Commissioner, "Recommending revokation [sic] of ABC license issued to Times Square Garden & Grill," December 13, 1938, 31–37; Memo, Commanding Officer, 18th Precinct, to Police Commissioner, "Arrests in premises licensed by the New York State Liquor Authority," December 5, 1938, 38–39.

9. George Chappell, *The Restaurants of New York* (New York: Greenberg, 1925), 127.

10. Herbert Asbury, *The Great Illusion: An Informal History of Prohibition* (Garden City, NY: Doubleday, 1950), 193, 197.

11. On Times Square in the 1920s see Jack Poggi, *Theater in America: The Impact of Economic Forces, 1870–1967* (Ithaca, NY: Cornell University Press, 1968); Margaret M. Knapp, "A Historical Study of the Legitimate Playhouses on West Forty-second Street Between Seventh and Eighth Avenues in New York City." Un-

published Ph.D. diss., City University of New York, 1982; Irving Drutman, *Good Company: A Memoir, Mostly Theatrical* (Boston: Little, Brown, 1976), 1–74; Asbury, *Great Illusion*, 192–196; Lewis A. Erenberg's chapter in this volume and his article, "From New York to Middletown: Repeal and the Legitimization of Nightlife in the Great Depression," *American Quarterly* 38 (1986):761–778.

12. Charles G. Shaw, *Nightlife: Vanity Fair's Intimate Guide to New York After Dark* (New York: John Day, 1931), 22.

13. Richard Meeker, *Better Angel* (New York: Greenberg, 1933), 259.

14. Knapp, "A Historical Study," 389–390.

15. Tennessee Williams recalled cruising Times Square with Donald Windham in the early 1940s, where he made "very abrupt and candid overtures [to groups of sailors or GIs], phrased so bluntly that it's a wonder they didn't slaughter me on the spot. . . . They would stare at me for a moment in astonishment, burst into laughter, huddle for a brief conference, and, as often as not, would accept the solicitation, going to my partner's Village pad or to my room at the 'Y' " (Tennessee Williams, *Memoirs* [1975; New York: Bantam, 1976], 66, see also 123, 172). Some verification of their activity in Times Square is offered by a letter Williams wrote Windham on October 11, 1940, while he was visiting his family in Missouri: "Have to play jam [i.e., straight] here and I'm getting horny as a jackrabbit, so line up some of that Forty-second Street trade for me when I get back. Even Blondie would do!" (Donald Windham, ed., *Tennessee Williams' Letters to Donald Windham, 1940–1965* [New York: Holt, Rinehart and Winston, 1977], 17); see also Donald Windham, *Lost Friendships: A Memoir of Truman Capote, Tennessee Williams, and Others* (New York: William Morrow, 1987), 114.

16. Frank Thompson, interviewed June 1 and 2, 1988, reported this was still the case in the 1940s.

17. Dorr Legg, interviewed October 4, 1988; Shaw, *Nightlife*, 66.

18. Nathan Kirschenbaum report, SLA, November 30, 1938, included in *Times Square Record on Review*, 28 Kirschenbaum also reported that a gay man at the bar had told a plainclothes policeman on October 15 that the " 'Queers' [who] frequented the premises . . . were the same crowd that hung out in the Consolidated . . . and at Ryans" (p. 25).

19. Testimony of Morris Horowitz, *Times Square Record on Review* (1939), 245.

20. As one man who frequented the Astor in the thirties and forties recalled, it was his favorite bar "because it wasn't a gay bar. People didn't know you were gay. It was never raided" (interview with Martin Leonard, July 16, 1988).

21. Interview with Nat Fowler, August 13, 1986. Other accounts of the Astor were provided by Robert Mason, interviewed November 20 and December 4, 1985; Wayne Hendricks, interviewed August 19, 1986; Frank McCarthy, interviewed September 5, 1986; and Willy W., interviewed September 2 and 5, 1986. The Astor was so famous in the gay world that upon the demolition of the hotel in 1966, a gay magazine published in Philadelphia ran a tribute to it: Paul Forbes, "Mrs. Astor's Bar," *Drum*, No. 20 (n.d. [ca. 1966]): 11–12. See also Allan Berube's account of the Astor in *Coming Out Under Fire: The History of Gay Men and Women in World War Two* (New York: Free Press, 1990), which appeared after this chapter was written.

22. Dorr Legg interview; "An Evening with Beatrice Lillie," reviewed by John Mason Brown, *Saturday Review* (n.d. [1952?]); article on Lillie by T. B. F., *Town & Country* (December 1952): "And, inevitably, the fairies at the bottom of her garden are once more revisited. They are, she admits, '. . . growing elderly but people simply adore them. They always ask for them.' " Both in Lillie clipping file, Billy Rose Theatre Collection, New York Public Library, Lincoln Center. On the audiences at Judy Garland's concerts see Richard Dyer, "Judy Garland and Gay Men," in his *Heavenly Bodies: Film Stars and Society* (New York: St. Martin's Press, 1986), 141–194.

23. Donald Vining, *How Can You Come Out If You've Never Been In?* (Trumansburg, NY: Crossing Press, 1986), 57.

CHAPTER 16   Private Parts in Public Places

1. Quoted in Morton Minsky and Milt Machlin, *Minsky's Burlesque* (New York: Arbor House, 1986), 255.
2. Neil Norman, "London's Little New York," *London Evening Standard Magazine* (March 1988):50–54.
3. Steven Marcus: *The Other Victorians. A Study of Sexuality and Pornography in Mid-nineteenth-century England* (New York: Bantam Books, 1967), Chap. 7.
4. William Kornblum, ed., "West 42nd Street: 'The Bright Light Zone.'" Unpublished study, City University of New York, 1978, 75.
5. W. G. Rogers and Mildred Weston, *Carnival Crossroads: The Story of Times Square* (Garden City, NY: Doubleday, 1960), 63.
6. Clement Wood, *The Truth About New York's White Light Region* (Girard, KS: Haldeman-Julius, 1926), 78; Herbert Asbury, *The Gangs of New York. An Informal History of the Underworld* (Garden City, NY: Garden City Publishing, 1928), 177, 234; Earl Lind, *Autobiography of an Androgyne* (New York: Arno Press, 1975), 62; Bernard Cohen, *Deviant Street Networks. Prostitution in New York City* (Lexington, MA: Lexington Books, 1980), 32–33.
7. George J. Kneeland and Katharine Bennett Davis, *Commercialized Prostitution in New York City* (New York: Century, 1913), 4, 33–37.
8. Wood, *The Truth*, 47–51; Kneeland and Davis, *Commercialized Prostitution*, 22, 65–66.
9. George Rector, *The Girl from Rector's* (Garden City, NY: Doubleday, 1927), 217; Burns Mantle, "Lines That Live." Part 2, *Stage* (July 1936):58.
10. Wood, *The Truth*, 912.
11. "Adam Fitz-Adam," *The World* (London: March 1, 1753).
12. See Claudia Johnson, "That Guilty Third Tier: Prostitution in Nineteenth-century American Theatre," in D. W.

Howe, ed., *Victorian America* (Philadelphia, PA: University of Pennsylvania Press, 1976).
13. Wood, *The Truth*, 23.
14. Josh Alan Friedman, *Tales of Times Square* (New York: Delacorte Press, 1986), 181–182. See also Kornblum, "West 42nd Street," 63; Minsky and Machlin, *Minsky's Burlesque*, 133; Brooks McNamara, "'A Congress of Wonders': The Rise and Fall of the Dime Museum," *English Studies Quarterly* (1974):229. The best account of Heckler's Flea Circus appears in Bill Ballantine, *Wild Tigers & Tame Fleas* (New York: Rinehart, 1958), 229–259.
15. Rollin Lynde Hartt, *The People at Play. Excursions in the Humor and Philosophy of Popular Amusements* (Boston: Houghton Mifflin, 1909), 104, 108.
16. Heywood Broun and Margaret Leech, *Anthony Comstock, Roundsman of the Lord* (New York: Literary Guild of America, 1927), 250.
17. Quoted in Dan H. Laurence, ed., *Collected Letters 1898–1910* (London: Max Reinhardt, 1972), 573.
18. Irving Zeidman, *The American Burlesque Show* (New York: Hawthorn Books, 1967), 131.
19. See Stephen M. Vallillo, "Broadway Revues in the Teens and Twenties: Smut and Slime?" *Drama Review* 25 (March 1981): 25–34.
20. Bernard Sobel, *Burleycue* (New York: Farrar & Rinehart, 1931), 276.
21. Clippings in *Artists and Models* file, Shubert Archive, New York.
22. Brooks Atkinson, *Broadway* (New York: Macmillan, 1970), 247.
23. Quoted in Broun and Leech, *Anthony Comstock*, 266.
24. Kaier Curtin, *"We Can Always Call Them Bulgarians." The Emergence of Lesbians and Gay Men on the American Stage* (Boston: Alyson Publications, 1987), Chap. 4.
25. See Ernest Boyd, Foreword to *Maya, A Play in a Prologue, Nine Scenes and an Epilogue, translated from the French of Simon Gantillon by Ernest Boyd* (New York: Robert McBride, 1928), x–xiv; Atkinson, *Broadway*, 248.
26. Hiram Motherwell, "Sense and

Censorship," *Theatre Guild Magazine* (November 1928):12.

27. Zeidman, *American Burlesque*, 169.

28. Frances Park, "Burlesque's Last Stand," *Theatre Guild Magazine* (December 1931):34.

29. Zeidman, *American Burlesque Show*, 173.

30. Minsky and Machlin, *Minsky's Burlesque*, 134–135.

31. Brooks McNamara, "Reconstructing Broadway: The Times Square Entertainment District at the End of the 1930s." See Chapter 9 of this book.

32. Cohen, *Deviant Street Networks*, 2, my emphasis.

33. Burlesque clippings file, Lincoln Center Library of the Performing Arts, New York.

34. Zeidman, *American Burlesque*, 222.

35. Zeidman, *American Burlesque*, 231; Rogers and Weston, *Carnival Crossroads*, 175; Minsky and Machlin, *Minsky's Burlesque*, 139 et seq.

36. Abel Green and Joe Laurie, Jr., *Show Biz from Vaude to Video* (New York: Holt, 1951), 451.

37. Zeidman, *American Burlesque*, 247.

38. Kornblum, "West 42nd Street," 66.

39. "Vice in New York," *Fortune* (July 1939), in Milton Crane, ed., *Sins of New York* (New York: Grosset & Dunlap, 1947), 276–277.

40. Neil Harris, "Urban Tourism and the Commercial City." See Chapter 3 of this book.

41. Lind, *Autobiography*, 71.

42. Tennessee Williams, *Memoirs* (New York: Doubleday, 1975), 53.

43. This is clearly a more specific use than the earlier complaints that burlesque shows had a tendency to attract "undesirables," voiced in "Burlesque Houses Called Unsightly," *New York Times* (May 1, 1932).

44. Kornblum, "West 42nd Street," 72.

45. Rogers and Weston, *Carnival Crossroads*, 158–163.

46. Bruce Fisher, D. Kelly Weisberg, and Toby Marotta, *Report on Adolescent Male Prostitution* (San Francisco: Urban and Rural Systems Associates, 1982), 42.

47. Rogers and Weston, *Carnival Crossroads*, 123.

48. John Rechy, *City of Night* (New York: Grove Press, 1963), 23.

49. Alan Bowne, *Forty-Deuce, a Play* (New York: Sea Horse Press, 1983), 31.

50. Larry Clark, *Teenage Lust, an Autobiography* (New York: Larry Clark, 1983). Another artist's positive response to Times Square "deviancy" can be found in Hans Falk, *Transvestie. Zeichnungen, Gouachen und Collagen. Der silberne Cocon. Notizen zur Transvestiten-Szene in New York 1979–1985* (Zurich: ABC-Verlag, 1985).

51. "Vice in New York," 277.

52. John D'Emilio and Estelle B. Freedman, *Intimate Matters, a History of Sexuality in America* (New York: Harper & Row, 1988), 327–329.

53. Friedman, *Tales of Times Square*, 74–76.

54. Kornblum, "West 42nd Street," 105.

55. Charles A. Sundholm, "The Pornographic Arcade: Ethnographic Notes on Moral Men in Immoral Places," *Urban Life and Culture* 2 (April 1973):46.

56. David Allen Karp, "Public Sexuality and Hiding Behavior: A Study of Times Square Sexual Community." Unpublished Ph.D. diss., New York University, 1971.

57. Friedman, *Tales of Times Square*, 183.

58. Friedman, *Tales of Times Square*, 79–81; Kornblum, "West 42nd Street," 119; Cohen, *Deviant Street Networks*, 6.

59. Jean-Jacques Wunenberger, *La Fête, le jeu et le sacré* (Paris: Jean-Pierre Delargue, 1977), 292, note 2.

60. Will H. Jarvis, "Show World," *Prude* 4 (1987):14; the series was continued in the next issue.

61. Elisabeth B, *Das ist ja zum Peepen* (Frankfurt am Main: Eichhorn, 1983), 93, my translation in every case. The CUNY study makes the same point (Kornblum, "West 42nd Street," 117): "The 42nd Street audience is also not visibly deviant; the deviants in the area are not likely to be

paying customers of the entertainment establishments."

62. Elisabeth B, *Das ist ja zum Peepen*, 103.

63. Elisabeth B, *Das ist ja zum Peepen*, 37.

64. Elisabeth B, *Das ist ja zum Peepen*, 22.

65. Eric Partridge, *A Dictionary of Slang and Unconventional English* (London: Routledge & Kegan Paul, 1953), 959.

66. Gail Sheehy, "Cleaning Up Hell's Bedroom," *New York* magazine 5 (November 13, 1972):59; Friedman, *Tales of Times Square*, 141.

67. Sheehy, "Cleaning Up," 55. See also Sheehy's "The Landlords of Hell's Bedroom," *New York* magazine 5 (November 20, 1972):67–80.

68. Friedman, *Tales of Times Square*, 145.

69. Friedman, *Tales of Times Square*, 166.

70. Information from Minda Novek, Institute for the Humanities, New York University.

71. For a libertarian feminist approach see Varda Burstyn, ed., *Women Against Censorship* (Vancouver, Canada: Douglas & McIntyre, 1985).

72. See Barbara Meil Hobson, *Uneasy Virtue. The Politics of Prostitution and the American Reform Tradition* (New York: Basic Books, 1987), 218–222, 234–235.

73. City of New York Office of Midtown Enforcement, *Annual Report 1986* (New York: Mayor's Office of Correspondence Services, 1987).

74. City of New York Office of Midtown Enforcement, *Annual Report 1987* (New York: Mayor's Office of Correspondence Services, 1988). See also City of New York Police Department, *Crime Comparison Report and Statistics*, 1988.

75. Cohen, *Deviant Street Networks*, 5–6.

76. City of New York Office of Midtown Enforcement, 1987.

77. Mark Thomas Connelly, *The Response to Prostitution in the Progressive Era* (Chapel Hill, NC: University of North Carolina Press, 1980), 29–30.

78. Daniel S. Campagna and Donald L. Poffenberger, *The Sexual Trafficking in Children: An Investigation of the Child Sex Trade* (Dover, MA: Auburn House, 1988), and D. Kelly Weisberg, *Children of the Night. A Study of Adolescent Prostitution* (Lexington, MA: Lexington Books, 1985), both take the typical alarmist approach to the subject. For a more temperate view see Toby Marotta, Bruce Fisher, and Michael Pincus, *Adolescent Male Prostitution, Pornography and Other Forms of Sexual Exploitation* (San Francisco: Urban and Rural Systems Associates, 1982).

79. See Charles Terrot, *Traffic in Innocents. The Shocking Story of White Slavery in England* (New York: Dutton, 1960).

80. Donald J. Shoemaker, "The Teeniest Trollops: 'Baby Pros,' 'Chicken,' and Child Prostitutes," in Clifton D. Bryant, ed., *Sexual Deviancy in Social Context* (New York: New Viewpoints, 1977), 244–245.

81. See Hubert Lafont, "Les bandes des jeunes," in *Communications* 35 (1982): especially 156.

82. Marotta et al., *Adolescent Male Prostitution*, 6–23.

83. Bruce Ritter, *Sometimes God Has a Kid's Face. Letters from Covenant House* (New York: Covenant House, 1988), 119–121. See also Sara Rimer, "In Times Sq., Creating Hope for Young Lives," *New York Times* (December 31, 1985). Since this chapter was written, Father Ritter has been formally accused of sexual relationships with his charges and of financial malfeasance. He has denied these accusations, but confessed himself guilty of poor judgment.

84. See Elaine Pagels, *Adam, Eve and the Serpent* (New York: Random House, 1988), and Peter Brown, *The Body and Society: Men, Women and Sexual Renunciation in Early Christianity* (New York: Columbia University Press, 1988).

85. Ritter, *Sometimes God Has a Kid's Face*, 54.

86. Ned Polsky, *Hustlers, Beats and Others* (Chicago: Aldine, 1967), 188. See also Kingsley Davis, "Sexual Behavior," in Robert Merton and Robert Nisbet, eds., *Contemporary Social Problems*, 3rd ed. (New York: Harcourt Brace Jovanovich, 1971), 341–351.

87. Karp, "Public Sexuality," 87.

88. Quoted in Andrew C. Revkin, "At the Crossroads," in "A Times Square Album," *New York Daily News Magazine* (June 12, 1988):17.

89. Quoted in Kornblum, "West 42nd Street," 137. For ways in which morality is constructed by social institutions, see Jack D. Douglas, ed., *Deviance & Respectability. The Social Construction of Moral Meanings* (New York: Basic Books, 1970), especially 3–30.

AFTERWORD   Re-Inventing Times Square: 1990

1. The 42nd Street Development Project, an undertaking of the New York City and New York State Urban Development corporations, was announced in 1981. The plan is meant to rebuild and rehabilitate Times Square from Forty-second to Forty-third streets and West Forty-second Street from Seventh to Eighth avenues. Construction will be assisted by government purchase and demolition of property with write-down of land costs and tax benefits to developers. Its focus is four large office towers facing Times Square on Forty-second and Forty-third streets, for which the sponsor is George Klein of Park Tower Realty, and the buildings designed by John Burgee Architects with Philip Johnson (since retired); in the ensuing nine years the design has gone through a sea change from mansard postmodern to jazzy deconstructivist. Other elements of the plan are to be a merchandise mart and a hotel at the Eighth Avenue end of Forty-second Street, and the restoration of some of the historic theaters on the Forty-second Street block. Neither the mart nor the hotel has found sponsors to date.

2. In 1984 the Municipal Art Society of New York, partly in protest against the cavalier treatment of the landmark Times Tower in the city-state redevelopment plan for Times Square, held a "Times Tower Site Competition." The purpose was to dramatize the danger to Times Square as much as to seek proposals for the building's future within the sanitized skyscrapers of the Johnson/Burgee design. Suggestions ranged from restoring the original Eidlitz and MacKenzie facade of the tower, or stripping the building to its antique steel frame and painting it white, to replacing it with a scaffolding of lighted signs or a sculpture of a big apple. A report on the competition and articles on Times Square appeared in the Municipal Art Society's publication, *The Living City*, No. 10/1 (October 1986).

3. A. L. Huxtable, "Architecture: That Midtown Tower Standing Naked in the Wind. Skyscraper Buffs See Antique Skeleton," *New York Times* (March 20, 1964):30.

4. Robert Venturi and Denise Scott Brown, *Learning From Las Vegas* (Boston, MA: MIT Press, 1977).

5. Robert A. M. Stern, Gregory Gilmartin, and John Montague Massengale, *New York 1900, Metropolitan Architecture and Urbanism 1890–1915* (New York: Rizzoli International Publications, 1983).

6. A. L. Huxtable, "54-Story Hotel Expected to Revitalize Times Square," *New York Times* (July 11, 1973):43, 50; "More Bad News About Times Square," *New York Times* (February 9, 1975) Section 2, 32. Reprinted as "New York: Bad News About Times Square," *Kicked a Building Lately?* (New York: Quadrangle/New York Times Book, 1976), 112–115.

7. The Special Midtown Zoning District was created in May 1982, following a study completed by the Department of City Planning in 1981. In addition to offering incentives to growth and expansion west and south of the midtown East Side, it contained features meant to improve light, air, and pedestrian circulation. It also tightened provisions that had allowed much "negotiated" zoning, turning optional features into "as-of-right" provisions or requirements. Among special subdistricts was a Theater Subdistrict Core Area designated to protect existing theaters.

8. *Midtown Development Review* (New York: Department of City Planning, July 1987), 7.

9. John Tierney, "Era Ends as Times Square Drops Slashers for Shakespeare," *New York Times* (January 14, 1991).

10. *Times Square Urban Design Controls*, Department of City Planning study. Summary of controls adopted by the Board of Estimate as amendments to the Special Midtown Zoning District, enacted into law February 5, 1987. Loose-leaf notebook with plans, diagrams, and illustrations of the controls.

11. *Times Square Urban Design Controls*, introductory statement.

12. Paul Goldberger, building reviewed in "Architecture View," *New York Times* (February 10, 1991).

13. Promotional brochure, 1585 Broadway, Solomon Equities, New York, NY (n.d.).

14. Ada Louise Huxtable, "Rockefeller Plaza West," *Center* (magazine of Rockefeller Center, March-April, 1991).

CONTRIBUTORS

JEAN-CHRISTOPHE AGNEW teaches in the American studies and history departments at Yale University. He is the author of *Worlds Apart: The Market and the Theater in Anglo-American Thought, 1550–1750* (New York: Cambridge University Press, 1986).

BETSY BLACKMAR teaches history at Columbia University. She has written on the history of leisure and of land use and real estate law. Her work includes *Manhattan for Rent* (Ithaca, NY: Cornell University Press, 1989) and a forthcoming book, written with Roy Rosenzweig, on the history of Central Park.

PETER BUCKLEY teaches history at the Cooper Union for the Advancement of Science and Art in New York City and is a Fellow of the New York Institute for the Humanities. He has published articles on the development of antebellum urban cultures. His book, *To the Opera House*, will be published by Oxford University Press.

GEORGE CHAUNCEY, JR. is assistant professor of history at the University of Chicago. He has contributed articles to the *Journal of Social Science*, *Salmagundi*, and several scholarly anthologies; is coeditor of *Hidden from History: Reclaiming the Gay and Lesbian Past* (edited by Martin Duberman, Martha Vicinius, and George Chauncey, Jr. New York: New American Library, 1989); and is currently finishing a book, *Gay New York: Urban Culture and the Making of a Gay Male World, 1890–1970*.

PETER A. DAVIS is associate professor of theater history at the University of Illinois at Urbana-Champaign and the author of numerous articles and reviews on early American theater history. He is presently working on an economic study of colonial American theater and editing a collection of essays on American theater history. He is also completing work on an annotated anthology of eighteenth century American plays.

LEWIS A. ERENBERG is associate professor of history at Loyola University of Chicago. He is the author of *Steppin' Out: New York Nightlife and the Transformation of American Culture, 1890–1930* (Westport, CT: Greenwood, 1981) and numerous articles on cabarets and popular entertainment. He is now completing a study of big bands and popular music in the 1930s and 1940s.

RICHARD WIGHTMAN FOX is professor of history and director of American studies at Boston University. He is the author of *Reinhold Niebuhr: A Biography* (New York: Pantheon, 1986) and coeditor of *The Culture of Consumption: Critical Essays in American History* (New York: Pantheon, 1983). He is at work on a study of liberal Protestant culture in America.

PHILIP FURIA is professor of English and American studies at the University of Minnesota. He is the author of *The Poets of Tin Pan Alley: A History of America's Great Lyricists* (New York: Oxford University Press, 1990) and other books and essays on modern American poetry and the arts.

TIMOTHY J. GILFOYLE is currently assistant professor of history at Loyola University of Chicago. He has published articles on New York City history in *American Quarterly* and the *Journal of Urban History*. His book, *City of Eros: New York City, Prostitution, and the Commercialization of Sex, 1790–1920*, will be published by W. W. Norton in 1992.

GREGORY GILMARTIN is an architect with Peter Pennoyer Architects. He is the coauthor, with Robert A. M. Stern and John Massengale, of *New York 1990* (New York: Rizzoli, 1983) and, with Mr. Stern and Thomas Mellin, of *New York 1930* (Rizzoli, 1987). He is currently at work on *Shaping the City, a History of the Municipal Art Society*.

DAVID HAMMACK is professor of history at Case Western Reserve University and director of the Social Policy Ph.D. program. He is the author of *Power and Society: Greater New York at the Turn of the Century* (New York: Russell Sage Foundation, 1982) and many articles on New York.

NEIL HARRIS is professor of history at the University of Chicago. He has written extensively on the history of popular culture. His work includes his influential *Humbug: The Art of P. T. Barnum* (Boston: Little, Brown, 1973) and *Cultural Excursions: Marketing Appetites and Cultural Tastes in Modern Society* (Chicago: University of Chicago Press, 1990).

ADA LOUISE HUXTABLE has been architecture critic of the *New York Times* and a member of its editorial board. She is a former MacArthur Fellow and now serves as an architectural consultant to public institutions. She is the author of *The Tall Building Artistically Reconsidered: The Search for a Skyscraper Style* (New York: Pantheon, 1984) and many other books and articles of architectural history and criticism.

MARGARET KNAPP is associate professor of history and criticism in the theater department at Arizona State University. She has written and published extensively on the history of the American theater, and has served as a consultant to several private and public institutions, including the New York City Landmarks Preservation Commission and the New York State Urban Development Corporation.

ERIC LAMPARD is professor of history at the State University of New York at Stony Brook. He has written widely on urban history and the history of economics. He is the author of *The History of the City in Economically Advanced Areas* (1955) and *The Rise of the Dairy Industry in Wisconsin* (Madison, WI: State Historical Society, 1963).

WILLIAM R. LEACH is the author of *True Love and Perfect Union: The Feminist Reform of Sex and Society* (New York: Basic Books, 1981) and the editor of *The Wonderful Wizard of Oz by L. Frank Baum* (Belmont, CA: Wadsworth, 1991). He is completing a history of the rise of American consumer economics and culture.

BROOKS MCNAMARA is professor of performance studies in the Tisch School of the Arts at New York University and is director of the Shubert Archive. He has recently published *Shuberts of Broadway* (New York: Oxford University Press, 1991) and has written extensively on the history of popular performance.

WILLIAM WOOD REGISTER, JR. received his Ph.D. in American history from Brown University in 1991. He is currently completing a study of Frederic Thompson and American consumer culture at the turn of the century.

LAURENCE SENELICK is Fletcher Professor of Drama at Tufts University. His many articles have appeared in a wide array of journals, from *The Journal of Sexuality* to *Cuisine*. His most recent books are the award-winning *The Age and Stage of George L. Fox; Cabaret Performance: Europe 1890–1920* (Hanover, NH: University Press of New England, 1988); and *National Theatre in Northern and Eastern Europe, 1743–1900* (Cambridge, England, and New York: Cambridge University Press, 1991).

ROBERT W. SNYDER is the author of *Voice of the City: Vaudeville and Popular Culture in New York* (New York: Oxford University Press, 1989). He has taught at Princeton and Rutgers Universities and is now doing research on news reporting on crime and the changes in life in New York City neighborhoods since the 1940s.

WILLIAM R. TAYLOR teaches history at State University of New York at Stony Brook and is program director of the New York Institute for the Humanities at New York University. He is the author of *Cavalier and Yankee: The Old South and American National Character* (Cambridge, MA: Harvard University Press, 1979). He has written widely on urban popular cultures and on New York. A collection of his recent work on New York, *In Pursuit of Gotham*, will be published next year by Oxford University Press.

INDEX

A

Abbott, George, 184
Abe Lincoln in Illinois (R. Sherwood), 184
Able-Peterson, Trudee, 348
Abraham and Straus, 115
Absentee Ownership (T. Veblen), 241
Academy of Music, 298
A Christmas Carol, 187
actors, 64, 87–88, 91, 161; audience adaptation of, 144; criticism of, 96; earnings of, 122, 139; at Hippodrome, 259; in musical films, 203; talents of, 97
Actors' Equity, 64, 122, 184, 189, 216
actresses, 64; kept, 332; meeting places for, 161; walk-on, 332. *See also* chorus girls
acts, 122, 174; amount paid for, 139; arena, 251; blues, 176; circus, 253; Hollywood, 217; novelty, 162; sequence of, 137; vaudeville, 137–141, 145
Adams, Franklin Pierce (F.P.A.), 81, 82, 220
Adams, Maude, 263, 267
Addams, Jane, 97, 289
Ade, George, 213
adolescents, 349–350, 352
adults, 290, 318; toys for, 243, 261. *See also* entertainment; play
advertisers, 28, 237; direct mail, 27
advertising, 26, 33, 99, 109, 341; American, 110; automobile, 22; collision of architecture and, 281; confluence of entertainment and, 18, 30; electrical, 116, 235–237, 240, 243; "ether," 20; experts, 102; for Hippodrome, 243, 257, 261; with light, 111, 234, 239; more effective, 235; for New York, 75, 76; for nightclubs, 175; outdoor, 235–237, 242; outlays on, 28–29; personnel,

287; restrictions, 240; schemes developed by department stores, 248; self-, 29
Advertising Age, 38
Aeolian Building, 116
Aeolian Hall, 49
aesthetic, 71, 236, 240, 273, 294; architectural, 358–359; integration of, 242; modernist, 369; new kind of, 234; progressivism, 274. *See also* commercial aesthetic
African–Americans, 302. *See also* blacks
"After the Ball" (C.K. Harris), 192
agencies, 288, 363; advertising, 20; government, 42; leading professional, 26; metropolitan, 28; of moral policing, 316; private reform, 288; professional model, 101; regulatory, 296; state, 289
agents, 138–139; advertising, 101; booking, 46
agglomeration, 25
"Ah! Sweet Mystery of Life" (I. Berlin), 198
AIDS epidemic, 348
Albany, 288, 334
Albee, E.F., 123, 134–136, 142, 143; reputation of, 141. *See also* Keith-Albee booking offices
alcohol, 171, 173; consumption of, 288; control of, 168; dealers, 166; illegal, 166, 169; legal, 170; prohibition of, 294; sales of, 165, 331, 332; trade, 309; war against, 164. *See also* Prohibition
Alda, Frances, 202
Alexander, H.M., 185
Alexander, Willard, 176
"Alexander, Don't You Love Your Baby No More" (I. Berlin), 196
"Alexander's Ragtime Band" (I. Berlin), 195, 196, 198
Algonquin Hotel, 200, 215
Ali Baba, 253

Boomer, Lucius, 77
Boorstin, Daniel, 105
Booth's Theatre, 254, 298
bootleggers, 165–167, 171; control of alcohol by whites, 168; slang of, 212
Borden's Condensed Milk, 26
Boston, 25, 37, 89, 359; conventions in, 78; productions of J. Urban, 275; shows in, 265
Boston Opera House, 272, 275
boundaries, 59, 65, 286; of class, 63, 65; cultural, 57, 60; new, 296; to respectability, 287; of Times Square area, 8, 178–179, 357
Bourdet, Edouard, 334
Bowery, 59, 134, 191–193, 330, arcades, 293; concert saloons, 303; prostitution, 297
Bowman, John, 77
Bowne, Alan, 340, 351
box office receipts, 46
The Boys from Syracuse (G. Abbott, L. Hart, R. Rodgers), 184
Brace, Charles Loring, 289
Brady, Diamond Jim, 188
Brady, William A., 199
Breath of the Avenue, 102
brewers, 309, 310, 311
Brewers Board of Trade, 309
Brice, Fanny, 164, 195
bridges, 41–42
Brieux, Eugène, 334
Brill Building, 189, 191, 210, 216
Brisbane, Arthur, 221
Britain, 23. See also England
broadcast media, 157. See also radio
Broadcast Music Incorporated (BMI), 208
Broadway, 17, 175, 178–179, 212, 218; "angels," 128; "babies," 203; critique of, 80; decline of, 147–148, 157, 181, 183; differentiations marking, 178; effect of Depression on, 169–170; houses, 180; mythos, 222, 230; office buildings on, 190, 356, 367; prostitution on, 300; radio industry on, 49; reputation of, 44; Rialto section of, 47; spots, 173; study of, 3; subject, 220, 221; theater business, 183–185; in the thirties, 188; visitors of, 81. See also cafés; nightclubs; restaurants; specific issues

Broadway, 249, 250
Broadway Association, 110, 180, 181; and use of signs, 240
Broadway Melody, 203
Broadway stories (by D. Runyon), 213, 222, 225–230; plots of, 226; success of, 225–227, 230
Broadway Theatre, 121, 299
brokering, 7, 100, 111, 113, 120
brokers, 60, 99–101, 106, 117; capital, 101, 112, 116, 117; consulting, 103; image, 101, 104, 105, 117; new group of, 20, 100–101
"brokers in beauty," 253, 255, 259, 268, 361
Brook, H.J., 175
Brooklyn, 247; talking sign in, 243; transportation from, 40, 41
Brooklyn Bridge, 69, 76; photographs of, 70, 73
Brooklyn Eagle, 247
Brooks Costume Company, 189
brothels, 297, 299–301, 312; clients of, 303, 331; closings of, 306, 307; disorderly, 305–306; French-run, 299, 304; monthly profits of, 305; replacement of, 298, 311; row houses used as, 299
Broun, Haywood, 220
Brown, Denise Scott, 358
brownstones, 297, 298–299
Bryant movie house, 129
Bryant Park, 323; closing of, 338; "fairy" prostitutes at, 320, 322, 327–328
Buck, Eugene Edward (Gene), 212–213
Buck and Bubbles, 168
Buckley, Peter G., 59, 286
Budapest, 272
Buffalo, NY, 246
builders, 364, 367; tenement, 57; theater, 121; uptown, 59
Building Department, 250–251, 255
buildings: business, 234; electric signage on, 357, 366; height of, in Times Square, 49, 65; midtown, 65; new, 71, 74, 356–357, 367–370; new rules for size of, 363; office, 363, 364, 367, 369; requirements for new, 366; tall, 78; Times Square, 294, 358; types of, 281. See also skyscrapers; specific buildings
Bull Market, 128

Murphy, Charles, 293
Murray, John L., 159, 161
Murray Hill, 57, 61
Murray's restaurant, 332
Muschenheim, Frederick and William, 77
museum curators, 101
Museum of Natural History, 79
museums: contents of, 333; dime, 186, 297, 332–333; of New York City, 69
music, 197, 201; American, 191–192, 201, 208, 211; black, 170, 176, 208; Broadway show, 169; country, 208; industry, 133, 176, 208; in New York, 38
musical comedy, 197, 335
musicals, 124, 203, 210; Broadway, 129, 277; film, 203–204; "hillbilly," 209; Hollywood, 130; "integrated," 208; presented in 1938–39 season, 184
Music Box Theatre, 200, 205
Music Center, 278
Music Hall, 172, 173, 187, 330
Myers, Bernard A., 142
"My Mariuccia Take a Steamboat," 194
"My Wife Ethel" (D. Runyon), 221, 225, 228

N

National Association of Piano Tuners, 78
National City of New York, 32
National Collegiate Athletic Association, 313
National Film Board of Review, 293
National Football League, 313
National Theatre, 91, 261; "Uncle Tom's Cabin" at, 90
National Winter Garden Theatre, 295
NBC, 20
negotiations, political, 53
Negro Building, 246
Neighborhood Playhouse, 127
neighborhoods. *See* residential neighborhoods
Nelson, Stephen, 188
Net National Product (NNP), 28
networks, 20. *See also* radio
New Amsterdam Theatre, 47, 122, 277, 360; legitimate shows at, 179;

revue at, 197; roof theater of, 125, 161
New Deal, 169
New Englander, 97
"New Era," 29, 32
New Jersey, rail connections to, 39, 41, 75
New Journalism, 221
New Orleans, 75
New Republic, 143
news, 25, 223, 224, 229
New School for Social Research building, 282
newsmakers, 136
newspapers, 17, 103, 105, 201, 230, 333; advertising in, 175; essays in, 220; Hearst, 225; Hippodrome articles in, 252, 260–261; location of, 215, 218; New York, 38, 221; offices of, 214; relations between theater and, 205; slang in, 224; spending on, 29
New Stagecraft, 275
New Theatre, 254
Newton, Frankie, 176
New Year's Eve, 360
New York, 37–38, 360; advertised as summer resort, 75; appeals of, for tourism, 67, 69, 76; canal, 24; as capital of "dangerous love," 158; fiscal crisis, 131; gay world of, 315; growth of, as business center, 66; popularization of, 73; renditions of, 70–73; reputation of, 81, 82, 330
New York, 344
New York Brewers Association, 309, 311
New York Central, 39, 40
New York Clipper, 256
New York Commission on Amusements, 196
New York Convention and Visitors Bureau, 175
New York Dramatic Mirror, 123
New York Edison, 258
The New Yorker, 168, 215, 220, 336
New Yorker Hotel, 170
New Yorkers: concerns of, 70; effects of tourism on, 67, 79–81; at Hippodrome opening night, 262; middle-class, 59; needs of, 80; well-to-do, 64, 298; working-class, 59, 64

Library of Congress Cataloging-in-Publication Data

Inventing Times Square : commerce and culture at the crossroads of the world / edited by
    William R. Taylor.
        p.   cm.
    Originally published : New York : Russell Sage Foundation, c1991.
    Based on a series of six conferences held during 1988–89, sponsored by the New York
Institute for the Humanities, at New York University.
    Includes bibliographical references and index.
    ISBN 0-8018-5337-0 (pbk. : alk. paper)
    1. Times Square (New York, N.Y.)—History.   2. New York (N.Y.)—History—1898–1951.
3. Popular culture—New York (N.Y.)—History.
I. Taylor, William Robert, 1922–
[F128.65.T5158   1996]
974.7´1—dc20   95-43542